Management Information Systems

Managing Information Technology in the E-Business Enterprise

InformationTechnology

At McGraw-Hill Higher Education, we publish instructional materials targeted at the higher education market. In an effort to expand the tools of higher learning, we publish texts, lab manuals, study guides, testing materials, software, and multimedia products.

At McGraw-Hill/Irwin (a division of McGraw-Hill Higher Education), we realize technolgy will continue to create new mediums for professors and students to manage resources and communicate information with one another. We strive to provide the most flexible and complete teaching and learning tools available and offer solutions to the changing world of teaching and learning.

McGraw-Hill/Irwin is dedicated to providing the tools necessary for today's instructors and students to navigate the world of Information Technology successfully.

Seminar Series – McGraw-Hill/Irwin's Technology Connection seminar series, offered across the country every year, demonstrates the latest technology products and encourages collaboration among teaching professionals.

Osborne/McGraw-Hill – A division of the McGraw-Hill Companies known for its best-selling Internet titles, *Harley Hahn's Internet & Web Yellow Pages* and the *Internet Complete Reference*, offers an additional resource for certification and has strategic publishing relationships with corporations such as Oracle Corporation, Corel Corporation, and America Online. For more information, visit Osborne at **www.osborne.com**.

Digital Solutions – McGraw-Hill/Irwin is committed to publishing Digital Solutions. Taking your course online doesn't have to be a solitary venture. Nor does it have to be a difficult one. We offer several solutions, which will let you enjoy all the benefits of having course material online. For more information, visit **www.mhhe.com/digital_solutions**.

Packing Options – For more about our discount options, contact your local McGraw-Hill/Irwin sales representative at 1-800-338-3987, or visit our website at **www.mhhe.com/it**.

Management

Information

Systems

Managing Information Technology in the E-Business Enterprise

Fifth Edition

James A. O'Brien

College of Business Administration
Northern Arizona University

Boston   Burr Ridge, IL   Dubuque, IA   Madison, WI   New York   San Francisco   St. Louis
Bangkok   Bogotá   Caracas   Kuala Lumpur   Lisbon   London   Madrid   Mexico City
Milan   Montreal   New Delhi   Santiago   Seoul   Singapore   Sydney   Taipei   Toronto

McGraw-Hill Higher Education

A Division of The McGraw-Hill Companies

MANAGEMENT INFORMATION SYSTEMS:
MANAGING INFORMATION TECHNOLOGY IN THE E-BUSINESS ENTERPRISE

Published by McGraw-Hill, an imprint of The McGraw-Hill Companies, Inc. 1221 Avenue of the Americas, New York, NY, 10020. Copyright © 2002, 1999, 1996, 1993, 1990 by The McGraw-Hill Companies, Inc. All rights reserved. No part of this publication may be reproduced or distributed in any form or by any means, or stored in a database or retrieval system, without the prior written consent of The McGraw-Hill Companies, Inc., including, but not limited to, in any network or other electronic storage or transmission, or broadcast for distance learning.

Some ancillaries, including electronic and print components, may not be available to customers outside the United States.

This book is printed on acid-free paper.

domestic   1 2 3 4 5 6 7 8 9 0 VNH/VNH 0 9 8 7 6 5 4 3 2 1
international   1 2 3 4 5 6 7 8 9 0 VNH/VNH 0 9 8 7 6 5 4 3 2 1

ISBN 0-07-244078-3

Vice president/Editor in chief: *Robin J. Zwettler*
Publisher: *George Werthman*
Senior sponsoring editor: *Rick Williamson*
Developmental editor: *Kelly L. Delso*
Marketing manager: *Jeffrey Parr*
Project manager: *Christina Thornton-Villagomez*
Production supervisor: *Debra R. Sylvester*
Media producer: *Greg Bates*
Designer: *Matthew Baldwin*
Lead supplement producer: *Marc Mattson*
Photo research coordinator: *Judy Kausal*
Photo researcher: *Judy Mason*
Cover image: *Eartha™, The world's largest rotating and revolving globe at DeLorme Publishing Corporate Headquarters, Yarmouth, Maine. Copyright © Jeffrey Stevenson*
Typeface: *10/12 Janson text*
Compositor: *GTS Graphics, Inc.*
Printer: *Von Hoffmann Press, Inc.*

Library of Congress Cataloging-in-Publication Data

O'Brien, James A.
    Management information systems : managing information technology in the e-business
    enterprise / James A. O'Brien.—5th ed.
        p. cm.
    Rev. Ed. of: Management information systems: managing information technology in
    the internetworked enterprise / James A. O'Brien. 4th ed. c1999.
        Includes bibliographical references and index.
        ISBN 0-07-244078-3 (hbk.)
        1. Electronic commerce. 2. Information technology—Management. 3. Management
    information systems. 4. Business—Data processing. I. Title.

    HF5548.32 .O27 2002
    658.4'038—dc21   2001024808

INTERNATIONAL EDITION ISBN 0-07-112350-4

www.mhhe.com

To your love, happiness, and success

James A. O'Brien is an adjunct professor of Computer Information Systems in the College of Business Administration at Northern Arizona University. He completed his undergraduate studies at the University of Hawaii and Gonzaga University and earned an M.S. and Ph.D. in Business Administration from the University of Oregon. He has been coordinator of the CIS area at Northern Arizona University, professor of Finance and Management Information Systems and chairman of the Department of Management at Eastern Washington University, and a visiting professor at the University of Alberta, the University of Hawaii, and Central Washington University.

Dr. O'Brien's business experience includes working in the Marketing Management Program of the IBM Corporation, as well as serving as a financial analyst for the General Electric Company. He is a graduate of General Electric's Financial Management Program. He has also served as an information systems consultant to several banks and computer services firms.

Jim's research interests lie in developing and testing basic conceptual frameworks used in information systems development and management. He has written eight books, including several that have been published in multiple editions, as well as in Chinese, Dutch, French, Japanese, or Spanish translations. He has also contributed to the field of information systems through the publication of many articles in business and academic journals, as well as through his participation in academic and industry associations in the field of information systems.

An E-Business Enterprise Perspective

The transformation of business caused by E-business and E-commerce applications of the Internet and related technologies demonstrates that information systems and information technology are essential ingredients for business survival and success. Thus, this new Fifth Edition is designed for business students who are or will be managers, entrepreneurs, and business professionals in today's E-business enterprises. The goal of this text is to help business students learn how to use and manage information technologies to revitalize business processes, conduct electronic commerce, improve business decision making, and gain competitive advantage. Thus, it places a major emphasis on the role of the Internet, intranets, extranets, and other Internet technologies in providing a technology platform for electronic business, commerce, and collaboration within and among internetworked enterprises and global markets.

This is the E-business enterprise perspective that this text brings to the study of information systems. Of course, as in all my texts, this edition:

- Loads the text with **real world cases,** examples, and exercises about real people and companies in the business world.
- Organizes the text around a simple **five-area framework** that emphasizes the IS knowledge a business end user needs to know.
- Distributes and integrates IS foundation theory throughout the text instead of concentrating it in several early chapters.
- Places a major emphasis on the strategic role of information technology in gaining competitive advantage, supporting electronic business operations and decision making, and enabling electronic commerce and enterprise collaboration.

Audience

This text is designed for use in undergraduate or introductory MBA courses in Management Information Systems, which are required in many Business Administration or Management programs as part of the common body of knowledge for all business majors. Thus, this edition treats the subject area known as Information Systems (IS), Management Information Systems (MIS), or Computer Information Systems (CIS) as a major functional area of business that is as important to management education as are the areas of accounting, finance, operations management, marketing, and human resource management.

Key Features

The new Fifth Edition is the most comprehensive revision of this text since it was first published. Most chapters have been significantly "E-engineered," that is, text material has been radically restructured, eliminated, and augmented with new E-business and E-commerce topics and real world examples to provide students with a solid E-business foundation for their studies and work in business.

All New Real World Cases and Examples

This text provides all new up-to-date real world case studies. These are not fictional stories, but actual situations faced by business firms and other organizations as reported in current business and IS periodicals. This includes five real world case studies in each chapter that apply specifically to that chapter's contents.

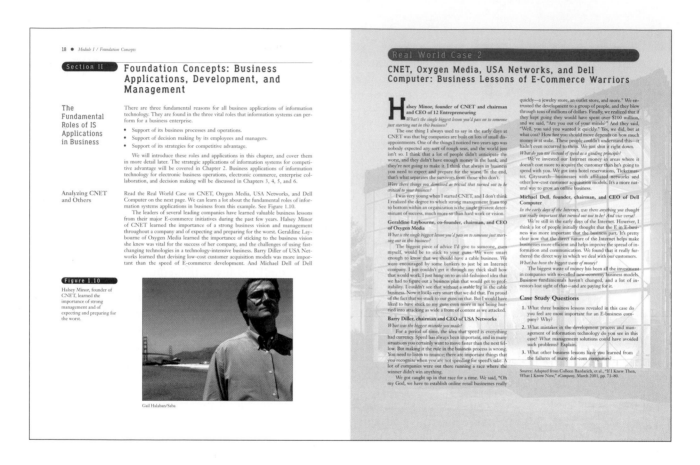

In addition, each chapter contains several application exercises, including two hands-on spreadsheet or database software assignments and new Internet-based real world assignments in most chapters. Also, many new highlighted in-text real world examples have been added to illustrate concepts in every chapter. The purpose of this variety of learning and assignment options is to give instructors and students many opportunities to apply each chapter's material to real world situations.

Boeing and Analog Devices: IT Failure and Success	The Boeing Company embarked on a major business process reengineering campaign in 1994, buying off-the-shelf enterprise resources planning (ERP) software to replace hundreds of mainframe legacy systems used to manufacture commercial aircraft. For example, Boeing bought Baan's manufacturing, finance, purchasing, and distribution ERP software suite; Metaphase's product data management package; CIMLINC's Linkage for process planning; and Trilogy's SalesBUILDER for configuration management, along with other software packages.
	Fast-forward to late 1998, when Boeing announced lousy financial results and major layoffs. It predicted a pathetic pretax profit margin of only 1 to 3 percent for its commercial aircraft group by the year 2000, up from 0 percent in 1998. A precipitous decline in airplane orders by Asian airlines is the culprit according to the company. But Wall Street analysts and others watching the company say production inefficiencies, poor planning, and a host of other internal failures bear part of the responsibility for the dismal margin and poor financial results, according to articles about the project in, among others, *The New York Times* and *The Wall Street Journal*.
	However, other ERP implementations have proved their worth through the positive results achieved. The ERP implementation at chip maker Analog Devices, Inc., for instance, helped the company weather tough times in 1998, when declining prices drove down revenues and otherwise put pressure on the entire semiconductor industry. Analog has continued to show progress in reducing costs in a variety of areas, including production, staffing, and inventory. Bottom line: If the right combination of ERP software, business processes, and managerial expertise are working together, there should be a substantial financial return, as there was for Analog [11].

New Chapters on Electronic Business and Commerce

This edition contains many thoroughly *E-engineered* chapters that emphasize how Internet and Web technologies provide the technological infrastructure and business tools that enable internetworked enterprises to engage in electronic business and commerce. This is demonstrated, not only in the text materials in Chapters 4 and 5, but in other chapters and Real World Cases and examples in the text. Examples include Kepler's Books and Magazines, Pepsi Cola Company, Uniglobe.com and Allfirst Bank, Siebel Systems and Telstra Corporation, Alcoa and Cisco Systems, Solectron Electronics, Hitachi Semiconductor and Dell Computer, eBay, Inc., Florist.com, Wal-mart, Kmart, Kingfisher and HMV, and Raytheon and Deere & Co., to name a few.

An Information Systems Framework

This text reduces the complexity of an introductory course in information systems by using a conceptual framework that organizes the knowledge needed by business students into five major areas (see Figure 1):

Figure 1

The five-area information systems framework.

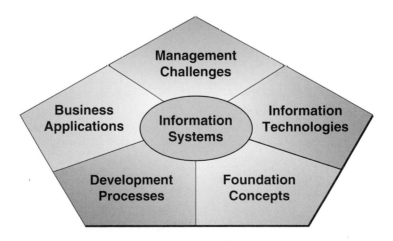

- **Foundation Concepts.** Fundamental business information systems concepts including trends, components, and roles of information systems (Chapter 1) and competitive advantage concepts and applications (Chapter 2). Other behavioral, managerial, and technical concepts are presented where appropriate in selected chapters.

- **Business Applications.** How the Internet, intranets, extranets, and other information technologies are used in E-business enterprises to support electronic business and commerce, team and enterprise collaboration, and business decision making (Chapters 3, 4, and 5).

- **Development Processes.** Developing and implementing E-business strategies and systems using several strategic planning and application development approaches (Chapters 7 and 8).

- **Management Challenges.** The challenges of E-business technologies and strategies, including security and ethical challenges and global IT management (discussed in many chapters, but emphasized in Chapters 9 and 10).

- **Information Technologies.** A review of major concepts, developments, and managerial implications involved in computer hardware, software, telecommunications networks, and data resource management technologies (Chapters 11, 12, 13, and 14). Other technologies used in computer-based information systems are discussed where appropriate in selected chapters.

Strategic, International, and Ethical Dimensions

This text also contains substantial text material and cases reflecting the strategic, international, and ethical dimensions of information systems. This can be found not only in Chapters 2, 9, and 10, but also in all other chapters of the text. This is especially evident in many real world cases and examples, such as General Electric Company, McDonald's and American Express, Oracle Corporation, E*Trade Bank, France Telecom, Siemens AG, Accel Partners, Merrill Lynch, University of Washington, the FBI and Resource Technologies, Visa, American Express, and GM, Axciom, Inc., TRW, Toyota, and Cendant, and many, many others. These examples repeatedly demonstrate the strategic and ethical challenges of managing E-business technologies for competitive advantage in global business markets and in the global information society in which we all live and work.

Modular Structure of the Text

The text is organized into five modules that reflect the five major areas of the framework for information systems knowledge mentioned earlier. See Figure 2. Also each chapter is organized into two distinct sections. This is done to avoid proliferation

Figure 2

The modular organization of the text.

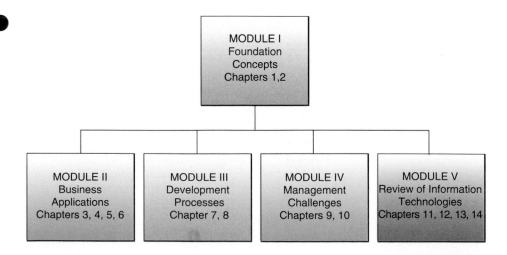

MODULE I
Foundation
Concepts
Chapters 1,2

MODULE II
Business
Applications
Chapters 3, 4, 5, 6

MODULE III
Development
Processes
Chapter 7, 8

MODULE IV
Management
Challenges
Chapters 9, 10

MODULE V
Review of Information
Technologies
Chapters 11, 12, 13, 14

of chapters, as well as to provide better conceptual organization of the text and each chapter. This organization increases instructor flexibility in assigning course material since it structures the text into modular levels (i.e., modules, chapters, and sections) while reducing the number of chapters that need to be covered.

Each chapter starts with Chapter Highlights and Learning Objectives and ends with a Summary, Key Terms and Concepts, a Review Quiz tied directly to the Key Terms and Concepts, Discussion Questions, and Application Exercises. Real World Cases are placed at the beginning of the two sections of each chapter (with a brief analysis), and at the end of each chapter, to help students understand the chapter material in the context of examples from the real world of business.

Changes to This Edition

As stated earlier, besides providing all new Real World Cases, this edition represents a comprehensive E-business revision of the text. This includes a major restructuring of the text's organization and sequence of chapters to better support its new E-business orientation. For example, the four chapters on hardware, software, data resource management, and telecommunications networks have been moved to an optional Review of Information Technologies module as Chapters 11, 12, 13, and 14. The chapter on strategic advantage has been brought forward to the Foundation Concepts module as Chapter 2, while coverage of systems development has been moved to a new module on Development Processes as Chapter 8. Highlights of other changes made to the Fourth Edition are found in the following Fifth Edition chapters:

Chapter 1: *Foundations of Information Systems in Business*
This chapter features a complete reorganization and major changes in content to present an overview of topics in the five areas of IS knowledge of the text. Much of the material formerly in Chapters 1 and 2 has been eliminated or concentrated in this chapter. Thus, Section I covers foundation concepts in information systems and technologies, and Section II presents concepts in E-business applications, the IS development process, and management challenges of IT.

Chapter 2: *Competing with Information Technology*
This was Chapter 12 in the previous edition. It was moved to the Foundation Concepts module at the urging of reviewers to emphasize the vital importance of using IT for competitive advantage. The strategic use of Internet technologies and E-business concepts are major content additions, along with revising previous coverage and replacing many in-text real world examples.

Chapter 3: *The Internetworked E-Business Enterprise*
Section I of this chapter features new topics and thoroughly revised content on E-business applications and the business use and value of the Internet. The chapter includes new material on intranet enterprise portals and technologies, and new in-text real world examples.

Chapter 4: *Electronic Business Systems*
This chapter has been completely E-engineered to provide students with two solid sections on E-business. Section I on E-business systems features major new content on cross-functional integrated enterprise applications, including enterprise application integration (EAI), enterprise resource planning (ERP), and customer relationship management (CRM), and supply chain management (SCM). Section II contains updated coverage of more traditional E-business applications that support activities in the functional areas of business. Much of the coverage of transaction processing systems formerly in Chapter 10 has now been concentrated in the treatment of online transaction processing (OLTP) in Section I.

Chapter 5: *Electronic Commerce Systems*
This chapter is a complete rewrite and expansion of the former edition's section on electronic commerce. Section I emphasizes the fundamental components and processes of E-commerce systems, while Section II explores key applications and issues in E-commerce, including B2C and B2B marketplaces, requirements for success, and clicks and bricks strategies.

Chapter 6: *E-Business Decision Support*
The focus of Section I of this chapter has been revised to emphasize the major trends and changes occurring in E-business decision support, which is empowering business professionals and knowledge workers (not just managers and executives) with Web-enabled decision support tools. The chapter also features new material on using data mining and enterprise portals for decision support, and new in-text real world examples.

Chapter 7: *Developing E-Business Strategies*
This chapter is a thorough revision of the material on IS planning and change management formerly in Chapter 14. Both chapter sections contain much new material and real world examples that emphasize the major changes needed in developing and implementing E-business strategies before new E-business applications can be successfully developed.

Chapter 8: *Developing E-Business Solutions*
This chapter (formerly Chapter 3), is thoroughly revised and reorganized at the urging of reviewers to stress an E-business systems development perspective, including prototyping, user interface, Web design, and end user development topics (Section I), and E-business system implementation (Section II). Most of the section on the systems approach, including the hypothetical case study example of Auto Shack Stores, has been moved to the text's online learning center.

Chapter 9: *Security and Ethical Challenges of E-Business*
This chapter is completely E-engineered to stress security, ethical, and societal challenges faced by E-businesses, including computer crime in Section I. Section II is a new, completely rewritten treatment that focuses on methods of E-business security management to counter the threats to E-business and E-commerce introduced in Section I.

Chapter 10: *Enterprise and Global Management of E-Business Technology*
The first section of this chapter is a completely E-engineered and new treatment of the impact of E-business on managers, organizations, and the management of information technologies and the IS function, eliminating much previous material that focused on more traditional approaches. Section II retains its global IT management structure, but includes new treatment and in-text real world examples on cultural and political challenges, E-business strategies, and data and Internet access issues in global E-business.

Chapter 11: *Computer Hardware*
Coverage of computer hardware has been updated and revised, including added content on information appliances and thin clients, and elimination of technical details on CPU components.

Chapter 12: *Computer Software*
Updated coverage of computer software, including business application software, the Windows 2000 and Linux operating systems, and the XML language.

Chapter 13: *Data Resource Management*
Includes new content on data resource management, data warehouses, and data mining, and new in-text real world examples.

Chapter 14: *Telecommunications and Networks*
Updated coverage of telecommunications network con,
the Internet, fiber optics and wireless technologies, P2P i.
width alternatives. Coverage of business applications of telec.
and the Internet has been moved to Chapter 3.

Teaching and Learning Resources

New to this edition, E-Tutor, authored by Ali Beza Montazemi of M
University, is an electronic tutor available free on CD-ROM that helps stu.
master basic key concepts before advancing to more complex topics. E-Tutor
an interactive electronic product, with content from the textbook embedded into
a software shell, that provides learning sessions in coordination with sections and
subsections from the textbook. It has the flexibility to allow students to work
through the material at their own pace. A **presentation manager Instructor
CD-ROM** is available to adopters and offers the following resources for course
presentation and management:

- An Instructor's Resource Manual, authored by Margaret Trenholm-Edmunds
  of Mount Allison University, contains suggestions for using the book in
  courses of varying lengths, detailed chapter outlines with teaching suggestions
  for use in lectures, and answers to all end-of-chapter questions, application
  exercises, and problems and case study questions. Teaching tips for incorporating the video clips are included for many chapters.

- A Test Bank, authored by Margaret Trenholm-Edmunds of Mount Allison
  University, containing true-false, multiple choice, fill-in-the-blank, and short
  essay questions.

- Computerized/Network Testing with Brownstone Diploma software is fully
  networkable for LAN test administration; tests also can be printed for standard
  paper delivery or posted to a website for student access.

- Slide shows in Microsoft PowerPoint, authored by Margaret Trenholm-
  Edmunds of Mount Allison University, are available for each chapter to
  support classroom discussion of chapter concepts and real world cases.

- Data/solutions files, authored by James N. Morgan of Northern Arizona
  University, for the database and spreadsheet application exercises in the text
  are included.

- Video clips are available that highlight how specific companies apply and use
  information technology.

The McGraw-Hill/Irwin Information Systems Video Library contains 14 10- to
12-minute videos on numerous companies demonstrating use of a variety of IT like
intranets, multimedia, or computer-based training systems, and concepts like
client/server computing and business process reengineering. This library is available
free to adopters. For further information, visit www.mhhe.com/business/mis/videos
or contact your local McGraw-Hill/Irwin sales representative. A video lecture guide
for all 14 videos is included in the Instructor's Resource Manual.

Digital Solutions

- Website/OLC—The book's website at http://www.mhhe.com/business/mis/
  obrien/obrien5e provides resources for instructors and students using the text.
  The Online Learning Center (OLC) builds on the book's pedagogy and features with self-assessment quizzes, extra material not found in the text, Web
  links, and other resources for students and instructors.

- Pageout—our Course Website Development Center. Pageout offers a syllabus
  page, website address, Online Learning Center content, online quizzing,
  gradebook, discussion forum, and student Web page creation.

...kaging Options The McGraw-Hill/Irwin *Advantage*, O'Leary, and Laudon Interactive computing series are collections of software application manuals and interactive computer-based training products for Microsoft Office. In addition, we offer several paperback Internet literacy books or CDs, perfect for introducing the World Wide Web, E-mail, and Web page design to students. These texts and CDs are available for discounted packaging options with any McGraw-Hill/Irwin title. For more about our discount options, contact your local McGraw-Hill/Irwin sales representative or visit our website at www.mhhe.com/it.

In addition, a software casebook—*Application Cases in MIS: Using Spreadsheet and Database Software and the Internet*, fourth edition, by James N. Morgan of Northern Arizona University—is available to supplement the hands-on exercises in this edition. This optional casebook contains an extensive number of hands-on cases, many of which include a suggested approach for solving each case with the Internet, spreadsheet, or database management software packages to develop solutions for realistic business problems.

Acknowledgments

The author wishes to acknowledge the assistance of the following reviewers whose constructive criticism and suggestions helped invaluably in shaping the form and content of this text.

Noushin Ashrafi, *University of Massachusetts–Boston*
Harry C. Benham, *Montana State University*
Karen E. Bland-Collins, *Morgan State University*
Warren Boe, *University of Iowa*
Gurpreet Dhillon, *University of Nevada–Las Vegas*
Sean B. Eom, *Southeast Missouri State University*
Dale Foster, *Memorial University of Newfoundland*
Robert Fulkerth, *Golden Gate University*
Michelle L. Kaarst-Brown, *University of Richmond*
Ronald J. Kizior, *Loyola University–Chicago*
Douglas M. Kline, *Sam Houston State University*
Andrew G. Kotulic, *York College of Pennsylvania*
Elizabeth E. Little, *The University of Central Oklahoma*
Stephen L. Loy, *Eastern Kentucky University*
Joan B. Lumpkin, *Wright State University*
Pam Milstead, *Louisiana Tech University*
Murli Nagasundaram, *Boise State University*
Margaret H. Neumann, *Governors State University*
Rene F. Reitsma, *St. Francis Xavier University*
Dolly Samson, *Weber State University*
Tod Sedbrook, *University of Northern Colorado*
Richard S. Segall, *Arkansas State University*
Dana V. Tesone, *University of Hawaii and Nova Southeastern University*
H. Joseph Wen, *New Jersey Institute of Technology*
Jennifer J. Williams, *University of Southern Indiana*
Karen L. Williams, *University of Texas–San Antonio*

My thanks also go to James N. Morgan of Northern Arizona University, who is the author of the software casebook that can be used with this text and who developed most of the hands-on Application Exercises in the text, as well as the data/solutions files on the Instructor CD-ROM. I am also grateful to Margaret Trenholm-Edmunds of Mount Allison University, the author of the Instructor's Resource Manual, for her revision of this valuable teaching resource.

Much credit should go to several individuals who played significant roles in this project. Thus, special thanks go to the editorial and production team at Irwin/McGraw-Hill, especially Rick Williamson, senior sponsoring editor; Christine Wright and Kelly Delso, developmental editors; Jeff Parr and Nicole Young, senior marketing managers; Christina Thornton-Villagomez and Claudia L. McCowan, project managers; and Matthew Baldwin, designer. Their ideas and hard work were invaluable contributions to the successful completion of the project. Thanks also to Kay Pinto, whose word processing skills helped me meet my manuscript deadlines. The contributions of many authors, publishers, and firms in the computer industry that contributed case material, ideas, illustrations, and photographs used in this text are also thankfully acknowledged.

A Special Acknowledgment

A special acknowledgment goes to Omar El Sawy, Arvind Malhotra, Sanjay Gosain, and Kerry Young for their award-winning *MIS Quarterly* article, "IT-Intensive Value Innovation in the Electronic Economy: Insights from Marshall Industries"; to Ravi Kalakota and Marcia Robinson for their groundbreaking book, *E-Business: Roadmap for Success;* and to Patricia Seybold for her best-selling book on E-commerce: *Customers.com: How to Create a Profitable Business Strategy for the Internet and Beyond.* Their pioneering works were invaluable sources for my coverage of E-business and E-commerce topics in this new edition.

Acknowledging the Real World of Business

The unique contribution of the hundreds of business firms and other computer-using organizations that are the subject of the real world cases, exercises, and examples in this text is gratefully acknowledged. The real-life situations faced by these firms and organizations provide the readers of this text with a valuable demonstration of the benefits and limitations of using the Internet and other information technologies to enable electronic business and commerce, and enterprise communications and collaboration in support of the business processes, managerial decision making, and strategic advantage of the E-business enterprise.

James A. O'Brien

Brief Contents

Module IV   Management Challenges

Module V   Review of Information Technologies

Contents

Module I Foundation Concepts

Chapter 2

Competing with Information Technology 43

Module II   Business Applications

Chapter 3

The Internetworked E-Business Enterprise 79

Chapter 4

Electronic Business Systems 123

Chapter 5

Electronic Commerce Systems 161

Chapter 6

E-Business Decision Support 199

Module III   Development Processes

Module IV   Management Challenges

Chapter 9

Chapter 10

Module V   Review of Information Technologies

Chapter 11

Computer Hardware 391

Chapter 12

Computer Software 429

Chapter 13

Data Resource Management 465

Chapter 14

Telecommunications and Networks 497

Appendix

Management Information Systems

Managing Information Technology in the E-Business Enterprise

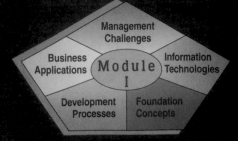

Management Challenges

Business Applications

Module I

Information Technologies

Development Processes

Foundation Concepts

Module I

Foundation Concepts

Why study information systems? Why do businesses need information technology? What do you need to know about the use and management of information technologies in business? The introductory chapters of Module I are designed to answer these fundamental questions about the role of information systems in E-business enterprises.

- **Chapter 1: Foundations of Information Systems in Business** presents an overview of the five basic areas of information systems knowledge needed by business professionals, including the conceptual system components and major types of information systems.

- **Chapter 2: Competing with Information Technology** introduces fundamental concepts of competitive advantage through information technology, and illustrates strategic applications of information systems that can gain competitive advantages for today's global E-business enterprises.

After completing these chapters, you can move on to study chapters on business applications (Module II), development processes (Module III), and the management challenges of information systems (Module IV), as well as selected chapters in a review of information technologies (Module V).

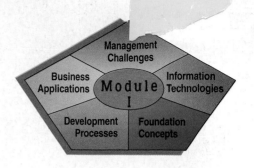

Management Challenges

Business Applications

Module I

Information Technologies

Development Processes

Foundation Concepts

Foundations of Information

Systems in Business

Chapter Highlights

Learning Objectives

After reading and studying this chapter, you should be able to:

1. Explain why knowledge of information systems is important for business professionals and identify five areas of information systems knowledge they need.

2. Give examples to illustrate how E-business, electronic commerce, or enterprise collaboration systems could support a firm's business processes, managerial decision making, and strategies for competitive advantage.

3. Provide examples of the components of real world information systems. Illustrate that in an information system, people use hardware, software, data, and networks as resources to perform input, processing, output, storage, and control activities that transform data resources into information products.

4. Provide examples of several major types of information systems from your experiences with business organizations in the real world.

5. Identify several challenges that a business manager might face in managing the successful and ethical development and use of information technology in a business.

Foundation Concepts: Information Systems and Technologies

Why Information Systems Are Important

The blending of Internet technologies and traditional business concerns is impacting all industries and is really the latest phase in the ongoing evolution of business. All companies need to update their business infrastructures and change the way they work to respond more immediately to customer needs [12].

Why study information systems and information technology? That's the same as asking why anyone should study accounting, finance, operations management, marketing, human resource management, or any other major business function. Information systems and technologies (including E-business and E-commerce technologies and applications) have become a vital component of successful businesses and organizations. They thus constitute an essential field of study in business administration and management. That's why most business majors must take a course in information systems. Since you probably intend to be a manager, entrepreneur, or business professional, it is just as important to have a basic understanding of information systems as it is to understand any other functional area in business.

The Real World of Information Systems

Let's take a moment to bring the real world into our discussion of the importance of information systems (IS) and information technology (IT). Read the Real World Case of Kepler's Books & Magazines on the next page. Then let's analyze it together. See Figure 1.1.

Figure 1.1

Clark Kepler provides a blend of traditional and E-commerce services to his bookstore's customers.

Robert Houser.

Kepler's Books and Magazines: Small Business Bricks-and-Clicks Strategies

I was chatting recently with Clark Kepler, a lifelong Silicon Valley local whose family has owned Kepler's Books and Magazines in Menlo Park for 40 years. We were having coffee at Cafe Borrone, an eclectic Valley hangout next door to his bookstore whose paper napkins have launched a thousand business plans. Not long ago, "there was a feeling that you'd better run hard or you were going to get run over," Kepler admits, and in some ways the slowdown is welcome. And yet, he fears that we're simply "in the eye of the storm" that the Internet has unleashed, and he's sure that more E-commerce and technological upheaval lies ahead.

By all rights, guys like Kepler are among the few that should be gloating a little bit here in Lake Wealthbegone. After all, they outlasted many of the dot-com vandals and visigoths who were licking their chops at the prospect of "distintermediating" books, pet supplies, groceries, gardening tools, and all that other charming stuff whose traditional merchants help make our communities tick. Fueled with seemingly endless supplies of venture capital and promising infinite selection at rock-bottom prices, dot-coms had local merchants in their E-commerce gun sights.

George Roberts, a third-generation grocer and owner of Roberts Market in tiny Woodside, listened to his prominent venture-capital customers and neighbors' grand plans for grocery delivery E-commerce outfits such as Webvan. "They had so much money, they were like the government. As long as you have somebody else's money, you're King Kong," he says, chuckling.

The pressure's off a bit now, but these merchants are far too smart to think the game is over and they've won. On the one hand, they did well by relying on the things they've always done best: Did Pets.com Inc. ever sneak your dog a cookie? Could Garden.com Inc. ever replicate the economics of the beloved local nursery, where you go to get watering advice from somebody with dirty fingernails and pay for it by buying plants and supplies you don't need? But successful merchants stuck to what they knew and embraced the best of what the E-commerce explosion offered to make their businesses work better, as they slowly morphed into bricks-and-clicks enterprises.

Quite a few local merchants, in fact, did not withstand the dot-com blitzkrieg, though they typically were not driven out by the success of outfits promising unprecedented service for unsustainable prices. Instead, they were ousted by the absurd rents the King Kongs were willing to pay for Silicon Valley office space. Some time ago, Kepler, for example, had to move his bookstore's business office several towns away to Belmont, because he simply couldn't justify paying the rent for the office space above his store.

Trimming costs like that helped Kepler add the E-commerce services the Internet was teaching customers to demand. Although Kepler's has long had one of the largest inventories in the San Francisco Bay area, customers suddenly started coming in carrying printouts from Amazon.com Inc.'s list of more than 2 million books, many of them out of print or otherwise rare. "It used to be people could come in and order those books, and I could get it for them in four to six weeks," he says. But online bookstores fundamentally changed his customers' expectations. "Now, I can usually get something in maybe three to seven days, but those same customers will wrinkle their noses and say, 'Gee, I don't know, I really need it today.'"

So now Kepler's has a storewide computer network and an E-commerce Web site where folks can order from their home or workplace, and Kepler works with a nearby E-commerce company (deliverEtoday.com) to get a book order of $50 or more to customers the same day if needed. "The lifestyles of my customers today have changed so much—it's go, go, go, and everyone is running. I have customers who say 'I want to hold a book, feel it, smell it.' But I look at my nephew and he and his generation don't have that attachment. Things are changing, and I have to adapt to it."

At least he now feels as if his competitors also have to make a profit. "We had a really wonderful Christmas selling season," Kepler says. Sales were good, but even more satisfying, he adds, was hearing "people say things like, 'It's so nice to see lines in here. That must mean Kepler's is doing O.K.' Another couple said, 'We could have ordered online, but we wanted to come in and support Kepler's.'"

Case Study Questions

1. What E-commerce challenges are facing small business retailers like Kepler's?

2. How can information technology and a bricks-and-clicks strategy help small retailers meet such challenges?

3. Visit the www.keplers.com web site. Evaluate the content of their site and the E-commerce strategies it reveals. What other E-commerce moves can you recommend to Kepler's? Defend your recommendations.

Source: Adapted from Joan Hamilton, "A Valley of Shopkeepers," *Business Week E. Biz*, February 19, 2001, pp. EB 18–19.

Analyzing Kepler's Books & Magazines

We can learn a lot about the importance of information technology and information systems from the Real World Case of Kepler's Books & Magazines.

This case dramatizes just one of the countless examples of the business challenges and opportunities created by the growth of the Internet and the World Wide Web. Like many business owners, Clark Kepler wondered if his bookstore would survive the onslaught of powerful dotcom competitors like Amazon.com. But Kepler's has survived and thrived by adding new E-commerce services to the traditional mix of products and services that its customers still wanted from their neighborhood bookstore. For example, Kepler's established its own E-commerce Web site and made arrangements with a nearby dotcom delivery company to provide same-day delivery service for customers who wanted it. Thus, Kepler's has transformed itself into a "bricks and clicks" enterprise, blending the best features of traditional and electronic commerce.

Thus, information technologies, including Internet-based information systems, are playing a vital and expanding role in business. Information technology can help all kinds of businesses improve the efficiency and effectiveness of their business processes, managerial decision making, and workgroup collaboration and thus strengthen their competitive positions in a rapidly changing marketplace. This is true whether information technology is used to support product development teams, customer support processes, interactive electronic commerce transactions, or any other business activity. Internet-based information technologies and systems are fast becoming a necessary ingredient for business success in today's dynamic global environment.

What You Need to Know

There is no longer any distinction between an IT project and a business initiative. IT at Marriott is a key component of the products and services that we provide to our customers and guests at our properties. As such, there's very little that goes on within the company that either I personally or one of my top executives is not involved in [13].

Those are the words of Carl Wilson, executive vice-president and CIO of Marriott International. So even top executives and managers must learn how to apply information systems and technologies to their unique business situations. In fact, business firms depend on all of their managers and employees to help them manage their use of information technologies. So the important question for any business professional or manager is: What do you need to know in order to help manage the hardware, software, data, and network resources of your business, so they are used for the strategic success of your company?

An IS Framework for Business Professionals

The field of information systems encompasses many complex technologies, abstract behavioral concepts, and specialized applications in countless business and nonbusiness areas. As a manager or business professional you do not have to absorb all of this knowledge. Figure 1.2 illustrates a useful conceptual framework that organizes the knowledge presented in this text and outlines what you need to know about information systems. It emphasizes that you should concentrate your efforts in five areas of knowledge:

- **Foundation Concepts.** Fundamental behavioral, technical, business, and managerial concepts about the components and roles of information systems. Examples include basic information system concepts derived from general systems theory, or competitive strategy concepts used to develop E-business applications of information technology for competitive advantage. Chapters 1 and 2 and other chapters of the text support this area of knowledge.

- **Business Applications.** The major uses of information systems for the operations, management, and competitive advantage of an E-business enterprise, including electronic business, commerce, collaboration and decision making using the Internet, intranets, and extranets are covered in Chapters 3 through 6.

Figure 1.2

This framework outlines the major areas of information systems knowledge needed by business professionals.

- **Development Processes.** How business professionals and information specialists plan, develop, and implement information systems to meet E-business opportunities using several strategic planning and application development approaches. Chapters 7 and 8 help you gain such knowledge as well as an appreciation of the E-business issues involved.

- **Management Challenges.** The challenges of effectively and ethically managing E-business technologies, strategies, and security at the end user, enterprise, and global levels of a business. Chapters 9 and 10 specifically cover these topics, but all of the chapters in the text emphasize the managerial challenges of information technology in today's global E-business environment.

- **Information Technologies.** Major concepts, developments, and management issues in information technology—that is, hardware, software, networks, data resource management, and many Internet-based technologies. Chapters 11 through 14 provide you with review coverage of such topics that supports this area of information systems knowledge.

In this chapter, we will discuss some of the foundation concepts of information systems and introduce other topics that give you an overview of the five areas of IS knowledge covered in this text.

What Is an Information System?

Let's begin with a simple definition of an information system, which we will expand in the next few pages. An **information system** can be any organized combination of people, hardware, software, communications networks, and data resources that collects, transforms, and disseminates information in an organization. See Figure 1.3. People have relied on information systems to communicate with each other using a variety of physical devices (*hardware*), information processing instructions and procedures (*software*), communications channels (*networks*), and stored data (*data resources*) since the dawn of civilization.

Information Technologies

Business professionals rely on many types of information systems. Some information systems use simple manual (paper-and-pencil) hardware devices and informal (word-of-mouth) communications channels. However, in this text, we will concentrate on *computer-based information systems* that use computer hardware and software, the Internet and other telecommunications networks, computer-based data resource management techniques, and many other **information technologies** to transform data resources into an endless variety of information products for consumers and business professionals. Now let's look at some of the basic foundation concepts of information systems.

Figure 1.3

Information systems rely on people, and a variety of hardware, software, data, and communications network technologies as resources to collect, transform, and disseminate information in an organization.

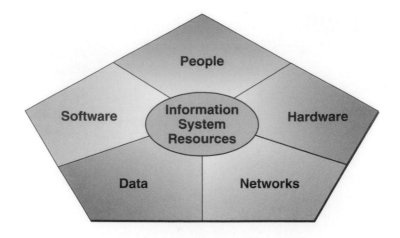

System Concepts: A Foundation

System concepts underlie the field of information systems. That's why we need to discuss how generic system concepts apply to business firms and the components and activities of information systems. Understanding system concepts will help you understand many other concepts in the technology, applications, development, and management of information systems that we will cover in this text. For example, system concepts help you understand:

- **Technology.** That computer networks are systems of information processing components that use a variety of hardware, software, data, and telecommunications technologies.
- **Applications.** That electronic business and commerce applications involve interconnected business information systems.
- **Development.** That developing ways to use information technology in business includes designing the basic components of information systems.
- **Management.** That managing information technology emphasizes the quality, strategic business value, and security of an organization's information systems.

What Is a System?

What is a *system*? A system can be most simply defined as a group of interrelated or interacting elements forming a unified whole. Many examples of systems can be found in the physical and biological sciences, in modern technology, and in human society. Thus, we can talk of the physical system of the sun and its planets, the biological system of the human body, the technological system of an oil refinery, and the socioeconomic system of a business organization.

However, the following generic system concept provides a more appropriate foundation concept for the field of information systems: a **system** is a group of interrelated components working together toward a common goal by accepting inputs and producing outputs in an organized transformation process.

Such a system (sometimes called a *dynamic* system) has three basic interacting components or functions:

- **Input** involves capturing and assembling elements that enter the system to be processed. For example, raw materials, energy, data, and human effort must be secured and organized for processing.
- **Processing** involves transformation processes that convert input into output. Examples are a manufacturing process, the human breathing process, or mathematical calculations.
- **Output** involves transferring elements that have been produced by a transformation process to their ultimate destination. For example, finished products, human services, and management information must be transmitted to their human users.

Example

A manufacturing system accepts raw materials as input and produces finished goods as output. An information system is a system that accepts resources (data) as input and processes them into products (information) as output. A business organization is a system where economic resources are transformed by various business processes into goods and services. •

Feedback and Control

The system concept becomes even more useful by including two additional components: feedback and control. A system with feedback and control components is sometimes called a *cybernetic* system, that is, a self-monitoring, self-regulating system.

- **Feedback** is data about the performance of a system. For example, data about sales performance is feedback to a sales manager.
- **Control** involves monitoring and evaluating feedback to determine whether a system is moving toward the achievement of its goal. The control function then makes necessary adjustments to a system's input and processing components to ensure that it produces proper output. For example, a sales manager exercises control when reassigning salespersons to new sales territories after evaluating feedback about their sales performance.

Example

A familiar example of a self-monitoring, self-regulating system is the thermostat-controlled heating system found in many homes; it automatically monitors and regulates itself to maintain a desired temperature. Another example is the human body, which can be regarded as a cybernetic system that automatically monitors and adjusts many of its functions, such as temperature, heartbeat, and breathing. A business also has many control activities. For example, computers may monitor and control manufacturing processes, accounting procedures help control financial systems, data entry displays provide control of data entry activities, and sales quotas and sales bonuses attempt to control sales performance. •

Other System Characteristics

Figure 1.4 uses a business organization to illustrate the fundamental components of a system, as well as several other system characteristics. Note that a system does not exist in a vacuum, rather, it exists and functions in an *environment* containing other systems. If a system is one of the components of a larger system, it is a *subsystem*, and the larger system is its environment.

Several systems may share the same environment. Some of these systems may be connected to one another by means of a shared boundary, or *interface*. Figure 1.5 also illustrates the concept of an *open system;* that is, a system that interacts with other systems in its environment. In this diagram, the system exchanges inputs and outputs with its environment. Thus, we could say that it is connected to its environment by input and output interfaces. Finally, a system that has the ability to change itself or its environment in order to survive is an *adaptive system*.

Example

Organizations such as businesses and government agencies are good examples of the systems in society, which is their environment. Society contains a multitude of such systems, including individuals and their social, political, and economic institutions. Organizations themselves consist of many subsystems, such as departments, divisions, process teams, and other workgroups. Organizations are examples of open systems because they interface and interact with other systems in their environment. Finally, organizations are examples of adaptive systems, since they can modify themselves to meet the demands of a changing environment. •

Figure 1.4

A business is an example of an organizational system where economic resources (input) are transformed by various business processes (processing) into goods and services (output). Information systems provide information (feedback) on the operations of the system to management for the direction and maintenance of the system (control) as it exchanges inputs and outputs with its environment.

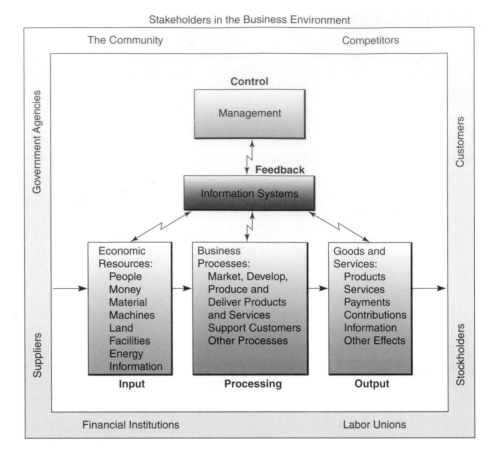

Components of an Information System

We are now ready to apply the system concepts we have learned to help us better understand how an information system works. For example, we have said that an information system is a system that accepts data resources as input and processes them into information products as output. How does an information system accomplish this? What system components and activities are involved?

Figure 1.5 illustrates an **information system model** that expresses a fundamental conceptual framework for the major components and activities of information systems. An information system depends on the resources of people (end users and IS specialists), hardware (machines and media), software (programs and procedures), data (data and knowledge bases), and networks (communications media and network support) to perform input, processing, output, storage, and control activities that convert data resources into information products.

This information system model highlights the relationships among the components and activities of information systems. It provides a framework that emphasizes four major concepts that can be applied to all types of information systems:

- People, hardware, software, data, and networks are the five basic resources of information systems.

- People resources include end users and IS specialists, hardware resources consist of machines and media, software resources include both programs and procedures, data resources can include data and knowledge bases, and network resources include communications media and networks.

- Data resources are transformed by information processing activities into a variety of information products for end users.

- Information processing consists of input, processing, output, storage, and control activities.

Figure 1.5

The components of an information system. All information systems use people, hardware, software, data, and network resources to perform input, processing, output, storage, and control activities that transform data resources into information products.

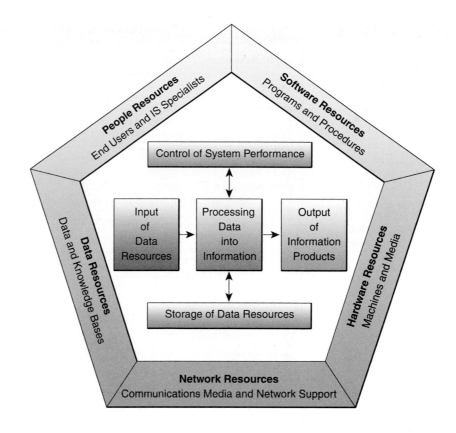

Information System Resources

Our basic IS model shows that an information system consists of five major resources: people, hardware, software, data, and networks. Let's briefly discuss several basic concepts and examples of the roles these resources play as the fundamental components of information systems. You should be able to recognize these five components at work in any type of information system you encounter in the real world. Figure 1.6 outlines several examples of typical information system resources and products.

People Resources

People are required for the operation of all information systems. These people resources include end users and IS specialists.

- **End users** (also called users or clients) are people who use an information system or the information it produces. They can be accountants, salespersons, engineers, clerks, customers, or managers. Most of us are information system end users. And most end users in business are **knowledge workers,** that is, people who spend most of their time communicating and collaborating in teams and workgroups and creating, using, and distributing information.
- **IS specialists** are people who develop and operate information systems. They include systems analysts, software developers, system operators, and other managerial, technical, and clerical IS personnel. Briefly, systems analysts design information systems based on the information requirements of end users, software developers create computer programs based on the specifications of systems analysts, and system operators help to monitor and operate large computer systems and networks.

Hardware Resources

The concept of **hardware resources** includes all physical devices and materials used in information processing. Specifically, it includes not only **machines,** such as computers and other equipment, but also all data **media,** that is, tangible objects on which data are recorded, from sheets of paper to magnetic or optical disks. Examples of hardware in computer-based information systems are:

Figure 1.6

Examples of information system resources and products.

Information Systems Resources and Products
People Resources Specialists—systems analysts, software developers, system operators. End Users—anyone else who uses information systems.
Hardware Resources Machines—computers, video monitors, magnetic disk drives, printers, optical scanners. Media—floppy disks, magnetic tape, optical disks, plastic cards, paper forms.
Software Resources Programs—operating system programs, spreadsheet programs, word processing programs, payroll programs. Procedures—data entry procedures, error correction procedures, paycheck distribution procedures.
Data Resources Product descriptions, customer records, employee files, inventory databases.
Network Resources Communications media, communications processors, network access and control software.
Information Products Management reports and business documents using text and graphics displays, audio responses, and paper forms.

- **Computer systems,** which consist of central processing units containing microprocessors, and a variety of interconnected peripheral devices. Examples are hand-held, laptop, or desktop microcomputer systems, midrange computer systems, and large mainframe computer systems.

- **Computer peripherals,** which are devices such as a keyboard or electronic mouse for input of data and commands, a video screen or printer for output of information, and magnetic or optical disks for storage of data resources.

Software Resources

The concept of **software resources** includes all sets of information processing instructions. This generic concept of software includes not only the sets of operating instructions called **programs,** which direct and control computer hardware, but also the sets of information processing instructions called **procedures** that people need.

It is important to understand that even information systems that don't use computers have a software resource component. This is true even for the information systems of ancient times, or the manual and machine-supported information systems still used in the world today. They all require software resources in the form of information processing instructions and procedures in order to properly capture, process, and disseminate information to their users.

The following are examples of software resources:

- **System software,** such as an operating system program, which controls and supports the operations of a computer system.

- **Application software,** which are programs that direct processing for a particular use of computers by end users. Examples are a sales analysis program, a payroll program, and a word processing program.

- **Procedures,** which are operating instructions for the people who will use an information system. Examples are instructions for filling out a paper form or using a software package.

Data Resources

Data are more than the raw material of information systems. The concept of data resources has been broadened by managers and information systems professionals.

They realize that data constitute valuable organizational resources. Thus, you should view data as **data resources** that must be managed effectively to benefit all end users in an organization.

Data can take many forms, including traditional alphanumeric data, composed of numbers and alphabetical and other characters that describe business transactions and other events and entities. Text data, consisting of sentences and paragraphs used in written communications; image data, such as graphic shapes and figures; and audio data, the human voice and other sounds, are also important forms of data.

The data resources of information systems are typically organized, stored, and accessed by a variety of data resource management technologies into:

- Databases that hold processed and organized data.
- Knowledge bases that hold knowledge in a variety of forms such as facts, rules, and case examples about successful business practices.

For example, data about sales transactions may be accumulated, processed, and stored in a web-enabled sales database that can be accessed for sales analysis reports by managers and marketing professionals. Knowledge bases are used by knowledge management systems and expert systems to share knowledge or give expert advice on specific subjects. We will explore these concepts further in later chapters.

Data versus Information. The word **data** is the plural of *datum*, though data commonly represents both singular and plural forms. Data are raw facts or observations, typically about physical phenomena or business transactions. For example, a spacecraft launch or the sale of an automobile would generate a lot of data describing those events. More specifically, data are objective measurements of the *attributes* (the characteristics) of *entities* (such as people, places, things, and events).

Example	Business transactions such as buying a car or an airline ticket can produce a lot of data. Just think of the hundreds of facts needed to describe the characteristics of the car you want and its financing, or the details for even the simplest airline reservation. ●

People often use the terms *data* and *information* interchangeably. However, it is better to view data as raw material resources that are processed into finished information products. Then we can define **information** as data that have been converted into a meaningful and useful context for specific end users. Thus, data are usually subjected to a value-added process (we call *data processing* or *information processing*) where (1) its form is aggregated, manipulated, and organized; (2) its content is analyzed and evaluated; and (3) it is placed in a proper context for a human user. So you should view information as processed data placed in a context that gives it value for specific end users.

Example	Names, quantities, and dollar amounts recorded on sales forms represent data about sales transactions. However, a sales manager may not regard these as information. Only after such facts are properly organized and manipulated can meaningful sales information be furnished, specifying, for example, the amount of sales by product type, sales territory, or salesperson. ●

Network Resources

Telecommunications technologies and networks like the Internet, intranets, and extranets have become essential to the successful electronic business and commerce operations of all types of organizations and their computer-based information systems. Telecommunications networks consist of computers, communications processors, and other devices interconnected by communications media and controlled by communications software. The concept of **network resources** emphasizes that communications technologies and networks are a fundamental resource component of all information systems. Network resources include:

- **Communications media.** Examples include twisted-pair wire, coaxial cable, and fiber-optic cable; and microwave, cellular, and satellite wireless technologies.
- **Network support.** This generic category includes the people and all of the hardware, software, and data technologies that directly support the operation and use of a communications network. Examples include communications processors such as modems and internetwork processors, and communications control software such as network operating systems and Internet browser packages.

Information System Activities

Let's take a closer look now at each of the basic **information processing** (or **data processing**) activities that occur in information systems. You should be able to recognize input, processing, output, storage, and control activities taking place in any information system you are studying. Figure 1.7 lists business examples that illustrate each of these information system activities.

Input of Data Resources

Data about business transactions and other events must be captured and prepared for processing by the **input** activity. Input typically takes the form of *data entry* activities such as recording and editing. End users typically enter data directly into a computer system, or record data about transactions on some type of physical medium such as a paper form. This usually includes a variety of editing activities to ensure that they have recorded data correctly. Once entered, data may be transferred onto a machine-readable medium such as a magnetic disk until needed for processing.

For example, data about sales transactions can be recorded on source documents such as paper sales order forms. (A **source document** is the original formal record of a transaction.) Alternately, salespersons can capture sales data using computer keyboards or optical scanning devices; they are visually prompted to enter data correctly by video displays. This provides them with a more convenient and efficient **user interface,** that is, methods of end user input and output with a computer system. Methods such as optical scanning and displays of menus, prompts, and fill-in-the-blanks formats make it easier for end users to enter data correctly into an information system.

Processing of Data into Information

Data are typically subjected to **processing** activities such as calculating, comparing, sorting, classifying, and summarizing. These activities organize, analyze, and manipulate data, thus converting them into information for end users. The quality of any data stored in an information system must also be maintained by a continual process of correcting and updating activities.

Figure 1.7

Business examples of the basic activities of information systems.

Information System Activities
● **Input.** Optical scanning of bar-coded tags on merchandise.
● **Processing.** Calculating employee pay, taxes, and other payroll deductions.
● **Output.** Producing reports and displays about sales performance.
● **Storage.** Maintaining records on customers, employees, and products.
● **Control.** Generating audible signals to indicate proper entry of sales data.

Example	Data received about a purchase can be (1) *added* to a running total of sales results, (2) *compared* to a standard to determine eligibility for a sales discount, (3) *sorted* in numerical order based on product identification numbers, (4) *classified* into product categories (such as food and nonfood items), (5) *summarized* to provide a sales manager with information about various product categories, and, finally, (6) used to *update* sales records. ●

Output of Information Products

Information in various forms is transmitted to end users and made available to them in the **output** activity. The goal of information systems is the production of appropriate **information products** for end users. Common information products include messages, reports, forms, and graphic images, which may be provided by video displays, audio responses, paper products, and multimedia. We routinely use the information provided by these products as we work in organizations and live in society. For example, a sales manager may view a video display to check on the performance of a salesperson, accept a computer-produced voice message by telephone, and receive a printout of monthly sales results.

Information Quality

What characteristics would make information products valuable and useful to you? One way to answer this important question is to examine the characteristics or attributes of **information quality.** Information that is outdated, inaccurate, or hard to understand would not be very meaningful, useful, or valuable to you or other end users. People want information of high quality, that is, information products whose characteristics, attributes, or qualities help to make the information more valuable to them. It is useful to think of information as having the three dimensions of time, content, and form. Figure 1.8 summarizes the important attributes of information quality and groups them into these three dimensions.

Storage of Data Resources

Storage is a basic system component of information systems. Storage is the information system activity in which data and information are retained in an organized manner for later use. For example, just as written text material is organized into words, sentences, paragraphs, and documents, stored data are commonly organized into fields, records, files, and databases. This facilitates its later use in processing or its retrieval as output when needed by users of a system. These logical data elements are shown in Figure 1.9 and are discussed further in Chapter 13.

Control of System Performance

An important information system activity is the **control** of its performance. An information system should produce feedback about its input, processing, output, and storage activities. This feedback must be monitored and evaluated to determine if the system is meeting established performance standards. Then appropriate system activities must be adjusted so that proper information products are produced for end users.

For example, a manager may discover that subtotals of sales amounts in a sales report do not add up to total sales. This might mean that data entry or processing procedures need to be corrected. Then changes would have to be made to ensure that all sales transactions would be properly captured and processed by a sales information system.

Recognizing Information Systems

As a business professional, you should be able to recognize the fundamental components of information systems you encounter in the real world. This means that you should be able to identify:

- The people, hardware, software, data, and network resources they use.
- The types of information products they produce.

Figure 1.8

A summary of the attributes of information quality. This outlines the attributes that should be present in high-quality information products.

Time Dimension

Timeliness	Information should be provided when it is needed
Currency	Information should be up-to-date when it is provided
Frequency	Information should be provided as often as needed
Time Period	Information can be provided about past, present, and future time periods

Content Dimension

Accuracy	Information should be free from errors
Relevance	Information should be related to the information needs of a specific recipient for a specific situation
Completeness	All the information that is needed should be provided
Conciseness	Only the information that is needed should be provided
Scope	Information can have a broad or narrow scope, or an internal or external focus
Performance	Information can reveal performance by measuring activities accomplished, progress made, or resources accumulated

Form Dimension

Clarity	Information should be provided in a form that is easy to understand
Detail	Information can be provided in detail or summary form
Order	Information can be arranged in a predetermined sequence
Presentation	Information can be presented in narrative, numeric, graphic, or other forms
Media	Information can be provided in the form of printed paper documents, video displays, or other media

- The way they perform input, processing, output, storage, and control activities.

This kind of understanding will help you be a better user, developer, and manager of information systems. And that, as we have pointed out in this chapter, is important to your future success as a manager, entrepreneur, or professional in business.

Analyzing Kepler's Information Systems

Refer back to the Real World Case on Kepler's Books and Magazines on page 5. Now let's try to recognize or visualize the resources used, activities performed, and information products produced by their information systems.

IS Resources. People resources include end users like Kepler's customers, employees, business partners, and owner Clark Kepler, and the IS specialists they must hire or contract with to develop and maintain their computer network and Web site. Hardware, software, and network resources include the PCs, servers, E-business and E-commerce software, and other network support components they need to operate their business and run their storewide computer network and E-commerce Web site. Data resources would include files and databases of data about their customers, products, sales, and inventory and other necessary business information.

Figure 1.9

Logical data elements. This
is a common method of
organizing stored data in
information systems.

■ A **field** is a grouping of characters that represent a
characteristic of a person, place, thing, or event.
For example, an employee's *name field*.

■ A **record** is a collection of interrelated fields. For
example, an employee's *payroll record* might
consist of a name field, a Social Security number
field, a department field, and a salary field.

■ A **file** is a collection of interrelated records. For
example, a *payroll file* might consist of the payroll
records of all employees of a firm.

■ A **database** is an integrated collection of interrelated
records or files. For example, the *personnel database*
of a business might contain payroll, performance review,
and career development files.

Information Products. The information products we can most easily visualize are
the displays on customer and employee PCs of information on customer accounts
and bookstore products and services provided by the E-commerce Web site or the
in-house E-business systems. Printouts from Amazon.com's book listings brought in
by customers are another form of information product.

IS Activities. Some of the input activities we can visualize are the input of Web
site navigation clicks and E-commerce and E-business data entries, selections, and
queries made by customers and employees. Processing activities are accomplished
whenever customer PCs and bookstore and Web site PCs and servers execute the
programs that constitute Kepler's E-commerce and E-business software. Output
activities primarily involve the display or printing of information products mentioned earlier. Storage activities take place whenever E-commerce or traditional
business data is stored in the files and databases on the disk drives of customer, bookstore, or Web site PCs and servers. Finally, we can visualize several control activities, including the use of passwords and other security codes by customers and
employees for entry into Kepler's Web site and bookstore databases.

So you see, analyzing an information system to identify its basic components is
not a difficult task. Just identify the resources that the information system uses, the
information processing activities it performs, and the information products it produces. Then you will be better able to identify ways to improve these components,
and thus the performance of the information system itself. That's a goal that every
business professional should strive to attain.

Foundation Concepts: Business Applications, Development, and Management

The Fundamental Roles of IS Applications in Business

There are three fundamental reasons for all business applications of information technology. They are found in the three vital roles that information systems can perform for a business enterprise.

- Support of its business processes and operations.
- Support of decision making by its employees and managers.
- Support of its strategies for competitive advantage.

We will introduce these roles and applications in this chapter, and cover them in more detail later. The strategic applications of information systems for competitive advantage will be covered in Chapter 2. Business applications of information technology for electronic business operations, electronic commerce, enterprise collaboration, and decision making will be discussed in Chapters 3, 4, 5, and 6.

Analyzing CNET and Others

Read the Real World Case on CNET, Oxygen Media, USA Networks, and Dell Computer on the next page. We can learn a lot about the fundamental roles of information systems applications in business from this example. See Figure 1.10.

The leaders of several leading companies have learned valuable business lessons from their major E-commerce initiatives during the past few years. Halsey Minor of CNET learned the importance of a strong business vision and management throughout a company and of expecting and preparing for the worst. Geraldine Laybourne of Oxygen Media learned the importance of sticking to the business vision she knew was vital for the success of her company, and the challenges of using fast-changing technologies in a technology-intensive business. Barry Diller of USA Networks learned that devising low-cost customer acquisition models was more important than the speed of E-commerce development. And Michael Dell of Dell

Figure 1.10

Halsey Minor, founder of CNET, learned the importance of strong management and of expecting and preparing for the worst.

Gail Halaban/Saba.

CNET, Oxygen Media, USA Networks, and Dell Computer: Business Lessons of E-Commerce Warriors

Halsey Minor, founder of CNET and chairman and CEO of 12 Entrepreneuring

What's the single biggest lesson you'd pass on to someone just starting out in this business?

The one thing I always used to say in the early days at CNET was that big companies are built on lots of small disappointments. One of the things I noticed two years ago was nobody expected any sort of rough seas, and the world just isn't so. I think that a lot of people didn't anticipate the worst, and they didn't have enough money in the bank, and they're not going to make it. I think that always in business you need to expect and prepare for the worst. In the end, that's what separates the survivors from those who don't.

Were there things you dismissed as trivial that turned out to be critical to your business?

I was very young when I started CNET, and I don't think I realized the degree to which strong management from top to bottom within an organization is the single greatest determinant of success, much more so than hard work or vision.

Geraldine Laybourne, co-founder, chairman, and CEO of Oxygen Media

What is the single biggest lesson you'd pass on to someone just starting out in this business?

The biggest piece of advice I'd give to someone, even myself, would be to stick to your guns. We were smart enough to know that we should have a cable business. We were encouraged by some bankers to just be an Internet company. I just couldn't get it through my thick skull how that would work. I just hung on to an old-fashioned idea that we had to figure out a business plan that would get to profitability. I couldn't see that without a stable leg in the cable business. Now it looks very smart that we did that. I'm proud of the fact that we stuck to our guns on that. But I would have liked to have stuck to my guns even more in not being hurried into attacking as wide a front of content as we attacked.

Barry Diller, chairman and CEO of USA Networks

What was the biggest mistake you made?

For a period of time, the idea that speed is everything had currency. Speed has always been important, and in many situations you certainly want to move faster than the next fellow. But making it the rule in the business process is wrong. You need to listen to nuance; there are important things that you recognize when you are not speeding for speed's sake. A lot of companies were out there running a race where the winner didn't win anything.

We got caught up in that race for a time. We said, "Oh my God, we have to establish online retail businesses really quickly—a jewelry store, an outlet store, and more." We entrusted the development to a group of people, and they blew through tens of millions of dollars. Finally, we realized that if they kept going they would have spent over $100 million, and we said, "Are you out of your minds?" And they said, "Well, you said you wanted it quickly." Yes, we did, but at what cost? How fast you should move depends on how much money is at stake. These people couldn't understand this—it hadn't even occurred to them. We just shut it right down.

What do you use instead of speed as a guiding principle?

We've invested our Internet money in areas where it doesn't cost more to acquire the customer than he's going to spend with you. We got into hotel reservations, Ticketmaster, Citysearch—businesses with affiliated networks and other low-cost customer acquisition models. It's a more natural way to grow an online business.

Michael Dell, founder, chairman, and CEO of Dell Computer

In the early days of the Internet, was there anything you thought was really important that turned out not to be? And vice versa?

We're still in the early days of the Internet. However, I think a lot of people initially thought that the E in E-business was more important that the business part. It's pretty clear now that the direct nature of the Internet helps make businesses more efficient and helps improve the spread of information and communication. We found that it really furthered the direct way in which we deal with our customers.

What has been the biggest waste of money?

The biggest waste of money has been all the investment in companies with so-called new-economy business models. Business fundamentals haven't changed, and a lot of investors lost sight of that—and are paying for it.

Case Study Questions

1. What three business lessons revealed in this case do you feel are most important for an E-business company? Why?

2. What mistakes in the development process and management of information technology do you see in this case? What management solutions could have avoided such problems? Explain.

3. What other business lessons have you learned from the failures of many dot-com companies?

Source: Adapted from Colleen Bazdarich, et al., "If I Knew Then, What I Know Now," *eCompany*, March 2001, pp. 71–80.

Figure 1.11

The three major roles of the business applications of information systems. Information systems provide an organization with support for business processes, operations, decision making, and competitive advantage.

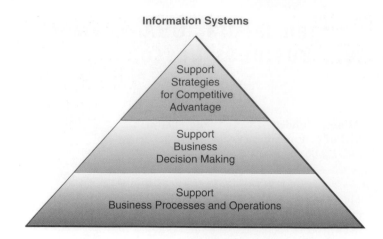

Information Systems

Support Strategies for Competitive Advantage

Support Business Decision Making

Support Business Processes and Operations

Computer learned that the Internet can significantly improve the efficiency, communications, and customer support provided by a business, and in his case, give his company a major competitive advantage.

Figure 1.11 illustrates the three major roles of the business applications of information systems. Let's look at a retail store as a good example of how these three fundamental roles can be implemented by a business.

Example

As a consumer, you have to deal regularly with the information systems that support business operations at the many retail stores where you shop. For example, most retail stores now use computer-based information systems to help them record customer purchases, keep track of inventory, pay employees, buy new merchandise, and evaluate sales trends. Store operations would grind to a halt without the support of such information systems.

Information systems also help store managers and other business professionals make better decisions and attempt to gain a competitive advantage. For example, decisions on what lines of merchandise need to be added or discontinued, or on what kind of investment they require, are typically made after an analysis provided by computer-based information systems. This not only supports the decision making of store managers, buyers, and others, but also helps them look for ways to gain an advantage over other retailers in the competition for customers. For example, Figure 1.12 illustrates a financial forecast report produced by a management information system.

Gaining a strategic advantage over competitors requires innovative use of information technology. For example, store management might make a decision to install touch-screen kiosks in all of their stores, with links to their E-commerce website for online shopping. This might attract new customers and build customer loyalty because of the ease of shopping and buying merchandise provided by such information systems. Thus, strategic information systems can help provide products and services that give a business a comparative advantage over its competitors. ●

Trends in Information Systems

The business applications of information systems have expanded significantly over the years. Figure 1.13 summarizes these changes.

Until the 1960s, the role of most information systems was simple: transaction processing, record-keeping, accounting, and other *electronic data processing* (EDP) applications. Then another role was added, as the concept of *management information systems* (MIS) was conceived. This new role focused on developing business applications that provided managerial end users with predefined management reports that would give managers the information they needed for decision-making purposes.

Figure 1.12

A financial forecast report produced by a management information system.

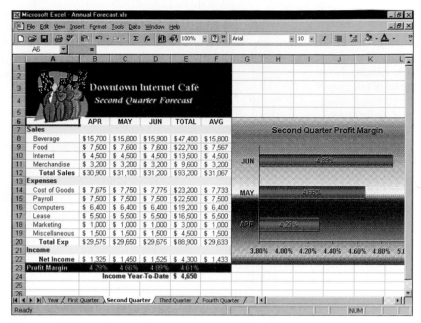

Courtesy of Microsoft.

By the 1970s, it was evident that the prespecified information products produced by such management information systems were not adequately meeting many of the decision-making needs of management. So the concept of *decision support systems* (DSS) was born. The new role for information systems was to provide managerial end users with ad hoc and interactive support of their decision-making processes. This support would be tailored to the unique decision-making styles of managers as they confronted specific types of problems in the real world.

In the 1980s, several new roles for information systems appeared. First, the rapid development of microcomputer processing power, application software packages, and telecommunications networks gave birth to the phenomenon of *end user computing*. Now, end users could use their own computing resources to support their job requirements instead of waiting for the indirect support of corporate information services departments.

Second, it became evident that most top corporate executives did not directly use either the reports of management information systems or the analytical modeling capabilities of decision support systems, so the concept of *executive information systems* (EIS) was developed. These information systems attempted to give top executives an easy way to get the critical information they want, when they want it, tailored to the formats they prefer.

Third, breakthroughs occurred in the development and application of artificial intelligence (AI) techniques to business information systems. *Expert systems* (ES) and other *knowledge-based systems* forged a new role for information systems. Today, expert systems can serve as consultants to users by providing expert advice in limited subject areas.

An important new role for information systems appeared in the 1980s and continued through the 1990s. This is the concept of a strategic role for information systems, sometimes called *strategic information systems* (SIS). In this concept, information technology becomes an integral component of business processes, products, and services that help a company gain a competitive advantage in the global marketplace.

Finally, the rapid growth of the Internet, intranets, extranets, and other interconnected global networks of the 1990s has dramatically changed the capabilities of information systems in business at the beginning of the twenty-first century. Internetworked enterprise and global **electronic business and commerce** systems are

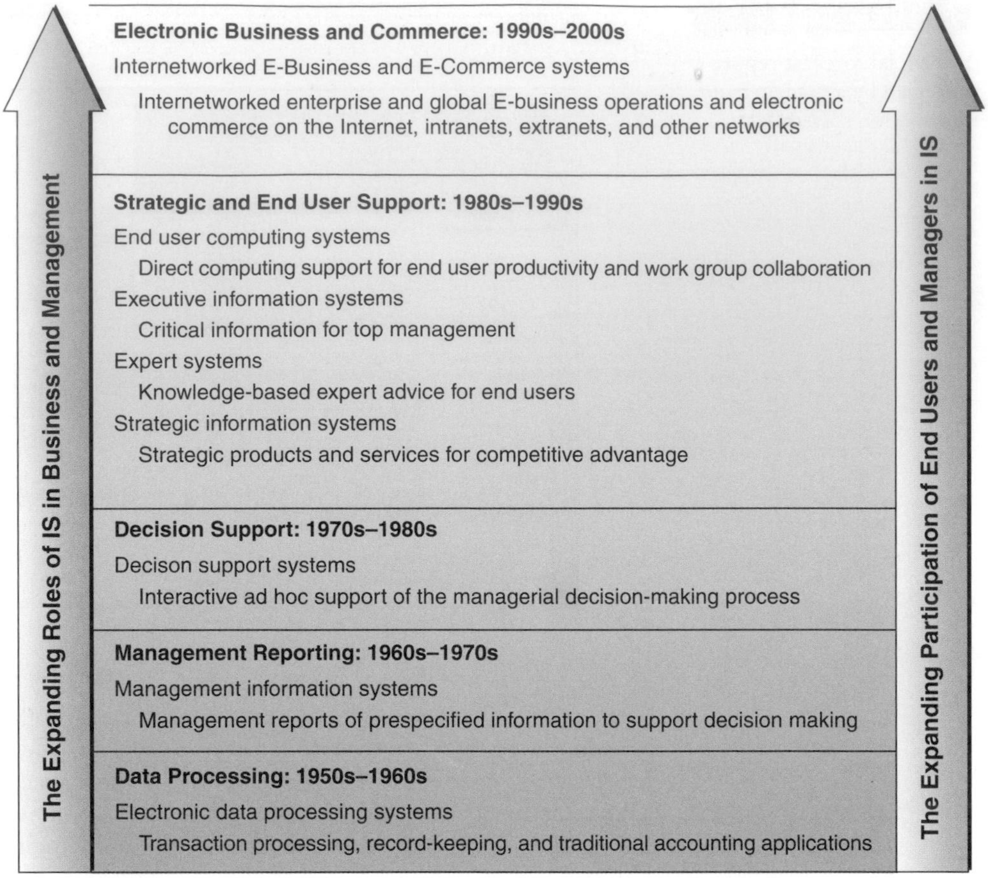

Figure 1.13

The expanding roles of the business applications of information systems. Note how the roles of computer-based information systems have expanded over time. Also, note the impact of these changes on the end users and managers of an organization.

The Expanding Roles of IS in Business and Management

The Expanding Participation of End Users and Managers in IS

Electronic Business and Commerce: 1990s–2000s

Internetworked E-Business and E-Commerce systems

Internetworked enterprise and global E-business operations and electronic commerce on the Internet, intranets, extranets, and other networks

Strategic and End User Support: 1980s–1990s

End user computing systems

Direct computing support for end user productivity and work group collaboration

Executive information systems

Critical information for top management

Expert systems

Knowledge-based expert advice for end users

Strategic information systems

Strategic products and services for competitive advantage

Decision Support: 1970s–1980s

Decison support systems

Interactive ad hoc support of the managerial decision-making process

Management Reporting: 1960s–1970s

Management information systems

Management reports of prespecified information to support decision making

Data Processing: 1950s–1960s

Electronic data processing systems

Transaction processing, record-keeping, and traditional accounting applications

revolutionizing the operations and management of today's business enterprises. Let's take a closer look at this development.

The E-Business Enterprise

There is an overriding change in information technology on whose importance business executives, academicians, and technologists all agree. The explosive growth of the Internet and related technologies and applications is revolutionizing the way businesses are operated and people work, and how information technology supports business operations and end user work activities.

Businesses are becoming **E-business enterprises.** The Internet and Internet-like networks—inside the enterprise **(intranets),** and between an enterprise and its trading partners **(extranets)**—have become the primary information technology infrastructure that supports the business operations of many companies. E-business enterprises rely on such technologies to (1) reengineer and revitalize internal business processes, (2) implement electronic commerce systems among businesses and their customers and suppliers, and (3) promote enterprise collaboration among business teams and workgroups. Figure 1.14 illustrates how an E-business enterprise depends on the Internet, intranets, extranets, and other information technologies to implement and manage E-business operations and electronic commerce and collaboration. Thus in this text, we can define **E-business** as the use of Internet technologies to internetwork and empower business processes, electronic commerce, and enterprise communication and collaboration within a company and with its customers, suppliers, and other business stakeholders.

Enterprise collaboration systems involve the use of groupware tools to support communication, coordination, and collaboration among the members of networked

Figure 1.14   An E-business enterprise depends on the Internet, intranets, and extranets to implement and manage electronic business operations, enterprise collaboration, and electronic commerce.

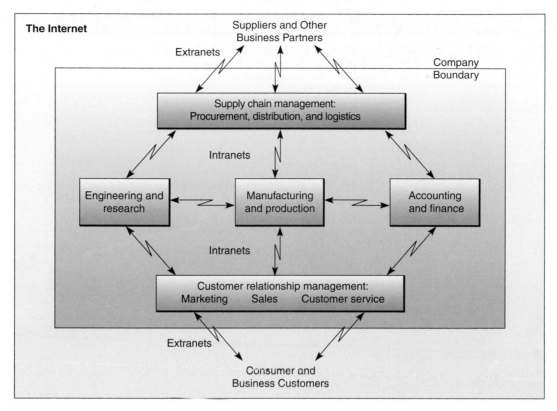

teams and workgroups. An E-business enterprise depends on intranets, the Internet, extranets, and other networks to implement such systems. For example, employees and external consultants may form a *virtual team* that uses a corporate intranet and an extranet for electronic mail, videoconferencing, electronic discussion groups, and Web pages of work-in-progress information to collaborate on business projects.

Electronic commerce is the buying and selling, and marketing and servicing of products, services, and information over a variety of computer networks. An E-business enterprise uses the Internet, intranets, extranets, and other networks to support every step of the commercial process. This might include everything from advertising, sales, and customer support on the World Wide Web, to Internet security and payment mechanisms that ensure completion of delivery and payment processes. For example, electronic commerce systems include Internet websites for online sales, extranet access of inventory databases by large customers, and the use of corporate intranets by sales reps to access customer records for customer relationship management.

Figure 1.15 is a sample of the E-commerce applications of several top-rated companies. Notice the broad range of products and services that these successful companies offer. This should give you a good idea of how versatile Internet technologies are as an information technology platform on which to base a variety of E-business strategies. Now let's look in more detail at how one company is using the Internet for electronic commerce.

Figure 1.15 The E-commerce applications of several top-rated companies. Notice the range of products and services they offer to their online customers.

E-Commerce Site	Markets	Types of Products
Amazon.com	Business-to-consumer	**Physical goods:** books, music, videos, toys, electronics, home improvement **Information content:** articles, chats **Services:** auctions, gift services
Barnes andnoble.com	Business-to-consumer	**Physical goods:** books, music, videos, software, magazines **Information content:** articles, chats **Services:** product recommendations, Northern Light search service
eBay.com	Consumer-to-consumer, business-to-consumer	**Services:** auction specialist
CVS.com	Business-to-consumer	**Physical goods:** health, beauty, wellness products; greeting cards **Services:** ordering and shipment of prescription drugs and other products, Kodak photo services
Drugstore.com	Business-to-consumer	**Physical goods:** health, beauty, wellness products **Services:** ordering, shipment of prescription drugs and other products
Cisco.com	Business-to-consumer	**Physical goods:** computer Web-based networking products **Information content:** company-related **Services:** international product ordering, distribution
Etrade	Business-to-consumer, business-to-business	**Information content:** stock quotes, investment information **Services:** financial services
Fidelity.com	Business-to-consumer, business-to-business	**Information content:** stock quotes, investment information **Services:** financial investments

Source: Adapted from Jacquiline Emigh, "E-Commerce Strategies," *Computerworld*, August 16, 1999, p. 53. Copyright 1999 by Computerworld, Inc., Framingham, MA 01701. Reprinted from *Computerworld*.

American Airlines: Moving into E-Commerce

Like many other companies, American Airlines offers a popular website (www.aa.com) that propelled them into electronic commerce on the Internet. First, American analyzed the compelling business reasons for a business website. Would it save money, improve customer service, build customer loyalty, shorten time to market, or transform distribution channels? Then, they decided to build a website that their customers would find useful, move them into E-commerce, and reduce the company's customer service costs. See Figure 1.16.

American Airlines spends millions of dollars each year to staff their toll-free customer service telephone systems. A large percentage of calls are not from customers wanting to book flights. Instead, many calls are from people wanting information such as how to get to the airport, how to travel with a pet, or whether they can take their skis along on a flight. American realized that many of their regular customers had computers at work or at home that were connected to the Internet. They assumed correctly that most of those customers would rather get the information they needed directly from the Web than call in and probably wait in line for answers.

So American's top-rated website posts travel-related information such as airport layouts and logistics, aircraft seating charts, listings of in-flight movies, city ticket office locations, and flight arrival and departure times. Frequent fliers can also check the status of their accounts. Then in a major move into full E-commerce, American added online booking and electronic ticketing, so their customers can make and pay for flight reservations on the Web [14].

Figure 1.16

The website home page (www.aa.com) of American Airlines.

Courtesy of American Airlines.

Types of Information Systems

Conceptually, the applications of information systems in the real world can be classified in several different ways. For example, several types of information systems can be classified as either operations or management information systems. Figure 1.17 illustrates this conceptual classification of information systems applications. Information systems are categorized this way to spotlight the major roles each plays in the operations and management of a business. Let's look briefly at some examples of how information systems exist in the business world.

Figure 1.17

Operations and management classifications of information systems. Note how this conceptual overview emphasizes the main purpose of information systems that support business operations and managerial decision making.

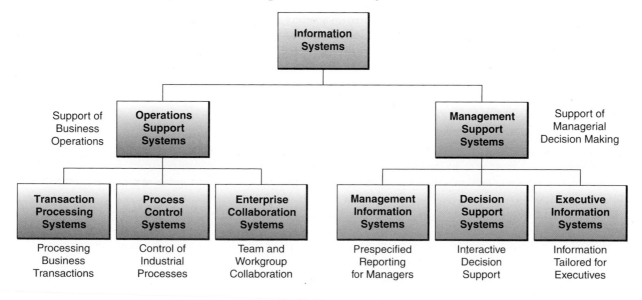

Operations Support Systems

Information systems have always been needed to process data generated by, and used in, business operations. Such **operations support systems** produce a variety of information products for internal and external use. However, they do not emphasize producing the specific information products that can best be used by managers. Further processing by management information systems is usually required. The role of a business firm's operations support systems is to efficiently process business transactions, control industrial processes, support enterprise communications and collaboration, and update corporate databases. See Figure 1.18.

Transaction processing systems are an important example of operations support systems that record and process data resulting from business transactions. They process transactions in two basic ways. In *batch processing*, transactions data are accumulated over a period of time and processed periodically. In *real-time* (or online) processing, data are processed immediately after a transaction occurs. For example, point-of-sale (POS) systems at many retail stores use electronic cash register terminals to electronically capture and transmit sales data over telecommunications links to regional computer centers for immediate (real-time) or nightly (batch) processing. See Figure 1.19.

Process control systems monitor and control physical processes. For example, a petroleum refinery uses electronic sensors linked to computers to continually monitor chemical processes and make instant (real-time) adjustments that control the refinery process. **Enterprise collaboration systems** enhance team and workgroup communications and productivity, and are sometimes called *office automation systems*. For example, knowledge workers in a project team may use electronic mail to send and receive electronic messages, and videoconferencing to hold electronic meetings to coordinate their activities.

Management Support Systems

When information system applications focus on providing information and support for effective decision making by managers, they are called **management support systems.** Providing information and support for decision making by all types of managers and business professionals is a complex task. Conceptually, several major types of information systems support a variety of decision-making responsibilities: (1) management information systems, (2) decision support systems, and (3) executive information systems. See Figure 1.20.

Management information systems provide information in the form of reports and displays to managers and many business professionals. For example, sales managers may use their networked computers and Web browsers to get instantaneous displays about the sales results of their products and to access their corporate intranet for daily sales analysis reports that evaluate sales made by each salesperson. **Decision support systems** give direct computer support to managers during the decision-making process. For example, advertising managers may use an electronic spreadsheet program to do what-if analysis as they test the impact of alternative advertising budgets on the forecasted sales of new products. **Executive information**

Figure 1.18   A summary of operations support systems with examples.

Operations Support Systems

- **Transaction processing systems.** Process data resulting from business transactions, update operational databases, and produce business documents. Examples: sales and inventory processing and accounting systems.
- **Process control systems.** Monitor and control industrial processes. Examples: petroleum refining, power generation, and steel production systems.
- **Enterprise collaboration systems.** Support team, workgroup, and enterprise communications and collaboration. Examples: E-mail, chat, and videoconferencing groupware systems.

Figure 1.19

Figure 1.19

QuickBooks is a popular accounting package that automates small business accounting transaction processing while providing business owners with management reports.

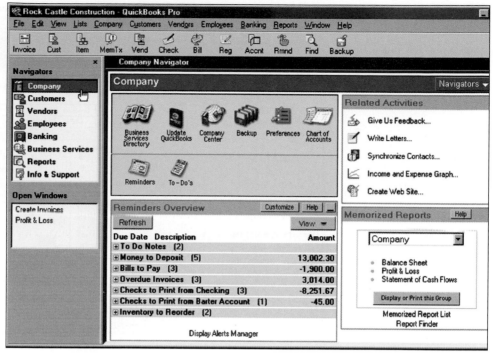

Courtesy of QuickBooks.

systems provide critical information from a wide variety of internal and external sources in easy-to-use displays to executives and managers. For example, top executives may use touchscreen terminals to instantly view text and graphics displays that highlight key areas of organizational and competitive performance. See Figure 1.21.

Other Classifications of Information Systems

Several other categories of information systems can support either operations or management applications. For example, **expert systems** can provide expert advice for operational chores like equipment diagnostics, or managerial decisions such as loan portfolio management. **Knowledge management systems** are knowledge-based information systems that support the creation, organization, and dissemination of business knowledge to employees and managers throughout a company. Information systems that focus on operational and managerial applications in support of basic business functions such as accounting or marketing are known as **functional business systems**. Finally, **strategic information systems** apply information technology to a firm's products, services, or business processes to help it gain a strategic advantage over its competitors.

Figure 1.20

A summary of management support systems with examples.

Management Suppor

- **Management Information systems.** Provide information in the form of prespecified reports and displays to support business decision making. Examples: sales analysis, production performance, and cost trend reporting systems.
- **Decision support systems.** Provide interactive ad hoc support for the decision-making processes of managers and other business professionals. Examples: product pricing, profitability forecasting, and risk analysis systems.
- **Executive information systems.** Provide critical information from many sources tailored to the information needs of executives. Examples: systems for easy access to analyses of business performance, actions of competitors, and economic developments to support strategic planning.

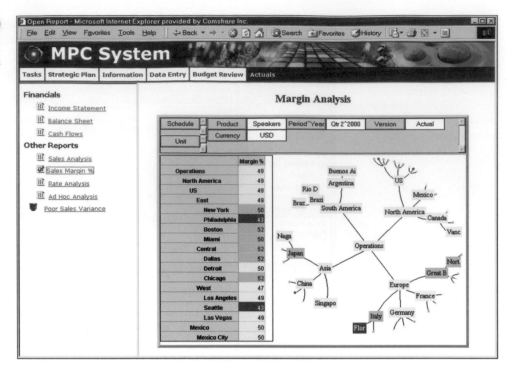

It is also important to realize that business applications of information systems in the real world are typically integrated combinations of several types of information systems we have just mentioned. That's because conceptual classifications of information systems are designed to emphasize the many different roles of information systems. In practice, these roles are combined into integrated or **cross-functional informational systems** that provide a variety of functions. Thus, most information systems are designed to produce information and support decision making for various levels of management and business functions, as well as do record-keeping and transaction processing chores. So whenever you analyze an information system, you will probably see that it provides information for a variety of managerial levels and business functions.

Figure 1.22 summarizes these categories of information system applications. We will explore many examples of the use of information systems in business in the chapters of Module II.

Figure 1.22 A summary of other categories of information systems with examples.

Other Categories of Information Systems

- **Expert systems.** Knowledge-based systems that provide expert advice and act as expert consultants to users. Examples: credit application advisor, process monitor, and diagnostic maintenance systems.
- **Knowledge management systems.** Knowledge-based systems that support the creation, organization, and dissemination of business knowledge within the enterprise. Examples: intranet access to best business practices, sales proposal strategies, and customer problem resolution systems.
- **Strategic information systems.** Support operations or management processes that provide a firm with strategic products, services, and capabilities for competitive advantage. Examples: online stock trading, shipment tracking, and E-commerce Web systems.
- **Functional business systems.** Support a variety of operational and managerial applications of the basic business functions of a company. Examples: information systems that support applications in accouting, finance, marketing, operations management, and human resource management.

Developing Business/IT Solutions

Developing information system solutions to business problems is a responsibility of many business professionals today. As a business professional, you will be responsible for proposing or developing new or improved uses of information technology for your company. As a business manager, you will also frequently manage the development efforts of information systems specialists and other business end users.

Most computer-based information systems are conceived, designed, and implemented using some form of systematic development process. Figure 1.23 shows that several major activities are involved in a complete IS development cycle. In this development process, end users and information specialists *design* information system applications based on an *analysis* of the business requirements of an organization. Examples of other activities include *investigating* the economic or technical feasibility of a proposed application, acquiring and learning how to use the software required to *implement* the new system, and making improvements to *maintain* the business value of a system.

Figure 1.24 also emphasizes that IS application development can involve producing several *prototypes* of an application, and concurrent or overlapping development processes, as illustrated by Netscape's developmental stages for a new version of its Navigator browser.

We will discuss the information systems development process further in Chapter 8. Many of the business and managerial challenges that arise in developing and implementing new uses of information technology will be explored in Chapters 7, 8, 9 and 10. Now let's look at an example of the challenges faced and overcome by a company that developed and installed a major new information system application. This example emphasizes how important good systems development practices are to a business.

A-DEC Inc.: Challenges in Systems Development

After turning on Baan Co.'s enterprise resource planning (ERP) software suite early in 1997, A-DEC expected it to automate much of their manufacturing, distribution, and financial information processing. But they soon fell behind on processing orders, building products, and then shipping the goods to dealers. "We lost a lot of business," said CIO Keith Bearden, who was brought in to manage A-DEC's information systems three months into the rollout. To get by, the Newberg, Oregon, dental equipment maker even had to fill some orders outside the system "because workers didn't understand it, and the performance was so bad," he said. At A-DEC, business changes initially were fought, Bearden said. End-user training also fell short at first, he said, and the IT department underestimated the processing power that Baan's software required.

After Beardon was hired, he pulled together a stabilization team from all parts of the company. It took about six months of systems development work to fix the performance issues by changing databases and upgrading A-DEC's servers and network. Another six months were spent redesigning business processes and training users. All that work basically doubled the cost of the project, Beardon said. "We spent a lot of money just cleaning up problems," he said. Even now, 50-plus key users spend 20 percent of their work time looking for ways to improve A-DEC's use of the software.

But the company now is getting some of the benefits it expected, Beardon said. For example, inventory levels have been cut by about 30 percent since the new system was put into use. And one of A-DEC's four product lines has been switched to a fast turnaround modular manufacturing approach that wasn't feasible before [17].

Figure 1.23

Developing information systems solutions to business problems can be viewed as a multistep process or cycle.

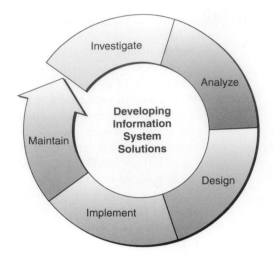

Managerial Challenges of Information Technology

Prospective managers and business professionals like you should become aware of the problems and opportunities presented by the use of information technology and learn how to effectively confront such managerial challenges. Today's internetworked E-business information systems play a vital role in the business success of an enterprise. For example, the Internet, intranets, and extranets can provide much of the IT infrastructure a business needs for E-business operations, effective management, and competitive advantage. However, Figure 1.25 emphasizes that information systems and their technologies must be managed to support the business strategies, business processes, and organizational structures and culture of an enterprise to increase its customer and business value.

Success and Failure with IT

That's because computer-based information systems, though heavily dependent on information technologies, are designed, operated, and used by people in a variety of organizational settings and business environments. Thus, the success of an informa-

Figure 1.24

Developing software and other components of an information system can be a concurrent application development process, as demonstrated by these timelines for the developmental stages and prototypes of a new version of the Navigator browser.

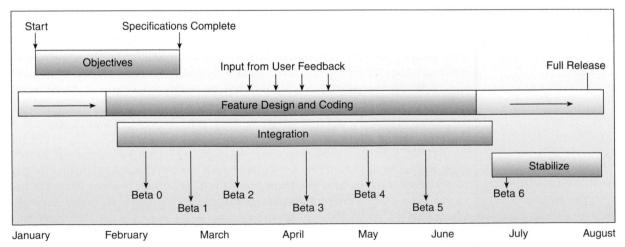

Source: Adapted and reprinted by permission of *Harvard Business Review* from Marco Iansiti and Alan MacCormack," Developing Products on Internet Time," September–October 1997, p. 112. Copyright © 1997 by the President and Fellows of Harvard College; all rights reserved.

Figure 1.25

Internetworked information systems and technologies must be managed to support E-business strategies, processes, and organizational structures and culture to increase the customer and business value of an E-business enterprise in a dynamic global business environment.

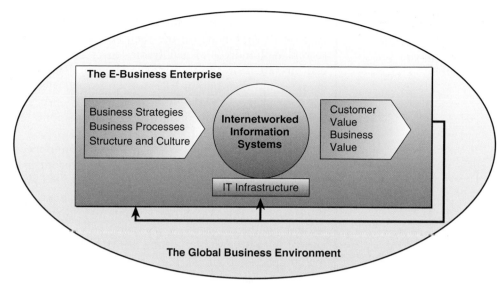

Source: Adapted from Mark Silver, M. Lynne Markus, and Cynthia Mathis Beath, "The Information Technology Interaction Model: A Foundation for the MBA Core Course," *MIS Quarterly*, September 1995, p. 366, and Allen Lee, "Inaugural Editor's Comments," *MIS Quarterly*, March 1999, pp. v–vi. Reprinted with permission from the *MIS Quarterly*.

tion system should not be measured only by its *efficiency* in terms of minimizing costs, time, and the use of information resources. Success should also be measured by the *effectiveness* of information technology in supporting an organization's business strategies, enabling its business processes, enhancing its organizational structures and culture, and increasing the customer and business value of the enterprise.

However, it is important that you realize that information technology and information systems can be mismanaged and misapplied so that IS performance problems create both technological and business failure. For example, Figure 1.26 outlines how information technology can contribute to business failure or success. Let's look at another business example.

Figure 1.26

Turning business failure i[...]cess with information technology.

From Failure to Success with IT	
The Boeing Company	**Thomson Consumer Electronics**
Business Failure Costly delays ($1.6 billion in 1997) in obtaining 6 million parts to build each aircraft with unintegrated IT systems.	**[Business] Failure** [...]s not getting quick replenishment of core [par]ts with old inventory systems.
New IT Solution Integrate entire supply chain into internal production systems.	**[New] IT Solution** [...]nand collaboration system with top retailers that link [dir]ectly into internal production and logistics systems.
Business Success Output capacity up 100% in 4 years. Aircraft lead times reduced by 60%.	**Business Success** Out of stock scenarios reduced to 1% with forecast accuracy now above 95%.

Source: Adapted from Peter Fingar, Harsha Kumar, and Tarun Sharma, *Enterprise E-commerce* (Tampa, FL: Meghan-Kiffer Press, 2000), p. 176.

Boeing and Analog Devices: IT Failure and Success	The Boeing Company embarked on a major business process reengineering campaign in 1994, buying off-the-shelf enterprise resources planning (ERP) software to replace hundreds of mainframe legacy systems used to manufacture commercial aircraft. For example, Boeing bought Baan's manufacturing, finance, purchasing, and distribution ERP software suite; Metaphase's product data management package; CIMLINC's Linkage for process planning; and Trilogy's SalesBUILDER for configuration management, along with other software packages.

The Boeing Company embarked on a major business process reengineering campaign in 1994, buying off-the-shelf enterprise resources planning (ERP) software to replace hundreds of mainframe legacy systems used to manufacture commercial aircraft. For example, Boeing bought Baan's manufacturing, finance, purchasing, and distribution ERP software suite; Metaphase's product data management package; CIMLINC's Linkage for process planning; and Trilogy's SalesBUILDER for configuration management, along with other software packages.

Fast-forward to late 1998, when Boeing announced lousy financial results and major layoffs. It predicted a pathetic pretax profit margin of only 1 to 3 percent for its commercial aircraft group by the year 2000, up from 0 percent in 1998. A precipitous decline in airplane orders by Asian airlines is the culprit according to the company. But Wall Street analysts and others watching the company say production inefficiencies, poor planning, and a host of other internal failures bear part of the responsibility for the dismal margin and poor financial results, according to articles about the project in, among others, *The New York Times* and *The Wall Street Journal*.

However, other ERP implementations have proved their worth through the positive results achieved. The ERP implementation at chip maker Analog Devices, Inc., for instance, helped the company weather tough times in 1998, when declining prices drove down revenues and otherwise put pressure on the entire semiconductor industry. Analog has continued to show progress in reducing costs in a variety of areas, including production, staffing, and inventory.

Bottom line: If the right combination of ERP software, business processes, and managerial expertise are working together, there should be a substantial financial return, as there was for Analog [11].

Ethics and IT

As a prospective manager, business professional, and knowledge worker, you should consider the **ethical responsibilities** generated by the use of information technology. For example, what uses of information technology might be considered improper, irresponsible, or harmful to other individuals or to society? What is the proper business use of the Internet and an organization's IT resources? What does it take to be a **responsible end user** of information technology? How can you protect yourself from computer crime and other risks of information technology? These are some of the questions that outline the ethical dimensions of information systems that we will discuss and illustrate with Real World Cases in Chapter 9 and other chapters of this text. Figure 1.27 outlines some of the ethical risks that may arise in the use of information technology. The following example illustrates some of the ethical challenges in the use of business resources to access the Internet.

3M Corp. and Others: Internet Ethics

Faced with international controversies over pornography and hate speech on the Internet, employers are setting policies to limit Internet usage to business purposes. They also are penalizing employees who send out abusive electronic mail, "flame" people on newsgroups, or visit inappropriate sites on the World Wide Web.

For most companies, an Internet usage policy is straightforward. It generally informs employees that their Internet access is a company resource that should be used only for their jobs. "3M's policy is simply put: that the Web must be used for business purposes. If people get on and abuse it, then you've got a problem with that individual and need to handle it," said Luke Crofoot, a marketing services supervisor at 3M in St. Paul, Minnesota.

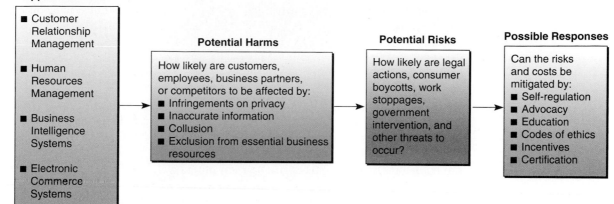

Figure 1.27 Ethical considerations of the potential harms or business risks in the business use of IT.

Firms that want more control over their employees develop detailed Internet usage policies. Companies that have detailed usage policies include the Chase Manhattan Bank NA; Johnson Controls, Inc.; Pioneer Hi-Bred International Inc.; and Monsanto Co. But some attorneys take a tougher stance. Says Neal J. Friedman, a Washington attorney who specializes in online law, "Employees need to know they have no right of privacy and no right of free speech using company resources" [18].

Challenges of IT Careers

Information technology and its uses in information systems have created interesting, highly paid, and challenging career opportunities for millions of men and women. So learning more about information technology may help you decide if you want to pursue an IT-related career. Employment opportunities in the field of information systems are excellent, as organizations continue to expand their use of information technology. However, this poses a resource management challenge to many companies, since employment surveys continually forecast shortages of qualified information systems personnel in a variety of job categories. Also, job requirements in information systems are continually changing due to dynamic developments in business and information technology. See Figure 1.28.

One major recruiter is the IT industry itself. Thousands of companies develop, manufacture, market, and service computer hardware, software, data and network products and services, or provide E-business and commerce applications and services, end user training, or business systems consulting. However, the biggest need for qualified people comes from the millions of businesses, government agencies, and other organizations that use information technology. They need many types of IS professionals to help them support the work activities and supply the information needs of their employees, managers, customers, suppliers, and other business partners. Let's take a look at IT career challenges at a leading E-commerce company.

Amazon.com: IT Career Challenges

John Vlastelca is the technical recruiting manager of Amazon.com Inc. in Seattle. He says: "We have a huge demand for people who have experience building relationships with customers online—people who bring together a retailing background and some IT background. We hire smart folks, and they are working their butts off. There is a heavy dose of informality. People aren't title-centric; the best idea wins and the career path is often vertical crossover to management or content areas.

Figure 1.28

Hiring and training people to provide IT consulting services to business is a major managerial challenge.

Index Stock Photography.

"The one thing that drives us is an obsession with the customer. What helps us make our selection decision is the question, 'Is this a technical person who views technology as a means to an end, where the end is the customer? Or does this person define him or herself as just a Java programmer?'

"But the bar is incredibly high here. It is really hard for my team to find the combination of skills—the software engineer who really understands the customer and the business. So half don't make it because they are not strong enough technically. Other reasons have to do with soft skills—being open to ideas, just raw smarts and not being passionate enough. The problem space we operate in is unexplored territory" [10].

The IS Function

In summary, successful management of information systems and technologies presents major challenges to business managers and professionals. Thus, the information systems function represents:

- A major functional area of business that is as important to business success as the functions of accounting, finance, operations management, marketing, and human resources management.

- An important contributor to operational efficiency, employee productivity and morale, and customer service and satisfaction.

- A major source of information and support needed to promote effective decision making by managers and business professionals.

- A vital ingredient in developing competitive products and services that give an organization a strategic advantage in the global marketplace.

- A dynamic, rewarding, and challenging career opportunity for millions of men and women.

- A key component of the resources, infrastructure, and capabilities of today's E-business enterprises.

Summary

- **Why Information Systems Are Important.** An understanding of the effective and responsible use and management of information systems and technologies is important for managers, business professionals, and other knowledge workers in today's internetworked enterprises. Information systems play a vital role in the E-business and E-commerce operations, enterprise collaboration and management, and strategic success of businesses that must operate in an internetworked global environment. Thus, the field of information systems has become a major functional area of business administration.

- **An IS Framework for Business Professionals.** The IS knowledge that a business manager or professional needs to know is illustrated in Figure 1.2 and covered in this chapter and text. This includes (1) *foundation concepts:* fundamental behavioral, technical, business, and managerial concepts like system components and functions, or competitive strategies; (2) *information technologies:* concepts, developments, or management issues regarding hardware, software, data management, networks, and other technologies; (3) *business applications:* major uses of IT for business processes, operations, decision making, and strategic/competitive advantage; (4) *development processes:* how end users and IS specialists develop and implement business/IT solutions to problems and opportunities arising in business; and (5) *management challenges:* how to effectively and ethically manage the IS function and IT resources to achieve top performance and business value in support of the business strategies of the enterprise.

- **System Concepts.** A system is a group of interrelated components working toward the attainment of a common goal by accepting inputs and producing outputs in an organized transformation process. Feedback is data about the performance of a system. Control is the component that monitors and evaluates feedback and makes any necessary adjustments to the input and processing components to ensure that proper output is produced.

- **An Information System Model.** An information system uses the resources of people, hardware, software, data, and networks to perform input, processing, output, storage, and control activities that convert data resources into information products. Data are first collected and converted to a form that is suitable for processing (input). Then the data are manipulated and converted into information (processing), stored for future use (storage), or communicated to their ultimate user (output) according to correct processing procedures (control).

- **IS Resources and Products.** Hardware resources include machines and media used in information processing. Software resources include computerized instructions (programs) and instructions for people (procedures). People resources include information systems specialists and users. Data resources include alphanumeric, text, image, video, audio, and other forms of data. Network resources include communications media and network support. Information products produced by an information system can take a variety of forms, including paper reports, visual displays, multimedia documents, electronic messages, graphics images, and audio responses.

- **Business Applications of Information Systems.** Information systems perform three vital roles in business firms. Business applications of IS support an organization's business processes and operations, business decision making, and strategic competitive advantage. Major application categories of information systems include operations support systems, such as transaction processing systems, process control systems, and enterprise collaboration systems, and management support systems, such as management information systems, decision support systems, and executive information systems. Other major categories are expert systems, knowledge management systems, strategic information systems, and functional business systems. However, in the real world, most application categories are combined into cross-functional information systems that provide information and support for decision making and also perform operational information processing activities. Refer to Figures 1.18, 1.20, and 1.22 for summaries of the major application categories of information systems.

Key Terms and Concepts

These are the key terms and concepts of this chapter. The page number of their first explanation is in parentheses.

1. Computer-based information system   (7)
2. Control   (9), 16
3. Data   (13)
4. Data or information processing   (14), 15
5. Data resources   (13), 15, 16
6. Developing business/IT solutions   (29)
7. E-business enterprise   (22), 23
8. Electronic business (21), 22
9. Electronic commerce   (23)
10. End user   (11)

11. Enterprise collaboration systems (22), 26

12. Extranet (22)

13. Feedback (9)

14. Hardware resources (11)

    a. Machines

    b. Media

15. Information (13)

    a. Products (15, 17)

    b. Quality (15)

16. Information system (7), 8

17. Information system activities (14)

    a. Input

    b. Processing

    c. Output

    d. Storage

    e. Control

18. Information system model (10)

19. Information technology (IT) (7)

20. Intranet (22)

21. IS knowledge needed by business professionals (4)

22. Knowledge workers (11)

23. Management challenges of IS (32)

    a. Ethics and IT (34)

    b. IT career challenges (35)

    c. IT success and failure (31)

24. Network resources (14)

25. People resources (11)

    a. IS specialists

    b. End users

26. Roles of IS applications in business (20)

    a. Support of business processes and operations

    b. Support of business decision making

    c. Support of strategies for competitive advantage

27. Software resources (12)

    a. Programs

    b. Procedures

28. System (17)

29. Trends in information systems (20)

30. Types of information systems (25)

    a. Cross-functional systems (28)

    b. Management support systems (26)

    c. Operations support systems (26)

Review Quiz

Match one of the previous key terms and concepts with one of the following brief examples or definitions. Look for the best fit for answers that seem to fit more than one key term or concept. Defend your choices.

_____ 1. You should know some fundamental concepts about information systems and their technologies, development processes, business applications, and management challenges.

_____ 2. People who spend most of their workday creating, using, and distributing information.

_____ 3. Computer hardware and software, networks, data management, and other technologies.

_____ 4. Information systems support an organization's business processes, operations, decision making, and strategies for competitive advantage.

_____ 5. Using IT to reengineer business processes to support E-business operations.

_____ 6. Using Web-based decision support systems to support sales managers.

_____ 7. Using information technology for electronic commerce to gain a strategic advantage over competitors.

_____ 8. A system that uses people, hardware, software, and network resources to collect, transform, and disseminate information within an organization.

_____ 9. An information system that uses computers and their hardware and software.

_____ 10. Anyone who uses an information system or the information it produces.

_____ 11. A company that uses the Internet, corporate intranets, and interorganizational extranets for electronic business operations, E-commerce, and enterprise collaboration.

_____ 12. The buying, selling, marketing, and servicing of products over the Internet and other networks.

_____ 13. The use of groupware tools to support collaboration among networked teams.

_____ 14. A group of interrelated components working together toward the attainment of a common goal.

_____ 15. Data about a system's performance.

_____ 16. Making adjustments to a system's components so that it operates properly.

_____ 17. Facts or observations.

_____ 18. Data that have been placed into a meaningful context for an end user.

_____ 19. The act of converting data into information.

_____ 20. An information system uses people, hardware, software, network, and data resources to perform input, processing, output, storage, and control activities that transform data resources into information products.

_____ 21. Machines and media.

_____ 22. Computers, disk drives, video monitors, and printers are examples.

_____ 23. Magnetic disks, optical disks, and paper forms are examples.

_____ 24. Programs and procedures.

_____ 25. A set of instructions for a computer.

_____ 26. A set of instructions for people.

_____ 27. End users and information systems professionals.

_____ 28. Using the keyboard of a computer to enter data.

_____ 29. Computing loan payments.

_____ 30. Printing a letter you wrote using a computer.

_____ 31. Saving a copy of the letter on a magnetic disk.

_____ 32. Having a sales receipt as proof of a purchase.

_____ 33. Information systems can be classified into operations, management, and other categories.

_____ 34. Includes transaction processing, process control, and end user collaboration systems.

_____ 35. Includes management information, decision support, and executive information systems.

_____ 36. Information systems that perform transaction processing and provide information to managers across the boundaries of functional business areas.

_____ 37. Information systems have evolved from a data processing orientation to the support of strategic decision making, end user collaboration, and electronic business and commerce.

_____ 38. Internet-like networks and websites inside a company.

_____ 39. Interorganizational Internet-like networks among trading partners.

_____ 40. You need to be a responsible end user of IT resources in your company.

_____ 41. Managing the IT resources of a company effectively and ethically to improve its business performance and value.

_____ 42. Using the Internet, intranets, and extranets as the IT platform for internal business operations, electronic commerce, and enterprise collaboration.

Discussion Questions

1. How can information technology support a company's business operations and decision making, and give them a competitive advantage? Give examples to illustrate your answer.

2. How does the use of the Internet, intranets, and extranets by an E-business enterprise support their E-commerce activities?

3. Refer to the Real World Case on Kepler's Books & Magazines in the chapter. Is a bricks-and-clicks strategy the best E-commerce model for a business today? Why or why not?

4. Why do big companies still fail in their use of information technology? What should they be doing differently?

5. How can a manager demonstrate that he or she is a responsible end user of information systems? Give several examples.

6. Refer to the Real World Case on CNET and other companies on in the chapter. What is the single biggest lesson you have learned from the failure of many pure E-commerce companies?

7. What is one major management challenge in developing IT solutions to solve business problems and meet new E-business opportunities?

8. Why are there so many conceptual classifications of information systems? Why are they typically integrated in the information systems found in the real world?

9. In what major ways have the roles of information systems applications in business expanded during the last 40 years? What is one major change you think will happen in the next 10 years?

10. Can the business use of Internet technologies help a company gain a competitive advantage? Give an example to illustrate your answer.

Application Exercises

Complete the following exercises as individual or group projects that apply chapter concepts to real world business situations.

1. Using the Internet for Business Research
Search the Internet for additional information and business examples about some of the topics or companies in this chapter. For example, use search engines like Google or Fast Search to research the latest developments in E-business, E-commerce, IT ethics and security, or IT careers. Or find and visit the websites of companies in the Real World Cases in this chapter. Look for examples of the business use of information technology in your search.
   a. Prepare a one- or two-page summary of some of your findings and the sources you used.
   b. End your paper with a few sentences describing one thing you have learned from your research that might help you in your future career in business.

2. Visiting the Smart Business Supersite
The Smart Business Supersite (www.smartbiz.com) is dubbed the "how-to resource for business" site. Nearly every colorful icon on the tool bar across the top of the home page leads to useful, relevant material such as columns on electronic privacy, violence in the workplace, and internal marketing. (See Figure 1.29.)

   You can also click on the browse button to call up a Windows-like menu of subjects. Then choose *Computing in Business* to get a precise index of all relevant material at the site. The Jobs/Careers section includes relevant articles and a message board. People Finder is a unique section that offers users a venue for locating speakers and consultants.
   a. Prepare a one- or two-page summary describing the *Computing in Business* material you found most interesting and relevant as a business end user.
   b. End your paper with a few sentences describing one thing you have learned from your research that might help you in your future career in business.

3. Jefferson State University: Recognizing IS Components
Students in the College of Business Administration of Jefferson State University use their desktop and laptop microcomputers for a variety of assignments. For example, a student may use a word processing program stored on the microcomputer system's hard disk drive and proceed to type a case study analysis. When the analysis is typed, edited, and properly formatted to an instructor's specifications, the student may save it on a floppy disk, E-mail a copy to the instructor via the Internet, and print out a copy on the system's printer. If the student tries to save the case study analysis using a file name he or she has already used for saving another document, the program will display a warning message and wait until it receives an additional command.
   Make an outline to identify the information system components in the preceding example.

Figure 1.29

The Smart Business Supersite.

Courtesy of Smart Business Supersite, © 2000.

a. Identify the people, hardware, software, network, and data resources and the information products of this information system.

b. Identify the input, processing, output, storage, and control activities that occurred.

4. Office Products Corporation: Recognizing IS Components

Office Products Corporation receives more than 10,000 customer orders a month, drawing on a combined inventory of over 1,000 office products stocked at the company's warehouse. About 60 PCs are installed at the Office Products headquarters and connected in a local area network to several IBM Netfinity servers. Orders are received by phone or mail and entered into the system by customer representatives at network computers, or they are entered directly by customers who have shopped at the electronic commerce website developed by Office Products. Entry of orders is assisted by formatted screens that help users follow data entry procedures to enter required information into the system, where it is stored on the magnetic disks of the Netfinity servers.

As the order is entered, a server checks the availability of the parts, allocates the stock, and updates customer and part databases stored on its magnetic disks. It then sends the order pick list to the warehouse printer, where it is used by warehouse personnel to fill the order. The company president has a networked PC workstation in her office, as do the controller, sales manager, inventory manager, and other executives. They use simple database management inquiry commands to get responses and reports concerning sales orders, customers, and inventory, and to review product demand and service trends.

Make an outline that identifies the information system components in Office Products' order processing system.

a. Identify the people, hardware, software, data, and network resources and the information products of this information system.

b. Identify the input, processing, output, storage, and control activities that occurred.

5. Western Chemical Corporation: Recognizing the Types and Roles of Information Systems

Western Chemical uses the Internet and an electronic commerce website to connect to its customers and suppliers, and to capture data and share information about sales orders and purchases. Sales and order data are processed immediately, and inventory and other databases are updated. Videoconferencing and electronic mail services are also provided. Data generated by a chemical refinery process are captured by sensors and processed by a computer that also suggests answers to a complex refinery problem posed by an engineer. Managers and business professionals access reports on a periodic, exception, and demand basis, and use computers to interactively assess the possible results of alternative decisions. Finally, top management can access text summaries and graphics displays that identify key elements of organizational performance and compare them to industry and competitor performance.

Western Chemical Corporation has started forming business alliances and using intranets, extranets, and the Internet to build a global electronic commerce website to offer their customers worldwide products and services. Western Chemical is in the midst of making fundamental changes to their computer-based systems to increase the efficiency of their E-business operations and their managers' ability to react quickly to changing business conditions. Make an outline that identifies:

a. How information systems support (1) business operations, (2) business decision making, (3) strategic advantage, (4) an E-business enterprise, and (5) electronic commerce at Western Chemical.

b. There are many different types of information systems at Western Chemical. Identify as many as you can in the preceding scenario. Refer to Figure 1.18, 1.20, and 1.22 to help you. Explain the reasons for your choices.

Pepsi Cola Co.: Web Marketing Strategies

Would you shop for a soft drink online? Seems like a silly question. Of all the products for sale in the universe, bottles and cans of sweet, carbonated liquid are probably the last things shoppers will want to buy on the Internet. Even frozen food has more E-potential. But soft drinks? They're cheap. They require no research to purchase. They're available on practically every street corner in the world.

So why is Pepsi-Cola Co. trying so hard online? While many traditional advertisers have dabbled in the Net, Pepsi has a range of programs on the virtual air, from music sites to banner ads to Internet sweepstakes. Though only about 3 percent of its estimated $400 million soft drink ad budget goes online, that belies the emphasis the company places on the Web. "This medium is here to stay, and we buy that," says John Vail, director of digital media and marketing for Pepsi-Cola.

One reason: Despite the difficulties in measuring on-line ad performance, Pepsi has crafted deals that already show benefits. In a barter arrangement with Yahoo! Inc. this summer, Pepsi plastered the portal's logo on 1.5 billion cans. In return, Yahoo took the cola company's already established loyalty program, Pepsi Stuff, to new heights. A co-branded web site, PepsiStuff.com let consumers collect points from bottle caps. The points were redeemable on the Web site for prizes—everything from electronic goods to concert tickets.

The results were considerable. Three million consumers logged on and registered at the PepsiStuff site, giving the cola company detailed consumer data that normally must be paid for in market research or gleaned from focus groups. Information that once took months to obtain could now be had in days. What's more, Vail was able to tweak the program while it was in progress, maintaining the right inventory of the most popular prizes. "Instead of lagtime data, we had real-time and we could react to it," says Vail. Sales volume rose 5 percent during the online promotion and the cost was about one-fifth what it had been as a mail-in project.

Pepsi has no intention of slowing its Internet rush. The Web is the medium of choice for Pepsi's prime demographic audience, those under 25. "They are going to where their customer hangs out and flashing their name," says Tom Pirko, a beverage consultant for Santa Barbara–based Bev-

mark uc. "This is aimed at flipping the next generation. For Pepsi, the Internet is serious. It's not a toy."

For consumer Shane Erstad, 29, that's good news. Intrigued by the prizes and the ability to collect the points online, he became devoted to Mountain Dew and a fan of the PepsiStuff site. Even now that the game has ended, he hasn't cut back. "I hope they repeat the promotion," he says. He can count on it, and much more.

For Pepsi knows that its E-commerce marketing strategies are a work in progress. Pepsi's online marketing road has been long and bumpy. On February 29, 1996, the company launched Pepsi World, a Web site of sponsored content designed to attract the youthful consumer. Sports and music news was mixed with online games and animation. A seven-figure publicity budget backed the debut. But it quickly became clear through focus groups and traffic numbers that Pepsi hadn't reached its target. Eyeballs were too fleeting, visitors too fickle. By the summer of 1997, Vail revamped the site to be less of a sports news digest and more of a vehicle to promote Pepsi-sponsored athletes, such as NASCAR driver Jeff Gordon.

Going forward, Pepsi plans to expand on its Web site–centric E-commerce marketing efforts. Although banner ads and other more traditional ad buys have had some success, it's the creation of engaging Pepsi Web sites that has given the brand the most traction online. For example, Vail would like to bring a virtual experience to many other Pepsi promotions, such as Choose Your Music, a current in-store create-your-own-CD promotion at participating music outlets. "We're looking ahead to the next evolution," says Vail.

Case Study Questions

1. What are the major business benefits of Pepsi's online marketing efforts?

2. Do you approve of Pepsi's "Web-centric" E-commerce marketing strategy? Why or why not?

3. Visit www.pepsistuff.com or other Pepsi websites. What else could Pepsi do to improve its web-based marketing efforts? Explain.

Source: Adapted from Ellen Neuborne, "Pepsi's Aim is True". *Business Week E.Biz*, January 22, 2001, p. EB 52.

Schilling Professional Staffing: E-Business Home Warrior

For nineteen years, Rick Schilling worked for one of the largest banks in the Philadelphia area, rising to vice president. He loved his job, he loved banking, and he intended to stay in the field for the rest of his working life. Then came the shakeout in the late 1980s as banks began to consolidate, and many bankers, including Rick Schilling, found themselves self-employed, like it or not.

He didn't—at first. But then he turned disappointment into opportunity. He now runs Schilling Professional Staffing Inc., a placement service for banking professionals, from his suburban Philadelphia home. And he's being paid so much by clients, including PNB, Summit Bank, and Sovereign Bank, that he's, well, laughing all the way to the bank.

Forty years ago, banks "had plenty of extra people around when they needed them," Schilling explains. "Today, they have no extra staff—they're being pushed too strongly for bottom line profits. So I saw a void, and I decided to try filling that void by providing professional staff on an interim basis," he says. "I began by thinking of myself as a business service which I could provide, rather than as a person needing a job," he adds. "If you market a service, rather than yourself, it's easier on the ego."

Schilling turned a bedroom of his seven-room split-level home into an office with a custom-built desk, a computer, a fax, a phone, and an Internet connection, and developed a simple marketing plan: Build on personal contacts and slowly expand. Today he has over 2,500 people in his computer's database, ready to work. He chooses to stay home-based and use his computer and the Internet to connect to customers and clients all over the globe. "I could have an office with a secretary, but I want to be virtual," he says. "I deal with people who are compatible and have the same background I do—ones who work to my high standards. When I assign somebody, it's like I'm doing the work myself. That's why I concentrated on banking—I know the people and know how they work."

Those people, he adds, are "highly trained, and hit the ground running—and are worth every penny I charge. Whenever someone says the price is too high, I graciously tell them I can't change it. Sometimes they take a few days to call back—but they do call back and we make the deal."

Schilling begins his day by going to the health club. "I'm home and working by 8:00 a.m. and then work till 6 or 7:00 p.m.," he says. "I love the freedom of working at home, doing my thing the way I want."

Doing his "thing" involves hours on his computer, the Internet, and the phone, placing his people. "When I get a possible job, I go through my computer database and decide who has the best qualifications," he explains. "Then I check by E-mail or phone to see if the person is available."

He also follows up and sees how their jobs are going, and "I call my banking clients to make sure all is well. I get e-mails all day long from people I've placed and people sending me their resumes," he adds.

At first Schilling worried that banks would hire his people full-time, which does happen in about one-third of his placements. But this has become a positive development. "I now have people that I've helped who are working in top positions all over the banking industry—and they call or E-mail me when they need someone," he says.

And since bankers tend to be conservative people who want to stay in the industry, he never seems to run out of names to add to his computer database. "I recently met a man with thirty years' experience as a bank trust security analyst working at a WaWa convenience store—and he's still hoping to get a new banking job." Shilling notes.

Being a somewhat conservative fellow himself, Schilling seems almost surprised by his good fortune. "I never approached this business as a way to make more money, but I am making more—a lot more—than when I was a vice president in the bank," he reveals. He also likes the security: "Banks always pay their bills on time, so I never have to deal with collection issues."

Case Study Questions

1. How would you rate Rick Shilling's strategies for his home E-business? Explain.

2. What information system resources and activities can you identify or visualize in Rick's E-business system?

3. If you had a home E-business, what products or services would you provide? How would information technology help you implement your E-business strategies?

Source: Adapted from Pam Blessinger, "Upfront: People," *House of Business*, January–February 2001, p. 48.

Sobeys, Reebok, and Home Depot: Success and Failure With IT

SAP AG's software applications for retailers continue to be stung by a series of high-profile installation problems that many say illustrate the complexity of trying to fit an integrated suite of enterprise resource planning (ERP) software into a retail operation. The latest example came late last month, when Canadian supermarket chain Sobeys Inc. abandoned an $89.1 million SAP Retail implementation.

"SAP Retail has insufficient core functionality . . . to effectively deal with the extremely high number of transactions in our retail operating environment," said Bill McEwan, president and CEO of the Stellarton, Nova Scotia–based retail chain.

Sobeys isn't alone. Jo-Ann Stores Inc. in Hudson, Ohio and pet supply retailer Petsmart Inc. in Phoenix last fall both attributed low financial results to problems with their SAP Retail rollouts. Both, however, said they're pleased with the system overall.

SAP officials continued to defend the capabilities of SAP Retail. Geraldine McBride, general manager of the consumer sector business unit at SAP America Inc., said the German vendor has signed up 264 retailers as customers, 128 of which have gone live.

But Greg Girard, an analyst at AMR Research Inc. in Boston, said most of the retailers are running SAP's financial and human resources applications, not SAP Retail itself. "I can't point to a single happy SAP Retail account in North America," said Girard.

SAP Retail is a good product, argues Kevin Restivo, a Canada-based analyst who works for IDC in Framingham, Massachusetts. But technology is never a "silver bullet, just part of a larger puzzle" that includes making sure internal business processes are in tune with the software's capabilities, Restivo said. That's especially true given the processing complexities faced by retailers, he added.

In late 1998, Reebok International Ltd. was the first U.S. company to go live with SAP Retail, which now supports 115 outlet stores run by the Stoughton, Massachusetts–based footwear maker. Peter Burrows, Reebok's chief technology officer, said the SAP system is producing "a very high level of stock accuracy" in the stores. But the year-long development and installation process wasn't easy and required some adjustments as the project went along, Burrows said.

The Home Depot Inc. recently completed an SAP R/3 installation in the company's Argentina operations. Gary Cochran, vice president of information services at the At-

lanta-based home improvement retailer, said he made "limited use" of SAP's consulting services. Instead Cochran put together a team of fifty top employees—IT personnel and end users. Because of the team's familiarity with their traditional legacy systems, he said, it didn't have to "face some of the configuration issues that have been problematic for other people." "It went so smoothly there was literally no ripple in corporate organization," Cochran said.

Canada's second largest supermarket chain abandoned the $89 million implementation of SAP AG's business applications for retailers after a five-day database and systems shutdown affected the company's business operations for nearly a month. McEwan said during a conference call last month that "growing pains" expected by the 1,400-store retail chain in the two-year-old project became "in fact systemic problems of a much more serious nature." McEwan, who inherited the SAP implementation when he joined Sobeys in November, added that it would have taken another two years to finish the software rollout.

The system shutdown in December resulted in "unprecedented" out-of-stock issues with products at many of Sobeys' corporate-owned stores, McEwan said. The SAP Retail software couldn't effectively deal with the "extremely high number of transactions in our retail operating environment," McEwan said. The disruption also forced Sobeys to implement work-arounds for its accounting department.

Sobeys plans to replace the SAP applications with software that can be installed more quickly and that "will fully meet all the business requirements" at the company, McEwan said.

Case Study Questions

1. What are some of the reasons retail companies are having major problems installing SAP's software?

2. What are several possible solutions to such problems? Explain.

3. What does this case demonstrate about the importance of proper development and management of IT solutions to business problems?

Source: Adapted from Lucas Merian, "Supermarket Dumps $89M SAP Project," *Computerworld*, February 5, 2001, pp. 77, and "Retailers Hit Installation Bumps With SAP Software," *Computerworld*, February 19, 2001, p. 36.

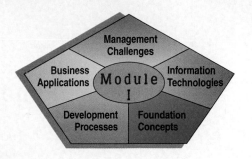

Management Challenges
Business Applications
Module I
Information Technologies
Development Processes
Foundation Concepts

Competing with Information Technology

Chapter Highlights

Learning Objectives

After reading and studying this chapter, you should be able to:

1. Identify several basic competitive strategies and explain how they can use information technologies to confront the competitive forces faced by a business.

2. Identify several strategic uses of information technologies for electronic business and commerce, and give examples of how they give competitive advantages to a business.

3. Give examples of how business process reengineering frequently involves the strategic use of E-business technologies.

4. Identify the business value of using E-business technologies for total quality management, to become an agile competitor, or to form a virtual company.

5. Explain how knowledge management systems can help a business gain strategic advantages.

6. Identify and evaluate several factors that could help a company sustain a strategic competitive advantage.

Fundamentals of Strategic Advantage

Strategic IT

Technology is no longer an afterthought in forming business strategy, but the actual cause and driver [23].

This chapter will show you that it is important that you view information systems as more than a set of technologies that support efficient business operations, workgroup and enterprise collaboration, or effective business decision making. Information technology can change the way businesses compete. So you should also view information systems strategically, that is, as vital competitive networks, as a means of organizational renewal, and as a necessary investment in technologies that help a company adopt strategies and business processes that enable it to reengineer or reinvent itself in order to survive and succeed in today's dynamic E-business environment.

Analyzing General Electric

Read the Real World Case on General Electric on the next page. We can learn a lot about the strategic business uses of Internet technologies from this case. See Figure 2.1.

Led by outgoing CEO Jack Welch and incoming CEO Jeff Immelt, General Electric is implementing a variety of E-business and E-commerce strategies designed to cut operating costs and grow revenues, while deepening its relationships with its customers. Welch has aimed his E-business initiatives at using Internet technologies to make drastic reductions in the cost of doing business. And he has led GE into a premier status in a lot of businesses—from GE Capital to GE Power Systems, from GE Appliance to GE Medical—and the list goes on. Jeff Immelt's mission is to design E-business and E-commerce strategies that will transform the way each of GE's businesses generate revenue. GE's challenge is to use Internet technologies to create Web-based information products and services with higher profit margins that will not only leverage its present competitive advantages but will significantly increase the revenue streams from the mix of products and services it offers its customers.

Figure 2.1

Jack Welch (left) and Jeff Immelt aim to transform GE with E-business initiatives.

Photo by Mark Peterson/Saba.

General Electric Company: Evaluating E-Business Strategies

Everything we've learned from the Internet says it plays to our strengths. It's transforming everything we do. And I think it's just the beginning," says GE's CEO-elect Jeff Immelt. Outgoing CEO Jack Welch has led GE's E-business initiatives. "This becomes the business," he said last year—a few months before he declared that the Web would save GE $10 billion in sales and overhead costs (a large chunk of which could come simply from layoffs, perhaps as many as 80,000 jobs). Critics have charged Welch with overstating the massive productivity gains that E-business is supposed to provide GE, while having scant evidence of it in his company's current financial statements. Yet it is really too early to make any conclusive judgments. The $7 billion of E-business at GE is a seemingly huge number—and it represents a massive increase over the $1 billion in on-line sales that GE booked in 1999—but at this point it's still too small a portion of the company's $230 billion in overall revenues to accurately gauge its impact on the bottom line.

But what has gone unrecognized in Welch's E-business strategy, is that when you get down to it, it is mainly just another way to drive costs out of the system by using the Internet to replace sales staff and back-office functions, as well as to automate transactions with customers and suppliers. That's a fine goal, but it represents only a portion of what the Internet can do for GE.

Immelt's chance to transform GE is to use the Internet to grow top-line revenues. One way he can do that is by encouraging GE's executives to use the Web to create new businesses that are information-intensive rather than capital-intensive. So far, most of the revenues GE has booked on the Web have come from existing customers. At GE Medical, for instance, Immelt's successor Joe Hogan figures that less than $250 million of last year's $1.5 billion in online sales came from new business. That could change, however, as he introduces more Web-based services. Already, GE Medical monitors 10,000 individual medical imaging machines electronically, often diagnosing problems before they become serious enough to shut down a piece of equipment, or downloading new software to upgrade the machines' capabilities.

GE Medical can provide other information services as well. For instance, it can inform an individual hospital how its use of equipment compares with benchmarks set by the best hospitals in the world, or it can recommend ways to run the machines more profitably. "As people use our equipment," explains Hogan, "we can feed information back to them." For example, a hospital could be running an MRI machine at full capacity, but an analysis by GE Medical might show that it is being used only for low-margin tests. Such Internet services are a negligible part of the business today but are growing rapidly.

Prudential Securities analyst Nicholas Heymann thinks these sorts of new E-businesses are the next phase of GE's growth. "Pricing will be based on the productivity savings GE can supply its customers," he predicts.

Hints of what is possible are already evident throughout GE's various businesses. Using sophisticated software tools availability via the Web, a power plant can now be designed in a matter of days instead of six months, resulting in time savings that yield additional revenues for GE Power System's utility customers.

GE is also well-positioned to take advantage of its existing physical assets to offer new Web-based services. For instance, GE Appliances already has an infrastructure in place that is ideally suited to the Web. It owns a nationwide appliance-delivery business aimed at homebuilders (a market that accounts for one-third of its revenues), complete with fleets of trucks, installers, warehouses, and other assets. Now, thanks to the Web, it can extend this home delivery service to individual consumers who order GE appliances from select retailers and reduces the amount of inventory that they have to carry on their books. The store doesn't have to touch anything; it just collects a bounty for each sale.

For instance, Heymann estimates that 62 percent of Home Depot's sales of GE appliances are made this way. "This is why Wal-Mart is so eager to get into appliances," he adds. Suddenly appliances are a high-margin category for GE's retail store customers, which of course makes them even more eager to do business with GE.

The more that GE can create new businesses that derive revenue from the Internet, the higher its overall profit margins will become. GE's operating margins on its manufacturing business are about 15 percent. When it is able to wrap services around its products, such as maintaining and repairing medical equipment or aircraft engines, its operating margins jump to around 25 or 30 percent. Now it has the opportunity to earn 60 or 70 percent operating margins by streaming valuable intellectual content to its customers. Heymann speculates that by mid-decade, GE's business mix could be 50 percent service, 20 percent intellectual content, and only 30 percent manufacturing.

Case Study Questions

1. Which of the strategic uses of IT summarized in Figures 2.3 and 2.5 do you recognize GE using in this case? Explain the reasons for your choices.

2. Do you agree with the case's evaluation of GE's past and potential E-business strategies? Why or why not?

3. If you were Jeff Immelt, what would be some of your first moves in E-business and E-commerce for GE? Explain the reasons for your proposals.

Source: Adapted from Erick Schonfeld, "A Bright Idea for GE," *eCompany*, March 2001, pp. 42–46.

Competitive Strategy Concepts

The strategic role of information systems involves using information technology to develop products, services, and capabilities that give a company major advantages over the competitive forces it faces in the global marketplace. This creates **strategic information systems,** information systems that support or shape the competitive position and strategies of an E-business enterprise. So a strategic information system can be any kind of information system (TPS, MIS, DSS, etc.) that helps an organization gain a competitive advantage, reduce a competitive disadvantage, or meet other strategic enterprise objectives [31]. Let's look at several basic concepts that define the role of such strategic information systems.

How should a business professional think about competitive strategies? How can competitive strategies be applied to the use of information systems by an E-business enterprise? Figure 2.2 illustrates an important conceptual framework for understanding and applying competitive strategies. A firm can survive and succeed in the long run if it successfully develops strategies to confront five **competitive forces** that shape the structure of competition in its industry. These are: (1) rivalry of competitors within its industry, (2) threat of new entrants, (3) threat of substitutes, (4) the bargaining power of customers, and (5) the bargaining power of suppliers [34].

Figure 2.2 also illustrates that businesses can counter the threats of competitive forces that they face by implementing five basic **competitive strategies** [31].

- **Cost Leadership Strategy.** Becoming a low-cost producer of products and services in the industry. Also, a firm can find ways to help its suppliers or customers reduce their costs or to increase the costs of their competitors.

- **Differentiation Strategy.** Developing ways to differentiate a firm's products and services from its competitors' or reduce the differentiation advantages of competitors. This may allow a firm to focus its products or services to give it an advantage in particular segments or niches of a market.

Figure 2.2

Businesses can develop competitive strategies to counter the actions of the competitive forces they confront in the marketplace.

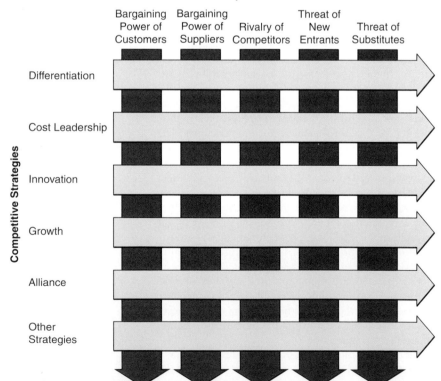

- **Innovation Strategy.** Finding new ways of doing business. This may involve the development of unique products and services, or entry into unique markets or market niches. It may also involve making radical changes to the business processes for producing or distributing products and services that are so different from the way a business has been conducted that they alter the fundamental structure of an industry.
- **Growth Strategies.** Significantly expanding a company's capacity to produce goods and services, expanding into global markets, diversifying into new products and services, or integrating into related products and services.
- **Alliance Strategies.** Establishing new business linkages and alliances with customers, suppliers, competitors, consultants, and other companies. These linkages may include mergers, acquisitions, joint ventures, forming of "virtual companies," or other marketing, manufacturing, or distribution agreements between a business and its trading partners.

Strategic Uses of Information Technology

How can business managers use investments in information technology to directly support a firm's competitive strategies? Figure 2.3 answers that question with a summary of the many ways that information technology could help a business implement the five basic competitive strategies. Figure 2.4 provides examples of how specific companies have used strategic information systems to implement each of these five basic strategies for competitive advantage. Note the major use of Internet technologies for electronic business and commerce applications. In the rest of this chapter, we will discuss and provide examples of many strategic uses of information technology.

Other Competitive Strategies

There are many other competitive strategies in addition to the five basic strategies of cost leadership, differentiation, innovation, growth, and alliance. Let's look at

---

Figure 2.3

A summary of how information technology can be used to implement the five basic competitive strategies. Many companies are using Internet technologies as the foundation for such strategies.

Basic Strategies in the Business Use of Information Technology

Lower costs
- Use IT to substantially reduce the cost of business processes.
- Use IT to lower the costs of customers or suppliers.

Differentiate
- Develop new IT features to differentiate products and services.
- Use IT features to reduce the differentiation advantages of competitors.
- Use IT features to focus products and services at selected market niches.

Innovate
- Create new products and services that include IT components.
- Develop unique new markets or market niches with the help of IT.
- Make radical changes to business processes with IT that dramatically cut costs, improve quality, efficiency, or customer service, or shorten time to market.

Promote Growth
- Use IT to manage regional and global business expansion.
- Use IT to diversify and integrate into other products and services.

Develop Alliances
- Use IT to create virtual organizations of business partners.
- Develop interenterprise information systems linked by the Internet and extranets that support strategic business relationships with customers, suppliers, subcontractors, and others.

Figure 2.4 Examples of how companies used information technology to implement five competitive strategies for strategic advantage. Note the use of Internet technologies for electronic business and commerce applications.

Strategy	Company	Strategic Information System	Business Benefit
Cost Leadership	Buy.com	Online price adjustment	Lowest price guarantee
	Priceline.com	Online seller bidding	Buyer-set pricing
	EBay.com	Online auctions	Auction-set prices
Differentiation	AVNET Marshall	Customer/Supplier E-commerce	Increase in market share
	Ross Operating Valves	Online customer design	Increase in market share
	Consolidated Freightways	Customer online shipment tracking	Increase in market share
Innovation	Charles Schwab & Co.	Online discount stock trading	Market leadership
	Federal Express	Online package tracking and flight management	Market leadership
	Amazon.com	Online full service customer systems	Market leadership
Growth	Citicorp	Global intranet	Increase in global market
	Wal-Mart	Merchandise ordering by global satellite network	Market leadership
	Toys 'Я' Us Inc.	POS inventory tracking	Market leadership
Alliance	Wal-Mart/Procter & Gamble	Automatic inventory replenishment by supplier	Reduced inventory cost/increased sales
	Cisco Systems	Virtual manufacturing alliances	Agile market leadership
	Airborne Express/ Rentrak Corp.	Online inventory management/ shipment tracking	Increase in market share

several key strategies that are also implemented with information technology. They are: locking in customers or suppliers, building switching costs, raising barriers to entry, and leveraging investment in information technology.

Investments in information technology can allow a business to **lock in customers and suppliers** (and lock out competitors) by building valuable new relationships with them. This can deter both customers and suppliers from abandoning a firm for its competitors or intimidating a firm into accepting less-profitable relationships. Early attempts to use information systems technology in these relationships focused on significantly improving the quality of service to customers and suppliers in a firm's distribution, marketing, sales, and service activities. Then businesses moved to more innovative uses of information technology.

Wal-Mart and Others

For example, Wal-Mart built an elaborate satellite network linking the point-of-sale terminals in all of its stores. The network was designed to provide managers, buyers, and sales associates with up-to-date sales and inventory status information to improve product buying, inventories, and store management. Then Wal-Mart began to use the operational efficiency of such information systems to offer lower cost, better-quality products and services, and differentiate itself from its competitors.

Companies like Wal-Mart began to extend their networks to their customers and suppliers in order to build innovative continous inventory replenishment systems that would lock in their business. This creates **interenterprise information systems** in which the Internet, extranets, and other networks electronically link the computers of businesses with their customers and suppliers, resulting in new business alliances and partnerships. Extranets between businesses and their suppliers are a prime example of such strategic linkages. An even stronger E-business link is formed by *stockless* inventory replenishment systems such as those between Wal-Mart and Procter & Gamble. In that system, Procter & Gamble automatically replenishes Wal-Mart's stock of Procter & Gamble products [6, 27].

A major emphasis in strategic information systems has been to find ways to build **switching costs** into the relationships between a firm and its customers or suppliers. That is, investments in information systems technology, such as those mentioned in the Wal-Mart example, can make customers or suppliers dependent on the continued use of innovative, mutually beneficial interenterprise information systems. Then, they become reluctant to pay the costs in time, money, effort, and inconvenience that it would take to change to a company's competitors.

By making investments in information technology to improve its operations or promote innovation, a firm could also erect **barriers to entry** that would discourage or delay other companies from entering a market. Typically, this happens by increasing the amount of investment or the complexity of the technology required to compete in an industry or a market segment. Such actions would tend to discourage firms already in the industry and deter external firms from entering the industry.

Investing in information technology enables a firm to build strategic IT capabilities that allow it to take advantage of strategic opportunities when they arise. In many cases, this results when a company invests in advanced computer-based information systems to improve the efficiency of its own business processes. Then, armed with this strategic technology platform, the firm can **leverage investment in information technology** by developing new products and services that would not be possible without a strong IT capability. An important current example is the development of corporate intranets and extranets by many companies, which enables them to leverage their previous investments in Internet browsers, PCs, servers, and client/server networks. Figure 2.5 summarizes the additional strategic uses of IT we have just discussed.

Merrill Lynch and Charles Schwab

Merrill Lynch is a classic example of several competitive strategies. By making large investments in information technology, along with a groundbreaking alliance with BancOne, they became the first securities brokers to offer a credit line, checking account, Visa credit card, and automatic investment in a money market fund, all in one account. This gave them major competitive advantage for several years before their rivals could develop the IT capability to offer similar services on their own. [31].

However, Merrill is now playing catch-up in online discount securities trading with Charles Schwab, E-Trade, and others. Schwab is now the leading online securities company with over 7.4 million customers in early 2001, far surpassing Merrill's online statistics. Thus, large investments in IT can make the stakes too high for some present or prospective players in an industry, but can evaporate over time as new technologies are employed by competitors [28].

The Value Chain and Strategic IS

Let's look at another important concept that can help you identify opportunities for strategic information systems. The value chain concept was developed by Michael Porter [34] and is illustrated in Figure 2.6. It views a firm as a series, chain, or network of basic activities that add value to its products and services, and thus add a

Figure 2.5   Additional ways that information technology can be used to implement competitive strategies.

Other Strategic Uses of Information Technology

- Develop interenterprise information systems whose convenience and efficiency create switching costs that lock in customers or suppliers.
- Make major investments in advanced IT applications that build barriers to entry against industry competitors or outsiders.
- Include IT components in products and services to make substitution of competing products or services more difficult.
- Leverage investment in IS people, hardware, software, databases, and networks from operational uses into strategic applications.

margin of value to the firm. In the value chain conceptual framework, some business activities are primary processes; others are support processes. This framework can highlight where competitive strategies can best be applied in a business. That is, managers and business professionals should try to develop a variety of strategic uses of Internet and other technologies for those basic processes that add the most value to a company's products or services, and thus to the overall business value of the company. Figure 2.6 provides examples of how and where information technologies can be applied to basic business processes using the value chain framework.

Value Chain Examples

Figure 2.6 emphasizes that collaborative workflow intranet-based systems can increase the communications and collaboration needed to dramatically improve administrative coordination and support services. A career development intranet can help the human resources management function provide employees with professional development training programs. Computer-aided engineering and design extranets enable a company and its business partners to jointly design products and processes. Finally, E-commerce auctions and exchanges can dramatically improve procurement of resources by providing an online marketplace for a firm's suppliers.

Figure 2.6   The value chain of a firm. Note the examples of the variety of strategic information systems that can be applied to a firm's basic business processes for competitive advantage.

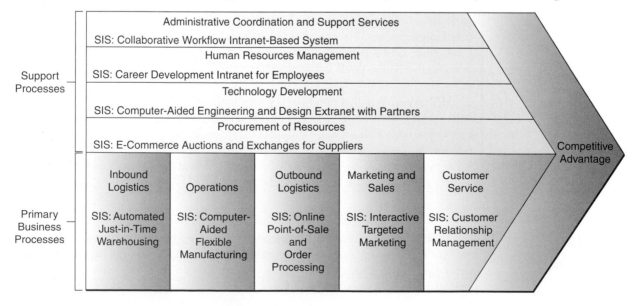

Other examples of strategic applications of information systems technology to primary business processes are identified in Figure 2.6. These include automated just-in-time warehousing systems to support inbound logistic processes involving storage of inventory, computer-aided flexible manufacturing (CAM) systems for manufacturing operations, and online point-of-sale and order processing systems to improve out-bound logistics processes that process customer orders. Information systems can also support marketing and sales processes by developing an interactive targeted marketing capability on the Internet and its World Wide Web. Finally, customer service can be dramatically improved by a coordinated and integrated customer relationship management system.

Internet-Based Value Chains

Value chains can also be used to strategically position a company's Internet-based applications to gain competitive advantage. Figure 2.7 is a value chain model that outlines several ways that a company's Internet connections with its customers could provide business benefits and opportunities for competitive advantage. For example, company-managed Internet newsgroups, chat rooms, and electronic commerce websites are powerful tools for market research and product development, direct sales, and customer feedback and support.

A company's Internet connections with its suppliers could also be used for competitive advantage. Examples are online auctions and exchanges at suppliers' E-commerce websites, and online shipping, scheduling, and status information at an E-commerce portal that gives employees immediate access to up-to-date information from a variety of vendors. This can substantially lower costs, reduce lead times, and improve the quality of products and services [8].

Thus, the value chain concept can help you decide where and how to apply the strategic capabilities of information technology. It shows how various types of information technologies might be applied to specific business processes to help a firm gain competitive advantages in the marketplace.

Figure 2.7

This Internet value chain demonstrates the strategic business value of Internet-based applications that focus on a company's relationships with its customers.

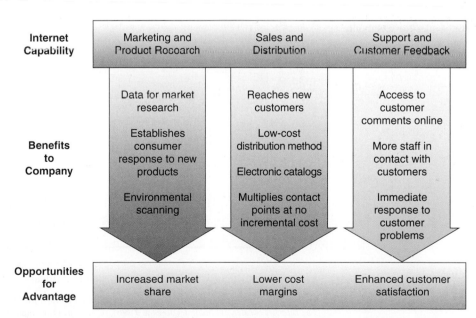

Source: Adapted from Mary Cronin, *Doing More Business on the Internet*, 2nd ed. (New York: Van Nostrand Reinhold, 1995), p. 61. Used by permission.

Identifying E-Business and E-Commerce Strategies

Companies need a strategic framework that can bridge the gap between simply connecting to the Internet and harnessing its power for competitive advantage. The most valuable Internet applications allow companies to transcend communication barriers and establish connections that will enhance productivity, stimulate innovative development, and improve customer relations [9].

E-business and E-commerce applications, and Internet technologies can be used strategically for competitive advantage, as this text will repeatedly demonstrate. However, in order to optimize this strategic impact, a company must continually assess the strategic value of such applications. Figure 2.8 is a strategic positioning matrix that can help a company identify where to concentrate its use of Internet technologies to gain a competitive advantage with E-business and E-commerce. Let's take a look at the strategies that each quadrant of this matrix represents [9].

- **Cost and Efficiency Improvements.** This quadrant represents a low amount of internal company, customer, and competitor connectivity and use of IT via the Internet and other networks. So one recommended strategy would be to focus on improving efficiency and lowering costs by using the Internet and the World Wide Web as a fast, low-cost way to communicate and interact with customers, suppliers, and business partners. The use of E-mail, chat systems, discussion groups, and a company website are typical examples.

- **Performance Improvement in Business Effectiveness.** Here a company has a high degree of internal connectivity and pressures to substantially improve its business processes, but external connectivity by customers and competitors is still low. A strategy of making major improvements in business effectiveness is recommended. For example, widespread internal use of Internet-based technologies like intranets and extranets can substantially improve information sharing and collaboration within the business and with its trading partners.

Figure 2.8

A strategic positioning matrix helps a company optimize the strategic impact of Internet technologies for electronic business and commerce applications.

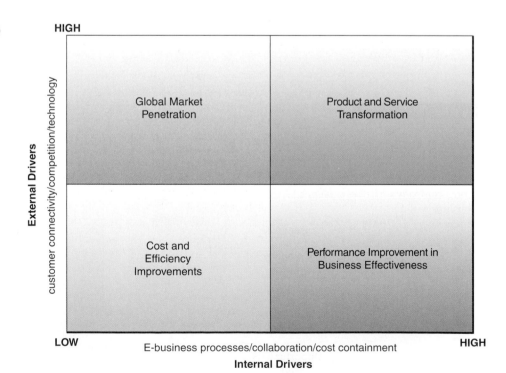

Source: Adapted and reprinted by permission of The Harvard Business School Press from Mary Cronin, *The Internet Strategy Handbook* (Boston: 1996), p. 20, and Don Tapscott, David Ticoll, and Alex Lowy, *Digital Capital: Harnessing the Power of Business Webs* (Boston, MA: 2000), p. 220. Copyright © 1996, 2000 by the President and Fellows of Harvard College, all rights reserved.

- **Global Market Penetration.** A company that enters this quadrant of the matrix must capitalize on a high degree of customer and competitor connectivity and use of IT. Developing E-business and E-commerce applications to optimize interaction with customers and build market share is recommended. For example, E-commerce websites with value-added information services and extensive online customer support would be one way to implement such a strategy.

- **Product and Service Transformation.** Here a company and its customers, suppliers, and competitors are extensively networked. Internet-based technologies, including E-commerce websites, and E-business intranets and extranets, must now be implemented throughout the company's operations and business relationships. This enables a company to develop and deploy new Internet-based products and services that strategically reposition it in the marketplace. Using the Internet for electronic commerce transaction processing with customers at company websites, and E-commerce auctions and exchanges for suppliers are typical examples of such strategic E-business applications. Let's look at a more specific example.

AVNET Marshall: E-Business and E-Commerce Strategies	AVNET Marshall exemplifies the major transformation in business strategies that Internet technologies enable in an E-business enterprise. AVNET Marshall is a business unit of AVNET Inc., and was a $1.7 billion electronics distributor company (Marshall Industries) before their acquisition by AVNET in October 1999. Their E-business initiatives include an electronic commerce website (www.avnet-marshall.com), an intranet called AVNET, and an extranet called PartnerNet that gives customers and suppliers customized entry into the company's intranets. Marshall's vision is to create a virtual distribution system where customers can learn about and buy products anytime and in any form. Figure 2.9 outlines the revolutionary changes in business strategies resulting from AVNET Marshall's transformation into an E-business enterprise.

The PartnerNet extranet creates personal profiles of selected customers and suppliers, which gives them customized views into AVNET Marshall's products, services, and inventory. The extranet provides customers and suppliers with personalized 24-hour access to AVNET Marshall's intranet resources. For example, suppliers can get point-of-sale and inventory status reports about their products at any time. Customers can also check the inventory status of items they want, as well as the status of orders they previously placed. AVNET Marshall reports that the extranet has helped them to increase sales and profits, while cutting sales staff and expenses.

AVNET Marshall's E-commerce website provides realtime news reports on the industry and its vendors, live audio feeds from industry trade shows, and online interactive seminars. They also created a TV and radio studio to host its online seminars and produce live reports from industry events. Their website is so popular in the industry that they sell advertising space on its web screens to their own vendors. The company is confident that increased sales have more than repaid its costs to develop the website [13].

Figure 2.9

The revolutionary changes in business strategies enabled by Internet technologies that transformed AVNET Marshall into an E-business enterprise.

Strategy Dimensions	Conventional Strategies	AVNET Marshall Strategies
Strategic Focus	To beat the competition—benchmark and improve. Benefits are marginal.	Don't use competitors as benchmarks. Go for the quantum leap in value. ● First in the industry with an E-commerce site on the Internet, open 24 hrs/day, 7 days/week ● First in the industry with laptops and intranet to connect employees
Customers	Expand and retain current customers through further segmentation.	Expand customer base through strategic alliances and new offerings: educational and international partner websites.
Assets and Capabilities	Leverage what you have.	Not constrained by what it already has—IT platforms or infrastructure—builds what complements the strategy: ● AVNET Marshall E-commerce website ● PartnerNet–Extranet ● AVNET–Intranet
Product and Service Offerings	The industry you are in determines the products and services you offer. The goal then is to add as much value as you can.	Not constrained by the industry boundaries. Thinks in terms of total solutions for the customer and supplier. Example: educational and entertainment Web services for the customers and suppliers.

Source: Adapted from Omar El Sawy, Arvind Malhotra, Sanjay Gosain, and Kerry Young, "IT-Intensive Value Innovation in the Electronic Economy: Insights from Marshall Industries," *MIS Quarterly*, September 1999, p. 328. Reprinted with permission from the *MIS Quarterly*.

Section II

Using Information Technology for Strategic Advantage

Strategic Uses of IT

There are many ways that organizations may view and use information technology. For example, companies may choose to use information systems strategically, or they may be content to use IT to support efficient everyday operations. But if a company emphasized strategic business uses of information technology, its management would view IT as a major competitive differentiator. It would then devise business strategies that would use IT to develop products, services, and capabilities that would give the company major advantages in the markets in which it competes. In this section, we will provide many examples of such strategic business applications of information technology.

Analyzing McDonald's and American Express

Read the Real World Case on McDonald's and American Express on the next page. We can learn a lot about electronic commerce strategies from this example. See Figure 2.10.

Large companies and venture capital firms are trying to develop a new business model for E-commerce that will be more successful than their past attempts to spin off dotcom entities from established traditional companies. Rather than spinning off digital versions of a company's core businesses, their strategy is to carve out

Figure 2.10

Gayle Sheppard is the CEO of Market Mile, an E-commerce company carved out of American Express.

Photo by Bryce Duffy/Saba.

McDonald's and American Express: E-Commerce Spinoff Strategies

A few weeks ago, Shaun Holliday was flipping burgers. Now flush with venture capital, he's searching Oak Brook, Illinois, for loft-like housing for his high-tech startup, eMac Digital. But this isn't another fairy tale from the days of Nasdaq 5,000. The majority shareholder in Holliday's new company is old-economy stalwart McDonald's. His venture capital comes from Accel-KKR, a firm formed last year with the goal of funding startups culled from old-economy cooperations. And strangest of all: Holliday, a former CEO of Guinness and Living.com, isn't relying on the kind of blockbuster IPO that first lured him to the online world. There's a chance that eMac will become nothing more than a small company selling software to restaurants. Which explains his burger-making: Holliday was employing the very old-economy trick of trying to learn the needs of eMac's potential customers—the 28,000 McDonald's locations he hopes will buy his company's software.

Welcome to the new, slow world of the Internet spinoff. For several years now, Fortune 500 companies have been trying to figure out what to do with their Web businesses. They were driven first by fear, as nimble, tech-savvy online upstarts rose to challenge them. Then, when the market gave their fledgling competitors outrageous valuations, that fear turned to greed. Corporations approached venture capitalists who, in return for a minority stake in the new company, would provide the business-building expertise and connections to the online world that the corporations felt they lacked. The new entities that resulted—often referred to as *carve-outs*—were going to become bigger than the parent corporations and reap vast rewards for those involved.

That never happened, of course. Net stocks collapsed. The speedy, agile competitors suddenly looked young and clueless. And the carve-outs were left questioning their existence. But instead of trashing the idea of the carve-out as just another relic of the dot-com era, both companies and venture capitalists have begun to rethink the whole process.

Now, companies are increasingly carving out businesses that are separate from, though complementary to, their core business. The less they tie in, the better their chance of remaining independent and keeping a smile on the faces of their VC partners. "The core should be something that a corporation owns," says eVolution's U.S. managing partner David Sanderson. "The Wal-mart.coms should remain a part of the Wal-Marts."

Sanderson's firm has even coined a consultant-style phrase, which he and his partners use at every opportunity, for the carve-outs in which it is willing to invest: "non-core but mission critical." That is how he describes eVolution's $16 million investment in MarketMile, a joint venture between American Express (which contributed $17 million) and Ventro ($13 million).

On the surface, MarketMile appears to be another of the increasingly ubiquitous online marketplaces. The new company will give midsized companies a single portal—the MarketMile online marketplace—from which to buy office supplies and other products from suppliers like Office Depot and Boise Cascade.

Amex's reasons for carving out MarketMile rather than developing it internally in many ways resemble those of earlier Internet spin-offs. "Given the other players in the market, it was far quicker for us to do it outside our walls, where the engineers would be free to create something on their own," says Jud Linville, Amex's executive vice president of corporate services. But Linville is quick to differentiate MarketMile from high-tech ventures the company chose to develop internally—programs, for instance, that keep track of card billing. "That's our core business," says Linville. "And it should be something we invest in within our own four walls."

Like many of the new carve-outs, MarketMile's goal is to succeed on its own while also fueling one of the company's businesses. "MarketMile is the new model," says CEO Gayle Sheppard. "Our relationship with Amex will enable both companies to prosper."

The business that needs boosting in this case is the American Express purchasing card, which has failed to capture the usage fees and overwhelming market share of its more glamorous sibling, the corporate travel card. MarketMile incorporated the languishing card into its exchange's purchasing process: Buy a stapler and the carve-out automatically bills your card. "We are certainly focused on the top- and-bottom-line growth of MarketMile," says Pierric Beckert, Amex's senior vice president of Interactive Business Development. "But this investment is also strategic. We believe that the growth of MarketMile will represent an opportunity for growth for Amex's purchasing-card business."

Case Study Questions

1. Which of the strategic uses of information technology summarized in Figures 2.3 and 2.5 do you see McDonald's and American Express using in this case? Explain the reasons for your choices.

2. Does the rationale of venture capital companies for "carve out" E-commerce spinoffs from large companies as outlined in this case make sound business sense? Why or why not?

3. Is there a strong business case for the E-commerce success of the eMac Digital and MarketMile carve-outs? Why or why not?

Source: Adapted from Nicholas Stein, "May We Offer You Our Net Business?" *Fortune*, March 5, 2001, pp. 167–172.

"non-core, but mission critical" parts of a business that have their own E-commerce model and set of competitive goals and strategies, but whose success will significantly support one or more of the parent company's strategic business initiatives. Thus, eMac Digital is a software company carve-out whose mission is to develop helpful business software, not only for McDonald's more than 28,000 restaurants worldwide, but for all other fast-food competitors as well. And MarketMile is a spinoff of an American Express strategic initiative to create an E-commerce marketplace for its corporate customers. But MarketMile's other strategic mission is to significantly improve the acceptance of the American Express corporate purchasing card by requiring its use for financing marketplace transactions.

Building a Customer-Focused E-Business

The driving force behind world economic growth has changed from manufacturing volume to improving customer value. As a result, the key success factor for many firms is maximizing customer value [9].

For many companies, the chief business value of becoming a **customer-focused E-business** lies in its ability to help them keep customers loyal, anticipate their future needs, respond to customer concerns, and provide top-quality customer service. This strategic focus on **customer value** recognizes that quality, rather than prices, has become the primary determinant in a customer's perception of value. From a customer's point of view, companies that consistently offer the best value are able to keep track of their customers' individual preferences, keep up with market trends, supply products, services, and information anytime, anywhere, and provide customer services tailored to individual needs [9]. And so electronic commerce has become a strategic opportunity for companies, large and small, to offer fast, responsive, high-quality products and services tailored to individual customer preferences.

Internet technologies can make customers the focal point of all E-business and E-commerce applications. Internet, intranet, and extranet websites create new channels for interactive communications within a company, with customers, and with the suppliers, business partners, and others in the external environment. This enables continual interaction with customers by most business functions and encourages cross-functional collaboration with customers in product development, marketing, delivery, service, and technical support [9].

Typically, E-commerce customers use the Internet to ask questions, air complaints, evaluate products, request support, and make and report their purchases. Using the Internet and corporate intranets, specialists in business functions throughout the enterprise can contribute to an effective response. This encourages the creation of cross-functional discussion groups and problem-solving teams dedicated to customer involvement, service, and support. Even the Internet and extranet links to suppliers and business partners can be used to enlist them in a way of doing business that ensures prompt delivery of quality components and services to meet a company's commitments to its customers [20]. This is how an E-business enterprise demonstrates its focus on customer value.

Figure 2.11 illustrates the interrelationships in a customer-focused E-business. Intranets, extranets, E-commerce websites, and web-enabled internal business processes form the invisible IT platform that supports this E-business model. This enables the E-business to focus on targeting the kinds of customers it really wants, and "owning" the customer's total business experience with the company. A successful E-business streamlines all business processes that impact their customers, and provides its employees with a complete view of each customer, so they can offer their customers top-quality personalized service. A customer-focused E-business helps their E-commerce customers to help themselves, while also helping them do their jobs. Finally, a successful E-business nurtures an online community of customers, employees, and business partners that builds great customer loyalty, while fostering cooperation to provide an outstanding customer experience [37]. Let's review a real world example.

Figure 2.11   How a customer-focused E-business builds customer value and loyalty in electronic commerce.

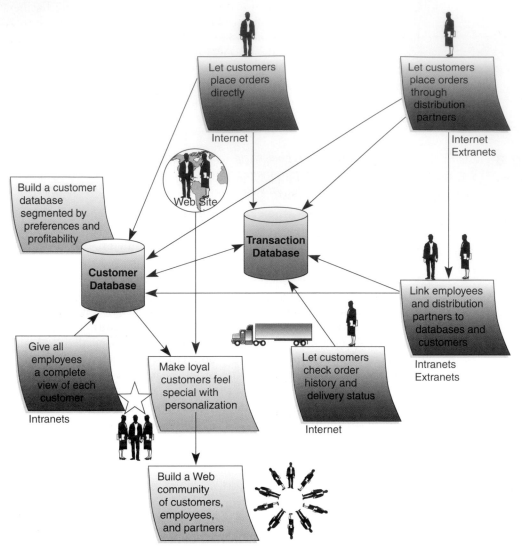

Source: Adapted from Patricia Seybold with Ronnie Marshak, *Customers.com: How to Create a Profitable Business Strategy for the Internet and Beyond* (New York: Times Books, 1998), p. 32.

**McAffee Associates:
Customer-Focused
E-Business**

Imagine a business model where you develop a product that many businesses need, offer it free on the Internet on a trial basis to anyone, and provide high-quality customer and technical support, so the product is easy to use and maintain. Then, after the fact, you try to collect site license fees from corporations and institutions that are using your product. That is the E-commerce business model of McAffee and Associates, the maker of McAffee VirusScan, one of the top antivirus programs for finding and eradicating computer viruses. The company and its products have been very successful. Their business gamble paid off and has been copied by many other companies [8]. See Figure 2.12.

Thus electronic distribution of software products over the Internet is a vital component of many companies' Internet strategy. This minimizes the cost of manufacturing, packaging, shipping, distributing, and marketing products. Such cost savings enable McAffee to make large investments to maximize what they consider to be the key to competitive advantage: customer satisfaction.

If customers are very satisfied with a product, they will increase their use of it, renew their licenses, and recommend the product to others. So McAffee relies heavily on the Web as the vehicle for distributing frequent, free product enhancements; encouraging customer participation in market research and product development; and providing top-quality customer service and technical support.

New software releases are made available for download to customers at the company's E-commerce website every six to eight weeks. The www.mcafee.com website also provides access to product information and ordering systems, bulletin boards, discussion groups, and customer service and technical support. McAffee specialists participate in all discussion groups on the Internet and online services like AOL, MSN, and CompuServe that relate to their product or its security and performance. This continual online interaction with their customers has made the entire company more customer-focused and responsive in product development and customer service, and given them a significant competitive advantage [8].

Reengineering Business Processes

One of the most important implementations of competitive strategies today is **business process reengineering** (BPR), most often simply called reengineering. Reengineering is a fundamental rethinking and radical redesign of business processes to achieve dramatic improvements in cost, quality, speed, and service. So BPR combines a strategy of promoting business innovation with a strategy of making major improvements to business processes so that a company can become a much stronger and more successful competitor in the marketplace.

However, Figure 2.13 points out that while the potential payback of reengineering is high, so is its risk of failure and level of disruption to the organizational environment [16]. Making radical changes to business processes to dramatically improve efficiency and effectiveness is not an easy task. For example, many

Figure 2.12

The home page of McAffee and Associates.

Courtesy of McAfee.com Corporation.

Figure 2.13

How business process reengineering differs from business improvement.

	Business Improvement	Business Reengineering
Definition	Incrementally improving existing processes	Radically redesigning business processes
Target	Any process	Strategic business processes
Primary Enablers	IT and work simplification	IT and organizational redesign
Potential Payback	10%–50% improvements	10-fold improvements
What Changes?	Same jobs, just more efficient	Big job cuts; new jobs; major job redesign
Risk of Failure and Level of Disruption	Low	High

companies have used cross-functional enterprise resource planning (ERP) software to reengineer, automate, and integrate their manufacturing, distribution, finance, and human resource business processes. While many companies have reported impressive gains with such ERP reengineering projects, many others have failed to achieve the improvements they sought (as we saw in the real world examples of Boeing, Analog Devices, and A-DEC in Chapter 1).

That's why *organizational redesign* approaches are an important enabler of reengineering, along with the use of information technology. For example, one common approach is the use of self-directed cross-functional or multidisciplinary *process teams*. Employees from several departments or specialties including engineering, marketing, customer service, and manufacturing may work as a team on the product development process. Another example is the use of *case managers*, who handle almost all tasks in a business process, instead of splitting tasks among many different specialists.

The Role of Information Technology

Information technology plays a major role in reengineering most business processes. The speed, information processing capabilities, and connectivity of computers and Internet technologies can substantially increase the efficiency of business processes, as well as communications and collaboration among the people responsible for their operation and management. For example, the order management process illustrated in Figure 2.14 is vital to the success of most companies [10]. Many of them are reengineering this process with enterprise resource planning software and Web-enabled electronic business and commerce systems. See Figure 2.15. Figure 2.16 dramatically illustrates the results of several reengineering projects at CIGNA Corporation. Now, let's take a look at an example from Ford Motor Company.

Ford Motor Company: Driving E-Engineering

Ford believes the Internet is ushering in an even bigger wave of business transformation than reengineering. Call it E-engineering. Ford realizes it's not enough to put up simple websites for customers, employees, and partners. To take full advantage of the Net, they've got to reinvent the way they do business—changing how they design, manufacture, and distribute goods, collaborate inside and outside the company, and deal with suppliers.

Ford is using Web technologies to reengineer its internal business processes as well as those between the company and its dealers, suppliers, and customers. For example, Ford's global intranet connects thousands of designers in the United States and Europe so they can collaborate on design projects. Also, extranet links

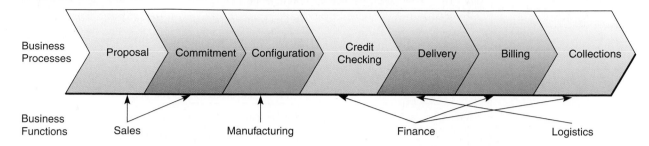

Figure 2.14 The order management process consists of several business processes and crosses the boundaries of traditional business functions.

enable suppliers from all over the world to collaborate on the design, manufacture, and assembly of automotive components. All of these E-engineering initiatives are designed to slash costs, reduce time to market, and lower inventory and workforce levels, while improving the sales, quality, and consistency of Ford's products. Ford's global intranet brings 4,500 engineers from labs in the United States, Germany, and England together in cyberspace to collaborate on automobile design projects. The idea is to break down the barriers between regional operations so basic auto components are designed once and used everywhere. When design plans conflict, the software automatically sends out E-mail alerts to members of design teams. When all of the pieces are in place, the company hopes to transform the way it designs and produces cars, so it can quickly build them to order [21, 40].

Improving Business Quality

Information technology can be used strategically to improve business performance in many ways other than in supporting reengineering initiatives. One important strategic thrust is continuous quality improvement, popularly called **total quality management** (TQM). Previous to TQM, quality was defined as meeting established standards or specifications for a product or service. Statistical *quality control* programs were used to measure and correct any deviations from standards [10].

Total Quality Management

Total quality management is a much more strategic approach to business improvement. Quality is emphasized from the customer's viewpoint, rather than the producer's. Thus, quality is defined as meeting or exceeding the requirements and expectations of customers for a product or service. This may involve many features and attributes, such as performance, reliability, durability, responsiveness, and aesthetics, to name a few [33].

Figure 2.15

Examples of information technologies that support reengineering the sales and order management processes.

- Customer relationship management systems using corporate intranets and the Internet.
- Supplier managed inventory systems using the Internet and extranets.
- Cross-functional ERP software for integrating manufacturing, distribution, finance, and human resource processes.
- Customer-accessible E-commerce websites for order entry, status checking, payment, and service.
- Customer, product, and order status databases accessed via intranets and extranets by employees and suppliers.

Figure 2.16

Some of the results of reengineering projects at CIGNA.

Business Unit	Accomplishments
CIGNA Re Division	• Staff reduced by 50%. • Operating expenses reduced by 42%. • 1,200% transaction time improvement. • Team-based organization. • Systems reduced from 17 mainframe-based systems to five PC-based systems.
CIGNA International Life and Employee Benefits–UK	• 30% improvement in cost. • 75% improvement in quality. • 100% improvement in cycle time. • 50% improvement in customer satisfaction.

Corporate Medical Presale Process

Before Reengineering	After Reengineering
• Seventeen-day cycle time.	• Three-day cycle time.
• Fourteen hand-offs—manual.	• Three hand-offs—all electronic.
• Seven authorization steps.	• Zero authorization steps.
• Six hours of total work.	• Three hours of total work.
• Four hours of value-added work.	• Three hours of value-added work.
• Two hours of rework.	• Zero hours of rework.

Source: Adapted from J. Raymond Caron, Sirkka Jarvenpaa, and Donna Stoddard, "Business Reengineering at CIGNA Corporation: Experiences and Lessons from the First Five Years," *MIS Quarterly*, September 1994, p. 240. Reprinted with permission from the *MIS Quarterly*.

TQM may use a variety of tools and methods to seek continuous improvement of quality, productivity, flexibility, timeliness, and customer responsiveness. According to quality expert Richard Schonberger, companies that use TQM are committed to:

1. Even better, more appealing, less-variable quality of the product or service.
2. Even quicker, less-variable response—from design and development through supplier and sales channels, offices, and plants all the way to the final user.
3. Even greater flexibility in adjusting to customers' shifting volume and mix requirement.
4. Even lower cost through quality improvement, rework reduction, and non-value-adding waste elimination [33].

GE's Six Sigma Quality Initiative

Six Sigma is the most fundamental, far-reaching and potentially significant initiative ever undertaken by General Electric (GE) to optimize its competitiveness.

Six Sigma is the mother of all quality efforts. To achieve it, GE will have to eliminate 9,999.5 of every 10,000 defects in its processes or only 3.4 defects per million opportunities. That's a tall order, but it's one that would add $8 billion to $12 billion to the bottom line.

GE's Superabrasives business, which produces industrial diamonds, has virtually completed the implementation of Six Sigma, giving a glimpse of what might be expected companywide in a few years. Figure 2.17 outlines the improvements that occurred between Six Sigma's start in 1995 and 1998.

Source: Adapted from Kathleen Melymuka, "GE's Quality Gamble," *Computerworld*, June 8, 1998, p. 64. Copyright 1998 by Computerworld, Inc., Framingham, MA 01701. Reprinted from *Computerworld*.

Figure 2.17

The results of GE's Six Sigma total quality management program in its Superabrasives division.

GE Superabrasives Business Process Results

- Operating margins rose from 9.8% to 25.5%.
- Variable manufacturing costs fell 50%.
- The number of carats per manufacturing run rose 500%.
- On-time deliveries improved 85%.
- Product quality improved 87%.
- Late deliveries to customers declined 85%.
- Billing mistakes fell 87%.
- Capital expenditures decreased 40%.

The Six Sigma mantra for approaching any process is "define, measure, analyze, improve, control," and information technology enables many of those activities. GE uses IT to collect baseline quality data, model defect-free Six Sigma processes, automate those processes to lock in improvements, and monitor them to assure they remain defect-free.

For example, a foundation of Six Sigma is that customers define a defect. GE developed an extranet website called the "customer dashboard" that invites more than 1,000 key customers to identify the most critical-to-quality (CTQ) aspects of GE products and services that define a good performance and a defect. For example, if a customer chose speedy product delivery as a CTQ aspect, it would then define a good performance—say, five days. Anything slower is a defect.

Having defined the CTQ aspects, customers use the dashboard to provide regular, precise, quantitative feedback on how GE's processes measure up, giving a snapshot of its performance at a given moment and a trend line over time.

GE also developed an intranet website that helps all employees focus on the Six Sigma process. It provides information and status reports on every project and shares best practices among 6,000 "black belt" Six Sigma experts, who work full-time on the effort, and 30,000 "green belts," who integrate Six Sigma projects into their regular workloads [29].

Becoming an Agile Company

We are changing from a competitive environment in which mass-market products and services were standardized, long-lived, information-poor, and exchanged in one-time transactions, to an environment in which companies compete globally with niche market products and services that are individualized, short-lived, information-rich, and exchanged on an ongoing basis with customers [19].

Agility in business performance is the ability of a company to prosper in rapidly changing, continually fragmenting global markets for high-quality, high-performance, customer-configured products and services. An **agile company** can make a profit in markets with broad product ranges and short model lifetimes, and can produce orders in arbitrary lot sizes. It supports *mass customization* by offering individualized products while maintaining high volumes of production. Agile companies depend heavily on Internet technologies to integrate and manage business processes, while providing the information processing power to treat masses of customers as individuals.

To be an agile company, a business must implement four basic strategies. First, customers of an agile company perceive products or services as solutions to their individual problems. Thus, products can be priced based on their value as solutions, not on their cost to produce. Second, an agile company cooperates with customers, suppliers, and other companies, even *coopetition* with competitors. This allows a business to bring products to market as rapidly and cost-effectively as possible, no matter where resources are located and who owns them. Third, an agile company organizes so that it thrives on change and uncertainty. It uses flexible organizational structures keyed to the requirements of different and constantly changing customer opportunities. Finally, an agile company leverages the impact of its people and the knowledge they possess. By nurturing an entrepreneurial spirit, an agile company provides powerful incentives for employee responsibility, adaptability, and innovation [19]. Now let's take another look at AVNET Marshall, which is a great example of an agile company.

AVNET Marshall: Agile for the Customer

Marshall realized that customers, if given a choice, wanted everything: products and services at the lowest possible cost, highest possible quality, greatest possible customization, and fastest possible delivery time. At the limit, this translates to the impossible goals of "Free.Perfect.Now" [13].

Figure 2.18 reveals the components of the Free.Perfect.Now business model that inspired the company then known as Marshall Industries to be an agile, customer-focused company. AVNET Marshall developed the model as a clear, simple, and powerful tool to focus its employees and its information technology platform on serving its customers in the most agile and responsive ways.

The Free dimension emphasizes that most customers want the lowest cost for value received, but are willing to pay more for a value-added services such as inventory management. The Perfect dimension stresses that AVNET Marshall's products and services should not only be defect-free, but that their quality can be enhanced by added features, customization, and anticipation of the future needs of the customer. Finally, the Now dimension of this business model emphasizes that customers want 24/7 accessibility to products and services, short delivery times, and consideration of the time-to-market for their own products [13].

As we saw in the example in Section I, AVNET Marshall's extensive use of Internet technologies for innovative Internet, intranet, and extranet E-commerce websites and services for its customers, suppliers, and employees is a cornerstone of their IT and E-business strategies. Such technologies are essential to the agility and customer responsiveness that have made them a successful E-business enterprise.

Creating a Virtual Company

These days, thousands of companies, large and small, are setting up virtual corporations that enable executives, engineers, scientists, writers, researchers, and other professionals from around the world to collaborate on new products and services without ever meeting face to face. Once the exclusive domain of Fortune 500 companies with banks of powerful computers and dedicated wide area networks, remote networking is now available to any company with a phone, a fax, and E-mail access to the Internet [36].

In today's dynamic global business environment, forming a **virtual company** can be one of the most important strategic uses of information technology. A virtual company (also called a *virtual corporation* or *virtual organization*) is an organization that uses information technology to link people, assets, and ideas.

Figure 2.19 illustrates that virtual companies typically use an organizational structure called a **network structure,** since most virtual companies are interlinked by the Internet, intranets, and extranets. Notice that this company has organized

Figure 2.18

The Free.Perfect.Now business model developed by AVNET Marshall to guide their transformation into an agile, customer-focused company.

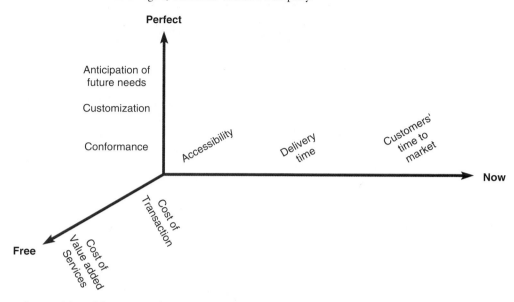

Source: Adapted from Omar El Sawy, Arvind Malhotra, Sanjay Gosain, and Kerry Young, "IT Intensive Value Innovation in the Electronic Economy: Insights from Marshall Industries," *MIS Quarterly*, September 1999, p. 311. Reprinted with permission from the *MIS Quarterly*.

internally into clusters of process and cross-functional teams linked by intranets. It has also developed alliances and extranet links that form **interorganizational information systems** with suppliers, customers, subcontractors, and competitors. Thus, network structures create flexible and adaptable virtual companies keyed to exploit fast-changing business opportunities [4].

Virtual Company Strategies

Why are people forming virtual companies? Several major reasons stand out and are summarized in Figure 2.20. People and corporations are forming virtual companies as the best way to implement key business strategies that promise to ensure success in today's turbulent business climate.

For example, in order to exploit a diverse and fast-changing market opportunity, a business may not have the time or resources to develop the manufacturing and distribution infrastructure, people competencies, and information technologies needed. Only by quickly forming a virtual company of all-star partners can it assemble the components it needs to provide a world-class solution for customers and capture the market opportunity. Of course, today, the Internet, intranets, extranets, and a variety of other Internet technologies are vital components in creating a successful solution.

Cisco Systems: Virtual Manufacturing

Cisco Systems is the world's largest manufacturer of telecommunications products. Jabil Circuit is the fourth largest company in the electronics contract manufacturing industry, with annual sales approaching $1 billion. Cisco has a *virtual manufacturing company* arrangement with Jabil and Hamilton Corporation, a major electronics parts supplier. Let's look at an example of how these three companies are involved in a typical business transaction.

An order placed for a Cisco 1600 series router (an internetwork processor used to connect small offices to networks) arrives simultaneously at Cisco in San Jose, California, and Jabil in St. Petersburg, Florida. Jabil immediately starts to build

Figure 2.19   A network structure facilitates the creation of virtual companies.

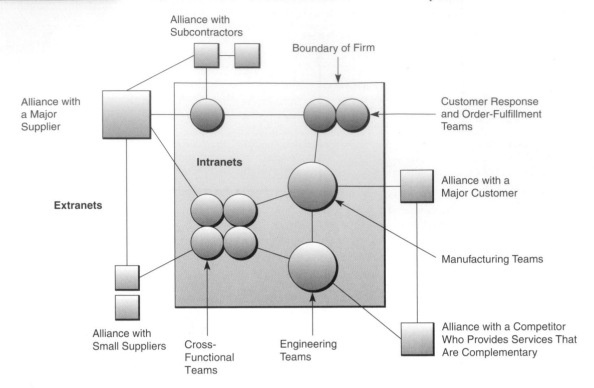

the router by drawing parts from three on-site inventories: Jabil's, one belonging to Cisco, and one owned and controlled by Hamilton. When completed, the router is tested and checked against the order in St. Petersburg by computers in San Jose, then shipped directly to the customer by Jabil. That triggers a Cisco invoice to the customer and electronic billings from Jabil and Hamilton to Cisco in San Jose. Thus, Cisco's virtual manufacturing company alliance with Jabil and Hamilton gives them an agile, build-to-order capability in the fiercely competitive telecommunications equipment industry [39].

Building a Knowledge-Creating Company

In an economy where the only certainty is uncertainty, the one sure source of lasting competitive advantage is knowledge. When markets shift, technologies proliferate, competitors multiply, and products become obsolete almost overnight, successful companies are those that consistently create new knowledge, disseminate it widely throughout the organization, and quickly embody it in new technologies and products. These activities define the "knowledge-creating" company, whose sole business is continuous innovation [32].

To many companies today, lasting competitive advantage can only be theirs if they become **knowledge-creating companies** or *learning organizations*. That means consistently creating new business knowledge, disseminating it widely throughout the company, and quickly building the new knowledge into their products and services.

Knowledge-creating companies exploit two kinds of knowledge. One is *explicit knowledge*—data, documents, things written down or stored on computers. The

Figure 2.20

The basic business strategies of virtual companies.

Strategies of Virtual Companies
● Share infrastructure and risk.
● Link complementary core competencies.
● Reduce concept-to-cash time through sharing.
● Increase facilities and market coverage.
● Gain access to new markets and share market or customer loyalty.
● Migrate from selling products to selling solutions.

other kind is tacit knowledge—the "how-tos" of knowledge, which reside in workers. Successful **knowledge management** creates techniques, technologies, and rewards for getting employees to share what they know and to make better use of accumulated workplace knowledge. In that way, employees of a company are leveraging knowledge as they do their jobs [32].

Knowledge Management Systems

New knowledge always begins with the individual. A brilliant researcher has an insight that leads to a new patent. A middle manager's intuitive sense of market trends becomes the catalyst for an important new products concept. A shop-floor worker draws on years of experience to come up with new process innovation. In each case, an individual's personal knowledge is transformed into organizational knowledge valuable to the company as a whole.

Making personal knowledge available to others is the central activity of the knowledge-creating company. It takes place continuously and at all levels of the organization [32].

Knowledge management has thus become one of the major strategic uses of information technology. Many companies are building **knowledge management systems** (KMS) to manage organizational learning and business know-how. The goal of such systems is to help knowledge workers create, organize, and make available important business knowledge, wherever and whenever it's needed in an organization. This includes processes, procedures, patents, reference works, formulas, "best practices," forecasts, and fixes. As you will see in Chapters 3 and 6, Internet and intranet websites, groupware, data mining, knowledge bases, and online discussion groups are some of the key technologies that may be used by a KMS.

Knowledge management systems facilitate organizational learning and knowledge creation. They use Internet and other technologies to collect and edit information, assess its value, disseminate it within the organization, and apply it as knowledge to the processes of a business. KMS are sometimes called *adaptive learning systems*, because they create cycles of organizational learning called *learning loops*, where the creation, dissemination, and application of knowledge produces an adaptive learning process within a company [12, 20].

Knowledge management systems are designed to provide rapid feedback to knowledge workers, encourage behavior changes by employees, and significantly improve business performance. As the organizational learning process continues and its knowledge base expands, the knowledge-creating company works to integrate its knowledge into its business processes, products, and services. This helps the company become a more innovative and agile provider of high-quality products and customer services, and a formidable competitor in the marketplace [35]. Now let's look at an example from the real world.

**Storage
Dimensions: A
Learning Company**

Storage Dimensions is a manufacturer and developer of high-availability RAID disk storage systems, high-capacity tape backup systems, and network storage management software. It markets and supports customers in Fortune 1000 companies in North America, Europe, and the Pacific Rim. Figure 2.21 illustrates the adaptive learning loop of Storage Dimensions' knowledge management system. This KMS is a key component of their TechConnect customer support management system, which has dramatically improved Storage Dimensions' customer service and support.

TechConnect relies on unique problem resolution software, use of the Internet and intranets, and online website knowledge base of hyperlinked solution documents. Customer problems are quickly analyzed and resolved by product managers, development engineers, technical support specialists, or the customers themselves. Solutions are incorporated into the TechConnect knowledge base as solutions documents. The new knowledge is automatically linked with related symptoms and solutions to update the knowledge base. TechConnect's software also automatically prioritizes solutions based on their usefulness or frequency of use in resolving specific kinds of problems. Thus, TechConnect learns, and new business knowledge is created each time it is used [12].

Figure 2.21

The adaptive learning loop of the knowledge management system used by Storage Dimensions' TechConnect customer support management system.

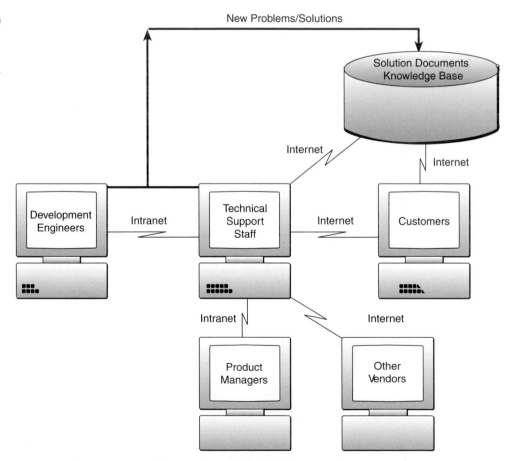

Source: Adapted from Omar El Sawy and Gene Bowles, "Redesigning the Customer Support Process for the Electronic Economy: Insights from Storage Dimensions," *MIS Quarterly*, December 1997, p. 467. Reprinted with permission from the *MIS Quarterly*.

Sustaining Strategic Success

We will close this chapter by looking at some of the factors that contribute to the success and sustainability of strategic information systems. Sustained success in using information technology strategically seems to depend on three sets of factors [25, 26]. See Figure 2.22.

- **The Environment.** A major environmental factor is the structure of an industry. For example, is it oligopolistic, that is, a closed structure with a few major players; or is it a wide open and level competitive playing field? Competitive restrictions and unique situations are environmental factors that involve political and regulatory restrictions to wide-open competition. For example, antitrust laws, patents, and government intervention can derail a company's plans for preemptive business use of IT.

- **Foundation Factors.** Unique industry position, organizational structure, alliances, assets, technological resources, and knowledge resources are foundation factors that can give a company a competitive edge in a market. If such a company develops a strategic business use of IT, they have a winning combination for strategic success.

- **Management Actions and Strategies.** None of the other factors mentioned will ensure success if a company's management does not develop and initiate successful actions and strategies that shape how information technology is actually applied in the marketplace. Examples include (1) preempting the market by being first and way ahead of competitors in strategic business uses of IT; (2) creating switching costs and barriers to entry; (3) implementing knowledge management and organizational learning; (4) developing strategies to quickly respond to the demands of customers and suppliers, and the catch-up moves of competitors; and (5) managing the business risks inherent in implementing any new or disruptive strategic IT initiatives [5].

Figure 2.22   Key factors for sustaining strategic success in the use of information technology.

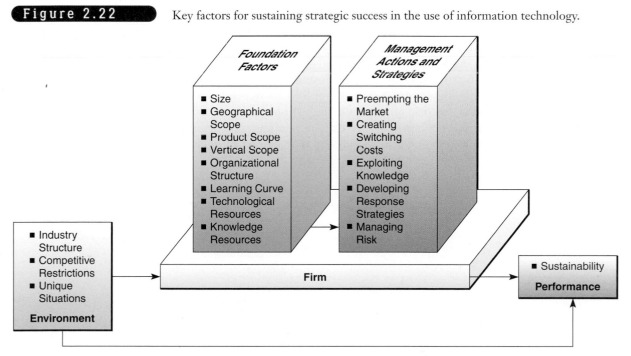

Source: Adapted from William Kettinger, Varun Grover, Subashish Guha, and Albert Segars, "Strategic Information Systems Revisited: A Study in Sustainability and Performance," *MIS Quarterly*, March 1994, p. 34. Reprinted with permission from the *MIS Quarterly*.

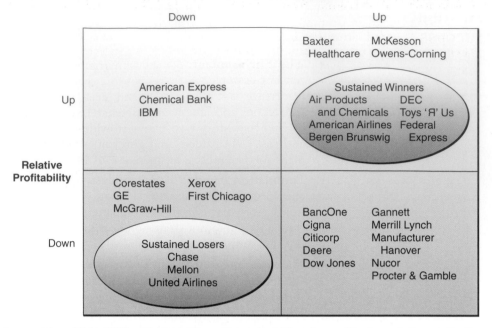

Source: Adapted from William Kettinger, Varun Grover, and Albert Segars, "Do Strategic Systems Really Pay Off? An Analysis of Classic Strategic IT Cases," *Information Systems Management* (New York: Auerbach Publications), Winter 1995, p. 39. © 1995 Research Institute of America. Used with permission.

Figure 2.23 provides an overview of research findings on companies that were winners or losers in their strategic use of information technology [26]. Sustained winners' investment in a specific strategic use of information technology continued to improve both their profitability and market share from 5 to 10 years after launching their strategic information systems. Sustained losers continued to suffer losses in profitability and market share for 5 to 10 years after making specific attempts to use IT strategically. As you can see, other companies had mixed success since they could not sustain profitability and market share for up to five years after introducing their strategic information systems.

So the lesson is clear. Sustained success in the strategic use of information technology is not a sure thing. Success depends on many environmental and foundation factors, but also on the actions and strategies of a company's management team. As a business manager, developing and defending against strategic business uses of information technology may be one of your biggest managerial challenges.

Summary

- **Strategic Uses of Information Technology.** Information technologies can support many competitive strategies. They can help a business cut costs, differentiate and innovate in its products and services, promote growth, develop alliances, lock in customers and suppliers, create switching costs, raise barriers to entry, and leverage its investment in IT resources. Thus, information technology can help a business gain a competitive advantage in its relationships with customers, suppliers, competitors, new entrants, and producers of substitute products. Refer to Figures 2.3 and 2.5 for summaries of the uses of information technology for strategic advantage.

- **Identifying E-Business and E-Commerce Strategies.** The Internet, intranets, extranets, and other Internet-based technologies can be used strategically for E-business and E-commerce capabilities that provide competitive advantage. This may result in major improvements in business efficiency and effectiveness, global market penetration, transforming products and services, and developing strategic applications and relationships with customers and business partners.

- **Building a Customer-Focused E-Business.** A key strategic use of Internet technologies is to build an E-business which develops its business value by making customer value its strategic focus. An E-business enterprise uses Internet, intranet, and extranet E-commerce websites and services to keep track of their customers' preferences; supply products, services, and information anytime, anywhere; and provide services tailored to the individual needs of their customers.

- **Reengineering Business Processes.** Information technology is a key ingredient in reengineering business operations by enabling radical changes to business processes that dramatically improve their efficiency and effectiveness. Internet technologies can play a major role in supporting innovative changes in the design of work flows, job requirements, and organizational structures in a company.

- **Improving Business Quality.** Information technology can be used to strategically improve the quality of business performance. In a total quality management approach, IT can support programs of continual improvement in meeting or exceeding customer requirements and expectations about the quality of products, services, customer responsiveness, and other features.

- **Becoming an Agile Company.** A business can use information technology to help it become an agile company. Then it can prosper in rapidly changing markets with broad product ranges and short model lifetimes in which it must process orders in arbitrary lot sizes, and can offer its customers customized products while maintaining high volumes of production. An agile company depends heavily on Internet technologies to help it be responsive to its customers with customized solutions to their needs and cooperate with its customers, suppliers, and other businesses to bring products to market as rapidly and cost-effectively as possible.

- **Creating a Virtual Company.** Forming virtual companies has become an important competitive strategy in today's dynamic global markets. Internet and other information technologies play an important role in providing computing and telecommunications resources to support the communications, coordination, and information flows needed. Managers of a virtual company depend on IT to help them manage a network of people, knowledge, financial, and physical resources provided by many business partners to quickly take advantage of rapidly changing market opportunities.

- **Building a Knowledge-Creating Company.** Lasting competitive advantage today can only come from innovative use and management of organizational knowledge by knowledge-creating companies and learning organizations. Internet technologies are widely used in knowledge management systems to support the creation and dissemination of business knowledge, and its integration into new products, services, and business processes.

- **The Challenge of Strategic IS.** Successful strategic information systems are not easy to develop and implement. They may require major changes in how a business operates internally and with external stakeholders. Sustained success depends on many environmental and fundamental business factors, and especially on the actions and strategies of a company's management team. So developing strategic uses of information technology is a major managerial challenge.

Key Terms and Concepts

These are the key terms and concepts of this chapter. The page number of their first explanation is in parentheses.

1. Agile company (63)
2. Business process reengineering (59)
3. Competitive forces (46)
4. Competitive strategies (46)
5. Creating switching costs (49)
6. Customer-focused E-business (57)
7. Identifying E-business and E-commerce strategies (52)
8. Knowledge-creating company (66)
9. Knowledge management system (67)
10. Leveraging investment in IT (49)
11. Locking in customers and suppliers (48)
12. Raising barriers to entry (49)
13. Strategic information systems (46)
14. Strategic uses of information technology (47)
15. Strategic uses of Internet technologies (44)
16. Sustaining competitive advantage (75)
17. Total quality management (61, 62)
18. Value chain (49)
19. Virtual company (64)

Review Quiz

Match one of the key terms and concepts listed previously with one of the brief examples or definitions that follow. Try to find the best fit for answers that seem to fit more than one term or concept. Defend your choices.

_____ 1. A business must deal with customers, suppliers, competitors, new entrants, and substitutes.

_____ 2. Cost leadership, differentiation of products, and new product innovation are examples.

_____ 3. Using investment in technology to keep firms out of an industry.

_____ 4. Making it unattractive for a firm's customers or suppliers to switch to its competitors.

_____ 5. Time, money, and effort needed for customers or suppliers to change to a firm's competitors.

_____ 6. Information systems that reengineer business processes or promote business innovation are examples.

_____ 7. Internet technologies enable a company to emphasize customer value as its strategic focus.

_____ 8. Highlights how strategic information systems can be applied to a firm's business processes and support activities for competitive advantage.

_____ 9. A business can find strategic uses for the computing and telecommunications capabilities it has developed to run its operations.

_____ 10. A business can use information systems to build barriers to entry, promote innovation, create switching costs, and so on.

_____ 11. Information technology can help a business make radical improvements in business processes.

_____ 12. Programs of continual improvement in meeting or exceeding customer requirements or expectations.

_____ 13. A business can prosper in rapidly changing markets while offering its customers individualized solutions to their needs.

_____ 14. A network of business partners formed to take advantage of rapidly changing market opportunities.

_____ 15. Many companies use the Internet, intranets, and extranets to achieve strategic gains in their competitive position.

_____ 16. Learning organizations that focus on creating, disseminating, and managing business knowledge.

_____ 17. Information systems that manage the creation and dissemination of organizational knowledge.

_____ 18. The competitive advantages of IT will disappear unless management implements strategies such as exploiting knowledge management.

_____ 19. Analyzing the strategic business value of E-business and E-commerce applications.

Discussion Questions

1. Suppose you are a manager being asked to develop E-business and E-commerce applications to gain a competitive advantage in an important market for your company. What reservations might you have about doing so? Why?

2. How could a business use information technology to increase switching costs and lock in its customers and suppliers? Use business examples to support your answers.

3. How could a business leverage its investment in information technology to build strategic IT capabilities that serve as a barrier to entry by new entrants into its markets?

4. Refer to the Real World Case on General Electric in the chapter. If you were a competitor of GE, what would you do to counter some of their E-business strategies? Use one of their businesses to illustrate your answer.

5. What strategic role can information play in business process reengineering and total quality management?

6. How can Internet technologies help a business form strategic alliances with its customers, suppliers, and others?

7. How could a business use Internet technologies to form a virtual company or become an agile competitor?

8. Refer to the Real World Case on McDonald's and American Express in the chapter. What strategic role should venture capital firms play to support E-business or E-commerce initiatives in today's economy?

9. Information technology can't really give a company a strategic advantage, because most competitive advantages don't last more than a few years and soon become strategic necessities that just raise the stakes of the game. Discuss.

10. MIS author and consultant Peter Keen says: "We have learned that it is not technology that creates a competitive edge, but the management process that exploits technology." What does he mean? Do you agree or disagree? Why?

Application Exercises

Complete the following exercises as individual or group projects that apply chapter concepts to real world business situations.

1. **Avnet Marshall and McAfee: Customer-Focused E-Business**

   Visit the top-rated websites of Avnet Marshall (www.avnetmarshall.com) and McAfee Associates (www.mcafee.com), which are highlighted in the chapter as examples of customer-focused E-business companies. Check out many of their website features and E-commerce services.

   a. Which site provided you with the best quality of service as a prospective customer? Explain.

   b. How could these companies improve their website design and marketing to offer even better services to their customers and prospective customers?

2. **Sabre's Travelocity and American Airlines: Competing for E-Travel Services**

   Visit the top-rated websites of Travelocity (www.travelocity.com), which is 70 percent owned by Sabre, and American Airlines (www.aa.com), the former corporate owner of Sabre. Check out their website features and E-commerce services.

   a. How do their E-commerce websites and business models seem to differ?

   b. Refer to the summaries of strategic uses of IT in Figures 2.3 and 2.5. Which strategies can you see each company using? Explain.

   c. How could each company improve their competitive position in travel services E-commerce?

3. Assessing Strategy and Business Performance

The latest annual figures for eBay.com's net revenue, stock price, and earnings per share at the time of publication of this book are shown below. eBay™ is one of the firms identified in Figure 2.4 as following a cost leadership strategy. Update the data for eBay™ if more recent annual figures are available and get comparable data for at least one other firm from the set of firms listed in Figure 2.4. (You can get financial data about most companies by looking on their website for a link called investor relations or about the company. If necessary search the index or site map.)

a. Create a spreadsheet based on these data. Your spreadsheet should include measures of percentage change in revenues, earnings per share and stock price. You should also compute the price earnings (PE) ratio, that is stock price divided by earnings per share. (Note that some companies may have no earning for a particular year so that the PE ratio cannot be computed for that year.

b. Create appropriate graphs highlighting trends in the performance of each company.

c. Write a brief (one page) report addressing how successful each company appears to be in maintaining strategic advantage? How important were general market conditions in affecting the financial performance of your companies.

Table 2.1

eBay's financial performance.

Year	Net Revenue (in millions)	Earnings per Share	Stock Price (at Year End)
1998	$186.129	$0.05	$40.21
1999	$224.724	$0.08	$62.59
2000	$431.424	$0.17	$33.00

4. Just-in-Time Inventory Systems for Pinnacle Manufacturing

Pinnacle Manufacturing is evaluating a proposal for the development of a new inventory management system that will allow it to use just-in-time techniques to manage the inventories of key raw materials. It is estimated that the new system will allow Pinnacle to operate with inventory levels for gadgets, widgets, and sprockets equaling 10 days of production and with inventories equaling only 5 days of production for cams and gizmos. In order to estimate the inventory cost savings from this system, you have been asked to gather information about current inventory levels at all of Pinnacle's production facilities. You have received estimates of the current inventory level of each raw material the amount of each raw material used in a typical production day, and the average dollar value of a unit of each raw material. These estimates are shown below.

a. Create a spreadsheet based on estimates below. Your spreadsheet should include a column showing the number of days of inventory of each raw material currently held (inventory value divided by inventory used per production day). It should also include columns showing the inventory needed under the new system (inventory used per day times 10 or 5) and the reduction in inventory under the new system for each raw material. Finally you should include columns showing the dollar value of existing inventories, the dollar value of inventories under the new system and the reduction in dollar value of the inventories held.

b. Assume that the annual cost of holding inventory is 10 percent times the level of inventory held. Add a summary showing the overall annual savings from the new system.

Table 2.2

Pinnacle's inventory estimates.

Item	Inventory (units)	Units Used per Day	Cost per Unit
Gadget	2,437,250	97,645	$2.25
Widget	3,687,450	105,530	$0.85
Sprocket	1,287,230	29,632	$3.25
Cam	2,850,963	92,732	$1.28
Gizmo	6,490,325	242,318	$2.60

Oracle Corporation: E-Business Catch-up Strategies

If you're a laggard in the Internet revolution, is it too late to catch up? Not yet—if your transition is as smart, targeted, and relentless as Oracle's.

In 1995 and 1996 a handful of digital pioneers like Cisco, Dell, Schwab, and Cemex were already putting in place new strategic options and building profitability through their use of digital technologies. Software giant Oracle was nowhere to be found. At least not until 1998, when founder and CEO Larry Ellison became dissatisfied with his company's performance. Oracle was recording profit margins of 16 percent—healthy in most industries, but lagging those of archrival Microsoft and other software firms. Ellison realized that Oracle had been slow to harness the Internet, to integrate and streamline business processes, and to create value for customers. So he launched a digital lightning attack. In two years Oracle was able to accomplish what took Cisco and other digital pioneers four years. So let's try to understand the basic principles that went into Ellison's revolution, and how those principles hold for any firm looking to become a digital company quickly.

1. Don't innovate, emulate. The first generation of digital innovators had already invented the wheel. So Ellison and his team were able to save precious time by emulating the best, most appropriate digital moves and strategies.

Dell had already linked its customers and suppliers in a digital network. Cisco had already shifted most purchasing, sales, customer service, and other business processes online. Oracle began moving its processes online in similar fashion and adapted other ideas from each of the pioneers. By unifying its internal processes and building self-service systems for customers, employees and suppliers, Oracle trimmed expenses by hundreds of millions of dollars, all while improving accuracy, speed, and convenience. For example, the cost of the typical service call was $350. The same query handled over the Internet: under $20.

Now that we're five years into the era of the digital business, there are some two dozen smart, tested and debugged digital moves ready to be copied. Brilliant emulation can be far more profitable than brilliant innovation.

2. Be unreasonable. Oracle created an all-or-nothing mentality around digitization. The message: Everything has to change. The internal computer network was rapidly consolidated, with 44 data centers reduced to one. Employees realized that they had to move fast to define their roles in the new Oracle. The company helped by sponsoring many training seminars on digitization.

Having Ellison as your CEO doesn't hurt. Ellison used such get-your-undivided-attention tactics as setting outrageous, mushrooming goals for his digital initiatives: April 1999, "We'll save half a billion dollars"; June 1999, "Make that a billion"; June 2000, "No, make it two billion." Was all of the economic improvement achieved through productivity? No, some came through revenue enhancement. Whatever the mix of these two factors, however, laying out the goals created tremendous psychological momentum. Says one Oracle alumnus, "The message from management was simple: 'We know things change rapidly in our business. Now we have to do it ourselves.'"

3. Get top customers involved. Oracle asked its most important customers to define the new benefits they wanted the digital side to produce; then it provided them. The most important benefit customers sought was the integration of their business systems, reducing the typical jigsaw puzzle of information modules into a single package. During 1999, Oracle built such a system for its own use. The modules, released as E-Business Suite 11i in the year 2000, offered the first integrated Internet package of ERP, supply-chain management, and database software. Then Oracle entered the fast-growing application service provider market with Business OnLine.

The new products are solid hits with customers, who report that they're spending less on hardware and staffing and say they're dealing with a new style at Oracle (which used to leave customer information scattered in different databases). Notes one customer: "now, as soon as I call, they know exactly who I am and what I have."

Oracle also used its website to connect and satisfy customers more efficiently. A "See, Try, Buy" function lets customers research and test Oracle products for free, then buy them online.. Real-time pricing eliminates haggling on all purchases under $500,000, saving customers (and Oracle) weeks of time and aggravation.

4. Faster is easier. Just as moving all your possessions into a new home in one day is easier than lugging one carton a day for a month, digitizing quickly can be less disruptive. Speed creates an unmistakable sense of urgency, underscoring the message to your people: "This isn't optional." When everyone starts to move, things happen more quickly, and at a certain point the chain reaction becomes irreversible.

Case Study Questions

1. Do you agree that the strategies outlined in this case are necessary for any company that wants to transform themselves into an E-business enterprise? Why or why not?

2. Which of the four E-business catch-up strategies described in this case would be the easiest to implement? The most difficult? Why?

3. What are several problems that could arise for a company that tries to implement the strategies in this case? How could such problems be solved?

Source: Adapted from Adrian Slywotzky, "Four Lessons From Larry", *Fortune*, March 5, 2001, pp. 178–80.

E*Trade Bank and Others: Evaluating Online Banking Strategies

Web-based banks figured their pitch was irresistible: By eliminating physical branches, tellers, and bankers' hours, they could slash costs and offer customers higher interest rates and more convenience. But in reality, customers want human contact, or at least an ATM. They're voting with their dollars.

Online banks are still struggling to attract business. E*Trade Bank, the largest Internet-only bank, counts around 290,000 customers, while no others claim more than 100,000 customers. The first online-only bank, Security First Network Bank, sold out in 1998 to the Royal Bank Financial Group of Canada, and even Citibank's Net-only offering, Citi f/I, flopped.

Many of the remaining entrants now own up to the fact that they need some of the physical presence they earlier denounced as too costly. Last May, E*Trade Bank bought more than 9,600 ATMs, and is testing an ATM with an E*Trade kiosk inside a Target store in Roswell, Georgia. In October, the Bank One–backed WingspanBank.com partnered with an ATM network to give customers 30,000 places to deposit checks and cash, and is also testing deposit kiosks within Bank One branches. Some online banks, such as Massachusetts-based directbanking.com, have even opened branches where customers can walk in and talk with a real banker.

"The multichannel strategy is what's important to people. They want to be able to use the Web, but it's not like 1996 rolled around and everyone forgot about the real world," says James Van Dyke, a senior analyst with Jupiter Research. "Money is too important to people. Most are not going to switch banks for a couple of percentage points."

Online banks have also learned that convenience means more than just twenty-four-hour banking. In fact, some aspects of the virtual banking model are flat-out inconvenient. For example, online banks require that deposits be made by check or money order eliminating the cash option available at traditional banks. "We heard from people that didn't know how to get money into the bank," says Kevin Watters, WingspanBank.com's senior vice president of marketing. "We asked customers, and 80 percent said they would like to deposit into an ATM."

Adding physical infrastructure, though, adds to an online bank's operating costs and may force it to lower interest rates paid on savings. Online banks maintain that they still run more efficiently than traditional banks because of practices such as online account managers, loan officers, and so on. That allows them to manage a branch with a smaller staff than a traditional bank would have.

Still, the additional costs of maintaining even a limited network of ATMs kiosks or branches might force online banks to pull back from the high interest rates they initially promised on savings. "A physical connection is going to be critical to online banks taking off," says Jamie Punishill, a senior analyst with Forrester Research. "And it may mean instead of 6 percent interest, customers get 4 percent interest."

Although a multchannel approach may appeal to customers, the strategy undermines the very premise of online-only institutions and makes them less distinguishable from traditional banks that also offer Web-banking services. It's a lot easier and cheaper for an existing bank to roll out Internet services than it is for a Net bank to buy enough ATMs or branches to compete on a national level.

So rather than competing head-to-head with big banks, some online banks, like directbanking.com, are choosing a regional strategy. And E*Trade Bank can lean on its relationship with the E*Trade brokerage to handle cash tied to customers' investments.

Some online banks, such as Atlanta-based NetBank, are set on remaining broadly focused. So far, NetBank does not offer any products or services that require a physical channel, says CEO D.R. Grimes. He insists that the bank is thriving with its lean online business model. NetBank has 10 consecutive quarters of profits to bolster the argument.

But for all its success, NetBank has only about 95,000 customers. To attract more, it has to convince people to give up some of the convenience of real-world banking when other Internet banks are offering more.

That's why most analysts remain skeptical that online-only banks will ever rise above boutique status. "It's very difficult for a start-up to market to a generic audience and become an online-only, broad player," says Van Dyke of Jupiter. "Those going up against fairly Net-ready, savvy organizations such as Bank of America and Wells Fargo are going to be in trouble."

Case Study Questions

1. What went wrong with the E-commerce strategies of Internet-only banks?

2. How are online banks changing their business strategies to survive? Will they be successful? Why or why not?

3. What else can all banks do to grow their online banking business? Provide a business case for your proposals.

Source: Adapted from Sean Donahue, "Don't Bank on It," *Business 2.0*, January 9, 2001, p. 35.

Dell Computer Corp.: Failure in B2B E-Commerce Strategy

Michael Dell has developed an attitude. He isn't as ornery as Oracle's Larry Ellison yet, but give the thirty-five-year-old chairman and CEO of Dell Computer some time. Mr. Dell has had to face growing criticism on Wall Street for his company's poor forecast of growth and an overall slowdown of PC sales. But Dell is defiant: "We have a very strong cash flow engine in our business, and the first thing I would tell you is I don't think there is anything wrong with a business that generates a lot of cash flow."

But sandwiched between Sun Microsystems on the high end and handheld appliances on the low end, Dell's growth isn't what it once was. Some think Dell needs to make an acquisition. "Bunk," says Mr. Dell. "We're acquiring our competitors, but we're doing it one customer at a time. We've looked at a number of potential acquisitions, and I can say that 99 percent of the time we made the right decision in not buying our competitors."

Dell makes few apologies for his company's performance. And in his fall 2000 Comdex keynote speech, he laughed at dot-coms and the free-PC crowd with business models that weren't "Y2K-compliant." But he still has to prove that Dell's present business plan is Wall Street–compliant.

Analysts said Dell Computer Corp.'s sudden shutdown of a business-to-business (B2B) exchange it launched with great fanfare just four months ago is more evidence that companies need to be sure of what they're doing before they dive into Internet-based business strategies.

Like many participants in B2B exchanges, Round Rock, Texas–based Dell was lured by predictions that online marketplaces would make good sales channels, said Ronald Exler, an analyst at Robert Frances Group in Westport, Connecticut. "They got caught up in the hype," he said. "I think they probably didn't realize the nature of what they were getting into."

So the PC maker confirmed that Dell Marketplace, the exchange it launched in October 2000, was closed in early January 2001. Dell had teamed with Mountain View, California–based Ariba Inc. and other software vendors to set up the exchange as a site where users could shop for products from Dell and other companies. But it pulled the plug after only three suppliers—3M Co., Motorola Inc. and Pitney Bowes Inc.—joined the exchange.

Rob Rosenthal, an analyst at IDC in Framingham, Massachusetts, said the speed with which Dell gave up on the venture is noteworthy. "They might not have realized up front that is was going to be a longer-term venture to make the exchange a success," he said. The exchange's shutdown came two weeks after Dell warned that profits would fall below expectations in its fiscal fourth quarter.

Dell spokesman Ken Bissell declined to say how much the company had invested in the venture. The decision to close the exchange wasn't based on the small number of participants, Bissell said, but he acknowledged that the collaborative commerce showcase that Dell had in mind is "somewhat immature." The company quickly discovered that customers aren't ready to use exchanges such as Dell Marketplace in droves, he said. Some users had asked Dell to develop a Web site with the capabilities that the exchange offered, Bissell said, "but as things sometimes go, you recognize that situations can change."

Dell will now use Supplier Advantage, a program it set up with Microsoft Corp. to market business-to-business technology to users who want to create their own online marketplaces. That offering bundles Dell's servers with software from Microsoft and consulting services from Chicago-based Lante Corp.

Bissell insisted that prospective Supplier Advantage customers shouldn't view Dell's pullout from its exchange as an ominous sign for their online venture. "I don't see it as a mixed message at all," he said.

Case Study Questions

1. Do you agree with some Wall Street analysts' concerns about Dell Computer's business performance or prospects? Why or why not?

2. Why did the Dell Marketplace fail? How could this failure have been avoided? Explain.

3. Was Dell Marketplace a strategic failure, or a reasonable business gamble whose loss Dell can absorb and learn from in other E-commerce ventures? Explain your reasoning.

Source: Adapted from Dean Takahashi and Michael Fitzgerald, "Michael Dell: Billionaire, Chief Executive, Weatherman," *Red Herring*, January 30, 2001, and Todd Weiss, "Dell Closes Marketplace After Four Months," *Computerworld*, February 12, 2001, p. 25.

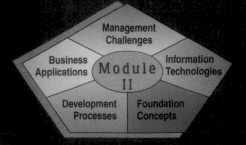

Module II

Business Applications

How do Internet technologies and other forms of IT support electronic business operations, electronic commerce, enterprise communications and collaboration, and business decision making? The four chapters of this module show you how such business applications of information systems are accomplished in today's internetworked enterprises.

- **Chapter 3: The Internetworked E-Business Enterprise,** explores how the Internet, intranets, and extranets provide the technology platform for electronic business and commerce applications, and enterprise communications and collaboration in the E-business enterprise.

- **Chapter 4: Electronic Business Systems,** describes how information systems integrate and support the enterprise-wide business processes and business functions of marketing, manufacturing, human resource management, accounting, and finance.

- **Chapter 5: Electronic Commerce Systems,** introduces the basic process components of E-commerce systems, and discusses important trends, applications, and issues in E-commerce.

- **Chapter 6: E-Business Decision Support,** shows how management information systems, decision support systems, executive information systems, expert systems, and artificial intelligence technologies can be applied to decision-making situations faced by business managers and professionals in today's E-business environment.

Technical Note: At the option of your instructor, you may be assigned one or more of the chapters in **Module V: Review of Information Technologies,** before being assigned the chapters in this module. Module V contains material on computer hardware (Chapter 11), computer software (Chapter 12), data resource management (Chapter 13), and telecommunications and networks (Chapter 14), some of which you may have previously covered in other computer courses, but may be asked to review to refresh your knowledge of these important aspects of information technology.

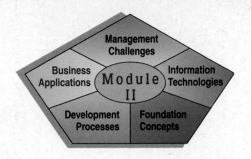

Management
Challenges

Business
Applications M o d u l e Information
II Technologies

Development Foundation
Processes Concepts

The Internetworked E-Business

Enterprise

Chapter Highlights

Learning Objectives

After reading and studying this chapter, you should be able to:

1. Identify the major types of electronic business applications supported by the Internet, intranets, and extranets in an E-business enterprise.

2. Give several examples of how companies are using the Internet, intranets, and extranets for communication and collaboration, information publishing and sharing, and business operations and management.

3. Identify several of the hardware, software, data, and network components of an intranet's information technology architecture.

4. Identify several ways that the use of the Internet, intranets, and extranets can provide cost savings or other business benefits to a company.

5. Identify several groupware tools for electronic communications, conferencing, and work management, and give examples of how they can enhance the collaboration of teams and workgroups in a business enterprise.

Section I

The Internet, Intranets, and Extranets in Business

The Internetworked E-Business Enterprise

In the emerging economy there is a new infrastructure, based on the Internet, that is causing us to scrutinize most of our assumptions about the firm. As a skin of networks—growing in ubiquity, robustness, bandwidth, and function—covers the skin of the planet, new models of how wealth is created are emerging [18].

Businesses have become **internetworked E-business enterprises.** The Internet and Internet-like networks inside the enterprise (intranets), between an enterprise and its trading partners (extranets), and other types of networks are now the primary information technology infrastructure of many organizations. An internetworked E-business enterprise enables mangers, business professionals, teams, and workgroups to electronically exchange data and information anywhere in the world with other end users, customers, suppliers, and business partners. Companies and workgroups can thus collaborate more creatively, manage their business operations and resources more effectively, and compete successfully in today's fast-changing global economy.

Analyzing Uniglobe.com and Allfirst Bank

Read the Real World Case on Uniglobe.com and Allfirst Bank on the next page. We can learn a lot about the challenges and opportunities that E-commerce presents to businesses concerning the care and management of their online customer relationships. See Figure 3.1.

Providing effective service and support to customers before, during, and after the sale has always been a major challenge. But customer care has become even more crucial with the advent of electronic commerce, which has added a vast electronic marketplace in which companies must compete for online customers, who can switch in an instant to their competitors. Uniglobe has responded with a new call center which integrates phone, E-mail, and chat systems for communicating with online

Figure 3.1

Mike Dauberman, Senior Vice-President of Business Operations for Uniglobe.com, established a call center that provides phone, E-mail, and chat support to customers.

Brian Smale.

Uniglobe.com and Allfirst Bank: Online Customer Care Alternatives

Pop quiz for E-commerce website managers: When a customer goes to a website and has a question he can't get answered—"Does your coffeemaker come in white?"—what does that customer do? Answer: He probably E-mails his question to the site, waits a few minutes and then goes to another site, where he finds what he's looking for and buys the coffeemaker. Case closed. Oh, and eventually an E-mail response from the first company shows up, the delay proving to the consumer that he made the right choice by shopping elsewhere.

Today's Web retailers are increasingly wise to the impatience and fickleness of many online shoppers. Numerous studies report shopping-cart abandonment rates of 20% to 60% per transaction. That's why retailers are investing in improved customer-care technologies such as Internet telephone, dynamic lists of frequently asked questions (FAQ), and text chat systems to get customers the answers they need to buy goods right away. Retailers are also paying to integrate previously disparate E-mail, phone, and chat systems. Integration means shorter response times, which can lead to greater sales.

In the cruise industry, quick responses to potential cruise buyers mean everything. That's because booking a cruise is an impulse buy, says Mike Dauberman, Senior Vice President of Business Operations of Vancouver, British Columbia-based Uniglobe.com of Canada, a subsidiary of Uniglobe Travel (International). Dauberman, who works at the U.S. headquarters in Renton, Washington, says, "If you can grab a customer while they're on their peak of interest in a cruise, they're considerably more likely to buy it."

That's why Uniglobe tries to respond to every customer E-mail within twenty minutes and to have phone representatives standing by to answer calls. But in mid-1999, the company was growing quickly, and the twenty-minute mark was hard to maintain. With Y2K approaching and Uniglobe's call center nearing the end of its five-year amortization, Dauberman says he wanted an all-in-one call center that would route not just incoming phone calls but also chat and E-mail to all of its agents' desks, one at a time. So now, if an agent doesn't have any phone calls in his queue, the software assigns him a text chat or an E-mail.

In October 1999, Uniglobe had a new call center from Avaya Inc. for 110 people up and running in five days, with no maintenance needed for the first twelve months. Uniglobe is about to upgrade the call center software and add capacity for 50 more people. The software cost $50,000 to $60,000 and coordinates all phone, E-mail, and chat traffic.

Avaya also made computer and telecom hardware recommendations, and "we went overboard," says Dauberman. "They said you could run this thing off a $400 Pentium, but we decided to get some fairly sophisticated Web servers." Uniglobe bought six Windows NT servers to run the phone system. Add networking costs and cable, and the extra equipment cost $30,000 to $40,000, he says. Uniglobe had considered building its own call center software to handle E-mail, phone, and chat traffic by contacting the individual suppliers for such capabilities. "It would have been considerably less expensive," says Dauberman—possibly as little as $15,000—"but it would not have been integrated." And integration was the critical selling point, he says.

Today Uniglobe's goal is to have a customer care system that enables it to staff its call center with people who only need to know how to use Microsoft Outlook. "My call center staff isn't technical. If they can use E-mail, they can use our call center," he says.

Other companies are taking the plunge into voice-over IP (a way to converse with another online user by telephone via an Internet connection, while also browsing the same Web pages). Visitors to the Web site of Allfirst Bank, a subsidiary of Allfirst Financial in Baltimore, can use their PCs to carry on phone conversations with the bank's salespeople. Java Script software, downloaded when the user hits a "live talk" link, creates a voice-over IP session. But users need a computer equipped with a sound card, a microphone, speakers, and a fast modem.

The goal is to make the customer's experience more intimate. "We're trying to humanize what we do. You go back to the brand. Chat was a way of humanizing customer care, but voice is a heck of a way of humanizing it," says Bill Murray, Senior Vice President of E-commerce at Allfirst. Murray says he was drawn to voice-over IP because unlike shopping for CDs or books, people often want to talk over their options before signing up for new bank accounts.

The bottom line for many E-business companies is reflected in a survey conducted by the Meta Group that indicates that live customer service can cut shopping-cart abandonment rates by 10% to 45% because company representatives can walk customers through problems or immediately answer their questions.

Case Study Questions

1. Why do you think so many online users abandon their shopping carts before completing their purchases?

2. Do you agree with how UniGlobe and Allfirst are moving to solve this problem? Why or why not?

3. What online communications methods would you prefer as an online customer at an E-commerce website? Why?

Source: Adapted from Mathew Schwartz, "The Care and Keeping of Online Customers," *Computerworld*, January 8, 2001, pp. 58–59.

and offline customers. Allfirst has added an Internet telephone capability to their customer support ineractions because they found that their customers prefer a more personal type of communications to discuss their banking matters. Studies show that such strategies do contribute significantly to improving a company's acquistion and retention of online customers.

E-Business

We defined **E-business** in Chapter 1 as the use of Internet technologies to internetwork and empower business process, electronic commerce, and enterprise communications and collaboration within a company and with its customers, suppliers, and other business stakeholders. Figure 3.2 shows how an E-business enterprise can use the Internet to interconnect its E-commerce websites, intranets for internal services within the company, and extranets to customers and suppliers. In this chapter, we will see how the Internet, intranets, and extranets support electronic business applications and enable enterprise communications and collaboration.

Overview of E-Business Applications

Figure 3.3 illustrates some of the many possible electronic business applications of an internetworked enterprise. It groups E-business applications into the major categories of enterprise communication and collaboration, electronic commerce, and internal business systems. Notice that these applications rely on the Internet, intranets, extranets, and other types of enterprise and interorganizational telecommunications networks. We will discuss the role of the Internet, intranets, and extranets in this section and cover enterprise communication and collaboration in Section II. Electronic commerce is covered in Chapter 5, and internal E-business applications will be discussed in Chapters 4 and 6.

Enterprise communications and collaboration applications support communication, coordination, and collaboration among the members of business teams

Figure 3.2

An E-business enterprise uses the Internet to interconnect its World Wide Web sites, intranets to other company locations, and extranets to business partners.

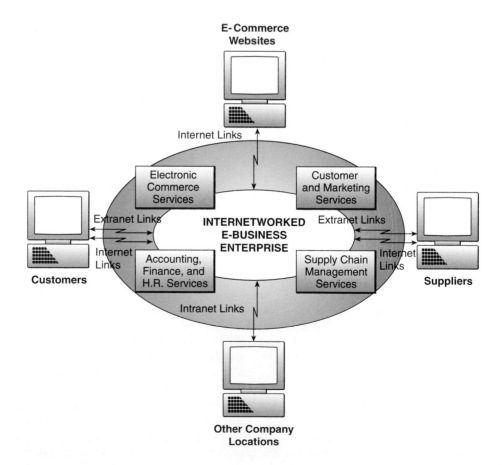

Figure 3.3

An overview of the E-business applications of the internetworked enterprise. Note the many types of applications for enterprise communication and collaboration, electronic commerce, and internal business operations.

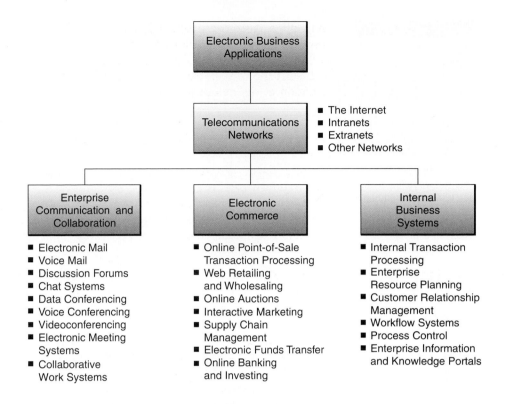

and workgroups. For example, employees and external consultants on a project team may use the Internet, intranets, and extranets to support electronic mail, videoconferencing, electronic discussion groups, and project websites to communicate and collaborate on business projects. **Electronic commerce** applications support the buying and selling of products, services, and information over the Internet and extranets. For example, many businesses use E-commerce websites for business-to-business and business-to-consumer sales and support, use extranets so large customers can access the company's inventory databases, and use a corporate intranet so employees can easily look up customer records stored on intranet servers.

Internal business applications of an E-business enterprise support a company's internal business processes and operations. For example, employees may use an intranet *enterprise information portal* to access benefits information on a human resource department server. Or a company may link an intranet to the Internet so managers can make inquiries, generate reports, and access corporate databases from anywhere in the world.

Business Use of the Internet

As Figure 3.4 illustrates, business use of the Internet has expanded from an electronic information exchange to a broad platform for strategic business applications. Notice how applications like collaboration among business partners, providing customer and vendor support, and electronic commerce have become major business uses of the Internet. Other studies of leading corporations and organizations show that they are also using Internet technologies for marketing, sales, and customer relationship management applications. However, these studies also show the strong growth of cross-functional business applications and the emergence of applications in engineering, manufacturing, human resources, and accounting.

Companies are using the Internet for business in a variety of ways, including enterprise communications and collaboration, electronic commerce, and strategic business alliances. Let's look at a real world example.

Figure 3.4 Examples of how a company can use the Internet for business.

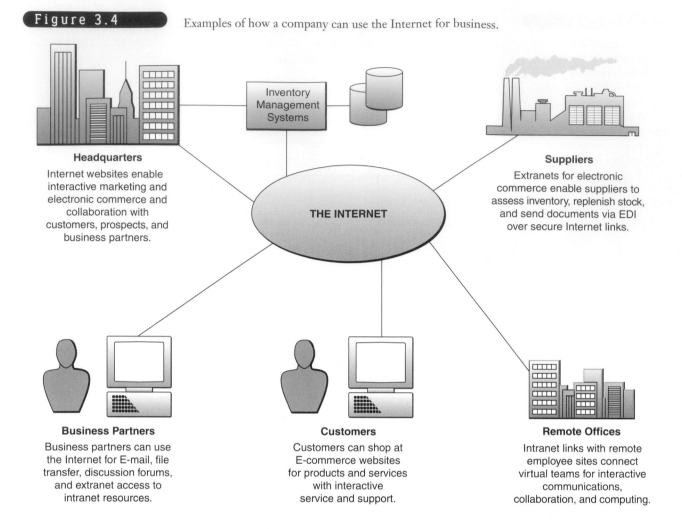

Headquarters
Internet websites enable interactive marketing and electronic commerce and collaboration with customers, prospects, and business partners.

Inventory Management Systems

THE INTERNET

Suppliers
Extranets for electronic commerce enable suppliers to assess inventory, replenish stock, and send documents via EDI over secure Internet links.

Business Partners
Business partners can use the Internet for E-mail, file transfer, discussion forums, and extranet access to intranet resources.

Customers
Customers can shop at E-commerce websites for products and services with interactive service and support.

Remote Offices
Intranet links with remote employee sites connect virtual teams for interactive communications, collaboration, and computing.

GE Power Systems: Using the Internet

General Electric Co. (GE) provides a fascinating glimpse of how the Net changes things. At GE Power Systems, customers and designers can use intranets, extranets, the Internet, and project collaboration technology to help construct a power plant from the ground up on the Web, says Jose A. Lopez, the subsidiary's general manager of E-business.

GE and customer engineers can now hold virtual meetings in which blueprints can be exchanged and manipulated in real time. Then customers can use the Web to watch from anywhere in the world as a turbine is built and moves down the production line, ordering last-minute changes as needed. Because the turbines cost an average of $35 million each and contain about 18,000 parts, catching changes—and errors—early is priceless. And after the turbine is delivered, a new Net-powered system called the Turbine Optimizer lets both customers and GE compare the performances of the turbines with other GE turbines around the world.

While GE's new systems should give the company a 20 percent to 30 percent reduction in the time it takes to build a turbine and could improve the annual output of each turbine by 1 percent to 2 percent, that's just the beginning. "Sure, there are productivity gains for us, but this is mainly a competetive advantage," says

Lopez. "If customers find this helps them, they'll come back." So far, so good: Sales at GE Power Systems increased to about $13 billion in 2000, up 30 percent from 1999 [31].

The Business Value of the Internet

The Internet provides a synthesis of computing and communication capabilities that adds value to every part of the business cycle [10].

What business value do companies derive from their business applications on the Internet? Figure 3.5 summarizes how many companies perceive the business value of the Internet for electronic commerce. Substantial cost savings can arise because applications that use the Internet and Internet-based technologies (like intranets and extranets) are typically less expensive to develop, operate, and maintain than traditional systems. For example, American Airlines saves money every time customers use their website instead of their customer support telephone system.

Other primary reasons for business value include attracting new customers with innovative marketing and products, and retaining present customers with improved customer service and support. Of course, generating revenue through electronic commerce applications is a major source of business value, which we will discuss in Chapter 5. To summarize, most companies are building E-commerce websites to achieve six major business values:

- Generate new revenue from online sales.
- Reduce costs through online sales and customer support.
- Attract new customers via Web marketing and advertising and online sales.
- Increase the loyalty of existing customers via improved Web customer service and support.
- Develop new Web-based markets and distribution channels for existing products.
- Develop new information-based products accessible on the Web [18].

Figure 3.5

How companies are deriving business value from their E-commerce applications.

Milacron Inc.: Business Value of E-Commerce	Manufacturing equipment vendor Milacron Inc. launched an ambitious, multi-million-dollar electronic commerce site aimed at thousands of new business customers. There are about 117,000 metalworking shops with 50 or fewer employees in the United States. According to Milacron market research, about half those shops already are on the Internet.

The Milacron site, called Milpro (www.milpro.com), was designed for machine shops that previously were considered too small to merit the attention of a Milacron salesperson. Milacron customers frequently require a lot of time from the company's sales engineers for help in selecting and setting up the company's complex industrial equipment. Now, Milacron's sales force and field-service engineers have two territories: their regular, geographic regions and new "cyberterritories." Salespeople now receive commissions for any orders secured in their cyberterritories—even if they never made actual contact with those shops.

The website offers customers a lot of advice on how to select and use Milacron's products, as well as a multimedia catalog of more than 50,000 items.

But Milacron officials are most proud of the website's Milpro Wizard, a knowledge-based expert system, developed in-house, that helps their customers decide which equipment, fluids, and peripherals are best for various manufacturing processes. It also offers advice for setting up the machine tools they buy from Milacron [21].

Applications of Intranets

Many companies have sophisticated and widespread intranets, offering detailed data retrieval, collaboration tools, personalized customer profiles, and links to the Internet. Investing in the intranet, they feel, is as fundamental as supplying employees with a telephone [25].

Before we get any futher, let's redefine the concept of an intranet, to specifically emphasize how intranets are related to the Internet and extranets. An **intranet** is a network inside an organization that uses Internet technologies (such as Web browsers and servers, TCP/IP network protocols, HTML hypermedia document publishing and databases, and so on) to provide an Internet-like environment within the enterprise for information sharing, communications, collaboration, and the support of business processes. An intranet is protected by security measures such as passwords, encryption, and fire walls, and thus can be accessed by authorized users through the Internet. A company's intranet can also be accessed through the intranets of customers, suppliers, and other business partners via *extranet* links.

Organizations of all kinds are implementing a broad range of intranet uses. One way that companies organize intranet applications is to group them conceptually into a few user services categories that reflect the basic services that intranets offer to their users. These services are provided by the intranet's portal, browser, and server software, as well as by other system and application software and groupware that are part of a company's intranet software environment [2]. Figure 3.6 illustrates how intranet applications support communication and collaboration, Web publishing, business operations and management, and intranet portal management. Notice also how these applications can be integrated with existing IS resources and applications, and extended to customers, suppliers, and business partners via the Internet and extranets.

Communications and Collaboration. Intranets can significantly improve communications and collaboration within an enterprise. For example, you can use your intranet browser and your PC or NC workstation to send and receive E-mail, voice-mail, paging, and faxes to communicate with others within your organization, and externally through the Internet and extranets. You can also use intranet groupware features to improve team and project collaboration with services such as discussion groups, chat rooms, and audio- and videoconferencing.

Figure 3.6

Intranets can provide an enterprise information portal for applications in communication and collaboration, business operations and management, Web publishing, and intranet portal management.

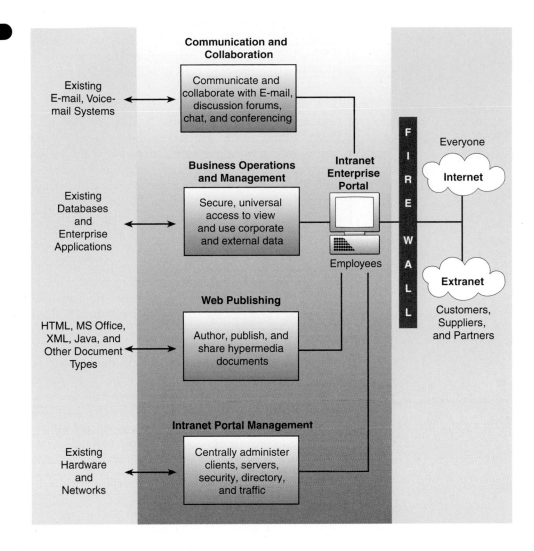

Web Publishing. The advantages of developing and publishing hyperlinked multimedia documents to hypermedia databases accessible on World Wide Web servers has moved to corporate intranets. The comparative ease, attractiveness, and lower cost of publishing and accessing multimedia business information internally via intranet websites have been the primary reasons for the explosive growth in the use of intranets in business. For example, information products as varied as company newsletters, technical drawings, and product catalogs can be published in a variety of ways, including hypermedia Web pages, E-mail, and net broadcasting, and as part of in-house business applications. Intranet software browsers, servers, and search engines can help you easily navigate and locate the business information you need.

Business Operations and Management. Intranets have moved beyond merely making hypermedia information available on Web servers, or pushing it to users via net broadcasting. Intranets are also being used as the platform for developing and deploying critical business applications to support business operations and managerial decision making across the internetworked enterprise. For example, many companies are developing custom applications like order processing, inventory control, sales management, and executive information systems that can be implemented on intranets, extranets, and the Internet. Many of these applications are designed to interface with, and access, existing company databases and legacy systems. The software for such business uses is then installed on intranet Web servers. Employees within the company, or external business partners, can access and run such applications using Web browsers from anywhere on the network whenever needed.

Now let's look at one company's use of an intranet in more detail to get a better idea of how intranets are used in business.

Cadence OnTrack: Business Value of an Intranet	Cadence Design Systems is the leading supplier of electronic design automation (EDA) software tools and professional services for managing the design of semiconductors, computer systems, networking and telecommunications equipment, consumer electronics, and other electronics-based products. The company employs more than 3,000 people in offices worldwide to support the requirements of the world's leading electronics manufacturers. Cadence developed an intranet for 500 managers, sales reps, and customer support staff. Called OnTrack, the intranet project provides sales support for a Cadence product line of over 1,000 products and services.
	The OnTrack system uses a home page with links to other pages, information sources, and other applications to support each phase of the sales process with supporting materials and reference information. For example, at any point in the sales process, such as one called "Identify Business Issues," a sales rep can find customer presentations, sample letters, and the internal forms needed to move effectively through this step. See Figure 3.7.
	With OnTrack, sales reps now use the intranet as a single tool that provides all of the information and data needed to go through the sales process, from prospecting, to closing a deal, to account management. In addition, global account teams have their own home page where they can collaborate and share information. Information on customers or competitors is now available instantly through access to an outside provider of custom news. The sales rep simply searches using a company name to get everything from financial information to recent news articles and press releases about the customer or competitor [7].

Enterprise Information Portals

A user checks his E-mail, looks up the current company stock price, checks his available vacation days, and receives an order from a customer—all from the browser on his desktop. That is the next-generation intranet, also known as a corporate or enterprise information portal. With it, the browser becomes the dashboard to daily business tasks [26].

Enterprise information portals are a growing trend in the design and deployment of intranets in business. An enterprise information portal (EIP) is a Web-based interface and integration of intranet and other technologies that gives all intranet users and selected extranet users access to a variety of internal and external business applications and services. For example, internal applications might include access to E-mail, project websites, and discussion groups; human resources Web self-services; customer, inventory, and other corporate databases; decision support systems, and knowledge management systems. External applications might include industry, financial, and other Internet news services; links to industry discussion groups; and links to customer and supplier Internet and extranet websites. Enterprise information portals are typically tailored or personalized to the needs of individual business users or groups of users. See Figure 3.8.

The business benefits of enterprise information portals include providing more specific and selective information to business users, providing easy access to key corporate intranet website resources, delivering industry and business news, and providing better access to company data for selected customers, suppliers, or business partners. Enterprise information portals can also help avoid excessive surfing by

Figure 3.7

The home page of the OnTrack intranet application.

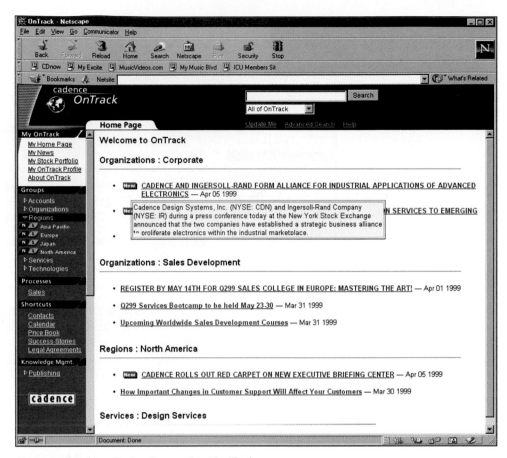

Courtesy of Cadence Design Systems, Inc./On Track.

employees across company and Internet websites by making it easier for them to receive or find the information and services they need, thus improving the productivity of a company's workforce [27].

However, in order to present something as simple as a Web page with links to useful internal and external information sources, applications, and services, an EIP must integrate many information technologies. So full-fledged corporate portals are proving to be a challenge to build. Figure 3.9 outlines many of the diverse technologies, applications, and services that developers are attempting to provide to business users through the use of an enterprise information portal. EIP software packages are now available from many sources that offer simple to full-fledged capabilities, and are thus being used by many companies [27]. Let's take a look at a real world example.

Figure 3.8

A display of a personalized Web page provided to a business user by an enterprise information portal.

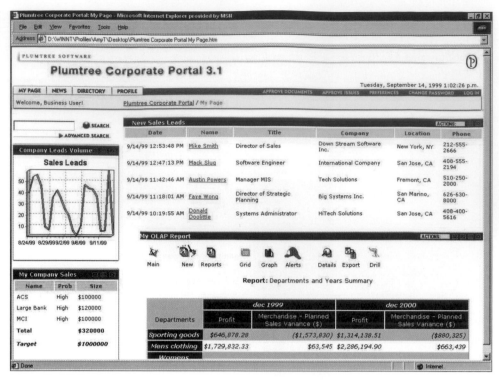

Courtesy of Plumtree Software.

Advantage Sales and Marketing: Enterprise Information Portal

Advantage Sales and Marketing, a food wholesaler in Irvine, California, was stretching its E-mail system and corporate wide area network to the limit and needed a different way to distribute information to the right people. The reason for the problem? The only way to get updated marketing presentations to its 1,000-member nationwide sales staff was to E-mail giant presentation files to each person or have users access the files on slow shared drives on their wide area network. That was often happening on a daily basis.

At first, the answer seemed to be simply building a corporate intranet. But the idea of a corporate portal seemed the next logical step for the company's 6,800 employees, because it went further in organizing the information for easier access by all employees. So Advantage bought RIO DataChannel from DataChannel Corp., a server-based enterprise information portal system that groups all data into different channels that are accessible to selected users.

Then Advantage began to organize the data they wanted into different categories called channels, and asked their four business groups to define all the channels out there and create "channel managers." Now, CIO Kevin Paugh says their portal gives his company's 6,800 employees easy access to the corporate and food industry data they need [27].

Intranet Technology Resources

Since intranets are Internet-like networks within organizations, they depend on all the information technologies that make the Internet possible. For example, companies using intranets must have or install TCP/IP client/server networks and related hardware and software, such as Web browser and server suites, HTML Web publishing software, and network management and security programs. Thus, intranets depend on the same Web browser/server capabilities, TCP/IP client/server networks, and hypermedia database access available on the Internet and the World Wide Web. Figure 3.10 illustrates the components of the information technology architecture of a typical intranet.

Figure 3.9

Examples of enterprise information portal applications and se~

Enterprise Information Portal Services		
• Personal Services		
Electronic mail	Calendaring/scheduling	Persona~
Discussion groups	Distance learning	Persona~
Chat systems	Pager messaging	Search e~
• Basic Services		
Internet access	Corporate databases	Directories
Custom Web links	Corporate knowledge bases	Document repositories
Intranet access	Mainframe reporting	Image/fax repositories
• Advanced Services		
Internal business application	Knowledge management	Videoconferencing
Data warehouse access	Document management	Web publishing
Decision support tools	Workflow systems	Push publishing

Source: Adapted from Gerry Murray, "Making Connections with Enterprise Knowledge Portals," White Paper, *Computerworld*, September 6, 1999, p. 3. Copyright 1999 by Computerworld, Inc., Framingham, MA 01701. Reprinted from *Computerworld*.

Notice in Figure 3.10 that Web browser and server software, search engines, Web software tools, and network management software are key components of an open intranet. It is these software components that give intranet users the same kind of easy point-and-click navigation of hyperlinked multimedia websites that they enjoy on the Internet. For example, Figure 3.11 outlines some of the services provided by an intranet software server for an enterprise information portal, provided by iPlanet, a joint venture of Sun Microsystems and Netscape Communications.

The Business Value of Intranets

The preliminary results from IDC's return on investment study of intranets found the typical ROI well over 1,000 percent—far higher than usually found with any technology investment. Adding to the benefit, with payback periods ranging from six to twelve weeks, the cost of an intranet is quickly recovered—making the risk associated

Figure 3.10

An example of the components of an intranet's information technology architecture.

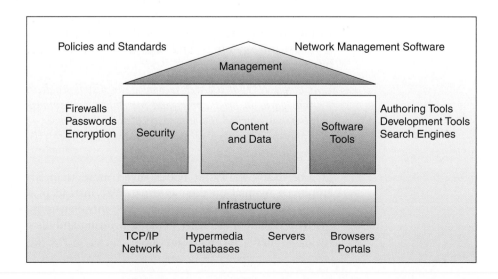

.11

...e of the
...se information
...l services provided by a
...ll-featured intranet
software server.

iPlanet Portal Server Intranet Services
● **Membership Services**—Establishes a portal community via user registration and policy-based access to services. Includes iPlanet Directory Server.
● **Presentation and Aggregation**—Provides portal page layout and creation using customizable channels. Includes iPlanet Web Server
● **Personalization Services**—Delivers multi-tiered personalization of content (such as stock quotes, weather, news), applications and other services as predefined by the portal user or administrator, or through dynamic interactions with the portal itself based on previous usage.
● **Security Services**—Extranet and remote access security via user authentication, on-demand virtual private network and single sign-on. Enables extended communication and collaboration beyond E-mail and calendaring.
● **Integration Services**—Integrates with HTML/XML applications (i.e., E-mail and file access) and Windows, Unix, and Mainframe applications.

Source: Adapted from iPlanet E-commerce Solutions, "iPlanet Portal Server Product Brief," at www.iplanet.com, March 3, 2000.

with an intranet project low. The results to date clearly show that for any company, not just those already contemplating an intranet, the best strategy is to begin an intranet deployment today. The sooner an intranet becomes a core component of the corporate technology infrastructure, the sooner the company can reap the benefits [7].

The impressive returns, quick payback, and endorsement of intranets by IT research groups have not gone unnoticed. Other intranet adopters report similar high paybacks at low cost. So the consensus advice of many corporate intranet users and consultants to the global business community has been that companies should quickly expand any current intranet initiatives [7].

Examples of Business Value

Many companies have derived business value from their intranet applications. Intranet-using companies report cost reductions, revenue increases, or other benefits after they replaced traditional methods of accomplishing information publishing and other business processes with intranet-based methods. Let's look at some examples.

Publication Cost Savings. Many companies are replacing the publication of paper documents, company newsletters, and employee manuals with electronic multimedia versions published on intranet Web servers. Elimination of printing, mailing, and distribution costs is a major source of cost savings. Companies are also electronically publishing telephone directories, human resource materials, company policies, job openings, and many other former paper-based communications on intranet websites.

Companies that use web technology to distribute documents may experience momentous gains in productivity and incredible cost savings. Like the reengineering craze that has marked the other half of the client/server revolution, converting many paper-based systems to web systems can save both labor and overhead costs within an organization [4].

For example, Tyson Foods saved more than $50,000 by just publishing their employee manual on their internal Web instead of spending $10 per employee for a paper version for each of their 5,000 intranet users. Lockheed Martin reports saving over $600,000 per year in paper printing and distribution costs no longer needed for over 70,000 intranet users [22].

Training and Development Cost Savings. Developing information access and Web publishing applications for an intranet is a lot easier than many traditional methods. Learning how to use a Web browser for the company intranet is fast and easy. Many employees already know how to use a browser anyway, from surfing the World Wide Web. So training and development costs for many intranet applications are low, especially for communication, collaboration, and information sharing. For example, here's what Dave Lambe, CIO of US West Communications, said about the minimal development and training time needed for a new intranet-based customer service application they recently implemented:

The most exciting aspects of this application are that it was developed in less than three months and was deployed with relative ease to our 6,000 service representatives. In fact, training time was cut down to five minutes of coaching. I have never seen such a large-scale system built and deployed so quickly. That shows the power of using this technology for software applications development [20].

In addition, putting electronic versions of training materials on intranet websites can reduce the amount of costly classroom training in business. For example, AT&T was able to cut classroom time in half for 4,500 customer service reps because they were provided with access to intranet-based instruction [22].

Measuring Costs and Benefits. For most businesses, the benefits to be gained from intranets outweigh their limitations. See Figure 3.12. Justifying the initial cost of investing in an intranet does not seem to be a problem for many organizations. For example, the Port of Los Angeles spent about $100,000 creating an intranet for 18 field offices worldwide. Payback time is estimated at three months, because one new sale attributed to the effectiveness of the intranet can justify the cost of the project. FedEx justified an intranet project by exceeding the company's minimum return on investment (ROI) criteria with projected savings from only four applications. These included cost savings from putting help desk call logs, corporate newsletters, employee benefit plan changes, and customer queries on intranet Web servers [22].

Figure 3.12

Some of the benefits and limitations of intranets.

Intranet Benefits	Intranet Limitations
Global, enterprisewide in scope	New evolving technology
Easy, intuitive GUI access via browsers	Lack of security features
Low-cost access	Lack of performance management
Low- or no-cost software	Minimal user support
Low-cost hardware	May require network upgrades
Runs on all platforms	Browser/server software incompatibilities between versions
Standardized file transfer	
Standardized document creation	May not scale for large enterprises with intense interactive applications
Standardized network protocol, TCP/IP	Difficult to maintain content over time
Reduces paper/printing cost	Animation, video, and audio are slow
Reduces marketing/sales costs	Unfiltered information may overwhelm users
Increases productivity via faster information access and easier collaboration	Not all employees may have personal computers

Source: Adapted from Nancy Cox, *Building and Managing a Web Services Team* (New York: Van Nostrand Reinhold, 1997), p. 13. Used by permission.

The Role of Extranets

As businesses continue to use open Internet technologies [extranets] to improve communication with customers and partners, they can gain many competitive advantages along the way—in product development, cost savings, marketing, distribution, and leveraging their partnerships [3].

As we have explained earlier, **extranets** are network links that use Internet technologies to interconnect the intranet of a business with the intranets of its customers, suppliers, or other business partners. Companies can establish direct private network links between themselves, or create private secure Internet links between them called *virtual private networks.* Or a company can use the unsecured Internet as the extranet link between its intranet and consumers and others, but rely on encryption of sensitive data and its own fire wall systems to provide adequate security. Thus, extranets enable customers, suppliers, consultants, subcontractors, business prospects, and others to access selected intranet websites and other company databases. See Figure 3.13.

Business Value of Extranets

The business value of extranets is derived from several factors. First, the Web browser technology of extranets makes customer and supplier access of intranet resources a lot easier and faster than previous business methods. Second, as you will see in two upcoming examples, extranets enable a company to offer new kinds of interactive Web-enabled services to their business partners. Thus, extranets are another way that a business can build and strengthen strategic relationships with its customers and suppliers. Also, extranets can enable and improve collaboration by a business with its customers and other business partners. Extranets facilitate an online, interactive product development, marketing, and customer-focused process that can bring better-designed products to market faster [3].

Countrywide and Snap-on: Extranet Examples

Countrywide Home Loans has created an extranet called Platinum Lender Access for its lending partners and brokers. About 500 banks and mortgage brokers can access Countrywide's intranet and selected financial databases. The extranet gives them access to their account and transaction information, status of loans, and company announcements. Each lender or broker is automatically identified by the extranet and provided with customized information on premium rates, discounts, and any special business arrangements they have negotiated with Countrywide [1, 3].

Snap-on Incorporated spent $300,000 to create an extranet link to their intranet called the Franchise Information Network. The extranet lets Snap-on's 4,000 independent franchises for automotive tools access a secured intranet website for customized information and interactive communications with Snap-on employees and other franchisees. Franchisers can get information on sales plus marketing updates. Tips and training programs about managing a franchise operation and discussion forums for employees and franchisees to share ideas and best practices are also provided by the extranet. Finally, the Franchise Information Network provides interactive news and information on car racing and other special events sponsored by Snap-on, as well as corporate stock prices, business strategies, and other financial information [28].

The Future of Intranets and Extranets

Research and consulting projects with many companies show not only their success with intranets, but that intranets and extranets will become even more pervasive in the business future. Figure 3.14 outlines what companies are expecting from enterprise information portals and intranet/extranet technologies [17].

One recurring theme for the future of intranets and extranets is the need to move beyond information publishing applications into enterprise information portal-enabled applications. For example, companies are planning more inquiry processing and trans-

Figure 3.13

Extranets connect the internetworked enterprise to consumers, business customers, suppliers, and other business partners.

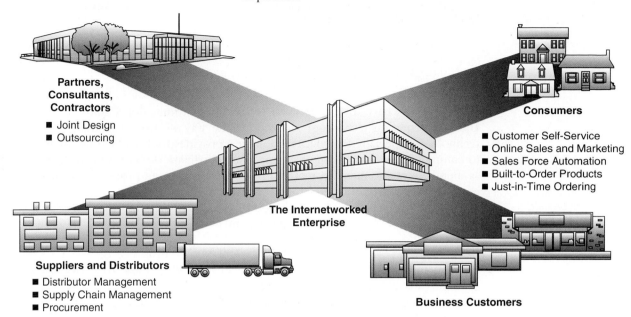

Partners, Consultants, Contractors
■ Joint Design
■ Outsourcing

Consumers
■ Customer Self-Service
■ Online Sales and Marketing
■ Sales Force Automation
■ Built-to-Order Products
■ Just-in-Time Ordering

The Internetworked Enterprise

Suppliers and Distributors
■ Distributor Management
■ Supply Chain Management
■ Procurement

Business Customers

action processing applications that tie the Internet, intranets, and extranets to mainframe and other legacy systems and databases. Though such applications are more costly and difficult to develop, many companies are forging ahead. These intranet-using companies are in the process of web-enabling operational and managerial support applications, including online transaction processing, database integration, and executive information and decision support. For example, a sales-inventory application might accept an order at a company's World Wide Web site, and then trigger an intranet search engine to search an internal inventory database for the product's stock status. Then a picking list and shipping notice would be prepared at the company's warehouse intranet site. Finally, an E-mail meassage and invoice would be generated and sent via extranet to the customer's own enterprise information portal.

Figure 3.14

What companies are expecting from their future use of intranets, extranets, and enterprise information portals.

The Future of Intranets and Extranets
● More and more information and applications will be accessible on the company intranet via an enterprise information portal.
● The Web browser and the intranet Web portal will be the ubiquitous, universal user interface for timely access to business information.
● Data analysis applications and legacy systems will be front-ended by a company's enterprise information portal.
● The intranet will become the primary vehicle for delivery of employee and company news, and the main source of information in the company worldwide.
● All applications, including cross-platform transaction processing, will be Web-enabled or will be entered via the Internet, the intranet, or extranets.
● More processes will be added to turn information into knowledge to increase the value the intranet delivers to each employee.
● Extranets will enable a significant degree of electronic bonding with customers and suppliers by allowing them to connect to company intranets.

Enterprise Communication and Collaboration

Enterprise Collaboration

The Internet phenomenon has permanently changed the computing mentality of business-people. Today's users expect any computing experience to include on-demand Internet access and tools for collaborating with other people [28].

Most of us have to interact with others to get things done. And as you already know, information technology is changing the way we work together. Information technology, especially Internet technologies, provides tools to help us collaborate—to communicate ideas, share resources, and coordinate our cooperative work efforts as members of the many formal and informal process and project teams and workgroups that make up many of today's organizations.

The goal of enterprise collaboration systems is to enable us to work together more easily and effectively by helping us to:

- **Communicate:** Sharing information with each other.
- **Coordinate:** Coordinating our individual work efforts and use of resources with each other.
- **Collaborate:** Working together cooperatively on joint projects and assignments.

Analyzing Groove Networks

Read the Real World Case on Groove networks on the next page. We can learn a lot about the business value and challenges of enterprise communication and collaboration technologies from this example. See Figure 3.15.

Ray Ozzie created Lotus Notes, the premier groupware product for corporate client/server networks. Now he has produced Groove, a peer-to-peer software product for business collaboration over the Internet. This time Ozzie claims Groove will be the foundation for supporting and managing instant peer-to-peer Internet communications and collaboration by teams and workgroups via all types of media for

Figure 3.15

Ray Ozzie developed Groove software to bring peer-to-peer collaboration via the Internet to business.

Craig Bromley.

Groove Networks: The Business Case for Peer-to-Peer Collaboration

Ray Ozzie didn't need to do it again. Back in the days before the Internet explosion, back when Web sites were still unknown and desktop software was all the rage, Ozzie invented Lotus Notes, one of the most elegant client-server applications ever. Then known as groupware, Notes helped people collaborate at work and quickly spread knowledge and information across organizations. In 1995, IBM bought Lotus for $3.5 billion just to get its hands on Notes. Now more than 68 million Notes licenses have been sold.

A lot has happened in the interim. The World Wide Web, for one thing, which makes it even easier to exchange data and share ideas. After IBM swallowed Lotus, Ray Ozzie left to pursue a dream: to harness the Internet with an amazing new program that does Notes one better. His creation is Groove, software that enables small ad-hoc groups of workers to get together quickly online to collaborate on projects. Three years in the making, Groove is emerging just in time to supercharge the trend toward peer-to-peer computing, the first great evolution of software beyond the Web.

Thus, Ray Ozzie wants to unlock once again the technology chains that bind you. After those three years of monastic silence, the software cult hero has pulled the wraps off his latest creation: peer-to-peer collaboration software. Mr. Ozzie, 44, and his band of merry conspirators at Groove Networks are betting that Groove will become as ubiquitous as E-mail or the Web browser.

Lest you think this is just another Web huckster blowing smoke, consider what others think of Ozzie and his creation. Industry godmother Esther Dryson says, "I would bet on it, and I was disappointed not to be allowed to invest." Publisher and software expert Tim O'Reilly calls Groove's design "prescient" and says it will "prefigure an awful lot of other software." Bill Gates has declared Ozzie "one of the best programmers in the universe," and calls Groove "a deep and innovative software product that is a great indicator of where the Internet is going"—even though some observers expect Microsoft to try to squash Groove eventually.

Think of Groove as Napster for business. The famous outlaw software connects one PC directly to another so that their owners can share music. Groove links workers via their PCs without the assistance of a central Web server so they can share all kinds of digital data. Such on-the-fly collaboration holds huge promise in today's ever-faster business environment. Although much Web software is great for automating projects, it falls short when human interaction must be involved. Groove fills that gap, which is why companies like General Electric and Intel, among others, are thinking of adding Groove to their Web-based supply-chain projects.

That's the theory. So exactly how does Groove work? When you download Groove onto your PC (a test version is available at www.groove.net), the software creates a space on your PC that can be accessed by other Groove users whom you invite in. That space appears exactly the same on the screen of every member of your group and includes tools to support collaboration: sharing Microsoft Office documents, text chat, live-voice chat, photo viewing, a drawing pad, and a browser. Whenever two or more people are online at the same time, they can use Groove to work on a document or brainstorm. Any changes they make to the document are transmitted live over the Net to other members' PCs. If the other members aren't online, the modifications are stored on a relay server; as soon as a member plugs back in, his Groove space is updated. The software is designed to work best for groups of 25 people or fewer but can be adapted for larger get-togethers.

Others will extend Groove in different ways—a key part of Ozzie's plan is to encourage other companies to write special applications on top of the Groove platform. (Inside the company they call such software "Groovy.") For example, Phil Stanhope, who until January ran an E-consulting unit for Perot Systems, has started Componentry Solutions to build Groove applications for managing insurance claims and other group tasks. At Beaumonde, which hosts Web sites for modeling and talent agencies, ten employees in the Boston and New York City offices who need to share documents securely now do so. Technical architect John Siqueira had spent months trying to set up a virtual private network to achieve the same result; setting up Groove took about a day. Hong Kong's Inlooktech.com is using Groove for collaboration on software projects that include contributors from Taiwan and China. And since Groove is a kind of blank slate, it may well be the platform for a variety of consumer E-commerce and home applications too.

Case Study Question

1. Why could Groove be thought of as "the Napster for business"?

2. What is the business value of the Groove approach to enterprise collaboration?

3. What consumer E-commerce and home applications can you envision for Groove? Defend the economic feasibility and business value of one of your proposals.

Source: Adapted from David Kirkpatrick, "Software's Humble Wizard Does it Again," *Fortune*, February 19, 2001, pp. 137–142.

all types of projects. Early reviews and business experiences are promising, and several major companies are testing Groove for use in a variety of E-business initiatives. But more time is needed for companies to experiment with final versions of Groove before the effectiveness of Ozzie's model of P2P Internet collaboration for E-business and consumer applications can be fully determined.

Teams, Workgroups, and Collaboration

There are many types of teams and workgroups, each with its own work styles, agendas, and computing needs. A **workgroup** can be defined as two or more people working together on the same task or assignment. A **team** can be defined as a *collaborative workgroup*, whose members are committed to **collaboration,** that is, working with each other in a cooperative way that transcends the coordination of individual work activities found in a typical workgroup. So collaboration is the key to what makes a group of people a team, and what makes a team successful.

> *Collaboration is about working together to produce a product that's much greater than the sum of its parts. Collaborators develop a shared understanding that's much deeper than they could have developed working on their own or contributing pieces to the product. The power is so great that unless you've experienced it, it's really hard to understand. The process taps into the collective wisdom, knowledge, and even subconscious minds of the collaborators. This powerful phenomenon is becoming a requirement to effectively compete in today's marketplace* [16].

Teams and workgroups can be as formal and structured as a traditional business office or department. Or they can be less formal and structured like the members of *process teams* in a manufacturing environment. Or they can be as informal, unstructured, and temporary as an ad hoc task force or a *project team* whose members work for different organizations in different parts of the world.

Thus, the members of a team or workgroup don't have to work in the same physical location. They can be members of a **virtual team,** that is, one whose members are united by the tasks on which they are collaborating, not by geography or membership in a larger organization. In sociology and cultural anthropology, these workgroups are called *social fields*—semiautonomous and self-regulating associations of people with their own work agendas, rules, relationships, and norms of behavior. Enterprise collaboration systems make *electronic social fields* possible. Computers, groupware, and telecommunications networks allow end users to work together in virtual teams without regard to time constraints, physical location, or organizational boundaries. See Figure 3.16.

Enterprise Collaboration System Components

Figure 3.17 emphasizes that an **enterprise collaboration system** is an *information system.* Therefore, it uses hardware, software, data, and network resources to support communication, coordination, and collaboration among the members of business teams and workgroups. For example, engineers, business specialists, and external consultants may form a virtual team for a project. The team may rely on intranets and extranets to collaborate via E-mail, videoconferencing, discussion forums, and a multimedia database of work-in-progress information at a project website. The enterprise collaboration system may use PC workstations networked to a variety of servers on which project, corporate, and other databases are stored. In addition, network servers may provide a variety of software resources, such as Web browsers, groupware, and application packages, to assist the team's collaboration until the project is completed.

Groupware for Enterprise Collaboration

> *Groupware is one of the most poorly defined terms in computing. Its most general definition—software that enables multiple users to share information with one another and work together on multiple projects—can include products of many disparate types, from contact management and E-mail to document-sharing programs* [15].

Figure 3.16

A virtual team can include members from other teams, departments, organizations, and locations interconnected by information technology.

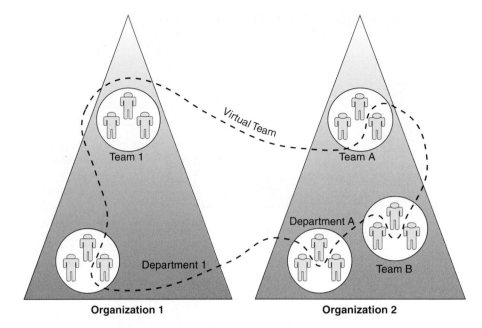

Organization 1   **Organization 2**

- Temporary, fluid, collaborating to achieve an objective
- Connected by shared interests and complementary expertise
- Communication and collaboration supported by information technology

Source: Adapted and reprinted from Don Mankin, Susan Cohen, and Tora Bikson, *Teams and Technology: Fulfilling the Promise of the New Organization* (Boston: Harvard Business School Press, 1996), p. 33, by permission of Harvard Business School Press. Copyright © 1996 by The President and Fellows of Harvard College; all rights reserved.

Groupware can be simply defined as *collaboration software*, that is, software tools that help teams and workgroups work together in a variety of ways to accomplish joint projects and group assignments. For example, groupware products like Lotus Notes, Novell GroupWise, Microsoft Exchange, and Netscape Communicator support collaboration through E-mail, data and audioconferencing, discussion forums, scheduling and calendaring, and so on. You should also be aware that groupware is changing as developers attempt to tailor it for use over the Internet or corporate intranets and extranets. In addition, application software suites like Microsoft Office, Lotus SmartSuite, and Corel WordPerfect Office are adding Internet/intranet access, joint document creation, and other collaborative capabilities that provide users with some groupware features.

Groupware is designed to make communication and coordination of workgroup activities and cooperation among end users significantly easier, no matter where the members of a team are located. So though groupware packages provide a variety of software tools that can accomplish many important jobs, the team and workgroup cooperation and coordination they make possible are their key feature. Groupware helps the members of a team collaborate on group projects, at the same or different times, and at the same place, or at different locations.

Many industry analysts believe that the capabilities and potential of the Internet, as well as intranets and extranets, are driving the demand for enterprise collaboration tools in business. On the other hand, it is Internet technologies like Web browsers and servers, hypermedia documents and databases, and intranets and extranets that are providing the hardware, software, data, and network platforms for many of the groupware tools for enterprise collaboration that business users want. Figure 3.18 provides an overview of some of the groupware tools we will discuss in this section. Notice that groupware provides software tools for electronic communication, electronic conferencing, and collaborative work management.

Figure 3.17 The components of an enterprise collaboration system.

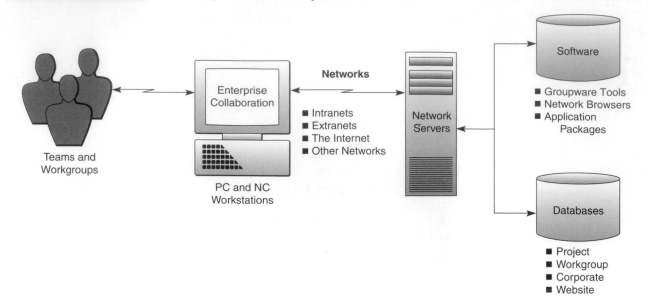

Electronic Communication Tools

Electronic communication tools include electronic mail, voice mail, faxing, Web publishing, bulletin board systems, paging, and Internet phone systems. These tools enable you to electronically send messages, documents, and files in data, text, voice, or multimedia over computer networks. This helps you share everything from voice and text messages to copies of project documents and data files with your team members, wherever they may be. The ease and efficiency of such communications are major contributors to the collaboration process.

Electronic Mail

Your choice of Internet E-mail software will have a growing impact on your working and other communications. Ideally, your mail client should be an active ally that will do a lot more than shuffle messages from one place to another. It should help you organize your burgeoning store of messages, filter out unwanted junk mail, transfer files, put an elegant face on your correspondence, and keep your private messages private [19].

Figure 3.18

Groupware for electronic communications, conferencing, and collaborative work provides software tools for enterprise collaboration.

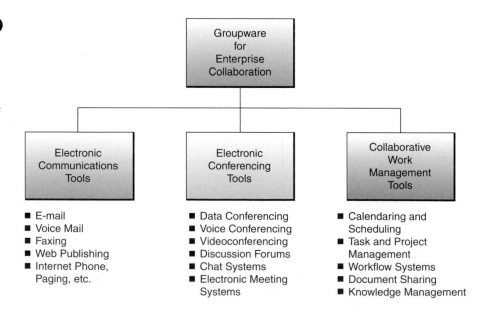

E-mail has become a vital, fast, and convenient way to communicate and build strategic relationships in business. E-mail has also been transformed into an important medium for transporting electronic copies of documents, data files, and multimedia content. This includes net broadcasters automatically *pushing* information from Internet and intranet sources into your E-mail in-box.

The downside of the E-mail phenomenon is the *information overload* caused by too many messages from too many sources. Especially controversial is the torrent of unsolicited *junk E-mail* (called *spamming*) that is flooding many users' Internet E-mail boxes. Many solutions for this problem are being tried, including legal action and organizational restrictions on E-mail use. But experts agree that using E-mail software with good E-mail management capabilities should be every user's first line of defense.

Internet Phone and Fax

The Internet isn't just for sending E-mail and surfing the Web anymore. It's turning into a low-cost and nearly universal communications medium, helping to send faxes, retrieve voicemail, and carry two-way conversations [9].

You can now use the Internet for telephone, voice mail, faxing, and paging services. All you need is a suitably equipped PC and software such as Internet Phone by Vocal-Tech, or Netscape Conference or Microsoft NetMeeting (which are part of Netscape Communicator and Microsoft Internet Explorer).

Depending on your PC's configuration (and that of the person you're calling) and the speed of your Internet connection, the sound quality of your phone call can vary from poor to very good. Internet voice mail and faxing work better, as does paging. In fact, many companies now offer unified Internet messaging services that will collect all your voice, fax, and E-mail in one website box (or *virtual office*) you can access with your browser. For an additional fee, you can be paged when new messages arrive [11]. See Figure 3.19.

Web Publishing

Web publishing can be viewed as an important electronic communications tool for enterprise collaboration. Application software suites like Microsoft Office, browser suites like Netscape Communicator, and other Web publishing and website development programs now enable you to publish hyperlinked documents in HTML directly to Internet or intranet websites. As Figure 3.20 illustrates a team member can publish a project report or other hyperlinked document directly to an intranet/extranet Web server for viewing and comments by other members of a

Courtesy of JFax.

Figure 3.20

The traditional versus the intranet/extranet way of Web publishing to share team and workgroup information.

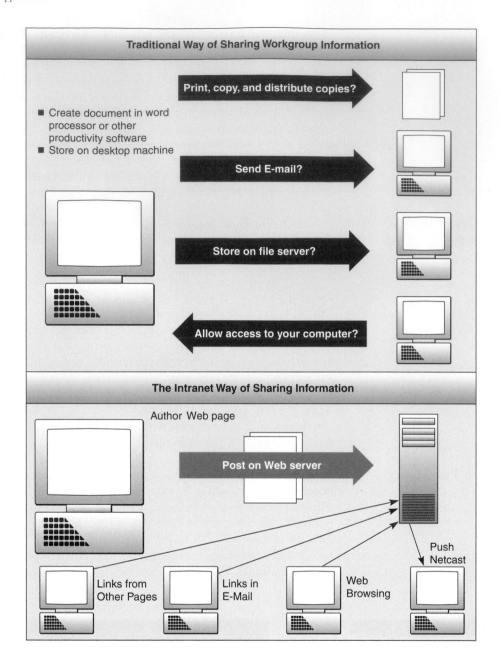

project team. Other project messages and news can be broadcast (pushed) to team members' video screens or E-mail boxes [5]. Thus, intranet web publishing has become a much more efficient and effective way of communicating among teams and workgroups than previous paper or electronic methods.

Electronic Conferencing Tools

Electronic conferencing tools help people communicate and collaborate while working together. A variety of conferencing methods enable the members of teams and workgroups at different locations to exchange ideas interactively at the same time, or at different times at their convenience. Electronic conferencing options also include *electronic meeting systems*, where team members can meet at the same time and place in a *decision room* setting. Let's take a brief look at these collaboration tools, which include data and voice conferencing, videoconferencing, chat systems, discussion forums, and electronic meeting systems.

Data and Voice Conferencing

Data and voice conferencing are frequently mentioned together because they are frequently used together in work situations. **Voice conferencing** formerly relied on speaker-phone systems, but now can be accomplished with browser modules like Netscape Conference or Microsoft NetMeeting, and other Internet telephone software and groupware. These packages support telephone conversations over the Internet or intranets between your PC and other voice-enabled networked PCs.

Data conferencing is also popularly called **whiteboarding.** In this method, a groupware package connects two or more PCs over the Internet or intranets so a team can share, mark up, and revise a *whiteboard* of drawings, documents, and other material displayed on their screens. For example, groupware like Netscape Conference or Microsoft NetMeeting lets you have a voice and data conference with other networked team members. You can all view the same document or graphic image on your PCs; mark it up in real time with painting, drawing, and highlighting tools; and save the annotated document file in your project database. See Figure 3.21.

Videoconferencing

Videoconferencing is an enterprise collaboration tool that enables real-time video/audio conferences among (1) networked PCs, known as **desktop videoconferencing,** or (2) networked conference rooms or auditoriums in different locations, called *teleconferencing.* In either case, team and enterprise collaboration can be enhanced with a full range of interactive video, audio, document, and whiteboard communications among the online participants. Desktop videoconferencing can now take place over the Internet, intranets, extranets, as well as public telephone and other networks. Desktop videoconferencing software such as White Pine's CU-SeeMe and Intel's ProShare are popular examples. See Figure 3.22.

Teleconferencing is an important form of enterprise collaboration. Sessions are held in real time, with major participants being televised while participants at remote sites may only take part with voice input of questions and responses. See Figure 3.23. Teleconferencing can also consist of using closed-circuit television to reach multiple small groups, instead of using television broadcasting to reach large groups at multiple sites. Several major communications carriers offer teleconferencing services for such events as sales meetings, new product announcements, and employee education and training. However, some organizations have found that teleconferencing may not be

Figure 3.21

Data conferencing supports team collaboration using a shared whiteboard of project information.

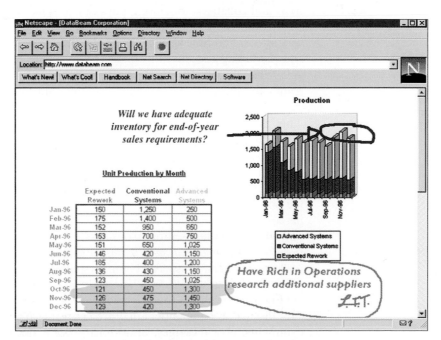

Courtesy of DataBeam Corporation.

Figure 3.22

Using a laptop computer for desktop videoconferencing.

John Feingersh/The Stock Market.

as effective as face-to-face meetings, especially when important participants are not trained in how to communicate using their systems. Also, the cost of providing teleconferencing services and facilities can be substantial and make teleconferencing not as cost effective as expected.

Desktop videoconferencing has a few limitations as well. Complaints include jerky motions of video images and the lack of nonverbal communications from "talking heads" displays of videoconference participants. These complaints are being addressed by improvements in the software compression of video images, and the use of higher-speed communications access technologies like DSL and cable modems. Using more of the display screen to show more complete images of the conferencing participants is another recommended solution [6].

However, desktop videoconferencing over the Internet, intranets, and extranets is proving to be an efficient, economical, and effective way of supporting communications and collaboration among physically displaced teams and workgroups. Reducing travel time and money to attend meetings results in increased team productivity as well as cost and time savings. For example, a product development team of engineers and marketing executives from several company locations will typically use desktop videoconferencing for weekly project status meetings, as well as ad hoc meetings of team subgroups to review detailed product drawings and proposed specifications.

Discussion Forums

This category of collaboration tools enables Internet and intranet *newsgroups* and other discussion groups. Discussion forums are an extension of the earlier concept of online *bulletin board systems* (BBS), which allowed users to post messages and download data and program files from online services and businesses. Discussion forums in business are an outgrowth of the widespread use of *newsgroups* to provide a forum for online text discussions by members of special interest user groups on the Internet and the major online services. As we will see in Chapter 5, discussion forums and newsgroups can be used by E-business enterprises to create and encourage *communities of interest* or *virtual communities* in support of their E-commerce initiatives. Customers, suppliers, prospects, company representatives, and others can develop a rapport that strengthens their relationship and loyalty to a company and its products.

Figure 3.24 shows the use of discussion groupware, which encourages and manages discussion by members of a project team. Team members can ask for and make comments, post messages, brainstorm, review documents, and even vote and make decisions online. Discussion forums are a good tool for collaboration when you don't

Figure 3.23 Teleconferencing in action.

Kinko's.

really need to get a team together for meeting, but still want to encourage and share the contribution of everyone on the project team.

Discussion groupware like Lotus Notes and Instant Teamroom significantly improves the collaboration capabilities of discussion forums by providing for *threaded discussions, virtual discussion groups, discussion tracking*, and *discussion databases*. What this means is that the groupware can keep track of the discussion contributions of each participant, organize them by a variety of key word discussion topics, and store them in a discussion database. This creates threads of discussion contributions on each topic over a period of time that can be tracked and retrieved from the discussion database for analysis.

For example, a company could use discussion groupware to monitor a customer service discussion group they created on the Internet. A sales rep could select only the discussion contributions of the employees of a particular business customer to evaluate their feedback. Or a customer service analyst could create a *virtual discussion group*. The groupware could track any discussion contributions about the company and its products across several Internet, intranet, extranet, and online service discussion groups. Thus, the discussion groupware would create a virtual discussion group by weaving together the threads of contributions on the same topic by people who had really been participants in other online discussion groups [2].

Chat Systems

Chat capabilities are built into many groupware products, including Microsoft NetMeeting and Netscape Conference. Chat software by ichat Inc. is licensed to companies like Yahoo! and Merrill Lynch and bundled into Lotus Notes. These tools are a groupware version of the Internet's Internet Relay Chat (IRC) and the *chat rooms* of America Online and the other online services. Chat enables two or more people to carry on online real time text conversations. With chat, you can converse

Figure 3.24

Lotus QuickPlace Team 2000 discussion forum groupware also helps manage project team collaboration.

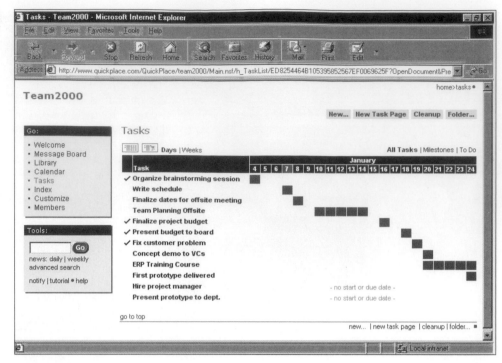

Courtesy of Lotus QuickPlace.

and share ideas interactively by typing in your comments and seeing the responses on your display screen. In addition, *instant messaging* services like AOL Instant Messenger or Yahoo Messenger add instant chat features to your online experience. Thus you are notified and can respond instantly to electronic messages received from group participants who are also online. See Figure 3.25.

Chat is an important tool for enterprise collaboration on corporate intranets, especially where voice and videoconferencing have not been implemented. One advantage of chat is that it records and stores the dialogues of all participants, so that other team members can review them later. Chat rooms are frequently added to Internet and intranet websites as another way to encourage participation and collaboration by customers or employees. For example, companies like K-Swiss, Kendall-Jackson Wines, and Nations Bank have created regularly scheduled and moderated chat rooms at their Internet websites. Even Microsoft Corporation has scheduled and moderated chat rooms on their corporate intranet to replace events like executive question-and-answer sessions at employee meetings [8, 30].

Electronic Meeting Systems

Organizations frequently schedule meetings as decision-making situations that require interaction among groups of people. The success of group decision making during meetings depends on such factors as (1) the characteristics of the group itself, (2) the characteristics of the task on which the group is working, (3) the organizational context in which the group decision-making process takes place, (4) the use of information technology such as electronic meeting systems, and (5) the communication and decision-making processes the group utilizes.

Information technology can provide a variety of tools to increase the effectiveness of group decision making. Known generically as *group support systems* (GSS), these technologies include an information systems category known as *electronic meeting systems* (EMS). Research studies indicate that electronic meeting systems produce several important benefits. For example, computer support makes group communications

Figure 3.25

An example of a team chat session supported by Lotus QuickPlace groupware.

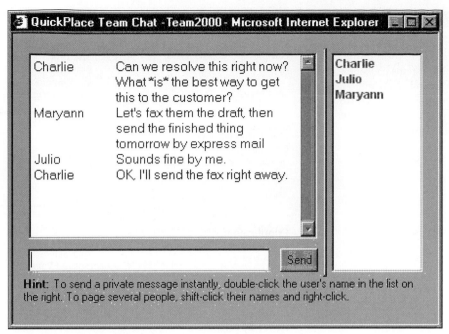

Courtesy of Lotus QuickPlace.

easier, protects the anonymity of participants, and provides a public recording of group communications (*group memory*). This significantly improves the efficiency, creativity, and quality of communications, collaboration, and group decision making in business meetings.

Electronic meeting systems packages are available that facilitate the group decision-making activities that take place in a computer-based *decision room* setting. Other types of group support systems, known as *group decision support systems* (GDSS) may be designed to support a specific application or task. Examples are groupware packages for labor/management negotiations, or GDSS software that supports anonymous voting on issues and proposals during an online collaborative process. Figure 3.26 illustrates the activities supported by the software tools in the GroupSystems EMS software package. Figure 3.27 shows a typical EMS decision room in action.

Collaborative Work Management Tools

Collaborative work management tools help people accomplish or manage group work activities. This category of groupware includes calendaring and scheduling tools, task and project management, workflow systems, and knowledge management tools. Other tools for joint work, such as joint document creation, editing, and revision, are found in the software suites discussed in Chapter 12. The groupware tools in this category are so diverse that we need to explain them individually in order to understand how they support enterprise collaboration.

Calendaring and Scheduling

Calendaring and scheduling tools are a groupware extension of many of the capabilities provided by *time management* software such as *desktop accessory* packages, personal information managers, and mainframe *office automation systems*. These packages enable you to use electronic versions of a variety of office tools such as a calendar, appointment book, contact list, and task to-do list.

Groupware calendaring and scheduling tools are included in packages like Novell GroupWise, Netscape Communicator, and Microsoft Exchange. They can automatically check the electronic calendar of team members for open time slots, propose

Figure 3.26

An example of the use of the software tools in the GroupSystems package for conducting electronic meetings. Note the various group activities supported by this EMS package.

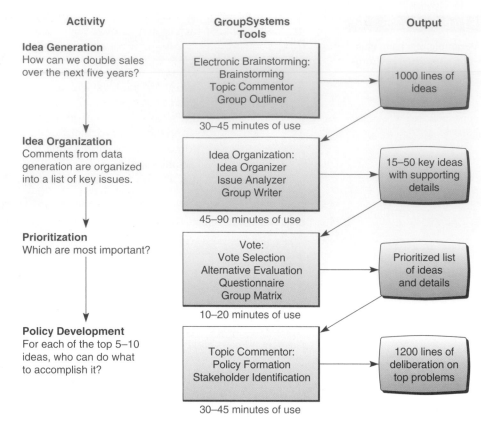

Activity	GroupSystems Tools	Output
Idea Generation How can we double sales over the next five years?	Electronic Brainstorming: Brainstorming Topic Commentor Group Outliner *30–45 minutes of use*	1000 lines of ideas
Idea Organization Comments from data generation are organized into a list of key issues.	Idea Organization: Idea Organizer Issue Analyzer Group Writer *45–90 minutes of use*	15–50 key ideas with supporting details
Prioritization Which are most important?	Vote: Vote Selection Alternative Evaluation Questionnaire Group Matrix *10–20 minutes of use*	Prioritized list of ideas and details
Policy Development For each of the top 5–10 ideas, who can do what to accomplish it?	Topic Commentor: Policy Formation Stakeholder Identification *30–45 minutes of use*	1200 lines of deliberation on top problems

Source: Adapted from H. Chen, P. Hsu, R. Orwig, L. Hoopes, and J. F. Nunamaker, "Automated Classification from Electronic Meetings," *Communications of the ACM*, October 1994, p. 57, Copyright 1994, Association for Computing Machinery, Inc. By Permission.

alternative meeting times, schedule team meetings or appointments, and notify and remind participants by E-mail. Some intranet packages even let you schedule meeting rooms and presentation equipment. Most calendaring and scheduling groupware can also send meeting notices containing a detailed agenda along with individual to-do lists to help each participant prepare for a meeting [17]. See Figure 3.28.

Figure 3.27

Using an electronic meeting system in a decision room setting.

Ventana Corporation.

Task and Project Management

Project management and personal information packages can be used to do task and project management on your PC. Examples are Microsoft Project and Outlook, Lotus Organizer, and CA-Super Project. However, groupware packages like Lotus Notes and Netscape Communicator are adding this capability to their repertoire, while Microsoft is integrating Outlook's task management feature into its Exchange groupware product.

Project management groupware helps project teams work together, and helps team members keep track of the many tasks and timelines involved. These tools produce project schedules, program reports, and automatic reminders of due dates for project tasks. Task and project management groupware also produces charts to help plan and track projects. One is the Gantt chart that specifies the times allowed for the various activities required in a business project. Other charts use network methodologies such as CPM (critical path method) and the PERT system (Program Evaluation and Review Technique), which develop a network diagram of required activities. These techniques view a project as a series or network of distinct tasks and milestones, and specify the amount of time budgeted for the completion of each task. Figure 3.29 is an example of a Gantt chart prepared by a project management groupware package.

Workflow Systems

Workflow systems are related to task and project management, as well as a type of electronic document processing called *document image management*. However, workflow systems involve helping knowledge workers collaborate to accomplish and manage structured work tasks within a knowledge-based business process. Workflow systems are typically based on rules that govern the flow of tasks and task information contained in business forms and other documents.

For example, you could fill out an electronic application form for a bank loan at a bank's website and download it to a bank loan officer's networked PC. Then the application could be completed by the loan officer during an interview with you and routed to other loan specialists' networked PCs for a credit check and the preparation

Figure 3.28

Lotus Organizer can maintain electronic calendars for individuals and projects at Internet or intranet websites.

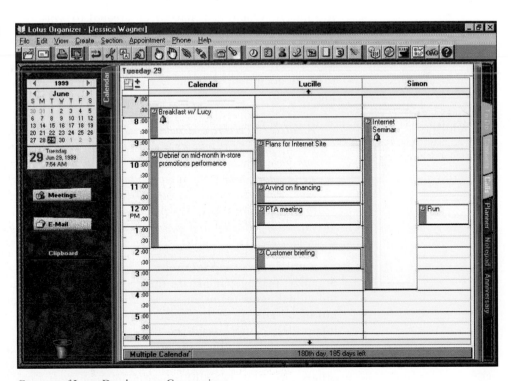

Courtesy of Lotus Development Corporation.

Figure 3.29

A Gantt chart for a business project produced by Microsoft Project.

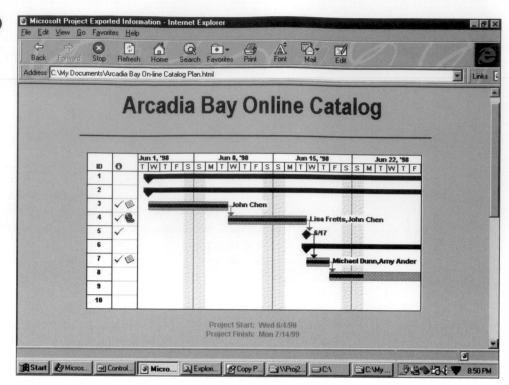

Courtesy of Microsoft Corporation.

of additional electronic forms and documents. Finally, your loan application could be electronically rerouted to the loan officer's workstation where the loan decision would be made.

Workflow systems tools are found in groupware like Novell GroupWise, Lotus Notes, and Microsoft Exchange. Some groupware workflow products, like Livelink Intranet by Open Text, have been created to work on corporate intranets. Workflow software includes forms designers to help you create electronic forms and workflow engines to process rules for completing and routing the forms. Workflow systems may access document image management databases or send E-mail to route documents to their next destination in the business process [6, 5, 16]. See Figure 3.30.

Knowledge Management

What is knowledge and how do you capture and share it? We've found over the years that we can take data and put it in reports, but to make it truly useful, someone must interpret the data and do something with it. In the past few years, we've added tools to turn data into information by identifying trends. With knowledge, we move forward another step. We capture more than just the numbers and their potential impact. We capture the organization's expertise to share with everyone. . . . Collecting and maintaining that knowledge is one of the many roles of groupware [16].

Knowledge management is an application that uses groupware tools to organize, manage, and share the diverse forms of business information created by individuals and teams in an organization. In Chapter 6, we will discuss how intranets, enterprise information portals, and enterprise knowledge portals are integrating many groupware tools and other technologies to provide easy, personalized access to business knowledge from many different data sources. Groupware such as Lotus Notes, Microsoft Exchange, Novell GroupWise, and many others store business information in document libraries, discussion databases,

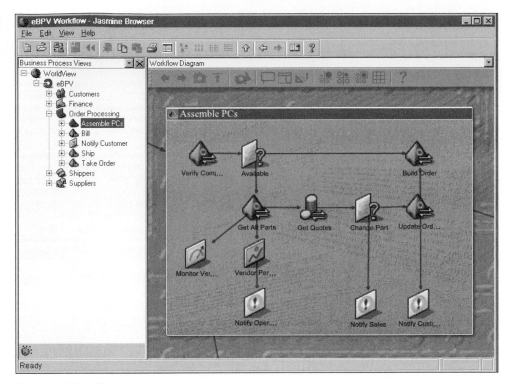

Courtesy of Novell.

Figure 3.30

Using eBVP Workflow by Computer Associates to view a workflow diagram of business processes.

knowledge repositories, and website hypermedia databases. These forms of stored information help create a *knowledge base* or *organizational memory* of strategic business information to be shared within the organization. Knowledge bases are part of the *knowledge management systems* being developed by many companies, which we discussed in Chapter 2.

For example, Compaq Computer Corporation's AltaVista Forum groupware package creates a *knowledge repository* at an intranet website to share documents and organize a team's project knowledge. Team members can store information they want to share (such as memos, reports, spreadsheets, and multimedia presentations) in shared folders. Forum can manage multiple versions of project files for different team members and time periods. Team members can also use a search tool to find project information and receive automatic notification whenever new documents are added to the knowledge repository.

Figure 3.31

Livelink by Open Text enables you to search a document management library at an intranet website for project information.

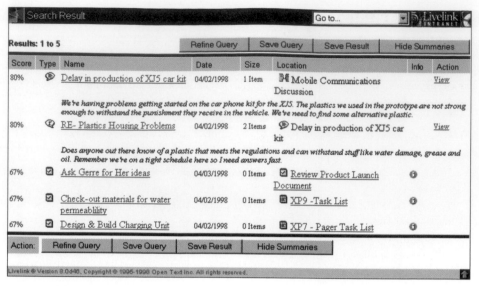

Courtesy of Open Text Corporation.

Another example is provided by the Livelink Intranet groupware package. With Livelink you can create a *document management library* for an enterprise information portal or intranet. Livelink lets you check in and check out project documents of all kinds and use a browser and search engine to find project information you need. This groupware also has a *version control* capability to manage multiple versions of project documents prepared or revised over time by team members [16]. See Figure 3.31.

Figure 3.32 closes this section with a summary of the major categories of groupware tools that many businesses are using for enterprise communication and collaboration. Remember that this summary is not intended to be a list of technical definitions. Instead, it briefly expresses how these tools can contribute to collaboration between teams and workgroups within an E-business enterprise.

Figure 3.32 A summary of the major categories of groupware tools for enterprise communication and collaboration.

Electronic Communication Tools

Electronic communication tools help you to communicate and collaborate with others by electonically sending messages, documents, and files in data, text, voice, or multimedia over the Internet, intranets, extranets, and other computer networks.

- **Electronic Mail.** Widely used to send and receive text messages between networked PCs over telecommunications networks. E-mail can also include data files, software, and multimedia messages and documents as attachments.
- **Voice Mail.** Unanswered telephone messages are digitized, stored, and played back to you by a voice messaging computer.
- **Faxing.** Transmitting and receiving images of documents over telephone or computer networks using PCs or fax machines.
- **Web Publishing.** Creating, converting, and storing hyperlinked documents and other material on Internet or intranet Web servers so they can easily be shared via Web browsers or netcasting with teams, workgroups, or the enterprise.

Electronic Conferencing Tools

Electronic conferencing tools help networked computer users share information and collaborate while working together on joint assignments, no matter where they are located.

- **Data Conferencing.** Users at networked PCs can view, mark up, revise, and save changes to a shared whiteboard of drawings, documents, and other material.
- **Voice Conferencing.** Telephone conversations shared among several participants via speaker phones or networked PCs with *Internet telephone* software.
- **Videoconferencing.** Real-time video- and audioconferencing (1) among users at networked PCs (desktop videoconferencing) or (2) among participants in conference rooms or auditoriums in different locations (teleconferencing). Videoconferencing can also include whiteboarding and document sharing.
- **Discussion Forums.** Provide a computer network discussion platform to encourage and manage online text discussions over a period of time among members of special interest groups or project teams.
- **Chat Systems.** Enable two or more users at networked PCs to carry on online, real-time text conversations.
- **Electronic Meeting Systems.** Using a meeting room with networked PCs, a large-screen projector, and EMS software to facilitate communication, collaboration, and group decision making in business meetings.

Collaborative Work Management Tools

Collaborative work management tools help people accomplish or manage joint work activities.

- **Calendaring and Scheduling.** Using electronic calendars and other groupware features to automatically schedule, notify, and remind the computer networked members of teams and workgroups of meetings, appointments, and other events.
- **Task and Project Management.** Managing team and workgroup projects by scheduling, tracking, and charting the completion status of tasks within a project.
- **Workflow Systems.** Help networked knowledge workers collaborate to accomplish and manage the flow of structured work tasks and electronic document processing within a business process.
- **Knowledge Management.** Organizing and sharing the diverse forms of business information created within an organization. Includes managing and providing personalized access to project and enterprise document libraries, discussion databases, hypermedia website databases, and other types of knowledge bases.

Summary

- **Electronic Business Applications.** Internetworked E-business enterprises are now deploying a range of applications that give them strategic capabilities in electronic business operations, enterprise communications and collaboration, and electronic commerce with businesses and consumers, and enable strategic alliances with their business partners. Refer to Figure 3.3.

- **The Business Value of the Internet.** Companies are deriving strategic business value from the Internet, which enables them to disseminate information globally, communicate and trade interactively with customized information and services for individual customers, and foster collaboration of people and integration of business processes within the enterprise and with business partners. These capabilities allow them to generate cost savings from using Internet technologies, revenue increases from electronic commerce, and better customer service and relationships through interactive marketing and customer relationship management.

- **Applications of Intranets.** Businesses are rapidly installing and extending intranets and enterprise information portals throughout their organizations (1) to improve communications and collaboration among individuals and teams within the enterprise; (2) to publish and share valuable business information easily, inexpensively, and effectively via enterprise information portals and intranet websites and other intranet services; and (3) to develop and deploy critical applications to support business operations and management decision making.

- **Intranet Technology Resources.** Intranets depend on all of the information technologies that make the Internet possible. Thus, companies must have or install Web browsers and servers, TCP/IP client/server networks, hypermedia database management systems, HTML Web publishing software, and network management and security software servers as part of the technology platform for their corporate intranets.

- **The Business Value of Intranets.** The early intranet applications of companies have demonstrated

impressive returns, quick payback, and other strategic benefits. Major cost savings come from replacing company publications and documents on paper with electronic multimedia versions published to Web servers. Intranet-based employee training and customer service programs are also proving much more cost-effective than traditional methods.

- **The Role of Extranets.** The primary role of extranets is to link the intranet resources of a company to the intranets of its customers, suppliers, and other business partners. Extranets can also provide access to operational company databases and legacy systems to business partners, as well as limited access to intranet resources by consumers and others over the Internet. Thus, extranets provide significant business value by facilitating and strengthening the business relationships of a company with customers and suppliers, improving collaboration with its business partners, and enabling the development of new kinds of Web-based service for its customers, suppliers, and others.

- **Enterprise Collaboration Systems.** The goal of enterprise collaboration systems is to help us work together more efficiently and effectively as members of the many process and project teams and workgroups that make up many organizations today. Collaboration technologies help us to share information with each other (communication), coordinate our work efforts and resources with each other (coordination), and work together cooperatively on joint assignments (collaboration).

- **Groupware Tools for Enterprise Collaboration.** Groupware is collaborative software that helps teams and workgroups work together in a variety of ways. Groupware provides many software tools for electronic communications, electronic conferencing, and collaborative work management. Refer to Figure 3.32 for a summary of the groupware tools we covered in this chapter.

Key Terms and Concepts

These are the key terms and concepts of this chapter. The page number of their first explanation is in parentheses.

1. Applications of extranets (86)
2. Applications of intranets (86)
3. Business uses of the Internet (86)
4. Business value of extranets (91)
5. Business value of intranets (91)
6. Business value of the Internet (91)
7. Calendaring and scheduling (107)
8. Chat systems (105)
9. Collaborative work management tools (107)
10. Data conferencing (103)
11. Desktop videoconferencing (103)
12. Discussion forums (104)
13. Electronic business applications (82)
14. Electronic commerce (83)
15. Electronic communication tools (100)
16. Electronic conferencing tools (102)
17. Electronic mail (100)
18. Electronic meeting systems (102)
19. Enterprise collaboration (96)
20. Enterprise information portal (88)
21. Extranets (94)
22. Faxing (101)
23. Groupware (98)
24. Internetworked E-business enterprise (80)
25. Intranets (86)
26. Intranet technology resources (90)
27. Knowledge management (110)
28. Task and project management (109)
29. Team (98)
30. Teleconferencing (103)
31. Videoconferencing (114)
32. Virtual teams (98)
33. Voice conferencing (100)
34. Voice mail (100)
35. Web publishing (101)
36. Whiteboarding (103)
37. Workflow system (109)
38. Workgroup (98)

Review Quiz

Match one of the key terms and concepts listed previously with one of the brief examples or definitions that follow. Try to find the best fit for answers that seem to fit more than one term or concept. Defend your choices.

_____ 1. A company that is interconnected internally and externally by the Internet, intranets, and other networks with its business partners.

_____ 2. Applications include enterprise communication and collaboration, electronic commerce, and internal business systems.

_____ 3. Companies are using the Internet for electronic commerce and enterprise collaboration.

_____ 4. Companies are cutting costs, generating revenue, improving customer service, and forming strategic business alliances via the Internet.

_____ 5. Using websites to buy and sell products and services.

_____ 6. A Web-based interface helps intranet and extranet users access internal and external resources and services.

_____ 7. An Internet-like network within a company.

_____ 8. Networks that link some of the Internet resources of a company to the intranets of their customers or suppliers.

_____ 9. Intranets use Web browsers and servers, TCP/IP client/server networks, hypermedia databases at networked websites, and so on.

_____ 10. Intranets are being used to improve communications and collaboration, publish and share informations, and develop applications to support business operations and managerial decision making.

_____ 11. Extranets provide access to a company's operational databases and legacy systems by its customers and suppliers.

_____ 12. Extranets can facilitate and strengthen the collaboration and relationships between a company and its business partners.

_____ 13. Intranets have demonstrated impressive returns, quick payback, and other strategic benefits.

_____ 14. Enables you to automatically check the electronic calendars of team members to schedule a meeting.

_____ 15. Two or more users at networked PCs can carry on online, interactive text conversations.

_____ 16. Includes calendaring and scheduling, tasks and project management, and workflow systems.

_____ 17. Users at networked PCs can view, mark up, revise, and save changes to a shared whiteboard of drawings and documents.

_____ 18. Same as data conferencing.

_____ 19. Enables real-time audio and video conferences.

_____ 20. Videoconferencing among networked PC users.

_____ 21. Videoconferencing among participants in conference rooms or auditoriums.

_____ 22. Encourages online text discussions over a period of time among members of teams or special-interest groups.

_____ 23. Includes E-mail, voice mail, faxing, and Web publishing.

_____ 24. Includes data conferencing, videoconferencing, voice conferencing, and discussion forums.

_____ 25. Widely used to send electronic text messages between networked PCs.

_____ 26. Helps to facilitate communication, collaboration, and group decision making in business meetings.

_____ 27. Information systems that use hardware, software, data, and network resources to help us work together more efficiently and effectively.

_____ 28. Transmitting or receiving images of documents.

_____ 29. Collaboration software for teams, workgroups, and the enterprise.

_____ 30. Organizing and sharing business information created within or imported into an organization.

_____ 31. Helps you schedule, track, and chart the status of tasks within a project.

_____ 32. A collaborative workgroup.

_____ 33. Telephone conversations shared among several participants.

_____ 34. Telephone messages to you are digitized, stored, and played back at your convenience.

_____ 35. Enterprise collaboration systems enable people from various business functions, locations, or companies to work together on a project.

_____ 36. Two or more people working together on the same task or assignment.

_____ 37. Creating, converting, and storing hyperlinked documents on Web servers.

_____ 38. Helps knowledge workers accomplish and manage the flow of structured work tasks and electronic documents in a business process.

Discussion Questions

1. The internetworked E-business enterprise is the best model for the business use of information technology today. Do you agree or disagree? Why?

2. Do you think that business use of the Internet, intranets, and extranets has changed what businesspeople expect from information technology in their jobs? Explain.

3. What is the business value driving so many companies to rapidly install and extend intranets and enterprise information portals throughout their organizations?

4. Refer to the Real World Case on Uniglobe and Allfirst Bank in the chapter. What other steps can E-commerce retailers take to reduce the abandonment of shopping processes by online visitors to a website?

5. What might be some of the limitations of using intranets in business today?

6. What strategic competitive benefits do you see in a company's use of extranets?

7. Refer to the Real World case on Groove Networks in the chapter. Is a product like Groove really necessary for collaboration on the Internet? Why or why not?

8. Do you agree that "today's users expect any computing experience to include on-demand Internet access and tools for collaborating with other people"? Why or why not?

9. Which of the 14 groupware tools summarized in Figure 3.32 do you feel are essential for any business to have today? Which of them do you feel are optional, depending on the type of business or other factor? Explain.

10. Do you use E-mail or Internet chat, or take part in any newsgroups or discussion forums? How well do any of those tools help your communication and collaboration with others? Explain.

Application Exercises

Complete the following exercises as individual or group projects that apply chapter concepts to real world business situations.

1. Microsoft Newsgroups: Collaboration for Technical Support.

Microsoft provides technical support to its customers through an assortment of online resources including newsgroups available only on Microsoft's own server (http://support.microsoft.com). Anyone on the Internet can ask technical questions about a multitude of Microsoft products and programming languages.

There are hundreds of newsgroups that cover Microsoft's Internet-related products, including Windows 2000, Office, Front Page, ActiveX, and Internet Explorer. The newsgroups are monitored by Microsoft employees for accuracy, although the bulk of the tech-support questions are answered by MVPs (most valuable professionals)—volunteers who have proven their value as support personnel on other online services.

a. Do you have a question or need help with a Microsoft software product? Check out the Microsoft newsgroups for help, or just to view the newsgroup postings if you do not want to participate.

b. Evaluate the Microsoft newsgroups as a business user. Do they provide a helpful service to Microsoft's customers? Do they provide business benefits to Microsoft? Do you have any suggestions for improvement for Microsoft? Explain your position.

2. Xilinx, Inc.: Using Intranets and Extranets for Enterprise Collaboration

Xilinx is the world's leading supplier of programmable logic microprocessors and related development software, with a website at www.xilinx.com.

Intranet

Xilinx's corporate intranet, Xilinx Crossroads, was developed by a team led by Sandy Sully, vice president and chief information officer. The intranet supports Xilinx work groups with groupware and workflow solutions and allows the company's global workforce to collaborate and share information easily through E-mail and discussion groups.

Employees use the Xilinx intranet to find competitive marketing information, sales materials, legal documents, product-specific information, and project information from the company's various departments and groups. Xilinx also built a seamless interface between its corporate intranet and the Internet to avoid replicating information that is already available. Xilinx Crossroads simply points to information that exists in another Internet location.

In the last few months, the intranet's capabilities have expanded to include workflow applications. For example, executive approvals for products are conducted through the intranet. Product specifications are posted to the intranet and the workflow/approval process is controlled by a workflow software application.

Extranet

Getting information, much of it confidential, out to sales partners often proved challenging before Xilinx developed its extranet. Xilinx needs to distribute materials such as updated product-status information, sales presentations, technical newsletters, competitive information, order lead time information, and selling tips in a timely manner while ensuring the utmost security.

Sales partners can now get a wealth of information from the Xilinx extranet, including sales tools on demand. "Our sales consultants can get in-depth customer information, such as the number of problems reported to technical support, or even request a quote for special types of products," says Sully. Xilinx protects its confidential information by authenticating users with Netscape security software.

Xilinx also uses its extranet to better collaborate with its manufacturing partners. The complex, graphically rich manufacturing specifications for Xilinx's products change frequently. Says Sully, "Our extranet provides the ideal way to give our manufacturing partners real-time information access. We have partners in Japan, Taiwan, and Korea and the worldwide acceptance of Web browser technology is what allows us to share website information seamlessly."

a. Choose an intranet application at Xilinx. What is its business value to the company?

b. Choose an extranet application at Xilinx. What is its business value to Xilinx and its business partners?

c. Visit the Xilinx website. Check out their Silicon Xpresso Cafe E-commerce site and other services. Sign their guestbook to register to visit more of the site. How would you rate the customer services and opportunities for collaboration of the Xilinx website? Explain your evaluation.

Source: Adapted from "Xilinx Succeeds at Being a Virtual Enterprise," from www.netscape.com/solutions/business/profiles, March 1999. Copyright 1999 Netscape Communications Corp. Used with permission. All Rights Reserved.

3. A Gantt Chart for an Intranet Development Project

Gantt charts are used primarily as a scheduling tool to determine the length of time required to complete a project and the steps in the project that are most critical to its timely completion. A Gantt chart identifies the shortest time in which a project can be completed. It begins each step as soon as all of its predecessor steps (those which must be compete in order to perform the current step) have been completed. By plotting the timing of elements in a project in a manner similar to that shown in Figure 3.29, a Gantt chart shows interdependencies among steps in a project and makes clear which steps are most critical to completing a project on time.

The data below list a hypothetical set of steps needed to complete an intranet project. Step A is to begin at week 1 of the project. Since steps B, C, and E have A as a predecessor step, they can only begin at week 4 after step A has been completed. Step D requires that steps B and C both be completed, so it can only begin at week 8, and so on.

If you do not have access to project management software, a Gantt chart can be presented on a standard spreadsheet by laying out a set of columns of equal width to represent elapsed weeks of project time. You can use cell outlining and filling to illustrate the timing of each step. A portion of this type of layout is illustrated below.

a. Using project planning software or a spreadsheet create an appropriate Gantt chart for this project. How will the completion of this project be affected if the time to complete step B runs 2 weeks longer than planned? If step C runs 2 weeks longer?

b. Prepare a brief presentation of your results using PowerPoint or similar presentation software. Be sure that your presentation highlights the steps that are most critical to rapid completion of the project. (Be sure to keep a copy of your work for this project because it is used again in a later exercise.)

Steps Required for an Intranet Development Project

Project Step	Description of Step	Weeks Required	Predecessor Steps	Elapsed Weeks 1	2	3	4
A	Gather Site Requirements	3	None	▓	▓	▓	
B	Design Navigation Structure	2	A				▓
C	Develop Prototype Content	4	A				
D	Create/Test/Revise Prototype Site	3	B and C				
E	Design Supporting Database	2	A				▓
F	Create/Test Supporting Database	3	E				
G	Link Site Pages to Database	2	F and D				
H	Test/Revise/Implement Completed Site	3	G				

4. Tracking Website Visits

The number of website visitors and the number of pages they look at can be important measures of the success of a commercial website. The data below show the 10 most popular websites in the U.S. for a week in March of 2001 measured on a sample basis. Data for both number of unique visitors and number of pages viewed are provided. A larger listing of the top 25 sites (measured by number of unique users) is provided in a database file on the website for this textbook. The textbook website is www.mhhe.com/business/mis/obrien/obrien5e/index.html. Click on downloads under the student resources section of that page.

a. Create a database file and enter the sample data shown or download the file listed for this exercise from the course website. Write queries to determine the average number of pages viewed per unique visitor, the maximum number of pages per visitor, and the minimum number of pages per visitor.

b. Produce a report that lists sites whose pages viewed per visitor is higher than average. The report should be sorted in descending order by the number of pages viewed per visitor.

c. From the Web (using the TrafficRanking.com™ site or a similar website ranking site) retrieve and print out a current listing of the top 10 websites based on either number of users or pages viewed. Write a brief memorandum to your instructor discussing the types of websites that are most frequently visited, the degree of change in the sites that are most visited, and the characteristics of sites that tend to have many pages viewed per user.

Website	Pages Viewed	Unique Visitors
msn.com	99029	6184
yahoo.com	123340	5526
passport.com	8195	2568
geocities.com	10835	1615
google.com	12700	1409
microsoft.com	13698	1300
aol.com	11897	1073
burstnet.com	8081	1051
Starship Traders (Interactive game site)	4956	1046
altavista.com	7645	1026

The marketing research data displayed above was provided by TrafficRanking.com™.

Zagat Survey and Ace Hardware: The Business Value of Online Communities

Has there ever been an Internet buzzword that has been more abused and confused than **community?** Remember back in the naïve 90s, when theglobe.com's stock rose 606 percent on its first day of trading—an IPO record at the time—because it supposedly was the hot place to chat? Or how about GeoCities, which offered free "homesteads" in online subdivisions complete with street addresses, as if the first thing you'd do after creating your free homepage would be to hop over to the neighbors' for a cup of digital coffee? In a $4 billion deal, Yahoo! paid more than $100 for every piddling dollar of revenue that GeoCities had from its inception in 1996 through the spring of 1999. But does anyone believe these "communities" would fetch any premium today?

Yet there really is something quite powerful and valuable behind the concept of online community, provided it is used to support a real business objective. The mistake such startups made was in believing that community was a business model unto itself. Interactive tools that allow people with common interests to exchange information work as a revenue opportunity only when they are attached to an established business model. When that's the case, communities can help a real business acquire and retain customers at a lower cost for a longer time.

Take Zagat Survey. The business behind it started more than twenty years ago, when husband and wife Tim and Nina Zagat created a system they called "organized word of mouth" and recruited thousands or reviewers to rate restaurants. The couple compiled the surveys into guidebooks for the world's top cities and sold millions of copies. Then they expanded their review system to hotels, resorts, and spas, and licensed their content for use on early online services. But it wasn't until May 1999 and the launch of Zagat's own Web site that the community of reviewers really blossomed.

Zagat will often award prizes for the wittiest comments, and it devotes a special section of the site to reviews that weren't tasteful enough to make the guidebook. Favorites include "Also known as Ebola Café," "Wear black and bring Maalox," "Grandma cooked like this, Grandpa died young," and "Still sleazy after all these years." Who wouldn't want to belong to such a fun-loving community?

Skeptics wondered why Zagat was giving away its content online. But sales of the printed guidebooks increased 70% between January and November last year. As a low-cost way to acquire new reviewers, the site boosts the value of the company's content, which leads to more online visitors in the market for printed guidebooks (and the new Palm and mobile WAP edition). And guidebook owners are more likely to return to the site for updated ratings and to submit reviews. The New York guide remains the number one book in the city (it outsells the Bible), even as site traffic increases about 10% each month.

Another example of the business value of community comes from the business-to-business domain. Ace Hardware's commercial and industrial IS division created an online community so the 325 licensed dealers of its paint, construction, and hardware products could exchange sales tips while ordering products. In one instance, a dealer in Arizona asked peers for advice on selling a new kind of industrial paint that bonds well on metal. The resulting discussion led to new sales of the Ace product totaling $1.7 million, according to the company. So far, Ace has achieved a nearly 600 percent return on its investment in these community tools.

"The Internet has to be about allowing people to collaborate and work better together," says Allen Warms, CEO and President of Participate.com, the software company that installed and manages Ace Hardware's online community as well as similar discussion forums for Cisco Systems, Hewlett-Packard, and E*Trade Securities. Corporations have invested more than $300 million in setting up and managing online communities, according to a study by The Yankee Group. Yet much of that money is wasted because companies have done a poor job in designing and implementing these tools.

And the lessons by now are well known. First, community is not an end in itself: Attach it to a working business model and give people a reason to participate. Only if they see a clear benefit will they do it. If it all works as planned, expect your customer acquisition costs to plunge and customer retention rates to surge. That's real business value.

Case Study Questions

1. What business value can be derived from the collaboration that occurs in online communities?

2. Why have many attempts to establish online communities as viable E-business models failed?

3. How can online communities help the success of a business venture? Give an example to illustrate your answer.

Source: Adapted from Evan Schwartz, "Real Community is Possible," *Business 2.0*, March 6, 2001, p. 64.

France Telecom: Internet, Intranet, and Extranet Services for Business

With operations in 75 countries, over 165,000 employees, and an annual revenue of Fr 156.7 billion, France Telecom is one of the world's largest telecommunications carriers. Specializing in voice- and data-transmission products and services, the company offers a wide range of E-business telecom services. France Telecom sets up and operates data networks and intranets and extranets for its customers, and also offers Internet access, electronic data exchange (EDI), E-mail and other electronic messaging services, as well as Web site development and hosting services.

France Telecom found that many small- to medium-sized companies throughout the world do not have the resources to develop and maintain their own corporate intranets and extranets to other companies. So it decided to create, define, and configure customer intranets and extranets and host them on its own network system.

France Telecom's hosting services are part of the worldwide Global One network, which was jointly developed by France Telecom, Deutsche Telekom, and Sprint to offer E-mail, discussion forums, and business applications over the Internet in a security-enhanced "virtual private network" environment. France Telecom also relies on Sun Microsystems servers and iPlanet software for intranet, extranet, and E-commerce management, including iPlanet's BuyerXpert, ECXpert, and TradingXpert E-commerce software products. IPlanet is a joint venture of Sun Microsystems and Netscape Communications.

"There were few doubts as to the improvements in productivity and the reduction in costs brought by an intranet," says Georges Even, Marketing Manager for France Telecom's Intranet Business Unit. "Small- and medium-sized companies in France are greatly attracted to the simplified management and reduced costs that a hosted intranet or extranet offers." According to Even, customers fall into three categories: those who want a simple intranet with email and discussion forms, those who want an intranet that offers information-sharing among employees and partner organizations, and those who want applications with a wide range of offerings—from intranet and extranet technology to online selling and customer service.

That's why France Telecomm also developed their Buyers' Network, which brings together buyers and sellers of business products and services the world over on a secure, hosted extranet site. This new E-commerce marketplace is the result of a business alliance between France Telecom and iPlanet E-Commerce Solutions. Dorothee Masse, E-Procurement Product Manager for the France Telecom Buyers Service Network, emphasized that one of the major reasons it chose iPlanet's E-commerce product line was their "open standards" design, which enables France Telecom to serve more business markets and reach more business partners of all sizes, no matter what computing platform they employ.

The France Telecom Buyers' Network is built on three levels of E-commerce processes and three network platforms, each with its own levels of security to protect customer and supplier transactions. The first level is The Buyers' Network Internet portal (www.ftcommerce.com), which is accessible for any company to visit to obtain public information about the trading exchange process and its participating companies. Companies who register at the portal can then gain access to the Buyers' Network secure extranet to access product catalogs and communicate with suppliers. Finally, companies can link their own intranets (which may be hosted by France Telecom) to the Buyers Network extranet to perform the E-commerce transaction processes required to complete purchases from suppliers.

Thus, Buyers' Network allows corporate buyers to quickly find new products and suppliers, negotiate terms, and authorize employees to place orders from their desktops, using only a Web browser. At the same time, suppliers can economically transmit their product catalogues to a large market of high-volume, global buyers. For both buyers and sellers, E-commerce processes are automated and transaction costs are reduced by using the extranet marketplace. And by offering intranet, extranet, and other Internet-based services, France Telecom has rapidly gained a large number of new business customers.

Case Study Questions

1. What are the business benefits and limitations of having companies like France Telecom host a company's Internet Web site and corporate intranets and extranets?

2. How has the business alliance between France Telecom and iPlanet benefited both companies?

3. What new E-business or E-commerce services would you recommend that France Telecom offer to its business customers? Defend your proposals.

Source: Adapted from iPlanet Corporation, "iPlanet Helps France Telecom Build Hosted Global Procurement Service," iPlanet.com, March 9, 2001.

Covisint and Others: Collaborative Product Development in E-Commerce

Companies using business-to-business (B2B) exchanges are gearing up for B2B's next frontier: collaborative development. Collaborative development, which involves sharing product design and engineering documents, improves operations, cuts costs, and saves time for the collaborating companies. Early users report that such E-business collaboration enables product design, development, and improvement processes to be coordinated and more tightly integrated before, during, and after a product is manufactured.

Covisint LLC, the automotive procurement exchange launched one year ago by the Big Three automakers, has begun to augment its online transaction-oriented E-commerce marketplace to include collaborative product development processes. Covisint is building a collaborative design portal that's expected to trim vehicle development times from 42 months down to 12 to 18 months and cut about $3.5 million in paper-based costs from the design process, Covisint spokesman Dan Jankowski said.

But the need for collaborative development goes beyond swapping documents and drawings between buyers and sellers. After a supplier or contractor wins a bid, these systems enable changes in product development and design to be communicated to all involved parties. Aerospace and defense B2B exchange Exostar LLC in Reston, Virginia, is in the midst of adding collaborative product design capabilities to the exchange's trading platform, using Windchill ProjectLink software by Parametric Technology Corp. An Exostar founder, defense giant Lockheed Martin Corp. also said that it will be using Windchill to revamp its supply-chain operations to speed up the time it takes to develop projects, which means making the collaborative software accessible internally and to potential customers and suppliers after a bid has been won.

"This type of collaboration will speed development by some 20% to 30%, and that's being conservative," said Tony Ellis, Managing Director of Commercial Systems Engineering at Bethesda, Maryland–based Lockheed Martin. To speed up the deployment of collaborative development among its business partners, Lockheed Martin has established a systems integration unit to install these types of systems for customers and small suppliers, Ellis said.

But it's not only the large B2B exchanges and biggest manufacturers that are implementing collaborative commerce initiatives. Intermet Corp., a $1 billion maker of automotive castings in Troy, Michigan, established a collaborative design Web site using ActiveProject software from Framework Technologies Corp. Russ Blaesing, Director of Automotive Business Development at Framework, said the software tracks incoming quotes from customers through the various stages of development as well as all of the drawings and specifications that accompany the proposals. And one of Covisint's founders, DaimlerChrysler AG in Stuttgart, Germany, is involved in its first large pilot project of networked design engineering, called FastCar.

Putting collaborative systems in place is of growing importance as increasing numbers of companies outsource the production of products and services to a variety of suppliers and subcontractors, all of which must be coordinated. But the automotive industry has been slow to take on the IT challenge, said Gary Dilts, DaimlerChrysler's Senior Vice President of U.S. E-commerce. Part of the problem is the usual inertia behind any major change from old ways to new ways of doing business. Another is the sheer scope of the many supply chain interrelationships and participants that many companies must learn to communicate and work with in a collaborative design and development endeavor. Yet another big barrier for some participants is that collaborative development requires investing in robust network resources and bandwidth capacities in order to properly share design specifications and drawings in realtime.

"It's an industry malady that is going to change as network technology allows us to talk to a community of business partners about a development decision rather than using point-to-point communications," said Dilts. "This is going to let us look into and understand what the impact of product development decisions are on all of the suppliers, subcontractors, and others in the supply chain."

Case Study Questions

1. What is the business value of online collaborative product development versus traditional development methods?

2. What are the business benefits and limitations of collaborative development via online exchanges like Covisint and Exostar?

3. What are some solutions to overcome the barriers to collaborative development outlined in this case? Defend one of your proposals.

Source: Adapted from Lee Copeland Gladwin, "Exchanges Racing to Add Product Design Collaboration," *Computerworld*, March 12, 2001, p.7.

Management
Challenges

Business
Applications

Module
II

Information
Technologies

Development
Processes

Foundation
Concepts

Electronic Business Systems

Chapter Highlights

Learning Objectives

After reading and studying this chapter, you should be able to:

1. Identify each of the following cross-functional E-business systems and give examples of how they can provide significant business value to a company and its customers and business partners.

    a. Enterprise resource planning

    b. Customer relationship management

    c. Enterprise application integration

    d. Supply chain management

    e. Online transaction processing

2. Give examples of how Internet and other information technologies support business processes within the business functions of accounting, finance, human resource management, marketing, and production and operations management.

Cross-Functional E-Business Systems

E-Business Applications

It's happening right before our eyes: a vast and quick reconfiguration of commerce on an evolving E-business foundation. What is the difference between E-commerce and E-business? We define E-commerce as buying and selling over digital media. E-business, in addition to encompassing E-commerce, includes both front- and back-office applications that form the engine for modern business. E-business is not just about E-commerce transactions; it's about redefining old business models, with the aid of technology, to maximize customer value [17].

This chapter explores the fast-changing world of electronic business applications of information technology. Remember that **E-business** is the use of the Internet and other networks and information technologies to support electronic commerce, enterprise communications and collaboration, and Web-enabled business processes both within an internetworked enterprise, and with its customers and business partners.

In this chapter, we will spotlight some of the major applications of E-business. We will focus on examples of cross-functional E-business applications like enterprise resource planning and enterprise application integration in Section I, and more traditional E-business applications that support activities in the functional areas of business in Section II.

Analyzing Siebel Systems and Telstra

Read the Real World Case on Siebel Systems and Telstra Corporation on the next page. We can learn a lot from this case about how information technologies are transforming and improving the management of customer relationships of E-business enterprises. See Figure 4.1.

Siebel Systems is a leading developer of customer relationship management software and other E-business systems. Siebel has exploited the intense competition for customers that is occurring in business today. Companies like Telstra are transforming themselves into customer-focused E-business enterprises, where customer aquisition, care, and retention have become key strategic goals and

Figure 4.1

Thomas Siebel, CEO of Siebel Systems, leads the development of customer relationship management systems.

Richard Morgan.

Siebel Systems and Telstra Corporation: Benefits of Customer Relationship Management

Appearances matter to Thomas M. Siebel. Although he is a brash Silicon Valley CEO who flies his own jet to his Montana ranch, he prefers his namesake software company sans flash—buttoned-up and tranquil, more IBM than Oracle. But don't mistake calm for complacency. Last year, just seven years after he founded the company in a dingy office in low-rent East Palo Alto, California, Siebel Systems Inc. passed the $1-billion-a-year sales milestone. It was a new record for a software maker.

How did he do it? By betting that the customer would be king in the business marketplace. Seven years ago, there were nearly 400 companies competing to sell programs that help keep track of customers, a niche known as customer relationship management (CRM). Today, only half of those vendors survive, with Siebel Systems on top of the heap with 35% market share. And Siebel has a ready explanation for the company's growth: his well-known obsession with customer service. No software gets written until customers are consulted. Outside consultants routinely poll clients on their satisfaction, and employee compensation is heavily based on those reports.

For example, take Australia's Telstra Corporation, which provides fixed, wireless, and E-commerce services to a customer base in nineteen countries. In addition, Telstra offers voice, data, Internet, multimedia, managed communications services, and customer-contact center solutions globally through its strategic alliances and partnerships. The Melbourne company is Australia's largest communications carrier and the clear market leader, with annual revenues of U.S. $9.5 billion.

To succeed in transforming its relationship with its customers, Telstra determined that it needed a CRM solution that would provide both its customer-facing employees and channel partners a single view of each customer relationship. The solution would also require the integration of more than twenty core legacy billing and operations databases across all of its product lines. After exploring several options, Telstra chose a variety of Siebel Systems products to provide its E-business solution.

For its initial deployment, Telstra rolled out Siebel Call Center to more than 250 telesales representatives and 150 telephone account managers in its outbound call centers, which are geographically dispersed throughout Australia. "This was where we could most quickly impact our business," explains Ross Riddoch, General Manager of Retail Technology Products. "We rolled out account, contact and opportunity management modules." This Siebel CRM product was deployed in approximately three months, on time and on budget.

User acceptance and business benefits quickly followed. "Users found Siebel Call Center's Web-based interface to be extremely intuitive and easy to use," says Riddoch. "This enabled us to reduce our training time and get our users up to speed in record time. Within four months of employing Siebel Call Center, our account management team doubled its weekly revenue, and we achieved a threefold gain in employee productivity."

The success of Telstra's initial CRM implementation led the company to expand its E-business deployment to target four work streams: sales and account management, commissions, order fulfillment, and marketing. Based on this strategy, Telstra is now managing seven concurrent projects and rolling out Siebel applications to the majority of its field sales, call center, telesales, and business partners.

Within its marketing organization, for example, Telstra has deployed Siebel Marketing and Siebel eAnalytics applications to more than 80 marketing professionals. These E-business applications enable Telstra's marketing managers to perform customer segmentation using customer information from across all touchpoints and create targeted campaigns that effectively reach their customers through call centers, direct mail, and email. Siebel Marketing helps Telstra manage, analyze, and track channel and marketing effectiveness through real-time reporting, enabling the company to continually refine its marketing efforts across all channels.

To better integrate partners into its channel system, Telstra also is deploying Siebel eChannel—a Web-based portal for communication of customer and sales data between Telstra and its business partners. By integrating its channel partners into its E-business system, Telstra wants to ensure that it maintains a seamless view of the customer across all points of interaction.

Case Study Questions

1. Why do you think the market for CRM software has expanded so dramatically in the past few years?

2. What do you see as the major business benefits of Telstra's CRM and other E-business initiatives?

3. What would you recommend as the next customer-based E-business initiative for Telstra? Why? Visit the Siebel Systems Web site (www.siebel.com) to view their ideas on E-business solutions for companies today.

Source: Adapted from "The Top 25 Managers of the Year," *Business Week*, January 8, 2001, pp. 63, and "Communications Leader Becomes Customer-focused E-business," siebel.com, March 12, 2001, pp.39–40.

competitive differentiators. Thus, Telstra uses a variety of Siebel customer relationship management and E-business systems to significantly improve the flow of customer information their employees and business partners need to effectively sell services and provide support to their customers. Telstra also is implementing Siebel marketing systems to perform in-depth marketing analyses that further support their customer focus.

E-Business Application Architecture

The world-class enterprise of tomorrow is built on the foundation of world-class application clusters implemented today. [17]

Figure 4.2 presents an **E-business application architecture,** which illustrates the application components, interrelationships, and interfaces with customers, employees, business partners, and other stakeholders of an E-business enterprise. Notice how many E-business applications are integrated into cross-functional *enterprise application clusters* like enterprise resource planning, customer relationship management, decision support, supply chain management, and selling chain management. We will discuss such applications in this section and in Chapters 5 and 6. Other applications fall into more traditional clusters, like management control (finance, accounting, and auditing) and administrative control (human resource management and procurement), which we will cover in Section II. Thus, Figure 4.2 gives you a good overview of the interrelatedness, interdependence, and integration of the E-business applications that are vital components of the successful operations and management of an E-business enterprise.

Figure 4.2

This E-business application architecture presents an overview of E-business applications and their interrelationships within an E-business enterprise.

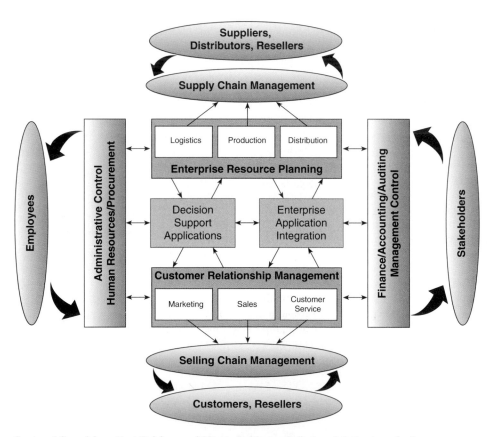

Source: Adapted from Ravi Kalakota and Marcia Robinson, *E-Business 2.0: Roadmap for Success* (Reading, MA: Addison-Wesley, 2001), p. 164. © 2001 Addison-Wesley Publishing Company, Inc. Reprinted by permission of Addison-Wesley Longman, Inc.

Cross-Functional Enterprise Systems

Integration of the enterprise has emerged as a critical issue for organizations in all business sectors striving to maintain competitive advantage. Integration is the key to success. It is the key to unlocking information and making it available to any user, anywhere, anytime [17].

As we emphasized in Chapter 1, information systems in the real world typically are integrated combinations of cross-functional business systems. Such systems support **business processes,** such as product development, production, distribution, order management, customer support, and so on. Many organizations are using information technology to develop integrated **cross-functional enterprise systems** that cross the boundaries of traditional **business functions** (such as marketing and finance), in order to reengineer and improve vital business processes all across the enterprise [3]. These organizations view cross-functional enterprise systems as a strategic way to use IT to share information resources and improve the efficiency and effectivenes of business processes, thus helping an E-business attain its strategic objectives. See Figure 4.3.

For example, as we have seen in the Real World Cases in previous chapters, business firms are turning to Internet technologies to help them reengineer and integrate the flow of information among their internal business processes and their customers and suppliers. Companies are using the World Wide Web and their intranets and extranets as a technology platform for their cross-functional and interorganizational enterprise systems.

In addition, many companies have moved from functional mainframe-based *legacy systems* to integrated cross-functional *client/server* applications. This typically has involved installing *enterprise resource planning* (ERP), *supply chain management* (SCM), or *customer relationship management* (CRM) software from SAP America, Baan, PeopleSoft, Oracle, and others. Instead of focusing on the information processing requirements of business functions, such enterprise software focuses on supporting integrated clusters of business processes involved in the operations of a business.

Enterprise Resource Planning

ERP is the backbone of E-business. In other words, ERP is a business operating system, the equivalent of the Windows operating system for back-office operations [17].

Enterprise resource planning (ERP) is a cross-functional enterprise system that serves as a framework to integrate and automate many of the business processes that must be accomplished within the manufacturing, logistics, distribution, accounting, finance, and human resources functions of a business. ERP software is a family of software modules that supports the business activities involved in these vital *back-office* processes. For example, ERP software for a manufacturing company will typically track the status of sales, inventory, shipping, and invoicing, as well as forecast raw material and human resource requirements. Figure 4.4 illustrates the major application components of an ERP system.

Many companies began installing ERP systems as a vital conceptual foundation for reengineering their business processes, and as the software engine required to accomplish these new cross-functional processes. Now ERP is being recognized as a necessary ingredient for the efficiency, agility, and responsiveness to customers and suppliers that an E-business enterprise needs to succeed in the dynamic world of E-commerce. Companies are finding major business value in installing ERP software in two major ways:

- ERP creates a framework for integrating and improving their back-office systems that results in major improvements in customer service, production, and distribution efficiency.

- ERP provides vital cross-functional information quickly on business performance to managers to significantly improve their ability to make better business decisions across the enterprise [17, 20, 25].

Figure 4.3 The new product development process in a manufacturing company. This business process must be supported by cross-functional information systems that cross the boundaries of several business functions.

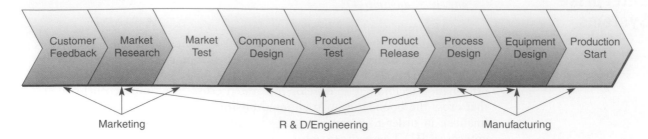

Figure 4.5 illustrates some of the cross-functional business processes and supplier and customer information flows supported by ERP systems. As we will see several times in this text, installing ERP systems successfully is not an easy task because of the major changes to a company's business processes required by ERP software. Now let's look at how a global corporation views the business value of ERP systems.

Colgate-Palmolive: The Benefits of ERP	Colgate-Palmolive is a global consumer products company that implemented the SAP R/3 enterprise resource planning system. Colgate embarked on an implementation of SAP R/3 to allow the company to access more timely and accurate data, get the most out of working capital, and reduce manufacturing costs. An important factor for Colgate was whether it could use the software across the entire spectrum of the business. Colgate needed the ability to coordinate globally and act locally. The implementation of SAP across the Colgate supply chain contributed to increased profitability. Now installed in operations that produce most of Colgate's worldwide sales, SAP will be expanded to all Colgate divisions worldwide by 2001. Global efficiencies in purchasing—combined with product and packaging standardization—also produced large savings.

- Before ERP, it took Colgate U.S. anywhere from one to five days to acquire an order, and another one to two days to process the order. Now, order acquisition and processing combined takes four hours, not up to seven days. Distribution planning and picking used to take up to four days; today, it takes 14 hours. In total, the order-to-delivery time has been cut in half.

- Before ERP, on-time deliveries used to occur only 91.5 percent of the time, and cases ordered were delivered correctly 97.5 percent of the time. After R/3 the figures are 97.5 percent and 99.0 percent, respectively.

- After ERP, domestic inventories have dropped by one-third and receivables outstanding have dropped to 22.4 days from 31.4. Working capital as a percentage of sales has plummeted to 6.3 percent from 11.3 percent. Total delivered cost per case has been reduced by nearly 10 percent [17].

Customer Relationship Management

- *It costs six times more to sell to a new customer than to sell to an existing one.*

- *A typical dissatisfied customer will tell eight to ten people about his or her experience.*

- *A company can boost its profits 85 percent by increasing its annual customer retention by only 5 percent.*

- *The odds of selling a product to a new customer are 15 percent, whereas the odds of selling a product to an existing customer are 50 percent.*

Figure 4.4

The major application components of enterprise resource planning demonstrate the cross-functional approach of ERP systems.

Source: Adapted from Ravi Kalakota and Marcia Robinson, *E-Business 2.0: Roadmap for Success* (Reading, MA: Addison-Wesley, 2001), p. 243. © 2001 Addison-Wesley Publishing Company, Inc. Reprinted by permission of Addison-Wesley Longman, Inc.

Figure 4.5

Some of the enterprise process flows and customer and supplier information flows supported by cross-functional ERP systems.

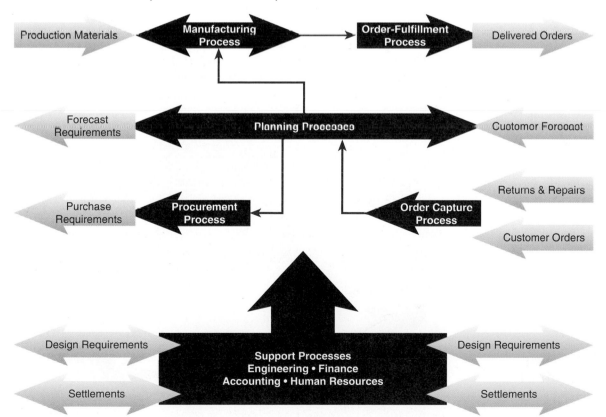

Source: Adapted from Grant Norris, James Hurley, Kenneth Hartley, John Dunleavy, and John Balls, *E-Business and ERP: Transforming the Enterprise*, p. 83. Copyright © 2000 by John Wiley & Sons, Inc. Reprinted by permission.

- *Seventy percent of complaining customers will do business with the company again if it quickly takes care of a service snafu.*
- *More than 90 percent of existing companies don't have the necessary sales and service integration to support E-commerce* [17].

That's why businesses are turning to **customer relationship management** (CRM) as a major *customer centric* business strategy. CRM uses information technology to create a cross-functional enterprise system that integrates and automates many of the *customer serving* processes in sales, marketing, and product services that interact with a company's customers. CRM systems also create an IT framework that integrates all of these processes with the rest of a company's business operations. CRM systems consist of a family of software modules that perform the business activities involved in such *front office* processes. CRM software provides the tools that enable a business and its employees to provide fast, convenient, dependable, and consistent service to its customers. Figure 4.6 illustrates some of the major application components of a CRM system.

For example, CRM programs typically include:

- **Sales.** CRM software tracks customer contacts and other business and life cycle events of customers for cross-selling and up-selling. For example, CRM would alert a bank sales rep to call customers who make large deposits to sell them premier credit programs or investment services.

- **Direct Marketing and Fulfillment.** CRM software can automate tasks such as qualifying leads, managing responses, scheduling sales contacts, and providing information to prospects and customers.

- **Customer Service and Support.** CRM helps customer service managers quickly create, assign, and manage service requests. *Help desk* software assists customer service reps in helping customers who are having problems with a product or service, by providing relevant service data and suggestions for resolving problems.

The business benefits of customer relationship management are many. For example, CRM allows a business to identify and target their best customers; those who are the most profitable to the business, so they can be retained as lifelong customers for

Figure 4.6

The major application clusters in customer relationship management.

Source: Adapted from Ravi Kalakota and Marcia Robinson, *E-Business 2.0: Roadmap for Success* (Reading, MA: Addison-Wesley, 2001), p. 180. © 2001 Addison-Wesley Publishing Company, Inc. Reprinted by permission of Addison-Wesley Longman, Inc.

greater and more profitable services. It enables real-time customization and personalization of products and services based on customer wants, needs, buying habits, and life cycles. CRM can also keep track of when a customer contacts the company, regardless of the contact point. And CRM enables a company to provide a consistent customer experience and superior service and support across all the contact points a customer chooses. All of these benefits provide strategic business value to a company and major customer value to its customers [12, 15, 16].

American Express: The Business Value of CRM	When a major airline announced two years ago that it would be leaving American Express Co.'s Membership Rewards program, customer relationship management technology flew to the rescue, recalls Dave Towers, who was the marketing manager for the program at the time. The program awards customers points toward frequent-flier miles for the purchases they charge to their American Express cards. Amex feared that if the airline flew the coop, its customers who used their points for travel on the airline would take off as well. "It was a real challenge because the value proposition we were selling to those customers had the potential to disappear overnight," Towers says. "We had to take quick action to make sure the airline wouldn't leave and that customers wouldn't leave." So Towers, who is now director of CRM at J. Crew Group Inc. in New York, piloted a multifaceted campaign using American Express' CRM systems to persuade the airline to remain in the program. From its database, the company identified cardholders in each of the airline's hub cities, including frequent users of the airline. It extracted data revealing their overall spending patterns and air travel charges. Then, via direct telephone surveys of these customers, Amex solicited customer reaction to the announcement and tracked it in a database. Coupling the feedback with the spending data, Amex was able to "prove the value of the partnership" to the airline, Towers says. "We showed them the benefits and convinced them to stay" [12].

Enterprise Application Integration

Enterprise application integration (EAI) software is becoming available which interconnects several E-business application clusters. See Figure 4.7. EAI software enables users to model the business processes involved in the interactions that should occur between business applications. EAI also provides *middleware* that performs data conversion and coordination, application communication and messaging services, and access to the application interfaces involved. Thus, EAI software can integrate a variety of enterprise application clusters by letting them exchange data according to rules derived from the business process models developed by users. For example, a typical rule might be:

> *When an order is complete, have the order application tell the accounting system to send a bill and alert shipping to send out the product.*

Thus, as Figure 4.7 illustrates, EAI software can integrate the front-office and back-office applications of an E-business, so they work together in a seamless, integrated way. This is a vital capability that provides real business value to an E-business enterprise that must respond quickly and effectively to business events and customer demands. For example, the integration of enterprise application clusters has been shown to dramatically improve customer call center responsiveness and effectiveness. That's because EAI integrates access to all of the customer and product data customer reps need to quickly serve customers. EAI also streamlines sales order processing so products and services can be delivered faster. Thus, EAI improves customer and supplier experience with the business because of its responsiveness [8, 17, 22].

Figure 4.7

Enterprise application integration software interconnects front-office and back-office applications clusters like customer relationship management and enterprise resource planning.

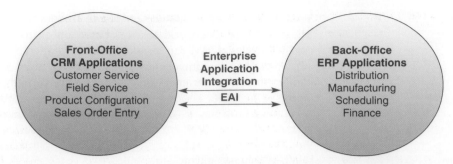

Source: Adapted from Ravi Kalakota and Marcia Robinson, *E-Business 2.0: Roadmap for Success* (Reading, MA: Addison-Wesley, 2001), p. 160. © 2001 Addison-Wesley Publishing Company, Inc. Reprinted by permission of Addison-Wesley Longman, Inc.

Nortel Networks: Enterprise Application Integration	Nortel Networks provides a complete line of products that meet the connectivity requirements of corporate enterprises, service providers, and telecommunications carriers. Nortel sells its products through multiple channels: resellers, field sales, and support personnel. Nortel resellers include network and systems integrators, value-added resellers (VARs), distributors, and original equipment manufacturers (OEMs). Nortel leverages sales channels to provide appropriate coverage, integration services, and specialized vertical market support.
	In support of their global customer service operations, Nortel built a custom interface between their customer relationship management application (Clarify) and enterprise resource planning application (SAP). This Enterprise Application Integration interface ensured that product deliveries to customers recorded in SAP were recorded in the installed product base information that resides in Clarify for contract and warranty validation. This custom EAI interface processes over 10,000 new delivery records per day [17].

Supply Chain Management

Legacy supply chains are clogged with unnecessary steps and redundant stockpiles. For instance, a typical box of breakfast cereal spends an incredible 104 days getting from factory to supermarket, struggling its way through an unbelievable maze of wholesalers, distributors, brokers, and consolidators, each of which has a warehouse.

The E-commerce opportunity lies in the fusing of each company's internal systems to those of its suppliers, partners, and customers. This fusion forces companies to better integrate interenterprise supply chain processes to improve manufacturing efficiency and distribution effectiveness [17].

So that's why many companies are making **supply chain management** (SCM) a top strategic objective of their E-business initiatives. Its an absolute requirement if they want to meet their E-commerce customer value imperative: *what the customer wants, when and where it's wanted, at the lowest possible cost.* Companies are reengineering their supply chain processes, aided by Internet technologies and supply chain management software. See Figure 4.8.

What is a company's supply chain? Let's suppose a company wants to build and sell a product to other businesses. Then it must buy raw materials and a variety of contracted services from other companies. The interrelationships with other businesses needed to build and sell a product make up a network of business relationships that is called the **supply chain.** Cross-functional E-business systems like supply chain management reengineer and streamline traditional supply chain processes.

For example, the demands of E-commerce are pushing manufacturers to use their intranets, extranets, and E-commerce Web portals to help them reengineer their relationships with their suppliers, distributors, and retailers. The objective is to significantly reduce costs, increase efficiency, and improve their supply chain

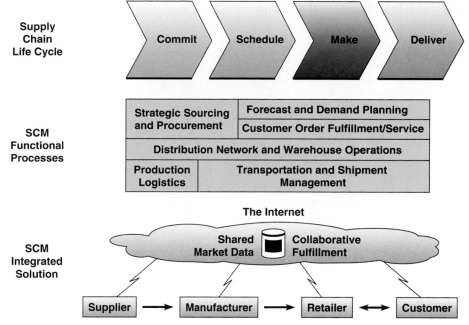

Figure 4.8

Internet technologies and supply chain management software can help companies reengineer and integrate the functional processes in the supply chain life cycle.

Source: Adapted from Ravi Kalakota and Marcia Robinson, *E-Business 2.0: Roadmap for Success* (Reading, MA: Addison-Wesley, 2001) pp. 280–289. © 2001 Addison-Wesley Publishing Company, Inc. Reprinted by permission of Addison-Wesley Longman, Inc.; and Craig Fellenstein and Ron Wood, *Exploring E-commerce, Global E-business, and E-societies* (Upper Saddle River, NJ: Prentice-Hall, 2000), p. 192.

cycle times. SCM software can also help to improve interenterprise coordination among supply chain process players. The result is much more effective distribution and channel networks among business partners. All of the objectives of supply chain management are aimed at achieving agility and responsiveness in meeting the demands of a company's customers and the needs of their business partners [2, 6, 17]. See Figure 4.9.

Sun Microelectronics: Web-Based SCM

Sun Microelectronics is a division of $116.5 billion Sun Microsystems. It custom-orders processors, chips, and circuit boards for Sun's desktop, server, and storage products. Sun doesn't actually *make* any of its microelectronic gear itself. As a "fabless" manufacturer, Sun contracts equipment fabrication to outside manufacturers, who in turn rely on components from their own subcontracted suppliers. All told, it's a supply chain with 150 "links"—suppliers in places such as Canada, Japan, Taiwan, and the United Kingdom. Somehow, no hard goods ever sit in Sun's inventory or touch the hands of any one of Sun's 29,000 employees.

Here's how it works: The microelectronics division gathers chip demand forecasts based on projected sales and Sun's internal demands, and loads them into i2 Technologies' Web-based supply chain management software. Instantly, every supplier has access to those forecasts via Sun's extranet. Contract manufacturers check Sun's demand against inventory and capacity, then enter components and materials needs into the system. That lets so-called second-tier suppliers (of memory and CPUs) see exactly what they must deliver to manufacturers. Once Sun places its demands online, each supplier's commitment to deliver materials or chips propagates back through the supply chain, giving Sun a picture of its upcoming product flow.

By entrusting its supply chain and fulfillment needs to i2's SCM software, Sun expects to lower operations costs by reducing the planning staff headcount, squeeze the most efficient production out of its manufacturing contractors, and shorten product cycles [5].

Figure 4.9

Achieving the objectives of
supply chain management
enables a company to reach
its E-business and customer
value goals.

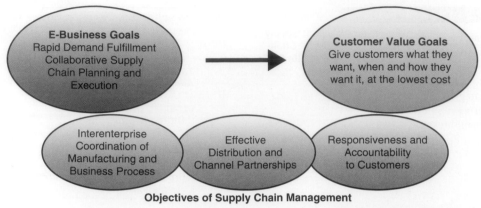

Objectives of Supply Chain Management

Source: Adapted from Ravi Kalakota and Marcia Robinson, *E-Business 2.0: Roadmap for Success* (Reading, MA: Addison-Wesley, 2001), pp. 273–79. © 2001 Addison-Wesley Publishing Company, Inc. Reprinted by permission of Addison-Wesley Longman, Inc.

Online Transaction Processing

Transaction processing systems (TPS) are cross-functional information systems that process data resulting from the occurrence of business transactions. We introduced transaction processing systems in Chapter 1 as one of the major application categories of information systems in business.

Transactions are events that occur as part of doing business, such as sales, purchases, deposits, withdrawals, refunds, and payments. Think, for example, of the data generated whenever a business sells something to a customer on credit, whether in a retail store or at an E-commerce site on the Web. Data about the customer, product, salesperson, store, and so on, must be captured and processed. This in turn causes additional transactions, such as credit checks, customer billing, inventory changes, and increases in accounts receivable balances, that generate even more data. Thus, transaction processing activities are needed to capture and process such data, or the operations of a business would grind to a halt. Therefore, transaction processing systems play a vital role in supporting the operations of an E-business enterprise.

Online transaction processing systems play a strategic role in electronic commerce. Many firms are using the Internet, extranets, and other networks that tie them electronically to their customers or suppliers for online transaction processing (OLTP). Such *real-time* systems, which capture and process transactions immediately, can help them provide superior service to customers and other trading partners. This capability adds value to their products and services, and thus gives them an important way to differentiate themselves from their competitors.

Syntellect's Online Transaction Processing

For example, Figure 4.10 illustrates an online transaction processing system for cable pay-per-view systems developed by Syntellect Interactive Services. Cable TV viewers can select pay-per-view events offered by their cable companies using the phone or the World Wide Web. The pay-per-view order is captured by Syntellect's interactive voice response system or Web server, then transported to Syntellect database application servers. There the order is processed, customer and sales databases are updated, and the approved order is relayed back to the cable company's video server, which transmits the video of the pay-per-view event to the customer. Thus, Syntellect teams with over 700 cable companies to offer a very popular and very profitable service [27].

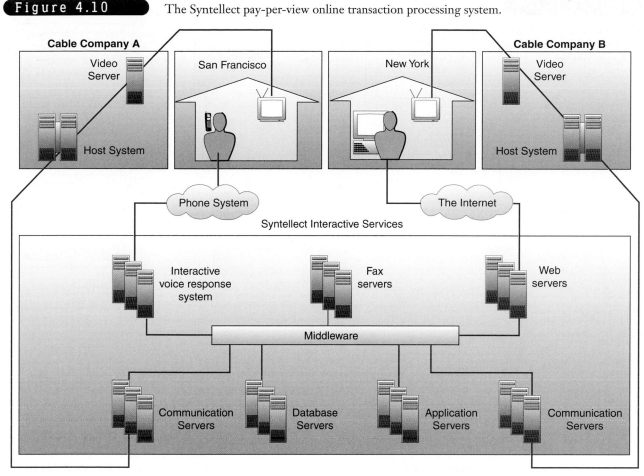

Figure 4.10 The Syntellect pay-per-view online transaction processing system.

Source: Adapted from Jay Tucker, "The New Money: Transactions Pour across the Web," *Datamation*, April 1997, p. 74. © 1997 by Cahners Publishing Co.

The Transaction Processing Cycle

Transaction processing systems, such as Syntellect's, capture and process data describing business transactions, update organizational databases, and produce a variety of information products. You should understand this as a **transaction processing cycle** of several basic activities, as illustrated in Figure 4.11.

- **Data Entry.** The first step of the transaction processing cycle is the capture of business data. For example, transaction data may be collected by point-of-sale terminals using optical scanning of bar codes and credit card readers at a retail store or other business. Or transaction data can be captured at an electronic commerce website on the Internet. The proper recording and editing of data so they are quickly and correctly captured for processing is one of the major design challenges of information systems discussed in Chapter 8.

- **Transaction Processing.** Transaction processing systems process data in two basic ways: (1) **batch processing,** where transaction data are accumulated over a period of time and processed periodically, and (2) **real-time processing** (also called online processing), where data are processed immediately after a transaction occurs. All online transaction processing systems incorporate real-time processing capabilities. Many online systems also depend on the capabilities of *fault tolerant* computer systems that can continue to operate even if parts of the system fail. We will discuss this fault tolerant concept in Chapter 9.

Figure 4.11

The transaction processing cycle. Note that transaction processing systems use a five-stage cycle of data entry, transaction processing, database maintenance, document and report generation, and inquiry processing activities.

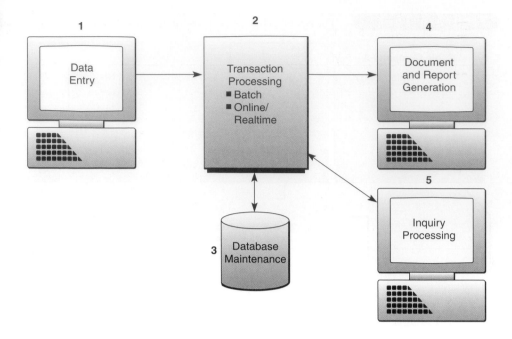

- **Database Maintenance.** An organization's database must be maintained by its transaction processing systems so that they are always correct and up-to-date. Therefore, transaction processing systems update the corporate databases of an organization to reflect changes resulting from day-to-day business transactions. For example, credit sales made to customers will cause customer account balances to be increased and the amount of inventory on hand to be decreased. Database maintenance ensures that these and other changes are reflected in the data records stored in the company's databases.

- **Document and Report Generation.** Transaction processing systems produce a variety of documents and reports. Examples of transaction documents include purchase orders, paychecks, sales receipts, invoices, and customer statements. Transaction reports might take the form of a transaction listing such as a payroll register, or edit reports that describe errors detected during processing.

- **Inquiry Processing.** Many transaction processing systems allow you to use the Internet, intranets, extranets, and Web browsers or database management query languages to make inquiries and receive responses concerning the results of transaction processing activity. Typically, responses are displayed in a variety of prespecified formats or screens. For example, you might check on the status of a sales order, the balance in an account, or the amount of stock in inventory and receive immediate responses at your PC.

Section II   Functional E-Business Systems

**Functional
Business
Systems**

Business managers are moving from a tradition where they could avoid, delegate, or ignore decisions about IT to one where they cannot create a marketing, product, international, organization, or financial plan that does not involve such decisions [18].

There are as many ways to use information technology in business as there are business activities to be performed, business problems to be solved, and business opportunities to be pursued. As a business professional, you should have a basic understanding and appreciation of the major ways information systems are used to support each of the functions of business. Thus, in this section, we will discuss **functional business systems,** that is, a variety of types of information systems (transaction processing, management information, decision support, etc.) that supports the business functions of accounting, finance, marketing, operations management, and human resource management.

**Analyzing Alcoa and
Cisco Systems**

Read the Real World Case on Alcoa and Cisco Systems on the next page. We can learn a lot from this case about how companies are using E-business systems to support realtime production and supply chain processes. See Figure 4.12.

Alcoa and Cisco Systems demonstrate the value of using new work methods and Internet technologies to move toward realtime manufacturing and supply chain management. The Internet, and company intranets and extranets, help to distribute live production information within the companies and with their business partners in the production process. New work methods also simplify realtime production decision making. The results are dramatic reductions in production cycle times, capital equipment, and inventory levels required for both companies. However, as we will see demonstrated in Real World Case 3 on Solectron Electronics at the end of the chapter, realtime production and supply chain systems can still be undermined by incorrect or overoptimistic product demand forecasts by human decision makers, and fail to deliver the business benefits they are capable of producing.

Figure 4.12

This production control specialist monitors aluminum refining processes from an automated control room that overlooks the production areas of an aluminum mill.

Charles Thatcher/Stone.

Alcoa and Cisco Systems: Real-time Manufacturing and Supply Chain Management

How did Alcoa reduce inventories by more than a quarter of a billion dollars in one year, while increasing sales by just under $1 billion? Credit goes to the Alcoa Business System, an E-business adaptation of Toyota's production methods that took more than $1.1 billion out of the aluminum maker's cost base. A big piece of it: getting Alcoa, as much as possible, to operate in real time.

Managing in real time—making decisions now, on the basis of accurate, live information delivered via the Internet and corporate intranets and extranets; eliminating filters and emptying catch basins for information and resources; producing to actual demand rather than to forecast or budget—is changing how business works. Both Alcoa and Cisco demonstrate the benefits that result.

Alcoa, already the aluminum industry's cost leader, began rolling out its new manufacturing methods in 1998, aiming to cut costs and improve responsiveness. "We were ill-prepared to meet customers' needs," says executive vice president P. Keith Turnbull, who leads the effort. "We'd ship out a pile of dead stuff"—inventory—"and if we didn't have what the customer wanted, we'd make the pile bigger." Inventories are a hedge against inefficiency, your own or that of your supplier or customer. Alcoa CEO Alain Belda calls them "monuments to incompetence."

Managing in real time is central to Alcoa's process. First, it's how Alcoa fixes plants. As at Toyota, any worker who has any problem—a machine out of kilter or a product defect—or has an idea pulls a cord summoning a leader, with the aim of fixing the problem or implementing the idea then and there. One problem, one cause, one time, at once—that's how the plant gets better, rather than by batching tasks off to engineers. Second, inside the plants, real demand dictates production as much as possible; that is, a worker upstream responds to live "pull" signals from workers downstream—ideally workers he can actually see. Says Turnbull, "Workers need to have the authority to buy and sell. Joe says to Marie, 'I need three extrusions by such and such a time'; Marie says yes or no; then she in turn buys what she needs."

The results show up all over the company. A plant in Sorocaba, Brazil turns its inventory 60 times a year. A Hernando, Mississippi extrusion plant, a money-loser when it was acquired in 1998, delivers custom orders in two days (versus three weeks previously) and makes money. In Portland, Australia, producing molten metal to real-time demand from an adjacent ingot mill raised asset utilization so much that the plan eliminated ten of twenty-four vacuum crucibles, saving about $60 million a year. All this—$832 million so far toward the $1.1 billion target—has taken just over two years.

Cisco's manufacturing couldn't be more different, or more similar. Alcoa owns 228 plants; Cisco uses 36, of which it owns but two. One of them is downstairs from the San Jose office of Randy Pond, Senior Vice President for Operations. The rest belong to top contract manufacturers like Jabil Circuit and Solectron. It's "virtual manufacturing," Pond says, made possible by a "suite of tools and processes that lets me manage an extended enterprise I don't own as if I do own it."

The key, says Pond, is "real-ime data on a real-time basis so my partners know what goes on in my business every single day." As much as possible, Cisco and a partner work with the same stream of information, doubling its value. Every day Cisco compiles its inventory, forecast for each model, order backlog, and thirteen weeks of daily data about parts and subassemblies; every day its partner compiles data on in-process inventory, cycle time by process step, optimal lot size, and yield; every night computers combine the Internet data streams into a river of information; every morning everyone knows what to build that day.

Cisco works the other end of the process—selling—the same way. Eighty-seven percent of Cisco's sales are entered directly from the Net and available instantaneously. Except for commodity parts, Cisco's E-business supply chain is as visible and as live as a televised football game. Validation and testing are also online and real-time. Autotest, a home-made tool, tests machines as they are built and won't print a packing label for a machine unless every test has been done and passed. Another tool checks a customer's order as he enters it, to make sure that he hasn't asked for incompatible gear.

The benefits of real-time E-business add up to about $400 million a year, by Pond's reckoning, plus up to a $1 billion saving in capital costs—from equipment Cisco doesn't carry on its books, improved utilization by suppliers, and minimal inventory.

Case Study Questions

1. How important is the use of Internet technologies to support Alcoa and Cisco's real-time E-business processes? Give an example to illustrate your answer.

2. What are the business benefits of their real-time E-business initiatives?

3. What are several limitations and potential pitfalls of a real-time E-business approach?

Source: Adapted from Thomas Stewart, "How Cisco and Alcoa Make Realtime Work," *Fortune*, May 29, 2000, pp. 284–86, and Ravi Kalakota and Marcia Robinson, *E-Business 2.0: Roadmap for Success*, (Reading, MA: Addison-Wesley, 2001), pp. 235–37.

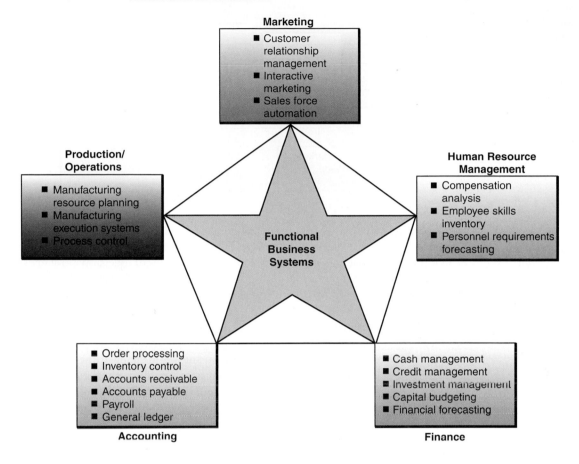

Figure 4.13

Examples of functional business information systems. Note how they support the major functional areas of business.

Marketing
- Customer relationship management
- Interactive marketing
- Sales force automation

Production/Operations
- Manufacturing resource planning
- Manufacturing execution systems
- Process control

Human Resource Management
- Compensation analysis
- Employee skills inventory
- Personnel requirements forecasting

Functional Business Systems

- Order processing
- Inventory control
- Accounts receivable
- Accounts payable
- Payroll
- General ledger

Accounting

- Cash management
- Credit management
- Investment management
- Capital budgeting
- Financial forecasting

Finance

IS in Business

As a business professional, it is important that you have a specific understanding of how information systems affect a particular business function—marketing, for example—or a particular industry (e.g., banking) that is directly related to your career objectives. For example, someone whose career objective is a marketing position in banking should have a basic understanding of how information systems are used in banking and how they support the marketing activities of banks and other firms.

Figure 4.13 illustrates how information systems can be grouped into business function categories. Thus, information systems in this section will be analyzed according to the business function they support to give you an appreciation of the variety of functional business systems that both small and large business firms may use.

Marketing Systems

The business function of marketing is concerned with the planning, promotion, and sale of existing products in existing markets, and the development of new products and new markets to better serve present and potential customers. Thus, marketing performs a vital function in the operation of a business enterprise. Business firms have increasingly turned to information technology to help them perform vital marketing functions in the face of the rapid changes of today's environment.

Figure 4.14 illustrates how **marketing information systems** provide information technologies that support major components of the marketing function. For example, Internet/intranet websites and services make an *interactive marketing* process possible where customers can become partners in creating, marketing, purchasing, and improving products and services. *Sales force automation* systems use mobile computing and Internet technologies to automate many information

Figure 4.14

Marketing information systems provide information technologies to support major components of the marketing function.

processing activities for sales support and management. Other marketing information systems assist marketing managers in customer relationship management, product planning, pricing, and other product management decisions, advertising, sales promotion, and targeted marketing strategies, and market research and forecasting. Let's take a closer look at some of the newer marketing applications.

Interactive Marketing

The term **interactive marketing** has been coined to describe a customer focused marketing process that is based on using the Internet, intranets, and extranets to establish two-way transaction between a business and its customers or potential customers. The goal of interactive marketing is to enable a company to profitably use those networks to attract and keep customers who will become partners with the business in creating, purchasing, and improving products and services.

In interactive marketing, customers are not just passive participants who receive media advertising prior to purchase, but are actively engaged in a network-enabled proactive and interactive process. Interactive marketing encourages customers to become involved in product development, delivery, and service issues. This is enabled by various Internet technologies, including chat and discussion groups, Web forms and questionnaires, and E-mail correspondence. Finally, the expected outcomes of interactive marketing are a rich mixture of vital marketing data, new product ideas, volume sales, and strong customer relationships.

Targeted Marketing

Targeted marketing has become an important tool in developing advertising and promotion strategies for a company's electronic commerce websites. As illustrated in Figure 4.15 targeted marketing is an advertising and promotion management concept that includes five targeting components.

Figure 4.15

The five major components of targeted marketing for electronic commerce on the World Wide Web.

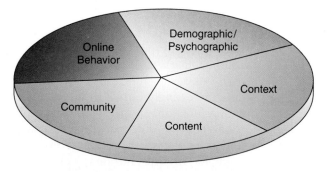

Source: Adapted from Chuck Martin, *The Digital Estate: Strategies for Competing, Surviving, and Thriving in an Internetworked World* (New York: McGraw-Hill, 1997), pp. 124–25, 206.

- **Community.** Companies can customize their Web advertising messages and promotion methods to appeal to people in specific communities. These can be *communities of interest*, such as *virtual communities* of online sporting enthusiasts or arts and crafts hobbyists, or geographic communities formed by the websites of a city or local newspaper.

- **Content.** Advertising such as electronic billboards or banners can be placed on various website pages, in addition to a company's home page. These messages reach the targeted audience. An ad for a movie on the opening page of an Internet search engine is a typical example.

- **Context.** Advertising appears only in Web pages that are relevant to the content of a product or service. So advertising is targeted only at people who are already looking for information about a subject matter (vacation travel, for example) that is related to a company's products (car rental services, for example).

- **Demographic/Psychographic.** Marketing efforts can be aimed only at specific types or classes of people: unmarried, twenty-something, middle income, male college graduates, for example.

- **Online Behavior.** Advertising and promotion efforts can be tailored to each visit to a site by an individual. This strategy is based on a variety of tracking techniques, such as "Web cookie" files recorded on the visitor's disk drive from previous visits. This enables a company to track a person's online behavior at a website so marketing efforts can be instantly developed and targeted to that individual at each visit to their website.

Sales Force Automation

Increasingly, computers and networks are providing the basis for **sales force automation.** In many companies, the sales force is being outfitted with notebook computers, Web browsers, and sales contact management software that connect them to marketing websites on the Internet, extranets, and their company intranets. This not only increases the personal productivity of salespeople, but dramatically speeds up the capture and analysis of sales data from the field to marketing managers at company headquarters. In return, it allows marketing and sales management to improve the delivery of information and the support they provide to their salespeople. Therefore, many companies are viewing sales force automation as a way to gain a strategic advantage in sales productivity and marketing responsiveness. See Figure 4.16.

For example, salespeople use their PCs to record sales data as they make their calls on customers and prospects during the day. Then each night, sales reps in the field can connect their computers by modem and telephone links to the Internet and extranets, which can access intranet or other network servers at their company. Then, they can upload information on sales orders, sales calls, and other sales statistics, as well as send electronic mail messages and access website sales support information. In return, the network servers may download product availability data, prospect lists of information on good sales prospects, and E-mail messages.

Manufacturing Systems

Manufacturing information systems support the *production/operations* function that includes all activities concerned with the planning and control of the processes producing goods or services. Thus, the production/operations function is concerned with the management of the operational processes and systems of all business firms. Information systems used for operations management and transaction processing support all firms that must plan, monitor, and control inventories, purchases, and the flow of goods and services. Therefore, firms such as transportation companies, wholesalers, retailers, financial institutions, and service companies must use production/operations information systems to plan and control their operations. In this section, we will concentrate on computer-based manufacturing applications to illustrate information systems that support the production/operations function.

Figure 4.16

This Web-based sales force automation package supports sales lead management of qualified prospects, and management of current customer accounts.

Courtesy of SalesForce.com.

Computer-Integrated Manufacturing

A variety of manufacturing information systems are used to support **computer-integrated manufacturing** (CIM). See Figure 4.17. CIM is an overall concept that stresses that the objectives of computer-based systems in manufacturing must be to:

- **Simplify** (reengineer) production processes, product designs, and factory organization as a vital foundation to automation and integration.

- **Automate** production processes and the business functions that support them with computers, machines, and robots.

- **Integrate** all production and support processes using computers, telecommunications networks, and other information technologies.

The overall goal of CIM and such manufacturing information systems is to create flexible, agile, manufacturing processes that efficiently produce products of the highest quality. Thus, CIM supports the concepts of *flexible manufacturing systems, agile manufacturing*, and *total quality management*. Implementing such manufacturing concepts enables a company to quickly respond to and fulfill customer requirements with high-quality products and services.

Manufacturing information systems help companies simplify, automate, and integrate many of the activities needed to produce products of all kinds. For example, computers are used to help engineers design better products using both *computer-aided engineering* (CAE) and *computer-aided design* (CAD) systems, and better production processes with *computer-aided process planning*. They are also used to help plan the types of material needed in the production process, which is called *material requirements planning* (MRP), and to integrate MRP with production scheduling and shop floor operations, which is known as *manufacturing resource planning*. Many of the processes within manufacturing resource planning systems are included in the manufacturing module of enterprise resource planning (ERP) software discussed earlier. See Figure 4.18.

Figure 4.17

Manufacturing information systems support computer-integrated manufacturing. Note that manufacturing resources planning systems are one of the application clusters in an ERP system.

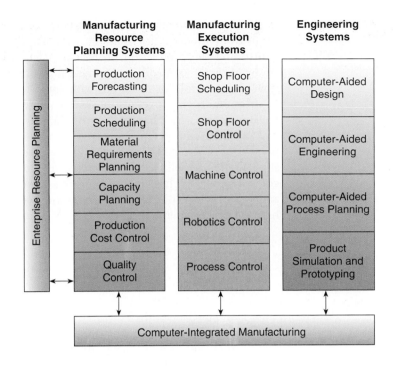

Figure 4.18

A display of a manufacturing resource planning package.

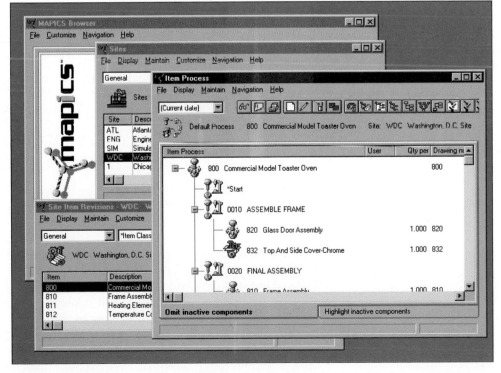

Courtesy of Mapics, Inc.

Computer-aided manufacturing (CAM) systems are those that automate the production process. For example, this could be accomplished by monitoring and controlling the production process in a factory (manufacturing execution systems) or by directly controlling a physical process (process control), a machine tool (machine control), or machines with some humanlike work capabilities (robots).

Manufacturing execution systems (MES) are performance monitoring information systems for factory floor operations. They monitor, track, and control the five essential components involved in a production process: materials, equipment, personnel, instructions and specifications, and production facilities. MES includes shop floor scheduling and control, machine control, robotics control, and process control systems. These manufacturing systems monitor, report, and adjust the status and performance of production components to help a company achieve a flexible, high-quality manufacturing process.

Johnson Controls: Collaborative Manufacturing Networks	Manufacturing processes like computer-aided engineering and design, production control, production scheduling, and procurement management typically involve a collaborative process. Increasingly, companies are using the Internet, intranets, and extranets to link the workstations of engineers and other specialists with their colleagues at other sites. These **collaborative manufacturing networks** may link employees within a company, or include representatives from a company's suppliers or customers wherever they may be located.
	For example, Johnson Controls uses the Internet, intranets and extranets to link the workstations of employees at their Automotive Systems Group with their counterparts at Ford and Chrysler and other companies worldwide. The engineers and other specialists use E-mail, chat, newsgroups, file transfer, and other Internet groupware tools to collaborate on a range of assignments, including car seat design, production issues, and delivery schedules [13].

Process Control

Process control is the use of computers to control an ongoing physical process. Process control computers control physical processes in petroleum refineries, cement plants, steel mills, chemical plants, food product manufacturing plants, pulp and paper mills, electric power plants, and so on. Many process control computers are special-purpose minicomputer systems. A process control computer system requires the use of special sensing devices that measure physical phenomena such as temperature or pressure changes. These continuous physical measurements are converted to digital form by analog-to-digital converters and relayed to computers for processing.

Process control software uses mathematical models to analyze the data generated by the ongoing process and compare them to standards or forecasts of required results. Then the computer directs the control of the process by adjusting control devices such as thermostats, valves, switches, and so on. The process control system also provides messages and displays about the status of the process so a human operator can take appropriate measures to control the process. See Figure 4.19.

Machine Control

Machine control is the use of a computer to control the actions of a machine. This is also popularly called *numerical control*. The control of machine tools in factories is a typical numerical control application, though it also refers to the control of type-setting machines, weaving machines, and other industrial machinery.

Numerical control computer programs for machine tools convert geometric data from engineering drawings and machining instructions from process planning into a numerical code of commands that control the actions of a machine tool. Machine control may involve the use of special-purpose microcomputers called programmable logic controllers (PLCs). These devices operate one or more machines accord-

Figure 4.19

Logs at Gulf States Paper's highly automated Alabama mill get measured by Machine Vision Process Control Systems, a business application of robotics and process control. Mindful of market conditions, a computer then calculates and displays the most profitable combination of boards to cut.

Paul Sumners.

ing to the directions of a numerical control program. Manufacturing engineers use computers to develop numerical control programs, analyze production data furnished by PLCs, and fine-tune machine tool performance.

Robotics

An important development in machine control and computer-aided manufacturing is the creation of smart machines and robots. These devices directly control their own activities with the aid of microcomputers. **Robotics** is the technology of building and using machines (robots) with computer intelligence and computer-controlled human-like physical capabilities (dexterity, movement, vision, etc.). Robotics has also become a major field of artificial intelligence (AI), which we will cover in Chapter 6.

Robots are used as "steel-collar workers" to increase productivity and cut costs. For example, a robot might assemble compressor valves with 12 parts at the rate of 320 units per hour, which is 10 times the rate of human workers. Robots are also particularly valuable for hazardous areas or work activities. Robots follow programs distributed by servers and loaded into separate or on-board special-purpose microcomputers. Input is received from visual and/or tactile sensors, processed by the microcomputer, and translated into movements of the robot. Typically, this involves moving its arms and hands to pick up and load items or perform some other work assignment such as painting, drilling, or welding. Robotics developments are expected to make robots more intelligent, flexible, and mobile by improving their computing, visual, tactile, and navigational capabilities. Refer to Figure 4.19.

Human Resource Systems

The human resource management (HRM) function involves the recruitment, placement, evaluation, compensation, and development of the employees of an organization. The goal of human resource management is the effective and efficient use of the human resources of a company. Thus, **human resource information systems** are designed to support (1) planning to meet the personnel needs of the business, (2) development of employees to their full potential, and (3) control of all personnel policies and programs. Originally, businesses used computer-based information systems to (1) produce paychecks and payroll reports, (2) maintain personnel records, and (3) analyze the use of personnel in business operations. Many firms have gone beyond these traditional *personnel management* functions and have developed human resource information systems (HRIS) that also support (1) recruitment, selection, and hiring; (2) job placement; (3) performance appraisals; (4) employee benefits analysis; (5) training and development; and (6) health, safety, and security. See Figure 4.20.

HRM and the Internet

The Internet has become a major force for change in human resource management. For example, online HRM systems may involve recruiting for employees through recruitment sections of corporate websites. Companies are also using commercial recruiting services and databases on the World Wide Web, posting messages in selected Internet newsgroups, and communicating with job applicants via E-mail.

The Internet has a wealth of information and contacts for both employers and job hunters. Figure 4.21 outlines top websites for job hunters and employers on the World Wide Web. These websites are full of reports, statistics, and other useful HRM information, such as job reports by industry, or listings of the top recruiting markets by industry and profession. Of course, you may also want to access the job listings and resource databases of commercial recruiting companies on the Web.

HRM and Corporate Intranets

Intranet technologies allow companies to process most common HRM applications over their corporate intranets. Intranets allow the HRM department to provide around-the-clock services to their customers: the employees. They can also disseminate valuable information faster than through previous company channels. Intranets can collect information online from employees for input to their HRM files, and they can enable employees to perform HRM tasks with little intervention by the HRM department.

Figure 4.20

Human resource information systems support the strategic, tactical, and operational use of the human resources of an organization.

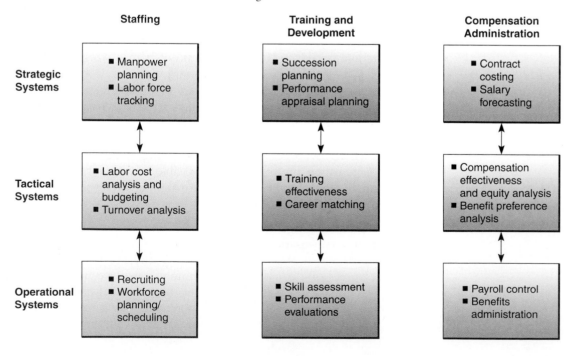

Figure 4.21

Some of the top job hunting/recruiting sites on the Web.

Top Web Job Sites
• **CareerPath.com** (www.careerpath.com) More than 80 newspapers have come together on this site to offer the bulk of their employment classifieds online. Job posts don't stay up for more than two weeks, so listings are always up-to-date. Users should also checkout the chat section, which buzzes with career advice at all hours.
• **FreeAgent.com** (www.freeagent.com) FreeAgent.com makes life easier for independent workers by matching them with appropriate freelance jobs. In addition to providing jobs and general information, FreeAgent.com also provides group-rate health insurance and 401K plans to freelancers who find work through its site.
• **Jobtrak** (www.jobtrak.com) Having partnered with more than 900 college and university career centers, Jobtrak is quickly becoming the essential site for many college grads. More than 35,000 job-seekers consult the site daily, and last year, more than 440,000 job openings were posted on the site.
• **Jobweb** (www.jobweb.org) Like Jobtrak, Jobweb aims at recent college graduates. It provides job-seekers with massive amounts of information and research—from job out-look statistics to career library resources to employer profiles. Jobweb also offers help with resumes and interviews.

Source: Adapted from "Your Body, Your Job," Technology Buyers Guide, *Fortune*, Winter 2000, pp. 264–66. © 2000 Time Inc. All rights reserved.

For example, *employee self-service (ESS)* intranet applications allow employees to view benefits, enter travel and expense reports, verify employment and salary information, access and update their personal information, and enter data that has a time constraint to it. Through this completely electronic process, employees can use their Web browsers to look up individual payroll and benefits information online, right from their desktop PCs, mobile computers, or intranet kiosks located around a work site.

Another benefit of the intranet is that it can serve as a superior training tool. Employees can easily download instructions and processes to get the information or education they need. In addition, employees using new technology can view training videos over the intranet on demand. Thus, the intranet eliminates the need to loan out and track training videos. Employees can also use their corporate intranets to produce automated paysheets, the online alternative to time cards. These electronic forms have made viewing, entering, and adjusting payroll information easy for both employees and HRM professionals [15].

Staffing the Organization

The staffing function must be supported by information systems that record and track human resources within a company to maximize their use. For example, a personnel record-keeping system keeps track of additions, deletions, and other changes to the records in a personnel database. Changes in job assignments and compensation, or hirings and terminations, are examples of information that would be used to update the personnel database. Another example is an employee skills inventory system that uses the employee skills data from a personnel database to locate employees within a company who have the skills required for specific assignments and projects.

A final example involves forecasting personnel requirements to assure a business an adequate supply of high-quality human resources. This application provides forecasts of personnel requirements in each major job category for various company departments or for new projects and other ventures being planned by management. Such long-range planning may use a computer-based simulation model to evaluate alternative plans for recruitment, reassignment, or retraining programs.

Training and Development

Information systems help human resource managers plan and monitor employee recruitment, training, and development programs by analyzing the success history of present programs. They also analyze the career development status of each employee to determine whether development methods such as training programs and periodic performance appraisals should be recommended. Computer-based multimedia training programs and appraisals of employee job performance are available to help support this area of human resource management. See Figure 4.22.

Accounting Systems

Accounting information systems are the oldest and most widely used information systems in business. They record and report business transactions and other economic events. Accounting information systems are based on the double-entry bookkeeping concept, which is hundreds of years old, and other, more recent accounting concepts such as responsibility accounting and activity-based costing. Computer-based accounting systems record and report the flow of funds through an organization on a historical basis and produce important financial statements such as balance sheets and income statements. Such systems also produce forecasts of future conditions such as projected financial statements and financial budgets. A firm's financial performance is measured against such forecasts by other analytical accounting reports.

Operational accounting systems emphasize legal and historical record-keeping and the production of accurate financial statements. Typically, these systems include transaction processing systems such as order processing, inventory control, accounts receivable, accounts payable, payroll, and general ledger systems. Management accounting systems focus on the planning and control of business operations. They emphasize cost accounting reports, the development of financial budgets and projected financial statements, and analytical reports comparing actual to forecasted performance.

Figure 4.23 illustrates the interrelationships of several important accounting information systems commonly computerized by both large and small businesses. Many accounting software packages are available for these applications. Let's briefly review how several of these systems support the operations and management of a business firm. Figure 4.24 summarizes the purpose of six common, but important, accounting information systems.

Figure 4.22

An example of a performance evaluation display.

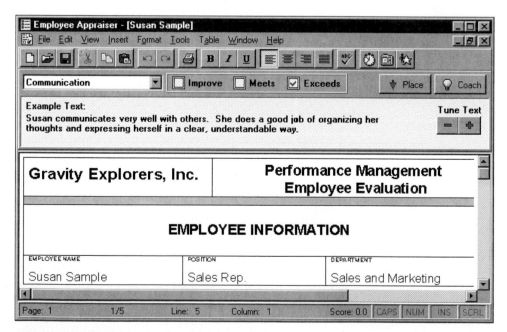

Courtesy of Austin-Hayne.

Online Accounting Systems

It should come as no surprise that the accounting information systems illustrated in Figures 4.23 and 4.24 are being affected by Internet technologies. Using the Internet, intranets, extranets, and other networks changes how accounting information systems monitor and track business activity. The online, interactive nature of such networks calls for new forms of transaction documents, procedures, and controls. This particularly applies to systems like order processing, inventory control, accounts receivable, and accounts payable. These systems are directly involved in the processing of transactions between a business and its customers and suppliers. So naturally, many companies are using Internet and other network links to these trading partners for such online transaction processing systems, as discussed in Section I.

Order Processing

Order processing, or sales order processing, is an important transaction processing system that captures and processes customer orders and produces data needed for sales analysis and inventory control. In many firms, it also keeps track of the status of customer orders until goods are delivered. Computer-based sales order processing systems provide a fast, accurate, and efficient method of recording and screening customer orders and sales transactions. They also provide inventory control systems with information on accepted orders so they can be filled as quickly as possible. See Figure 4.25.

Inventory Control

Inventory control systems process data reflecting changes to items in inventory. Once data about customer orders are received from an order processing system, a computer-based inventory control system records changes to inventory levels and prepares appropriate shipping documents. Then it may notify managers about items that need reordering and provide them with a variety of inventory status reports. Computer-based inventory control systems thus help a business provide high-quality service to customers while minimizing investment in inventory and inventory carrying costs.

Figure 4.23

Important accounting information systems for transaction processing and financial reporting. Note how they are related to each other in terms of input and output flows.

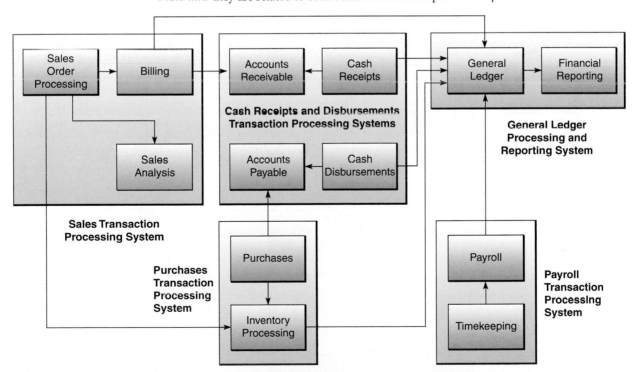

Source: Adapted from Joseph W. Wilkinson and Michael J. Cerullo, *Accounting Information Systems: Essential Concepts and Applications,* 3rd ed., p. 10. Copyright © 1997 by John Wiley & Sons, Inc. Reprinted by permission.

Figure 4.24 A summary of six widely used accounting information systems.

Common Business Accounting Systems
● **Order Processing**   Captures and processes customer orders and produces data for inventory control and accounts receivable.
● **Inventory Control**   Processes data reflecting changes in inventory and provides shipping and reorder information.
● **Accounts Receivable**   Records amounts owed by customers and produces customer invoices, monthly customer statements, and credit management reports.
● **Accounts Payable**   Records purchases from, amounts owed to, and payments to suppliers, and produces cash management reports.
● **Payroll**   Records employee work and compensation data and produces paychecks and other payroll documents and reports.
● **General Ledger**   Consolidates data from other accounting systems and produces the periodic financial statements and reports of the business.

Accounts Receivable

Accounts receivable systems keep records of amounts owed by customers from data generated by customer purchases and payments. They produce invoices to customers, monthly customer statements, and credit management reports. Computer-based accounts receivable systems stimulate prompt customer payments by preparing accurate and timely invoices and monthly statements to credit customers. They provide managers with reports to help them control the amount of credit extended and the collection of money owed. This activity helps to maximize profitable credit sales while minimizing losses from bad debts.

Accounts Payable

Accounts payable systems keep track of data concerning purchases from and payments to suppliers. They prepare checks in payment of outstanding invoices and produce cash management reports. Computer-based accounts payable systems help

Figure 4.25

Using the sales order processing of MYOB, a popular accounting package.

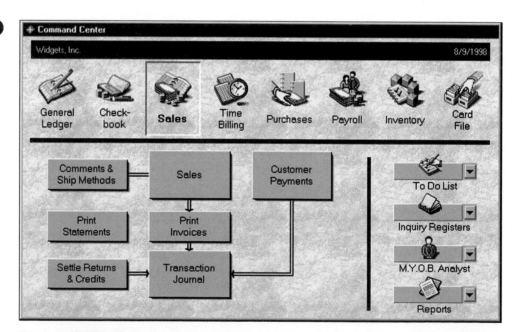

Courtesy of MYOB US, Inc.

ensure prompt and accurate payment of suppliers to maintain good relationships, ensure a good credit standing, and secure any discounts offered for prompt payment. They provide tight financial control over all cash disbursements of the business. They also provide management with information needed for the analysis of payments, expenses, purchases, employee expense accounts, and cash requirements.

Payroll

Payroll systems receive and maintain data from employee time cards and other work records. They produce paychecks and other documents such as earning statements, payroll reports, and labor analysis reports. Other reports are also prepared for management and government agencies. Computer-based payroll systems help businesses make prompt and accurate payments to their employees, as well as reports to management, employees, and government agencies concerning earnings, taxes, and other deductions. They may also provide management with reports analyzing labor costs and productivity.

General Ledger

General ledger systems consolidate data received from accounts receivable, accounts payable, payroll, and other accounting information systems. At the end of each accounting period, they close the books of a business and produce the general ledger trial balance, the income statement and balance sheet of the firm, and various income and expense reports for management. Computer-based general ledger systems help businesses accomplish these accounting tasks in an accurate and timely manner. They typically provide better financial controls and management reports and involve fewer personnel and lower costs than manual accounting methods.

Financial Management Systems

Computer-based **financial management systems** support financial managers in decisions concerning (1) the financing of a business and (2) the allocation and control of financial resources within a business. Major financial management system categories include cash and investment management, capital budgeting, financial forecasting, and financial planning. See Figure 4.26.

Cash Management

Cash management systems collect information on all cash receipts and disbursements within a company on a realtime or periodic basis. Such information allows businesses to deposit or invest excess funds more quickly, and thus increase the income generated by deposited or invested funds. These systems also produce daily, weekly, or monthly forecasts of cash receipts or disbursements (cash flow forecasts) that are used to spot future cash deficits or surpluses. Mathematical models frequently can determine optimal cash collection programs and determine alternative financing or investment strategies for dealing with forecasted cash deficits or surpluses.

Figure 4.26

Examples of important financial management systems.

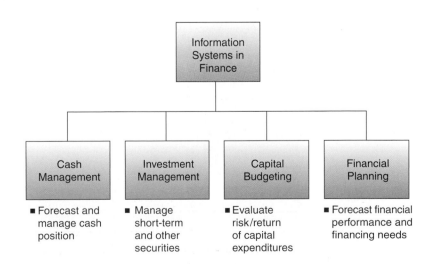

Online Investment Management

Many businesses invest their excess cash in short-term low-risk marketable securities (such as U.S. Treasury bills, commercial paper, or certificates of deposit) or in higher-return/higher-risk alternatives, so that investment income may be earned until the funds are required. The portfolio of such securities can be managed with the help of portfolio management software packages. Investment information and securities trading are available from hundreds of online sources on the Internet and other networks. Online investment management services help a financial manager make buying, selling, or holding decisions for each type of security so that an optimum mix of securities is developed that minimizes risk and maximizes investment income for the business. See Figure 4.27.

Capital Budgeting

The **capital budgeting** process involves evaluating the profitability and financial impact of proposed capital expenditures. Long-term expenditure proposals for plants and equipment can be analyzed using a variety of techniques. This application makes heavy use of spreadsheet models that incorporate present value analysis of expected cash flows and probability analysis of risk to determine the optimum mix of capital projects for a business.

Financial Forecasting and Planning

Financial analysts typically use electronic spreadsheets and other **financial planning** software to evaluate the present and projected financial performance of a business. They also help determine the financing needs of a business and analyze alternative methods of financing. Financial analysts use financial forecasts concerning the economic situation, business operations, types of financing available, interest rates, and stock and bond prices to develop an optimal financing plan for the business. Electronic spreadsheet packages, DSS software, and Web-based groupware can be used to build and manipulate financial models. Answers to what-if and goal-seeking questions can be explored as financial analysts and managers evaluate their financing and investment alternatives. We will discuss such applications further in Chapter 6.

Figure 4.27

The Red Herring online investment site offers free securities and portfolio analysis and charting tools.

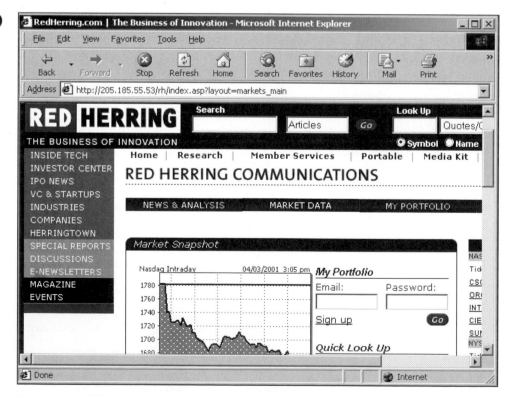

Courtesy of Red Herring.

Summary

- **Cross-Functional E-Business Applications.** Major E-business applications and their interrelationships are summarized in the E-business application architecture of Figure 4.2. Many E-business applications are integrated into cross-functional enterprise application clusters like enterprise resource planning (ERP), customer relationship management (CRM), and supply chain management (SCM), which also reengineers the business processes involved. Thus, ERP integrates and automates many of the business processes within the manufacturing, logistics, distribution, accounting, finance, and human resources functions of a business. CRM integrates and automates many of the customer serving processes in sales, marketing, and product services that interact with a company's customers, while SCM reengineers and automates many traditional supply chain processes.

  In addition, these clusters themselves are being interconnected with enterprise application integration (EAI) software so that the business users of these applications can easily access all the information resources they need to support the needs of customers and the management of an E-business enterprise. Refer to Figures 4.4, 4.6, 4.7 and 4.8 for summary views of the E-business application in EAI, ERP, CRM, and SCM systems.

- **Online Transaction Processing.** Online transaction processing system play a vital role in E-commerce. Transcation processing involves the basic activities of (1) data entry, (2) transaction processing, (3) database maintenance, (4) document and report generation, and (5) inquiry processing. Many firms are using the Internet, intranets, extranets, and other networks for online transaction processing to provide superior service to their customers and suppliers. See Figure 4.11.

- **Functional Business Systems.** Functional business information systems support the business functions of marketing, production/operations, accounting, finance, and human resource management through a variety of E-business operational and management information systems summarized in Figure 4.13.

- **Marketing.** Marketing information systems support traditional and E-commerce processes and management of the marketing function. Major types of marketing information systems include interactive marketing at E-commerce websites, sales force automation, customer relationship management, sales management, product management, targeted marketing, advertising and promotion, and market research. Thus, marketing information systems assist marketing managers in electronic commerce product development and customer relationship decisions, as well as in planning advertising and sales promotion strategies and developing the E-commerce potential of new and present products, and new channels of distribution.

- **Manufacturing.** Computer-based manufacturing information systems help a company achieve computer-integrated manufacturing (CIM), and thus simplify, automate, and integrate many of the activities needed to quickly produce high-quality products to meet changing customer demands. For example, computer-aided design using collaborative manufacturing networks helps engineers collaborate on the design of new products and processes. Then manufacturing resource planning systems help plan the types of resources needed in the production process. Finally, manufacturing execution systems monitor and control the manufacture of products on the factory floor through shop floor scheduling and control systems, controlling a physical process (process control), a machine tool (numerical control), or machines with some humanlike work capabilities (robotics).

- **Human Resource Management.** Human resource information systems support human resource management in organizations. They include information systems for staffing the organization, training and development and compensation administration. HRM websites on the Internet or corporate intranets have become important tools for providing HR services to present and prospective employees.

- **Accounting and Finance.** Accounting information systems record, report, and analyze business transactions and events for the management of the business enterprise. Examples of common accounting information systems include order processing, inventory control, accounts receivable, accounts payable, payroll, and general ledger systems. Information systems in finance support financial managers in decisions regarding the financing of a business and the allocation of financial resources within a business. Financial information systems include cash management, online investment management, capital budgeting, and financial forecasting and planning.

Key Terms and Concepts

These are the key terms and concepts of this chapter. The page number of their first explanation is in parentheses.

1. Accounting systems (148)
2. Accounts payable (150)
3. Accounts receivable (150)
4. Batch processing (135)
5. Collaborative manufacturing networks (144)
6. Computer-aided manufacturing (144)
7. Computer-integrated manufacturing (142)
8. Cross-functional enterprise systems (127)
9. Customer relationship management (130)
10. E-business (124)
    a. Application architecture (126)
11. Enterprise application integration (131)
12. Enterprise resource planning (127)
13. Financial management systems (151)
14. Functional business systems (137)
15. General ledger (151)
16. Human resource systems (145)
17. Interactive marketing (142)
18. Inventory control (149)
19. Machine control (144)
20. Manufacturing execution systems (144)
21. Manufacturing systems (141)
22. Marketing systems (139)
23. Online accounting systems (149)
24. Online HRM systems (146)
25. Online investment systems (152)
26. Online transaction processing systems (134)
27. Order processing (149)
28. Payroll (151)
29. Process control (144)
30. Real-time processing (135)
31. Robotics (145)
32. Sales force automation (141)
33. Supply chain (132)
34. Supply chain management (132)
35. Targeted marketing (140)
36. Transaction processing cycle (135)

Review Quiz

Match one of the key terms and concepts listed previously with one of the brief examples or definitions that follow. Try to find the best fit for the answers that seem to fit more than one term or concept. Defend your choices.

_____ 1. Using the Internet and other networks for E-commerce, collaboration, and business processes.

_____ 2. Information systems that cross the boundaries of the functional areas of a business in order to integrate and automate business processes.

_____ 3. Information systems that support marketing, production, accounting, finance, and human resource management.

_____ 4. E-business applications can be grouped into clusters of cross-functional enterprise applications.

_____ 5. Software that interconnects enterprise application clusters.

_____ 6. A cross-functional enterprise application that integrates and automates key back-office processes.

_____ 7. Information systems for customer relationship management, sales management, and promotion management.

_____ 8. Collaborating interactively with customers in creating, purchasing, servicing, and improving products and services.

_____ 9. Using mobile computing networks to support salespeople in the field.

_____ 10. A cross-functional enterprise system that integrates and automates many customer serving processes.

_____ 11. Information systems that support manufacturing operations and management.

_____ 12. A conceptual framework for simplifying and integrating all aspects of manufacturing automation.

_____ 13. Using computers in a variety of ways to help manufacture products.

_____ 14. Engineers and other specialists use the Internet and other networks to participate in product or process design.

_____ 15. Using computers to operate a petroleum refinery.

_____ 16. Using computers to help operate machine tools.

_____ 17. Computerized devices with work capabilities that enable them to take over some production activities from human workers.

_____ 18. Information systems to support staffing, training and development, and compensation administration.

_____ 19. Using the Internet for recruitment and job hunting is an example.

_____ 20. Accomplishes legal and historical record-keeping and gathers information for the planning and control of business operations.

_____ 21. An example is using the Internet and extranets to do accounts receivable and accounts payable activities.

_____ 22. Handles sales orders from customers.

_____ 23. Keeps track of items in stock.

_____ 24. Keeps track of amounts owed by customers.

_____ 25. Keeps track of purchases from suppliers.

_____ 26. Produces employee paychecks.

_____ 27. Produces the financial statements of a firm.

_____ 28. Information systems for cash management, investment management, capital budgeting, and financial forecasting.

_____ 29. Using the Internet and other networks for investment research and trading.

_____ 30. Performance monitoring and control systems for factory floor operations.

_____ 31. Customizing advertising and promotion methods to fit their intended audience.

_____ 32. Data entry, transaction processing, database maintenance, document and report generation, and inquiry processing.

_____ 33. Collecting and periodically processing transaction data.

_____ 34. Processing transaction data immediately after they are captured.

_____ 35. Systems that immediately capture and process transaction data and update corporate databases.

_____ 36. A network of business relationships between a business that produces a product or service and business partners involved in the processes that are required.

_____ 37. Integrates the management functions involved in promoting efficient and effective supply chain processes.

Discussion Questions

1. How is E-business "redefining old business models, with the aid of technology, to maximize customer value"?

2. Why is there a trend toward cross-functional integrated enterprise systems in business?

3. What are the benefits and limitations of interactive marketing for a business?

4. Refer to the Real World Case on Siebel Systems and Telstra in the chapter. How could CRM or other E-business systems help a company build customer value and loyalty? Give an example to illustrate your answer.

5. How do you think sales force automation affects salesperson productivity, marketing management, and competitive advantage?

6. How can Internet technologies be involved in improving a process in one of the functions of business? Choose one example and evaluate its business value.

7. How can Internet technologies improve customer relationships and service for a business?

8. Refer to the Real World Cases on Alcoa and Cisco Systems and Solectron and Others in the chapter. What can the companies involved do in the future to avoid the problems revealed in the Solectron case?

9. Do you agree that "ERP is the backbone of E-business"? Why or why not?

10. What is the role and business value of using Internet technologies in supply chain management?

Application Exercises

Complete the following exercises as individual or group projects that apply chapter concepts to real world business situations.

1. Apps.com and Smart Online: Online Business Applications

Why build a power plant when you can pay someone else for electricity? This is the logic behind the recent emergence of Web-based software companies known as application service providers, or ASPs, that hope to become an essential part of the Internet economy. Instead of providing electric power, ASPs aim to deliver software applications over the Internet for monthly or per-user fees.

Today's ASPs provide browser-based, Web-native applications—meaning the software and data exist on the Web—and generally require high-speed Internet access. Service providers create enterprise-level software and charge customers a monthly per-user service fee, which includes all installations, upgrades, and maintenance, so small businesses can automate such critical functions as accounting, human resources, and customer management.

Apps.com (www.apps.com) lists and rates online software application sites for businesses in categories such as business research, human resources, and ASPs. Each application is given a brief description and rated on a five-star scale. See Figure 4.28.

Smart Online (www.smartonline.com) provides online services in four areas—finance, legal, human re-

sources, and sales and marketing. The apps can help you create a business plan or conduct market research. There are also lots of standard forms for contracts, letters, etc.

a. Check out Apps.com and several online application software Websites such as Smart Online that are rated by Apps.com.

b. Do you agree with Apps.com's evaluations? Use Smart Online or another online application service provider (ASP) to illustrate your answer.

c. Would you use or recommend any of the online application services to a small business? Why or why not?

Source; "Apps on Tap", Technology Buyers Guide. *Fortune*, Winter 2001, pp. 217–218.

2. eLance.com and Others: Online Job Matching and Auctions

The online job boards are keeping pace with the Internet-time needs of recruiters and job hunters alike. "Custom-tailored" is the catch phrase characterizing what many of the sites provide: Applicants are well screened to meet job requirements and to ensure that all parties find what they are looking for.

Thousands of opportunities await those who troll the big job boards, the free-agent sites, the auction services where applicants bid for projects, and the niche

---

Figure 4.28

Apps.com provides a variety of information services, including ratings for business application software.

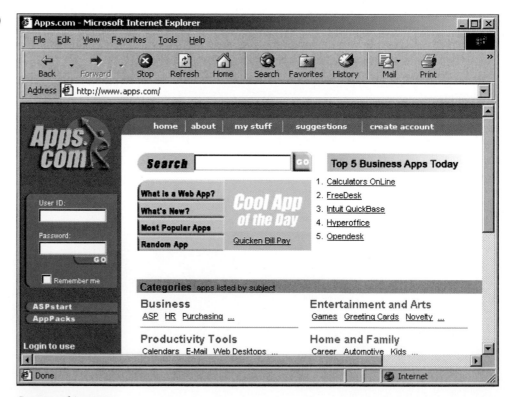

Courtesy of Apps.com.

sites for specialized jobs and skills. Wherever they may be, employers are electronically privy to a bountiful workforce and job seekers have the work world at their fingertips. Refer to Figure 4.21 in the chapter for a list of some of the top job hunting/recruiting sites on the Web. Examples of top job matching and auction sites are eWork Exchange and eLance.com.

eWork Exchange (www.eworkexchange.com). No more sifting through irrelevant search results: Fill out a list of your skills and let eWork Exchange's proprietary technology find the most suitable projects for you—no bidding required.

eLance.com (www.elance.com). This global auction marketplace covers more than just IT jobs; it runs the gamut, from astrology and medicine to corporate work and cooking projects. Register a description of your services or go straight to browsing the listings of open projects—and then start bidding. A feedback section lets both employers and freelancers rate one another.

a. Check out eWork Exchange and eLance, and other online job sites on the Web like those mentioned in Figure 4.21.

b. Evaluate several sites based on their ease of use and their value to job seekers and employers.

c. Which website was your favorite? Why?

Source: "Browse, Click, Career," Technology Buyers Guide, *Fortune*, Winter 2001, pp. 224–226.

3. Job Search Database

a. Create a database table to store key characteristics of jobs. Include all of the job characteristics shown in the list and sample record below as fields in your table, but feel free to add additional fields of interest to you. Use web sites like those listed in Figure 4.21 to gather information about available jobs. Look up and record the relevant data for at least 10 current job openings that are of interest to you or that meet criteria provided by your instructor. If data are not available for some fields (such as, salary range) for a particular job, leave that field blank.

b. Write queries that will enable you to retrieve a) just those jobs in a specified location, and b) just those jobs in a specified job category.

c. Create a report that groups jobs by Location and sorts jobs within each group by Job category.

List of Fields for the Job Search Database

Job title:	Systems Analyst
Employer:	Techron Inc.
Location:	Springfield, MA
Job Category:	Data and Information Services
Job Description:	Work with team to analyze, design, and develop E-Commerce Systems. Skills in systems analysis, relation database design, and Programming in Java are required.
Qualifications:	Bachelors degree in Information Systems or Computer Science
Salary Range:	$48,000-$60,000 depending on experience.

4. Performing an Industry Financial Analysis

Select an industry of interest to you and at least 3 prominent firms in that industry which you would like to investigate. Go to an online investment management web site (as illustrated in Figure 4.27) and/or the web sites of the firms you are investigating and obtain information about financial operations including at least net sales (or net revenue) and net after tax income for the 3 most recent years available. Also, search the web for current information affecting your firms and the industry.

a. Create a simple spreadsheet of the net sales and after tax income data you collected. Your spreadsheet should include percentage changes between years to facilitate comparisons between companies that are of unequal size. Also, you should show the rate of after tax income as a percentage of net sales. Add charts comparing trends in net revenue and net income for the firms you are investigating. Include a projection for net revenue and net income for the next year.

b. Write a brief report describing the income statistics of your spreadsheet, discussing current trends affecting your firms, and justifying your projections for the upcoming year.

Solectron Electronics and Others: Failures in Supply Chain Management

The scene was a conference room at a the Anaheim Marriott booked by consulting firm Technology Forecasters Inc. Seated around a square of long tables, thirty-three executives from across the electronics industry—big telecom networking companies, distributors, component makers, software providers, contract manufacturers big and small—gathered in early 2001 to mull the once-again hot topic of supply-chain management.

But in no time, the sparks were flying. At issue: Why, in this supposed age of just-in-time delivery and razzle-dazzle E-business technology, is the U.S. electronics industry sitting on an inventory pile-up that could take at least six months to flush out? Moreover, who will end up footing the bill for carrying all that stuff now that the line between buyer and seller has been blurred by outsourcing and virtual alliances? "I'm alarmed about the lack of ownership of the massive build-up of inventories," said Harriet Green, an executive at distribution giant Arrow Electronics Inc., which saw its own inventory double last year to $8 billion. "Everyone says it's yours."

It's undeniable that the revolution in information technology and management practices over the past decade has made U.S. industry vastly more efficient. But beneath all the boasts of flexible manufacturing and transparent supply chains, a lot needs to be done to improve the workings of the New Economy. The problems include flawed flows of information, software tools that are too difficult and costly to use, and confused lines of responsibility.

Yet, just a year ago, Wall Street was intoxicated by the idea that technological advances would help companies achieve the nirvana of business management: zero inventory. But today, with warehouses starting to bulge despite millions spent on inventory management efforts, investors and CEOs alike are left with a bitter taste in their mouths.

The theory contended that technologically driven improvements in inventory management—like "just-in-time" production, direct online sales, and supply-chain management software—would prompt increased efficiency and allow managers to tailor output to match demand exactly. That, in turn, would increase working capital, boost margins, and help companies smooth out the ups and downs in the business cycle.

Lesson one is that killer software aps can't compensate for old-fashioned business judgment. There's a flaw in the premise that technology can synchronize every party in the product chain by providing a transparent view of supply and demand: The forecasts driving the entire flow of work are still concocted by people, not by real-time blips of data from retail shelves. No matter how mechanized the system becomes, sales managers and CEOs still shoot for the moon in a boom and don't share internal market intelligence with outsiders.

The experience of Solectron Corp., the world's biggest electronics contract manufacturer, is a case in point. Last fall, company officials say they could tell a supply glut of telecom equipment was brewing. Each of their big customers, which include Cisco, Ericsson, and Lucent, was expecting explosive growth for wireless phones and networking gear. But since Solectron supplies every major player, it knew the numbers didn't add up, even under the rosiest scenario.

Nevertheless, the telecom giants told Solectron and other contractors to produce flat out, assuring them that they would pay for excess materials. But when the bottom finally fell out and its clients ordered production cutbacks, it was too late for Solectron to halt orders from all of its 4,000 suppliers. Now, Solectron has $4.7 billion in inventory.

There is also a real problem integrating the plethora of software used throughout the supply chain. Software companies like SAP, Oracle, and i2 sell a host of tools that link materials suppliers to purchasing departments to engineers to factory floors. Problem is, "the tools are overhyped, underdeveloped when they are sold, and require immense resources to bolt them together," says Bob Flowers, Senior Sales Manager of chipmaker Xilinx Inc.

Lots of better Web-based software solutions are in the pipeline. But technology still won't cure the problem of sloppy management and forecasts. If nothing else, the shake-out, which will surely feature hefty write-downs for whoever ends up stuck with the inventory hot potato, will underscore the financial risks of accepting overly optimistic estimates and lacking the willpower to curb production. It also will send a message to companies that let wishful thinking get the better of them: Efficient supply chains cannot cure unreal demand forecasts.

Case Study Questions

1. Who should accept responsibility for the huge inventory build-ups among U.S. electronics companies revealed in this case? Why?

2. Why didn't E-business supply-chain management systems prevent this problem from occurring?

3. What should be done to keep this problem from occurring again? Defend your proposed solution.

Source: Adapted from Pete Engardio, "Why the Supply Chain Broke Down," *Business Week*, March 19, 2001, p. 41, and J. P. Vincente, "A Myth Debunked," *Red Herring*, March 6, 2001, p. 130.

Hitachi Semiconductor and Dell Computer: Benefits of Enterprise Application Integration

Girish Mharre, Director of E-business at Hitachi Semiconductor, had some of the finest, most up-to-date information technology that money could buy. He had a super powerful Sun server nearly the size of a telephone booth. He had a sprawling collection of business software from SAP. His programmers had custom-built an array of specialized applications running on an industrial-strength Oracle database. The logistics people, the marketing department, procurement, sales—all of them were tied together in one seamless operation.

There was one big problem in Mharre's system: It couldn't talk to outsiders fluently. More specifically, the system wasn't integrated with those of Hitachi's customers and suppliers. While it could communicate electronically, it relied on sending out batches of information to partners every few hours. But that wasn't good enough for many transactions, so one of the company's biggest distributors wound up sending information by fax. And so, after investing millions in all that automation, Mharre found his people entering faxed information by hand.

The amazing thing about Mharre's story is how common it is. There are a lot of businesses out there that have spent millions of dollars and thousands of hours automating every aspect of their operation, only to discover that their wondrous new systems stopped cold whenever their business touched their customers, suppliers, and partners.

Meanwhile, there is a seemingly infinite variety of incompatible back-office computer systems embedded across corporate America. In a survey of just 75 companies it deals with, Dell Computer found eighteen different software packages, says Terry Klein, vice president of E-business for Dell's "relationship group." This lack of integration means that companies aren't getting the seamless processing that reduces costs and speeds up customer responsiveness.

Fortunately, there's a way out of this mess: application-integration software. This technology essentially serves as a universal translator. Rather than making a company's computers learn how to communicate with scores of different systems at other companies, the enterprise application integration (EAI) software transforms information into a common language before sending it across the Internet. Then software on the other end gets the message and translates it into something the receiving company's systems can understand.

The biggest name in application-integration software is WebMethods. Phillip Merrick, its CEO, has built a $4 billion company on his vision of transforming the lumbering back-end systems of big customers—Lands' End and Poly-One, a plastics manufacturer, to cite two examples—into nodes in intricate webs of business partners transmitting orders back and forth across the Internet.

Another major customer is Dell. Dell knew that figuring out how to get its system to talk to each of those eighteen different systems in its partners' back offices, one at a time, would be impractical, to say the least. Instead Dell used WebMethods software to build links to 40 or so of its biggest customers, allowing a customer to buy, say, a truckload of new laptops online while Dell simultaneously enters the order for those laptops into the customer's procurement system. Think of it as one-click shopping for corporate buyers. Just as Amazon.com automates the process of entering credit-card information to speed purchases by consumers, Dell is able to update its customers' procurement tracking systems every time they make a purchase.

Once you decide on an EAI software package, your troubles aren't necessarily over. Integration requires a big investment of time and money. The up-front costs of an integration software system can start in the low six figures, because often a company must first install an enterprise resource planning application package just to get its own applications talking to each. So integration is not for companies afraid of complex projects. Implementing even the best integration software requires the help of skilled programmers.

Girish Mharre says it took Hitachi Semiconductor three months and roughly $250,000, not including the price of the software, to get its application integration in place. Now, rather than faxing new product-design registrations to Hitachi, distributors can zap the information electronically into Hitachi's system. Mharre says he doesn't expect a clear return on his investment until more distributors gets with the program. But he says he's pleased with the results so far. "This was a totally manual process in the past," Mharre says. "As we put more and more distributors on, it will be a tremendous benefit for us."

Case Study Questions

1. What business problems are caused by the technological inadequacies revealed in this case?

2. How can EAI systems help to solve such problems?

3. What are the limitations of the EAI approach?

Source: Adapted from Brian Caulfield, "Systems That Talk Together, Kick Butt Together," *eCompany*, January/February 2001, pp. 92–93.

GE Capital and Others: E-Business Challenges of Chief Financial Officers

Walter Leen still remembers the days when the IT department was called data processing and it reported to the chief financial officer. "A computer was just used as a big, fast calculator and a fast typewriter," Leen said, who is a former vice president of internal auditing at Enesco Group Inc. "But the CFOs had no idea of its capabilities to provide management information."

Now the CFOs—whose focus is often on the bottom-line results of specific markets but not the technological arcana that affect them—need to understand new tools that can give them a clearer picture of their companies' financial health. E-commerce and capital-intensive IT investments also require the CFO to stay on top of the latest technology trends. But a surprisingly high number of companies, especially so-called Old Economy firms, continue to be wary about braving the E-business waters. In a poll of the more than 100 executives at an annual meeting of CFOs held recently, 24% of the respondents said their companies aren't yet involved in any online business activities. That includes even relatively mundane functions such as electronic invoicing.

Part of the problem, according to many of the CFOs, is that it's probably going to take at least another few years before successful E-business models have been firmly established and can be easily implemented by companies. That's true even at some businesses that have their feet in both the brick-and-mortar and online worlds. "We're going to have to wait a few years to see how all these electronic business models shake out," says Ray Arthur, CFO at Toysrus.com Inc., the online affiliate of Paramus, New Jersey–based retailer Toys R Us Inc.

Other companies that have been aggressive about championing E-business strategies have run into some snags. For example, James Parke, Vice Chairman and CFO at General Electric Capital Corp., said the Stamford, Connecticut–based firm has faced challenges in getting its "hands around the systems that worked well in the legacy world but had to be Web-enabled."

In addition, Parke said, "a lot of process and cultural changes were needed" before GE Capital was ready to conduct business online, and that effort is still continuing, even though the financial services arm of General Electric Co. has successfully implemented some E-business initiatives. For example, in one case, it took less than six months to achieve a return on a $1.5 million software investment that was made to Web-enable data gathered from private-label credit cards GE Capital supports for Atlanta-based The Home Depot Inc. and other corporate clients.

But Parke acknowledged that it's hard to quantify how much such moves are contributing to GE Capital's bottom line. "The industries that we're in have not been transformed by E-business," he said.

But others have. Patrick J. Spain, chairman and CEO of Hoover's Inc., in Austin, Texas, said the provider of company-specific research is now generating 98% of its sales online, compared with zero just a few years ago. But that hasn't come easily. Spain said it has "been a continuing challenge" to get writers and researchers to conceptualize their work from an online standpoint.

San Rafael, California–based Autodesk Inc., which sells AutoCAD and other design software, gets half of its business through the Web, said CFO Steve Cakebread. In addition, about a third of the company's suppliers take payments in electronic form. "And we're always talking to our suppliers—'You need to get more automated; your money is going to get to you faster,'" he said.

One of the fundamentals that financial executives are emphasizing about E-business is that the same principles apply as in the physical world: Companies still need to make money. "The laws of economics have not been repealed, and the basic methods for making money have not really changed," said Thomas W. Malone, Professor of Information Systems at the MIT Sloan School of Management. But what is changing, Malone added, is that CFOs are being asked to act as "process architects" for their companies. That emerging role focuses on developing profitable E-business plans for reengineering internal processes that cut across different departments. In that way, CFOs can ensure that customers, suppliers, and other business partners are linked together in mutually profitable E-business relationships.

Case Study Questions

1. Why are many companies still reluctant to move into E-business applications? Do you agree with their positions? Why or why not?

2. What are some of the challenges faced by companies that did move successfully into new E-business?

3. How can CFOs help their companies successfully meet such challenges and implement E-business initiatives?

Source: Adapted from Marie Trombly, "CFOs Race to Keep Up With New Technology," *Computerworld*, February 26, 2001, p. 32, and Thomas Hoffman, "CFOs Not So Fast To Implement E-Business Strategies," *Computerworld*, March 12, 2001, p. 36.

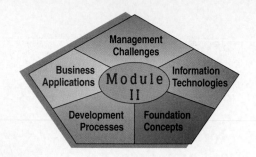

Management Challenges

Business Applications

Module II

Information Technologies

Development Processes

Foundation Concepts

Electronic Commerce Systems

Chapter Highlights

Section I
Electronic Commerce Fundamentals

Introduction to E-Commerce

Real World Case: eBay Inc. and Amazon.com: Lessons from an E-Commerce Leader

The Scope of E-Commerce

Essential E-Commerce Processes

Electronic Payment Processes

Section II
E-Commerce Applications and Issues

E-Commerce Application Trends

Real World Case: MarthaStewart.com: Building an E-Commerce Website

Business to Consumer E-Commerce

Web Store Requirements

Business-to-Business E-Commerce

E-Commerce Marketplaces

Clicks and Bricks in E-Commerce

Learning Objectives

After reading and studying this chapter, you should be able to:

1. Identify the major categories and trends of E-commerce applications.

2. Identify the essential processes of an E-commerce system, and give examples of how they are implemented in E-commerce applications.

3. Identify and give examples of several key factors and Web store requirements needed to succeed in E-commerce.

4. Identify and explain the business value of several types of E-commerce marketplaces.

5. Discuss the benefits and trade-offs of several E-commerce clicks and bricks alternatives.

Electronic Commerce Fundamentals

Introduction to E-Commerce

Few concepts have revolutionized business more profoundly than E-commerce. E-commerce is changing the shape of competition, the speed of action, and the nature of leadership. Simply put, the streamlining of interactions, products, and payments from customers to companies and from companies to suppliers is causing an earthquake in many boardrooms [17].

For E-business enterprises in the age of the Internet, electronic commerce is more than just buying and selling products online. Instead, it encompasses the entire online process of developing, marketing, selling, delivering, servicing, and paying for products and services transacted on internetworked, global marketplaces of customers, with the support of a worldwide network of business partners. As we will see in this chapter, electronic commerce systems rely on the resources of the Internet, intranets, extranets, and other technologies to support every step of this process.

Analyzing eBay Inc.

Read the Real World Case on eBay Inc. on the next page. We can learn a lot about the challenges and opportunities of electronic commerce from this example. See Figure 5.1.

The lessons learned in the last few years by the leader of one of the few profitable large E-commerce companies are worth hearing. CEO Meg Whitman credits eBay's innovative "community commerce" business model for a large part of its success. Thus, eBay is more than a global collection of consumer-to-consumer electronic marketplaces. eBay brings E-commerce to millions of consumer and small business participants who congregate in thousands of communities of interest that provide the critical mass of buyers and sellers required for the success of the countless electronic auctions taking place daily. Whitman also credits basic business requirements such as financial discipline, understanding and serving diverse customer needs, building an outstanding management team, and hiring committed employees for eBay's success. Her biggest concern for the future is properly managing the growth of eBay as it expands globally. Whitman also believes that Amazon.com will finally achieve profitability if it can master its inventory and fulfillment management challenges.

Figure 5.1

Meg Whitman, CEO of eBay, leads one of the few profitable large E-commerce companies today.

Christopher Smith.

eBay Inc. and Amazon.com: Lessons from an E-Commerce Leader

An Interview with Margaret C. Whitman, CEO, eBay Inc.

Why eBay? You worked for a variety of traditional companies—Procter & Gamble, Stride Rite, Hasbro. What tempted you to an Internet company like eBay?

When I first got a call from the headhunter to come to eBay, I said: "Absolutely not. I'm not thinking about living 3,000 miles across the country, uprooting my neurosurgeon husband, and taking my two boys out of school to go to the West Coast for this no-name Internet company." So I said no. To the credit of the headhunter, he called me back about three weeks later and he said: "eBay is perfect for you and you are perfect for eBay. I beg you to get on an airplane to go meet the founder, Pierre Omidyar."

What changed your mind?

EBay had two main things that really spoke to me. In enabled individuals to do things that they could not have done without the Web. The second thing was what Pierre said: "People have met their best friends on eBay. What this has enabled is truly online community." I recognized the land-based equivalent, which is that whatever your interest is—whether it's bowling or dance—you tend to like people who like the same things you do. And so I saw it had the makings of a great brand.

Why has eBay's business model been successful?

It was a business model and a concept uniquely suited to the Web and took advantage of the characteristics of the Web. The second thing is that it really is the first community commerce model. People ask me, how is managing in the New Economy different from managing in the Old Economy? Actually, it's a lot the same. It's about the financial discipline of the bottom line, understanding your customers, segmenting your customers by their needs, and building a world-class management team.

Even so, the stock has declined by 70%. Why?

The last two years in our economy will not be repeated again in our lifetime. This was an extraordinary event funded by very significant access to capital, and a lot of the economic reality of running businesses was suspended. So the pendulum swung all the way to the right. Now the pendulum is swinging all the way to the left. I think it will ultimately come back to the middle. We have fared better than just about everyone on the Net. So we're not too worried about that. The ethos of the company is: "You know what we can control? We can control the results." And as long as we continue to put the results on the board, I think the market cap will take care of itself.

I think the investors that own eBay understand the promise of what has been created here. We have truly created a global-trading platform where practically anyone can sell practically anything. It might be the only entirely new concept that's been born out of the Web. This can be a very big, very profitable model. Our gross margins are in the mid-80's. Our operating margins reached 20% in the fourth quarter of last year. We said for a long time that our long-term business model has 30% to 35% operating margins. And our estimate of the market that we can address is $1.7 trillion on a global basis.

How has the depressed stock price affected employee retention and morale?

There's no question that people are disappointed that a lot of their initial stock grants are under water. But we tried to hire people because they believed in what the company was doing. We were looking for what we call missionaries, as opposed to mercenaries. In Silicon Valley, a lot of companies were founded by mercenaries, and they were not built to last.

What is it you worry about most?

I worry about the ability to grow a company at the rate that we have been growing on a global basis. When I joined the company in January, 1998, we had just finished a year where we did $4.5 million in sales. There were 20 people in the company in a small office in Silicon Valley. Today, we have almost 2000 individuals, we've just finished a year where we did about $430 million in sales, and the sun now never sets on eBay's offices. Just growing at 50% a year, with offices all over the world, is a huge challenge. How do you keep core values? How do you train people? How do you make sure that you don't repeat mistakes? Also, we're building a site to handle $30 billion of gross merchandise sales in 25 countries, 16 languages, 24-7.

What is your prognosis for Amazon.com?

I think Amazon is a great consumer concept. It has an unbelievable user interface. It's easy, it's friendly. Their customer support is terrific. And they really set the standard in many ways for buying on the Net. I think the difficulty is the back end-inventory, warehouses, fulfillment, returns, obsolescence. I think they're a smart group of managers, and I think they will get there because they have built a tremendous consumer franchise. But I think a lot of blocking and tackling and heavy lifting—Old Economy skills—are going to be required to ultimately make money there.

Case Study Questions

1. What are several possible reasons for the success of the eBay business model, besides those given by Margaret Whitman?

2. What are several things eBay could do to increase the success and value of their business? Visit www.ebay.com to get ideas to help you formulate an answer.

3. Do you agree with Whitman's evaluation of Amazon's performance and prospects? Why or why not?

Source: Adapted from Steven Shepard, "A Talk with Meg Whitman," *Business Week*, March 19, 2001, pp. 98–99.

Figure 5.2

E-commerce involves accomplishing a range of business processes to support the electronic buying and selling of goods and services.

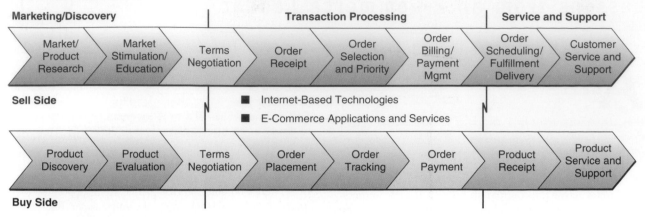

Source: Adapted from Craig Fellenstein and Ron Wood, *Exploring E-Commerce, Global E-Business, and E-Societies* (Upper Saddle River, N.J.: Prentice-Hall), 2000, p. 28.

The Scope of E-Commerce

Figure 5.2 illustrates the range of business processes involved in the marketing, buying, selling, and servicing of products and services in companies that engage in E-commerce. Companies involved in E-commerce as either buyers or sellers rely on Internet-based technologies, and E-commerce applications and services to accomplish marketing, discovery, transaction processing, and product and customer service processes. For example, electronic commerce can include interactive marketing, ordering, payment, and customer support processes at E-commerce catalog and auction sites on the World Wide Web, extranet access of inventory databases by customers and suppliers, intranet access of customer relationship management systems by sales and customer service reps, and customer collaboration in product development via E-mail exchanges and Internet newsgroups.

Many companies today are participating in or sponsoring three basic categories of electronic commerce applications: business-to-consumer, business-to-business, and consumer-to-consumer E-commerce. Note: We will not explicitly cover business-to-government (B2G) and *E-government* applications in this text. However, many E-commerce concepts apply to such applications.

Business-to-Consumer (B2C) E-Commerce. In this form of electronic commerce, businesses must develop attractive electronic marketplaces to entice and sell products and services to consumers. For example, many companies offer E-commerce websites that provide virtual storefronts and multimedia catalogs, interactive order processing, secure electronic payment systems, and online customer support.

Business-to-Business (B2B) E-Commerce. This category of electronic commerce involves both electronic business marketplaces and direct market links between businesses. For example, many companies offer secure Internet or extranet E-commerce catalog websites for their business customers and suppliers. Also very important are B2B E-commerce portals that provide auction and exchange marketplaces for businesses. Others may rely on electronic data interchange (EDI) via the Internet or extranets for computer-to-computer exchange of E-commerce documents with their larger business customers and suppliers.

Consumer-to-Consumer (C2C) E-Commerce. The huge success of online auctions like eBay, where consumers (as well as businesses) can buy and sell with each other in an auction process at an auction website, makes this E-commerce model an important E-commerce business strategy. Thus, participating in or sponsoring consumer or business auctions is an important E-commerce alternative for B2C or B2B E-commerce. Electronic personal advertising of products or services to buy or sell by consumers at electronic newspaper sites, consumer E-commerce portals, or personal websites is also an important form of C2C E-commerce.

Electronic Commerce Technologies

What technologies are necessary for electronic commerce? The short answer is that most information technologies and Internet technologies that we discuss in this text are involved in electronic commerce systems. A more specific answer is illustrated in Figure 5.3.

Figure 5.3 illustrates an electronic commerce architecture developed by Sun Microsystems and its business partners. This architecture emphasizes that:

- The Internet, intranets, and extranets are the network infrastructure or foundation of electronic commerce.
- Customers must be provided with a range of secure information, marketing, transaction processing, and payment services.

Figure 5.3

The software components and functions of an integrated E-commerce system. This architecture would enable a business to use the Internet, intranets, and extranets to accomplish E-commerce transactions with consumers, business customers, and business partners.

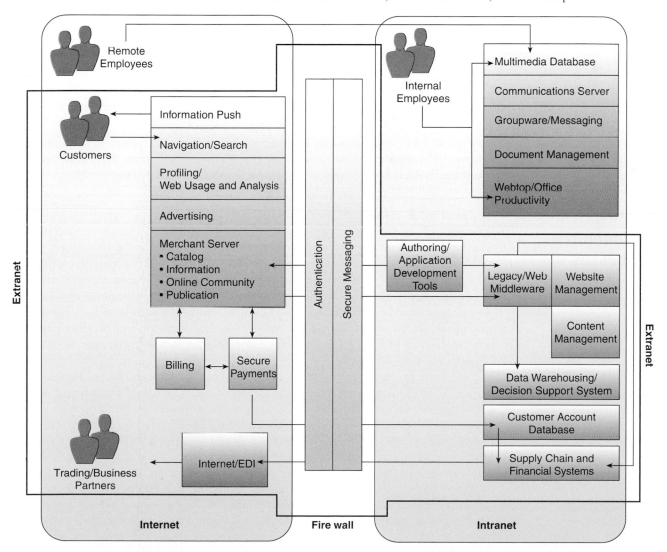

Adapted courtesy of Sun Microsystems.

Figure 5.4

The E-commerce technology architecture of the Holt Educational Outlet (holt.com), a top retailer of educational toys with over 20,000 products online.

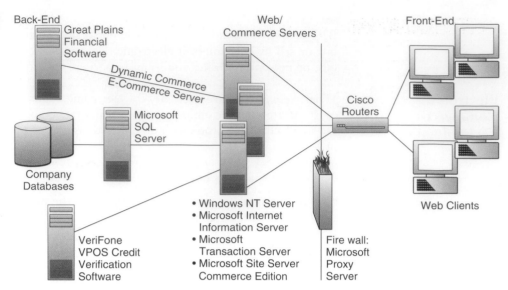

Source: Adapted from Steffano Korper and Juanita Ellis, *The E-Commerce Book: Building the E-Empire* (San Diego: Academic Press, 2000), p. 114.

- Trading and business partners rely on the Internet and extranets to exchange information and accomplish secure transactions, including electronic data interchange (EDI) and other supply chain and financial systems and databases.

- Company employees depend on a variety of Internet and intranet resources to communicate and collaborate in support of their EC work activities.

- IS professionals and end users can use a variety of software tools to develop and manage the content and operations of the websites and other EC resources of a company.

Figure 5.4 is an example of the technology resources required by E-commerce systems. The figure illustrates some of the hardware, software, data, and network components used by a company to provide E-commerce services.

Essential E-Commerce Processes

The essential **E-commerce processes** required for the successful operation and management of E-commerce activities are illustrated in Figure 5.5. This figure outlines the nine key components of an *E-commerce process architecture* that is the foundation of the E-commerce initiatives of many companies today [15]. We will concentrate on the role these processes play in E-commerce systems, but you should recognize that many of these components may also be used in internal, noncommerce E-business applications. An example would be an intranet-based human resource system used by a company's employees, which might use all but the catalog management and product payment processes shown in Figure 5.5. Let's take a brief look at each essential process category.

Access Control and Security

E-commerce processes must establish mutual trust and secure access between the parties in an E-commerce transaction by authenticating users, authorizing access, and enforcing security features. For example, these processes establish that a customer and E-commerce site are who they say they are through user names and passwords, encryption keys, or digital certificates and signatures. The E-commerce site must then authorize access to only those parts of the site that an individual user needs needs to accomplish his or her particular transactions. Thus, you usually will be given access to all resources of an E-commerce site except for other people's accounts, restricted company data, and webmaster administration areas. Other security processes protect the resources of an E-commerce site from threats such as hacker attacks, theft of passwords or credit card numbers, and system failures. We discuss some of these security threats and features in Chapter 9.

Figure 5.5   This E-commerce process architecture highlights nine essential categories of E-commerce processes.

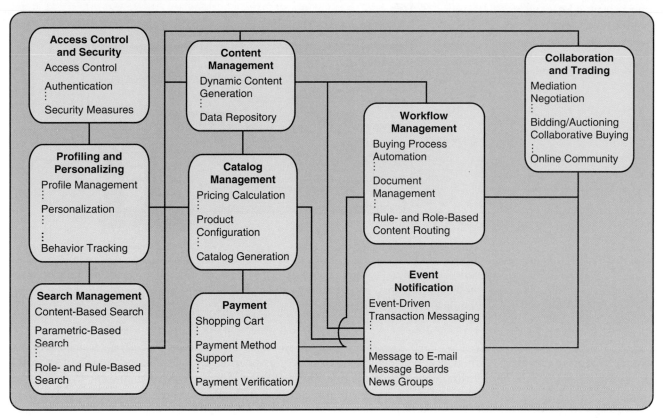

Source: Adapted from Faisal Hoque, *E-Enterprise: Business Models, Architecture, and Components* (Cambridge, UK: Cambridge University Press, 2000), p. 207.

Profiling and Personalizing

Once you have gained access to an E-commerce site, profiling processes can occur that gather data on you and your website behavior and choices, and build electronic profiles of your characteristics and preferences. User profiles are developed using profiling tools such as user registration, cookie files, website behavior tracking software, and user feedback. These profiles are then used to recognize you as an individual user and provide you with a personalized view of the contents of the site, as well as product recommendations and personalized Web advertising as part of a *one-to-one marketing* strategy. Profiling processes are also used to help authenticate your identity for account management and payment purposes, and to gather data for customer relationship management, marketing planning, and website management. Some of the ethical issues in user profiling are discussed in Chapter 9. See Figure 5.6.

E.piphany Corporation: Personalizing E-Commerce

One of the main drawbacks of replacing brick-and-mortar commerce with E-commerce is that websites lack the personal assistance of a floor salesperson who can guide customers to appropriate products. E.piphany (www.epiphany.com) developed an E.4 software suite that is used by many E-commerce companies to reduce this problem. E.4 helps companies to personalize the online shopping experience through a real-time analysis of each customer's website inquiries and transactions. So E.4 analyzes all kinds of customer data to let companies know who their customers are and how they navigate their websites. This analysis combines Web sales data, purchase history information, and click stream data with marketing, operational, and supplier information. Also, the 16 Web-based modules of E.4 are

Figure 5.6

E.piphany's E.4 software gathers and analyzes the behavior of visitors to a website to help companies personalize a customer's Web shopping experience.

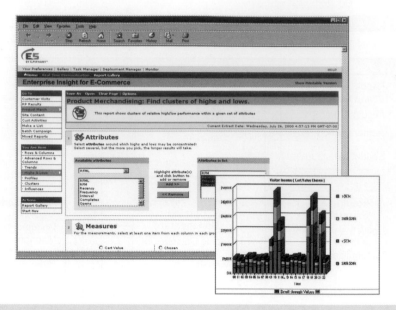

compatible with leading database software and customer relationship management applications, so E-commerce data from E.4 can be integrated into a company's E-business processes [21].

Search Management

Efficient and effective search processes provide a top E-commerce website capability that helps customers find the specific product or service they want to evaluate or buy. E-commerce software packages can include a website search engine component, or a company may acquire a customized E-commerce search engine from search technology companies like Excite and Requisite Technology. Search engines may use a combination of search techniques, including searches based on content (a product description, for example), or by parameters (above, below, or between a range of values for multiple properties of a product, for example).

Content and Catalog Management

Content management software helps E-commerce companies develop, generate, deliver, update, and archive text data, and multimedia information at E-commerce websites. For example, German media giant Bertelsmann, part owner of BarnesandNoble.com, uses StoryServer content manager software to generate Web page templates that enable online editors from six international offices to easily publish and update book reviews and other product information, which are sold (syndicated) to other E-commerce sites.

E-commerce content frequently takes the form of multimedia catalogs of product information. So generating and managing catalog content is a major subset of content management. For example, W.W. Grainger & Co. a multibillion-dollar industrial parts distributor, uses the CenterStage catalog management software suite to retrieve data from more than 2,000 supplier databases, standardize the data and translate it into HTML or XML for Web use, and organize and enhance the data for speedy delivery as multimedia Web pages at their www.grainger.com website.

Content and catalog management software work with the profiling tools we mentioned earlier to personalize the content of Web pages seen by individual users. For example, Travelocity.com uses OnDisplay content manager software to push personalized promotional information about other travel opportunities to users while they are involved in an online travel-related transaction.

Finally, content and catalog management may be expanded to include *product configuration* processes that support Web-based customer self-service and the *mass customization* of a company's products. Configuration software helps online customers select the optimum feasible set of product features that can be included in a finished product. For example, both Dell Computer and Cisco Systems use configuration software to sell build-to-order computers and network processors to their online customers [6].

Cabletron Systems: E-Commerce Configuration

When $3 billion network equipment maker Cabletron Systems began selling its wares online, its sales reps knew full well that peddling made-to-order routers was not as simple as the mouse-click marvel of online book selling. Cabletron's big business customers—whether ISP EarthLink or motorcycle maker Harley-Davidson—did not have the technical expertise to build their own router (which can be as small as a breadbox or as large as a television, depending upon the customer, and can include hundreds of components). Worse, Cabletron's website listed thousands of parts that presented users with nearly infinite combinations, most of which would work only when assembled in a certain way.

That's why part of Cabletron's new online sales team consists of a set of complex Web-based product configuration tools made by Calico Commerce of San Jose, California. Called eSales Configuration Workbench, it prompts customers the same way a salesperson might: It walks them through product features; analyzes their needs, budgets, and time constraints; and considers only components and options compatible with existing systems. The configurator also suggests various options—different kinds of backup power, the number of parts, types of connecting wires—and generates price quotes for up to 500 concurrent online users. When a customer clicks the Buy button, the configurator generates an order that is passed on to Cabletron's back-end order fulfillment systems, which update inventory, accounting, and shipping databases.

Within a year of completing a six-month implementation of Calico's software, Cabletron saw staggering results. Some 60 percent of the businesses using its website now use the configurator. Kirk Estes, Cabletron's director of E-commerce estimates Calico's software saved $12 million in one year by whittling down the percentage of misconfigured orders—and subsequent returns—to nearly nothing. "We think it's 99.8 percent accurate," Estes says. Order processing costs also dropped 96 percent, and customers can now place online orders in 10 to 20 minutes—a fraction of the two to three days it takes through a sales rep. [5].

Workflow Management

Many of the business processes in E-commerce applications can be managed and partially automated with the help of workflow management software. We introduced workflow systems for enterprise collaboration in Chapter 3. Such E-business workflow systems help employees electronically collaborate to accomplish structured work tasks within knowledge-based business processes. Workflow management in both E-business and E-commerce depends on a *workflow software engine* containing software models of the business processes to be accomplished. The workflow models express the predefined sets of business rules, roles of stakeholders, authorization requirements, routing alternatives, databases used, and sequence of tasks required for each E-commerce process. Thus, workflow systems ensure that the proper transactions, decisions, and work activities are performed, and the correct data and documents are routed to the right employees, customers, suppliers, and other business stakeholders.

For example, Figure 5.7 illustrates the E-commerce procurement processes of the MS Market system of Microsoft Corporation. Microsoft employees use their global intranet and the catalog/content management and workflow management software engines built into MS Market to electronically purchase more than $3 billion annually of business supplies and materials from approved suppliers connected to the MS Market system by their corporate extranets [17].

Figure 5.7

The role of catalog/content management and workflow management in a Web-based procurement process: the MS Market system used by Microsoft Corporation.

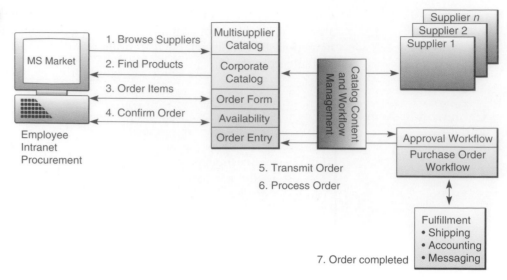

Source: Adapted from Ravi Kalakota and Marcia Robinson, *E-Business: Roadmap for Success* (Reading, MA: Addison-Wesley, 1999), p. 243. © 1999 Addison-Wesley Publishing Company, Inc. Reprinted by permission of Addison-Wesley Longman Inc.

Microsoft Corporation: E-Commerce Purchasing Processes

MS Market is an internal E-commerce purchasing system that works on Microsoft's intranet. MS Market drastically reduced the personnel required to manage low-cost requisitions and gives employees a quick, easy way to order materials without being burdened with paperwork and bureaucratic processes. These high-volume, low-dollar transactions represent about 70 percent of total volume, but only 3 percent of Microsoft's accounts payable. Employees were wasting time turning requisitions into purchase orders (POs) and trying to follow business rules and processes. Managers wanted to streamline this process, so the decision was made to create a requisitioning tool that would take all the controls and validations used by requisition personnel and push them onto the Web. Employees wanted an easy-to-use online form for ordering supplies that included extranet interfaces to procurement partners, such as Boise Cascade and Marriott.

How does this system work? Let's say a Microsoft employee wants a technical book. He goes to the MS Market site on Microsoft's intranet, and MS Market immediately identifies his preferences and approval code through his log-on ID. The employee selects the Barnes & Noble link, which brings up a catalog, order form, and a list of hundreds of books with titles and prices that have been negotiated between Microsoft buyers and Barnes & Noble. He selects a book, puts it in the order form, and completes the order by verifying his group's cost center number and manager's name.

The order is transmitted immediately to the supplier, cutting down on delivery time as well as accounting for the payment of the supplies. Upon submission of the order, MS Market generates an order tracking number for reference, sends notification via E-mail to the employee's manager, and transmits the order over the Internet to Barnes & Noble for fulfillment. In this case, since the purchase total is only $40, the manager's specific approval is not required. Two days later, the book arrives at the employee's office. Thus, MS Market lets employees easily order low-cost items in a controlled fashion at a low cost, without going through a complicated PO approval process [17].

Event Notification

Most E-commerce applications are *event-driven* systems that respond to a multitude of events—from a new customer's first website access, to payment and delivery processes, and to innumerable customer relationship and supply chain management activities. That is why **event notification** processes play an important role in E-commerce systems, since customers, suppliers, employees, and other stakeholders must be notified of all events that might affect their status in a transaction. Event notification software works with the workflow management software to monitor all E-commerce processes and record all relevant events, including unexpected changes or problem situations. Then it works with user-profiling software to automatically notify all involved stakeholders of important transaction events using appropriate user-preferred methods of electronic messaging, such as E-mail, newsgroup, pager, and fax communications. This includes notifying a company's management so they can monitor their employees' responsiveness to E-commerce events and customer and supplier feedback.

For example, when you purchase a product at a retail E-commerce website like Amazon.com, you automatically receive an E-mail record of your order. Then you may receive E-mail notifications of any change in product availability or shipment status, and finally, an E-mail message notifying you that your order has been shipped and is complete.

Collaboration and Trading

This major category of E-commerce processes are those that support the vital collaboration arrangements and trading services needed by customers, suppliers, and other stakeholders to accomplish E-commerce transactions. Thus, in Chapter 2, we discussed how a customer-focused E-business like McAffee Associates uses tools such as E-mail, chat systems, and discussion groups to nurture online *communities of interest* among employees and customers to enhance customer service and build customer loyalty in E-commerce. The essential collaboration among business trading partners in E-commerce may also be provided by Internet-based trading services. For example, B2B E-commerce Web portals provided by companies like Ariba and Commerce One support matchmaking, negotiation, and mediation processes among business buyers and sellers. In addition, B2B E-commerce is heavily dependent on Internet-based trading platforms and portals that provide online exchange and auctions for E-business enterprises. Therefore, the online auctions and exchange developed by companies like FreeMarkets are revolutionizing the procurement processes of many major corporations. We will discuss these and other E-commerce applications in Section II.

Electronic Payment Processes

Payment for the products and services purchased is an obvious and vital set of processes in electronic commerce transactions. But payment processes are not simple, because of the near-anonymous electronic nature of transactions taking place between the networked computer systems of buyers and sellers, and the many security issues involved. Electronic commerce payment processes are also complex because of the wide variety of debit and credit alternatives and financial institutions and intermediaries that may be part of the process. Therefore, a variety of **electronic payment systems** have evolved over time. In addition, new payment systems are being developed and tested to meet the security and technical challenges of electronic commerce over the Internet.

Web Payment Processes

Most E-commerce systems on the Web involving businesses and consumers (B2C) depend on credit card payment processes. But many B2B E-commerce systems rely on more complex payment processes based on the use of purchase orders, as was illustrated in Figure 5.7. However, both types of E-commerce typically use an electronic *shopping cart* process, which enables customers to select products from website catalog displays and put them temporarily in a virtual shopping basket for later

Figure 5.8

An example of a secure electronic payment system with many payment alternatives.

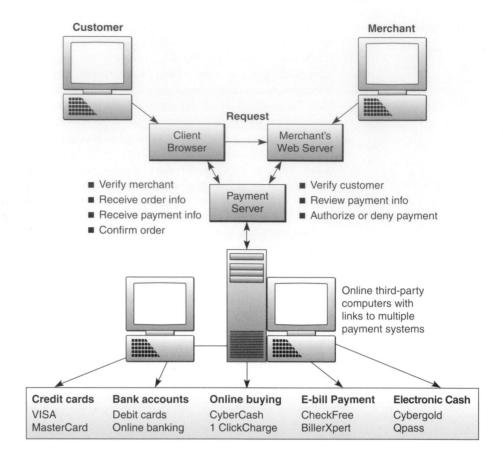

Customer

Merchant

Request

Client Browser

Merchant's Web Server

Payment Server

- Verify merchant
- Receive order info
- Receive payment info
- Confirm order

- Verify customer
- Review payment info
- Authorize or deny payment

Online third-party computers with links to multiple payment systems

Credit cards	Bank accounts	Online buying	E-bill Payment	Electronic Cash
VISA	Debit cards	CyberCash	CheckFree	Cybergold
MasterCard	Online banking	1 ClickCharge	BillerXpert	Qpass

checkout and processing. Figure 5.8 illustrates and summarizes a B2C electronic payment system with several payment alternatives.

Electronic Funds Transfer

Electronic funds transfer (EFT) systems are a major form of electronic payment systems in banking and retailing industries. EFT systems use a variety of information technologies to capture and process money and credit transfers between banks and businesses and their customers. For example, banking networks support teller terminals at all bank offices and automated teller machines (ATMs) at locations throughout the world. Banks may also support pay-by-phone and Web-based bill payment services, which enable bank customers to use their telephones or networked PCs to electronically pay bills. In addition, most point-of-sale terminals in retail stores are networked to bank EFT systems. This makes it possible for you to use a credit card or debit card to instantly pay for gas, groceries, or other purchases at participating retail outlets.

Micropayment Systems

Other electronic payment systems include *micropayment* systems like Cybergold and Qpass. Some of these technologies create *electronic scrip* or *digital cash*, sometimes called e-cash, for making payments that are too small for credit card transactions. Encryption and authentication techniques are used to generate strings of data that can be handled like currency for making cash payments. For example, websites like ESPNET SportsZone, Discovery Online, and *The Wall Street Journal Interactive Edition* let you chat with superstars, download video segments, or pay for business reports by using digital cash micropayment systems [1, 27].

Secure Electronic Payments

When you make an online purchase on the Internet, your credit card information is vulnerable to interception by *network sniffers*, software that easily recognizes credit card number formats. Several basic security measures are being used to solve this security problem: (1) encrypt (code and scramble) the data passing between the customer and merchant, (2) encrypt the data passing between the customer and the company authorizing the credit card transaction, or (3) take sensitive information offline. (Note: Because encryption and other security issues are discussed in Chapter 9, we will not explain how they work in this section.)

For example, many companies use the Secure Socket Layer (SSL) security method developed by Netscape Communications that automatically encrypts data passing between your Web browser and a merchant's server. However, sensitive information is still vulnerable to misuse once it's decrypted (decoded and unscrambled) and stored on a merchant's server. So a digital wallet approach such as the CyberCash payment system was developed. In this method, you add security software add-on modules to your Web browse: That enables your browser to encrypt your credit card data in such a way that only the bank that authorizes credit card transactions for the merchant gets to see it. All the merchant is told is whether your credit card transaction is approved or not.

The Secure Electronic Transaction, or SET, standard for electronic payment security extends the CyberCash digital wallet approach. In this method, EC software encrypts a digital envelope of digital certificates specifying the payment details for each transaction. SET has been agreed to by VISA, MasterCard, IBM, Microsoft, Netscape, and most other industry players. Therefore, SET is expected to eventually become the dominant standard for secure electronic payments on the Internet. However, SET has been stalled by the reluctance of companies to incur its increased hardware, software, and cost requirements [28]. See Figure 5.9.

Figure 5.9

CyberCash provides electronic payment services on the World Wide Web including a digital wallet system for secure credit card transactions.

Courtesy of Cyber Cash, © 2000.

E-Commerce Applications and Issues

**E-Commerce
Application
Trends**

E-commerce is here to stay. In the new millennium, the Web and E-commerce are key industry drivers. It's changed how many companies do business. It's created new channels for our customers, making leaders in many different industries sit up and take notice. Managers everywhere are feeling the heat: their companies are at the E-commerce crossroads and there are many ways to go [17].

Thus, E-commerce is changing how companies do business both internally and externally with their customers, suppliers, and other business partners. How companies apply E-commerce to their business is also subject to change as their managers confront a variety of E-commerce alternatives. The applications of E-commerce by many companies have gone through several major stages as E-commerce matures in the world of business. For example, E-commerce between businesses and consumers (B2C) moved from merely offering multimedia company information at corporate websites *(brochureware)*, to offering products and services at Web storefront sites via electronic catalogs and online sales transactions. B2B E-commerce, on the other hand, started with website support to help business customers serve themselves, and then moved toward automating intranet and extranet procurement systems. But before we go any further, let's look at a real world example.

**Analyzing
MarthaStewart.com**

Read the Real World Case on MarthaStewart.com on the next page. We can learn a lot about the challenges that companies face as they develop a major E-commerce Website. See Figure 5.10.

Martha Stewart practices a top-level, close-quarters kind of executive oversight and leadership over the development and design of the E-commerce website for her Martha Stewart Living Omnimedia company. However, she relies on her IT staff to develop design proposals and work out the technical details of their implementation, and seeks advice about building a first class site from top contacts at Microsoft and other

Figure 5.10

Martha Stewart, CEO of Martha Stewart Living Omnimedia, has played a leading role in the development of her company's E-commerce Web site.

John Hryriuk/Corbis Sygma.

MarthaStewart.com: Building an E-Commerce Website

Martha Stewart is running behind schedule. But then, Martha is a busy woman. There is much to do to keep the machinery humming in the billion dollar lifestyle empire that she has created—Martha Stewart Living Omnimedia (MSLO). But all of that is put on hold, if only momentarily. Microsoft CEO Steve Ballmer is on the phone.

Yes, Martha Stewart, guru of laborious decorating tips and arbiter of God-is-in-the-details perfectionism, is rushing off to talk technology with Ballmer. Not every executive can simply pick up the phone and speed-dial Mr. Microsoft, but all sharp managers need top-notch sounding boards. And Stewart knows where to turn when it comes to translating her vision of simple perfection to her website.

In the past three years, Stewart has turned MarthaStewart .com into an online destination that boasts 1.5 million registered users who can sift through MSLO content from her television programming, radio shows, newspaper columns, and magazines, or buy gifts and housewares from her online merchandising business. With $33 million in revenue for the first nine months of 2000, Internet and direct commerce are the fastest-growing segment of Stewart's company.

She didn't do this all by herself, of course—the site has been overseen by an army of Internet experts. But as with every other aspect of her business, it is Stewart who is running the show. That's a good thing, because close-quarters, top-level executive oversight is a key to success in all web business ventures. The technology is too green, the choices too complex, and the cost of failure too high to leave web effort to subordinates.

Martha also surrounded herself with some of the tech world's best teachers—among them her friend Charles Simonyi, who has the title "distinguished engineer" at Microsoft Research—in order to gain a grasp of the issues surrounding building a site, if not how to build a site herself. And she states what should be the mantra of every business manager or professional: "I don't have time to learn all of the technology and how many miles of wires we have running under the floors. But I understand the process."

As one might expect from the crafts-and-lifestyle expert, Stewart wants to create a site that's beautiful, elegant, and useful. "The bottom line is," she says, "is it working, is it providing a service, is it something good, does it do what I want it to do?"

Stewart has also kept tight control over costs. From the outset, she has avoided making huge expenditures on building new technology, preferring to depend on what is proven and readily available. Stewart has also saved money by tapping the partnerships she has created off-line. Thanks in part to Stewart's connections at the company, Microsoft built MarthaStewart.com's platform for almost nothing. MSLO got the architecture, and Microsoft got the publicity for building the site.

No decision is made without first passing Stewart's desk. "The Internet can become a little fiefdom," she says. "I don't want that to happen here. Some companies just don't know what's going on." At a recent off-site conference to discuss the migration to new shopping cart technology, her team put together three navigation options on storyboards. "Martha studied them and said, 'This is how my consumer wants to shop,'" says Sheila Beauchesne, her chief information officer.

"I'm the critiquer," Martha says of her website design involvement. "I'll say, you know, I can't get from here without getting switched off, I can't return, I can't do this, I can't do that. I'll give them all my critiques. I do that all the time. That's my job."

But that's not to say Stewart has not been involved in the technology decisions. For instance, it became clear that the site would be much easier to use if it shared a shopping cart with Kmart's BlueLight.com, where her Martha Stewart Everyday line is available. Stewart moved quickly to work out the changes with Mark Goldstein, CEO of BlueLight.

And her desire to keep an eye on things extends beyond her employees to nearly everyone she deals with. Stewart has one employee whose job is simply to inform her about what is going on with all of her strategic partners. "I want to know what's happening to everybody we do business with. You know, what the hell's going on with Ask Jeeves?"

Yet despite her desire for control, even Stewart has had to acknowledge that the Internet is something that at times might be beyond her grasp. "Nothing happens as quickly as you hope," she says. "I'm a terribly logical person, and terribly, terribly practical. And I think all this stuff should be that way, but it isn't. You have to constantly remember that it has to evolve, day by day, minute to minute." But she remains hopeful: "Ultimately," she says, "we're going to have a site that really is practical and simple, easy to navigate and beautiful to look at. It's not there yet."

Case Study Questions

1. Visit MarthaStewart.com. What are several reasons why E-commerce is one of the fastest growing parts of Stewart's MSLO empire? Defend your choices.

2. What is your evaluation of the style and substance of Stewart's management of her E-commerce business?

3. Do you approve of Stewart's role in the development and design process of her website? Why or why not?

Source: Adapted from Stacy Perman, "E-Business the Martha Stewart Way," *eCompany*, January/February, 2001, pp. 86–87.

companies. Stewart keeps tight control over costs and sticks with proven technology, including the minimal-cost development of her site by Microsoft, and the sharing of a shopping cart system with Kmart's BlueLight.com. She also reviews and critiques all website design decisions, and monitors the performance of her company's business partners. Stewart's leadership is a key ingredient in the success of the site, as it moves closer to her vision of simplicity and beauty in a practical, easy to navigate online experience.

E-Commerce Trends

Figure 5.11 illustrates some of the trends taking place in E-commerce applications that we introduced at the beginning of this section. Notice how B2C E-commerce moves from simple Web storefronts to interactive marketing capabilities that provide a personalized shopping experience for customers, and then toward a totally integrated Web store that supports a variety of customer shopping experiences. B2C E-commerce is also moving toward a self-service model where customers configure and customize the products and services they wish to buy, aided by configuration software and online customer support as needed.

B2B E-commerce participants moved quickly from self-service on the Web to configuration and customization capabilities and extranets connecting trading partners. As B2C E-commerce moves toward full-service and wide-selection retail Web portals, B2B is also trending toward the use of E-commerce portals that provide catalog, exchange, and auction markets for business customers within or across industries. Of course, both of these trends are enabled by E-business capabilities like customer relationship management and supply chain management, which are the hallmarks of the customer-focused and internetworked supply chains of the successful E-business enterprise [30].

Figure 5.11   Trends in B2C and B2B E-commerce, and the business strategies and value driving these trends.

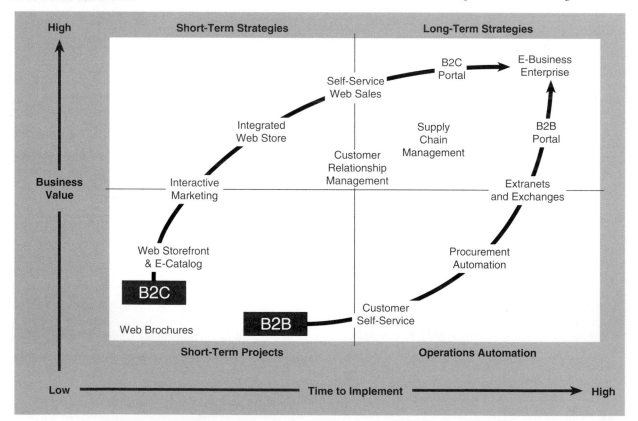

Source: Adapted from Jonathan Rosenoer, Douglas Armstrong, and J. Russell Gates, *The Clickable Corporation: Successful Strategies for Capturing the Internet Advantage* (New York: The Free Press, 1999), p. 24.

Business-to-Consumer E-Commerce

E-commerce applications that focus on the consumer share an important goal: to attract potential buyers, transact goods and services, and build customer loyalty through individual courteous treatment and engaging community features [15].

What does it take to create a successful B2C E-commerce business venture? That's the question that many are asking in the wake of the failures of many pure B2C *dot-com* companies. One obvious answer would be to create a Web business initiative that offers attractive products or services of great customer value, and whose business plan is based on realistic forecasts of profitability within the first year or two of operation—a condition that was lacking in many failed dotcoms. But such failures have not stemmed the tide of millions of businesses, both large and small, that are moving at least part of their business to the Web. So let's take a look at some essential success factors and website capabilities for companies engaged in either B2C or B2B E-commerce. Figure 5.12 provides examples of a few top-rated retail Web companies.

E-Commerce Success Factors

On the Internet, the barriers of time, distance, and form are broken down, and businesses are able to transact the sale of goods and services 24 hours a day, 7 days a week, 365 days a year with consumers all over the world. In certain cases, it is even possible to convert a physical good (CDs, packaged software, a newspaper) to a virtual good (MP3 audio, downloadable software, information in HTML format) [15].

A basic fact of Internet retailing *(E-tailing)* is that all retail websites are created equal as far as the "location, location, location" imperative of success in retailing is concerned. No site is any closer to its Web customers, and competitors offering similar goods and services may be only a mouse click away. This makes it vital that businesses find ways to build customer satisfaction, loyalty, and relationships, so customers keep coming back to their Web stores. Thus the key to E-tail success is to optimize several key factors such as selection and value, performance and service efficiency, the look and feel of the site, advertising and incentives to purchase, personal attention, community relationships, and security and reliability. Let's briefly examine each of these factors that are essential to the success of a B2C Web business. See Figure 5.13.

Figure 5.12

Examples of a few top-rated retail websites.

Top Retail Websites
● **Amazon.com   www.amazon.com** Amazon.com is the exception to the rule that consumers prefer to shop "real-world" retailers online. The mother of all shopping sites, Amazon features a vast selection of books, videos, DVDs, CDs, toys, kitchen items, electronics, and even home and garden goods sold to millions of loyal customers.
● **eBay   www.ebay.com** The fabled auction site operates the world's biggest electronic flea market, with everything from antiques, computers, and coins to Pez dispensers and baseball cards. This site boasts billions of page views per month, and millions of items for sale in thousands of categories supported by thousands of special-interest groups.
● **Eddie Bauer   www.eddiebauer.com** Sportswear titan Eddie Bauer has integrated its retail channels-store, Website, and catalog. Shoppers can return an item to any Eddie Bauer store, no matter where it was purchased—a policy other merchants should follow.
● **Lands' End   www.landsend.com** With several seasons as an online retailer, Lands' End is a pro at meeting shoppers' expectations. One of the best features: Specialty Shoppers. A customer service rep will help you make your selections and answer questions by phone or via a live chat.

Source: Adapted from "Tech Lifestyles: Shopping," Technology Buyers Guide, *Fortune*, Winter 2001, pp. 288–90. © 2001 Time Inc. All rights reserved.

E-Commerce Success Factors
● **Selection and Value.** Attractive product selections, competitive prices, satisfaction guarantees, and customer support after the sale.
● **Performance and Service.** Fast, easy navigation, shopping, and purchasing, and prompt shipping and delivery.
● **Look and Feel.** Attractive Web storefront, website shopping areas, multimedia product catalog pages, and shopping features.
● **Advertising and Incentives.** Targeted Web page advertising and E-mail promotions, discounts and special offers, including advertising at affiliate sites.
● **Personal Attention.** Personal Web pages, personalized product recommendations, Web advertising, and E-mail notices, and interactive support for all customers.
● **Community Relationships.** Virtual communities of customers, suppliers, company representatives, and others via newsgroups, chat rooms, and links to related sites.
● **Security and Reliability.** Security of customer information and website transactions, trustworthy product information, and reliable order fulfillment.

Selection and Value. Obviously, a business must offer Web shoppers a good selection of attractive products and services at competitive prices or they will quickly click away from a Web store. But a company's prices don't have to be the lowest on the Web if they build a reputation for high quality, guaranteed satisfaction, and top customer support while shopping and after the sale. For example, top-rated E-tailer REI.com helps you select quality outdoor gear for hiking and other activities with a "How to Choose" section, and gives a money-back guarantee on your purchases.

Performance and Service. People don't want to be kept waiting when browsing, selecting, or paying in a Web store. A site must be efficiently designed for ease of access, shopping, and buying, with sufficient server power and network capacity to support website traffic. Web shopping and customer service must also be friendly and helpful, as well as quick and easy. In addition, products offered should be available in inventory for prompt shipment to the customer.

Look and Feel. B2C sites can offer customers an attractive Web storefront, shopping areas, and multimedia product catalogs. This could range from an exciting shopping experience with audio, video, and moving graphics, to a more simple and comfortable look and feel. Thus, most retail E-commerce sites let customers browse product sections, select products, drop them into a virtual shopping cart, and go to a virtual checkout station when they are ready to pay for their order.

Advertising and Incentives. Some Web stores may advertise in traditional media, but most advertise on the Web with targeted and personalized banner ads and other Web page and E-mail promotions. Most B2C sites also offer shoppers incentives to buy and return. Typically, this means coupons, discounts, special offers, and vouchers for other Web services, sometimes with other E-tailers at cross-linked websites. Many Web stores also increase their market reach by being part of Web banner advertising exchange programs with thousand of other Web retailers.

Personal Attention. Personalizing your shopping experience encourages you to buy and make return visits. Thus, E-commerce software can automatically record details of your visits and build user profiles of you and other Web shoppers. Many sites also encourage you to register with them and fill out a personal interest profile. Then, whenever you return, you are welcomed by name or with a personal Web page, greeted with special offers, and guided to those parts of the site that you are most interested in. This *one-to-one marketing* and relationship building power is one of the major advantages of personalized Web retailing.

Community Relationships. Giving online customers with special interests a feeling of belonging to a unique group of like-minded individuals helps build customer loyalty and value. Thus, website relationship and affinity marketing programs build and promote virtual communities of customers, suppliers, company representatives, and others via a variety of Web-based collaboration tools. Examples include discussion forums or newsgroups, chat rooms, message board systems, and cross-links to related website communities.

Security and Reliability. As a customer of a successful Web store, you must feel confident that your credit card, personal information, and details of your transactions are secure from unauthorized use. You must also feel that you are dealing with a trustworthy business, whose products and other website information you can trust to be as advertised. Having your orders filled and shipped as you requested, in the time frame promised, and with good customer support are other measures of an E-tailer's reliability.

Amazon.com: Tops in B2C Retailing	Amazon (www.amazon.com) is rated as one of the biggest and best virtual retailers on the Web, though it has lost its luster with investors because it has yet to make a profit. See Figure 5.14. The site is designed to speed you through the process of browsing and ordering merchandise, while giving you reassuring, personal service at discount prices. For example, the search engine for finding the products you want is quick and accurate, and the ordering process easy and fast. Confirmation is quick, notifications are accurate and friendly, and delivery is prompt. Buyers are E-mailed both when their order is confirmed, as well as the day their order is shipped. The company also offers customers a complete money-back guarantee.

In creating this potential powerhouse of shopping services and offerings, Amazon.com wants to be not simply a Wal-Mart of the Web but rather a next-generation retail commerce portal. Imagine a customized site where — through a personalized shopping service and communities of other shoppers—you will not only shop easily with a trusted brand for books, videos, gifts, and more, but you will also research the features, price, and availability of millions of products from a single storefront that has Amazon's—and your—name on it.

That's what has gotten Amazon this far in its first years of business: exhaustive focus on convenience, selection, and personalization. It lived up to its billing as "Earth's Biggest Selection" by building an inventory of millions of products. It was also among the first Net stores to facilitate credit-card purchases; greet customers by name and offer customized home pages; send purchase recommendations via E-mail; and number and explain each step in the purchasing process. This combination of vast selection, efficiency, discount prices, and personal service is why Amazon is frequently mentioned as the top retailer on the Web [6, 36]. |

Web Store Requirements

Most business-to-consumer E-commerce ventures take the form of retail business sites on the World Wide Web. Whether a huge retail Web portal like Amazon.com, or a small specialty Web retailer, the primary focus of such E-tailers is to develop, operate, and manage their websites so they become high-priority destinations for consumers who will repeatedly choose to go there to buy products and services. Thus, these websites must be able to demonstrate the key factors for E-commerce success that we have just covered. In this section, let's discuss the essential Web store requirements that you would have to implement to support a successful retail business on the Web, as summarized and illustrated in Figure 5.15.

Figure 5.14

The home page of Amazon.com.

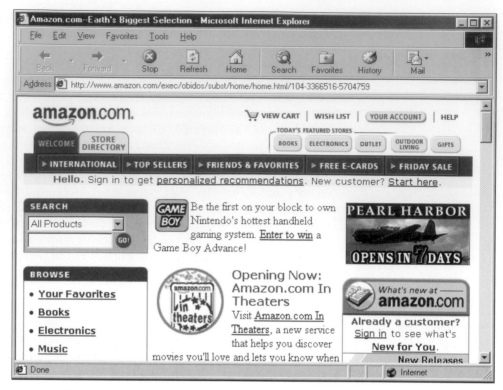

Courtesy of Amazon.com, © 2000.

Developing a Web Store

Before you can launch your own retail store on the Internet, you must build an E-commerce website. Many companies use simple website design software tools and predesigned templates provided by their website hosting service to construct their Web retail store. That includes building your Web storefront and product catalog Web pages, as well as tools to provide shopping cart features, process orders, handle credit card payments, and so forth. Of course, larger companies can use their own software developers or hire an outside website development contractor to build a custom-designed E-commerce site. Also, like most companies, you can contract with your ISP (Internet service provider) or a specialized Web hosting company to operate and maintain your B2C website.

Once you build your website, it must be developed as a retail Web business by marketing it in a variety of ways that attract visitors to your site and transform them into loyal Web customers. So your website should include Web page and E-mail advertising and promotions for Web visitors and customers, and Web advertising exchange programs with other Web stores. Also, you can register your Web business with its own domain name (for example, yourstore.com), as well as registering your website with the major Web search engines and directories to help Web surfers find your site more easily. In addition, you might consider affiliating as a small business partner with large Web portals like Yahoo! and Netscape, large E-tailers and auction sites like Amazon and eBay, and small business Web centers like Microsoft bCentral and Prodigy Biz.

Freemerchant and Prodigy Biz: Getting Started

Freemerchant and Prodigy Biz are examples of the many companies that help small businesses get on the Web. Freemerchant.com enables you to set up a Web store for free by choosing from nearly 60 design templates. That includes Web hosting on secure networks, shopping cart and order processing, and providing common database software for importing your product catalog data. Fee-based

Figure 5.15   These Web store requirements must be implemented by a company or its website hosting service, in order to develop a successful E-commerce business.

Developing a Web Store

● **Build**
Website design tools
Site design templates
Custom design services
Website hosting

● **Market**
Web page advertising
E-mail promotions
Web advertising exchanges with affiliate sites
Search engine registrations

Serving Your Customers

● **Serve**
Personalized web pages
Dynamic multimedia catalog
Catalog search engine
Integrated shopping cart

● **Transact**
Flexible order process
Credit card processing
Shipping and tax calculations
E-mail order notifications

● **Support**
Website online help
Customer service E-mail
Discussion groups and chat rooms
Links to related sites

Managing a Web Store

● **Manage**
Website usage statistics
Sales and inventory reports
Customer account management
Links to accounting system

● **Operate**
24x7 website hosting
Online tech support
Scalable network capacity
Redundant servers and power

● **Protect**
User password protection
Encrypted order processing
Encrypted website administration
Network fire walls and security monitors

services include banner ad exchanges, domain and search engine registrations, and enabling product data to be listed on eBay and sales data to be exported to the Quickbooks accounting system.

Prodigybiz.com is designed to serve small E-tail businesses with a full range of Web store development services. Prodigy Biz features both free and fee-based site design and Web publishing tools, website hosting and site maintenance, full E-commerce order and credit card processing, Internet access and E-mail services, and a variety of management reports and affiliate marketing programs [34]. See Figure 5.16.

Serving Your Customers

Once your retail store is on the Web and receiving visitors, the website must help you welcome and serve them personally and efficiently so that they become loyal customers. So most E-tailers use several website tools to create user profiles, customer files, and personal Web pages and promotions that help them develop a one-to-one relationship with their customers. This includes creating incentives to encourage visitors to register, developing *Web cookie files* to automatically identify returning visitors, or contracting with website tracking companies like DoubleClick and others for software to automatically record and analyze the details of the website behavior and preferences of Web shoppers.

Of course, your website should have the look and feel of an attractive, friendly, and efficient Web store. That means having E-commerce features like a dynamically changing and updated multimedia catalog, a fast catalog search engine, and a convenient shopping cart system that is integrated with Web shopping, promotions, payment, shipping, and customer account information. Your E-commerce order processing software should be fast and able to adjust to personalized promotions and customer options like gift handling, special discounts, credit card or other payments,

Figure 5.16

Prodigy Biz is one of many companies offering retail website development and hosting services.

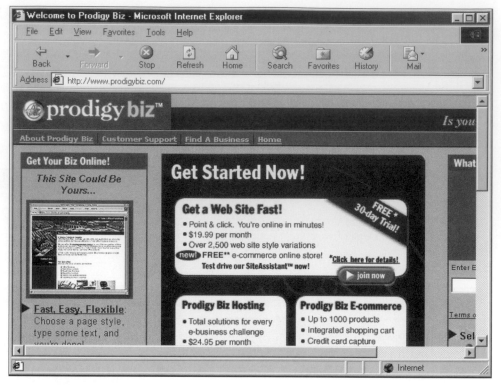

Courtesy of Prodigy Biz.

and shipping and tax alternatives. Also, automatically sending your customers E-mail notices to document when orders are processed and shipped is a top customer service feature of E-tail transaction processing.

Providing customer support for your web store is an essential web site capability. So many E-tail sites offer help menus, tutorials, and lists of FAQs (frequently asked questions) to provide self-help features for Web shoppers. Of course, E-mail correspondence with customer service representatives of your Web store offers more personal assistance to customers. Establishing website discussion groups and chat rooms for your customers and store personnel to interact helps create a more personal community that can provide invaluable support to customers, as well as building customer loyalty. Providing links to related websites from your Web store can help customers find additional information and resources, as well as earning commission income from the affiliate marketing programs of other Web retailers. For example, the Amazon.com Affiliate program pays commissions of up to 15 percent for purchases made by Web shoppers clicking to their Web store from your site.

Managing a Web Store

A Web retail store must be managed as both a business and a website, and most E-commerce hosting companies offer software and services to help you do just that. For example, companies like Freemerchant, Prodigy Biz, and Verio provide their hosting clients with a variety of management reports that record and analyze Web store traffic, inventory, and sales results. Other services build customer lists for E-mail and Web page promotions, or provide customer relationship management features to help retain Web customers. Also, some E-commerce software includes links to download inventory and sales data into accounting packages like Quickbooks for bookkeeping and preparation of financial statements and reports.

Of course, Web hosting companies must enable their Web store clients to be available online twenty-four hours a day and seven days a week all year. This requires them to build or contract for sufficient network capacity to handle peak

Web traffic loads, and redundant network servers and power sources to respond to system or power failures. Most hosting companies provide E-commerce software that uses passwords and encryption to protect Web store transactions and customer records, and employ network fire walls and security monitors to repel hacker attacks and other security threats. Many hosting services also offer their clients twenty-four hour tech support to help them with any technical problems that arise. We will discuss these and other E-commerce security management issues in Chapter 9.

| Verio Inc.: Website Management | Verio Inc. (www.verio.com) is an example of one of the world's leading Web hosting companies. Verio provides complete software, computing, and network resources to Web hosting companies, as well as offering E-commerce development and hosting services to Web retailers. Verio also offers a Web startup and development service for small businesses called SiteMerlin (www.sitemer-lin.com). Verio guarantees 99.9 percent website uptime to its E-commerce customers, with 24 × 7 server monitoring and customer support. Verio hosts more than 10,000 small and medium-sized Web businesses; has a network hosting alliance with Sun Microsystems, an Oracle Web database application service; and provides hosting services to Lycos and other Web hosting companies [34]. |

Business-to-Business E-Commerce

Business-to-business electronic commerce is the wholesale and supply side of the commercial process, where businesses buy, sell, or trade with other businesses. B2B electronic commerce relies on many different information technologies, most of which are implemented at E-commerce websites on the World Wide Web and corporate intranets and extranets. B2B applications include electronic catalog systems, electronic trading systems such as exchange and auction portals, electronic data interchange, electronic funds transfers, and so on. All of the factors for building a successful retail website we discussed earlier also apply to wholesale websites for business-to-business electronic commerce.

In addition, many businesses are integrating their Web-based E-commerce systems with their E-business systems for supply chain management, customer relationship management, and online transaction processing, as well as to their traditional, or legacy, computer-based accounting and business information systems. This ensures that all electronic commerce activities are integrated with E-business processes and supported by up-to-date corporate inventory and other databases, which in turn are automatically updated by Web sales activities. Let's look at a successful example.

| Cisco Systems: B2B Marketplace Success | The E-commerce website Cisco Connection Online enables corporate users to purchase routers, switches, and other hardware that enables customers to build high-speed information networks. Over 70% of Cisco's sales take place at this site.
So what has made Cisco so successful? Some would argue that its market—networking hardware—is a prime product to sell online because the customer base is composed almost entirely of IT department staffers and consultants. To |

some degree, this is certainly true. On the other hand, competitors initially scoffed at Cisco's efforts due to the inherent complexity of its product. However, it's difficult to dispute that Cisco has built an online store with functionality and usefulness that is a model of success in the B-to-B commerce world.

Cisco was able to achieve success largely due to the variety of service offerings made available throughout its purchasing process. In addition to simply providing a catalog and transaction processing facilities, Cisco includes a personalized interface for buyers, an extensive customer support section with contact information, technical documents, software updates, product configuration tools, and even online training and certification courses for Cisco hardware. Also, Cisco provides direct integration with its internal back-end systems for frequent customers, and makes software available that customers can use to design custom links to their own line-of-business software from such players as SAP America, PeopleSoft, and Oracle.

Cisco has also made a concerted effort to ensure that post-sale customer support is available to buyers of every kind. For most large corporations, this means diligent account management and dedicated support representatives to troubleshoot problems and aid in complex network design. For smaller businesses that may be installing their first routers or switches, Cisco includes recommended configurations and simple FAQs to get users up and running.

Like any mature virtual marketplace, Cisco Connection Online integrates directly with Cisco's internal applications and databases to automatically manage inventory and production. Cisco even allows vendors such as HP, PeopleSoft, and IBM to exchange design data to enable easy network configuration troubleshooting online [15].

E-Commerce Marketplaces

The latest E-commerce transaction systems are scaled and customized to allow buyers and sellers to meet in a variety of high-speed trading platforms: auctions, catalogs, and exchanges [23].

Businesses of any size can now buy everything from chemicals to electronic components, excess electrical energy, construction materials, or paper products at business to business **E-commerce marketplaces.** Figure 5.17 outlines five major types of E-commerce marketplaces used by businesses today. However, many B2B **E-commerce portals** provide several types of marketplaces. Thus they may offer an electronic **catalog** shopping and ordering site for products from many suppliers in an industry. Or they may serve as an **exchange** for buying and selling via a bid-ask process, or at negotiated prices. Very popular are electronic **auction** websites for business-to-business auctions of products and services. Figure 5.18 illustrates a B2B trading system that offers exchange, auction, and reverse auction (where sellers bid for the business of a buyer) electronic markets.

Many of these B2B **E-commerce portals** are developed and hosted by third-party *market maker* companies who serve as **infomediaries** that bring buyers and sellers together in catalog, exchange, and auction markets. Infomediaries are companies that serve as intermediaries in E-business and E-commerce transactions. Examples are Ariba, Commerce One, VerticalNet, and FreeMarkets, to name a few. All provide E-commerce marketplace software products and services to power their Web portals for E-commerce transactions. See Figure 5.19.

These B2B E-commerce sites make business purchasing decisions faster, simpler, and more cost effective, since companies can use Web systems to research and

Figure 5.17

Types of E-commerce Marketplaces.

E-Commerce Marketplaces
● **One to many:** Sell-side marketplaces. Host one major supplier, who dictates product catalog offerings and prices. Examples: Cisco.com and Dell.com.
● **Many to one:** Buy-side marketplaces. Attract many suppliers that flock to these exchanges to bid on the business of a major buyer like GE or AT&T.
● **Some to many:** Distribution marketplaces. Unite major suppliers who combine their product catalogs to attract a larger audience of buyers. Examples: VerticalNet and Works.com
● **Many to some:** Procurement marketplaces. Unite major buyers who combine their purchasing catalogs to attract more suppliers and thus more competition and lower prices. Examples: the auto industry's Covisint and energy industry's Pantellos.
● **Many to Many:** Auction marketplaces used by many buyers and sellers, which can create a variety of buyers' or sellers' auctions to dynamically optimize prices. Examples are eBay and FreeMarkets.

Source: Adapted from Edward Robinson, "Battle to the Bitter End (-to-End)," *Business2.0*, July 25, 2000, pp. 140-141.

transact with many vendors. Business buyers get one-stop shopping and accurate purchasing information. They also get impartial advice from infomediaries that they can't get from the sites hosted by suppliers and distributors. Thus, companies can negotiate or bid for better prices from a larger pool of vendors. And of course, suppliers benefit from easy access to customers from all over the globe [23, 25]. Figure 5.20 illustrates the huge B2B procurement marketplaces formed by consortiums of major corporations in various industries to trade with their thousands of suppliers. Now, let's look at a real world example.

Figure 5.18

This is an example of a B2B E-commerce Web portal that offers exchange, auction, and reverse auction electronic markets.

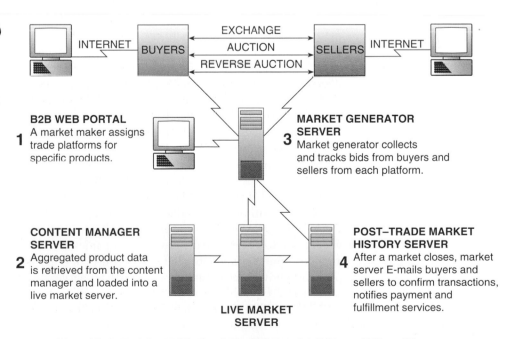

Source: Adapted from Mark Leon, "Trading Spaces," *Business 2.0*, February 2000, p. 129.

FreeMarkets.com: B2B E-Commerce Auctions	Auction sites like e-Steel, MetalSite, and PlasticsNet.com create lively global spot markets for standard processed materials like steel, chemicals, and plastics. On MetalSite, for example, Weirton or LTV can put sheet or rolled steel on the block anytime the market looks hungry. Buyers then enter their bids over two or three days, and the highest price wins. This is called a sellers' auction: Think of it as the business version of the familiar estate sale for rugs or antiques.

The FreeMarkets online auction model takes the Internet into a much bigger, far more complex kind of corporate purchase: the individually crafted parts—the motors, gears, circuit boards, and plastic casings that producers forge into their finished automobiles, washing machines, and locomotives—that are purchased on contracts typically running three or four years, and there is nothing standard about them.

However, the FreeMarkets model standardizes absolutely every item in a buyer's RFQ or "request for quotation" that documents the specifications for a part. To participate in a FreeMarkets auction, suppliers must offer not only to deliver the same part but also to do it on the same schedule, with the same payment terms, inventory arrangements, and everything else. That way each package is practically the same; plastic refrigerator shelves and automobile bumpers become almost as much a commodity as bushels of wheat. All that remains is to find the lowest price, and the best way to do that is through an auction.

The auction itself is a tense, 20-to-30-minute sweepstakes. The events are called buyers' or reverse auctions because, unlike the exchange sponsored by e-Steel, the price starts high and moves downward. Linked over the Internet, the sellers don't have to guess at their competitors' bids as they do with RFQs. They see exactly what the opposition is bidding, in real time—and how low they must go to pocket the order.

General Motors, United Technologies, Raytheon, and Quaker Oats have saved more than 15 percent on average buying parts, materials, and even services at FreeMarkets auctions. Says Kent Brittan, vice president of supply management for United Technologies: "This FreeMarkets auction idea is revolutionizing procurement as we know it" [41].

Electronic Data Interchange	**Electronic data interchange** (EDI) was one of the earliest forms of electronic commerce. EDI involves the electronic exchange of business transaction documents over the Internet and other networks between supply chain trading partners (organizations and their customers and suppliers). Data representing a variety of business transaction documents (such as purchase orders, invoices, requests for quotations, and shipping notices) are automatically exchanged between computers using standard document message formats. Typically, EDI software is used to convert a company's own document formats into standardized EDI formats as specified by various industry and international protocols. Thus, EDI is an example of the almost complete automation of an E-commerce supply chain process. And EDI over the Internet, using secure *virtual private networks*, is a growing B2B E-commerce application.

Formatted transaction data are transmitted over network links directly between computers, without paper documents or human intervention. Besides direct network links between the computers of trading partners, third-party services are widely used. Value-added network companies like GE Global Exchange Services and Computer Associates offer a variety of EDI services. Many EDI service providers now offer secure, lower cost EDI services over the Internet. Figure 5.21 illustrates a typical EDI system [33].

EDI is still a popular data-transmission format among major trading partners, primarily to automate repetitive transactions. It automatically tracks inventory changes; triggers orders, invoices, and other documents related to transactions; and

Figure 5.19

VerticalNet provides B2B marketplaces for over 50 industries.

Courtsey of VerticalNet.

schedules and confirms delivery and payment. By digitally integrating the supply chain, EDI streamlines processes, saves time, and increases accuracy. And by using Internet technologies, lower cost Internet-based EDI services are now available to smaller businesses [37, 39].

Telefónica's TSAI: Internet EDI

Telefónica is Spain's largest supplier of telecommunications services, serving the Spanish-speaking and Portuguese-speaking world with affiliates in Latin America and the United States. Telefónica Serviciós Avanzados de Información (TSAI) is a subsidiary of Telefónica that handles 60 percent of Spain's electronic data interchange (EDI) traffic. TSAI's customers are supply chain trading partners—merchants, suppliers, and others involved in business supply chains from design to delivery.

To tap into the sizable market of smaller businesses that can't afford standard EDI services, TSAI offers an Internet EDI service, InfoEDI, based on Netscape ECXpert electronic commerce software. InfoEDI allows transactions to be entered and processed on the Internet, so smaller trading partners no longer have to buy and install special connections, dedicated workstations, and proprietary software. Instead, they can access the EDI network through the Internet via TSAI's Web portal.

InfoEDI's forms-based interface lets businesses connect with InfoEDI simply by using modems and Web browsers. They can then interact with the largest suppliers and retailers to send orders, issue invoices based on orders, send invoice summaries, track document status, and receive messages. InfoEDI also provides a product database that lists all details of trading partners' products. Once a trading relationship has been established, each partner has encrypted access to details of its own products. Because those details remain accessible on TSAI's Web server, users need enter only minimal information to create links to that data, which is then plugged in as needed [39].

Figure 5.20 Examples of the B2B procurement marketplaces formed by major corporations in various industries.

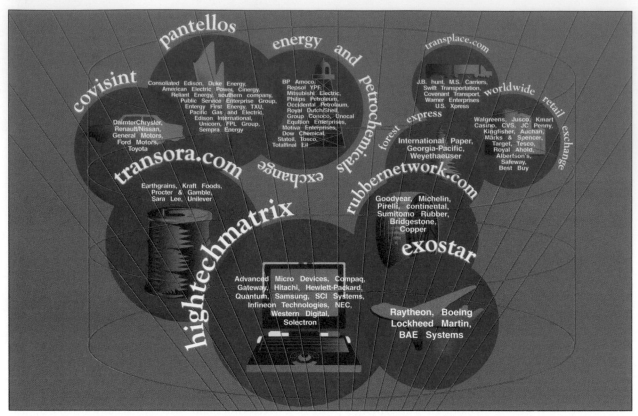

Source: Adapted from Peter Henig, "Revenge of the Bricks," *Red Herring*, August 2000, p. 123.

Figure 5.21 A typical example of electronic data interchange activities, an important form of business-to-business electronic commerce. EDI over the Internet is a major B2B E-commerce application.

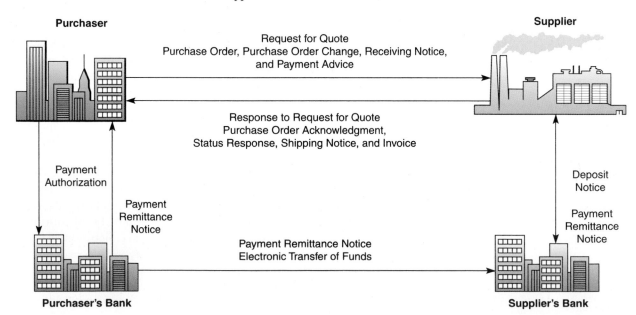

Clicks and Bricks in E-Commerce

Companies are recognizing that success in the new economy will go to those who can execute clicks-and-mortar strategies that bridge the physical and virtual worlds. Different companies will need to follow very different paths in deciding how closely—or loosely—to integrate their Internet initiatives with their traditional operations [13].

Figure 5.22 illustrates the spectrum of alternatives and benefit trade-offs that E-business enterprises face when choosing an E-commerce "clicks and bricks" strategy. E-business managers must answer this question: Should we integrate our E-commerce virtual business operations with our traditional physical business operations, or keep them separate? As Figure 5.22 shows, companies have been implementing a range of integration/separation strategies and made key benefits trade-offs in answering that question. Let's take a look at several alternatives [13].

E-Commerce Integration

The Internet is just another channel that gets plugged into the business architecture [13].

So says CIO Bill Seltzer of office supply retailer Office Depot, which fully integrates their OfficeDepot.com E-commerce venture into their traditional business operations. Thus, Office Depot is a prime example of why many companies have chosen integrated clicks and bricks strategies, where their E-commerce business is integrated in some major ways into the traditional business operations of a company. The business case for such strategies rests on:

- Capitalizing on any unique strategic capabilities that may exist in a company's traditional business operations that could be used to support an E-commerce business.

- Gaining several strategic benefits of integrating E-commerce into a company's traditional business; such as the sharing of established brands and key business information, and joint buying power and distribution efficiencies.

For example, Office Depot already had a successful catalog sales business with a professional call center and a fleet of over 2,000 delivery trucks. Its 1,825 stores and

---

Figure 5.22   Companies have a spectrum of alternatives and benefits trade-offs when deciding upon an integrated or separate E-commerce business.

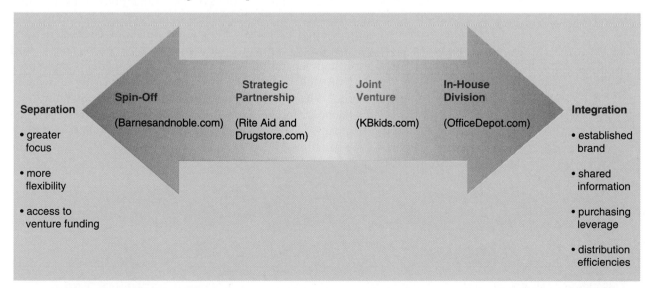

Source: Adapted from Ranjay Gulati and Jason Garino, "Get the Right Mix of Bricks and Clicks," *Harvard Business Review*, May–June 2000, p. 110.

30 warehouses were networked by a sophisticated information system that provided complete customer, vendor, order, and product inventory data in real time. These business resources made an invaluable foundation for coordinating Office Depot's E-commerce activities and customer services with its catalog business and physical stores. Thus, customers can shop at OfficeDepot.com at their home or business, or at in-store kiosks. Then they can choose to pick up their purchases at the stores or have them delivered. In addition, the integration of Web-enabled E-commerce applications within Office Depot's traditional store and catalog operations has helped to increase the traffic at their physical stores and improved the catalog operation's productivity and average order size.

Other Clicks and Bricks Strategies

As Figure 5.22 illustrates, other clicks and bricks strategies range from partial E-commerce integration using joint ventures and strategic partnerships, to complete separation via the spin-off of an independent E-commerce company. For example, Kbkids.com is an E-commerce joint venture created by toy retailer KB Toys and Brain-Play.com, formerly an E-tailer of children's products. The company is 80 percent owned by KB Toys, but has independent management teams and separate distribution systems. However, Kbkids.com has successfully capitalized on the shared brand name and buying power of KB Toys, and the ability of its customers to return purchases to over 1,300 KB Toys stores, which also heavily promote their E-commerce site.

The strategic partnership of the Rite-Aid retail drugstore chain and Drugstore.com is a good example of a less integrated E-commerce venture. Rite-Aid only owns about 25 percent of Drugstore.com, which has an independent management team and a separate business brand. However, both companies share the decreased costs and increased revenue benefits of joint buying power, an integrated distribution center, co-branded pharmacy products, and joint prescription fulfillment at Rite-Aid stores.

Finally, let's look at an example of the benefits and challenges of a completely separate clicks and bricks strategy. Barnesandnoble.com was created as an independent E-commerce company that was spun off by the Barnes & Noble book retail chain. This enabled it to gain several hundred million dollars in venture capital funding, create an entrepreneurial culture, attract quality management, maintain a high degree of business flexibility, and accelerate decision making. But the book E-retailer has done poorly since its founding, and has failed to gain market share from Amazon.com, its leading competitor. Many E-commerce analysts say that the failure of Barnes & Noble to integrate some of the marketing and operations of Barnesandnoble.com within their thousands of bookstores forfeited a strategic business opportunity in E-commerce.

The previous examples emphasize that there is no universal clicks and bricks E-commerce strategy for every company, industry, or type of business. Both E-commerce integration and separation have major business benefits and shortcomings. Thus, deciding on a clicks and bricks strategy depends heavily on whether or not a company's unique business operations provide strategic capabilities and resources to successfully support integration with an E-commerce venture. As these examples show, most companies are implementing some measure of clicks and bricks integration, because "the benefits of integration are almost always too great to abandon entirely" [13].

Summary

- **Electronic Commerce.** Electronic commerce encompasses the entire online process of developing, marketing, selling, delivering, servicing, and paying for products and services. The Internet and related technologies and E-commerce websites on the World Wide Web and corporate intranets and extranets serve as the business and technology platform for E-commerce marketplaces for consumers and businesses in the basic categories of business-to-consumer (B2C), business-to-business (B2B), and consumer-to-consumer (C2C) E-commerce. The essential processes that should be implemented in all E-commerce applications—access control and security, personalizing and profiling, search management, content management, catalog management, payment systems, workflow management, event notification, and collaboration and trading—are summarized in Figure 5.5.

- **E-Commerce Issues.** Many E-business enterprises are moving toward offering full-service B2C and B2B E-commerce portals supported by integrated customer-focused processes and internetworked supply chains as illustrated in Figure 5.11. In addition, E-business companies must evaluate a variety of E-commerce integration or seperation alternatives and benefit trade-offs when choosing a clicks and bricks strategy, as summarized in Figure 5.22.

- **B2C E-Commerce.** Business typically sell products and services to consumers at E-commerce websites that provide attractive Web pages, multimedia catalogs, interactive order processing, secure electronic payment systems, and online customer support. However, successful E-tailers build customer satisfaction and loyalty by optimizing factors outlined in Figure 5.13, such as selection and value, performance and service efficiency, the look and feel of the site, advertising and incentives to purchase, personal attention, community relationships, and security and reliability. In addition, a Web store has several key business requirements, including building and marketing a Web business, serving and supporting customers, and managing a Web store, as summarized in Figure 5.15.

- **B2B E-Commerce.** Business-to-business applications of E-commerce involve electronic catalog, exchange, and auction marketplaces that use Internet, intranet, and extranet websites and portals to unite buyers and sellers, as summarized in Figure 5.17 and illustrated in Figure 5.18. Many B2B E-commerce portals are developed and operated for a variety of industries by third-party market-maker companies called infomediaries, which may represent consortiums of major corporations. B2B E-commerce also includes applications like electronic data interchange, which automates the exchange of business documents on the Internet.

Key Terms and Concepts

These are the key terms and concepts of this chapter. The page number of their first explanation is in parentheses.

1. Clicks and bricks alternatives (189)
2. E-commerce marketplaces (184)
   a. Auction (184)
   b. Catalog (184)
   c. Exchange (184)
   d. Portal (184)
3. E-commerce success factors (176)
4. E-commerce technologies (162)
5. Electronic commerce (162)
   a. Business-to-business (164)
   b. Business-to-consumer (164)
   c. Consumer-to-consumer (164)
6. Electronic data interchange (186)
7. Electronic funds transfer (172)
8. Essential E-commerce processes (164)
   a. Access control and security (166)
   b. Catalog management (168)
   c. Collaboration and trading (171)
   d. Content management (168)
   e. Electronic payment systems (171)
   f. Event notification (171)
   g. Profiling and personalizing (167)
   h. Search management (168)
   i. Workflow management (169)
9. Infomediaries (180)
10. Trends in E-commerce (176)
11. Web store requirements (179)

Review Quiz

Match one of the key terms and concepts listed previously with one of the brief examples or definitions that follow. Try to find the best fit for the answers that seem to fit more than one term or concept. Defend your choices.

_____ 1. The online process of developing, marketing, selling, delivering, servicing, and paying for products and services.

_____ 2. Business selling to consumers at retail Web stores is an example.

_____ 3. Using an E-commerce portal for auctions by business customers and their suppliers is an example.

_____ 4. Using an E-commerce website for auctions among consumers is an example.

_____ 5. E-commerce depends on the Internet and the World Wide Web, and on other networks of browser-equipped client/server systems and hypermedia databases.

_____ 6. E-commerce applications must implement several major categories of interrelated processes such as search management and catalog management.

_____ 7. Helps to establish mutual trust between you and an E-tailer at an E-commerce site.

_____ 8. Tracks your website behavior to provide you with an individualized Web store experience.

_____ 9. Develops, generates, delivers, and updates information to you at a website.

_____ 10. Ensures that proper E-commerce transactions, decisions, and activities are performed to better serve you.

_____ 11. Sends you an E-mail when what you ordered at an E-commerce site has been shipped.

_____ 12. Includes matchmaking, negotiation, and mediation processes among buyers and sellers.

_____ 13. Companies that serve as intermediaries in E-commerce transactions.

_____ 14. A website for E-commerce transactions.

_____ 15. An E-commerce marketplace that may provide catalog, exchange, or auction service for businesses or consumers.

_____ 16. Buyers bidding for the business of a seller.

_____ 17. Marketplace for bid (buy) and ask (sell) transactions.

_____ 18. The most widely used type of marketplace in B2C E-commerce.

_____ 19. The exchange of business documents between the networked computers of business partners.

_____ 20. The processing of money and credit transfers between businesses and financial institutions.

_____ 21. Ways to provide efficient, convenient, and secure payments in E-commerce.

_____ 22. E-businesses are increasingly developing full-service B2C and B2B E-commerce portals.

_____ 23. E-businesses can evaluate and choose from several E-commerce integration alternatives.

_____ 24. Successful E-tailers build customer satisfaction and loyalty in several key ways.

_____ 25. Successful E-commerce ventures must build, market, and manage their Web businesses while serving their customers.

Discussion Questions

1. Most businesses should engage in electronic commerce on the Internet. Do you agree or disagree with this statement? Explain your position.

2. Are you interested in owning, managing, or working for a business that is primarily engaged in electronic commerce on the Internet? Explain your position.

3. Refer to the Real World Case on eBay Inc. in the chapter. How could eBay's community commerce model be used to improve other companies' E-commerce ventures?

4. Why do you think there have been so many business failures among "dotcom" companies that were devoted only to retail E-commerce?

5. Do the E-commerce success factors listed in Figure 5.13 guarantee success for an E-commerce business venture? Give a few examples of what else could go wrong and how you would confront such challenges.

6. If personalizing a customer's website experience is a key success factor, then electronic profiling processes to track visitor website behavior are necessary. Do you agree or disagree with this statement? Explain your position.

7. All corporate procurement should be accomplished in E-commerce auction marketplaces, instead of using B2B websites that feature fixed-price catalogs or negotiated prices. Explain you position on this proposal.

8. Refer to the Real World Case on MathaStewart.com in the chapter. Do you agree that "Close-quarters, top-level executive oversight is a key to success in all Web ventures?" Why or why not?

9. If you were starting an E-commerce Web store, which of the business requirements summarized in Figure 5.15 would you primarily do yourself, and which would you outsource to a Web development or hosting company? Why?

10. Which of the E-commerce clicks and bricks alternatives illustrated in Figure 5.22 would you recommend to Barnes & Noble? Amazon.com? Wal-Mart? Any business? Explain your position.

Application Exercises

Complete the following exercises as individual or group projects that apply chapter concepts to real world business situations.

1. BCentral.com: Small Business E-Commerce Portals

On the net, small businesses have become big news. And a really big business, Microsoft, wants a piece of the action. The company's BCentral Web portal (www.bcentral.com) is one of many sites offering advice and services for small businesses moving online. Most features, whether free or paid, are what you'd expect: lots of links and information along the lines established by Excite's Work.com, and other competitors like ECongo.com or GoBizGo.com. BCentral, however, stands out for its affordable advertising and marketing services. See Figure 5.23.

Figure 5.23

Microsoft's BCentral is a small business E-commerce portal.

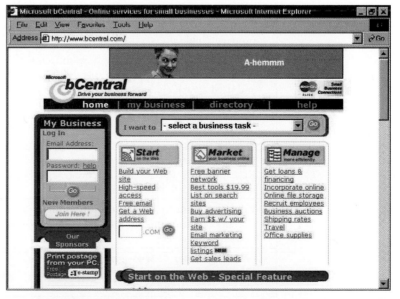

Courtesy of Microsoft Corporation.

One BCentral program allows you to put banner ads on other sites in exchange for commissions from click-throughs and sales. As on other sites, a banner ad exchange program lets you place one ad on a member site in exchange for displaying two ads on your own. For as little as $20 a month, you can buy a marketing package that includes ads on sites such as Yahoo and Excite, and get help with direct E-mail campaigns, as well as track all activities on your personal "my business" page.

a. Check out BCentral and the other E-commerce portals mentioned. Identify several benefits and limitations for a business using their websites.

b. Which is your favorite. Why?

c. Which site would you recommend or use to help a small business wanting to get into E-commerce? Why?

Source: Adapted from Anush Yegazarian, "BCentral.com Puts Your Business on the Web," *PC World*, December 1999, p. 64.

2. Ford, Microsoft, GM, and Others: E-Commerce Websites for Car Buying

Ford and Microsoft—leaders in their respective industries—have forged an alliance that may have a big impact on the future of online car buying. Customers will be able to configure the car of their dreams on Microsoft's CarPoints Website. While the giants share the spotlight, other online car sellers have begun to offer similar innovations. See Figure 5.24.

For now, the majority of car buyers are still using the Internet as a place to research rather than buy. Most auto sites simply put consumers in touch with a local dealer, where they test drive a vehicle and negotiate a price. Autobytel.com of Irvine, Calif., for example, has been referring buyers to new and used car dealers since 1995, as well as offering online financing and insurance. General Motors' BuyPower site provides access to a vast inventory of cars, though shoppers still have to go to a dealer to close the sale.

The Microsoft-Ford alliance will make consumers less dependent on what cars a dealer has on the lot. At CarPoint and Ford.com, buyers can customize a car—any car as long as it's a Ford—by selecting trim, paint color, and other options before purchase. Buyers will still pick up and pay for the cars at local dealerships.

a. Check out several of the websites shown in Figure 5.24. Evaluate them based on ease of use, response times, relevance of information provided, and other criteria you feel are important. Don't forget the classic: "Did they make you want to buy?"

b. Which sites would you use or recommend if you or a friend actually wanted to buy a car? Why?

Source: Adapted from "E-Commerce Cars," in Technology Review, *Fortune*, Winter 2000, p. 42. © 2000 Time Inc. All rights reserved.

Figure 5.24

Some of the top E-commerce websites for car buying and researching.

Top Car Buying Websites
● **Autobytel.com**   www.autobytel.com Enter make and model, and a local dealer will contact you with a price offer. Home delivery is an option.
● **AutoNation**   www.autonation.com Every make and model available, as well as financing and insurance information, home delivery, and test drives.
● **carOrder.com**   www.carorder.com Configure, price, and directly order a car. If no partner dealership has it, the manufacturer will build it.
● **Microsoft CarPoint**   www.carpoint.com Auto reviews, detailed vehicle specifications, safety ratings, and buying services for new and used cars, including customizing your very own Ford.
● **cars.com**   www.cars.com Research tools include automotive reviews, model reports, dealer locators, and financing information.
● **CarsDirect.com**   www.carsdirect.com Research price and design, then order your car. CarsDirect will deliver it to your home—wrapped, if you like, in a bow.
● **Edmunds.com**   www.edmunds.com For an objective opinion, Edmunds.com provides reviews, safety updates, and rebate news for car buyers.
● **GM BuyPower**   www.gmbuypower.com With access to nearly 6,000 GM dealerships, car shoppers can get a price quote, schedule a test drive, and buy.

3. Comparing E-Commerce Sites

In this exercise you will experiment with electronic shopping and compare alternative electronic commerce sites. First you will need to select a category of product widely available on the web, such as books, CDs, toys, etcetera. Next select 5 specific products to price on the Internet, e.g., 5 specific CDs you might be interested in buying. Search three prominent electronic commerce sites selling this type of product and record the price charged for each product by each site.

a. Using a spreadsheet record a set of information similar to that shown below for each product. (categories describing the product will vary depending upon the type of product you select—CDs might require the title of the CD and the Performer(s), while toys or similar products would require the name of the product and its description.)

b. For each product rank each company based on the price charged. Give a rating of 1 for the lowest price and 3 for the highest and split the ratings for ties—two sites tying for 1st and 2nd lowest price would each receive a 1.5. If a site does not have one of the products available for sale, give that site a rating of 4 for that product. Add the ratings across your products to produce an overall price/availability rating for each site.

c. Based on your experience with these sites rate them on their ease of use, completeness of information, and order-filling and shipping options. As in part B, give a rating of 1 to the site you feel is best in each category, a 2 to the second best and a 3 to the poorest site.

d. Prepare a set of power point slides or similar presentation materials summarizing the key results and including an overall assessment of the sites you compared.

Title of Book	Author	Price at:			Rating		
		Site A	Site B	Site C	A	B	C
The Return of Little Big Man	Berger, T.	$15.00	$16.95	$14.50	2	3	1
Learning Perl/Tk	Walsh, N & Mui, L	$26.36	$25.95	$25.95	3	1.5	2
Business at the Speed of Thought	Gates, W.	$21.00	$22.95	$21.00	1.5	3	2
Murders for the Holidays	Smith, G.		$8.25	$7.95	4	2	1
Design for Dullards	Jones, .	$17.95	$18.50	$18.50	1	2.5	3
Sum of ratings (low score represents most favorable rating)					12	12	8

4. Evaluating the Market for B 2 C Electronic Commerce

In assessing the potential for business to consumer, B to C, electronic commerce, it is important to know how many people are using the Internet for business transactions and what segments of the population are using the Internet in this manner. In August of 2000 the US Census Bureau asked a number of questions about Internet use as a part of its monthly Current Population Survey. This survey is administered to over 100,000 individuals and its results are used to create projected rates of use for the full population. Among the questions was one, which asked each respondent whether they used the Internet to shop, to pay bills or for other commercial purposes. A number of general demographic characteristics, such as age, education level and household income level are also gathered for each respondent.

The sample table below shows summary results for different education levels. Data showing the distribution of Internet use for shopping across age categories and levels of family income have also been collected from this survey data and are available as a download file for this application exercise in the web site for this textbook. The textbook website is www.mhhe.com/business/mis/obrien/obrien5e/index.html. Click on downloads under the student resources section of that page.

a. download the initial spreadsheet file for this exercise and modify it to include percentage use calculations for each age, education level and income category.

b. Create appropriate graphs to illustrate how the distribution of use of Internet for shopping varies across age, income, and education level categories.

c. Write a short memorandum to your instructor summarizing your results and describing their implications for a web-based retailer that is designing a marketing strategy.

Education Level	Have Used Internet to Shop / Pay Bills		% Using Internet to Shop / Pay Bills
	Yes	No	
Less Than High School	598824	32354711	1.8%
High School Grad	5104952	60930000	7.7%
Some College No Degree	6613400	32290000	17.0%
Associate Degree	7840540	38855612	16.8%
Bachelors Degree	9581979	22830000	29.6%
Masters Degree or Higher	5196040	10280934	33.6%

Compucision and International Cellulose: Challenges of B2B Marketplaces

Talk to an average American business owner and you'll see that while B2B E-commerce has potential, it's hardly the miracle it's been made out to be. "What it did do was give our business some stability," says George Blass, partner in Compucision, a small New Milford, Connecticut, machine shop that builds parts for various industries, including aerospace and automotive. Eight months ago, Blass logged onto FreeMarkets.com, an online exchange where buyers and sellers bid on goods and services. "We would never have had the resources to generate this amount of work," he says of the three-year, $1.1 million contract that Compucision won on FreeMarkets—allowing the shop to double its employee count and invest in expensive, specialized machinery.

However, Compucision had to do what most supply-side exchange participants must do: shave profit margins to compete. "You have to know what your capabilities are—including what kind of profit margin you need—before you bid," says Blass.

Compucision's experience was a typical result for the small to midsize businesses that experimented with e-commerce last year. Although companies have seen benefits such as reduced procurement costs and growth of their customer base, the one major advantage of B2B E-commerce is that it results in new and improved lines of communication between customers and suppliers. E-procurement, especially of nonstrategic materials, is the easiest way to get started in B2B E-commerce. Most companies first buy office supplies online and progress to purchasing computer components, machine parts, and other supplies not needed for manufacture of their products.

The hype surrounding the market-based B2B models obscures the fact that most E-commerce doesn't happen on public Internet exchanges, but on private marketplaces, whether built on enterprise software or a hosted web platform which connect strategic business partners. These E-commerce networks can be either one-to-one project management and transaction facilitators that mimic the benefits normally associated with electronic data interchange (but for a fraction of the cost), or they can be one-to-many with a single business connecting to a network of preferred partners.

In some industries the possibilities that web-based private marketplaces create are rapidly changing business practices. "This was something we had to become part of or lose access to a part of our marketplace," says Dan Kirk, executive vice president of International Cellulose, a midsize recycled-paper recovery firm in Atlanta that uses Fibermarket.com primarily "as an Internet platform to communicate with our customers." In addition, International Cellulose used

Fibermarket.com as a shortcut to e-business. "It's very easy to have a web site that says here we are and here's what we have, but in the end it has to integrate into your data systems," Kirk says. "Those were huge programming costs that were totally out of our league."

When International Cellulose joined Fibermarket.com for instance, it was less by choice than on demand. The paper industry is so dominated by big players like Georgia-Pacific and International Paper, Kirk says, that the big boys are able to force smaller players to move online. Similarly Covisint, the auto-industry consortium founded by GM, DaimlerChyrsler, and Ford Motor Company, has made participating in its e-commerce site mandatory for all suppliers.

As a result, the benefits of online commerce for smaller enterprises—cost savings and increased customer reach—don't necessarily extend to industries where a few large players dominate. "No, the Internet doesn't level the playing field," says Kirk, explaining that recycled paper is basically a commodity. "The ultimate consuming marketplace is well defined and actually getting smaller, so I really don't see the Internet as a vehicle for expanding markets. It's really just an efficiency mechanism." However, Kirk adds that Fibermarket.com has provided important process improvements. "There's only so many phone calls and faxes I can deal with in a day, but if I can get my offers out to the marketplace and to the regular customers that we deal with [online], it just improves my business."

Still, large corporations will continue to drive the spread of E-commerce. "It's a forced solution," says KPMG Consulting's director of digital marketplaces, Jerry Maginnis, "but when the equity founders of a marketplace are major players, they're telling suppliers, 'If you want to do business with us, you have to do it in this marketplace.'"

Case Study Questions

1. What are the major benefits of B2B marketplaces to both business buyers and suppliers?

2. Why do you think most B2B E-commerce transactions happen on private rather than public marketplaces? Visit fibermarket.com (private), and freemarkets.com (public) to help you answer the question.

3. Dan Kirk of International Cellulose says that the Internet is just an efficiency mechanism, does not level the business playing field, and is not a vehicle for expanding markets. Do you agree or disagree? Defend your position.

Source: Adapted from Kayte Vanscoy, "B2B Bust," *Smart Business*, March, 2001, pp. 101–109.

Florist.com and Others: The Success of Small Business E-Commerce

When Aaron Benon founded Florist.com in 1996, his strategy couldn't have been more different from the many dot-coms then exploding onto the Web scene. Instead of raising millions of dollars in venture capital, he converted half his tiny Beverly Hills California flower shop, Floral & Hardy, into a threadbare online operation and hired just four employees, including his wife. Still pinching pennies, he told his Florist.com employees to bring cell phones to work the week before Valentine's Day so they wouldn't tie up the company's barebones phone system.

Roughing it paid off big time for the online small fry. Last year, Florist.com turned a $1 million profit on $3 million in sales. Benon's success stands in stark contrast to the fast rise and even faster failure of other, more high-profile gift sites such as Send.com, which bit the dust in January, a year after blowing $20 million on a quirky ad campaign. "I knew the bubble was going to burst," says Benon. "I said, 'No, I'm going to keep it grassroots.' We take one baby step at a time. Only when the business proves itself to us will we spend the money to get bigger."

Dot-coms may be going down in flames every day, but a surprising group of web survivors is emerging unscathed: small business, the might mini-dots. With just a handful of employees and annual sales of $5 million or less, these intrepid independents are doing what almost none of their venture-capital-funded brethren could: make real money online.

Who would have thought? After the rise of big dot-coms such as Amazon.com and the later arrival to the Web of big retail chains such as Wal-Mart Stores Inc., a lot of experts predicted the Web giants would crush small businesses like bugs. Instead it was other dot-coms—all playing high-stakes, get-big-fast games with multimillion-dollar portal deals and TV ads—that got slammed. Thousands of small businesses, flying under the radar, are turning modest but healthy profits. Already, the evidence is coming in. According to ActivMedia Research, 44% of companies with fewer than 10 employees turn a profit on their web sales, compared with 26% of companies with 100 employees or more.

Unlike dot-coms with inexperienced executives, the mini-dots are succeeding by employing the same strategies that small-business owners have relied on for centuries: They're sticking to niches they know well. They scrimp on expenses, forgoing expensive portal deals and using net resources, from e-mail to customer-sharing arrangements, to save money. And they're banding together on the Web, presenting a bigger face to the online world. With its vast reach, the Internet can enhance any small business that uses it properly.

How so? First, they're using the Net's access to a global customer base to zero in on defensible niches, instead of offering all things to all web surfers. Pets.com Inc., for instance, went bust in December 2000 partly because it tried to sell all kinds of pet supplies—even huge bags of inexpensive dog food with high shipping costs and margins under 10%. By contrast, Lee (Massachusetts)-based Waggin Tails sells scarce items such as Provi-Tabs dog vitamins and Hi-Tor prescription cat food. That allows the Web store to charge high enough prices to turn a 30% profit margin on well under $5 million in annual sales. "Are we the cheapest game in town? No," admits founder John Gigliotti. "But our customers typically can't find a full-blown selection of super-premium pet products in their local pet shop, so they're not very price-sensitive."

Then, small companies are taking advantage of websites, e-mail and chat groups as new marketing channels for their businesses. And no online marketing channel has proved more effective than online auctions, pioneered by eBay in 1996. Besides spurring the formation of thousands of new small businesses online, online auctions have given many small businesses a new outlet for their wares.

Finally, the Net has allowed farflung small businesses to gang up and pool their resources against their bigger and louder competition in ways they can't do in the physical world. For example, the American Booksellers Assn., which promotes independent bookstores, runs a program called BookSense.com that allows members to offer amenities only big chains could offer before, such as gift certificates good at any member store. Moreover, their online customers can order any book in print from their site, even if they don't stock it themselves. Thus, Kerry Slattery, owner of Skylight Books in Los Angeles, partly credits the program for a higher-than-expected 15% rise in her store's sales in 2000 to $1 million.

Case Study Questions

1. Why do you think that many small business E-commerce ventures have been more successful than many well-financed dotcoms?

2. What should venture capital funded E-commerce startups like Pets.com have done differently to survive and succeed?

3. Do you think that the E-commerce spinoffs of large traditional retailers like Wal-Mart, or a possible resurgence of pure dotcoms like Amazon.com, will drive small E-tailers out of business in the future? Why or why not?

Source: Adapted from Eileen Weintraub, "The Mighty Mini-Dots," *Business Week E.Biz*, March 19, 2001, pp. 45–48.

Wal-Mart, Kmart, Kingfisher and HMV: Retail Bricks and Clicks Strategies

Now that so many dot-coms are floundering or failing, some retailers are rethinking the separation of their online and brick and mortar operations, given that many of the advantages of spinning off online units have either dissolved or become less important.

Wal-Mart

When Walmart.com announced plans to lay off about 10% of its workforce, the online retailer's CEO insisted that top brass has "more confidence than ever in our potential for this business." CEO Jeanne Jackson continues to see reasons to keep her dot-com arm separate. But like most online retailers that have a physical presence, Walmart.com expects to see greater synergies between the online and physical stores' IT staffs during the coming year. "They work closer and closer every day," Jackson says.

Though Walmart.com has chosen to stay separate from Wal-Mart Stores Inc.'s brick and mortar operations, Jackson said the Brisbane, California–based dot-com operation continues to reap benefits from its close proximity to the Silicon Valley labor pool for web design and engineering talent. She noted that her company plans more hiring in the site design and technology areas, dismissing last week's layoffs as a "readjustment" for resources spent on projects that weren't producing adequate returns.

The prospect of folding the online operation into the parent company is "not on anybody's radar screen now," Jackson said. "Clearly, for the foreseeable future, Silicon Valley is a preferable place to incubate the business than Bentonville, Arkansas," she added. Jackson also noted the expert advice her company receives from its joint owner, Accel Partners in Palo Alto, California, which potentially saves it millions in consulting fees.

But that's not to say her company doesn't recognize the need to work with its parent. Jackson noted that her company also receives ""incredibly valuable" help—particularly with logistics and fulfillment—from its Bentonville, Arkansas–based parent. IT staffers make weekly visits to California, and she predicted that cooperation will increase.

Kmart

Mark Goldstein, CEO of BlueLight.com LLC, the online spin-off of Kmart Corp., said key staffers from the Troy, Michigan-based parent company are spending increasing levels of time with his online arm. CIO Randy Allen serves as BlueLight's chairman of the board, and since the holiday season, she has been spending at least one day per week at the San Francisco-based online company. Rich Blunck, Kmart's chief technology officer, is now based in both California and Michigan, Goldstein added.

BlueLight is also "integrating more and more each day" to better leverage Kmart's assets, particularly its supply chain and technology licenses, he said. Yet separation continues to have its advantages, such as helping the company act swiftly, Goldstein claimed. "The external reasons to create separate entities—stock options and incremental market valuation—have all but disappeared over the course of the last year," he said, but he insisted that the internal reasons remain the same. "At the point in time when it becomes clear that integration is everything, then one might question separation," Goldstein said.

Kingfisher

Ian Cheshire, CEO of e-Kingfisher, the e-commerce arm of London-based Kingfisher PLC, a $16 billion seller of home improvement supplies, consumer electronics and general merchandise, said his company always knew the electronic and physical operations would fuse someday. They now have separate staffs with "human middleware" joining the two sides, but the companies envision complete reintegration within the next two years, he said.

Unless you have 100% focus on it, it doesn't get done. That's what led us to separate it," Cheshire said. "But we were also conscious that we bought into the multichannel idea for the future, so we couldn't go too far away . . . If you go too far, why would these parent companies, who you need for products, systems, all the other bits, ever support you?"

HMV

HMV UK Ltd.'s online arm started out with an independent staff, building on technology from Microsoft Corp. But when the E-commerce operation recognized that it would be better off using the business applications on the IBM AS/400 computer systems its parent used, integration began in earnest, said Stuart Rowe, general manager at HMV Direct & E-Commerce in London.

The online and brick-and-mortar operations of the music, video and computer games retailer are "now integrating fast," Rowe said. "The fact that we're using the same supply chain as the record store, the same systems and actually, the fact that I've been put onto the HMV Europe board, is an indication that we're bringing it into the fold."

Case Study Questions

1. Is the independent spinoff status of walmart.com and bluelight.com the best E-commerce strategy for these companies? Why or why not?

2. Is the planned reintegration of the independent spin-offs of Kingfisher and HMV the best E-commerce strategy for these companies? Why or why not?

3. Can a pure online retail business with no relationships to any traditional retailer succeed in both revenue and profitability? Defend your position.

Source: Adapted from Carol Sliwa, "E-Tailers: Back to the Fold?," *Computerworld*, March 5, 2001, pp. 1, 61.

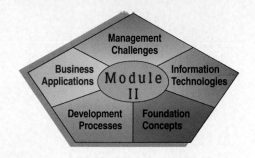

Management Challenges

Business Applications

Module II

Information Technologies

Development Processes

Foundation Concepts

Chapter 6

E-Business Decision Support

Chapter Highlights

Learning Objectives

After reading and studying this chapter, you should be able to:

1. Identify the changes taking place in the form and use of decision support in E-business enterprises.

2. Identify the role and reporting alternatives of management information systems.

3. Describe how online analytical processing can meet key information needs of managers.

4. Explain the decision support system concept and how it differs from traditional management information systems.

5. Explain how executive information systems can support the information needs of executives and managers.

6. Identify how neural networks, fuzzy logic, genetic algorithms, virtual reality, and intelligent agents can be used in business.

7. Give examples of several ways expert systems can be used in business decision-making situations.

Section I   Decision Support in E-Business

E-Business and Decision Support

Conventional wisdom says knowledge is power, but knowledge harvesting without focus can render you powerless. As companies migrate toward responsive E-business models, they are investing in new data-driven decision support application frameworks that help them respond rapidly to changing market conditions and customer needs [32].

So to succeed in E-business and E-commerce, companies need information systems that can support the diverse information and decision-making needs of their managers and business professionals. In this section, we will explore in more detail how this is accomplished by several types of management information, decision support, and executive information systems. We will concentrate our attention on how the Internet, intranets, and other Web-enabled information technologies have significantly strengthened the role information systems play in supporting the decision-making activities of every manager and knowledge worker in the E-business enterprise.

Analyzing Siemens AG

Read the Real World Case on Siemens AG on the next page. We can learn a lot from this case about how Internet and intranet technologies have become key components of successful knowledge management systems. See Figure 6.1.

Knowledge management systems (KMS) have great promise, but face problems with employee resistance to sharing their workplace knowledge. Siemens is a huge global conglomerate which has developed an Internet/intranet KMS called ShareNet, which has been successful in encouraging employees to share their knowledge in several key business situations. ShareNet is being implemented on a phased basis, starting with its $10.5 billion Information and Communications Networks Group, where employees from several different country units have used ShareNet to help each other win major business contracts. Siemens is meeting the challenge of employee disinterest or resistance to using knowledge management systems by rewarding participation

Figure 6.1

Joachim Doring is a skydiver, and vice president of Siemens AG, who leads their worldwide knowledge management initiative.

Peter Schinzler/Agency Ann Hamann.

Siemens AG: The Business Case for Global Knowledge Management

Joachim Doring is a Siemens vice president in charge of creating a high-tech solution to the age-old problem of getting employees to stop hoarding their knowhow. His grand plan: Use the Internet to spread the knowledge of 461,000 co-workers around the globe so that people could build off one another's expertise. "People who give up knowhow get knowhow back," says Doring, a hyperactive 31-year old who likes to spend his free time skydiving.

At the heart of his vision is a web site called ShareNet. The site combines elements of a chat room, a database, and a search engine. An online entry form lets employees store information they think might be useful to colleagues—anything from a description of a successful project to a PowerPoint presentation. Other Siemens workers can search or browse by topic, then contact the authors via e-mail for more information.

So far, the payoff has been a dandy: Since its inception in April, 1999, ShareNet has been put to the test by nearly 12,000 salespeople in Siemens' $10.5 billion Information & Communications Networks Groups, which provides tele com equipment and services. The tool, which cost only $7.8 million, has added $122 million in sales. For example, it was crucial to landing a $3 million contract to build a pilot broadband network for Telecom Malaysia. The local salespeople did not have enough expertise to put together a proposal, but through ShareNet they discovered a team in Denmark that had done a nearly identical project. Using the Denmark group's expertise, the Malaysia team won the job.

Better yet, the system lets staffers post an alert when they need help fast. In Switzerland, Siemens won a $460,000 contract to build a telecommunications network for two hospitals even though its bid was 30% higher than a competitor's. The clincher: Via ShareNet, colleagues in the Netherlands provided technical data to help the sales rep prove that Siemens' system would be substantially more reliable.

ShareNet is a case study in knowledge management systems, which are gaining a foothold in corporations around the world. Advocates preach that the collective expertise of workers is a company's most precious resource, so executives need to tear down the walls between departments and individuals. By using the Net, companies can quickly and easily unlock the profit potential of the knowledge tucked away in the brains of their best employees. While only 6% of global corporations now have company-wide knowledge management programs, that will surge to 60% in five years, according to a 2000 survey by the Conference Board. Among the early birds: Chevron, Johnson & Johnson, Royal Dutch/Shell, Ford Motor and Whirlpool.

Siemens has had little choice but to lead the knowledge management parade. The $73 billion conglomerate, which makes everything from X-ray machines to high-speed trains, is under intense pressure because of uncertainty about the global economy and shrinking profit margins. But Chief Executive Heinrich von Pierer is trying to prove big can work—and might even be an advantage in the Information Age. The CEO wants to take the ShareNet approach beyond the telecom unit to every nook and cranny of the Siemens empire. Next up: people who service telecom equipment and scientists in research and development.

Even though the advantages are clear, getting employees to change their ways and share is the toughest obstacle to overcome. "You have to go in and change processes around. It take s a lot of time," says Greg Dyer, a senior research analyst of knowledge management services at International Data Corporation. Siemens has tackled this problem through a three-pronged effort. It has anointed 100 internal evangelists drawn from all its country units, who are responsible for training, answering questions, and monitoring the system. Siemens' top management has shown that it's behind the projects. And the company is providing incentives to overcome employees' resistance to change.

Siemens uses the carrot and the stick. Managers get bonuses if they use ShareNet and generate additional sales. But CEOs and CFOs of the company's country business units can't collect all their performance-linked bonus unless they demonstrate that they either gave information over ShareNet or borrowed information from it to build sales. Employees get prizes such as trips to professional conferences if they contribute knowledge that proves valuable to someone else.

But the real incentive is much more basic. Commission-driven salespeople have learned that drawing on the expertise of their far-flung colleagues can be crucial in winning lucrative contracts. "They realize very soon that people using ShareNet have an advantage, and that convinces them to join the club," says Roland Koch, CEO of Siemens' telecom unit.

Case Study Questions

1. What is the business value of knowledge management systems to companies like Siemens? To any company?

2. Why do you think there is a reluctance to share knowledge and use knowledge management systems in Siemens and many organizations?

3. Do you approve of how Siemens is implementing and encouraging employees to use their ShareNet knowledge management system? Why? What else could Siemens do to encourage employee participation?

Source: Adapted from Jack Ewing, "Sharing the Wealth," *Business Week E-Biz*, March 19, 2001, pp. 36–40.

in ShareNet, and making some forms of managerial compensation dependent on sharing or using knowledge via the KMS. And Siemens salespeople have begun to realize that using the knowledge gathered in ShareNet from their colleagues around the world can help them win lucrative contracts in competetive business situations.

E-Business Decision Support Trends

The emerging class of applications focus on personalized decision support, modeling, information retrieval, data warehousing, what-if scenarios, and reporting [32].

As we discussed in Chapter 1, using information systems to support business decision making has been one of the primary thrusts of the business use of information technology. However, the E-commerce revolution spawned by the Internet and the World Wide Web is expanding the information and decision support uses and expectations of a company's employees, managers, customers, suppliers, and other business partners. But this change was noticed even earlier, as both academic researchers and business practitioners began reporting that the traditional managerial focus originating in classic management information systems (1960s), decision support systems (1970s), and executive information systems (1980s) was expanding. The fast pace of new information technologies like PC hardware and software suites, client/server networks, and networked PC versions of DSS/EIS software made decision support available to lower levels of management, as well as to non-managerial individuals and self-directed teams of business professionals [25, 46, 50].

This trend has accelerated with the Internet and E-commerce revolutions, and the dramatic growth of intranets and extranets that internetwork E-business enterprises and their stakeholders. Figure 6.2 illustrates that all E-commerce participants expect easy and instant access to information and Web-enabled self-service data analysis. Internetworked E-business enterprises are responding with a variety of personalized and proactive Web-based analytical techniques to support the decision-making requirements of all of their stakeholders. Figure 6.3 highlights several of the major E-business decision support applications that are being customized, personalized, and Web-enabled for use in E-business and E-commerce [24, 25, 32, 46]. We will emphasize the trend toward such E-business decision support applications in all of the various types of information and decision support systems that are discussed in this chapter.

Target Corporation: E-Business DSS

Target Corporation's decision support system is composed of several applications known collectively as the Decision Maker's Workbench, which use Decision Suite and WebOLAP software from Information Advantage. The DSS and Target's corporate intranet support more than 1,700 active users creating more than 60,000 ad-hoc online analytical processing (OLAP) reports each month. During the Christmas season, more than 20,000 analytic OLAP reports are produced each day. By integrating the Web with its corporate data warehouse, Target Stores enabled its vendors to access its data warehouse to monitor the sales and performance of their own products via secure extranet links across the Internet.

With the Target Stores system complete, the corporation has standardized it as a model for the entire company. Already the standardized warehouse has enabled Target Corporation to obtain more accurate data on how items are performing across divisions, across the company. This has improved vendor negotiations considerably by enabling the different divisions to consolidate orders and receive a better price. The standardized DSS applications also allow for cross-referencing of fashion trends across divisions, and they have helped validate merchandising hunches through the analysis of cross-company data [14, 43].

Figure 6.2

An E-business enterprise must meet the information and data analysis requirements of customers and companies in E-commerce with more personalized and proactive Web-based decision support.

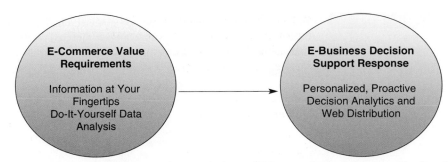

Source: Adapted from Ravi Kalakota and Marcia Robinson, *E-Business: Roadmap for Success* (Reading, MA: Addison-Wesley, 1999), p. 270. © 1999 Addison-Wesley Publishing Company, Inc. Reprinted by permission of Addison-Wesley Longman, Inc.

Information, Decisions, and Management

Figure 6.4 emphasizes that the type of information required by decision makers in a company is directly related to the **level of management decision making** and the amount of structure in the decision situations they face. You should realize that the framework of the classic *managerial pyramid* shown in Figure 6.4 applies even in today's *downsized* organizations and *flattened* or nonhierarchical organizational structures. Levels of management decision making still exist, but their size, shape, and participants continue to change as today's fluid organizational structures evolve. Thus, the levels of managerial decision making that must be supported by information technology in a successful organization are:

- **Strategic Management.** Typically, a board of directors and an executive committee of the CEO and top executives develop overall organizational goals, strategies, policies, and objectives as part of a strategic planning process. They also monitor the strategic performance of the organization and its overall direction in the political, economic, and competitive business environment.

- **Tactical Management.** Increasingly, business professionals in self-directed teams as well as business unit managers develop short- and medium-range plans, schedules, and budgets and specify the policies, procedures, and business objectives for their subunits of the company. They also allocate resources and monitor the performance of their organizational subunits, including departments, divisions, process teams, project teams, and other workgroups.

Figure 6.3

Examples of E-business decision support applications available to employees, managers, customers, suppliers, and other business partners of an internetworked E-business enterprise.

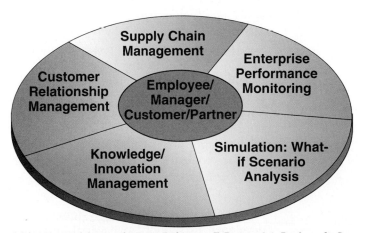

Source: Adapted from Ravi Kalakota and Marcia Robinson, *E-Business 2.0: Roadmap for Success* (Reading, MA: Addison-Wesley, 2001), p. 361. © 2001 Addison-Wesley Publishing Company, Inc. Reprinted by permission of Addison-Wesley Longman, Inc.

Figure 6.4

Information requirements of decision makers. The type of information required by directors, executives, managers, and members of self-directed teams is directly related to the level of management decision making involved and the structure of decision situations they face.

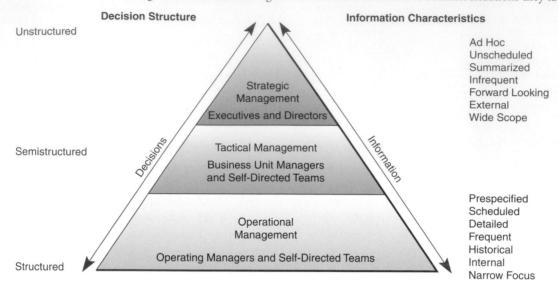

Decision Structure

Unstructured

Semistructured

Structured

Information Characteristics

Strategic Management

Executives and Directors

Tactical Management

Business Unit Managers and Self-Directed Teams

Operational Management

Operating Managers and Self-Directed Teams

Decisions

Information

Ad Hoc
Unscheduled
Summarized
Infrequent
Forward Looking
External
Wide Scope

Prespecified
Scheduled
Detailed
Frequent
Historical
Internal
Narrow Focus

- **Operational Management.** The members of self-directed teams or operating managers develop short-range plans such as weekly production schedules. They direct the use of resources and the performance of tasks according to procedures and within budgets and schedules they establish for the teams and other workgroups of the organization.

Decision Structure

Decisions made at the operational management level tend to be more *structured*, those at the tactical level more *semistructured*, and those at the strategic management level more *unstructured*. Structured decisions involve situations where the procedures to follow when a decision is needed can be specified in advance. The inventory reorder decisions faced by most businesses are a typical example. Unstructured decisions involve decision situations where it is not possible to specify in advance most of the decision procedures to follow. At most, many decision situations are semistructured. That is, some decision procedures can be prespecified, but not enough to lead to a definite recommended decision. For example, decisions involved in starting a new line of E-commerce services or making major changes to employee benefits would probably range from unstructured to semistructured. Figure 6.5 provides a variety of examples of business decisions by type of decision structure and level of management [27].

Therefore, information systems must be designed to produce a variety of information products to meet the changing needs of decision makers throughout an organization. For example, decision makers at the strategic management level require more summarized, ad hoc, unscheduled reports, forecasts, and external intelligence to support their more unstructured planning and policy-making responsibilities. Decision makers at the operational management level, on the other hand, may require more prespecified internal reports emphasizing detailed current and historical data comparisons that support their more structured responsibilities in day-to-day operations.

Management Information Systems

Management information systems were the original type of information system developed to support managerial decision making. An MIS produces information products that support many of the day-to-day decision-making needs of managers and business professionals. Reports, displays, and responses produced by such

Figure 6.5   Examples of decisions by the type of decision structure and by level of management.

Decision Structure	Operational Management	Tactical Management	Strategic Management
Unstructured	Cash management	Business process reengineering	New E-commerce initiatives
		Work group performance analysis	Company reorganization
Semistructured	Credit management	Employee performance appraisal	Product planning
	Production scheduling	Capital budgeting	Mergers and acquisitions
	Daily work assignment	Program budgeting	Site location
Structured	Inventory control	Program control	

management support systems provide information that these decision makers have specified in advance as adequately meeting their information needs. Such predefined information products satisfy the information needs of decision makers at the operational and tactical levels of the organization who are faced with more structured types of decision situations. For example, sales managers rely heavily on sales analysis reports to evaluate differences in performance among salespeople who sell the same types of products to the same types of customers. They have a pretty good idea of the kinds of information about sales results they need to manage sales performance effectively.

Managers and other decision makers use an MIS to request information at their networked workstations that supports their decision-making activities. This information takes the form of periodic, exception, and demand reports and immediate responses to inquiries. Web browsers, application programs, and database management software provide access to information in the intranet and other operational databases of the organization. Remember, operational databases are maintained by transaction processing systems. Data about the business environment are obtained from Internet or extranet databases when necessary.

Management Reporting Alternatives

Management information systems provide a variety of information products to managers. Four major reporting alternatives are provided by such systems.

- **Periodic Scheduled Reports.** This traditional form of providing information to managers uses a prespecified format designed to provide managers with information on a regular basis. Typical examples of such periodic scheduled reports are daily or weekly sales analysis reports and monthly financial statements.

- **Exception Reports.** In some cases, reports are produced only when exceptional conditions occur. In other cases, reports are produced periodically but contain information only about these exceptional conditions. For example, a credit manager can be provided with a report that contains only information on customers who exceed their credit limits. Exception reporting reduces *information overload*, instead of overwhelming decision makers with periodic detailed reports of business activity.

- **Demand Reports and Responses.** Information is available whenever a manager demands it. For example, Web browsers and DBMS query languages and report generators enable managers at PC workstations to get immediate responses or find and obtain customized reports as a result of their requests for the information they need. Thus, managers do not have to wait for periodic reports to arrive as scheduled.

- **Push Reporting.** Information is *pushed* to a manager's networked workstation. As we discussed in Chapter 3, many companies are using webcasting software to selectively broadcast reports and other information to the networked PCs of managers and specialists over their corporate intranets [12, 49]. See Figure 6.6.

Online Analytical Processing

At a recent stockholder meeting, the CEO of PepsiCo, D. Wayne Calloway, said: "Ten years ago I could have told you how Doritos were selling west of the Mississippi. Today, not only can I tell you how well Doritos sell west of the Mississippi, I can also tell you how well they are selling in California, in Orange County, in the town of Irvine, in the local Vons supermarket, in the special promotion, at the end of Aisle 4, on Thursdays" [55].

The competitive and dynamic nature of today's global business environment is driving demands by business managers and analysts for information systems that can provide fast answers to complex business queries. The IS industry has responded to these demands with developments like analytical databases, data marts, data warehouses, data mining techniques, and multidimensional database structures (discussed in Chapter 13), and with specialized servers and Web-enabled software products that support **online analytical processing** (OLAP).

Online analytical processing enables managers and analysts to interactively examine and manipulate large amounts of detailed and consolidated data from many perspectives. OLAP involves analyzing complex relationships among thousands or even millions of data items stored in multidimensional databases to discover patterns, trends, and exception conditions. An OLAP session takes place online in real time, with rapid responses to a manager's or analyst's queries, so that their analytical or decision-making process is undisturbed [21]. See Figure 6.7.

Online analytical processing involves several basic analytical operations, including consolidation, "drill-down," and "slicing and dicing" [20]. See Figure 6.8.

- **Consolidation.** Consolidation involves the aggregation of data. This can involve simple roll-ups or complex groupings involving interrelated data. For

---

Figure 6.6

An example of the push components in a marketing intelligence system that uses the Internet and a corporate intranet system to provide information to employees.

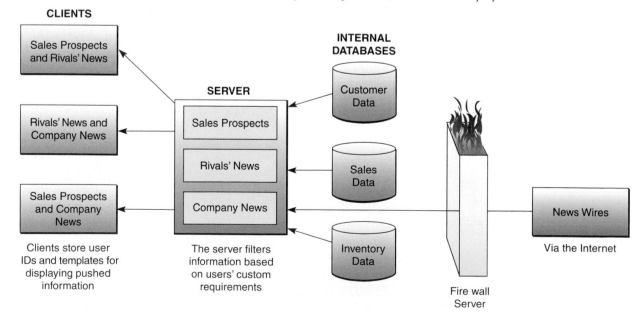

Figure 6.7

Online analytical processing may involve the use of specialized servers and multidimensional databases. OLAP provides fast answers to complex queries posed by managers and analysts using traditional and Web-enabled OLAP software.

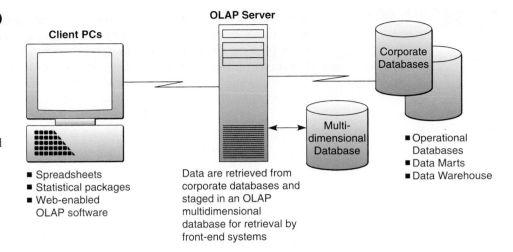

Client PCs

- Spreadsheets
- Statistical packages
- Web-enabled OLAP software

OLAP Server

Data are retrieved from corporate databases and staged in an OLAP multidimensional database for retrieval by front-end systems

Multi-dimensional Database

Corporate Databases

- Operational Databases
- Data Marts
- Data Warehouse

example, sales offices can be rolled up to districts and districts rolled up to regions.

- **Drill-Down.** OLAP can go in the reverse direction and automatically display detail data that comprise consolidated data. This is called drill-down. For example, the sales by individual products or sales reps that make up a region's sales totals could be easily accessed.

- **Slicing and Dicing.** Slicing and dicing refers to the ability to look at the database from different viewpoints. One slice of the sales database might show all sales of product type within regions. Another slice might show all sales by sales channel within each product type. Slicing and dicing is often performed along a time axis in order to analyze trends and find patterns.

Figure 6.8

An example of a display produced by a Web-enabled online analytical processing package.

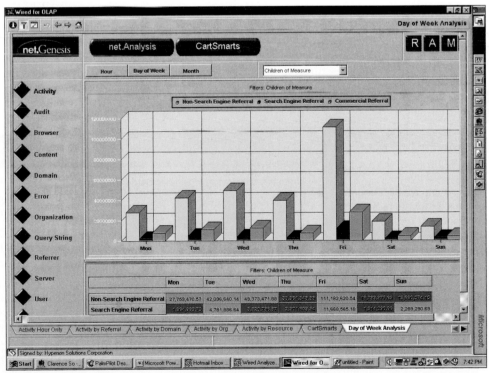

Courtesy of Actuate.

A marketing manager or analyst might use online analytical processing to access a multidimensional database consisting of sales data that have been aggregated by region, product type, and sales channel. In a typical OLAP query, a manager might access a multigigabyte/multiyear sales database in order to find all product sales in each region for each product type. After reviewing the results, the manager might refine his or her query to find the sales volume of each marketing channel within each sales region and product classification. Finally, the marketing manager might perform quarter-to-quarter or year-to-year comparisons of each marketing channel. ●

OLAP at MasterCard International

MasterCard International developed OLAP software called Market Advisor, which enables members to query a data warehouse and drill down into information to analyze transactions and trends online. Market Advisor also provides a 13-month historical database, extended report graphing, and triggered marketing alerts based on above- or below-average merchant or cardholder activity.

In a typical application, a marketing analyst can examine a trend in spending at aggregate levels for a particular merchant category, such as hardware store, restaurant, car rental agency, or gas station. By using Market Advisor, analysts can determine which states or provinces accounted for the volume and identify which merchants accounted for the greatest volume. An analyst can even drill into the data to find which cardholder accounts were used at a particular store over a period of time. The analyst can then find common spending patterns among certain categories of cardholders, and tailor marketing promotions appropriately [22].

Decision Support Systems

Decision support systems are computer-based information systems that provide interactive information support to managers and business professionals during the decision-making process. Decision support systems use (1) analytical models, (2) specialized databases, (3) a decision maker's own insights and judgments, and (4) an interactive, computer-based modeling process to support the making of semistructured and unstructured business decisions. See Figure 6.9.

Figure 6.9

Comparing decision support systems and management information systems. Note the major differences in the information and decision support they provide.

	Management Information Systems	Decision Support Systems
● Decision support provided	Provide information about the performance of the organization	Provide information and decision support techniques to analyze specific problems or opportunities
● Information form and frequency	Periodic, exception, demand, and push reports and responses	Interactive inquiries and responses
● Information format	Prespecified, fixed format	Ad hoc, flexible, and adaptable format
● Information processing methodology	Information produced by extraction and manipulation of business data	Information produced by analytical modeling of business data

Example

An example might help at this point. Sales managers typically rely on management information systems to produce sales analysis reports. These reports contain sales performance figures by product line, salesperson, sales region, and so on. A decision support system, on the other hand, would also interactively show a sales manager the effects on sales performance of changes in a variety of factors (such as promotion expense and salesperson compensation). The DSS could then use several criteria (such as expected gross margin and market share) to evaluate and rank several alternative combinations of sales performance factors. ●

Therefore, DSS are designed to be ad hoc, quick-response systems that are initiated and controlled by business decision makers. Decision support systems are thus able to directly support the specific types of decisions and the personal decision-making styles and needs of individual executives, managers, and business professionals.

**DSS Models
and Software**

Unlike management information systems, decision support systems rely on **model bases** as well as databases as vital system resources. A DSS model base is a software component that consists of models used in computational and analytical routines that mathematically express relationships among variables. For example, a spreadsheet program might contain models that express simple accounting relationships among variables, such as Revenue − Expenses = Profit. Or a DSS model base could include models and analytical techniques used to express much more complex relationships. For example, it might contain linear programming models, multiple regression forecasting models, and capital budgeting present value models. Such models may be stored in the form of spreadsheet models or templates, or statistical and mathematical programs and program modules. See Figure 6.10.

DSS software packages can combine model components to create integrated models that support specific types of decisions. DSS software typically contains

Figure 6.10

Components of a Web-enabled marketing decision support system. Note the hardware, software, model, data, and network resources involved.

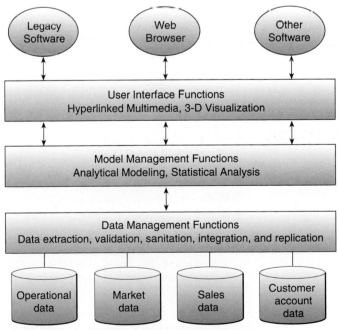

Data Marts and Other Databases

Source: Adapted from Ravi Kalakota and Andrew Whinston, *Electronic Commerce: A Manager's Guide* (Reading, MA: Addison-Wesley, 1997), p. 343. © 1997 by Addison-Wesley Publishing Company, Inc. Reprinted by permission of Addison-Wesley Longman, Inc.

built-in analytical modeling routines and also enables you to build your own models. Many DSS packages are now available in microcomputer and Web-enabled versions (e.g., PC/FOCUS, IFPS Personal, and Decision-Web). Of course, electronic spreadsheet packages also provide some of the model building (spreadsheet models) and analytical modeling (what-if and goal-seeking analysis) offered by more powerful DSS software. See Figure 6.11.

Web-Enabled DSS at PepsiCo	PepsiCo and Sedgwick James Inc., the world's second largest insurance broker, developed a risk management DSS to help minimize PepsiCo's losses from accidents, theft, and other causes. Every week, Sedgwick loads the latest casualty claims data from the nation's leading insurance carriers into a DSS database resident on IBM RS/6000 servers in the PepsiCo intranet. The database is then accessed by managers and analysts using desktop PCs and remote laptops equipped with the INFORM risk management system. Both the RS/6000 servers and local PCs use Information Builders' middleware to provide PepsiCo managers and business analysts with transparent data access from a variety of hardware/ software configurations.
	The INFORM risk management system combines the analytical power of FOCUS decision support modeling with the graphical analysis capabilities of FOCUS/EIS for Windows. As a result, PepsiCo managers and business analysts at all levels can pinpoint critical trends, drill down for detailed backup information, identify potential problems, and plan ways to minimize risks and maximize profits [41].

Geographic Information and Data Visualization Systems

Geographic information systems (GIS) and *data visualization systems* (DVS) are special categories of DSS that integrate computer graphics with other DSS features. A geographic information system is a DSS that uses *geographic databases* to construct and display maps and other graphics displays that support decisions affecting the geographic distribution of people and other resources. Many companies are using GIS technology along with *global positioning system* (GPS) devices to help them choose new retail store locations, optimize distribution routes, or analyze the demographics of their target audiences. For example, companies like Levi Strauss, Arby's, Consolidated Rail, and Federal Express use GIS packages to integrate maps, graphics, and other geographic data with business data from spreadsheets and statistical packages. GIS software such as MapInfo and Atlas GIS is used for most business GIS applications [36].

Figure 6.11

Examples of special-purpose DSS packages.

DSS Packages

- **Retail:** Information Advantage and Unisys offer the Category Management Solution Suite, an OLAP decision support system and industry-specific data model.

- **Insurance:** Computer Associates offers RiskAdvisor, an insurance risk decision support system whose data model stores information in insurance industry specific tables designed for optimal query performance.

- **Telecom:** NCR and SABRE Decision Technologies have joined forces to create the NCR Customer Retention program for the communications industry including data marts for telephone companies to use for decision support in managing customer loyalty, quality of service, network management, fraud, and marketing.

Source: Adapted from Charles B. Darling, "Ease Implementation Woes with Packaged Data Marts," *Datamation*, March 1997, p. 103. © 1997 by Cahners Publishing Co.

Data visualization systems represent complex data using interactive three-dimensional graphical forms such as charts, graphs, and maps. DVS tools help users to interactively sort, subdivide, combine, and organize data while it is in its graphical form. This helps users discover patterns, links, and anomalies in business or scientific data in an interactive knowledge discovery and decision support process. Business applications like data mining typically use interactive graphs that let users drill down in real time and manipulate the underlying data of a business model to help clarify its meaning for business decision making. [15, 28]. Figure 6.12 is an example of business data displayed by a data visualization system.

OshKosh B'Gosh Uses Data Visualization	OshKosh B'Gosh, Inc., the Oshkosh, Wis.-based maker of children's clothing, uses the data visualization tools built into Cognos PowerPlay DSS software. Visualizing data helps them pinpoint data anomalies and intuitively see what's happening in their business data. The tools have been particularly helpful for analyzing canceled orders and returns. Business analysts drill into graphs and models to see the underlying cause of their results. "Say, for example, we're getting lots of items returned from retailers," says CIO Jon Dell'Antonia. "We can drill into the visual model for the data about what plants made the items that are being returned. If they primarily came from one plant, then we may have a manufacturing problem. But if the returns are coming primarily from one retailer, then we know we don't have a product quality issue, but instead might need to talk to that customer. This type of analysis used to take us days and days to do. Now it can take minutes" [15].

Using Decision Support Systems

Using a decision support system involves an interactive **analytical modeling** process. For example, using a DSS software package for decision support may result in a series of displays in response to alternative what-if changes entered by a manager.

Figure 6.12

Displays of business data for sales analysis by a data visualization system.

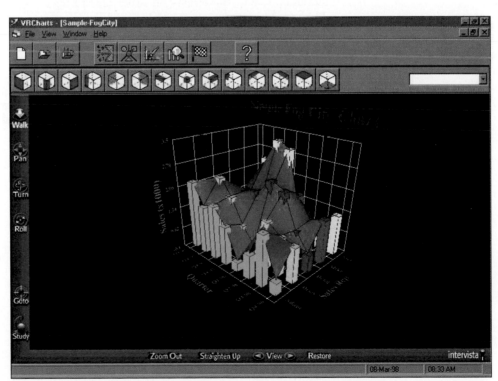

Courtesy of AlterVue Systems, Inc. (www.vrcharts.com).

This differs from the demand responses of management information systems, since decision makers are not demanding prespecified information. Rather, they are exploring possible alternatives. Thus, they do not have to specify their information needs in advance. Instead, they use the DSS to find the information they need to help them make a decision. That is the essence of the decision support system concept.

Using a decision support system involves four basic types of analytical modeling activities: (1) what-if analysis, (2) sensitivity analysis, (3) goal-seeking analysis, and (4) optimization analysis. Let's briefly look at each type of analytical modeling that can be used for decision support. See Figure 6.13.

What-If Analysis

In **what-if analysis,** an end user makes changes to variables, or relationships among variables, and observes the resulting changes in the values of other variables. For example, if you were using a spreadsheet, you might change a revenue amount (a variable) or a tax rate formula (a relationship among variables) in a simple financial spreadsheet model. Then you could command the spreadsheet program to instantly recalculate all affected variables in the spreadsheet. A managerial user would be very interested in observing and evaluating any changes that occurred to the values in the spreadsheet, especially to a variable such as net profit after taxes. To many managers, net profit after taxes is an example of *the bottom line*, that is, a key factor in making many types of decisions. This type of analysis would be repeated until the manager was satisfied with what the results revealed about the effects of various possible decisions. Figure 6.14 is an example of what-if analysis.

Sensitivity Analysis

Sensitivity analysis is a special case of what-if analysis. Typically, the value of only one variable is changed repeatedly, and the resulting changes on other variables are observed. So sensitivity analysis is really a case of what-if analysis involving repeated changes to only one variable at a time. Some DSS packages automatically make repeated small changes to a variable when asked to perform sensitivity analysis. Typically, sensitivity analysis is used when decision makers are uncertain about the assumptions made in estimating the value of certain key variables. In our previous spreadsheet example, the value of revenue could be changed repeatedly in small increments, and the effects on other spreadsheet variables observed and evaluated. This would help a manager understand the impact of various revenue levels on other factors involved in decisions being considered.

Figure 6.13

Activities and examples of the major types of analytical modeling.

Type of Analytical Modeling	Activities and Examples
What-if analysis	Observing how changes to selected variables affect other variables. *Example:* What if we cut advertising by 10 percent? What would happen to sales?
Sensitivity analysis	Observing how repeated changes to a single variable affect other variables. *Example:* Let's cut advertising by $100 repeatedly so we can see its relationship to sales.
Goal-seeking analysis	Making repeated changes to selected variables until a chosen variable reaches a target value. *Example:* Let's try increases in advertising until sales reach $1 million.
Optimization analysis	Finding an optimum value for selected variables, given certain constraints. *Example:* What's the best amount of advertising to have, given our budget and choice of media?

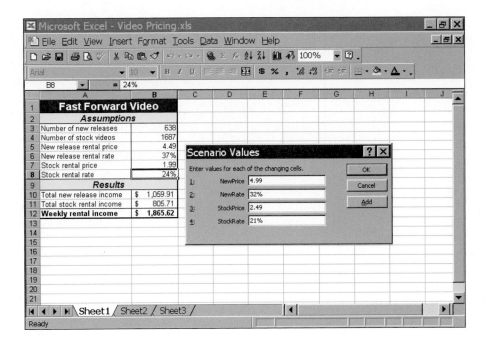

Figure 6.14

What-if analysis involves the development of alternative scenarios based on changing assumptions as part of the decision-making process.

Goal-Seeking Analysis

Goal-seeking analysis reverses the direction of the analysis done in what-if and sensitivity analysis. Instead of observing how changes in a variable affect other variables, goal-seeking analysis (also called *how can* analysis) sets a target value (a goal) for a variable and then repeatedly changes other variables until the target value is achieved. For example, you could specify a target value (goal) of $2 million for net profit after taxes for a business venture. Then you could repeatedly change the value of revenue or expenses in a spreadsheet model until a result of $2 million is achieved. Thus, you would discover what amount of revenue or level of expenses the business venture needs to achieve in order to reach the goal of $2 million in after-tax profits. Therefore, this form of analytical modeling would help answer the question, "How can we achieve $2 million in net profit after taxes?" instead of the question, "What happens if we change revenue or expenses?" Thus, goal-seeking analysis is another important method of decision support.

Optimization Analysis

Optimization analysis is a more complex extension of goal-seeking analysis. Instead of setting a specific target value for a variable, the goal is to find the optimum value for one or more target variables, given certain constraints. Then one or more other variables are changed repeatedly, subject to the specified constraints, until the best values for the target variables are discovered. For example, you could try to determine the highest possible level of profits that could be achieved by varying the values for selected revenue sources and expense categories. Changes to such variables could be subject to constraints such as the limited capacity of a production process or limits to available financing. Optimization typically is accomplished by special-purpose software packages for optimization techniques such as linear programming, or by advanced DSS generators.

Lexis-Nexis: Web Tools for Decision Support

"Our new subscribers will grow geometrically with Web-based access to our information services," explains Keith Hawk, vice president of sales for the Nexis division of Lexis-Nexis. "And therefore our business model is changing from selling primarily to organizations to selling to individual users." To track their 1.7

million subscribers of legal and news documents, Lexis-Nexis replaced its old decision support system with new DSS tools and an NCR Teradata data warehouse system. The new customer data warehouse lets 475 salespeople and in-house analysts use the corporate intranet and Web browsers to look up daily detailed customer usage data.

The type of data that the company's salespeople sort through and analyze includes subscriber usage patterns—what they look up, what sources they use most often, when they're connecting—along with customer contract details. To get to that data, Lexis-Nexis uses decision support software from MicroStrategy Inc. Field sales representatives who need ad hoc reporting capabilities use MicroStrategy DSS WebPE, a Web-based reporting tool. Power users, such as market research analysis, use DSS Agent, an analytical modeling tool with Web access, to closely analyze and model business processes [16, 24].

Data Mining for Decision Support

We discuss data mining and data warehouses in Chapter 13 as applications of data resource management. However, data mining's main purpose is knowledge discovery leading to decision support. Data mining software analyzes the vast stores of historical business data that have been prepared for analysis in corporate data warehouses. Data mining attempts to discover patterns, trends, and correlations hidden in the data that can give a company a strategic business advantage.

Data mining software may perform regression, decision tree, neural network, cluster detection, or market basket analysis for a business. See Figure 6.15. The data mining process can highlight buying patterns, reveal customer tendencies, cut redundant costs, or uncover unseen profitable relationships and opportunities. For example, many companies use data mining to find more profitable ways to perform successful direct mailings, including E-mailings, or to discover better ways to display products in a store, design a better E-commerce website, reach untapped profitable customers, or recognize customers or products that are unprofitable or marginal [18].

Key Corp. and Peoples Bank: Data Mining DSS

Quick payback and support for some surprising, counterintuitive decisions have been among the benefits early users found with IBM's DecisionEdge for Relationship Marketing decision support software. "We had a full return on our investment 14 months after installing the data mining component," said Jo Ann Boylan, an executive vice president in the Key Technology Service division at Key Corp., the nation's 13th largest retail bank with 7 million customers. She added that the data mining and analysis system helped raise the bank's direct-mail response rate from 1 to as high as 10 percent. It also helped identify unprofitable product lines.

The DecisionEdge decision support package includes application suites, analytical tools, a mining data tool, industry-specific data models, and consulting services. Pricing begins at around $150,000.

Peoples Bank & Trust Co. in Indianapolis used the DecisionEdge for Relationship Marketing to delve into some highly profitable bank offerings that turned out to be prohibitively expensive, said Bob Connors, a senior vice president of information services. The DSS pointed out how much it actually costs to bring in each highly profitable home equity loan customer. "Because those loans can be so profitable, it seems like a no-brainer that you'd want to market them," Connors explained. "But we found that the costs to bring them in were far too high, so we've cut way back on that spending. We still offer the loans, but we don't spend so much on advertising or direct mail any more" [17].

Figure 6.15

A display of a data mining software package.

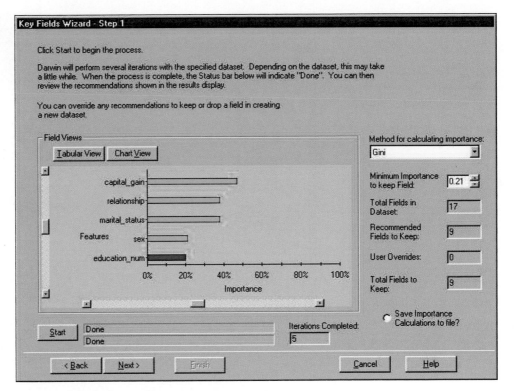

Courtesy of Oracle Corporation.

Executive Information Systems

Executive information systems (EIS) are information systems that combine many of the features of management information systems and decision support systems. When they were first developed, their focus was on meeting the strategic information needs of top management. Thus, the first goal of executive information systems was to provide top executives with immediate and easy access to information about a firm's *critical success factors* (CSFs), that is, key factors that are critical to accomplishing an organization's strategic objectives. For example, the executives of a retail store chain would probably consider factors such as its E-commerce versus traditional sales results, or its product line mix to be critical to its survival and success.

However, executive information systems are becoming so widely used by managers, analysts, and other knowledge workers that they are sometimes humorously called "everyone's information systems." More popular alternative names are enterprise information systems (EIS) and executive support systems (ESS). These names also reflect the fact that more features, such as Web browsing, electronic mail, groupware tools, and DSS and expert system capabilities, are being added to many systems to make them more useful to managers and business professionals [23, 25, 50].

In an EIS, information is presented in forms tailored to the preferences of the executives using the system. For example, most executive information systems stress the use of a graphical user interface and graphics displays that can be customized to the information preferences of executives using the EIS. Other information presentation methods used by an EIS include exception reporting and trend analysis. The ability to *drill down*, which allows executives to quickly retrieve displays of related information at lower levels of detail, is another important capability. And of course, the growth of Internet and intranet technologies has added Web browsing to the list of EIS capabilities.

Figure 6.16 shows an actual display provided by the Hyperion executive information system. Notice how simple and brief this display is. Also note how it provides

Figure 6.16

Displays provided by an executive information system. Note the simplicity and clarity in which key information is provided, and the ability to drill down to lower levels of detail.

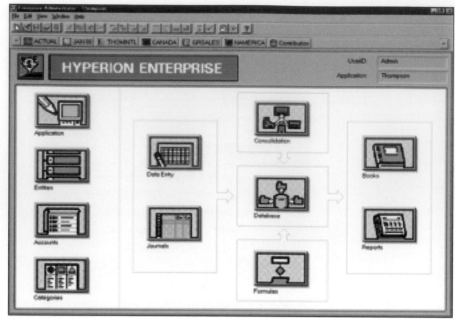

Courtesy of Comshare, Inc.

users of the system with the ability to drill down quickly to lower levels of detail in areas of particular interest to them. Beside the drill-down capability, the Hyperion EIS also stresses trend analysis and exception reporting. Thus, a business user can quickly discover the direction key factors are heading and the extent to which critical factors are deviating from expected results [53].

EIS have spread into the ranks of middle management and business professionals as they recognized their feasibility and benefits, and as less-expensive systems for client/server networks and corporate intranets became available. For example, one popular EIS software package reports that only 3 percent of its users are top executives. Another example is the EIS of Conoco, one of the world's largest oil companies. Conoco's EIS is used by most senior managers, and by over 4,000 employees located at corporate headquarters in Houston and throughout the world [4, 51, 54].

EIS at Conoco and KeyCorp

As we just mentioned, Conoco, Inc., has a widely used EIS. Conoco's EIS is a large system with 75 different applications and hundreds of screen displays. Senior executives and over 4,000 managers and analysts worldwide use EIS applications ranging from analyzing internal operations and financial results to viewing external events that affect the petroleum industry. Conoco's EIS is popular with its users and has resulted in improved employee productivity and decision making, and significant cost savings compared to alternative methods of generating information for managers and analysts [4].

KeyCorp is a large banking and financial services holding company. It developed Keynet, a corporate intranet that transformed their mainframe-based EIS into a new EIS—a Web-enabled system they call "everyone's information system." Now more than 1,000 managers and analysts have web access to 40 major business information areas within Keynet, ranging from sales and financial statistics to human resource management.

Enterprise Portals and Decision Support

Don't confuse portals with the executive information systems that have been used in some industries for many years. Portals are for everyone in the company, and not just for executives. You want people on the front lines making decisions using browsers and portals rather than just executives using specialized executive information system software [45].

We began this chapter by observing that major changes and expansion are taking place in traditional MIS, DSS, and EIS tools for providing the information and modeling managers need to support their decision making. Decision support in business is changing, driven by rapid developments in end user computing and networking; Internet, Web browser, and related technologies, and the explosion of E-commerce activity. The growth of corporate intranets, extranets, as well as the Web, has accelerated the development and use of "executive class" information delivery and decision support software tools by lower levels of management and by individuals and teams of business professionals. In addition, the dramatic expansion of E-commerce has opened the door to the use of such E-business DSS tools by the suppliers, customers, and other business stakeholders of a company for customer relationship management, supply chain management, and other E-business applications.

Enterprise Information Portals

Figure 6.17 illustrates how companies are developing **enterprise information portals** as a way to provide Web-enabled information, knowledge, and decision support to their executives, managers, employees, suppliers, customers, and other business partners. We introduced the enterprise information portal (EIP) in Chapter 3 as a customized and personalized Web-based interface for corporate intranets, which gives users easy access to a variety of internal and external business applications, databases, and services. For example, the EIP in Figure 6.17 might give a qualified user secure access to DSS, data mining, and OLAP tools, the Internet and the Web, the corporate intranet, supplier or customer extranets, operational and analytical databases, a data warehouse, and a variety of business applications [43, 44, 45].

Amway, Inc.: Using an EIP

Amway, the direct-sales organization based in Ada, Michigan, turned to an enterprise information portal to address problems associated with managing its distributed computing environment. Basically, the various systems it had adopted over the years to contend with the company's growth weren't integrated, and the steady pace of software upgrades was resulting in a lower return on investment.

Amway began to search for a way to integrate the systems and provide tailored retrieval from multiple information resources. These resources included IBM mainframe-based document management and planning systems, Sybase database tables stored in the corporate data warehouse, customer client/server-based financial applications and various other locally managed applications.

The primary goal of the new EIP—a Web-based Lotus Notes and Domino groupware application—is to reduce the time spent logging onto multiple applications and switching from one to another to retrieve product information. "Our objective is to shave the weekly workload for our scientists, engineers, and managers by reducing the time spent wading through existing systems trying to find information we already know about our products," Steve Klemm, director of engineering R&D, explains.

Now, freed from logging onto multiple systems to produce routine reports and updates, most of the current users report that they're saving a significant amount of time each week. "The information delivered by Artemis is tailored for our use, which allows us to focus more of our time on developing better products for our customers," says Klemm [57].

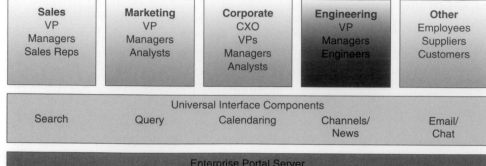

Figure 6.17

The components of this enterprise information portal identify it as an E-business decision support system that can be personalized for executives, managers, employees, suppliers, customers, and other business partners.

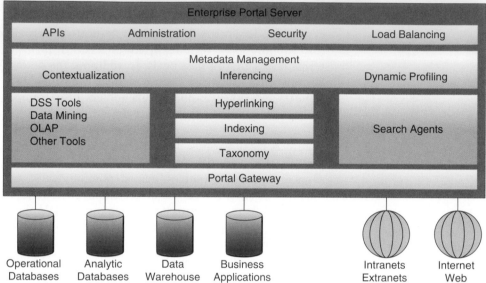

Source: Adapted from Gerry Murray, "Making Connections with Enterprise Knowledge Portals," White Paper, *Computerworld*, September 6, 1999, p. 6. Copyright 1999 by Computerworld, Inc., Framingham, MA 01701. Reprinted from *Computerworld*.

Enterprise Knowledge Portals

It should also be emphasized that an enterprise information portal is the entry to corporate intranets that serve as the primary **knowledge management systems** for many companies. That's why they are called **enterprise knowledge portals** by some vendors. We introduced knowledge management systems in Chapters 2 and 3 as the use of information technology to help gather, organize, and share business knowledge within an organization. In many organizations, hypermedia databases at corporate intranet websites have become the *knowledge bases* for storage and dissemination of business knowledge. This frequently takes the form of best practices, policies, and business solutions at the project, team, business unit, and enterprise levels of the company. Thus, the enterprise knowledge portal can play a major role in helping a company use its intranets as knowledge management systems to share and disseminate knowledge in support of its business decision making [29, 43]. See Figure 6.18.

Shiva Corporation: Web Knowledge Management

Shiva Corporation is in the business of connecting employees, customers, and partners to business networks via remote access technology. Using Verity's Information Server and CD-Web Publisher software, Shiva built a knowledge management application for their corporate intranet and company site on the Web. The solution provides customers and employees with Web-based answers to their technical support questions, access to online peer groups, CD-ROM-based product documentation, and a quarterly CD-ROM containing time-saving information.

The Knowledge Management solution took three months to develop. Within 45 days of use, it surpassed its financial break-even point. Shiva experienced a 22 percent drop in customer support calls in the first three months. Shiva's Knowledgebase area is now the second-most-accessed section of the company's website, with 110,000 people hitting the site every month, including Shiva's 500-plus employees worldwide, most of whom access the site through the corporate intranet.

Shiva's knowledgebase is updated primarily by the company's technical support and engineering departments, although anyone in the company can enter a knowledgebase article into the system via the corporate intranet. It then becomes accessible to everyone else on the company's intranet before being placed on the Web. Within the Knowledge Management application, the Lotus Notes knowledgebase is converted to HTML and uploaded to a server. Then, the Verity software indexes all of the available documents and ties all the information together, where it's available to customers via the Web.

The Knowledge Management application has helped foster a corporate culture in which technical information is shared fully via the company intranet and site on the Web, rather than kept under lock and key. In-house staff can track common technical problems and determine what areas need improvement. And customers can obtain instant answers to their questions [29].

Figure 6.18   An example of the capabilities and components of an enterprise knowledge portal.

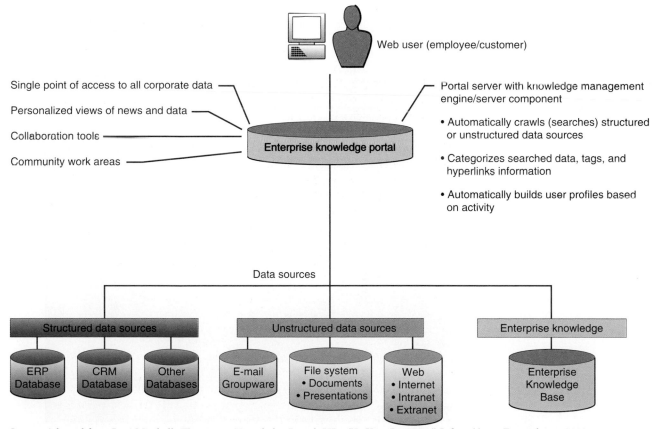

Source: Adapted from Lori Mitchell, "Enterprise Knowledge Portals Wise Up Your Business," *Infoworld.com*, December 1, 2000.

Artificial Intelligence Technologies in Business

Artificial intelligence is making its way back to the mainstream of corporate technology. Designed to leverage the capabilities of humans rather than replace them, today's AI technology enables an extraordinary array of applications that forge new connections among people, computers, knowledge, and the physical world. AI-enabled applications are at work in information distribution and retrieval, database mining, product design, manufacturing, inspection, training, user support, surgical planning, resource scheduling, and complex resource management.

Indeed, for anyone who schedules, plans, allocates resources, designs new products, uses the Internet, develops software, is responsible for product quality, is an investment professional, heads up IT, uses IT, or operates in any of a score of other capacities and arenas, new AI technologies already may be in place and providing competitive advantage [56].

Analyzing RivalWatch.com and Others

Read the Real World Case on RivalWatch.com and others on the next page. We can learn a lot about the business value of using the Internet and artificial intelligence technologies from this example. See Figure 6.19.

Companies are using the Internet and competitive intelligence (CI) software tools to gather information on their competitors' traditional business and E-commerce activities. This is especially important in the dynamic world of E-commerce, where the customers of online businesses are only a few mouse clicks away from comparing prices, product features, and deals with those of other business competitors. So

Figure 6.19

Ann Hsu is a co-founder of RivalWatch.com and vice president of business development for its competitive intelligence Web-based services.

Jenny Thomas.

RivalWatch.com and Others: AI Tools for Competitive Business Intelligence

Gathering competitive intelligence over the Internet is a deadly serious game that can be played in many ways. There's a wealth of information readily available, and it can offer a surprising amount of insight into the competition's next move. Savvy companies are keeping close tables on competitors in a variety of ways.

Ross Stapleton-Gray is the head of competitive intelligence at Sandstorm Enterprises, a Cambridge, Massachusetts–based computer security firm. His job is to watch companies whose products might knock Sandstorm's out of the market. He spends his days trolling the Internet for often small bits of information that might add up to deeper insights. He says that the marketplace is responding to the need for competitive intelligence. Websites that focus on providing specialized data are popping up, along with products that help people search the Internet for information about rivals.

John Fisk is director of business development at Caesius Software, a Seattle company that has developed a web-searching tool called WebQL. The product is a sophisticated pattern recognition engine that will download a collection of web pages and search for particular patterns. "The functions or commands are based on a combination of Perl and other expressions to find patterns in the HTML," he explains.

Fisk says that some Fortune 500 companies use his tool to watch their competitors. "Let's say you had a retail site out there and you were competing with the big brick-and-mortar and on-line sites. We've already written queries that track the product mix, the price or the percentage discounts. We can categorize it by stock-keeping units or product or anything," he says.

Another firm, RivalWatch.com in Santa Clara, California, has proprietary software that downloads information for its customers from competitors' web sites and then produces reports. RivalWatch focuses on adding some analysis and presenting the data in a useful form. It specializes in surveying digital commerce sites so customers can be sure they're pricing items competitively. "We present the data in a form [that let's you] make a business decision," says Ann Hsu, vice president for business development and a co-founder of RivalWatch. "Just giving you a spreadsheet with the prices of 10,000 products is not helpful. Only 5,000 may direct overlap with your site, and out of these, we summarize the price differences.

Hsu says the Web has tipped the scales in the consumers' favor and has forced e-retail sites to rethink their business models. Consumers know where to get the best deals. Hsu says brick-and-mortars and internet pure-lays are playing catch-up. Collecting competitive intelligence is one way to narrow the gap. "The sellers need to know as much as the buyers know, so they don't lose out without knowing why," Hsu says. "In any business, everybody keeps an eye on the competition. RivalWatch will help retailers deal with information that is in high volume and dynamic."

Although some potential clients have bristled at RivalWatch's flat fee—$150,000 for a one-year subscription—Hsu says that collecting this level of competitive intelligence would require businesses to dedicate staff to this purpose, which in her opinion, would be less comprehensive and more costly than RivalWatch. The Santa Clara, California company's customers include national pharmacy chain Eckerd drugs and outdoor sporting good supplier Recreational Equipment Incorporated (REI).

RivalWatch's main offering is called the eMerchandising Platform for retailers, which breaks into three main categories—product assortment analysis, pricing analysis and promotions analysis. This enables clients to compare its assortment, pricing, quantity and promotions of selected products with those of its competitors. For the same subscription fee RivalWatch also offers a manufacturing version of the service, which uses the above categories to track manufacturers' products in retail stores.

Before RivalWatch can go to work, clients must set their parameters: which products or categories to monitor, which websites to search, how often to search (daily, weekly, monthly) and what kind of reporting to be done. Setup may take anywhere from a few days to four weeks. RivalWatch's software, which uses web crawler/spider technology (programs that perform automated searches on the Web), scours websites for this information, analyzes it with the aid of artificial intelligence routines, and formats the data into a customized or canned report, which can be accessed through the client's interface at a RivalWatch.com secured website.

Of course, gathering and reporting the data is only half of the formula. The rest is up to you. "We provide the information," Hsu says. "You're the expert in your field. You should now what to do with it."

Case Study Questions

1. How do WebQL and RivalWatch gather competitive intelligence? Visit the caesius.com and rivalwatch.com websites to help you answer.

2. Which product would you prefer for gathering competitive business information? Why?

3. Do you have any reservations about the use of such competitive intelligence products as a business professional? As a consumer? Explain.

Source: Adapted from Jon Surmacz, "RivalWatch.com," *darwinmag.com*, January 24, 2001, and Peter Wayner, "I Spy," *Computerworld*, February 5, 2001, pp. 60–61.

several Fortune 500 companies and retailers like Eckerd Drugs and REI are using Web-based competitive intelligence software tools and services with artificial intelligence (AI) features like WebOL from Caesius Software, and eMerchandising Platform from RivalWatch.com. These tools can scour the websites of competitors for information on products, pricing, and promotions being offered each day, and analyze them using sophisticated pattern recognition and other AI technologies. Caesius sells WebOL as a CI software product to large companies, while RivalWatch offers its CI technology as an expensive web-based service. For example, RivalWatch subscribers can check a secure website at any time for the latest information on the competitors' E-commerce activities.

An Overview of Artificial Intelligence

What is artificial intelligence? **Artificial intelligence** (AI) is a field of science and technology based on disciplines such as computer science, biology, psychology, linguistics, mathematics, and engineering. The goal of AI is to develop computers that can think, as well as see, hear, walk, talk, and feel. A major thrust of artificial intelligence is the development of computer functions normally associated with human intelligence, such as reasoning, learning, and problem solving, as summarized in Figure 6.20. That's why the term *artificial intelligence* was coined by John McCarthy at MIT in 1956. Besides McCarthy, AI pioneers included Herbert Simon and Allen Newell at Carnegie-Mellon, Norbert Wiener and Marvin Minsky at MIT, Warren McCulloch and Walter Pitts at Illinois, Frank Rosenblatt at Cornell, Alan Turing at Manchester, Edward Feigenbaum at Stanford, Roger Shank at Yale, and many others.

Debate was raged around artificial intelligence since serious work in the field began in the 1950s. Not only technological, but moral and philosophical questions abound about the possibility of intelligent, thinking machines. For example, British AI pioneer Alan Turing in 1950 proposed a test for determining if machines could think. According to the Turing test, a computer could demonstrate intelligence if a human interviewer, conversing with an unseen human and an unseen computer, could not tell which was which [37, 50].

Though much work has been done in many of the subgroups that fall under the AI umbrella, critics believe that no computer can truly pass the Turing test. They claim that developing intelligence to impart true humanlike capabilities to computers is simply not possible. But progress continues, and only time will tell if the ambitious goals of artificial intelligence will be achieved and equal the popular images found in science fiction.

The Domains of Artificial Intelligence

Figure 6.21 illustrates the major domains of AI research and development. Note that AI applications can be grouped under three major areas: cognitive science, robotics, and natural interfaces, though these classifications do overlap each other, and other

---

Figure 6.20

Some of the attributes of intelligent behavior. AI is attempting to duplicate these capabilities in computer-based systems.

Attributes of Intelligent Behavior
● Think and reason.
● Use reason to solve problems.
● Learn or understand from experience.
● Acquire and apply knowledge.
● Exhibit creativity and imagination.
● Deal with complex or perplexing situations.
● Respond quickly and successfully to new situations.
● Recognize the relative importance of elements in a situation.
● Handle ambiguous, incomplete, or erroneous information.

Figure 6.21

The major application areas of artificial intelligence. Note that the many applications of AI can be grouped into the three major areas of cognitive science, robotics, and natural interfaces.

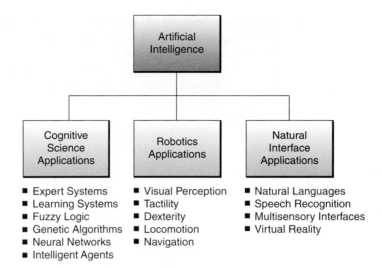

classifications can be used. Also note that expert systems are just one of many important AI applications. Let's briefly review each of these major areas of AI and some of their current technologies. Figure 6.22 outlines some of the latest developments in commercial applications of artificial intelligence.

Figure 6.22

Examples of some of the latest commercial applications of AI.

Commercial Applications of AI
Decision Support
• Intelligent work environment that will help you capture the *why* as well as the *what* of engineered design and decision making
• Intelligent human-computer interface (HCI) systems that can understand spoken language and gestures, and facilitate problem solving by supporting organizationwide collaborations to solve particular problems
• Situation assessment and resource allocation software for uses that range from airlines and airports to logistics centers
Information Retrieval
• AI-based intra- and Internet systems that distill tidal waves of information into simple presentations
• Natural language technology to retrieve any sort of online information, from text to pictures, videos, maps, and audio clips, in response to English questions
• Database mining for marketing trend analysis, financial forecasting, maintenance cost reduction, and more
Virtual Reality
• X-ray-like vision enabled by enhanced-reality visualization that allows brain surgeons to "see through" intervening tissue to operate, monitor, and evaluate disease progression
• Automated animation and haptic interfaces that allow users to interact with virtual objects via touch (i.e., medical students can "feel" what it's like to suture severed aortas)
Robotics
• Machine vision inspections systems for gauging, guiding, identifying, and inspecting products and providing competitive advantage in manufacturing
• Cutting-edge robotics systems from micro robots and hands and legs to cognitive robotic and trainable modular vision systems

Source: Adapted from Patrick Winston, "Rethinking Artificial Intelligence," Program Announcement: Massachusetts Institute of Technology, September 1997, p. 3.

Cognitive Science. This area of artificial intelligence is based on research in biology, neurology, psychology, mathematics, and many allied disciplines. It focuses on researching how the human brain works and how humans think and learn. The results of such research in *human information processing* are the basis for the development of a variety of computer-based applications in artificial intelligence.

Applications in the cognitive science area of AI include the development of *expert systems* and other *knowledge-based systems* that add a knowledge base and some reasoning capability to information systems. Also included are *adaptive learning systems* that can modify their behaviors based on information they acquire as they operate. Chess-playing systems are primitive examples of such applications, though many more applications are being implemented. *Fuzzy logic* systems can process data that are incomplete or ambiguous, that is, *fuzzy data*. Thus, they can solve unstructured problems with incomplete knowledge by developing approximate inferences and answers, as humans do. *Neural network* software can learn by processing sample problems and their solutions. As neural nets start to recognize patterns, they can begin to program themselves to solve such problems on their own. *Genetic algorithm* software uses Darwinian (survival of the fittest), randomizing, and other mathematics functions to simulate evolutionary processes that can generate increasingly better solutions to problems. And *intelligent agents* use expert system and other AI technologies to serve as software surrogates for a variety of end user applications.

Robotics. AI, engineering, and physiology are the basic disciplines of robotics. This technology produces robot machines with computer intelligence and computer-controlled, humanlike physical capabilities. This area thus includes applications designed to give robots the powers of sight, or visual perception; touch, or tactile capabilities; dexterity, or skill in handling and manipulation; locomotion, or the physical ability to move over any terrain; and navigation, or the intelligence to properly find one's way to a destination [37]. The use of robotics in computer-aided manufacturing was discussed in Chapter 4.

Natural Interfaces. The development of natural interfaces is considered a major area of AI applications and is essential to the natural use of computers by humans. For example, the development of *natural languages* and speech recognition are major thrusts of this area of AI. Being able to talk to computers and robots in conversational human languages and have them "understand" us as easily as we understand each other is a goal of AI research. This involves research and development in linguistics, psychology, computer science, and other disciplines. This area of AI drives developments in the voice recognition and response technology discussed in Chapter 11 and the natural programming languages discussed in Chapter 12. Other natural interface research applications include the development of multisensory devices that use a variety of body movements to operate computers. This is related to the emerging application area of *virtual reality*. Virtual reality involves using multisensory human-computer interfaces that enable human users to experience computer-simulated objects, spaces, activities, and "worlds" as if they actually exist.

Neural Networks

Neural networks are computing systems modeled after the brain's meshlike network of interconnected processing elements, called *neurons*. Of course, neural networks are a lot simpler in architecture (the human brain is estimated to have over 100 billion neuron brain cells!). However, like the brain, the interconnected processors in a neural network operate in parallel and interact dynamically with each other. This enables the network to "learn" from data it processes. That is, it learns to recognize patterns and relationships in the data it processes. The more data examples it receives as input, the better it can learn to duplicate the results of the examples it processes. Thus, the neural network will change the strengths of the interconnections between the processing elements in response to changing patterns in the data it receives and the results that occur [8, 50].

For example, a neural network can be trained to learn which credit characteristics result in good or bad loans. Developers of a credit evaluation neural network could provide it with data from many examples of credit applications and loan results to process, and opportunities to adjust the signal strengths between its neurons. The neural network would continue to be trained until it demonstrated a high degree of accuracy in correctly duplicating the results of recent cases. At that point it would be trained enough to begin making credit evaluations of its own.

Neural networks can be implemented on microcomputers and other traditional computer systems by using software packages that simulate the activity of a neural network. Specialized neural network coprocessor circuit boards for PCs are also available that provide significantly greater processing power. In addition, special-purpose neural net microprocessor chips are being used in specific application areas such as military weapons systems, image processing, and voice recognition. However, most business applications depend primarily on neural net software packages to accomplish applications ranging from credit risk assessment to check signature verification, investment forecasting, data mining, and manufacturing quality control [8, 55]. See Figure 6.23.

Neural Nets at Infoseek	Infoseek has developed a targeted marketing service that more closely targets advertising on its Internet search engine to users' interests by keeping track of every search that a user makes. The service uses neural network technology from Aptex Software to observe all the searches users run every time they visit the Infoseek search engine. The neural net software then calculates a numeric value, or "vector," that describes users' interests. Infoseek uses that information to match users to the online ads it sells to advertisers on its Web search pages.

Other commercial World Wide Web sites use this technology to build up the usefulness of their websites or encourage repeat business. Many electronic commerce websites use customizing software to track user behavior and predict what a user will be interested in seeing in the future. For example, Aptex has a version of its neural net software designed for sites that sell products and services online. Select Cast for Commerce Servers analyzes customer buying patterns, and predicts products and services the customer will be likely to buy, based on past behavior [52]. |

Fuzzy Logic Systems

In spite of the funny name, **fuzzy logic** systems represent a small, but serious and growing, application of AI in business. Fuzzy logic is a method of reasoning that resembles human reasoning since it allows for approximate values and inferences (fuzzy logic) and incomplete or ambiguous data (fuzzy data) instead of relying only on *crisp data*, such as binary (yes/no) choices. For example, Figure 6.24 illustrates a partial set of rules (fuzzy rules) and a fuzzy SQL query for analyzing and extracting credit risk information on businesses that are being evaluated for selection as investments.

Notice how fuzzy logic uses terminology that is deliberately imprecise, such as *very high, increasing, somewhat decreased, reasonable*, and *very low*. This enables fuzzy systems to process incomplete data and quickly provide approximate, but acceptable, solutions to problems that are difficult for other methods to solve. Fuzzy logic queries of a database, such as the SQL query shown in Figure 6.24, promise to improve the extraction of data from business databases. Queries can be stated more naturally in words that are closer to the way business specialists think about the topic for which they want information [11, 31].

Fuzzy Logic in Business

Examples of applications of fuzzy logic are numerous in Japan, but rare in the United States. The United States has tended to prefer using AI solutions like expert systems

Figure 6.23

A display of a data mining software package that uses neural network technology.

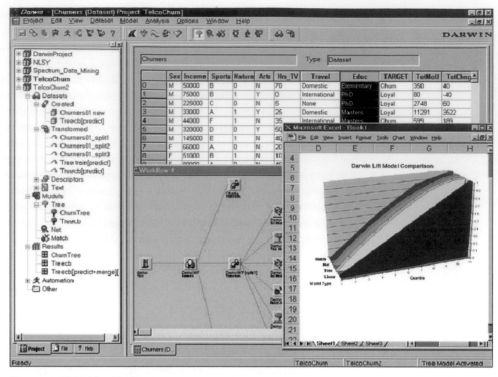

Courtesy of Thinking Machines.

or neural networks. But Japan has implemented many fuzzy logic applications, especially the use of special-purpose fuzzy logic microprocessor chips, called fuzzy process controllers. Thus, the Japanese ride on subway trains, use elevators, and drive cars that are guided or supported by fuzzy process controllers made by Hitachi and Toshiba. They can even trade shares on the Tokyo Stock Exchange using a stock-trading program based on fuzzy logic rules. Many new models of Japanese-made products also feature fuzzy logic microprocessors. The list is growing, but includes auto-focus cameras, auto-stabilizing camcorders, energy-efficient air conditioners, self-adjusting washing machines, and automatic transmissions [42].

Figure 6.24

An example of fuzzy logic rules and a fuzzy logic SQL query in a credit risk analysis application.

Fuzzy Logic Rules

Risk should be acceptable
If debt-equity is very high
   then risk is positively increased
If income is increasing
   then risk is somewhat decreased
If cash reserves are low to very low
   then risk is very increased
If PE ratio is good
   then risk is generally decreased

Fuzzy Logic SQL Query

Select companies
  from financials
     where revenues are very large
     and pe_ratio is acceptable
     and profits are high to very high
     and (income/employee_tot) is reasonable

Genetic Algorithms

The use of **genetic algorithms** is a growing application of artificial intelligence. Genetic algorithm software uses Darwinian (survival of the fittest), randomizing, and other mathematical functions to simulate an evolutionary process that can yield increasingly better solutions to a problem. Genetic algorithms were first used to simulate millions of years in biological, geological, and ecosystem evolution in just a few minutes on a computer. Now genetic algorithm software is being used to model a variety of scientific, technical, and business processes [3, 26].

Genetic algorithms are especially useful for situations in which thousands of solutions are possible and must be evaluated to produce an optimal solution. Genetic algorithm software uses sets of mathematical process rules *(algorithms)* that specify how combinations of process components or steps are to be formed. This may involve trying random process combinations *(mutation)*, combining parts of several good processes *(crossover)*, and selecting good sets of processes and discarding poor ones *(selection)* in order to generate increasingly better solutions. Figure 6.25 illustrates a business use of genetic algorithm software.

GE's Engeneous

General Electric's design of a more efficient jet engine for the Boeing 777 is a classic example of a genetic algorithm application in business. A major engineering challenge was to develop more efficient fan blades for the engine. GE's engineers estimated that it would take billions of years, even with a supercomputer, to mathematically evaluate the astronomical number of performance and cost factors and combinations involved. Instead, GE used a hybrid genetic algorithm/expert system, called Engeneous, that produced an optimal solution in less than a week [3].

Figure 6.25

Using genetic algorithm software for business problem solving.

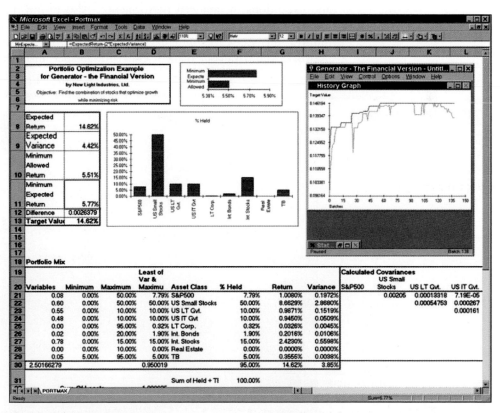

Courtesy of New Light Industries.

Virtual Reality

Virtual reality (VR) is a computer-simulated reality. Virtual reality is a fast-growing area of artificial intelligence that had its origins in efforts to build more natural, realistic, multisensory human-computer interfaces. So virtual reality relies on multisensory input/output devices such as a tracking headset with video goggles and stereo earphones, a *data glove* or jumpsuit with fiber-optic sensors that track your body movements, and a *walker* that monitors the movement of your feet. Then you can experience computer-simulated "virtual worlds" three-dimensionally through sight, sound, and touch. Thus, virtual reality is also called *telepresence*. For example, you can enter a computer-generated virtual world, look around and observe its contents, pick up and move objects, and move around in it at will. Thus, virtual reality allows you to interact with computer-simulated objects, entities, and environments as if they actually exist [2, 48]. See Figure 6.26.

VR Applications

Current applications of virtual reality are wide ranging and include computer-aided design (CAD), medical diagnostics and treatment, scientific experimentation in many physical and biological sciences, flight simulation for training pilots and astronauts, product demonstrations, employee training, and entertainment, especially 3-D video arcade games. CAD is the most widely used industrial VR application. It enables architects and other designers to design and test electronic 3-D models of products and structures by entering the models themselves and examining, touching, and manipulating sections and parts from all angles. This scientific-visualization capability is also used by pharmaceutical and biotechnology firms to develop and observe the behavior of computerized models of new drugs and materials, and by medical researchers to develop ways for physicians to enter and examine a virtual reality of a patient's body.

VR designers are creating everything from virtual weather patterns and virtual wind tunnels to virtual cities and virtual securities markets. For example, by converting stock market and other financial data into three-dimensional graphic form, securities analysts can use VR systems to more rapidly observe and identify trends and exceptions in financial performance. Also promising are applications in information technology itself. This includes the development of 3-D models of telecommunications networks and databases. These virtual graphical representations of networks and databases make it easier for IS specialists to visualize the structure and

Figure 6.26

This environmental designer uses a virtual reality system to design the interiors of an office building.

Image Bank.

relationships of an organization's telecommunications networks and corporate databases, thus improving their design and maintenance.

VR becomes *telepresence* when users who can be anywhere in the world use VR systems to work alone or together at a remote site. Typically, this involves using a VR system to enhance the sight and touch of a human who is remotely manipulating equipment to accomplish a task. Examples range from virtual surgery, where surgeon and patient may be on either side of the globe, to the remote use of equipment in hazardous environments such as chemical plants or nuclear reactors.

VR Limitations. The use of virtual reality seems limited only by the performance and cost of its technology For example, some VR users develop *cybersickness*, such as eyestrain and motion sickness, from performance problems in the realism of VR systems. The cost of a virtual reality system is another limitation. A VR system consisting of a headset with goggles and headphones, a fiber-optic data glove, motion-sensing devices, and a powerful engineering workstation with top-quality 3-D modeling software can exceed $50,000. If you want less cumbersome devices, more realistic displays, and a more natural sense of motion in your VR world, costs can escalate into several hundred thousand dollars. CAVEs *(cave automatic virtual environments)*, virtual reality rooms that immerse you in a virtual reality experience, cost several million dollars to set up [10, 48].

Organizations such as NASA, the U.S. Department of Defense, IBM, Lockheed, Matsushita Electric, Caterpillar, and several universities are investing millions of dollars in virtual reality R&D projects involving the use of supercomputers, complex modeling software, and custom-made sensing devices. However, the cost of highly realistic multisensory VR systems is dropping each year. In the meantime some VR developers are using the VRML *(virtual reality modeling language)* to develop 3-D hypermedia graphics and animation products that provide a primitive VR experience for PC users on the World Wide Web and corporate intranets. Further advances in these and other VR technologies are expected to make virtual reality useful for a wide array of business and end user applications [2, 5, 48].

VR at Morgan Stanley	The Market Risks Department of Morgan Stanley & Co. uses Discovery virtual reality software by Visible Decisions to model risks of financial investments in varying market conditions. Discovery displays three-dimensional results using powerful Silicon Graphics workstations.
	Morgan Stanley also uses VRML (virtual reality modeling language) as a way to display the results of risk analyses in three dimensions on PCs in their corporate intranet. (VRML allows developers to create hyperlinks between 3-D objects in files and databases on the World Wide Web and corporate intranets.) 3-D results are displayed on ordinary PCs in a virtual reality experience over an intranet connection to a Sun Microsystems SPARCstation server running a Sun VRML browser. Seeing data in three dimensions and experiencing relationships among data in a virtual reality process make it easier for analysts to make intuitive connections than it would be with a 2-D chart or table of numbers [53].

Intelligent Agents

Intelligent agents are growing in popularity as a way to use artificial intelligence routines in software to help users accomplish many kinds of tasks in E-business and E-commerce. An intelligent agent is a *software surrogate* for an end user or a process that fulfills a stated need or activity. An intelligent agent uses its built-in and learned knowledge base about a person or process to make decisions and accomplish tasks in a way that fulfills the intentions of a user. Sometimes an intelligent agent is given a graphic representation or persona, such as Einstein for a science advisor, Sherlock Holmes for an information search agent, and so on. Thus, intelligent agents (also called *software robots* or "bots") are special-purpose knowledge-based information systems that accomplish specific tasks for users. Figure 6.27 summarizes major types of intelligent agents [30, 40].

One of the most well-known uses of intelligent agents is the wizards found in Microsoft Office and other software suites. These wizards are built-in capabilities that can analyze how an end user is using a software package and offer suggestions on how to complete various tasks. Thus, wizards might help you change document margins, format spreadsheet cells, query a database, or construct a graph. Wizards and other software agents are also designed to adjust to your way of using a software package so that they can anticipate when you will need their assistance. See Figure 6.28.

The use of intelligent agents is growing rapidly as a way to simplify software use, search websites on the Internet and corporate intranets, and help customers do comparison shopping among the many E-commerce sites on the Web. Intelligent agents are becoming necessary as software packages become more sophisticated and powerful, as the Internet and the World Wide Web become more vast and complex, and as information sources and E-commerce alternatives proliferate exponentially. In fact, some commentators forecast that much of the future of computing will consist of intelligent agents performing their work for users. So instead of using agents to help us accomplish computing tasks, we will be managing the performance of intelligent agents as they perform computing tasks for us [34].

Dow Jones & Co.: Intelligent Web Agents	Websites such as Amazon.com's Shop the Web, Excite's Jango.com, and MySimon's MySimon.com use intelligent agent technology to help users compare prices for fragrances, book titles, or other items on multiple sites. Other types of agents can answer E-mail, conduct intelligent searches, or help users find news reports and useful sites based on stated preferences.
	For example, dozens of sites can show you the news, but Dow Jones & Co.'s Dow Jones Interactive (www.djinteractive.com) is different. Nearly 600,000 customers pay to search through stories from its 6,000 licensed and internal publications. That's a huge amount of data to filter and the company has applied intelligent agent and other artificial intelligence (AI) technologies to manage the task.
	One of the site's most important features is Custom Clips, which allows users to create folders based on predefined topics—such as agribusiness or IBM—or to build their own using custom key words. When the site IS agent retrieves relevant articles, it can post them to a database-generated Web page or send the stories to the user's E-mail address [39, 40].

Expert Systems

One of the most practical and widely implemented applications of artificial intelligence in business is the development of expert systems and other knowledge-based information systems. A *knowledge-based information system* (KBIS) adds a knowledge base to the major components found in other types of computer-based information systems. An **expert system** (ES) is a knowledge-based information system that uses its knowledge about a specific, complex application area to act as an expert consultant to end users. Expert systems provide answers to questions in a very specific problem area by making humanlike inferences about knowledge contained in a specialized knowledge base. They must also be able to explain their reasoning process and conclusions to a user. So expert systems can provide decision support to end users in the form of advice from an expert consultant in a specific problem area [19, 37].

Components of an Expert System

The components of an expert system include a knowledge base and software modules that perform inferences on the knowledge and communicate answers to a user's questions. Figure 6.29 illustrates the interrelated components of an expert system. Note the following components:

Figure 6.27

Examples of different types of intelligent agents.

Types of Intelligent Agents

User Interface Agents

- **Interface Tutors.** Observe user computer operations, correct user mistakes, and provide hints and advice on efficient software use.

- **Presentation Agents.** Showing information in a variety of reporting and presentation forms and media based on user preferences.

- **Network Navigation Agents.** Discover paths to information and provide ways to view information that are preferred by a user.

- **Role-Playing Agents.** Play what-if games and other roles to help users understand information and make better decisions.

Information Management Agents

- **Search Agents.** Help users find files and databases, search for desired information, and suggest and find new types of information products, media, and resources.

- **Information Brokers.** Provide commercial services to discover and develop information resources that fit the business or personal needs of a user.

- **Information Filters.** Receive, find, filter, discard, save, forward, and notify users about products received or desired, including E-mail, voice mail, and all other information media.

- **Knowledge Base.** The knowledge base of an expert system contains (1) facts about a specific subject area (for example, *John is an analyst*) and (2) heuristics (rules of thumb) that express the reasoning procedures of an expert on the subject (for example: IF John is an analyst, THEN he needs a workstation). There are many ways that such knowledge is represented in expert systems. Examples are *rule-based*, *frame-based*, *object-based*, and *case-based* methods of knowledge representation. See Figure 6.30.

Figure 6.28

Intelligent agents like those in Ask Jeeves help you find information in a variety of categories from many online sources.

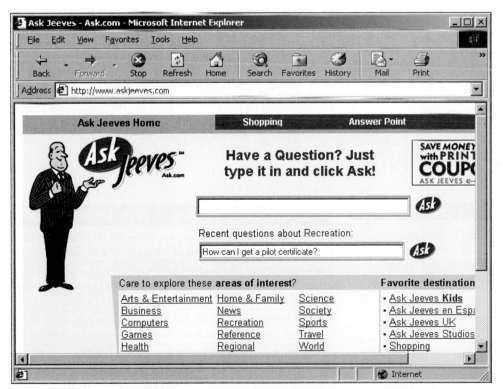

Courtesy of Ask Jeeves, Inc., © 2000.

Figure 6.29

Components of an expert system. The software modules perform inferences on a knowledge base built by an expert and/or knowledge engineer. This provides expert answers to an end user's questions in an interactive process.

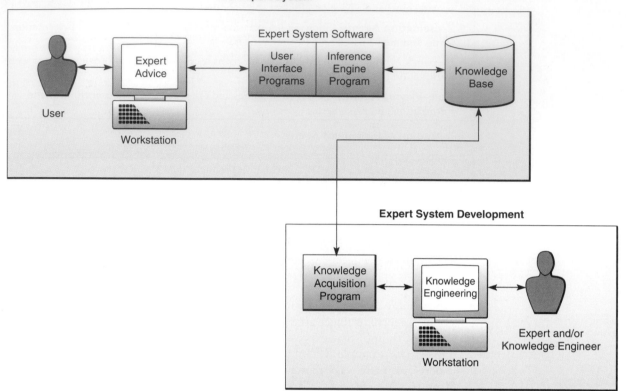

- **Software Resources.** An expert system software package contains an inference engine and other programs for refining knowledge and communicating with users. The **inference engine** program processes the knowledge (such as rules and facts) related to a specific problem. It then makes associations and inferences resulting in recommended courses of action for a user. User interface programs for communicating with end users are also needed, including an explanation program to explain the reasoning process to a user if requested. Knowledge acquisition programs are not part of an expert system but are software tools for knowledge base development, as are *expert system shells*, which are used for developing expert systems.

Figure 6.30

A summary of four ways that knowledge can be represented in an expert system's knowledge base.

Methods of Knowledge Representation
• **Case-Based Reasoning.** Representing knowledge in an expert system's knowledge base in the form of cases, that is, examples of past performance, occurrences, and experiences.
• **Frame-Based Knowledge.** Knowledge represented in the form of a hierarchy or network of *frames*. A frame is a collection of knowledge about an entity consisting of a complex package of data values describing its attributes.
• **Object-Based Knowledge.** Knowledge represented as a network of objects. An object is a data element that includes both data and the methods or processes that act on those data.
• **Rule-Based Knowledge.** Knowledge represented in the form of rules and statements of fact. Rules are statements that typically take the form of a premise and a conclusion such as: If (condition), Then (conclusion).

Expert System Applications

Using an expert system involves an interactive computer-based session in which the solution to a problem is explored, with the expert system acting as a consultant to an end user. The expert system asks questions of the user, searches its knowledge base for facts and rules or other knowledge, explains its reasoning process when asked, and gives expert advice to the user in the subject area being explored. For example, Figure 6.31 illustrates one of the displays of an expert system.

Expert systems are being used for many different types of applications, and the variety of applications is expected to continue to increase. However, you should realize that expert systems typically accomplish one or more generic uses. Figure 6.32 outlines six generic categories of expert system activities, with specific examples of actual expert system applications. As you can see, expert systems are being used in many different fields, including medicine, engineering, the physical sciences, and business. Expert systems now help diagnose illnesses, search for minerals, analyze compounds, recommend repairs, and do financial planning. So from a strategic business standpoint, expert systems can and are being used to improve every step of the product cycle of a business, from finding customers to shipping products to providing customer service.

ES for Advertising Strategy

ADCAD (ADvertising Communications Approach Designer) is an expert system that assists advertising agencies in setting marketing and communications objectives, selecting creative strategies, and identifying effective communications approaches. In particular, it is designed to help advertisers of consumer products with the development of advertising objectives and ad copy strategy, and the selection of communications techniques. ADCAD's knowledge base consists of rules derived from various sources, including consultations with the creative staff of the Young & Rubicam advertising agency. Figure 6.33 gives examples of two of the hundreds of rules in ADCAD's knowledge base [6].

Figure 6.31

This expert system helps a bank analyze and score customers based on various profiles, thus helping it manage the compostion and attrition of its customer base.

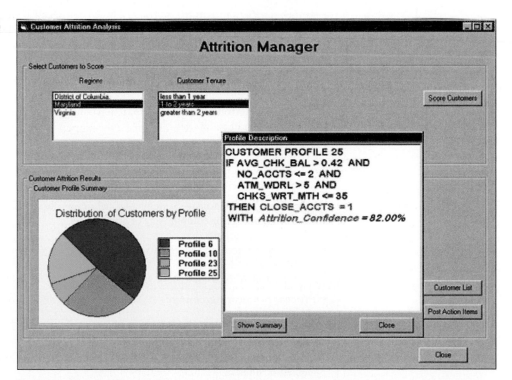

Courtesy of Gensym Corporation.

ADCAD uses a question-and-answer format, asking the user a series of questions about the advertising problem. It then searches through its knowledge base, matching user answers against its rules to draw inferences. Then ADCAD presents its recommendations, along with a rationale for each recommendation if asked. For example, Figure 6.33 shows how ADCAD responded when asked to explain its recommendation to use a celebrity to present an ad on television for a shampoo product.

ADCAD has been popular with advertising and brand managers since it provides them with a rationale for their current advertising, as well as ideas for new communications approaches. Another benefit of ADCAD is its support of what-if analysis of advertising options. ADCAD allows users to easily change their responses to questions and investigate the impact of alternative product or market assumptions. This feature has also made ADCAD a valuable training tool for students and novice advertising managers [6].

Figure 6.32

Major application categories and examples of typical expert systems. Note the variety of applications that can be supported by such systems.

Application Categories of Expert Systems

- **Decision management**—Systems that appraise situations or consider alternatives and make recommendations based on criteria supplied during the discovery process:
    Loan portfolio analysis
    Employee performance evaluation
    Insurance underwriting
    Demographic forecasts

- **Diagnostic/troubleshooting**—Systems that infer underlying causes from reported symptoms and history:
    Equipment calibration
    Help desk operations
    Software debugging
    Medical diagnosis

- **Maintenance/scheduling**—Systems that prioritize and schedule limited or time-critical resources:
    Maintenance scheduling
    Production scheduling
    Education scheduling
    Project management

- **Design/configuration**—Systems that help configure equipment components, given existing constraints:
    Computer option installation
    Manufacturability studies
    Communications networks
    Optimum assembly plan

- **Selection/classification**—Systems that help users choose products or processes, often from among large or complex sets of alternatives:
    Material selection
    Delinquent account identification
    Information classification
    Suspect identification

- **Process monitoring/control**—Systems that monitor and control procedures or processes:
    Machine control (including robotics)
    Inventory control
    Production monitoring
    Chemical testing

Figure 6.33

Examples of the rules and explanations of the ADCAD expert system for developing advertising strategies.

Examples of ADCAD's Rules

- **IF** ad objective = convey brand image or reinforce brand image
  AND brand purchase motivation = sensory stimulation
  AND message processing motivation = high
  THEN emotional tone = elation.

- **IF** ad objective = change brand beliefs
  AND message processing motivation = low
  AND purchase anxiety = low
  AND brand use avoids fearful consequences = yes
  THEN emotional tone = high fear.

Example of an ADCAD explanation of its recommendation to use a celebrity.

- Just a moment please . . .
  The advertising objective is to communicate or reinforce your brand's image, mood, or an associated lifestyle to consumers who are not highly motivated to process your ad message. A celebrity presenter can attract the consumer's attention, enhance your brand's image, and become a memorable cue for brand evaluation.

Developing Expert Systems

The easiest way to develop an expert system is to use an **expert system shell** as a developmental tool. An expert system shell is a software package consisting of an expert system without its kernel, that is, its knowledge base. This leaves a *shell* of software (the inference engine and user interface programs) with generic inferencing and user interface capabilities. Other development tools (such as rule editors and user interface generators) are added in making the shell a powerful expert system development tool.

Expert system shells are now available as relatively low-cost software packages that help users develop their own expert systems on microcomputers. They allow trained users to develop the knowledge base for a specific expert system application. For example, one shell uses a spreadsheet format to help end users develop IF-THEN rules, automatically generating rules based on examples furnished by a user. Once a knowledge base is constructed, it is used with the shell's inference engine and user interface modules as a complete expert system on a specific subject area. Other software tools may require an IT specialist to develop expert systems. See Figure 6.34.

Knowledge Engineering

A **knowledge engineer** is a professional who works with experts to capture the knowledge (facts and rules of thumb) they possess. The knowledge engineer then builds the knowledge base (and the rest of the expert system if necessary), using an iterative, prototyping process until the expert system is acceptable. Thus, knowledge engineers perform a role similar to that of systems analysts in conventional information systems development.

Once the decision is made to develop an expert system, a team of one or more domain experts and a knowledge engineer may be formed. Or experts skilled in the use of expert system shells could develop their own expert systems. If a shell is used, facts and rules of thumb about a specific domain can be defined and entered into a knowledge base with the help of a rule editor or other knowledge acquisition tool. A limited working prototype of the knowledge base is then constructed, tested, and evaluated using the inference engine and user interface programs of the shell. The knowledge engineer and domain experts can modify the knowledge base, then retest the system and evaluate the results. This process is repeated until the knowledge base and the shell result in an acceptable expert system.

ES Development at MacMillan Bloedel

MacMillan Bloedel Corp. is a forest products conglomerate in British Columbia, Canada, that produces particleboard used in building items such as bookshelves, furniture, and kitchen cupboards. Due to high staff turnover and a reorganization of divisional personnel at the particleboard plant, only two senior employees had the comprehensive, operational know-how and training needed to operate the facility. After they retired, MacMillan had to call back a former manager, named Herb, as a very expensive consultant to keep the mill running. So MacMillan decided to develop an expert system to capture his knowledge of plant operations. The expert system that resulted documents the procedures needed to efficiently run the facility, and is also used for training and upgrading employees.

Knowledge engineers used the ACQUIRE expert system shell from Acquired Intelligence to develop the system. The ACQUIRE knowledge-based acquisition system was used to pick Herb's brain for his knowledge of how to start up, clean up, and set up the particleboard coating line. The line consisted of machines whose operations parameters changed according to the coating to be applied. Herb was able to provide expert information, in the form of facts and rules, that was captured in the expert system's knowledge base. The resulting expert system consistently provides quality maintenance and operations advice to the mill operators [19].

The Value of Expert Systems

Obviously, expert systems are not the answer to every problem facing an organization. People using other types of information systems do quite well in many problem situations. So what types of problems are most suitable to expert system solutions? One way to answer this is to look at examples of the applications of current expert systems, including the generic tasks they can accomplish, as were summarized in Figure 6.32. Another way is to identify criteria that make a problem situation suitable for an expert system. Figure 6.35 outlines some important criteria.

Figure 6.35 should emphasize that many real-world situations do not fit the suitability criteria for expert system solutions. Hundreds of rules may be required to capture the assumptions, facts, and reasoning that are involved in even simple problem situations. For example, a task that might take an expert a few minutes to accomplish might require an expert system with hundreds of rules and take several months to develop. A task that may take a human expert several hours to do may require an expert system with thousands of rules and take several years to build [1, 9].

Figure 6.34

Using the Visual Rule Studio and Visual Basic to develop rules for a credit management expert system.

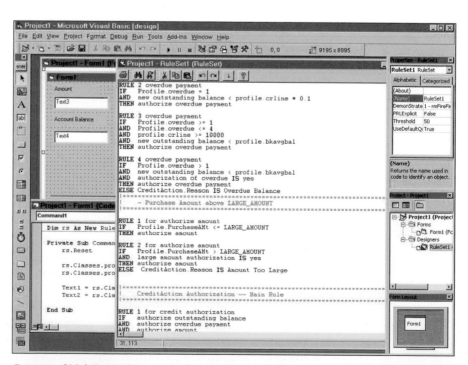

Courtesy of MultiLogic, Inc.

Figure 6.35

Criteria for applications that are suitable for expert systems development.

Suitability Criteria for Expert Systems

- **Domain:** The domain, or subject area, of the problem is relatively small and limited to a well-defined problem area.
- **Expertise:** Solutions to the problem require the efforts of an expert. That is, a body of knowledge, techniques, and intuition is needed that only a few people possess.
- **Complexity:** Solution of the problem is a complex task that requires logical inference processing, which would not be handled as well by conventional information processing.
- **Structure:** The solution process must be able to cope with ill-structured, uncertain, missing, and conflicting data, and a problem situation that changes with the passage of time.
- **Availability:** An expert exists who is articulate and cooperative, and who has the support of the management and end users involved in the development of the proposed system.

Benefits of Expert Systems

An expert system captures the expertise of an expert or group of experts in a computer-based information system. Thus, it can outperform a single human expert in many problem situations. That's because an expert system is faster and more consistent, can have the knowledge of several experts, and does not get tired or distracted by overwork or stress.

Expert systems also help preserve and reproduce the knowledge of experts. They allow a company to preserve the expertise of an expert before she leaves the organization. This expertise can then be shared by reproducing the software and knowledge base of the expert system. This allows novices to be trained and supported by copies of an expert system distributed throughout an organization. Finally, expert systems can have the same competitive advantages as other types of information technology. That is, the effective use of expert systems can allow a firm to significantly improve the efficiency of its business processes, or produce new knowledge-based products and services.

Limitations of Expert Systems

The major limitations of expert systems arise from their limited focus, inability to learn, maintenance problems, and developmental cost. Expert systems excel only in solving specific types of problems in a limited domain of knowledge. They fail miserably in solving problems requiring a broad knowledge base and subjective problem solving. They do well with specific types of operational or analytical tasks, but falter at subjective managerial decision making. For example, an expert system might help a financial consultant develop alternative investment recommendations for a client. But it could not adequately evaluate the nuances of current political, economic, and societal developments, or the personal dynamics of a session with a client. These important factors would still have to be handled by the human consultant before a final investment decision could be reached.

Expert systems may also be difficult and costly to develop and maintain properly. The costs of knowledge engineers, lost expert time, and hardware and software resources may be too high to offset the benefits expected from some applications. Also, expert systems can't maintain themselves. That is, they can't learn from experience but must be taught new knowledge and modified as new expertise is needed to match developments in their subject areas. However, some of these limitations can be overcome by combining expert systems with AI technologies such as fuzzy logic and neural networks or by the use of expert system developmental tools that make the job of development and maintenance easier.

Summary

- **E-Business Decision Support Trends.** Major changes are taking place in traditional MIS, DSS, and EIS tools for providing the information and modeling managers need to support their decision making. Decision support in business is changing, driven by rapid developments in end user computing and networking; Internet, Web browser, and related technologies; and the explosion of E-commerce activity. The growth of corporate intranets, extranets, as well as the Web, has accelerated the development of "executive class" interfaces like enterprise information portals, enterprise knowledge portals, and Web-enabled decision support software tools, and their use by lower levels of management and by individuals and teams of business professionals. In addition, the dramatic expansion of E-commerce has opened the door to the use of enterprise portals and DSS tools by the suppliers, customers, and other business stakeholders of a company for customer relationship and supply chain management and other E-business applications.

- **Information, Decisions, and Management.** Information systems can support a variety of management decision-making levels and decisions. These include the three levels of management activity (strategic, tactical, and operational decision making) and three types of decision structures (structured, semistructured, and unstructured). Information systems provide a wide range of information products to support these types of decisions at all levels of the organization.

- **Management Information Systems.** Management information systems provide prespecified reports and responses to managers on a periodic, exception, demand, or push reporting basis, to meet their need for information to support decision making.

- **OLAP and Data Mining.** Online analytical processing interactively analyzes complex relationships among large amounts of data stored in multidimensional databases. Data mining analyzes the vast amounts of historical data that have been prepared for analysis in data warehouses. Both technologies discover patterns, trends, and exception conditions in a company's data that support their business analysis and decision making.

- **Decision Support Systems.** Decision support systems are interactive, computer-based information systems that use DSS software and a model base and database to provide information tailored to support semistructured and unstructured decisions faced by individual managers. They are designed to use a decision maker's own insights and judgments in an ad hoc, interactive, analytical modeling process leading to a specific decision.

- **Analytical Modeling.** Using a decision support system is an interactive, analytical modeling process, consisting of what-if analysis, sensitivity analysis, goal-seeking analysis, and optimization analysis activities. Decision support system applications may be institutional or ad hoc but are typically developed to support the types of decisions faced by specific industries, functional areas, and decision makers.

- **Executive Information Systems.** Executive information systems are information systems originally designed to support the strategic information needs of top management. However, their use is spreading to lower levels of management. EIS are easy to use and enable executives to retrieve information tailored to their needs and preferences. Thus, EIS can provide information about a company's critical success factors to executives to support their planning and control responsibilities.

- **Artificial Intelligence.** The major application domains of artificial intelligence (AI) include a variety of applications in cognitive science, robotics, and natural interfaces. The goal of AI is the development of computer functions normally associated with human physical and mental capabilities, such as robots that see, hear, talk, feel, and move, and software capable of reasoning, learning, and problem solving. Thus, AI is being applied to many applications in business operations and managerial decision making, as well as in many other fields.

- **AI Technologies.** The many application areas of AI are summarized in Figure 6.21, including neural networks, fuzzy logic, genetic algorithms, virtual reality, and intelligent agents. Neural nets are hardware or software systems based on simple models of the brain's neuron structure that can learn to recognize patterns in data. Fuzzy logic systems use rules of approximate reasoning to solve problems where data are incomplete or ambiguous. Genetic algorithms use selection, randomizing, and other mathematics functions to simulate an evolutionary process that can yield increasingly better solutions to problems. Virtual reality systems are multisensory systems that enable human users to experience computer-simulated environments as if they actually existed. Intelligent agents are knowledge-based software surrogates for a user or process in the accomplishment of selected tasks.

- **Expert Systems.** Expert systems are knowledge-based information systems that use software and a knowledge base about a specific, complex application area to act as expert consultants to users in many business and technical applications. Software includes an inference engine program that makes inferences based on the facts and rules stored in the knowledge base. A knowledge base consists of facts about a specific subject area and heuristics (rules of thumb) that express the reasoning procedures of an expert. The benefits of expert systems (such as preservation and replication of expertise) must be balanced with their limited applicability in many problem situations.

Key Terms and Concepts

These are the key terms and concepts of this chapter. The page number of their first explanation is in parentheses.

1. Analytical modeling (211)
   a. Goal-seeking analysis (213)
   b. Optimization analysis (213)
   c. Sensitivity analysis (212)
   d. What-if analysis (212)
2. Artificial intelligence (222)
   a. Application areas (223)
   b. Domains (222)
3. Data mining (214)
4. Data visualization system (211)
5. Decision structure (204)
6. Decision support versus management reporting (208)
7. Decision support system (208)
8. DSS software (209)
9. E-business DSS (202)
10. E-business decision support trends (202)
11. Enterprise information portal (217)
12. Executive information system (215)
13. Expert system (230)
    a. Applications (233)
    b. Benefits and limitations (237)
    c. Components (230)
    d. System development (235)
14. Expert system shell (235)
15. Fuzzy logic (225)
16. Genetic algorithms (227)
17. Geographic information system (210)
18. Inference engine (232)
19. Intelligent agent (229)
20. Knowledge base (231)
21. Knowledge engineer (235)
22. Knowledge management system (216)
23. Level of management decision making (203)
24. Management information system (204)
25. Management support system (205)
26. Model base (209)
27. Neural network (224)
28. Online analytical processing (206)
29. Reporting alternatives (205)
30. Robotics (224)
31. Virtual reality (228)

Review Quiz

Match one of the key terms and concepts listed previously with one of the brief examples or definitions that follow. Try to find the best fit for answers that seem to fit more than one term or concept. Defend your choices.

_____ 1. Internet technologies and E-commerce developments have expanded the form and use of decision support in business.

_____ 2. A Web-enabled system of decision support for E-business managers, employees, and business partners.

_____ 3. A CEO and a production team may have different needs for decision making.

_____ 4. Decision-making procedures cannot be specified in advance for some complex decision situations.

_____ 5. An information system category that includes management information systems, decision support systems, and executive information systems.

_____ 6. Systems that produce predefined reports for management.

_____ 7. Managers can receive reports periodically, on an exception basis, or on demand.

_____ 8. Provide an interactive modeling capability tailored to the specific information needs of managers.

_____ 9. Interactive responses to ad hoc inquiries versus prespecified information.

_____ 10. A collection of mathematical models and analytical techniques.

_____ 11. Analyzing the effect of changing variables and relationships and manipulating a mathematical model.

_____ 12. Changing revenues and tax rates to see the effect on net profit after taxes.

_____ 13. Changing revenues in many small increments to see revenue's effect on net profit after taxes.

_____ 14. Changing revenues and expenses to find how you could achieve a specific amount of net profit after taxes.

_____ 15. Changing revenues and expenses subject to certain constraints in order to achieve the highest profit after taxes.

_____ 16. Information systems for the strategic information needs of top and middle managers.

_____ 17. Real-time analysis of complex business data.

_____ 18. Attempts to find patterns hidden in business data in a data warehouse.

_____ 19. Represents complex data using three-dimensional graphical forms.

_____ 20. A customized and personalized Web interface to company resources available through a corporate intranet.

_____ 21. Using intranets to gather, store, and share a company's best practices.

_____ 22. Information technology that focuses on the development of computer functions normally associated with human physical and mental capabilities.

_____ 23. Applications in cognitive science, robotics, and natural interfaces.

_____ 24. Development of computer-based machines that possess capabilities such as sight, hearing, dexterity, and movement.

_____ 25. Computers can provide you with computer-simulated experiences.

_____ 26. An information system that integrates computer graphics, geographic databases, and DSS capabilities.

_____ 27. A knowledge-based information system that acts as an expert consultant to users in a specific application area.

_____ 28. Applications such as diagnosis, design, prediction, interpretation, and repair.

_____ 29. These systems can preserve and reproduce the knowledge of experts but have a limited application focus.

_____ 30. A collection of facts and reasoning procedures in a specific subject area.

_____ 31. A software package that manipulates a knowledge base and makes associations and inferences leading to a recommended course of action.

_____ 32. A software package consisting of an inference engine and user interface programs used as an expert system development tool.

_____ 33. One can either buy a completely developed expert system package, develop one with an expert system shell, or develop one from scratch by custom programming.

_____ 34. An analyst who interviews experts to develop a knowledge base about a specific application area.

_____ 35. AI systems that use neuron structures to recognize patterns in data.

_____ 36. AI systems that use approximate reasoning to process ambiguous data.

_____ 37. Knowledge-based software surrogates that do things for you.

_____ 38. Software that uses mathematical functions to simulate an evolutionary process.

Discussion Questions

1. Is the form and use of information and decision support in E-business changing and expanding? Why or why not?

2. Has the growth of self-directed teams to manage work in organizations changed the need for strategic, tactical, and operational decision making in business?

3. What is the difference between the ability of a manager to retrieve information instantly on demand using an MIS and the capabilities provided by a DSS?

4. Refer to the Siemens/ShareNet Real World Case in the chapter. How could Siemens improve ShareNet so it could be a more useful knowledge management system? Explain your reasoning.

5. In what ways does using an electronic spreadsheet package provide you with the capabilities of a decision support system?

6. Why is the use of executive information systems expanding into the ranks of middle management and throughout an organization?

7. Refer to the Real World Case on RivalWatch.com and Others in the chapter. What other information would you like to know about your business competitors? How might AI technologies obtain it from the Web?

8. Can computers think? Will they ever be able to? Explain why or why not.

9. What are some of the most important applications of AI in business? Defend your choices.

10. What are some of the limitations or dangers you see in the use of AI technologies such as expert systems, virtual reality, and intelligent agents? What could be done to minimize such effects?

Application Exercises

Complete the following exercises as individual or group projects that apply chapter concepts to real world business situations.

1. BizRate: E-Commerce Website Reviews
Visit *www.bizrate.com* and you instantly have information about hundreds of online stores and what thousands of previous shoppers at those stores think about them. See Figure 6.36.

Looking to buy a Miles Davis music CD, I entered *CDnow.com* at BizRate.com's Rapid Reports section.

What I got back was an overall customer satisfaction rating of four and a half stars out of a possible five. I scrolled down farther to find individual ratings of the online music store's product selection, pricing, customer support, and on-time delivery record. The rating was based on reports from 22,034 shoppers who had already been to the CDnow site.

BizRate.com users who don't know the name of an online music retailer can go to the site's categories section. Here, I typed in *music* and was given the choice of shopping by product, store, or personal preferences. I wanted to pay by check and receive my CD the next day. Two sites—Cdconnection.com and Playback.com— met my criteria. The first had been reviewed by more than 1,200 shoppers. The other had received 911 reviews.

a. Check out the reviews of online stores for a product you want to buy at the bizrate.com site. How thorough, valid, and valuable were they to you? Explain.

b. How could similar Web-enabled reporting systems be used in other business situations? Give an example.

Source: Adapted from Julia King, "Infomediary," *Computerworld*, November 1, 1999, p. 58. Copyright 1999 by Computerworld, Inc., Framingham, MA 01701. Reprinted from *Computerworld*.

2. Jango and mySimon: Intelligent Web Price Comparison Agents

Jango/Excite Product Finder

The Jango award-winning intelligent agent software is used in the Excite shopping area. This agent can use presupplied templates to search categories or adapt new templates from past experiences. The Excite shopping area at www.excite.com covers a range of product categories, although the merchant list in the standard categories is a bit shorter than some others. One nice touch is that some of Jango's price comparisons also list shipping costs along with the product price, so you can compare the total price. You also can search for product reviews in addition to finding merchants that sell a given product.

mySimon

The mySimon site (http://www.mysimon.com) starts from a category listing that covers many different kinds of merchandise. After you find the subcategory that interests you, you can search by manufacturer and product keywords. mySimon also offers shopping guides for areas such as Winter Sports or product guides such as Coffeemaker/Espresso. You can register with the site to receive its newsletter, use the talk forums, and save your searches.

a. Visit the Jango and mySimon sites. Which price comparison agent do you prefer? Why?

b. Are these sites examples of Web-enabled decision support systems? Why or why not?

c. How could this technology be used in business situations? Give an example.

Source: Adapted from Jennifer Powell, "Streamline Your Shopping," *Smart Computing*, February 2000, pp. 88–90.

Figure 6.36

The BizRate website offers customer reviews of online stores.

Courtesy of BizRate.com, © 2000.

3. Retail Electronic Commerce System for Pinnacle Products

Pinnacle Products is considering a developing a strategic system to allow it to sell products through its web site. None of Pinnacle's direct competitors currently utilize electronic retailing, but the President of Pinnacle feels that business to consumer electronic commerce is appropriate for Pinnacle's industry and wants to be in leadership position. You have been asked to assist in preparing a preliminary feasibility study for the system. Your analysis is to be restricted to the first five years of operation

The Information Systems and Marketing departments have developed estimates for your use. The marketing department estimates that sales will be $1,000,000 in year 2 (the system is expected to take 1 full year for initial development) and that sales will grow 50 percent per year thereafter. The department also estimates that each dollar of electronic sales will contribute 25 cents to profit. The IS department has estimated the cost of developing and maintaining this system across it first five years of operation, as shown below.

	Year 1	Year 2	Year 3	Year 4	Year 5
System Cost:	$900,000	$400,000	$400,000	$500,000	$600,000
Projected Sales $:		$2,000,000 (50 percent growth per year)			
Sales Contribution Rate:		(25 percent contribution to profits in all years 1–5)			

a. Based upon these figures construct a spreadsheet to analyze the costs and benefits of the proposed system. Projected sales for year 3 will be 1.5 times year 2 sales, year 4's sales will be 1.5 times year 3's and so on. The benefits of the system are equal to new sales times the 25 percent contribution to profits. Your spreadsheet should include a column showing the net contribution (benefits minus system cost) for each year.

b. Assume that ABC Company requires a return of 25 percent on this type of investment. Add an internal rate of return estimate to your spreadsheet and determine whether the return exceeds the 25 percent requirement.

c. This type of investment is risky largely because sales growth is very hard to predict. To assess risk, marketing has been asked to provide worst-case and best-case estimates for the rate of growth in sales. Their worst-case estimate is a growth of only 10 percent per year while their best-case estimate is 100 percent growth per year. Calculate the returns under best case and worst case assumptions and add these estimates to your spreadsheet.

d. Prepare a set of PowerPoint slides or similar presentation materials summarizing your key results and including a recommendation as to whether this project should be pursued.

4. Palm City Police Department

The Palm City Police Department has 8 defined precincts. The Police Station in each precinct has primary responsibility for all activities in its precinct area. The current population of each precinct, the number of violent crimes committed in each precinct, and the number of officers assigned to each precinct are shown below. The department has established a goal of equalizing access to police services. Ratios of population per police officer and violent crimes per police officer should be calculated for each precinct. These ratios for the city as a whole are shown below.

a. Build a spreadsheet to perform the analysis described above and print it out.

Currently, no funds are available to hire additional officers. Based on the citywide ratios the department has decided to develop a plan to shift resources as needed in order to ensure that no precinct has more than 1100 residents per police officer and no precinct has more than 7 violent crimes per police officer. The department will transfer officers from precincts, which easily meet these goals to precincts that violate one or both of these ratios.

b. Use goal seeking on your spreadsheet to move police officers between precincts until the goals are met. (You can use the goal seek function to see how many officers would be required to bring each precinct into compliance and then judgmentally reduce officers in precincts that are substantially within the criteria.) Print out a set of results that allow the department to comply with these ratios and a memorandum to your instructor summarizing your results and the process you used to develop them.

Precinct	Population	Violent Crimes	Police Officers
Shea Blvd.	96,552	318	85
Lakeland Heights	99,223	582	108
Sunnydale	68,432	206	77
Old Town	47,732	496	55
Mountainview	101,233	359	82
Financial District	58,102	511	70
Riverdale	78,903	537	70
Cole Memorial	75,801	306	82
Total	625,978	3,315	629
Per Officer	995.196	5.270	

Procter & Gamble: The Business Case for Enterprise Portals

Back in 1996, when a portal was just a fancy name for a door, Procter & Gamble Co.'s IT division began developing a rudimentary system for sharing documents and information over the company's intranet. As the demands of users and the number of web pages supported by the system grew, the IT team expanded the scope of this Global Knowledge Catalog. The larger system is a storehouse of information that lets all 97,000 Procter & Gamble employees worldwide find information specific to their needs.

But although the system helped make sense of volumes of data, it still led to information overload. What Procter & Gamble really needed was a way to personalize the information for each employee, based on his or her job, says Dan Gerbus, project manager for the personalized portal project in the Cincinnati company's IT division. "Users wanted one tool on their browser that would consolidate and deliver all the information they needed to do their work without having to navigate through 14 web sites," he says.

Thus Gerbus and his team set out to build a portal to their intranet that would provide Procter & Gamble employees with a more personalized information experience. What Gerbus soon discovered, is that building a portal isn't easy. So in January 2000, Procter & Gamble awarded a contract to Plumtree Software for 100,000 seats of the Plumtree Corporate Portal. Procter & Gamble, which became an investor in Plumtree, uses the portal to deliver marketing, product, and strategic information, as well as industry-news documents in thousands of Lotus Notes databases to its employees. The portal's document directory pulls data from more than 1 million web pages.

By early 2001, Procter & Gamble's enterprise-wide portal included web links to the company's SAP R/3 enterprise resource planning system and a wide range of Oracle data-warehousing and decision support products, including Oracle Discoverer, Oracle Express and Oracle Sales Analyzer. Customer data analyzed by E.piphany's customer relationship management application is also incorporated. The idea, Gerbus says, is to give employees one place to get the information and applications they need. "They used to have to scan multiple intranet sites to find ways to get that. The portal is one-stop shopping," he says.

Gerbus says that by the time the enterprise portal becomes fully operational this year, Procter & Gamble employees will be able to glance at their "dashboard," which will deliver a preset view into various information sources, and find all the up-to-date information they need to make decisions about new products, advertising campaigns, or other initiatives. "If a business manager always needs to track some key pieces of information, we'll be able to build a dashboard for that," Gerbus says. "But we'll also provide the tools for them to get to the application or data source for a more in-depth analysis."

The enterprise information portal (EIP) is the latest stage in the intranet's evolution, and it's one that should be embraced by all companies, says Mark O'Connor, Yankee Group's associate director for enterprise knowledge management, because the benefits far outweigh the hassle of implementing and maintaining the technology. Executives are demanding that data be readily accessible by common business users, rather than being stored indiscriminately, so it can have a daily impact.

Enterprise portals function as electronic doorways into a company or one of its parts. They help employees access appropriate data, collaborate with one another, distribute reports, and monitor indicators of market performance. Portals let users select content and subscribe to information, all of which is presented in a consistent format. "My taxonomy of information—or topics and categories—might always be displayed on the left, decision-support graphs in the middle, my news feeds on the right, my company-news ticker tape at the top, and my toolbox at the bottom," says Jonathan Harding, executive VP of Viador. "What I actually see in each of these windows will be determined by who I am, what I do, and by my preferences."

The main advantages of enterprise portals, analysts and users say, are increased productivity and job satisfaction. If, for example, a manager gets a request for proposals from a big insurance company and has to respond in 10 days, he or she can use the portal to find the content and people that can help produce the RFP. The manager can also put out a request for help from someone who has experience preparing RFPs for insurance companies. Still, quantifying the benefits that IT managers, analysts, and portal software vendors insist come with portal use can be hard to do. "It's difficult to put a hard number on the value of a product-research person finding something on the intranet that they may not have been able to find before and, because of that, speeding up the development of a new product," Procter & Gamble's Gerbus says. "How do you even find out what happened, much less measure it?"

Case Study Questions

1. How does an enterprise information portal differ from an intranet in terms of technologies used and applications provided?

2. What is the business value of an EIP for a company like Procter and Gamble?

3. How might an EIP help you as a business professional or manager in your work activities? Give several examples to illustrate your answer?

Source: Adapted from Karen Schwartz, "Companies Spin Personalized Portals to Their Advantage," *Information Week Online*, July 3, 2000, and "Customer: Procter and Gamble," Plumtree.com, March 16, 2001.

EMI Group: Using OLAP for Strategic Decision Support

With more than 70 subsidiary companies and labels worldwide, including the EMI, Virgin, and Capitol labels, the EMI Group is currently the world's third largest music company. The company is setting its sights on being number one, and its business strategies support this objective. EMI aims to continually improve business operations and see efficiencies to drive down costs.

That's where Mike Hillerman, Director of Projects and Relationship Management for EMI Music Distribution (EMD) in Los Angeles, comes in. "The president at EMD, Richard Cottrell, wanted our sales and marketing people to have a shaping strategy—a strategy to achieve a competitive advantage. He felt business decisions should be made with relevant data about our customers and their overall habits."

In addition to limited knowledge of customers' buying behavior at different levels, Hillerman explains. "We didn't feel like our sales and marketing staff had a big picture view of what their goals were with our existing reporting systems. We were looking for a better way of measuring marketing plan effectiveness."

So EMD—together with software and development help from the SAS institute—implemented a new business intelligence strategy with a solution called SIS, for Sales Information System. Module one of SIS is a Multidimensional Database (MDDB) application that provides an intuitive method of analyzing sales and marketing data for EMD's U.S. markets. Taking advantage of Online Analytical Processing (OLAP) technology, SIS enables better decision making for EMD by giving business users unlimited views of multiple relationships in large quantities of summarized data.

Through SIS, more than 200 sales and marketing representatives and executive management can now track crucial sales information quickly and easily against established forecasts or goals. Using OLAP, they can view data on product lines, market teams, customers (Parent or Ship-to) and product or titles.

Built on an IBM Netfinity Winframe server, the hub-and-spoke design of SIS involved building a base of data (the hub) and then a spoke for each application so that EMD is always working from the same base data. "What we do is build a spoke file and the use multidimensional database (MDDB) code to build a cube off that spoke file," explains Hillerman. Before we actually build a cube, we do an incredible amount of analyzing and appraising of the data to make sure that we're capturing the most significant part. Doing that makes what we show more relevant. We look for the most important customers and most important products for the last 12 months. We have variables that drive that and our users actually determine what those variables will be."

The different organizational levels in the cube enable sales staff to drill down in different directions to find detailed views of product lines, market teams, customers, and titles.

For example, if users want a particular customer view of a product line, they can drill down and find out what titles that customer is buying. "Not only do we report what they buy, we also report what they don't buy," says Hillerman. "That way we can find out the top-selling items in each product line level. And at the bottom of the report we list those titles that the customer didn't buy, so if the customer didn't happen buy a couple of the top listed titles, we'll see that, and of course that's an opportunity for us."

SIS Modules II and III replace monthly sales tracking reports that were compiled to track basic customer sales performance. Now everyone from sales representatives to EMI's president uses the system to get up-to-date information any time they want it. "They're really amazed by it because they've never seen these levels of information before—it's very meaningful to them in a business sense," says Hillerman. "I think it was the right business perspective and that's what's so important with an application like this. It has to be the appropriate business perspective for the users you give it to."

Hillerman says that users are becoming more knowledgeable about their relationships with their customers and their habits, and the original goals of the project have been met as well. "Everyone feels more like they understand what they are expected to do and where they stand. Because of that, they are achieving their goals better because they know what they are—very specifically," Hillerman comments. With OLAP technology, EMD can now use SIS to find its most profitable customers and calculate their lifetime value, determine the best candidates for cross-selling opportunities, and decide who to target as new prospects.

Hillerman definitely sees SIS as a competitive advantage for EMD. "I don't know if our competitors have a similar application like this, but if they don't, they just aren't going to be able to maximize their position and their product as well as we can." He adds, "For the first time, EMD is building decision support systems to facilitate customer relationship management. We can really see what our customers' habits are and how effective we are in the way that we deal with them."

Case Study Question

1. How is EMI's Sales Information System helping their managers and business professionals?

2. How do the capabilities of a system like SIS differ from the reporting capabilities of a traditional management information system?

3. What competitive advantages does SIS provide to a company in the global music industry like EMI?

Source: Adapted from SAS Institute, "EMI Music Treats Customers Like Movie Stars," SAS.com, March 23, 2001.

Ford Motor Company: Using Natural Language Intelligent Agents

In October, 2000, Vic Nagy, hotline operations manager at Ford Motor Co. in Dearborn, Michigan, hired a new virtual service representative he dubbed "Ernie." Powered by software from San Francisco-based NativeMinds Inc. (www.nativeminds.com), Ernie answers questions over the Web about Ford's car problem analyzer, the Worldwide Diagnostic System (WDS), from repair technicians at 5,600 Ford dealerships nationwide.

"It has a uniqueness that we really like, a natural language interface," says Nagy. That means Ernie can answer questions posed in conversational format, such as "How do I run the WDS on a field test?" Ernie has been programmed to understand what a technician means by "WDS" and "Field test." Plus, it tracks the topic of a back-and-forth interaction with a technician, so if Ernie gets a follow-up question like "How do I hook it up?" it knows to what "it" refers.

Nagy says that context-sensitive capability and around-the-clock availability has made the system a valuable supplement to Ford's human-staffed help line, which is open only 12 hours a day, six days a week.

NativeMinds' NeuroServer is the brains behind Ernie, says Scott Benson, co-founder and chief technology officer at NativeMinds. Customers interact with NeuroServer via the Web, he says. A web service processes the questions, passing them to the NeuroServer, a natural language, intelligent agent program. When the NeuroServer finds an answer, it returns a web page to the questioner.

Chris Martins, an analyst at high-tech consulting firm Aberdeen Group Inc. in Boston, says NeuroServer's most important feature is its ability to step through a sequence of questions, where the follow-up question is based on the previous question. That context sensitivity makes it able to drill down to just the right answer, he says, and is significantly different from the more common search engines that web sites often use. NeuroServer doesn't take a question and search for multiple answers. Rather, Martins says, it finds the answer based on multiple questions.

Martins says effective applications of NeuroServer focus on a bounded set of questions. It's not meant to respond to any possible question, but to act as a guided interactive tool. Users teach NeuroServer its initial set of knowledge through a wizard-driven authoring environment. A web-based interface allows companies to update NeuroServer's information set while the intelligent agent is up and running. But NeuroServer isn't limited to tapping that data stored in its internal database.

At Ford, Ernie will search the WDS manual for information not found in its internal knowledge base, Nagy says. Linking directly to that database instead of loading duplicate information into Ernie means lower maintenance costs and no problems synchronizing two sets of data. Plus, when Ernie is truly stumped, the application automatically routes the customer's question and contact information to customer service for a callback, saving a Ford technician the effort of starting over with the customer's question, says Nagy.

Martins says the external data links make NeuroServer useful in areas where the questions are general but the answers are customer-specific. For example, he points to financial services, where many people have the same questions, but the answers need to bring in data from individual investment files.

Walter A. Tackitt, cofounder and CEO of NativeMinds, says NeuroServer is best suited to answering "how-to" type questions. These questions can often cost $25 per incident when handled by a human operator over the phone, he estimates; using just e-mail or live chat only brings the price down to $10. With NeuroServer, he claims, companies can answer these how-to questions for only 50 cents each, when all costs are amortized. Product pricing is not cheap, running $300,000 on average for software and services.

Two main competitors of NativeMinds are Boston's Artificial Life Inc.(www.artificial-life.com) and eGain Communications Corp. of Sunnyvale, California (www.egain.com). Artificial Life's virtual agents have natural language processing capabilities, can carry on interactive conversations, and will escalate incidents to a human upon reaching the limits of their knowledge. An eGain Assistant intelligent agent can also conduct interactive conversations, gather customer intelligence, and provide an online brand and personality, while allowing companies to analyze their customer interactions.

Besides Ford, NativeMinds customers include Glaxo-SmithKline, Deutsche Telecom, and Western Provident Association, and their investors include the Oracle Venture Fund. The company is working on internationalizing NeuroServer, says Benson, allowing it to enter the Spanish, Dutch and French markets in the immediate future. Another focus of improvement is adding voice recognition so that customers can ask questions as well as type them.

Case Study Questions

1. What AI technologies do you recognize in NeuroServer and Ernie? Explain your choices.

2. What business problems is Ernie solving for Ford?

3. Is NeuroServer worth the price NativeMinds is charging its customers? Use Ford's experience to illustrate your answer.

Source: Adapted from Amy Helen Johnson, "Web Tool Makes for Good Conversation," *ComputerWorld*, February 26, 2001, p. 60.

Management
Challenges

Business
Applications

Module
III

Information
Technologies

Development
Processes

Foundation
Concepts

Module III

Development Processes

How can business professionals plan, develop, and implement
E-business strategies and solutions to meet the challenges and
opportunities faced by today's E-business enterprises? Answering that
question is the goal of the chapters of this module, which focus on the
processes for planning, developing, and implementing E-business strategies
and applications.

- Chapter 7, **Developing E-Business Strategies,** emphasizes the importance of the planning process in developing E-business strategies, and the
implementation challenges that arise when introducing new E-business
strategies and applications into an organization.

- Chapter 8, **Developing E-Business Solutions,** introduces the
traditional, prototyping, and end user approaches to the development of
E-business systems, and discusses the processes and managerial issues in
the implementation of new E-business applications.

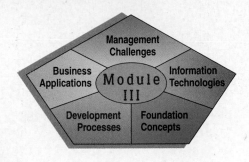

Management Challenges

Business Applications

Module III

Information Technologies

Development Processes

Foundation Concepts

Chapter

Developing E-Business

Strategies

Chapter Outline

Learning Objectives

After reading and studying this chapter, you should be able to:

1. Discuss the role of planning in an E-business enterprise using the scenario approach and planning for competitive advantage as examples.

2. Discuss the role of E-business planning in the development of E-business strategies, architectures, and applications.

3. Identify several change management solutions for end user resistance to the implementation of new E-business strategies and applications.

Section I E-Business Planning Fundamentals

Introduction

Imagine taking a caravan of thousands of people on a journey with no map, no plan, no one in charge, no logistical support, no way to keep everyone informed, no scouting reports to assess and update progress, and no navigational instruments. Sheer madness, yet that's how most companies are handling the transition to E-business.

E-business technology has created a seismic shift in the way companies do business. Just knowing the importance and structure of E-business is not enough. You need to create and implement an action plan that allows you to make the transition from an old business design to a new E-business design [18].

That is why you need to learn about E-business planning, which is the goal of this section. We will first discuss several strategic planning concepts, and then talk more specifically about developing E-business strategies and other planning issues. In Section II, we will discuss the process of implementing E-business plans, and the challenges that arise when introducing new E-business strategies and applications into a company. Now let's look at an E-business planning example.

Analyzing Accel Partners

Read the Real World Case on Accel Partners on the next page. We can learn a lot about the past mistakes and future prospects of E-commerce from that case. See Figure 7.1.

Accel Partners was one of the few Silicon Valley venture capital firms that did not take part in the wide-scale rush to fund pure play dot coms. Instead, they concentrated on carve-out E-commerce strategies with traditional companies, such as their partnership with Wal-Mart to develop Wal-Mart.com, and insisted that E-commerce business plans clearly meet traditional measures of profitability. Managing partner Jim Breyer scoffed at the "first mover" advantage, emphasizing that second and third movers like Microsoft, Cisco Systems, Dell Computers, and Siebel Systems usually end up dominating their markets.

Figure 7.1

Jim Breyer is managing partner of venture capital firm Accel Partners, a leading investor in the second wave of E-commerce.

Peter Stember.

Accel Partners: The Past, Present, and Future of E-Commerce

He who hesitates is not always lost. Sometimes, he is not only prudent but downright savvy. Such is the case with Jim Breyer, the youthful-looking managing partner of Accel Partners, the heavy-hitting Silicon Valley venture-capital firm. A few years ago, Breyer was criticized for not joining the massive early investment in e-retailing start-ups. He was derided in the press as a venture capitalist who "didn't get it." Today, because he refused to be rushed along with the herd, he is being hailed as a major force in Silicon Valley.

His strategy was deceptively simple: In retrospect, it seems completely obvious. Breyer decided that, despite all the hype about a New Economy with new rules, he was going to invest only in businesses that met a traditional measure of profitability. Breyer didn't worry he'd miss the chance to participate in what everyone else seemed to view as a land grab. He was confident that the "first-mover advantage" was a myth. He said history shows the second or third movers, such as Dell Computer and Cisco Systems, usually end up dominating their markets.

So Breyer patiently put together a strategy for "carve-outs," taking the assets of big companies and putting them into standalone businesses that could act with the nimbleness of startups. Among his biggest projects as a venture capitalist, Breyer formed Wal-Mart.com with Wal-Mart Stores. Now, let's evaluate Breyer's analysis of what companies might learn and include in their E-commerce planning.

Past Lessons

We tried to remain very consistent in our analysis and really look to how the math came together. We focused on gross margins. It's something we've always felt strongly about in core software and communications businesses.

Some 95% of the entrepreneurs we met with could not take us through a detailed analysis of their gross margin structure. Compare that with conversations we've had over the past year with Wal-Mart. We always start and end with gross-margin structure. It's a night-and-day difference.

I think there was unfounded belief that being first to market meant everything. In fact, as we've seen again and again, in particular where technology is concerned, leaders are not necessarily first to market. Whether it's Microsoft in operating systems, Dell in the personal-computer business, Cisco in the data-communications and router business, Siebel Systems in customer relationship management software—all of these companies were second or third to market but were able to capitalize on enormous opportunities.

There was simply too much emphasis on being first to market and on building a pre-emptive brand position. People confused those dynamics with what have historically been the real drivers of success.

Present Position

We're about where the personal-computer business was circa 1985. E-commerce has gone through the initial mass frenzy and surreal hype. We are now in the backlash days. I believe that we will go through a very rapid and very painful consolidation that will eliminate many of the pure-play E-commerce companies. But I have absolutely no doubt that we'll emerge and that there will be a handful of multibillion dollar E-commerce businesses that will be tomorrow's Microsofts and Ciscos.

Future Prospects

Companies such as Dell and Cisco were founded well after the introduction of the PC but were leaders of what might be called the second wave of that business. There are similar opportunities to lead in the second wave of e-commerce.

I think that with businesses that handle physical goods, the right approach is to do the sort of carve-out that we're doing with Wal-Mart, to take advantage of their physical presence, their logistics capabilities, and so on.

In businesses that aren't physical—music, entertainment, and financial services—there are huge opportunities to fundamentally change the industries' business models. I think we'll see the peer-to-peer model—exemplified by Napster's approach to sharing music files—become transcendent in numerous areas.

We'll also see the P2P model deeply influence businesses' supply chains, and we're very aggressively pursuing an investment strategy around that. For instance, we've invested in Ray Ozzie's new company, Groove Networks, which is based on the notion that peer-to-peer computing and communications sit at the heart of how business will be transacted going forward.

The venture-capital business is awash in new funds. We recently raised a new fund of $1.6 billion, and we're going to make bigger and bolder bets. Anybody who thinks the pace of innovation will slow is due for a rude awakening. In technology cycles, once you work your way through the backlash, the change that occurs always turns out to be greater than anyone expected, even in his wildest dreams.

Case Study Questions

1. Which important lessons from Jim Breyer's analysis of the past should companies include in their E-commerce planning?

2. Do you agree with Breyer's forecasts of the key opportunities in the future of E-commerce? Why or why not?

3. What types of new E-commerce business would you be willing to create, work for, or invest in? Defend the business value of your proposal.

Source: Adapted from Paul Carroll, "2nd and Foremost," *Context*, December 2000/January 2001, pp. 34–38.

Breyer sees E-commerce going through a backlash stage at present, with widespread consolidation of E-commerce companies. Then he forecasts the emergence of a "second wave" of E-commerce, with even greater technological innovations and business opportunities. He still recommends a carve-out strategy for E-commerce initiatives involving the sale of physical goods, but sees tremendous opportunities for successful new business models involving E-commerce in areas like music, entertainment, and financial services. For example, Breyer sees great opportunities in applying the peer-to-peer network model to these areas, as well as to E-business supply chain applications.

Organizational Planning

Figure 7.2 illustrates the components of an **organizational planning** process. This fundamental planning process consists of (1) team building, modeling, and consensus, (2) evaluating what an organization has accomplished and the resources they have acquired, (3) analyzing their business, economic, political, and societal environment, (4) anticipating and evaluating the impact of future developments, (5) building a shared vision and deciding on what goals they want to achieve, and (6) deciding what actions to take to achieve their goals.

The result of this planning process is what we call a *plan*, which formally articulates the actions we feel are necessary to achieve our goals. Thus, a plan is an action statement. Plans lead to actions, actions produce results, and part of planning is learning from results. In this context, the planning process is followed by implementation, which is monitored by control measures, which provide feedback for planning.

Strategic planning deals with the development of an organization's mission, goals, strategies, and policies. Corporations may begin the process by developing a shared vision using a variety of techniques, including team building, scenario modeling, and consensus creating exercises. Team planning sessions frequently include answering *strategic visioning* questions such as those shown in Figure 7.3 *Tactical planning* involves the setting of objectives and the development of procedures, rules, schedules, and budgets. *Operational planning* is planning done on a short-term basis to implement and control day-to-day operations. Typical examples are project planning and production scheduling. Now let's look at two popular methods of organizational planning.

The Scenario Approach

Planning and budgeting processes are notorious for their rigidity and irrelevance to management action. Rigid adherence to a process of rapid or efficient completion may only make the process less relevant to the true management agenda [8].

Figure 7.2   The components of an organizational planning process.

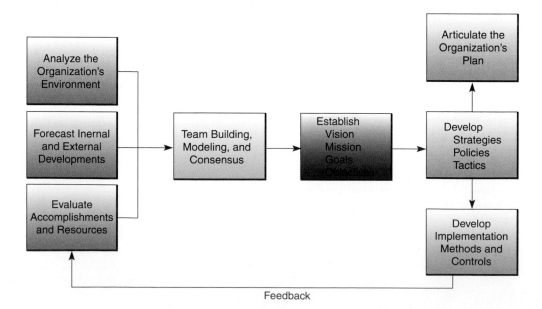

Feedback

Figure 7.3   Examples of strategic visioning questions for E-business planning.

Strategic E-Business Visioning	
● **Understanding the Customer**	Who are our customers? How are our customers' priorities shifting? Who should be our target customer? How will an E-business help reach our target customer segments?
● **Customer Value**	How can we add value for the customer with E-business sevices? How can we become the customer's first choice?
● **Competition**	Who are our real competitors? What is our toughest competitor's business model? What are they doing in E-business and E-commerce? Are our competitors potential partners, suppliers, or customers in an E-business venture?
● **Value Chain**	How would we design a value chain if we were just starting an E-business? Who would be our supply chain partners? What roles should we play: E-commerce website, B2C portal, B2B marketplace, or partner in an E-commerce alliance?

Source: Adapted from Ravi Kalakota and Marcia Robinson, *E-Business 2.0: Roadmap for Success* (Reading, MA: Addison-Wesley, 2001), p. 396, © 2001 Addison-Wesley Publishing Company, Inc. Reprinted by permission of Addison-Wesley Longman Inc. and Peter Fingar, Harsha Kumar, and Tarun Sharma, *Enterprise E-Commerce: The Software Component Breakthrough for Business to Business Commerce* (Tampa, FL: Meghan-Kiffer Press, 2000), p. 229.

Managers and planners continually try different approaches to make planning easier, more accurate, and more relevant to the dynamic, real world of business. The **scenario approach** to planning has gained in popularity as a less formal, but more realistic, strategic planning methodology for use by business professionals.

In the scenario approach, teams of managers and other planners participate in what management author Peter Senge calls *microworld*, or *virtual world*, exercises. A microworld is a simulation exercise that is a microcosm of the real world. In a microworld exercise, managers can safely create, experience, and evaluate a variety of scenarios of what might be happening, or what might happen in the real world.

> *When a work team goes white-water rafting or engages in some other outdoor team-building exercise, they are creating a microworld to reflect on and improve the way they work together. When personnel staff create a role-playing exercise to be used in a supervisory training, they are creating a microworld. Many team retreats serve as microworlds* [26].

Thus, in the scenario approach to strategic IS planning, teams of business and IS managers create and evaluate a variety of business scenarios. For example, they make assumptions on what a business will be like three to five years or more into the future, and the role that information technology can or will play in those future scenarios. Alternative scenarios are created by the teams or by business simulation software, based on combining a variety of developments, trends, and environmental factors, including political, social, business, and technological changes that might occur [11]. For example, Figure 7.4 outlines key business, political, and technological trends that are shaping E-business planning.

Royal Dutch Shell and Dennys: Scenario Planning

Royal Dutch Shell, one of the world's largest oil companies, changed their planning process to a scenario approach over 20 years ago. They shifted from the idea that planning involves "producing a documented view of the future," to a scenario approach where planning involves "designing scenarios so managers would question their own model of reality and change it when necessary." Royal Dutch Shell believes this change to scenario-based planning was a major reason for their successful business decisions during the oil market upheavals of the 1970s and 1980s [8, 9].

Denny's, the nationwide restaurant corporation, uses scenario-based planning to develop five-year plans for the business use of information technology. Department managers gather off-site for several days to create business and IS scenarios. They assess the success of scenarios from the past, to help them anticipate what the company might be like five years into the future. The managers create several most-likely business scenarios, and develop a high-level IS plan for the information technology needed to support each one. Then the IS director analyzes these IS plans to identify the common IT resources required by each one. The managers then reconvene to discuss these findings, and decide on one IS plan for Denny's [11].

Planning for Competitive Advantage

Betting on new IT innovations can mean betting the future of the company. Leading-edge firms are sometimes said to be on the "bleeding edge." Almost any business executive is aware of disastrous projects that had to be written off, often after large cost overruns, because the promised new system simply did not work [19].

Planning for competitive advantage is especially important in today's competitive E-business arena and complex information technology environment. So strategic E-business planning involves an evaluation of the potential benefits and risks a company faces when using E-business strategies and technologies for competitive advantage. In Chapter 2, we introduced a model of *competitive forces* (competitors, customers, suppliers, new entrants, and substitutes) and *competitive strategies* (cost leadership, differentiation, growth, innovation, and alliances), as well as a value chain model of basic business activities. These models can be used in a strategic planning process to help generate ideas for the strategic use of information technologies to support E-business initiatives.

Also popular in strategic E-business planning is the use of a *strategic opportunities matrix* to evaluate the strategic potential of proposed E-business opportunities, as measured by their risk/payoff probabilities. See Figure 7.5.

Figure 7.4 Converging business, political, and technological trends that are shaping E-business strategic planning.

Technology	**Deregulation**
• Electronic Commerce	• Regulated Markets Opening Up
• Customer Information Technology	• Fewer Regulatory Impediments in Business
• "Death of Distance"	• Single Currency Zones
• Digital Everything, Technology Convergence	• Regulators Outflanked by Changing Boundaries
• Information Content of Products and Services Increasing Steadily	and Unstoppable Forces (Internet and E-Business)

Converging Trends

Competitive Imperatives	**Customer Sophistication/ Expectations**
• Imperatives:	• Demand for Better and More Convenient Solutions
- Real Growth	• Increased Emphasis on Service
- Globalization	• Demand for Added Value
- Customer Orientation	• Less Tolerance for Poor Standards
- Knowledge and Capability as Key Assets	• Just-in-Time Delivery
- New Entrants	• Global Influences
• Enablers:	• Brand "Savvy"
- Alliances	
- Outsourcing	

Source: Adapted from Martin Diese, Conrad Nowikow, Patrick King, and Amy Wright, *Executive's Guide to E-Business: From Tactics to Strategy,* 2000, p. 139. Reprinted with permission of John Wiley & Sons, Inc. Copyright © 2000 by John Wiley & Sons, Inc.

Figure 7.5

A strategic opportunities matrix helps to evaluate the strategic risk/payoff potential of proposed E-business opportunities.

SWOT analysis (strengths, weaknesses, opportunities, and threats) is used to evaluate the impact that each possible strategic opportunity can have on a company and its use of information technology [7,19]. A company's strengths are its core competencies and resources in which it is one of the market or industry leaders. Weaknesses are areas of substandard business performance compared to others in their industry or market segments. Opportunities are the potential for new business markets or innovative breakthroughs that might greatly expand present markets. Threats are the potential for business and market losses posed by the actions of competitors and other competitive forces, changes in government policies, disruptive new technologies, and so on. Now let's look at a real world example of how a company used SWOT analysis to evaluate a strategic opportunity.

Dell Computer: Using SWOT Analysis

Dell Computer Corp. is a good example of how a company can use SWOT analysis to carve out a strong business strategy to meet a strategic opportunity: the huge demand for PCs by Internet-connected consumers and businesses. Dell recognized that its strength was selling directly to consumers and businesses and keeping its costs lower than those of other hardware vendors. As for weaknesses, the company acknowledged that it lacked solid dealer relationships.

Identifying opportunities was an easier task. Dell looked at the marketplace and saw that customers increasingly valued convenience and one-stop shopping and that they knew what they wanted to purchase. Dell also saw the Internet as a powerful marketing tool. On the threats side, Dell realized that competitors like IBM and Compaq Computer Corp. had stronger brand names, which put Dell in a weaker position with dealers.

Dell put together a business strategy that included mass customization and just-in-time manufacturing (letting customers use the Web to design their own computers, and then custom-building their systems). Dell also stuck with its direct sales plan and developed a world-class E-commerce website to showcase and sell its products [4].

E-Business Planning

Figure 7.6 illustrates the **E-business planning** process, which focuses on discovering innovative approaches to satisfying a company's customer value and business value goals. This planning process leads to development of strategies and business models for new E-business and E-commerce platforms, processes, products,

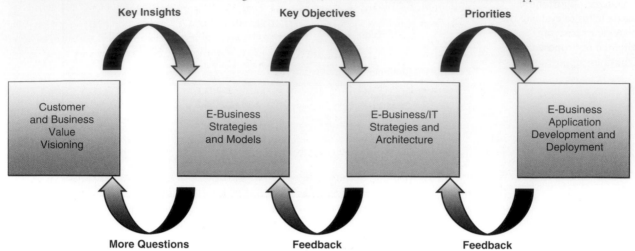

Figure 7.6

The E-business planning process emphasizes a customer and business value focus for devoloping E-business strategies and models, and an IT architecture for E-business applications.

Source: Adapted from Ravi Kalakota and Marcia Robinson, *E-Business: Roadmap for Success* (Reading, MA: Addison-Wesley, 1999), p. 305. © 1999 Addison-Wesley Publishing Company, Inc. Reprinted by permission of Addison-Wesley Longman Inc.

and services. Then a company can develop IT strategies and an IT architecture that supports building and implementing their newly planned E-business applications.

Both the CEO and the chief information officer (CIO) of a company must manage the development of complementary E-business and IT strategies to meet its customer value and business value vision. This *co-adaptation* process is necessary because as we have seen so often in this text, information technologies are a fast changing, but vital component in all E-business and E-commerce initiatives. The E-business planning process has three major components:

- **Strategy Development.** Developing E-business and E-commerce strategies that support a company's E-business vision. use information technology to create innovative E-business systems that focus on customer and business value.

- **Resource management.** Developing strategic plans for managing or outsourcing a company's IT resources, including IS personnel, hardware, software, data, and network resources.

- **Technology architecture.** Making strategic IT choices that reflect an information technology architecture designed to support a company's E-business and E-commerce initiatives.

Information Technology Architecture

The **IT architecture** that is created by the strategic E-business planning process is a conceptual design, or blueprint, that includes the following major components:

- **Technology platform.** The Internet, intranets, extranets, and other networks, computer systems, system software, and integrated enterprise application software provide a computing and communications infrastructure, or platform, that supports the strategic use of information technology for E-business and E-commerce.

- **Data resources.** Many types of operational and specialized databases, including data warehouses and Internet/intranet databases (as reviewed in Chapter 13) store and provide data and information for business processes and decision support.

- **Applications architecture.** Business applications of information technology are designed as an integrated architecture of enterprise systems that support strategic E-business initiatives, as well as cross-functional business processes. For example, an applications architecture should include support for developing and maintaining interenterprise supply chain applications, and integrated enterprise resource planning and customer relationship management applications we discussed in Chapter 4.

- **IT organization.** The organizational structure of the IS function within a company and the distribution of IS specialists are designed to meet the changing strategies of a business. The form of the IT organization depends on the managerial philosophy and business/IT strategies formulated during the strategic planning process. We will discuss the IT organization in Chapter 10.

The E-business planning process we have just described can produce many different E-business strategies. Let's look at several examples of the E-business strategies created and implemented by a variety of companies.

E-Business Strategy Examples	**Market creator.** Use the Internet to define a new market by identifying a unique customer need. This model requires you to be among the first to market and to remain ahead of competition by continuously innovating. Examples: Amazon.com and E*TRADE. **Channel reconfiguration.** Use the Internet as a new channel to directly access customers, make sales, and fulfill orders. This model supplements, rather than replaces, physical distribution and marketing channels. Example: Cisco and Dell. **Transaction intermediary.** Use the Internet to process purchases. This transactional model includes the end-to-end process of searching, comparing, selecting, and paying online. Examples: Microsoft Expedia and eBay. **Infomediary.** Use the Internet to reduce the search cost. Offer the customer a unified process for collecting information necessary to make a large purchase. Examples: HomeAdvisor and Auto-By-Tel. **Self-service innovator.** Use the Internet to provide a comprehensive suite of services that the customer's employees can use directly. Self-service affords employees a direct, personalized relationship. Examples: Employease and Healtheon. **Supply chain innovator.** Use the Internet to streamline the interactions among all parties in the supply chain to improve operating efficiency. Examples: McKesson and Ingram Micro. **Channel mastery.** Use the Internet as a sales and service channel. This model supplements, rather than replaces, the existing physical business offices and call centers. Example: Charles Schwab [18].

E-Business Application Planning

The **E-business application planning** process begins after the strategic phase of E-business planning has occurred. Figure 7.7 shows that the application planning process includes the evaluation of proposals made by the IT management of a company for using information technology to accomplish the strategic E-business priorities developed earlier in the planning process as was illustrated in Figure 7.6. Then, the business case for investing in proposed E-business development projects is evaluated by company executives and business unit managers based on the strategic E-business priorities that they decide are most desirable or necessary at that point in time. Finally, E-business application planning involves developing and implementing E-business applications, and managing their development projects. We will cover the application development and implementation process in Chapter 8. Now, let's examine a real world example.

Figure 7.7

An E-business application planning process includes consideration of IT proposals for addressing the strategic E-business priorities of a company and planning for E-business application development and implementation.

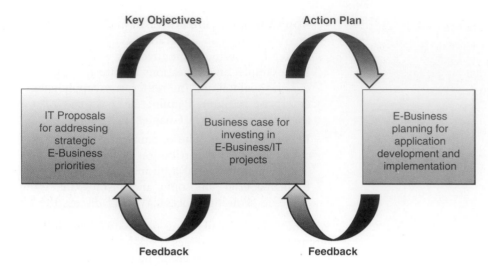

Source: Adapted from Ravi Kalakota and Marcia Robinson, *E-Business: Roadmap for Success* (Reading, MA: Addison-Wesley, 1999), p. 341. © 1999 Addison-Wesley Publishing Company, Inc. Reprinted by permission of Addison-Wesley Longman Inc.

Avnet Marshall: E-Business Planning

Figure 7.8 outlines Avnet Marshall's E-business strategic and application planning process, and compares it to conventional IT planning approaches. Avnet Marshall is the giant electronics distributor we first mentioned in Chapter 2. Avnet Marshall weaves both E-business and IT strategic planning together *co-adaptively* under the guidance of the CEO and the CIO, instead of developing IT strategy by just tracking and supporting business strategies. Avnet Marshall also locates IT application development projects within the business units that are involved in an E-business initiative to form centers of E-business/IT expertise throughout the company. Finally, Avnet Marshall uses an application development process with rapid deployment of E-business applications, instead of a traditional systems development approach. This application development strategy trades the risk of implementing incomplete applications with the benefits of gaining competitive advantages from early deployment of E-business services to employees, customers, and other stakeholders, and of involving them in the "fine-tuning" phase of E-business application development [12].

E-Business Architecture Planning

Another way to look at the E-business planning process, which is growing in acceptance and use in industry, is shown in Figure 7.9. **E-business architecture planning** combines contemporary strategic planning methods like SWOT analysis and alternative planning scenarios with more recent business modeling and application development methodologies like component-based development. As illustrated in Figure 7.9, E-business (and E-commerce) strategic initiatives, including strategic goals, constraints, and requirements, are developed based on SWOT analysis and other planning methods. Then application developers use business process engineering methods to define how strategic E-business requirements are to be implemented, using organizational, process, and data models to create new internal and interenterprise E-business processes among a company's customers, suppliers, and other business partners.

E-business and E-commerce component-based applications are then developed to implement the new business processes using application software and data components stored in a *repository* of reusable business models and application components. Of course, the business process engineering and component-based application development activities are supported by a company's technology infrastructure, which

Figure 7.8

Comparing conventional and E-business strategic and application planning approaches.

Conventional IT Planning	Avnet Marshall's E-Business Planning
• Strategic alignment: IT strategy tracks specified enterprise strategy • CEO endorses IT vision shaped through CIO • IT application development projects functionally organized as technological solutions to business issues • Phased application development based on learning from pilot projects	• Strategic improvisation: IT strategy and enterprise E-business strategy co-adaptively unfold based on the clear guidance of a focus on customer value • CEO proactively shapes IT vision jointly with CIO as part of E-business strategy • IT application development projects co-located with E-business initiatives to form centers of IT-intensive E-business expertise • Perpetual application development based on continuous learning from rapid deployment with incomplete functionality

Source: Adapted from Omar El Sawy, Arvind Malhotra, Sanjay Gosain, and Kerry Young, "IT-Intensive Value Innovation in the Electronic Economy: Insights from Marshal Industries," *MIS Quarterly*, September 1999, p. 324. Reprinted with permission from the *MIS Quarterly*.

includes all the resources of its IT architecture, as well as the necessary component development technologies. So E-business architecture planning links strategy development to business modeling and component development methodologies in order to rapidly produce the strategic E-business applications needed by a company [14].

Figure 7.9

E-business architecture planning integrates business strategy development and business process engineering to produce E-business and E-commerce applications using the resources of the IT architecture, component development technologies, and a repository of business models and application components.

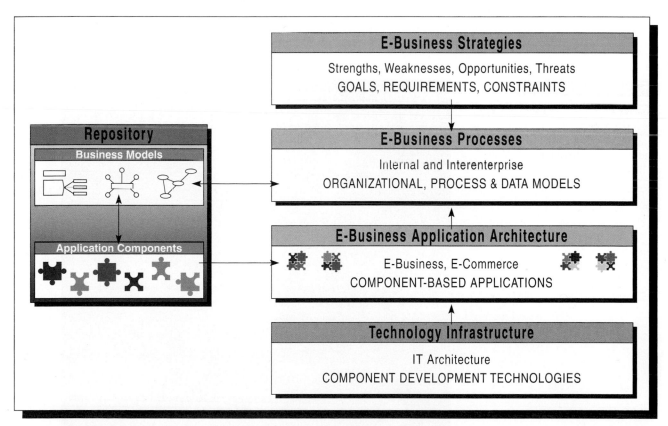

Source: Adapted from Peter Fingar, Harsha Kumar, and Tarun Sharma, *Enterprise E-Commerce: The Software Component Breakthrough for Business to Business Commerce* (Tampa, FL: Meghan-Kiffer Press, 2000), p. 68.

Implementing E-Business Strategies

Implementation

Many companies plan really well, yet few translate strategy into action, even though senior management consistently identifies E-business as an area of great opportunity and one in which the company needs stronger capabilities [18].

Implementation is an important managerial responsibility. Implementation is doing what you planned to do. You can view **implementation** as a process that carries out the plans for changes in E-business strategies and applications that were developed in the planning process we covered in Section I.

Analyzing Cross Engineering, Pitney-Bowes, and Emerson

Read the Real World Case on Cross Engineering, Pitney-Bowes, and Emerson on the next page. We can learn a lot from this case about the important implementation challenges that arise when implementing new E-business strategies. See Figure 7.10.

This case demonstrates the challanges of implementing major E-business strategies and applications, and the change management challenges that confront management. Customer relationship management (CRM) is a prime example of a key E-business application for many companies today. It is designed to implement an E-business strategy of using IT to support a total customer care focus for all areas of a company. Yet CRM projects have a history of a high rate of failure in meeting their objectives. For example, because Crane Engineering is still facing significant resistance from their sales force, more management involvement and peer pressure is being required to get reluctant sales people to use the company's new CRM system. But Pitney-Bowes discovered that an application development process that involved consulting with customer-facing employees resulted in a CRM system that helps sales people do their jobs, while meeting the other business objectives of CRM. And Emerson is finding success in implementing its new CRM system in stages within the company. IT staff meet regularly with customer-facing employees and executives to help plan E-business applications to support a new business strategy that focuses on the ultimate consumer as their true customer.

Figure 7.10

Charles Peterson is senior executive vice president of Emerson Corporation and leader of their drive into E-business.

Ferguson and Katzman.

Cross Engineering, Pitney Bowes, and Emerson: Change Management Challenges of CRM Systems

Why is there such a high failure rate for CRM implementations? According to a recent report from Meta Group a staggering 55% to 75% of CRM projects fail to meet their objectives, often as a result of sales force automation problems and "unaddressed cultural issues"—sales staffs are often resistant to, or even fearful of, using CRM systems.

"Our biggest challenge was our sales guys—changing their habits, getting them to use it for planning. They'd make comments like, 'I don't have time to enter the information.' Some are afraid of using Windows, not to mention CRM," says Jeff Koeper, vice president of operations at Crane Engineering, a Kimberly, Wisconsin-based industrial equipment distributor.

Crane initially had formed a cross-functional team with IT sales and customer service staffers to hear sales automation software vendors' presentations and mutually decide on the desired goals. After a vendor was chosen in 1999, a cross-functional pilot project was formed to iron out any kinks before the system was rolled out company wide. Two full-day training classes have been held since the initial implementation.

But now, Crane is requiring sales managers to ride herd on foot-draggers, and using peer pressure from salespeople selling different products to the same accounts. A cross-functional CRM steering committee meets monthly to discuss problem areas.

"Salespeople want to know what's in it for them; it's not enough to tell them they have to do it. But give them a panoramic view of what their customer is doing in call centers and on the company web site, such as buying other products or complaints. That's a very powerful motivator—they respond to revenue potential and growing their customer base," says Liz Shahnam, a Meta Group analyst.

But companies face a bigger challenge: CRM is a mindset—a business philosophy that reshapes a company's sales, marketing, customer service and analytics and presents a radical cultural shift for many organizations. "It's a change from a product-centered or internal focus to a customer-centered or external focus. It's a change from a monologue to a dialogue with the customer; with the advent of the Internet, customers want to converse with a company. Also, it's a change from targeting customers to becoming the target. Customers are now the hunters," says Ray McKenzie, Seattle-based director of management consulting at DMR Consulting.

"This switch means getting IT professionals to "think customer" and breaking down the barriers between IT and the employees who interact with customers. It also means structural changes in how the company operates, like sharing information and resources across departments and job functions, which translates into giving up control over who "owns" it; retraining employees in new roles, responsibilities and skills; and measuring their job performance, and even how they're paid.

Some IT organizations have tried to tackle these problems head-on. At Pitney Bowes Inc., a Stamford Connecticut-based business equipment manufacturer, IT staffers met with customer-facing employees and focus groups to solve problems and jointly develop a CRM system salespeople could live with.

"The IT people loved getting out of their cubicles," says Russ Wilson, vice president of customer process re-engineering at Pitney Bowes. "How you establish your requirements and initial design is crucial. You need to understand how sales reps need the tools to do their job, which means a user-friendly GUI. IT people love pull-down menus—salespeople look at it and go, 'Aarggh!'"

Emerson, a maker of electronics products ranging from air-conditioning system compressors to power-related supplies and tools, is deepening its customer relationships. Formerly known as Emerson Electric Co., the St. Louis-based firm held a three-day seminar for marketing staffers in 1999 that included an introduction to a CRM system the company launched last year. Six of Emerson's 60 divisions now use the system, and 20 more are about to go live with it.

The company's IT staffers and customer-facing employees and executives meet regularly to discuss opportunities to create new business models and how to rapidly deploy applications to enable them. "We try to follow the Jerry Maguire school of marketing: The customer is the money. Historically, we thought of the retailer, such as Sears, Roebuck, as our customer and totally depended on retailers to push our product out," says Charles Peters, senior executive vice president and E-business leader at Emerson. "But the Internet changes how we interface with the customer, how we manage internally, and makes it possible to do direct marketing. For the first time, we're talking to our true customer."

Case Study Questions

1. What are several major reasons why there is such a high failure rate in implementing CRM projects?

2. Do you agree with how Crane Engineering has been trying to solve their CRM implementation problems? Why or why not?

3. What are Pitney Bowes and Emerson doing that should help improve the implementation of CRM systems in business?

Source: Adapted from Sharon McDonnel, "Putting CRM to Work," *Computerworld*, March 12, 2001, pp. 48–49.

Implementing E-Business Change

Moving to an E-business environment involves a major organizational change. For many large, global companies, becoming an E-business is the fourth or fifth major organizational change they have undergone since the early 1980s. Many companies have gone through one or more rounds of business process reengineering (BPR); installation and major upgrades of an ERP system; upgrading legacy systems to be Y2K compliant; creating shared service centers; implementing just-in-time (JIT) manufacturing; automating the sales force; contract manufacturing; and the major challenges related to the introduction of Euro currency [24].

So implementing new E-business strategies and applications is only the latest catalyst for major organizational changes enabled by information technology. Figure 7.11 illustrates the impact and the levels and scope of business changes that E-business and other applications of information technology introduce into an organization. For example, implementing an E-business application like online transaction processing brings efficiency to single-function or core business processes. However, implementing E-business applications such as enterprise resource management or customer relationship management requires a reengineering of core business processes internally and with supply chain partners, thus forcing a company to model and implement business practices being implemented by leading firms in their industry. Of course, major new E-commerce initiatives can enable a company to redefine its core lines of business and precipitate dramatic changes within the entire interenterprise value chain of an E-business enterprise.

As we will see in this section, implementing new E-business strategies requires managing the effects of major changes in key organizational dimensions such as business processes, organizational structures, managerial roles, employee work assignments, and stakeholder relationships that arise from the deployment of new E-business systems. For example, Figure 7.12 emphasizes the variety and extent of the challenges reported by 100 companies that developed and implemented new enterprise information portals and ERP systems.

Figure 7.11   The impact and the levels and scope of business change introduced by E-business and other implementations of information technology.

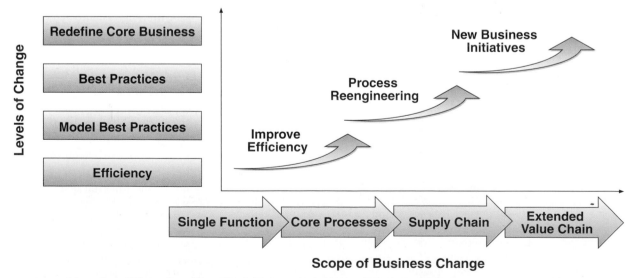

Source: Adapted from Craig Fellenstein and Ron Wood, *Exploring E-Commerce, Global E-Business and E-Societies* (Upper Saddle River, NJ: Prentice-Hall, 2000), p. 97.

Figure 7.12

The ten greatest challenges of developing and implementing intranet enterprise portals and enterprise resource planning systems reported by 100 E-business companies.

Intranet Enterprise Portal Challenges	Enterprise Resource Planning Challenges
● Security, security, security	● Getting end-user buy-in
● Defining the scope and purpose of the portal	● Scheduling/planning
● Finding the time and the money	● Integrating legacy systems/data
● Ensuring consistent data quality	● Getting management buy-in
● Getting employees to use it	● Dealing with multiple/international sites and partners
● Organizing the data	● Changing culture/mind-sets
● Finding technical expertise	● IT training
● Integrating the pieces	● Getting, keeping IT staff
● Making it easy to use	● Moving to a new platform
● Providing all users with access	● Performance/system upgrades

Source: Adapted from Kathleen Melymuka, "An Expanding Universe," *Computerworld*, September 14, 1998, p. 57; and Tim Ouellette, "Opening Your Own Portal," *Computerworld*, August 9, 1999. p. 79. Copyright 1998 and 1999 by Computerworld, Inc., Framingham, MA 01701, Reprinted from *Computerworld*.

End User Resistance and Involvement

Any new way of doing things generates some resistance by the people affected. Thus, the implementation of new E-business work support technologies can generate fear and resistance to change by employees. Let's look at a real world example that illustrates this phenomenon.

Automated Data Processing: Overcoming User Resistance to CRM

Senior managers at the accounting service firm Automated Data Processing Inc. (ADP) in Roseland, New Jersey, were thrilled at projections that a new CRM system would cut company costs by $450 million. But that wasn't the argument Howard Koenig used when he faced resistance from call center workers, sales representatives, and sales managers. Call center workers were worried about the increased stress of having to enter much more detailed data whenever a customer called—and also about Big Brother–type monitoring of their every move. Salespeople were worried that automating the submission of new customer contacts would get in the way of closing deals.

So rather than point out how the new system would help the company, Koenig focused on allaying fears. "We had to demonstrate that the technology was going to make their jobs better," said Koenig, corporate vice president of operations and client services at ADP. He showed call center workers how their managers would be able to better anticipate peak call times, thus improving staff scheduling. He showed them how having a history of each customer's interaction with the firm would lead to less-stressful encounters. Sales representatives, on the other hand, were shown that they never would have to make a call without knowing about any outstanding issues on an account, Koenig says. And salespeople, who wouldn't get their commissions until a contract was officially processed, could track the progress of a deal through the system.

In addition to meeting company objectives, turnover among call center workers has been cut by more than 10 percent—"We believe the job is actually less stressful," Koenig says—and sales representatives have improved the retention of existing accounts by 5 percent [22].

One of the keys to solving problems of **end user resistance** to new information technologies is proper education and training. Even more important is **end user involvement** in organizational changes, and in the development of new information systems. Organizations have a variety of strategies to help manage business change, and one basic requirement is the involvement and commitment of top management and all business stakeholders affected by the E-business planning process we described in Section I.

Direct end user participation in E-business planning and application development projects before a new system is implemented is especially important in reducing the potential for end user resistance. That is why end users frequently are members of E-business systems development teams or do their own development work. Such involvement helps ensure that end users assume ownership of a system, and that its design meets their needs. Systems that tend to inconvenience or frustrate users cannot be effective systems, no matter how technically elegant they are and how efficiently they process data. For example, Figure 7.13 illustrates some of the major obstacles to knowledge management systems in business. Notice that end user resistance to sharing knowledge is the biggest obstacle to the implementation of knowledge management applications. Let's look at a real world example that spotlights this problem and some of its solutions.

Context Integration: User Resistance to Knowledge Management	In a Web consulting firm, the whole business is pretty much locked away in the minds of employees. And Chairman Bruce Strong didn't feel that the consultants were sharing the ideas they had stored there. So he decided to design a knowledge-management system to help them unlock their thoughts and be more productive. After all, using technology to solve problems was what the company he had co-founded, Context Integration, was all about. Six months and half a million dollars later, he unveiled a new tool with a friendly acronym, IAN (Intellectual Assets Network). Just one snag: Few of his people actually wanted to use it.

The truth is that getting people to participate is the hardest part of knowledge management. Carla O'Dell, president of the American Productivity & Quality Center, says that of the companies trying knowledge management, less than 10 percent have succeeded in making it part of their culture.

Some reluctance surfaced at Context simply because IAN was a bother. Depositing notes or project records into the database was one more task in a consultant's busy day—and worse yet, it was a task that didn't have any obvious ugency. Even more important, IAN forced consultants to reveal their ignorance. Asking a trusted colleague a question is one thing; posting it for the whole company to see can be downright intimidating. Abdou Touray, who's been at Context even longer than IAN, says that consultants don't like admitting that they can't solve a problem. Moreover, they resented management's trying to impose what seemed like a rigid structure on their work.

But Strong made IAN usage part of everyone's job description. He even started paying them to use it. Each IAN task has now been assigned points, and the score accounts for 10 percent of a consultant's quarterly bonus. Before these metrics were introduced, only a third of Context employees were rated as good or better for IAN usage. Two months later, that IAN usage had almost doubled. "You don't want to be the person that doesn't use IAN at all," says Strong. "It's your performance—it's how we view you as a person in the company" [21].

Change Management

Figure 7.14 illustrates some of the key dimensions of **change management,** and the level of difficulty and business impact involved. Notice some of the people, process, and technology factors involved in the implementation of E-business strategies and applications, or other changes caused by introducing new information technologies

Figure 7.13

Obstacles to knowledge management systems. Note that end user resistance to knowledge sharing is the biggest obstacle.

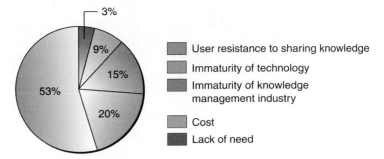

- User resistance to sharing knowledge
- Immaturity of technology
- Immaturity of knowledge management industry
- Cost
- Lack of need

Source: Adapted from Barb Cole-Gomolski, "Users Loathe to Share Their Know-How," *Computerworld*, November 17, 1997, p. 6. Copyright 1997 by Computerworld, Inc. Framingham, MA. 01701. Reprinted from *Computerworld*.

into a company. Some of the technical factors listed, such as systems integrators, outsourcing, and hardware and software technology selection, will be discussed in more detail in the next few chapters. For example, systems integrators are consulting firms or other outside contractors who may be paid to assume the responsibility for developing and implementing a new E-business application, including designing and leading its change management activities. And notice that people factors have the highest level of difficulty and longest time to resolve of any dimension of change management.

Thus, people are a major focus of organizational change management. This includes activities such as developing innovative ways to measure, motivate, and

Figure 7.14

Dimensions of change management. Examples of the people, process, and technology factors involved in managing the implementation of E-business or other IT-based changes to an organization.

	People	Process	Technology
Strategic (High Impact on Business)	• Change Leaders • Loose/Tight Controls • Executive Sponsorship and Support • Aligning on Conditions of Satisfaction	• Ownership • Design • Enterprisewide Processes • Interenterprise Processes	• Enterprise Architecture • Supplier Partnership • Systems Integrators • Outsourcing
Operational	• Recruitment • Retention • Training • Knowledge Transfer	• Change Control • Implementation Management • Support Processes	• Technology Selection • Technology Support • Installation Requirements

Impact on Business: Low → High

Level of Difficulty/Time to Resolve: Low → High

Source: Adapted from Grant Norris, James Hurley, Kenneth Hartley, John Dunleavy, and John Balls, *E-Business and ERP: Transforming the Enterprise*, p. 120. Copyright © 2000 by John Wiley & Sons, Inc. Reprinted by permission.

reward performance. So is designing programs to recruit and train employees in the core competencies required in a changing workplace. Change management also involves analyzing and defining all changes facing the organization, and developing programs to reduce the risks and costs and to maximize the benefits of change. For example, implementing a new E-business process such as customer relationship management might involve developing a *change action plan*, assigning selected managers as *change sponsors*, developing employee *change teams*, and encouraging open communications and feedback about organizational changes. Some key tactics change experts recommend include:

- Involve as many people as possible in E-business planning and application development.
- Make constant change an expected part of the culture.
- Tell everyone as much as possible about everything as often as possible, preferably in person.
- Make liberal use of financial incentives and recognition.
- Work within the company culture, not around it [23].

A Change Management Process

An eight-level process of change management is illustrated in Figure 7.15. This change management model is only one of many that could be applied to manage organizational changes caused by new E-business strategies and applications that transform a company into an E-business enterprise. For example, this model suggests that the E-business vision created in the strategic planning phase should be communicated in a compelling *change story* to the people in the organization. Evaluating the readiness for E-business changes within an organization and then developing change strategies and choosing and training change leaders and champions based on that assessment could be the next steps in the process.

These change leaders are the change agents that would then be able to lead change teams of employees and other business stakeholders in building a business case for E-business changes in technology, business processes, job content, and organizational structures. They could also communicate the benefits of these changes and lead training programs on the details of new E-business applications. Of course, many change management models include methods for performance measurement and rewards to provide financial incentives for employees and stakeholders to cooperate with changes that may be required. Fostering an E-business enterprise culture within the organization by establishing communities of interest for employees and other business stakeholders via Internet, intranet, and extranet discussion groups, for example, could also be a valuable change management strategy that provides stake-

Avnet Marshall: E-Business Transformation

Figure 7.16 illustrates how a company like Avnet Marshall can transform itself into an E-business enterprise. Notice how Avnet Marshall moved through several stages of organizational transformation as they implemented various E-business and E-commerce technologies. Throughout this change process, they were driven by their commitment to the customer value focus of the Free.Perfect.Now business model that we introduced in Chapter 2.

First, Avnet Marshall implemented an automated shipping and receiving system (AS/RS) and a quality order booking, resell application (QOBRA) as they focused on achieving customer value through cost savings generated by the efficiencies of automating these core business processes. Then they focused on achieving interconnectivity internally and building a platform for enterprise collaboration and knowledge management by implementing their AvNet intranet and a data warehouse. The second step was building an Avnet Marshall website on

Figure 7.15

The process of change management. Examples of the activities involved in successfully managing organizational change caused by the implementation of E-business strategies.

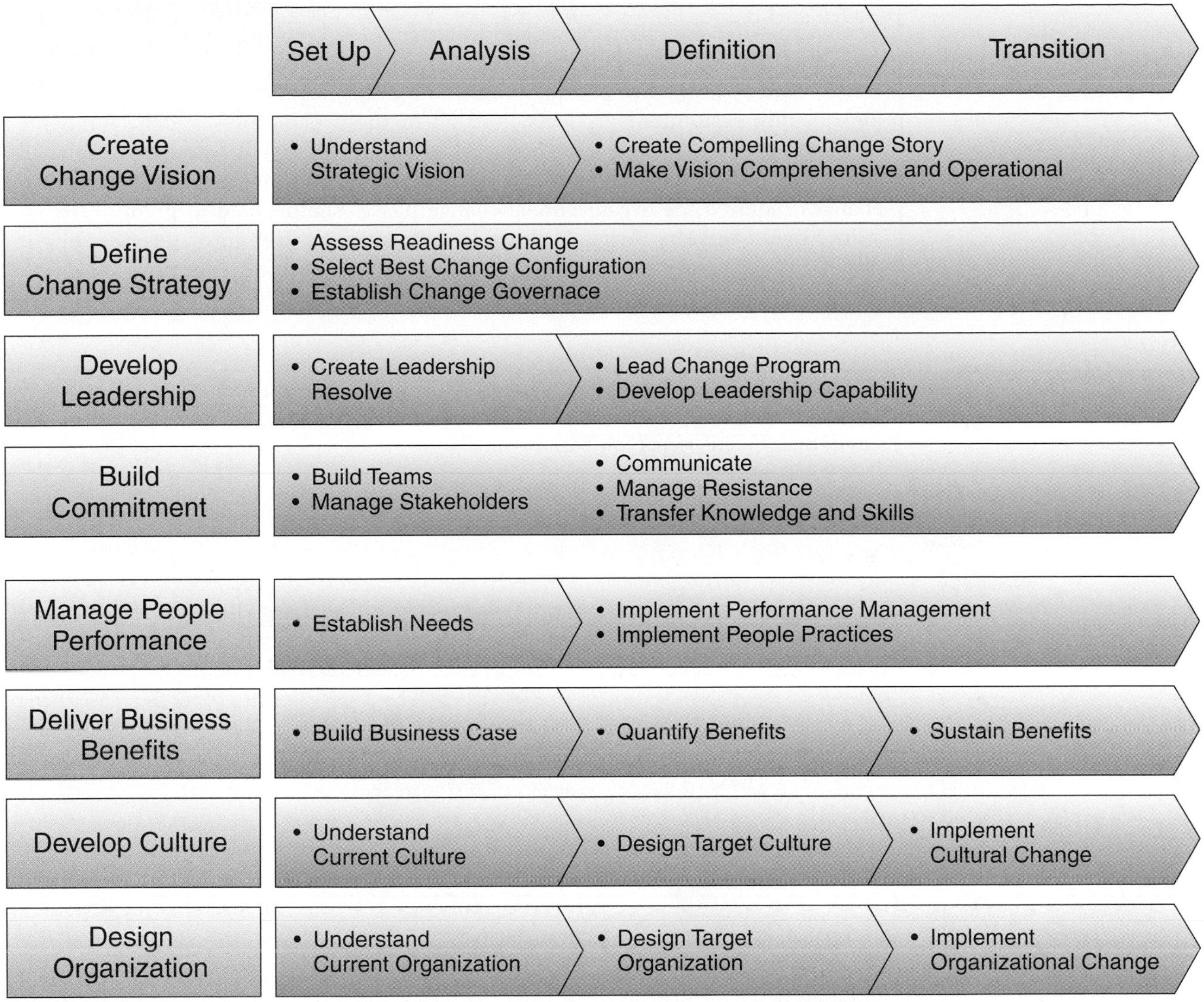

Source: Adapted from Martin Diese, Conrad Nowikow, Patric King, and Amy Wright, *Executive's Guide to E-Business: From Tactics to Strategy*, p. 190. Copyright © 2000 by John Wiley & Sons, Inc. Reprinted by permission.

the Internet to offer customers 24 × 7 online E-commerce transactions and customer support services. In addition, the company built a customized website for customers of its European partner SEI.

Next Avnet Marshall connected with their suppliers by building a Partnernet extranet and the Distribution Resource Planner (DRP) system, a supply chain management application that enables the company and its suppliers to help manage a customer's purchases and inventories. Avnet Marshall also implemented a customer relationship management and market intelligence system known as the Manufacturing Account Profile Planner (MAP), which integrates and uses all the customer information from other systems to better target its marketing activities and manage its customer contacts. As Figure 7.16 illustrates, Avnet Marshall's other innovative E-business applications help its customers (1) simulate online and design custom special-purpose microprocessor chips (Electronic Design Center), (2) design new products online with suppliers, as well as take online training classes using real-time streaming video and audio and online chat (NetSeminar), and (3) let customers themselves offer online seminars and push broadcasts to their employees and customers—the Education News and Entertainment Network (ENEN).

All of the E-business technologies and applications we have mentioned now enable Avnet Marshall to provide more value to its customers with fast delivery of high-quality customized products. And all of these E-business and E-commerce initiatives created many new internetworked business links between Avnet Marshall and its customers and business partners. These major technological and business changes required the organizational change phases summarized in Figure 7.16. In a little over five years, Avnet Marshall had transformed itself into a premier example of an internetworked, customer value focused, E-business enterprise [12].

Figure 7.16

Avnet Marshall moved through several stages of organizational transformation as they implemented various E-business and E-commerce technologies, driven by the customer value focus of their Free.Perfect.Now business model.

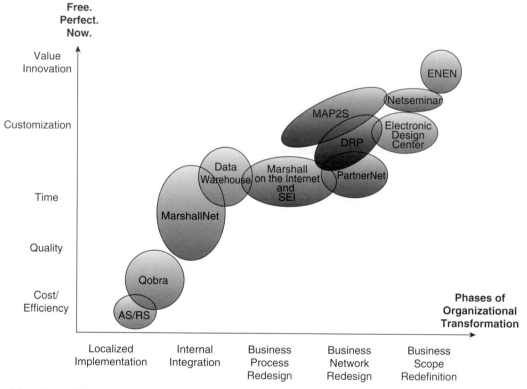

Source: Adapted from Omar El Sawy, Arvind Malhotra, Sanjay Gosain, and Kerry Young, "IT-Intensive Value Innovation in the Electronic Economy: Insights from Marshall Industries," *MIS Quarterly*, September 1999, p. 316. Reprinted by permission from the *MIS Quarterly*.

Summary

- **Organizational Planning.** Managing information technology requires planning for changes in business goals, processes, structures, and technologies. Planning is a vital organizational process that uses methods like the scenario approach and planning for competitive advantage to evaluate an organization's internal and external environments; forecast new developments; establish an organization's vision, mission, goals, and objectives; develop strategies, tactics, and policies to implement its goals; and articulate plans for the organization to act upon. A good planning process helps organizations learn about themselves and promotes organizational change and renewal.

- **E-Business Planning.** Strategic E-business planning involves aligning investment in information technology with a company's E-business vision and strategic goals such as reengineering business processes or gaining competitive advantages. It results in a strategic plan that outlines a company's E-business/IT strategies and technology architecture. The technology architecture is a conceptual blueprint that specifies a company's technology platform, data resources, applications architecture, and IT organization.

- **Implementing E-Business Change.** Implementation activities include managing the introduction and implementation of changes in business processes, organizational structures, job assignments, and work relationships resulting from E-business strategies and applications such as E-commerce initiatives, reengineering projects, supply chain alliances, and the introduction of new technologies. Companies use change management tactics such as user involvement in E-business planning and development to reduce end user resistance and maximize acceptance of E-business changes by all stakeholders. See Figures 7.14 and 7.15.

Key Terms and Concepts

These are the key terms and concepts of this chapter. The page number of their first explanation is in parentheses.

1. Change management (262)
2. E-business planning (255)
   a. Application planning (255)
   b. Architecture planning (256)
   c. Strategic planning (257)
3. End user involvement (262)
4. End user resistance (262)
5. Implementation (258)
6. Implementing E-business change (260)
7. Information technology architecture (254)
8. Organizational planning (250)
9. Planning for competitive advantage (252)
10. Scenario approach to planning (251)
11. SWOT analysis (253)

Review Quiz

Match one of the key terms and concepts listed previously with one of the brief examples or definitions that follow. Try to find the best fit for answers that seem to fit more than one term or concept. Defend your choices.

_____ 1. An organization should create a shared business vision and mission, and plan how it will achieve its strategic goals and objectives.

_____ 2. Outlines an E-business vision, E-business/IT strategies, and technical architecture for a company.

_____ 3. A blueprint for information technology in a company that specifies a technology platform, applications architecture, data resources, and IT organization structure.

_____ 4. Evaluating strategic E-business opportunities based on their risk/payoff potential for a company.

_____ 5. Planning teams simulate the role of information technology in various hypothetical business situations.

_____ 6. Evaluating IT proposals for new E-business application development projects.

_____ 7. Evaluating strategic E-business opportunities based on a company's capabilities and the competitive environment.

_____ 8. Accomplishing the strategies and applications developed during organizational planning.

_____ 9. Implementing new E-business strategies and applications within a company.

_____ 10. End users frequently resist the introduction of new technology.

_____ 11. End users should be part of planning for organizational change and E-business project teams.

_____ 12. Companies should try to minimize the resistance and maximize the acceptance of major changes in E-business and information technology.

Discussion Questions

1. Planning is a useless endeavor, because developments in E-business and E-commerce, and in the political, economic, and societal environment are moving too quickly nowadays. Do you agree or disagree with this statement? Why?

2. "Planning and budgeting processes are notorious for their rigidity and irrelevance to management action." How can planning be made relevant to the challenges facing an E-business enterprise?

3. Refer to the Real World Case on Accel Partners in the chapter. What new technologies do you think companies should include in their E-business and E-commerce planning? Give several examples and explain the possible impact of one of them.

4. What planning methods would you use to develop E-business and E-commerce strategies and applications for your own business? Explain your choices.

5. What are several E-business and E-commerce strategies and applications that should be developed and implemented by many companies today? Explain your reasoning.

6. Refer to the Real World Case on Cross Engineering, Pitney-Bowes, and Emerson in the chapter. "The Internet changes how we interface with the customer, how we manage internally . . ." What are several implications of this statement for E-business planning?

7. How can a company use change management to minimize the resistance and maximize the acceptance of changes in business and technology? Give several examples.

8. "Many companies plan really well, yet few translate strategy into action." Do you think this statement is true? Why or why not?

9. Review the real world examples on end user resistance to knowledge management (Context Integration) and customer relationship management (Automated Data Processing) in the chapter. What else would you recommend to encourage user acceptance in both cases? Explain your recommendations.

10. What major business changes beyond E-business and E-commerce do you think most companies should be planning for in the next ten years? Explain your choices.

Application Exercises

Complete the following exercises as individual or group projects that apply chapter concepts to real world business situations.

1. Business Insight: Analyzing Your Business Plan

Having a machine assess your revolutionary idea may seem like a bad idea. But Business Resource Software (www.brs-inc.com) wants to assess and screen business plans with something it calls Business Insight, a program that analyzes your model online or off. "There are a number of advantages over the more conventional method of actually asking a so-called knowledgeable human," says Jerry Spencer, a co-founder of BRS. "Human consultants often have a different agenda. They want to get more business, so they tell you what you want to hear." Business Insight and its database, however, have the advantage of being brutally honest. "We think it's better to tell you your weaknesses rather than your strengths," Spencer says.

Business Insight, the analysis software, includes 500 questions, costs $800, and has been sold to half of the Fortune 500 companies, according to Spencer. The program, which uses economic principles drawn from the works of business gurus Michael Porter of Harvard and Philip Kotler of Northwestern University, also has been sold to thousands of smaller business. The free online service, called Business Insight Online, is a scaled-down version.

Here's how it works: Clients answer 30 questions about their business plan, on such topics as the potential market, the company's experience, and the perceived competition. BRS's database then goes to work, spitting out your free summary analysis. See Figure 7.17.

a. Visit the BRS website, scroll to their Web Resources, and click on the "Analyze your business strategy" link. Register and begin answering the questions asked by the Business Insight software about a business idea you have.

b. Evaluate the list of 30 questions you are asked. How well do they cover the key points of business planning? Explain your reasoning.

c. Evaluate the analysis results you are given. How effective is the Business Insight service as a planning tool? Explain your answer.

Source: Adapted from Andy Goldberg, "Does Your Model Go?" *Business 2.0*, August 8, 2000, p. 35.

2. BRS Inc.: Evaluating Business Plans

The BRS website at www.brs-inc.com provides links to many business planning Web resources, including how to prepare and evaluate business plans, and examples of many business plans submitted in the Moot Corp. Competition by MBA students from top U.S. and international business schools.

a. Visit the BRS website. Click on Business Planning Resources and link to sites providing information you can review on preparing and evaluating business plans. Then click on Sample Business Plans and review the world champion and runner-up winning business plans, and any others you prefer.

b. How well do these plans meet the goal of presenting an outstanding business case for a business idea? Explain your answer.

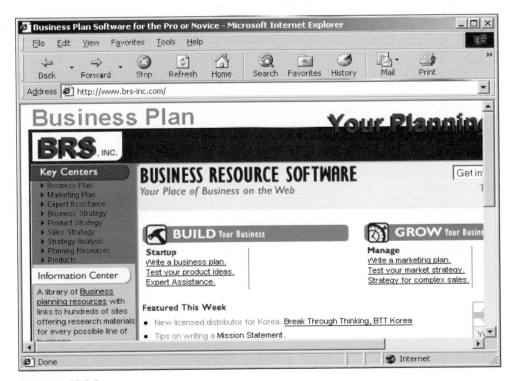

Figure 7.17

The Business Resource Software website provides a variety of business planning resources.

Courtesey BRS, Inc.

c. How could you improve any of the business ideas presented in the business plans you reviewed, or the business plans themselves? Give several examples to illustrate how you might be able to do so.

3. Developing an EDI System for Beta Business Products

Beta Business Products (BBP) sells business supplies directly to large corporations and wholesales its products to large business supply retailers. BBP has asked you to investigate the costs and benefits of developing an electronic data interchange system to connect with its customers.

You find that the cost of hardware and software to support this system would be approximately $540,000 the first year, with maintenance costs of $40,000 per year thereafter. Additional training and personnel costs in the IS department are estimated to be $200,000 the first year and $150,000 each year thereafter.

Benefits from the system will come from a reduction in the clerical time required to process orders and from improved market share. Since the impact on market share is difficult to quantify, you must base your quantitative analysis only on the savings in clerical time. BBP processes 275,000 orders per year. The processing time that could be saved by the EDI system is 20 minutes per order and the average cost of clerical labor is $12 including benefits. Turnover in clerical workers is currently running 40 percent per year. It is expected that the new system would process 20 percent of all orders the first year, 40 percent the second year, and 50 percent in the third and succeeding years.

a. Based on the data described above develop a spreadsheet comparing the costs and benefits of the EDI system over the first 5 years of operation. Use a column for each year and develop total cost and benefit estimates and net benefit (benefits minus costs) for each year based on the information above. Then compute an internal rate of return for this project.

b. Would you expect to see substantial resistance within the organization to this new system? Why or why not? Are there things the organization could do to reduce any resistance to the new system? Prepare a set of power point slides or similar presentation materials summarizing issues of resistance to the new system and measures that could be used to overcome this resistance.

4. Managing Salary Adjustments

You are director of IT services at a company that gives departments a great deal of flexibility in allocating merit raise funds. Departments are given a fixed pot of funds for merit raises and allowed to allocate them as they see fit. This year your department has received $55,000 to be distributed among your department's 25 employees. You, in consultation with your staff, have developed a process for allocating merit that contains three components.

1. Any employee completing a degree or a professional certificate during the year receives a $1,800 raise for that accomplishment.

2. 60% of the remaining merit funds are dispersed to employees receiving a good or excellent rating on their departmental annual evaluation. A fixed dollar amount is to be paid for good performance and those with an excellent performance will receive twice that amount.

3. The remaining merit funds, after step 2, are paid out by allocating a fixed dollar amount to each employee who received a peer evaluation of excellent.

An employee database table like the sample shown below, but including all 25 records is available to you from the website for this textbook. The textbook website is www.mhhe.com/business/mis/obrien/obrien5e/index.html. Click on downloads under the student resources section of that page.

a. Download the full employee table containing the records for all 25 of your employees from the website for this textbook. You may either perform a set of queries to determine the allocation of raises based on the criteria above, or you may copy the data to a spreadsheet and perform the manipulations to determine the amount of the various merit bonus components that will appropriately allocate the available pot of $55,000. Be sure to fully document the process you use—show all queries if you do your computations in the database—show appropriate intermediate result columns if you do your calculations in a spreadsheet.

b. Once you have determined the procedures needed to allocate the merit funds appropriately, write an updated query that will actually change each person's salary to reflect the merit raise they are to receive.

Employee_name	Employee_id	Salary	Performance_Eval	Team_Eval	Cert_Degree_Completed
Ann Adams	1234	$39,500.00	G	E	No
Bob Bates	2345	$43,250.00	A	G	No
Carl Combs	3456	$38,400.00	E	G	No
Dawn Davis	4567	$52,000.00	G	E	Yes
Ellen Eads	5678	$43,250.00	A	A	No

Merrill Lynch: Catch-up Leader in E-Commerce Technology

After Merrill Lynch stumbled embarrassingly late to offer online trading to its retail investors, America's premier brokerage firm vowed to get ahead in addressing the needs of its most valuable clients, institutional investors. To do it, the financial power house built an entirely separate software development division.

Merrill's e-commerce group is made up of around 150 software engineers. They have their own office a few blocks from the firm's New York headquarters. The team has spent the last 18 months converting the company's financial functions to the Internet. The challenges were clear-cut: provide institutional clients with the applications they want most, like trading applications and access to the firm's research reports over secure connections; make sure they never fail; and keep rolling out new applications and fixes for those already released. The answer was MLX.ML.com, a single web portal accessible by all institutional clients.

So far the move has worked remarkably well. A year and a half after the institutional e-commerce division's May 1999 launch, Merrill's institutional clients have direct electronic access to some of today's most sophisticated E-commerce applications. The firm's early struggles have been practically forgotten and now brokers industry wide hasten to keep pace with Merrill Lynch.

"Merrill is definitely ahead of the pack," says Todd Eyler, senior analyst of online financial services for Forrester Research. "Its institutional technologies are of the more advanced on the street."

Merrill Lynch is one of the world's largest full-service brokerage firms. It provides just about every imaginable financial service, from investment banking to debt and equity trading. The fact that its tech prowess is now mentioned in the same breath as that of Charles Schwab or ETrade is a testament to the work of the institutional e-commerce division, which made sure that the Web didn't happen to Merrill Lynch, again. It wasn't easy. It meant building and implementing web-based tolls for Merrill's huge corporate and institutional client group, which serves a myriad of customers, including banks and pension and endowment fund managers.

The institutional e-commerce division's various solutions are industry models. "Their applications are some of the most complex out there," says Dan Tsou, director of financial services at Proxicom, a web consultancy that helped Merrell Lynch go online. "The breadth of business lines and depth of technology involved are most demanding. "They're pushing the envelope of innovation."

The complexity of the required applications is mind-bending. Michael Packer, head of Merrill's institutional e-commerce team, points out that the firm's larger, more sophisticated clients want direct computer-to-computer links to ensure the highest level of security. That's not easy. Even more challenging is integrating the realtime updating of market data and sending it in real time. As the market flexes, Merrill Lynch must simultaneously receive and feed a massive amount of pricing information to a client's web browser, with full security, through multiple firewalls.

Thus far the team has built and implemented 50 new web-based applications, including several sophisticated trading applications and post trade applications that handle the logistics of settlement and clearance. The team also maintains a decade-old liquidity-management system through Boomberg, which processes as trillion in trades annually. "In terms of transaction volumes, security, data integrity, and the complexity of interactions with back-end systems, the demands we place on technology are unparalleled," Mr. Packer says.

However, the Merrill Lynch team knows that a mistake, even a split-second delay, could cost the firm not only a transaction but a customer. Or a lawsuit. Paradoxically, in this business playing it safe means walking the edge. The more advanced the technology, the more money the company can save itself and its clients. Implementing new technologies also brings in new business. That thinking inspired the ongoing shift of the company's institutional group from the phone to the Web.

The Merrill Lynch group has gotten some development help over the past two years from system integrator Proxicom. Once an application has been created, Merrill Lynch often turns over the ongoing management, testing, maintenance, and support to Fairfield, New Jersey, management service provider Aptegrity.

Merrill Lynch has accomplished what few others on the Street have—it has begun to think less like a bank and more like a development firm. It has restructured its team to better address its technological needs and transformed itself from the butt of industry jokes to an E-commerce leader.

Case Study Questions

1. What business challenges faced Merrill Lynch? How did they respond to those challenges?

2. What are several reasons why you think Merrill Lynch chose a strategy of concentrating more of their E-commerce catch-up efforts on serving their institutional investors, rather than their individual investors?

3. What is the business value and risk to Merrill of outsourcing ongoing management, testing, maintenance, and support?

Source: Adapted from Scott Tyler Shafer, "Trading on Innovation," *Red Herring*, January 16, 2001, pp. 76–78, and Melissa Solomon, "Look Who's Gaining," *Computerworld*, February 12, 2001, pp. 42–43.

Eastman Chemical and the Vanguard Group: Planning for Strategic E-Business Change

Only recently have CEOs begun to appreciate the impact of technology on their businesses. They have resisted spending money on IT for years because it was a tool that typically cost—but rarely made—lots of money. Instead, IT was viewed as a way to help the accounting departments keep better records or work faster, but the business could survive without it.

The Internet is the first technology to change that perception. If you sell on the Internet, you are completely dependent on technology. No Internet, no servers, no business.

Technology has never held that kind of sway before, and the opinion numbers show it. In 1998, only 55 percent of CEOs said that "technology decisions were an integral part of the decision making process." Today that number is 97 percent, according to a worldwide survey by the Chicago-based consultancy A.T. Kearney of more than 250 CEOs in 2000.

For example, executives at Eastman Chemical are planning for a strategic transition, and looking to IT as a key enabler. They want to take the company from a pure manufacturing company to a service organization. To help make that happen, they need to look outside their own industry for cues on technology strategies and spending levels, as they do their strategic planning.

Making these cross-industry analogies is how Gartner Group analyst Kurt Potter helps his clients get comfortable with big shifts in technology strategy. "To predict what you will spend on IT, figure out what industry you will look like in the future," says Potter, who is research director for Gartner's Management Strategies & Directions Service.

One planning model for Eastman to consider is The Vanguard Group, the Valley Forge, Pennsylvania-based mutual fund company. In 1986, Vanguard spent 12 percent of its operating budget on IT. In 2000, it will spend 42 percent, says Vanguard CIO Bob DiStefano. In those 14 years, Vanguard has gone from the ninth- to the second-largest mutual fund in terms of assets managed.

Along the way, DiStefano's company has endured a transformation that he sees coming for many other industries. The first change is in access. Vanguard's customers have demanded 24-hour phone access to accounts across an increasing number of different channels—online, phone and e-mail.

The second change has been breadth of services. Says DiStefano, "The question we've been asking ourselves since 1986 is, 'Do we want our product sold through other companies, or do we want to try to own the entire customer relationship ourselves?'" To grow in the mutual fund business, you have to choose the latter, he says.

So Vanguard has pulled together an entire range of financial products, all of them technology based. Why? Such products as brokerage services, individual retirement programs, increased financial advisory services and aggregated financial record keeping are all cheaper to provide online, he says. "After 14 years, we wouldn't be spending 42 percent of our operating budget on technology if the business and customers didn't like what they were getting. Technology has proven to be the most cost-effective way to expand our services and give customers better access to their accounts."

At Vanguard, business units don't just pay for their IT systems, they must also provide a senior executive to help IT projects full time. "You have to demand passionate sponsorship from the business," says Vanguard's DiStefano. "You can't leave it to the techies because they may not be connected well enough to the business to know what they should be providing. If the business units pull a senior person off the line to do a project, we know they are serious about it."

"Someone on the business side needs to own technology," says Gartner Group's Potter. "Companies need to do continuous cost/benefit analysis on IT projects, and businesspeople are the ones best suited to do that. They are the ones responsible for profit and loss."

And the quickest, easiest way to begin the shift to strategic IT spending is to create a direct line from IT to the CEO. That's what happened at Eastman Chemical last year when CIO Roger Mowen—whose background at the company is in sales and marketing—assumed the role of directing the company's E-commerce efforts. He eventually became CIO, reporting to the CEO. "We're an asset-intensive industry, and we've traditionally looked at technology as a cost," he says. "My proposition is that technology is an integral part of business today and should be represented at the table when deciding strategy, products and services to customers.

The question for the rest of the Fortune 500 is not whether they should spend significantly more on technology but rather how to ramp up technology spending quickly and wisely. Those that can use technology to transform their business practices and supply chains will become industry leaders. To do so, IT staff and businesspeople will need to forge a new partnership that alters the way they plan their IT investments. If non-IT executives become more responsible for technology spending—and IT executives are elevated to a peer adviser role rather than a subservient service function—companies will have the structure they need to transform themselves quickly and effectively.

Case Study Questions

1. Why has IT become such an integral part of most companies' business strategy?

2. How can Eastman Chemical and other companies use Vanguard's experience to transform themselves with the help of IT?

3. What role should business professionals and managers play in the planning and development of new IT/business applications?

Source: Adapted from Christopher Koch, "Sticker Shock," *Darwin*, February, 2001, pp. 37–42.

Brookfield Properties: Prototyping E-Commerce Strategies

The end of the dotcom mania doesn't mean that its underlying cause—the increasing pace of technological innovation—has disappeared. Far from it: Companies still have to cope with a world where change is occurring faster than they can plan for it. They know that the old, cautious planning process no longer works. If business strategies have a shelf life of only 20 months, companies can't spend 30 months fine-tuning and honing new businesses before launching them. What can old-line CEOs do other than tear out their hair in frustration?

Management strategist Michael Treacy thinks he has an answer. The co-founder of strategy technology firm Gen3 Partners and author of the now-classic Discipline of Market Leaders, Treacy thinks he has come up with a more sophisticated way for large companies to keep up with the changing business landscape. Treacy emphasizes that corporations must look at their existing assets—customer relationships, distribution channels, marketing muscle, patents, logistics expertise, manufacturing techniques—and try to come up with ways to rearrange those assets so that they support new strategies.

Then, rather than spending months deliberating, they should quickly test those new business strategies in small-scale ways. Sometimes the result of such strategic prototyping is a new and separate business, sometimes a complete revamping of the existing business—and sometimes, of course, the result is failure. But whatever the outcome, the point is not to spin off the new strategy but to hold onto the value it creates.

Once companies do that, Treacy says, it is important for them to try various approaches simultaneously to extract value from those assets. It is only through constant small-scale testing of business prototypes in the actual marketplace that you can determine what really works. You take a series of incremental steps, and as each one is successful, you up the ante.

For instance, Brookfield Properties, a Treacy client, owns or manages about 1200 million square free of real estate in commercial office towers and suburban office parks in North America, mostly in cities such as Boston, Denver, New York, and Toronto. As a landlord, Brookfield has established relationships with the thousands of businesses that are its tenants. But rather than simply provide well-lit, air-conditioned space to those tenants and leave it at that. Brookfield feels that it is in a position to help those businesses with many of their non-core functions—from procuring office supplies and computers to outsourcing payroll, health benefits, or the IT help desk. At least, that's the ultimate goal.

As its first step, Brookfield has created a new company, called OfficeTempo.com. Through OfficeTempo, office managers in Brookfield's buildings will be able to electronically purchase office supplies, computers, furniture, phones, high-speed Internet access, printing services, catering, flowers, corporate gifts, and more. The website is powered by Ariba e-commerce software and thus hooks into Ariba's existing network of suppliers.

By consolidating the purchases of Brookfield's many tenants, OfficeTempo hopes to be able to negotiate volume discounts with suppliers, especially those located near Brookfield's buildings. It also hopes to make the lives of office managers easier by giving them web software that can eliminate paper invoices, provide unified billing for everything they buy over the system, and help them better control the purchasing habits of other workers. Since Brookfield owns the buildings, it can also create central drop-off points for suppliers or modify the loading docks and freight elevators to accommodate the logistics that OfficeTempo will be orchestrating.

It seems like a smart idea—but that doesn't necessarily mean it's a workable one. So OfficeTempo is undergoing a test run: Brookfield is initially trying the business model on a small scale, open only to select tenants in Boston. A beta version of the site allows OfficeTempo to experiment with various offerings, see which suppliers are up to snuff, and refine its service through an interactive process of trial and error.

When the three-month trial period is over, Brookfield will expand the service to more buildings in the Boston market, going after other landlords' tenants as well (or bringing other landlords' in by offering them equity in OfficeTempo). Then, if Brookfield is still confident that the business can succeed, it will invest further to roll out the service to other cities.

Much is yet to be determined, but in this way, Brookfield will prototype its way to a new business that uses its existing assets and does not initially require substantial new resources in terms of capital or people (the three-month beta will cost less than $3 million and require about 25 people; serving the entire city of Boston would cost an additional $5 million). Yet OfficeTempo could potentially open an entirely new business to Brookfield.

Case Study Questions

1. What major E-commerce planning challenges are confronting many companies today?

2. What are the benefits and limitations of the planning and implementation approach for E-commerce projects recommended by Michael Treacy?

3. Do you approve of the E-commerce business model and planning and implementation approach chosen by Brookefield Properties? Why or why not?

Source: Adapted from Erik Schonfeld, "Trial and Error," *eCompany*, January/February 2001, pp. 76-76.

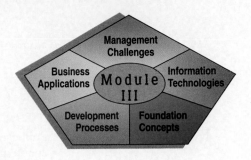

Management Challenges

Business Applications Module III Information Technologies

Development Processes Foundation Concepts

Developing E-Business

Solutions

Chapter Highlights

Learning Objectives

After reading and studying this chapter, you should be able to:

1. Use the systems development process outlined in this chapter, and the model of IS components from Chapter 1 as problem-solving frameworks to help you propose information systems solutions to simple business problems.

2. Describe and give examples to illustrate how you might use each of the steps of the information systems development cycle to develop and implement an E-business system.

3. Explain how prototyping improves the process of systems development for end users and IS specialists.

4. Identify the activities involved in the implementation of new information systems.

5. Describe several evaluation factors that should be considered in evaluating the acquisition of hardware, software, and IS services.

Developing E-Business Systems

IS Development

Suppose the chief executive of the company where you work asks you to find a Web-enabled way to get information to and from the salespeople in your company. How would you start? What would you do? Would you just plunge ahead and hope you could come up with a reasonable solution? How would you know whether your solution was a good one for your company? Do you think there might be a systematic way to help you develop a good solution to the CEO's request? There is. It's a problem-solving process called *the systems approach.*

When the systems approach to problem solving is applied to the development of information system solutions to business problems, it is called *information systems development* or *application development.* This section will show you how the systems approach can be used to develop E-business systems and applications that meet the business needs of a company and its employees and stakeholders.

Analyzing Raytheon, Cutter, GE, and Honeywell

Read the Real World Case on Raytheon, Cutter, GE, and Honeywell on the next page. We can learn a lot about different approaches to quality in E-business systems development. See Figure 8.1.

The conflict between speed and quality in developing new E-commerce applications is evident in this case. But as Eric Singleton of Raytheon indicates, the speed versus quality debate in the development of computer applications for business has been going on for a long time. Obviously, an E-business system developed quickly that performs badly, is a bad business investment. But so is a quality system whose development has taken so long, that it is delivered after a key business opportunity has passed. This is the essence of the debate being played out in this case.

Figure 8.1

Debby Sollenberger is an E-process leader who led the development of a digital desktop intranet portal for employees at GE Aircraft Engines.

Jim Callaway.

Raytheon, Cutter, GE, and Honeywell: Quality in E-Business Systems Development

People claim they're "flying by the seat of the pants and really being creative, saying this is a whole new world and we have to make it up as we go along," says Eric Singleton, director of electronic business at Raytheon Co. in Lexington, Massachusetts. "But that's the oldest argument in the world, and it's been proven wrong time and time again." In the 1990s, Singleton recalls, "there was subculture that said the development of Windows-based systems was such a fluid thing, it really didn't fit in with any type of process modeling." But it soon became clear that the old rules still applied, he says.

Singleton says he suspects that a no-rules approach to E-commerce systems development began in the early days, when people could still get away with it. "There did seem to be a proliferation of activity largely about creativity and look-and-feel," he says. "The emphasis in brochureware was on content, art, layout—soft, frilly stuff without many moving parts." Now the nature of E-commerce projects has changed from being content-oriented to more business-transaction-focused, says Jim Highsmith, a consultant at Cutter Consortium in Arlington, Massachusetts. "It's not cool to drop transactions, so the quality, in terms of defect levels, has got to be higher," he says.

But Highsmith says Web projects are different because of their high speed, changeability and uncertainty and require an approach to quality that he calls "light methodology." "In the past, we have equated discipline with formality and we've got to unlink those," Highsmith says. "Documentation is not understanding; formality is not discipline; process is not skill." He says the question for quality-oriented E-commerce and E-business project managers to ponder is, "How do I lighten up and maintain quality and improve speed and flexibility?"

The folks at GE Aircraft Engines (GEAE) in Cincinnati seem to have found an approach to quality that does just that. When E-process leader Debby Sollenberger put together a "digital desktop" intranet last year, she used a development methodology cobbled together from traditional GEAE quality processes, GE's company wide Six Sigma quality imitative, and E-business requirements.

The digital desktop allows GEAE employees to customize their access to any of 400,000 online files and interactive sites that they may need. Sollenberger's group had the site operational within one month. "This was very, very fast and very exciting," she says.

Sollenberger says the aircraft parts maker follows what it calls the New Product Introduction (NPI) process. The NPI is spelled out in "a huge notebook—about 2 inches thick—laying out step-by-step what you do, day to day, to introduce a new product or process," she says. "It's extremely rigorous and detailed and about a thorough as you can imagine."

But NPI wasn't designed for E-business, so GEAE condensed 2 inches of notebook pages and five years of Six Sigma experience into one page of deliverables, combining the speed of the Internet with the rigor of the Six Sigma program and NPI. The result was called a eNPI. "Of course, behind each deliverable is a checklist, so it's really longer," she says. "But the one-pager is the critical things an E-project needs to consider."

eNPI takes the angst out of lightening-speed Web application development, Sollenberger says. "We're confident that now that we have this in place, we're not going to miss something huge and let quality suffer," she says.

GEAE's eNPI quality program is designed to build quality into E-business application development projects that have to be done quickly. Here are some of the steps that less-disciplined developers might miss.

Prework. Analyze the project's scope by defining, measuring and analyzing the customer's requirements to clearly understand the whys behind the project.

Charter. Who's buying into the project? What's the current process, and what will the new e-process look like? What issues are critical to quality?

Reality check. Conduct an examination of issues such as resources, best-in-class technologies, options for outsourcing and build vs. buy.

One quality methodology doesn't fit all, and the Internet may require some flexibility. But whether your quality methodology is heavy, light or hybrid, it's a tool that's designed to save time, not consume it. Bill Sanders, CIO at Honeywell International Inc. in Morristown, New Jersey, says that good software development processes actually save time. "Speed doesn't always equal quality, but true quality always equals speed," he explains. "If you start with a true quality focus and a methodology, those actually help you do things faster," says Honeywell's Sanders. "They are fully consistent with speed and what we want to do in an Internet world."

Case Study Questions

1. Do you favor Eric Singleton's or Jim Highsmith's views on ensuring the quality of Web-based application development projects? Why?

2. Is GEAE's eNPI methodology the right approach for developing a personalized intranet portal application for their employees?

3. Would you recommend a more rigorous quality assurance approach for some E-business and E-commerce projects than others? Why or why not?

Source: Adapted from Kathleen Melymuka, "Ensuring E-Quality," *Computerworld*, January 29, 2001, pp. 44–45.

That's why Jim Highsmith of Cutter Consortium proposes a "light methodology" for some E-commerce projects, while Singleton insists that E-commerce development projects have moved beyond fast and easy Web "brochureware" applications to more mission-critical online transaction processing systems, where quality is essential. And Debby Sollenberger outlines a rapid development approach with quality safeguards used by GE Aircraft Engines to quickly develop an intranet portal application. Finally, Bill Sanders of Honeywell points out that a quality focus and methodology is fully consistent with the speed of development needed in an E-business environment.

The Systems Approach

The systems approach to problem solving uses a systems orientation to define problems and opportunities and develop solutions. Studying a problem and formulating a solution involves the following interrelated activities:

1. Recognize and define a problem or opportunity using *systems thinking*.
2. Develop and evaluate alternative system solutions.
3. Select the system solution that best meets your requirements.
4. Design the selected system solution.
5. Implement and evaluate the success of the designed system.

Systems Thinking

Using **systems thinking** to understand a problem or opportunity is one of the most important aspects of the systems approach. Management consultant and author Peter Senge calls systems thinking *the fifth discipline*. Senge argues that mastering systems thinking (along with the disciplines of personal mastery, mental models, shared vision, and team learning) is vital to personal fulfillment and business success in a world of constant change. The essence of the discipline of systems thinking is "seeing the forest *and* the trees" in any situation by:

- Seeing *interrelationships* among *systems* rather than linear cause-and-effect chains whenever events occur.
- Seeing *processes* of change among *systems* rather than discrete "snapshots" of change, whenever changes occur [32].

One way of practicing systems thinking is to try to find systems, subsystems, and components of systems in any situation you are studying. This is also known as using a *systems context*, or having a *systemic view* of a situation. For example, the business organization or business process in which a problem or opportunity arises could be viewed as a system of input, processing, output, feedback, and control components. Then to understand a problem and solve it, you would determine if these basic systems functions are being properly performed. See Figure 8.2.

Figure 8.2

An example of systems thinking. You can better understand a sales problem or opportunity by identifying and evaluating the components of a sales system.

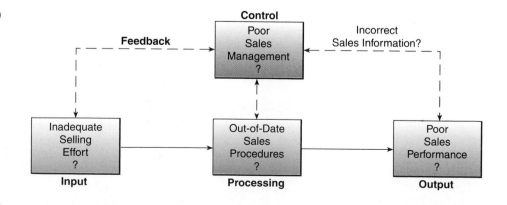

The sales process of a business can be viewed as a system. You could then ask: Is poor sales performance (output) caused by inadequate selling effort (input), out-of-date sales procedures (processing), incorrect sales information (feedback), or inadequate sales management (control)? Figure 8.2 illustrates this concept. ●

The Systems Development Cycle

Using the systems approach to develop information system solutions can be viewed as a multistep process called the **information systems development cycle,** also known as the *systems development life cycle* (SDLC). Figure 8.3 illustrates what goes on in each stage of this process, which includes the steps of (1) investigation, (2) analysis, (3) design, (4) implementation, and (5) maintenance.

You should realize, however, that all of the activities involved are highly related and interdependent. Therefore, in actual practice, several developmental activities can occur at the same time, so different parts of a development project can be at different stages of the development cycle. In addition, you and IS specialists may recycle back at any time to repeat previous activities in order to modify and improve a system you are developing.

Figure 8.3

The traditional information systems development cycle. Note how the five steps of the cycle are based on the stages of the systems approach. Also note the products that result from each step in the cycle, and that you can recycle back to any previous step if more work is needed.

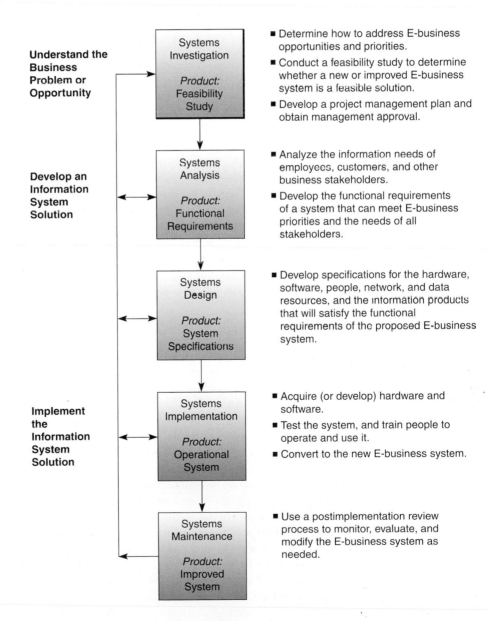

Understand the Business Problem or Opportunity

Systems Investigation
Product: Feasibility Study

- Determine how to address E-business opportunities and priorities.
- Conduct a feasibility study to determine whether a new or improved E-business system is a feasible solution.
- Develop a project management plan and obtain management approval.

Develop an Information System Solution

Systems Analysis
Product: Functional Requirements

- Analyze the information needs of employees, customers, and other business stakeholders.
- Develop the functional requirements of a system that can meet E-business priorities and the needs of all stakeholders.

Systems Design
Product: System Specifications

- Develop specifications for the hardware, software, people, network, and data resources, and the information products that will satisfy the functional requirements of the proposed E-business system.

Implement the Information System Solution

Systems Implementation
Product: Operational System

- Acquire (or develop) hardware and software.
- Test the system, and train people to operate and use it.
- Convert to the new E-business system.

Systems Maintenance
Product: Improved System

- Use a postimplementation review process to monitor, evaluate, and modify the E-business system as needed.

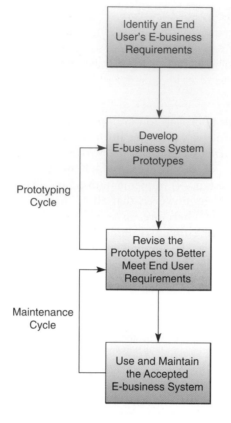

Figure 8.4

Application development using prototyping. Note how prototyping combines the steps of the systems development cycle and changes the traditional roles of IS specialists and end users.

Identify an End User's E-business Requirements

- **Investigation/Analysis.** End users identify their E-business needs and assess the feasibility of several alternative information system solutions.

Develop E-business System Prototypes

- **Analysis/Design.** End users and/or IS specialists use application development tools to interactively design and test prototypes of information system components that meet end user E-business needs.

Prototyping Cycle

Revise the Prototypes to Better Meet End User Requirements

- **Design/Implementation.** The E-business system prototypes are tested, evaluated, and modified repeatedly until end users find them acceptable.

Maintenance Cycle

Use and Maintain the Accepted E-business System

- **Implementation/Maintenance.** The accepted E-business system can be modified easily since most system documentation is stored on disk.

Prototyping

The systems development process frequently takes the form of, or includes, a *prototyping* approach. **Prototyping** is the rapid development and testing of working models, or **prototypes,** of new applications in an interactive, iterative process that can be used by both IS specialists and business professionals. Prototyping makes the development process faster and easier, especially for projects where end user requirements are hard to define. Thus, prototyping is sometimes called *rapid application design* (RAD). Prototyping has also opened up the application development process to end users because it simplifies and accelerates systems design. Thus prototyping has enlarged the role of end users and changed the methods of IS specialists in systems development. See Figure 8.4.

The Prototyping Process

Prototyping can be used for both large and small applications. Typically, large E-business systems still require using a traditional systems development approach, but parts of such systems can frequently be prototyped. A prototype of a business application needed by an end user is developed quickly using a variety of application development software tools. The prototype system is then repeatedly refined until it is acceptable.

As Figure 8.4 illustrates, prototyping is an iterative, interactive process that combines steps of the traditional systems development cycle. End users with sufficient experience with application development tools can do prototyping themselves. Alternatively, you could work with an IS specialist to develop a prototype system in a series of interactive sessions. For example, you could develop, test, and refine prototypes of management reports, data entry screens, or output displays.

Usually, a prototype is modified several times before end users find it acceptable. Any program modules that are not generated by application development software can then be coded by programmers using conventional programming languages. The final version of the application system is then turned over to its end users for operational use. Figure 8.5 outlines a typical prototyping-based systems development process for an E-business application.

Figure 8.5

An example of a typical prototyping-based systems development process for an E-business application.

Example of Prototyping Development
● **Team.** A few end users and IS developers form a team to develop an E-business application.
● **Schematic.** The initial prototype schematic design is developed.
● **Prototype.** The schematic is converted into a simple point-and-click prototype using prototyping tools.
● **Presentation.** A few screens and routine linkages are presented to users.
● **Feedback.** After the team gets feedback from users, the prototype is reiterated.
● **Reiteration.** Further presentations and reiterations are made.
● **Consultation.** Consultations are held with IT consultants to identify potential improvements and conformance to existing standards.
● **Completion.** The prototype is converted into a finished application.
● **Acceptance.** Users review and sign off on their acceptance of the new E-business system.
● **Installation.** The new E-business software is installed on network servers.

Amway, Inc.: Doing Prototyping

To keep development times to a minimum, Amway, Inc. sought to build an enterprise information portal that would essentially perform as an intelligent assistant, able to retrieve and format relevant information for employees in research and development. Craig Abbott, IT group leader, developed a Web-based application using Lotus Notes and Domino groupware systems.

After a series of prototypes and a pilot project, the portal (code-named Artemis) was rolled out to a cross-section of approximately 100 users in the product development and process development areas of the division. It retrieved information for costing, forecasting, and project management activities, and was slated to integrate with Amway's document management system.

To understand its business drivers, Amway set up a user development group that identified the information needed and how difficult it was to retrieve it. The initial prototype EIP was then tailored to help the project team meet its top three objectives: speed, accuracy, and ease of use. "The rapid development of prototypes (in a series of prototyping sessions with users) was important to help refine the system, because users sometimes have a hard time communicating the results they're looking for," says Steve Klemm, director of engineering R&D.

Artemis is still being phased in, but it's already having an impact. "The biggest benefit has been to provide a source of consistent information to the research and development staff," Klemm says. "There's less confusion during project discussions because everyone is looking at the same set of information" [36].

Starting the Systems Development Process

Do we have E-business opportunities? What are our E-business priorities? How can information technologies provide information system solutions that address our E-business priorities? These are the questions that have to be answered in the **systems investigation stage**—the first step in the systems development process. This stage may involve consideration of proposals generated by an E-business planning process, which we discussed in Chapter 7. The investigation stage also includes the preliminary study of proposed information system solutions to meet a company's E-business priorities and opportunities.

Feasibility Studies

Because the process of development can be costly, the systems investigation stage may require a preliminary study called a **feasibility study.** A feasibility study is a preliminary study where the information needs of prospective users and the resource

If management approves the recommendations of the feasibility study team, the development process can continue.

Jon Riley/Stone.

requirements, costs, benefits, and feasibility of a proposed project are determined. Then you might formalize the findings of this study in a written report that includes preliminary specifications and a developmental plan for a proposed E-business application. If management approves the recommendations of the feasibility study, the development process can continue. See Figure 8.6.

The goal of feasibility studies is to evaluate alternative system solutions and to propose the most feasible and desirable E-business application for development. The feasibility of a proposed E-business system can be evaluated in terms of four major categories, as illustrated in Figure 8.7.

The focus of **organizational feasibility** is on how well a proposed system supports the strategic E-business priorities of the organization. **Economic feasibility** is concerned with whether expected cost savings, increased revenue, increased profits, reductions in required investment, and other types of benefits will exceed the costs of developing and operating a proposed system. For example, if an E-business project can't cover its development costs, it won't be approved, unless mandated by government regulations or strategic business considerations.

Technical feasibility can be demonstrated if reliable hardware and software capable of meeting the needs of a proposed system can be acquired or developed by the business in the required time. Finally, **operational feasibility** is the willingness

Organizational, economic, technical, and operational feasibility factors. Note that there is more to feasibility than cost savings or the availability of hardware and software.

Organizational Feasibility	Economic Feasibility
• How well the proposed system supports the E-business priorities of the organization	• Cost savings • Increased revenue • Decreased investment requirements • Increased profits

Technical Feasibility	Operational Feasibility
• Hardware, software, and network capability, reliability and availability	• Employee, customer, supplier acceptance • Management support • Government or other requirements

Figure 8.8

Examples of how a feasibility study might measure the feasibility of a proposed E-commerce system.

Organizational Feasibility	Economic Feasibility
• How well a proposed E-commerce system fits the company's plans for integrating sales, marketing, and financial E-business systems	• Savings in labor costs • Increased sales revenue • Decreased investment in inventory • Increased profits
Technical Feasibility	**Operational Feasibility**
• Capability, reliability and availability of E-commerce hardware, software, and website management services	• Acceptance of employees • Management support • Customer and supplier acceptance

and ability of the management, employees, customers, suppliers, and others to operate, use, and support a proposed system. For example, if the software for a new E-commerce system is too difficult to use, customers or employees may make too many errors and avoid using it. Thus, it would fail to show operational feasibility. See Figure 8.8.

Cost/Benefit Analysis. Feasibility studies typically involve **cost/benefit analysis.** If costs and benefits can be quantified, they are called tangible; if not, they are called intangible. Examples of tangible costs are the costs of hardware and software, employee salaries, and other quantifiable costs needed to develop and implement an IS solution. **Intangible costs** are difficult to quantify; they include the loss of customer goodwill or employee morale caused by errors and disruptions arising from the installation of a new system.

Tangible benefits are favorable results, such as the decrease in payroll costs caused by a reduction in personnel or a decrease in inventory carrying costs caused by reduction in inventory. **Intangible benefits** are harder to estimate. Such benefits as better customer service or faster and more accurate information for management fall into this category. Figure 8.9 lists typical tangible and intangible benefits with examples. Possible tangible and intangible costs would be the opposite of each benefit shown.

Systems Analysis

What is **systems analysis?** Whether you want to develop a new application quickly or are involved in a long-term project, you will need to perform several basic activities of systems analysis. Many of these activities are an extension of those used in conducting a feasibility study. However, systems analysis is not a preliminary study. It is an in-depth study of end user information needs that produces *functional requirements* that are used as the basis for the design of a new information system. Systems analysis traditionally involves a detailed study of:

- The information needs of a company and end users like yourself.
- The activities, resources, and products of one or more of the present information systems being used.
- The information system capabilities required to meet your information needs, and those of other E-business stakeholders that may use the system.

Organizational Analysis

An **organizational analysis** is an important first step in systems analysis. How can anyone improve an information system if they know very little about the organizational environment in which that system is located? They can't. That's why the members of a development team have to know something about the organization, its management structure, its people, its business activities, the environmental systems it

Figure 8.9

Possible benefits of
E-commerce systems, with
examples. Note that an
opposite result for each of
these benefits would be a
cost or disadvantage of
E-commerce systems.

Tangible Benefits	Example
● Increase in sales or profits	● Development of E-commerce-based products
● Decrease in information processing costs	● Elimination of unnecessary documents
● Decrease in operating costs	● Reduction in inventory carrying costs
● Decrease in required investment	● Decrease in inventory investment required
● Increased operational efficiency	● Less spoilage, waste, and idle time

Intangible Benefits	Example
● Improved information availability	● More timely and accurate information
● Improved abilities in analysis	● OLAP and data mining
● Improved customer service	● More timely service response
● Improved employee morale	● Elimination of burdensome job tasks
● Improved management decision making	● Better information and decision analysis
● Improved competitive position	● Systems that lock in customers
● Improved business image	● Progressive image as perceived by customers, suppliers, and investors

must deal with, and its current information systems. Someone on the team must know this information in more detail for the specific business units or end user workgroups that will be affected by the new or improved information system being proposed. For example, a new inventory control system for a chain of department stores cannot be designed unless someone on a development team knows a lot about the company and the types of business activities that affect its inventory. That's why business end users are frequently added to systems development teams.

Analysis of the Present System

Before you design a new system, it is important to study the system that will be improved or replaced (if there is one). You need to analyze how this system uses hardware, software, network, and people resources to convert data resources, such as transactions data, into information products, such as reports and displays. Then, you should document how the information system activities of input, processing, output, storage, and control are accomplished.

For example, you might evaluate the format, timing, volume, and quality of input and output activities. Such *user interface* activities are vital to effective interaction between end users and a computer-based system. Then, in the systems design stage, you can specify what the resources, products, and activities should be to support the user interface in the system you are designing. Figure 8.10 presents a Web page from the analysis of an E-commerce website.

Panasonic.com: Evaluating an E-Commerce Website

Buying electronics direct from the manufacturer should be a cinch. But if you're looking for a VCR, don't go to Panasonic's online store, which sells a random selection of products (manicure sets and camcorder batteries were featured when I visited), but no VCRs. In addition to being very slow, the graphics-heavy pages don't provide the answers a customer needs to make a purchase.

The product catalog on Panasonic's home page is relegated to a pop-up menu that requires extensive scrolling. The menu has no entry for "VCR," although selecting "video" does lead to a page that lists VCRs as one of the choices. With two more clicks, you finally arrive at a product list that includes the PV–8400

("4-Head VHS Mono Video Cassette Recorder") and the PV–9400 ("4-Head VHS Mono VCR"). The latter is $40 cheaper. What's the difference? The site doesn't say—unless using acronyms saves money.

The page for the PV–S7680, the most expensive model, also fails to justify the price difference in terms that make sense to normal people. Are there any links to independent reviews that would be more credible than the manufacturer's own claim of "excellent picture quality"? No. Even though I'm in the market for a high-end VCR, I didn't buy this machine.

Most companies would do more business on the Internet if they fired their entire Web marketing department and replaced it with people who could produce interactive content that actually makes it easier for users to buy [26].

Functional Requirements Analysis

This step of systems analysis is one of the most difficult. You may need to work as a team with IS analysts and other end users to determine your specific business information needs. For example, first you need to determine what type of information each business activity requires; what its format, volume, and frequency should be; and what response times are necessary. Second, you must try to determine the information processing capabilities required for each system activity (input, processing, output, storage, control) to meet these information needs. *Your main goal is to identify what should be done, not how to do it.*

Finally, you should try to develop **functional requirements.** Functional requirements are end user information requirements that are not tied to the hardware, software, network, data, and people resources that end users presently use or might use in the new system. That is left to the design stage to determine. For example, Figure 8.11 shows examples of functional requirements for a proposed E-commerce application.

Figure 8.10

A Web page from Panasonic's E-commerce site at www.panasonic.com.

Courtesy of Panasonic Corporation.

Figure 8.11

Examples of functional requirements for a proposed E-commerce system.

Examples of Functional Requirements
● **User Interface Requirements** Automatic entry of product data and easy-to-use data entry screens for Web customers.
● **Processing Requirements** Fast, automatic calculation of sales totals and shipping costs.
● **Storage Requirements** Fast retrieval and update of data from product, pricing, and customer databases.
● **Control Requirements** Signals for data entry errors and quick E-mail confirmation for customers.

Systems Design

Systems analysis describes *what* a system should do to meet the information needs of users. **Systems design** specifies *how* the system will accomplish this objective. Systems design consists of design activities that produce system specifications satisfying the functional requirements that were developed in the systems analysis process.

A useful way to look at systems design is illustrated in Figure 8.12. This concept focuses on three major products, or *deliverables*, that should result from the design stage. In this framework, systems design consists of three activities: user interface, data, and process design. This results in specifications for user interface methods and products, database structures, and processing and control procedures. Let's take a closer look at user-interface design, since it is the system component closest to business end users, and the one they will most likely help design.

User Interface Design

The user interface design activity focuses on supporting the interactions between end users and their computer-based applications. Designers concentrate on the design of attractive and efficient forms of user input and output, such as easy-to-use Internet or intranet Web pages.

As we mentioned earlier, user interface design is frequently a *prototyping* process, where working models or prototypes of user interface methods are designed and modified several times with feedback from end users. The user interface design process produces detailed design specifications for information products such as display screens, interactive user/computer dialogues (including the sequence or flow of dialogue), audio responses, forms, documents, and reports. Figure 8.13 gives examples of user interface design elements and guidelines suggested for the multimedia Web pages of E-commerce websites. Figure 8.14 presents actual before and after screen displays of the user interface design process for a work scheduling application of State Farm Insurance Company [27].

Figure 8.12

Systems design can be viewed as the design of user interfaces, data, and processes.

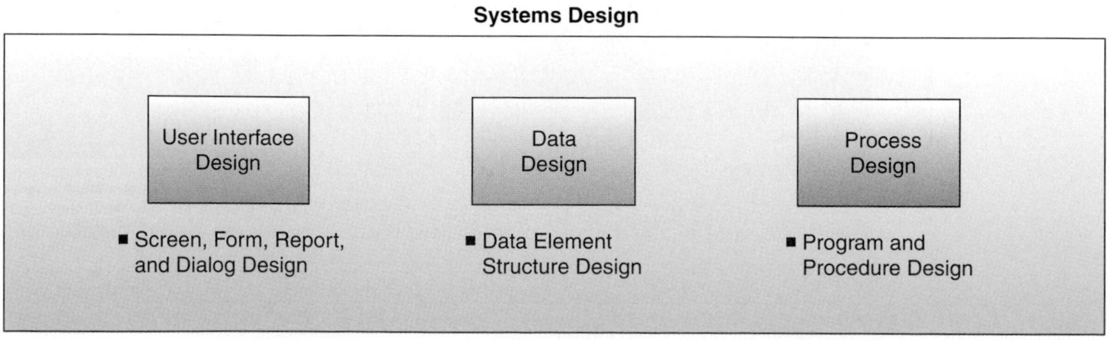

Systems Design

User Interface Design	Data Design	Process Design
■ Screen, Form, Report, and Dialog Design	■ Data Element Structure Design	■ Program and Procedure Design

Quicken Loans: Web Page Design

One yellow box. A measly 150 by 72 pixels on the QuickenLoans.com home page. Fifteen minutes of coding on a Tuesday afternoon. Yet it boosted Quicken Loans Inc.'s user return rates from 2 percent to 11 percent. Talk about an inexpensive way to recapture customer loyalty. That's the power of proper Web design. The problem isn't so much the coding but knowing what to code. And that's where Web redesign plans like those of QuickenLoans.com come in.

Creating a good design is a challenge all E-commerce sites face because a poor design can frustrate customers and have a bad financial impact. As studies from Zona Research have shown, more than one-third of online shoppers who have trouble finding a product just give up altogether. And really dissatisfied customers don't just stay away; they discourage their friends from visiting, too.

QuickenLoans.com, a leader in the booming online mortgage business, has been through the website redesign trenches and has deduced three key lessons: keep testing to see what works and what's wrong, keep tweaking (modifying features) to fix what's wrong and, when necessary, tell customers what they should buy instead of giving them too many choices [31].

System Specifications

System specifications formalize the design of an application's user interface methods and products, database structures, and processing and control procedures. Therefore, systems designers will frequently develop hardware, software, network, data, and personnel specifications for a proposed system. Figure 8.15 shows examples of system specifications that could be developed for an E-commerce system.

Computer-Aided Systems Engineering

Computer-aided systems engineering (CASE), which also stands for *computer-aided software engineering*, involves using software called CASE tools to perform many of the activities of the systems development life cycle. CASE provides many software tools for both the *front end* of the systems development life cycle (planning, analysis, and design) and the *back end* of systems development (implementation and maintenance). See Figure 8.16. For example, a *system repository* is a software tool to manage a special database for all of the analysis and design details of a system generated with other systems development tools. The repository helps to ensure consistency and compatibility in the design of the data elements, processes, user interfaces, and other aspects of the system being developed.

Figure 8.13 Useful guidelines for the user interface design of business websites.

Checklist for Corporate Websites

- **Remember the Customer:** Successful websites are built solely for the customer, not to make company vice presidents happy.
- **Aesthetics:** Successful designs combine fast-loading graphics and simple color palettes for pages that are easy to read.
- **Broadband Content:** The Web's coolest stuff can't be accessed by most Web surfers. Including a little streaming video isn't bad, but don't make it the focus of your site.
- **Easy to Navigate:** Make sure it's easy to get from one part of your site to another. Providing a site map, accessible from every page, helps.
- **Searchability:** Many sites have their own search engines; very few are actually useful. Make sure yours is.
- **Incompatibilities:** A site that looks great on a PC using Internet Explorer can often look miserable on an iBook running Netscape.
- **Registration Forms:** Registration forms are a useful way to gather customer data. But make your customers fill out a three-page form, and watch them flee.
- **Dead Links:** Dead links are the bane of all Web surfers—be sure to keep your links updated. Many Web-design software tools can now do this for you.

Source: Adapted from "Design Matters," Technology Buyers Guide, *Fortune*, Winter 2001, p. 186. © 2001 Time, Inc. All rights reserved.

Figure 8.14

An example of the user interface design process. State Farm developers changed this work scheduling and assignment application's interface after usability testing showed that end users working with the old interface (at left) didn't realize that they had to follow a six-step process. If users jumped to a new page out of order, they would lose their work. The new interface (at right) made it clearer that a process had to be followed.

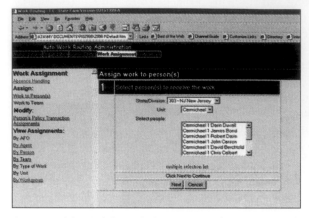 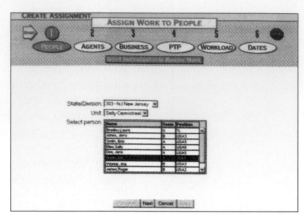

Courtesy of the Usability Lab, State Farm, and ComputerWorld.

Integrated CASE tools (called I-CASE) are now available that can assist all of the stages of systems development. Some of these CASE tools support *joint application design* (JAD), where a group of systems analysts, programmers, and end users can jointly and interactively design new applications. Finally, if the development of new systems can be called *forward engineering*, some CASE tools support *reverse engineering*. That is, they allow systems analysts to inspect the logic of a program code for old applications and convert it automatically into more efficient programs that significantly improve system effectiveness.

Figure 8.15

Examples of system specifications for a new E-commerce system.

Examples of System Specifications
● **User Interface Specifications** Use personalized screens that welcome repeat Web customers and make product recommendations.
● **Database Specifications** Develop databases that use object relational database management software to organize access to all customer and inventory data, and multimedia product information.
● **Software Specifications** Acquire an E-commerce software engine to process all E-commerce transactions with fast responses, i.e., retrieve necessary product data, and compute all sales amounts in less than one second.
● **Hardware and Network Specifications** Install redundant networked Web servers and sufficient high bandwidth telecommunications lines to host the company E-commerce website.
● **Personnel Specifications** Hire an E-commerce manager and specialists and a webmaster and Web designer to plan, develop, and manage E-commerce strategies.

Figure 8.16

Sharper Image used the WebObjects application development tool to create and test prototypes of dynamic Web pages for the catalog of products at their website.

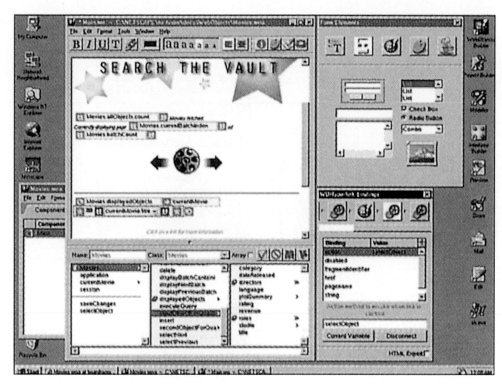

Courtesy of NeXT Software.

End User Development

In a traditional systems development cycle, your role as a business end user is similar to that of a customer or a client. Typically, you make a request for a new or improved system, answer questions about your specific information needs and information processing problems, and provide background information on your existing E business systems. IS professionals work with you to analyze your problem and suggest alternative solutions. When you approve the best alternative, it is designed and implemented. Here again, you may be involved in a prototyping design process or be on an implementation team with IS specialists.

However, in **end user development,** IS professionals play a consulting role, while you do your own application development. Sometimes a staff of user consultants may be available to help you and other end users with your application development efforts. This may include training in the use of application packages; selection of hardware and software; assistance in gaining access to organization databases; and, of course, assistance in analysis, design, and implementing your E-business application.

Focus on IS Activities

It is important to remember that end user development should focus on the fundamental activities of any information system: input, processing, output, storage, and control. Figure 8.17 illustrates these system components and the questions they address.

In analyzing a potential application, you should focus first on the **output** to be produced by the application. What information is needed and in what form should it be presented? Next, look at the **input** data to be supplied to the application. What data are available? From what sources? In what form? Then you should examine the **processing** requirements. What operations or transformation processes will be

Figure 8.17   End user development should focus on the basic information processing activity components of an information system.

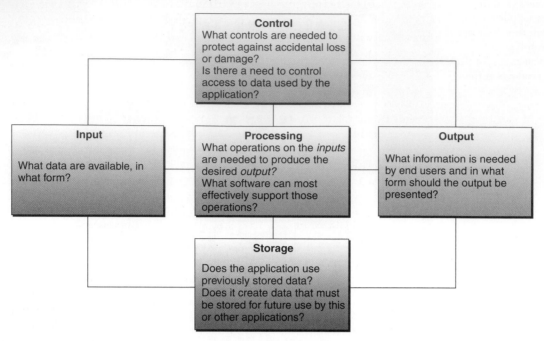

Source: Adapted from James N. Morgan, *Application Cases in MIS*, 3rd ed. (New York: Irwin/McGraw-Hill, 1999), p. 4.

required to convert the available inputs into the desired output? Among software packages the developer is able to use, which package can best perform the operations required?

You may find that the desired output cannot be produced from the inputs that are available. If this is the case, you must either make adjustments to the output expected, or find additional sources of input data, including data stored in files and databases from external sources. The **storage** component will vary in importance in end user applications. For example, some applications require extensive use of stored data or the creation of data that must be stored for future use. These are better suited for database management development projects than for spreadsheet applications.

Necessary **control** measures for end user applications vary greatly depending upon the scope and duration of the application, the number and nature of the users of the application, and the nature of the data involved. For example, control measures are needed to protect against accidental loss or damage to end user files. The most basic protection against this type of loss is simply to make backup copies of application files on a frequent and systematic basis. Another example is the cell protection feature of spreadsheets that protects key cells from accidental erasure by users.

Doing End User Development

In end user development, you and other business professionals can develop new or improved ways to perform your jobs without the direct involvement of IS specialists. The application development capabilities built into a variety of end user software packages have made it easier for many users to develop their own computer-based solutions. For example, you can use a website development tool to help you develop, update, and manage an intranet website for your business unit. Or you might use an electronic spreadsheet package as a tool to develop a way to easily analyze weekly sales results for the sales managers in a company. Or you could use a database management package to design data-entry displays to help sales clerks enter sales data, or to develop monthly sales analysis reports needed by district sales managers. Let's take a look at a real world example of how many companies are encouraging business end users to do their own website development. See Figures 8.18 and 8.19.

Providence Health Systems: End User Web Development	Business groups at Providence Health systems in Portland, Oregon, complained to information technology staff about the sometimes outdated and incorrect content of the company's intranet websites. That was especially frustrating to IT workers, because the content originated from and belonged to the business groups, says Erik Sargent, lead Internet developer at the health care provider. So Providence Health's IT and Web development group did what many companies are considering. They gave up some of their central power to let business personnel in different departments contribute directly to corporate Internet and intranet sites with the help of Web content development tools.

More IT groups can do this because the tools have made it easier for users to create, manage, and update websites without knowing the intricacies of the Internet programming language HTML. Sargent and his team at Providence Health used Microsoft FrontPage 98 on their development efforts. And because the company standardized on Microsoft Office productivity tools, it made sense to stay with FrontPage when allowing employees to do the intranet publishing duties.

One reason was that FrontPage maintained the same look and feel as Office, so there was a gentler learning curve. The other reason: FrontPage was cheaper to roll out to the 108 non-IT people now contributing to the intranet, rather than buying high-end tools with big price tags [28].

Figure 8.18

Microsoft FrontPage is an example of an easy-to-use end user website development tool.

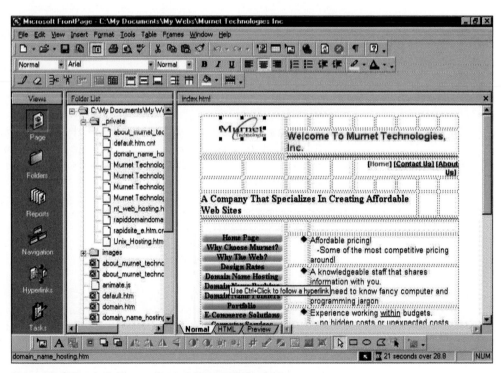

Courtesy of Microsoft Corporation and Murnet Technologies.

Figure 8.19

How companies are encouraging and managing intranet website development by business end users.

Encouraging End User Web Development

- **Look for Tools That Make Sense.**
  Some Web development tools may be too powerful and more costly than what your business end users really need.

- **Spur Creativity.**
  Consider a competition among business departments for the best website, to help spur users to more creative uses of their intranet sites.

- **Set Some Limits.**
  Yes, you have to keep some control. Consider putting limits on exactly what parts of a Web page users can change and who can change what pages. You still want some consistency across the organization.

- **Give Managers Responsibility.**
  Make business unit managers sign off on who will be Web publishing from their groups, and make the managers personally responsible for the content that goes on their websites. That will help prevent the publishing of inappropriate content by some users.

- **Make Users Comfortable.**
  Training users well on the tools will help users become confident in their ability to properly manage and update their sites—and save IT the trouble of fixing problems later on or providing continuous support for minor problems.

Source: Adapted from Tim Ouellette, "Giving Users the Key to Their Web Content," *Computerworld*, July 26, 1999, p. 67. Copyright 1999 by Computerworld, Inc., Framingham, MA 01701. Reprinted from *Computerworld*.

Section II   Implementing E-Business Systems

Implementation

Once a new E-business system has been designed, it must be implemented and maintained. The implementation process we will cover in this section follows the investigation, analysis, and design stages of the systems development cycle we discussed in Section I. Implementation is a vital step in the deployment of information technology to support the E-business systems by a company for employees, customers, and other business stakeholders.

Analyzing Select Comfort and VocalPoint

Read the Real World Case on Select Comfort and VocalPoint on the next page. We can learn a lot from this case about the importance of the implementation process in maintaining the quality and reliability of E-business systems. See Figure 8.20.

Managing the implementation of changes made to E-commerce systems is the focus of this case. Thus, Steve Etzell of Select Comfort believes that the need to make quick changes to improve or update an E-commerce Web site must be balanced with the need to keep rock-solid reliability an essential E-business requirement. He demonstrates this with an example where what seemed like a small unauthorized change to a Web page brought his E-commerce system down. Don Ursem of VocalPoint insists that his E-commerce services must be held to the same reliability standards as the telephone system, even though his fast-growing Web business requires frequent system changes as it expands. Therefore, Ursem demands total control of any changes made to his system by the managed service provider that hosts his Web-to-phone business, and monitors the system remotely to assure that this policy is implemented.

Figure 8.20

Don Ursem is vice president of network operations at VocalPoint, Inc., where system reliability is a key quality of their E-commerce services.

Kathrin Miller.

Select Comfort and VocalPoint: Implementing Web System Changes

Steve Etzell saw for himself how quickly a minor unauthorized change can foul up a web site. Etzell, director of web technology at Select Comfort Corp. in Minneapolis, was on vacation when he got a call telling him the bed maker and retailer's web site performance had gone "into the tank." The reason: A developer had let a business group user "twist his arm" into dynamically generating user-specific price quotes on a web page that showed an entire category of Select Comfort's products. The site had previously sent users to a cached page that showed the same prices to everyone.

That change "seemed fairly innocuous," Etzell recalls. But the page "is accessed potentially 100,000 times per day…and you'll bring the server to its knees" by forcing it to dynamically create the page for each visitor, he adds.

It's that kind of unplanned, untested change that web site managers hate and users love. Managing systems changes on the Web is a "balancing act" between the need to keep your very public web site up and running and the need to update it often enough to keep it attractive to visitors, says Etzell.

The Web environment is unique because users demand changes within hours, not weeks. Changes to web content aren't done by database administrators who first check the validity of the data and its effect on site performance, but by marketing managers. There's no single mainframe vendor to release software updates or patches on a regular schedule, but rather a half-dozen or more suppliers that find and fix flaws in their software products on their own schedules.

Then there's security, which can require major changes to sites as hackers discover new ways to bring them down. "There's a lot more changes going on in these web-facing systems, with most of those relating to security," says Jason Lochhead, co-founder and chief technology officer at Data Return Corp., a Dallas-based managed hosting company. "You didn't have to worry so much on legacy systems because they're isolated from public traffic."

Thus, when Don Ursem compares the reliability of his web site with that of the telephone system, he isn't kidding. Ursem is vice president of network operations at VocalPoint Inc., a San Francisco-based application service provider that lets consumers access web sites via phone by converting web data into voice responses. VocalPoint sells the service to telephone companies and in vertical markets such as health care. For the end user, "it's a telephone application," and "you expect your telephone to work all of the time," says Ursem. But that's easier said than done.

First, there's the volume: VocalPoint leases two telecom data lines, each of which can handle 644 simultaneous incoming calls and needs 135 servers to process them. Then there's growth: As he adds new lines, Ursem expects that he'll soon be managing about 650 servers across three sites.

VocalPoint also rolls out a new release of its voice web-browsing software every three months and is converting about 30 Windows NT servers to Linux to support a new text-to-speech engine. Then there are routine upgrades and maintenance of the databases, operating systems, network switches and storage-area networks. Each must be tested for its effect on the system, rolled out in a coordinated way and tracked so that if any updates backfire, the offending change can be pulled out of production.

Ursem, a former mainframe data center manager, ended up outsourcing his IT operations to Intira Corp., a managed service provider in Pleasanton, California. The selection came after a grueling examination of seven outsourcers to see how they matched up with his goals of outsourcing and automating change management of his systems.

Ursem wanted a service-level agreement that covered not only the servers and network, but also the incoming lines and their links to the servers. He insisted on choosing his server hardware and software, which ruled out many outsourcers that require customers to use standard offerings. He also insisted that the outsourcer's staff follow written procedures and that he have access to an online monitoring tool to ensure that those procedures were being followed. Ursem demanded and got contractual commitments "that there would be no changes made to my environment without my prior approval," including updates to network switches, storage environments or software drivers.

Intira monitors the operation of its systems with Hewlett-Packard's OpenView system monitor software, which would have bogged down if Ursem had also used it to do continuous, real-time monitoring for any changes in every server. So, using StatePoint Plus, change-management software developed by Westinghouse Electric, "I have the ability, from San Francisco, to link into the Intira data center and compare any set of servers against a reference server" to find and investigate any unexpected changes, Ursem says.

"I don't want changes done manually by gangs of people," says Ursem. "Then you would suffer from human inconsistencies. "I'm looking to reduce that. Anything I can automate, I will. Anything I can outsource, I will."

Case Study Questions

1. What types of changes are typically made to established Web systems? What is their business value?

2. What are the business problems and management challenges involved in implementing changes to established Web systems?

3. What are several ways that changes to established systems can be managed and properly implemented?

Source: Adapted from Robert Scheier, "You Want to Change What?," *Computerworld*, March 12, 2001, pp. 64–65.

Figure 8.21

An overview of the implementation process. Implementation activities are needed to transform a newly developed information system into an operational system for end users.

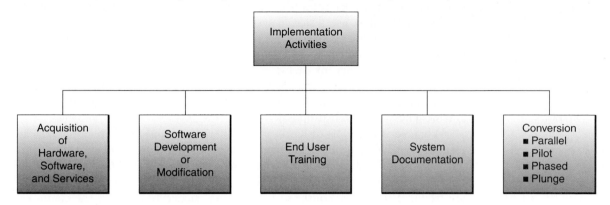

Implementing New Systems

Figure 8.21 illustrates that the **systems implementation** stage involves hardware and software acquisition, software development, testing of programs and procedures, development of documentation, and a variety of conversion alternatives. It also involves the education and training of end users and specialists who will operate a new system.

Implementation can be a difficult and time-consuming process. However, it is vital in ensuring the success of any newly developed system, for even a well-designed system will fail if it is not properly implemented. Figure 8.22 illustrates the activities and timelines that might be required to implement an intranet for a new employee benefits system in the human resources department of a company.

Evaluating Hardware Software, and Services

How do companies evaluate and select hardware and software? Large companies may require suppliers to present bids and proposals based on system specifications developed during the design stage of systems development. Minimum acceptable physical and performance characteristics for all hardware and software requirements are established. Most large business firms and all government agencies formalize these

Figure 8.22

An example of the implementation process activities and timelines for a company installing an intranet-based employee benefits system in its human resource management department.

Intranet Implementation Activities	Month 1	Month 2	Month 3	Month 4
Acquire and install server hardware and software	██			
Train administrators	██			
Acquire and install browser software	████			
Acquire and install publishing software	███			
Train benefits employees on publishing software	██			
Convert benefits manuals and add revisions	████			
Create Web-based tutorials for the intranet		████		
Hold rollout meetings				██

Source: Adapted from Melanie Hills, *Intranet Business Strategy* (New York: John Wiley & Sons, 1997), p. 193. Reprinted by permission of John Wiley & Sons, Inc. Copyright © 1997 by John Wiley & Sons, Inc.

requirements by listing them in a document called an RFP (request for proposal) or RFQ (request for quotation). Then they send the RFP or RFQ to appropriate vendors, who use it as the basis for preparing a proposed purchase agreement.

Companies may use a *scoring* system of evaluation when there are several competing proposals for a hardware or software acquisition. They give each **evaluation factor** a certain number of maximum possible points. Then they assign each competing proposal points for each factor, depending on how well it meets the specifications of the computer user. Scoring each evaluation factor for several proposals helps organize and document the evaluation process. It also spotlights the strengths and weaknesses of each proposal.

Whatever the claims of hardware manufacturers and software suppliers, the performance of hardware and software must be demonstrated and evaluated. Independent hardware and software information services (such as Datapro and Auerbach) may be used to gain detailed specification information and evaluations. Other users are frequently the best source of information needed to evaluate the claims of manufacturers and suppliers. That's why Internet newsgroups established to exchange information about specific software or hardware vendors and their products have become one of the best sources for obtaining up-to-date information about the experiences of users of the products. See Figure 8.23.

Large E-business companies frequently evaluate proposed hardware and software by requiring the processing of special *benchmark* test programs and test data. Benchmarking simulates the processing of typical jobs on several computers and evaluates their performances. Users can then evaluate test results to determine which hardware device or software package displayed the best performance characteristics.

Hardware Evaluation Factors

When you evaluate hardware for an E-business system, you should investigate specific physical and performance characteristics for each hardware component to be acquired. This is true whether you are evaluating microcomputers, mainframes, or peripheral devices. Specific questions must be answered concerning many important factors. Ten of these **hardware evaluation factors** and questions are summarized in Figure 8.24.

Notice that there is much more to evaluating hardware than determining the fastest and cheapest computing device. For example, the question of obsolescence must be addressed by making a technology evaluation. The factor of ergonomics is also very important. Ergonomic factors ensure that computer hardware and software are user-friendly, that is, safe, comfortable, and easy to use. Connectivity is another important evaluation factor, since so many network technologies and bandwidth alternatives are available to connect computer systems to the Internet, intranet, and extranet networks.

Software Evaluation Factors

You should evaluate software according to many factors that are similar to those used for hardware evaluation. Thus, the factors of performance, cost, reliability, availability, compatibility, modularity, technology, ergonomics, and support should be used to evaluate proposed software acquisitions. In addition, however, **the software evaluation factors** summarized in Figure 8.25 must also be considered. You should answer the questions they generate in order to properly evaluate software purchases. For example, some software packages are notoriously slow, hard to use, bug-filled, or poorly documented. They are not a good choice, even if offered at attractive prices.

Figure 8.23

Example of E-commerce hardware, software, and services offered by IBM and IPlanet, a joint venture of Sun Microsystems and Netscape. These are the kinds of hardware, software, and IS services that many E-business companies are evaluating and acquiring to support their moves into E-commerece.

IPlanet	IBM
Hardware	**Hardware**
Full range of Sun offerings, including low-end desktop and workgroup servers, midrange E3500, E4500, E5500, and E6500 servers and mainframe-class E10,000 server. Also has storage systems.	Full range of offerings, including Netfinity servers, AS/400 midrange for small and midsize businesses, RS6000 servers for UNIX customers and System 390 mainframes for large enterprises. Also has full range of storage options
Software	**Software**
Web server: IPlanet Web Server (formerly Netscape Enterprise Server).	**Web server:** Lotus DominoGo Web server.
Storefront: IPlanet MerchantXpert (formerly Netscape MerchantXpert).	**Storefront:** WebSphere Commerce Suite (formerly known as Net.Commerce) for storefront and catalog creation, relationship marketing and order management. Can add Commerce Integrator to integrate with back-end systems and Catalog Architect for content management.
Middleware/transaction services: IPlanet Application Server (Also NetDynamics Application Server, Netscape Application Server).	**Middleware/transaction services:** WebSphere application server manages transactions. MQ Series queues messages and manages connections. CICS processes transactions.
Database: None.	**Database:** DB2 Universal Database.
Tools: Recently acquired Forte tools and NetBeans for building Java components.	**Tools:** WebSphere Studio includes set of predefined templates and common business logic.
Other applications include: IPlanet Certificate Management Solution, IPlanet BillerXpert for Internet bill presentment and payment, IPlanet PublishingXpert for digital goods delivery and selling and IPlanet Portal Server to help companies set up personalized hub sites.	**Other applications include:** IBM Payment Suite for handling credit cards and managing digital certificates.
Services	**Services**
IPlanet Professional Services, Sun Professional Services. Also, Sun has "dotcom" practice to strategize and build E-commerce sites.	IBM Global Services, which includes groups organized by each major industry, including retail and financial. Can design, build and host E-commerce applications.

Source: Adapted from Carol Sliwa, "E-Commerce Solutions: How Real?" *Computerworld*, February 28, 2000, pp. 68–69. Copyright 2000 by Computerworld, Inc., Framingham, MA 01701. Reprinted from *Computerworld*.

Evaluating IS Services

Most suppliers of hardware and software products and many other firms offer a variety of **IS services** to end users and organizations. Examples include assistance during E-commerce website development, installation or conversion of new hardware and software, employee training, and hardware maintenance. Some of these services are provided without cost by hardware manufacturers and software suppliers.

Other types of IS services needed by a business can be outsourced to an outside company for a negotiated price. For example, *systems integrators* take over complete responsibility for an organization's computer facilities when an organization outsources its computer operations. They may also assume responsibility for developing and implementing large systems development projects that involve many vendors and

Figure 8.24

A summary of ten major hardware evaluation factors. Notice how you can use this to evaluate a computer system or a peripheral device.

Hardware Evaluation Factors	Rating
Performance What are its speed, capacity, and throughput?	
Cost What is its lease or purchase price? What will be its cost of operations and maintenance?	
Reliability What are the risk of malfunction and its maintenance requirements? What are its error control and diagnostic features?	
Compatibility Is it compatible with existing hardware and software? Is it compatible with hardware and software provided by competing suppliers?	
Technology In what year of its product life cycle is it? Does it use a new untested technology or does it run the risk of obsolescence?	
Ergonomics Has it been "human factors engineered" with the user in mind? Is it user-friendly, designed to be safe, comfortable, and easy to use?	
Connectivity Can it be easily connected to wide area and local area networks that use different types of network technologies and bandwidth alternatives?	
Scalability Can it handle the processing demands of a wide range of end users, transactions, queries, and other information processing requirements?	
Software Is system and application software available that can best use this hardware?	
Support Are the services required to support and maintain it available?	
Overall Rating	

subcontractors. Value-added resellers (VARs) specialize in providing industry-specific hardware, software, and services from selected manufacturers. Many other services are available to end users, including systems design, contract programming, and consulting services. Evaluation factors and questions for IS services are summarized in Figure 8.26.

Microsoft and IBM: Customer Service Satisfaction

Microsoft

The effectiveness of Microsoft's support depends on who you are, or whom you know, according to a recent *Computerworld* survey. The company is highly selective in determining who receives its Premier Support plan, the very attentive service it's using to get deeper into the corridors of Fortune 500 corporations. Very large—2,500 users or more—companies fortunate enough to be included in Premier Support receive Microsoft's undivided and very effective attention. But the mediocre grades Microsoft received from *Computerworld*'s survey come largely from the rank-and-file companies that don't quality for Premier class. These users, the vast majority of Microsoft business customers, are bounced to one of the company's many support partners.

One bright spot for Microsoft: Users really like its website support and gave it the highest grade of any in the survey. Respondents said that between its website and its TechNet informational CD-ROM service, Microsoft is the best at letting its users help themselves.

IBM

IBM's whatever-the-customer-wants approach to service has made it the benchmark by which other vendors are measured, according to several *Computerworld* survey respondents. Big Blue scored highest in six of eight rating categories and achieved the highest customer-satisfaction grade in the entire survey for its emergency and mission-critical service. IT managers gave the highest grades to the responsiveness and knowledge demonstrated by IBM's phone staff. IBM, they said, best follows the priorities users set when calling in problems. Priority 1 means a system is down. When that happens, IBM's goal is to connect the user to the person best qualified to fix the system within the hour.

IBM lost ground in *Computerworld*'s survey over website support, however. Surveyed managers said IBM's site is OK for logging minor problems into a queue but not among the best when users need to quickly locate specific solutions. IBM wasn't alone in the area of weak Web-based support, but it's certainly one place that IBM needs to work on [2].

Other Implementation Activities

Testing, documentation, and training are keys to successful implementation of a new E-business system. See Figure 8.27.

Testing

System testing may involve testing website performance, testing and debugging software, and testing new hardware.

An important part of testing is the review of prototypes of displays, reports, and other output. Prototypes should be reviewed by end users of the proposed systems

Figure 8.25

A summary of selected software evaluation factors. Note that most of the hardware evaluation factors in Figure 8.24 can also be used to evaluate software packages.

Software Evaluation Factors	Rating
Quality Is it bug free, or does it have many errors in its program code?	
Efficiency Is the software a well-developed system of program code that does not use much CPU time, memory capacity, or disk space?	
Flexibility Can it handle our E-business processes easily, without major modification?	
Security Does it provide control procedures for errors, malfunctions, and improper use?	
Connectivity Is it *Web-enabled* so it can easily access the Internet, intranets, and extranets, on its own, or by working with Web browsers or other network software?	
Language Is it written in a programming language that is familiar to our own software developers?	
Documentation Is the software well documented? Does it include help screens and helpful software agents?	
Hardware Does existing hardware have the features required to best use this software?	
Other Factors What are its performance, cost, reliability, availability, compatibility, modularity, technology, ergonomics, scalability, and support characteristics? (Use the hardware evaluation factor questions in Figure 8.24)	
Overall Rating	

Evaluation Factors for IS Services	Rating
Performance What has been their past performance in view of their past promises?	
Systems Development Are website and other E-business developers available? What are their quality and cost?	
Maintenance Is equipment maintenance provided? What are its quality and cost?	
Conversion What systems development and installation services will they provide during the conversion period?	
Training Is the necessary training of personnel provided? What are its quality and cost?	
Backup Are similar computer facilities available nearby for emergency backup purposes?	
Accessibility Does the vendor provide local or regional sites that offer sales, systems development, and hardware maintenance services? Is a customer support center at the vendor's website available? Is a customer hot line provided?	
Business Position Is the vendor financially strong, with good industry market prospects?	
Hardware Do they provide a wide selection of compatible hardware devices and accessories?	
Software Do they offer a variety of useful E-business software and application packages?	
Overall Rating	

for possible errors. Of course, testing should not occur only during the system's implementation stage, but throughout the system's development process. For example, you might examine and critique prototypes of input documents, screen displays, and processing procedures during the systems design stage. Immediate end user testing is one of the benefits of a prototyping process.

Documentation

Developing good user **documentation** is an important part of the implementation process. Sample data entry display screens, forms, and reports are good examples of documentation. When computer-aided systems engineering methods are used, documentation can be created and changed easily since it is stored in a CASE system repository. Documentation serves as a method of communication among the people responsible for developing, implementing, and maintaining a computer-based system. Installing and operating a newly designed system or modifying an established application requires a detailed record of that system's design. Documentation is extremely important in diagnosing errors and making changes, especially if the end users or systems analysts who developed a system are no longer with the organization.

Training

Training is a vital implementation activity. IS personnel, such as user consultants, must be sure that end users are trained to operate a new E-business system or its implementation will fail. Training may involve only activities like data entry, or it may also involve all aspects of the proper use of a new system. In addition, managers and end users must be educated in how the new technology impacts the company's business operations and management. This knowledge should be supplemented by training programs for any new hardware devices, software packages, and their use

Roger Tully/Stone.

for specific work activities. Figure 8.28 illustrates how one business coordinated its
E-business training program with each stage of its implementation process for developing intranet and E-commerce access within the company.

Clarke American Checks: Web-Based ERP Training	If it's 10 A.M., workers at Clarke American Checks Inc. are firing up their Web browsers for a collaborative training lesson on how to perform purchasing with their new SAP AG enterprise resource planning (ERP) software. During the daily sessions, end users in more than 20 locations either watch their colleagues perform simulated transactions with the software, or do it themselves.
	Self-paced ERP training delivered via the Web is becoming a popular concept. Users say training eats up 10 to 20 percent of an ERP project's budget and is one of the more vexing parts of an ERP development project. Many ERP systems have tricky user interfaces and are highly customized, making generic, computer-based training courses ineffective. Clarke American, a San Antonio-based check printer, is in a growing group of companies using Web-based training to get workers up to speed on enterprise resource planning applications. Doing so can trim up to 75 percent off the cost of traditional training methods, such as instructor-led sessions, users said [4].

Conversion Methods

The initial operation of a new E-business system can be a difficult task. This typically requires a **conversion** process from the use of a present system to the operation of a new or improved application. Conversion methods can soften the impact of introducing new information technologies into an organization. Four major forms of system conversion are illustrated in Figure 8.29. They include:

- Parallel conversion.
- Phased conversion.
- Pilot conversion.
- Plunge or direct cutover.

Figure 8.28 How one company developed E-business training programs for the implementation of Internet E-commerce and intranet access for its employees.

Conversions can be done on a *parallel* basis, whereby both the old and the new systems are operating until the project development team and end user management agree to switch completely over to the new system. It is during this time that the operations and results of both systems are compared and evaluated. Errors can be identified and corrected, and the operating problems can be solved before the old system is abandoned. Installation can also be accomplished by a direct cutover or *plunge* to a newly developed system.

Conversion can also be done on a *phased basis*, where only parts of a new application or only a few departments, branch offices, or plant locations at a time are converted. A phased conversion allows a gradual implementation process to take place within an organization. Similar benefits accrue from using a *pilot conversion*, where one department or other work site serves as a test site. A new system can be tried out at this site until developers feel it can be implemented throughout the organization.

IS Maintenance

Once a system is fully implemented and is being used in business operations, the maintenance function begins. **Systems maintenance** is the monitoring, evaluating, and modifying of operational E-business systems to make desirable or necessary improvements. For example, the implementation of a new system usually results in the phenomenon known as **the** *learning curve*. Personnel who operate and use the system will make mistakes simply because they are not familiar with it. Though such

Figure 8.29

The four major forms of conversion to a new system.

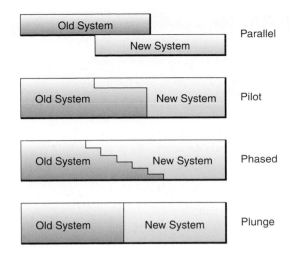

errors usually diminish as experience is gained with a new system, they do point out areas where a system may be improved.

Maintenance is also necessary for other failures and problems that arise during the operation of a system. End users and information systems personnel then perform a *troubleshooting* function to determine the causes of and solutions to such problems.

The maintenance activity includes a **postimplementation review** process to ensure that newly implemented systems meet the E-business objectives established for them. Errors in the development or use of a system must be corrected by the maintenance process. This includes a periodic review or audit of a system to ensure that it is operating properly and meeting its objectives. This audit is in addition to continually monitoring a new system for potential problems or necessary changes.

Maintenance also includes making modifications to an E-business system due to changes in the business organization or the business environment. For example, new tax legislation, company reorganizations, and new E-business and E-commerce ventures may require major changes to current E-business systems.

Farmland Industries and Lockheed Martin: Implementing ERP Systems	Farmland Industries, a $10.7 billion farmer-owned cooperative in Kansas City, Missouri, installed a version of the SAP R/3 enterprise resource planning (ERP) software tailored for oil and gas users two years ago. Farmland has had only minor problems with the software, said Dick Weaver, technology manager at its petroleum and crop production units. But changing the way the company does business to take full advantage of R/3 has been a sticky proposition. Because Farmland didn't do much of that work up front, its finance and order-entry operations didn't see the kind of savings they were looking for. Now the cooperative is going back and making the business-process changes that were put off earlier in the project. "If you just put in SAP, you haven't gained a whole lot," Weaver said. "Two years into it, we're getting a lot of value. The first year, we didn't."

At Lockheed Martin Aeronautics, 900 business users from its three aircraft manufacturing companies have been working to design common ways to enter orders and process other transactions in using R/3. When that's done, several hundred users will test the system for another six months. Lockheed Martin first rolled out R/3 at an aircraft maintenance operation, and installed SAP's human resources module a few months later, to get its feet wet before bigger installations at the manufacturing units. Its project team also sought advice from Pratt & Whitney Canada, an aircraft engine supplier that had previously done an R/3 rollout [34].

Summary

- **The Systems Development Cycle.** Business end users and IS specialists may use a systems approach to help them develop information system solutions to meet E-business opportunities. This frequently involves a systems development cycle where IS specialists and end users conceive, design, and implement E-business systems. The stages, activities, and products of the information systems development cycle are summarized in Figure 8.3.

- **Prototyping.** Prototyping is a major alternative methodology to the traditional information systems development cycle. It includes the use of prototyping tools and methodologies, which promote an iterative, interactive process that develops prototypes of user interfaces and other information system components. See Figure 8.4.

- **End User Development.** The application development capabilities built into many end user software packages have made it easier for end users to develop their own E-business applications. End users should

focus their development efforts on the system components of business processes that can benefit from the use of information technology, as summarized in Figures 8.19.

- **Implementing IS.** The implementation process for information system projects is summarized in Figure 8.30. Implementation involves acquisition, testing, documentation, training, installation, and conversion activities that transform a newly designed E-business system into an operational system for end users.

- **Evaluating Hardware, Software, and Services.** Business professionals should know how to evaluate the acquisition of information system resources. IT vendors' proposals should be based on specifications developed during the design stage of systems development. A formal evaluation process reduces the possibility of incorrect or unnecessary purchases of hardware or software. Several major evaluation factors, summarized in Figures 8.24, 8.25, and 8.26, can be used to evaluate hardware, software, and IS services.

Figure 8.30

An overview of the implementation process. Implementation activities are needed to transform a newly developed information system into an operational system for end users.

Implementing New Systems
● **Acquisition**   Evaluate and acquire necessary hardware and software resources and information system services. Screen vendor proposals.
● **Software Development**   Develop any software that will not be acquired externally as software packages. Make any necessary modifications to software packages that are acquired.
● **Training**   Educate and train management, end users, customers and other business stakeholders. Use consultants or training programs to develop user competencies.
● **Testing**   Test and make necessary corrections to the programs, procedures, and hardware used by a new system.
● **Documentation**   Record and communicate detailed system specifications, including procedures for end users and IS personnel and examples of input screens and output displays and reports.
● **Conversion**   Convert from the use of a present system to the operation of a new or improved system. This may involve operating both new and old systems in *parallel* for a trial period, operation of a *pilot* system on a trial basis at one location, *phasing* in the new system one location at a time, or an immediate *plunge* or *cutover* to the new system.

Key Terms and Concepts

These are the key terms and concepts of this chapter. The page number of their first explanation is in parentheses.

1. Computer-aided systems engineering   (287)
2. Conversion methods   (301)
3. Cost/benefit analysis   (283)
4. Documentation   (300)
5. Economic feasibility   (282)
6. End user development   (289)
7. Evaluation factors   (295)
   a. Hardware   (296)
   b. IS services   (297)
   c. Software   (296)
8. Feasibility study   (281)
9. Functional requirements   (285)
10. Implementation process   (293)
11. Intangible   (283)
    a. Benefits   (283)
    b. Costs   (283)
12. Operational feasibility   (282)
13. Organizational analysis   (283)
14. Organizational feasibility   (282)
15. Postimplementation review   (303)
16. Prototype   (280)
17. Prototyping   (280)
18. Systems analysis   (283)
19. Systems approach   (278)
20. Systems design   (286)
21. Systems development life cycle   (279)
22. Systems implementation   (295)
23. Systems investigation   (281)
24. Systems maintenance   (302)
25. Systems specifications   (287)
26. System testing   (299)
27. Systems thinking   (278)
28. Tangible   (283)
    a. Benefits   (283)
    b. Costs   (283)
29. Technical feasibility   (282)
30. User interface design   (286)

Review Quiz

Match one of the key terms and concepts listed previously with one of the brief examples or definitions that follow. Try to find the best fit for answers that seem to fit more than one term or concept. Defend your choices.

_____ 1. Using an organized sequence of activities to study a problem or opportunity using systems thinking.

_____ 2. Trying to recognize systems and the new interrelationships and components of systems in any situation.

_____ 3. Evaluating the success of a solution after it has been implemented.

_____ 4. Your evaluation shows that benefits outweigh costs for a proposed system.

_____ 5. The costs of acquiring computer hardware, software, and specialists.

_____ 6. Loss of customer goodwill caused by errors in a new system.

_____ 7. Increases in profits caused by a new system.

_____ 8. Improved employee morale caused by efficiency and effectiveness of a new system.

_____ 9. A multistep process to conceive, design, and implement an information system.

_____ 10. The first stage of the systems development cycle.

_____ 11. Determines the organizational, economic, technical, and operational feasibility of a proposed information system.

_____ 12. Cost savings and additional profits will exceed the investment required.

_____ 13. Reliable hardware and software are available to implement a proposed system.

_____ 14. Customers will not have trouble using a proposed system.

_____ 15. The proposed system supports the strategic plan of the business.

_____ 16. Studying in detail the information needs of users and any information systems presently used.

_____ 17. A detailed description of user information needs and the input, processing, output, storage, and control capabilities required to meet those needs.

_____ 18. The process that results in specifications for the hardware, software, people, network, and data resources and information products needed by a proposed system.

_____ 19. Systems design should focus on developing user-friendly input and output methods for a system.

_____ 20. A detailed description of the hardware, software, people, network, and data resources and information products required by a proposed system.

_____ 21. Acquiring hardware and software, testing and documenting a proposed system, and training people to use it.

_____ 22. Making improvements to an operational system.

_____ 23. Using software tools to computerize many of the activities in the systems development process.

_____ 24. A working model of an information system.

_____ 25. An interactive and iterative process of developing and refining information system prototypes.

_____ 26. Managers and business specialists can develop their own E-business applications.

_____ 27. Includes acquisition, testing, training, and conversion to a new system.

_____ 28. Performance, cost, reliability, technology, and ergonomics are examples.

_____ 29. Performance, cost, efficiency, language, and documentation are examples.

_____ 30. Maintenance, conversion, training, and business position are examples.

_____ 31. Operate in parallel with the old system, use a test site, switch in stages, or cut over immediately to a new system.

_____ 32. Checking whether hardware and software work properly for end users.

_____ 33. A user manual communicates the design and operating procedures of a system.

_____ 34. Modifying an operational system by adding E-commerce website access would be an example.

Discussion Questions

1. Why do you think prototyping has become a popular way to develop E-business applications?

2. Refer to the Real World Case on Raytheon, Cutter, GE, and Honeywell in the chapter. Do you agree that in the development of E-commerce systems, "speed doesn't always equal quality, but quality always equals speed"? Why or why not?

3. Review the Panasonic and Quicken Loans real world examples in the text. What design changes should Panasonic make to correct the design flaws at their site and bring their website design up to Quicken's standard? Explain your reasoning.

4. What are the three most important factors you would use in evaluating computer hardware? Explain why.

5. What are the three most important factors you would use in evaluating computer software? Explain why.

6. Assume that in your first week on a new job you are asked to use a type of software package that you have never used before. What kind of user training should your company provide to you before you start?

7. Refer to the Real World Case on Select Comfort and VocalPoint in the chapter. Should system reliability be such an overiding concern in E-commerce systems? Why or why not?

8. What is the difference between the parallel, plunge, phased, and pilot forms of IS conversion? Which conversion strategy is best? Explain why.

9. What are several key factors in designing a successful E-commerce or intranet website? Refer to Figure 8.13 as a starting point. Explain why the design factors you chose are important to Web success.

10. Pick a business task you would like to computerize. How could you use the steps of the information systems development cycle as illustrated in Figure 8.3 to help you? Use examples to illustrate your answer.

Application Exercises

Complete the following exercises as individual or group projects that apply chapter concepts to real world business situations.

1. Amazon and eBay: Evaluating E-Commerce Website Behavior

Stanford University communications professors and NetSage officers Byron Reeves and Clifford Nass evaluate E-commerce websites for their human interfaces and social behavior. Their position is that people dislike some websites not because they are badly designed, but because the sites behave badly during people's visits. Here's their evaluation of Amazon and eBay.

Amazon.com Inc.: Overall Grade = **A−**
Bottom Line: *Successfully applies social rules to create a bookstore rather than a warehouse or a library.*

Befitting its reputation as the premier E-commerce player, Amazon's book-buying site follows many social rules to great effect. The consistent style and tone throughout the site communicates a reliable personality that builds comfort and trust in the business relationship. Appropriate for its products, the tone of the site is casual.

For example, Amazon tells users, "For now, you just need to . . ." Visitors have a sense that the same person is communicating with them consistently throughout their visit at the site. This promotes a feeling that customers have a single personal assistant rather than a confusing group of merchants—all with different methods and personalities—to help with purchases. Amazon maximizes personalization with minimal information by offering suggestions based on previous purchases, discussing what people in geographic areas are buying and offering one-click shopping that uses information previously stored on the site.

It continually tells users where they are in the ordering and registration process, particularly when they're about to purchase something. A confirmation to customers that they're "doing the right things" to accomplish a transaction—commonplace in real-life transactions—is used effectively at Amazon.

Amazon also effectively uses physical places on its site to let people know what to expect of the information presented in those places. For example, the largest column of information (the middle two-thirds of each page from the top to the bottom) is devoted to product information. And regardless of whether a shopper is looking for books, music, or electronic gear, the function of the space is unchanged. Even the details of price, shipping, and discounts are identical among products.

Amazon-generated book reviews and postings from customers are mixed with book reviews (from, for example, *The New York Times*) to produce commentary relevant to many items. Through careful use of language for related groups of customers, (for example, *Purchase Circles* rather than, say, folksier *Neighbors*, and the avoidance of visual clutter around the buttons that execute the purchase, they remind the customer that this isn't a library.

eBay Inc.: Overall Grade = **D**
Bottom Line: *An expert auctioneer that doesn't behave like one.*

People labeled as experts, whether by others or themselves, are perceived as more competent, more trusting, and more likely to provide unique knowledge and expertise. But eBay's reputation as an expert suffers because it doesn't correct sellers' mistakes and is considered to be complicit in these errors. For example, typographical errors in product descriptions reduce credibility, yet eBay doesn't edit that text. There are trade-offs among image size, picture quality, and details of the background in product presentations, but eBay doesn't make suggestions or offer ways to improve them.

A lesson here is that people hopelessly confuse the errors of the "message" with the competence of the "messenger"; poor presentation undermines eBay as well as the sale items. eBay is also impolite. For example, signing up for an account can take as long as 24 hours for confirmation. eBay users also aren't alerted when they omit a field during registration. Instead of dismissing people during that period, eBay should invite customers to browse. A good social partner tries to own the problems and makes an attempt to resolution.

eBay also fails to carry through on the notion of a "personal" shopper. It's unclear how to submit the initial form that activates the personal shopper, and the shopper doesn't save a list of items on which the customer might want to bid. Having someone remember things for you is essential in personalization. Finally, eBay users must traverse many pages to find the personal shopper—the exact opposite of what a "personal" shopper should be. The idea of an automatic bidder, someone working on your behalf, is a social plus. However, eBay should place more attention and emphasis on making the bidding process personal rather than simply automatic.

a. Visit the Amazon.com and eBay.com websites. Do you agree with the evaluations of Professors Reeves and Nass? Why or why not?

b. How could Amazon improve the experience it offers its E-commerce shoppers? Give several examples.

c. What should eBay do to improve the experience it provides to customers at its auction site? Give several examples.

Source: Adapted from Kevin Fogarty, "Net Manners Matter: How Top Sites Rank in Social Behavior," *Computerworld*, October 18, 1999, pp. 40–41. Copyright 1999 by Computerworld, Inc., Framingham, MA 01701. Reprinted from *Computerworld*.

2. The Fortune 100: Poor Quality Website Maintenance

Anyone who has been online for more than a day has probably encountered at least one problem with a site. From the "Error: File Not Found" screens to pop-up Java-script warning windows and broken links—the Web still struggles with standards incompatibility, simple laziness, and sloppy upkeep. But one would think most of these errors would take place on personal pages, not on top corporate sites with their huge Internet teams, right?

Wrong. Website consultancy ParaSoft recently tested 95 sites out of the Fortune 100 and discovered that the sites had an average of one link error per 3.5 pages and more than 12 HTML coding errors per page when tested for these and other functional and aesthetic glitches. Some sites could not be accessed due to security issues, or simply did not exist. The industries deemed the most error-ridden were motor vehicles and parts, pharmaceuticals, general merchandisers, office equipment, and computers—including such heavy hitters as IBM, Intel, and Compaq.

For example, websites with the most Web link errors per Web page included Lockheed Martin, Fannie Mae, Bank One, Gap, Sara Lee, GTE, HP, Alcoa, Ameritech, and Johnson & Johnson. Websites with the most HTML errors per page included GI, IBM, Safeway, JC Penney, Compaq, Intel, Ford, Caterpillar, First Union, and MCI worldcom. Sites with no link errors included Citigroup, Target Corp., Albertsons, Kroger, UPS, Coca-Cola, Philip Morris, American Stores, and SuperValu. And the websites with the fewest HTML errors per page were Prudential, Cardinal Health, Target Corp., USX, Albertsons, Merrill Lynch, Bell Atlantic, CIGNA, and General Motors.

Arthur Hicken, executive vice president of Para-Soft, says he was shocked by the results, and points a finger at Web-coding tools. "One theory is that people are using tools to generate these pages, and in some cases the tools generate bad code. Tools don't necessarily look for bad links or, if they do, they only look for a certain category of bad links." Surprisingly, Hicken also throws some blame on the team approach to Web building: "Suddenly you have a group involved. One person used to be the webmaster, but now there are different sections of a site belonging to different people and the interconnects tend to be bad."

a. Visit the websites of several of the companies mentioned in this exercise. Compare websites with the most broken links and HTML errors with the sites of companies with no link errors and few HTML errors like Albertsons and Target Corp. Does your experience match that of ParaSoft? What else did you find in terms of the quality of website design and maintenance?

b. Do you agree with Arthur Hicken on the reasons for the high rate of link and HTML errors at some companies? Why or why not? What should be done to correct this website quality problem?

Source: Adapted from Elizabeth Millard, "Big Company Weakened," *Business 2.0,* January 2000, pp. 217–18.

3. E-Business System Report

Study an E-business system described in a case study in this text or one used by an organization to which you have access. Write up the results in an E-business system report. Make a presentation to the class based on the results of your study of an E-business system. Use the outline in Figure 8.31 as a table of contents for your report and the outline of your presentation. Use presentation software and/or overhead transparencies to display key points of your analysis.

4. Creating a Personal Web Page

Create a personal Web page for yourself using appropriate software recommended by your instructor. If you use Microsoft Word to create your Web page, a brief description of special features of Word that are particularly useful in developing Web pages is available on the website for my textbooks at www.mhhe.com/business/mis/obrien.

Or you may want to try the free website building and hosting services offered by sites like Homestead.com and Webprovider.com and many others, including those provided to members of online Web communities and services like AOL, GeoCities, Tripod, and EarthLink.

Your website should begin with an attractive home page that contains links to the other, more detailed pages. You may also want to include bookmarks within a page linking to other sections of the same page and/or links to the websites of others.

Figure 8.31   Outline of an E-business system report.

- **Introduction to the organization and E-business system.** Briefly describe the organization you selected and the type of E-business system you have studied.

- **Analysis of an E-business system.** Identify the following system components of a business use of the Internet, intranets, extranets, or electronic commerce.
  - Input, processing, output, storage, and control methods currently used.
  - Hardware, software, networks, and people involved.
  - Data captured and information products produced.
  - Files and databases accessed and maintained

- **Evaluation of the E-business system.**
  - **Efficiency:** Does it do the job right? Is the E-business system well organized? Inexpensive? Fast? Does it require minimum resources? Process large volumes of data, produce a variety of information products?
  - **Effectiveness:** Does it do the right job? The way the employees, customers, suppliers, or other end users want it done? Does it give them the information they need, the way they want it? Does it support the E-business objectives of the organization? Provide significant customer and business value?

- **Design and implementation of an E-business system proposal.**
  - Do end users need a new system or just improvements? Why?
  - What exactly are you recommending they do?
  - Is it feasible? What are its benefits and costs?
  - What will it take to implement your recommendations?

Southwest Airlines, Home Depot, and BlueLight.com: Alternative E-Commerce Website Strategies

A web site with no e-mail capability and no banner ads? At first glance, it might not spark much interest in the business community, but that model has turned into a billion-dollar baby for Southwest Airlines Inc. In August the discount carrier became the first airline to crack $1 billion in ticket revenue on its branded web site. It has done so with perhaps the simplest formula in the trade: The Dallas-based carrier doesn't seek to create new revenue streams or develop new types of business partnerships through its online operation; it sells tickets, keeps things simple and makes money.

"It's a low-cost distribution channel for Southwest," says Melanie Stillings, a marketing automations manager at the airline. "It costs us about $1 to book one. It costs us about $10 to book through a travel agency. What we try to avoid is spending ungodly amounts money on an Internet product if it's going to raise the price of our tickets."

Southwest is typical of businesses that will use the Internet in the coming year as a low-cost channel to streamline sales, not just as a reason to launch ad campaigns or a way to build brand recognition. The mandate for IT in 2001? Use the Internet to build a reliable customer base.

Southwest began selling tickets online in early 1996, and despite not having an e-mail button on its site, the airline has managed to keep its reputation for customer service. "If people need customer service, we want to do it right," Stillings says. "We want to give them an answer and a live person, not a wall. Airlines are still a people business."

Southwest has also forgone the banner advertisements that are common on many web pages. Stillings says the company isn't interested in bogging down its web page with peripheral information. Southwest wants the page to load quickly and customers to get the information they want with relative ease, she says.

We got a lot of comments about not having bells and whistles and the latest wireless technology," Stillings says. "Our customers want cheap airline tickets, and we'd be in trouble if we lost track of that."

At Southwest, its technical web crew is housed inside the company's marketing department. Stillings says Southwest wants those two groups to work in harmony. "We do all of our work on Southwest.com in-house," she says. "This is not just some technical offshoot of our business. It is our business."

As many Internet businesses have learned, you must establish a workable supply chain and reliable customer service before expanding. Many of the latest entrants to the Web arena have decided that they would rather take the mom-and-pop store approach and expand after they've enjoyed some success.

Atlanta-based The Home Depot Inc. went online in August 2, 2000, but decided to start small, web-enabling only its six stores in Las Vegas and making them the fulfillment centers for the company's line of more than 40,000 products. Online shoppers in that region can either pick up their purchases at one of the stores or have the items delivered by Home Depot or UPS directly to a job site.

Depending on the success of the Las Vegas rollout, Home Depot will launch similar online sales programs in San Antonio and Austin, Texas, before the end of 2001. Home Depot spokesman Jerry Shields says the web site will keep track of each Las Vegas store's inventory in real time. The company will then replicate that model for each new region it develops, he says.

Brian Sugar, chief web officer at BlueLight.com in San Francisco, says his company has prepared itself for the next wave of web customers—those who aren't PC savvy. BlueLight was founded in December 1999 by Kmart Corp. and Tokyo-based Softbank Corp. and was designed to succeed where Kmart.com failed.

BlueLight decided that it needed to offer more than Kmart's product line to make a splash on the Web. Specifically, it began offering free Internet access through a partnership with Yahoo Inc. in Santa Clara, California. Though its model is more complex than Southwest's proposition, BlueLight believes it needs to create a unique market to make money in the retail world, where profit margins are low.

More than 1 million customers have signed on for the service, many of them Internet neophytes. Yahoo acts as their internet service provider, while BlueLight runs pervasive advertising. The hope is that customers will think of BlueLight whenever they need to make a purchase. BlueLight is also selling its own branded low-price PCs—another initiative to increase the web savvy of its potential shoppers. "It's all an effort to bring customers to us," Sugar says. "We really target Mom, who is the Kmart shopper," Sugar says. "Anything we can do in web design to make buying online easier or more direct for Mom, we'll do it."

Case Study Questions

1. Do you agree with Southwest's website design strategy, and their decision not to accept E-mail queries from customers at their website? Why or why not? Visit Southwest.com to help you answer.

2. What are the benefits and limitations of Home Depot's implementation strategy for their entry into E-commerce?

3. Should BlueLight.com continue to offer free Internet access and sell low-priced PC's? Why or why not?

Source: Adapted from Michael Meehan, "Develop Your Web Content Strategy," *Computerworld*, January 1, 2001, p. S20.

The Sports Authority and Others: E-Commerce Website Design Requirements

Depending on which survey you choose, customers abandon online shopping carts at a rate of between 25 percent and 77 percent. "I think it's really indicative of consumer expectations not being met," says Christine Leber, a senior analyst with the Yankee Group. "Now that consumers have been online for a while the tolerance level isn't there. They expect online shopping to be more convenient than offline shopping. If not, why bother?"

Shoppers abandon their online carts for many reasons. Turn-offs include poor site navigation, hard-to-find shopping carts, and time-consuming checkouts. Let's look at how several companies are confronting this E-commerce problem.

Web Site Navigation

Consistent design throughout your site makes it easier for your customers to find their way: Users can always click on product images for most information. Buttons use a consistent color. Links are always underlined. If your site is simple for users to understand, they will happily keep moving toward the checkout. Walmart.com's recent redesign came under fire by industry critics for being too boring. However, the changes made the site cleaner, simpler, and easier for shoppers to master.

Shopping Cart Design

Whatever you do, make sure your site's shopping cart is a clearly identified link placed on the top right corner of the page, traditionally a high-click area. Moreover, make it available on every page in the same place.

Also try bringing your site's shopping cart area to life. Sports retailer The Sports Authority (*www.thesportsauthority.com*) does that with its dynamic shopping cart. The cart displays the latest item added, allowing the customer to keep a running tab more easily. The company also made sure customers could click on the cart icon to start shopping.

Don't expect people to instantly notice items added to a dynamic cart. When shoppers add items, route them to a cart summary page each time—even if it seems redundant. This page indicates confirmation and invites the shopper to check out.

Checkout Process

Shopping online is all about convenience, and nothing is a bigger pain than lengthy forms that extend the checkout process. No wonder people click away in disgust. While there may be no way around forms for the time being, keep information that you request to a minimum. Demographics are nice to know, but they can also kill sales.

A winning checkout system needs to be fast and easy. Any good checkout process makes a distinction between a repeat shopper and a first-time buyer. Greet returning customers by getting them as close as possible to single-click shopping process. Amazon.com leads in this area with the fastest possible checkout. The Gap (www.gap.com) also offers shoppers two clear shopping tracks, as well as an easy way to retrieve an account password.

Trust and Security

Shoppers demand more than security online. Getting customers to trust you must happen throughout the site, not just when they use their credit card. Establishing trust with your customers means making service a priority by giving them multiple ways to contact you and providing them with a timely reply.

The human touch, especially in a faceless online world, is important to customers. Land's End (www.landsend.com) has 250 sales reps ready to answer questions live online—and it pays: Their Internet orders end up averaging $10 more than catalog orders.

Ensure the privacy of your customer data in a clearly worded and easy-to-find policy. Also, make sure you spell out your encryption standard by using recognizable signs such as the VeriSign logo, and explain how credit card information is transmitted to your site's servers.

Website Speed

As long as shoppers use dial-up modems to access the Web, overall site speed will be a fundamental measurement to live and die by. Browse the top ten Media Metrix sites with stopwatch in hand and you can almost feel the wind in your hair. You won't get a gratuitous 20-second splash screen on Yahoo or wait for graphic after graphic to download. The fastest sites help you get in and get out by making each subsequent clock and page view as fast-loading as possible. How fast is fast enough? There is no set rule, but for a fast and free look at how your site's speed stacks up, visit Web Site Garage, a web site maintenance service, at websitegarage.netscape.com.

Case Study Questions

1. Visit the Walmart.com and SportsAuthority.com websites. Which one has the better website navigation and shopping cart design? Why?

2. Compare the Amazon.com website with one of the websites mentioned in this case. Which one has the fastest website and checkout processes? Defend your choices.

3. Evaluate the LandsEnd.com privacy and security policies at their website. Does this information help build trust in the security of their E-commerce transactions? Explain.

Source: Adapted from Alice Hill, "Top 5 Reasons Your Customers Abandon Their Shopping Carts," *Smart Business*, March 2001, pp. 80–84.

Spirit Airlines: Failure in Systems Implementation and Conversion

A problematic conversion to a new software system for managing staff and tracking flights grounded flight operations at Spirit Airlines Inc. to a halt, resulting in passengers stranded in cities such as New York, Detroit and Palm Beach, Florida. The system wide problems forced the Fort Lauderdale, Florida-based discount airline to book all available hotel rooms in many markets and to institute a nationwide disaster response program.

Spirit Airlines President and CEO Jacob Schorr said the crisis wasn't touched off by the new system crashing or other technical problems. Instead, the problems were caused by a lack of familiarity with the software on the part of Spirit's employees—a situation that snowballed at the airline after winter storms affected air travel in the Northeast.

While the new scheduling system had been run in parallel with the airline's old one from September through the end of last year, Schorr said users couldn't negotiate the software fast enough to keep pace after the storms began forcing flight cancellations. "The people who operated the software were no longer as fast with it, even though they were proficient and they were trained," Schorr said. "It's one of those situations where your fingers aren't connected to your brain anymore, and we weren't prepared for that." Flights were also booked to capacity because of the crush of holiday travelers, making it more difficult to accommodate stranded passengers after the problems merged, he said.

Compounding the situation even further was the fact that Spirit's CIO post is vacant, said Schorr, who held that position until he was promoted to CEO in mid-2000. The airline began interviewing potential CIO candidates last month but has yet to hire a replacement. A hands-on IT executive might have been able to foresee the impending crisis and steer Spirit's crew staffing department away from doing the software conversion at such a busy travel time, Schorr said. "The only way we could have avoided this problem was to have called off the conversion," he said. "But we obviously didn't see the problem coming."

Henry Harteveldt, an analyst at Forrester Research who follows the travel industry, faulted Spirit for its timing. "You never want to do a cutover to a new software system during a peak travel period," he said. Spirit's staffing department wanted the conversion to occur January 1 because the airline needs to track pilot and crew flight hours on a calendar basis in order to ensure that workers don't exceed flying limits set by the U.S. Federal Aviation Administration. Making the switch a week or two later would have required the initial records for this year to be moved from the old system to the new one.

"Up until now, it's been our policy to let individual departments manage their own projects and not involve the IT department," Schorr said. "That's going to change. We need to have our tech people more involved." Harteveldt said such a hand-off IT policy is recipe for danger. "You don't mess around with technology," he said. "It is not kind to the people who don't understand it."

Schorr said the airline will have to spend at least the rest of the month trying to win back passengers who were inconvenienced by the problems. Spirit, the largest privately held airline in the U.S., carried more than 200,000 passengers last year.

The airline will also have to mend its relationship with the New York & New Jersey Port Authority, which is considering pulling Spirit's landing permits at the LaGuardia and Newark airports in the wake of the ordeal. Port authority spokesman Steven Coleman said that at one point, New York police were called to LaGuardia to calm an unruly crowd of disgruntled passengers. "There were some near fistfights between some of the passengers who'd just had enough," he said.

The crisis also will lead to organizational restructuring at Spirit, Coleman said, although he added that specific changes haven't been decided on. A week ago, the airline announced that it had returned to "business-as-usual operation." Schorr said the new software remains in place. "It was a matter of knowing how to use it," he said.

Case Study Questions

1. What major problems in system implementation and conversion practices do you recognize in this case?

2. What major management problems do you recognize in this case?

3. What should Spirit Airlines have done to avoid its system problems? What steps should they take now?

Source: Adapted from Michael Meehan, "Software Conversion Creates Chaos for Spirit Airlines," *Computerworld*, January 15, 2001, p. 20

Module IV

Management Challenges

What managerial challenges do information systems pose for E-business enterprises? The two chapters of this module emphasize how managers and business professionals can manage the successful use of E-business technologies in a global information society.

Chapter 9, **Security and Ethical Challenges of E-Business,** discusses the threats against, and defenses needed for E-business performance and security, as well as the ethical implications and societal impacts of information technologies.

Chapter 10, **Enterprise and Global Management of E-Business Technology,** emphasizes the impact of E-business technologies on management and organizations, the components of information systems management, and the managerial implications of the use of information technology in global E-business.

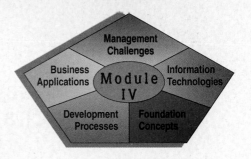

Chapter 9

Security and Ethical

Challenges of E-Business

Chapter Highlights

Learning Objectives

After reading and studying this chapter, you should be able to:

1. Identify several ethical issues in how the use of information technologies in E-business affects employment, individuality, working conditions, privacy, crime, health, and solutions to societal problems.

2. Identify several types of security management strategies and defenses, and explain how they can be used to ensure the security of E-business applications.

3. Propose several ways that business managers and professionals can help to lessen the harmful effects and increase the beneficial effects of the use of information technology.

Security, Ethical, and Societal Challenges of E-Business

Introduction

There is no question that the use of information technology in E-business operations presents major security challenges, poses serious ethical questions, and affects society in significant ways. Therefore, in this section we will explore the threats to E-business security posed by many types of computer crime and unethical behavior. In Section II, we will examine a variety of methods that companies use to manage the security and integrity of today's E-business enterprise. Now let's look at a real world example.

Analyzing the University of Washington and Others

Read the Real World Case on the University of Washington and others on the next page. We can learn a lot from this case about the ethical and security issues and challenges that surround the private and business use of Internet technologies. See Figure 9.1.

University security experts were the first to discover the threat of denial of service attacks hiding in the university computer systems. For example, David Dittrich of the University of Washington discovered denial of service program files stored on the university servers months before the first widely publicized attacks on E-commerce Web sites. Hackers later used such unsecured university systems as "zombie" machines to help launch massive distributed denial of service (DDOS) against Yahoo!, eBay, Amazon.com, and other popular Web sites. The potential threat continues because many university servers are purchased with government grants that do not provide funds for security. Also, probes of corporate networks by hackers have increased dramatically, and new strains of computer viruses that can be used in hacker attacks have been found. So security experts are warning companies to protect their networks and Web sites with proper security measures because the threat of destrictive denial of service attacks has increased significantly.

Figure 9.1

David Dittrich, a senior security engineer at the University of Washington, was one of the first to recognize the role of university servers in denial of service attacks on E-commerce Web sites.

Randall Scott.

University of Washington and Others: Vulnerability to Hacker Attacks on E-Commerce Websites

Remember February 7, 2000? That's when the first wave of distributed denial-of-service (DDOS) attacks hit Internet portal Yahoo. During the next few days, other high-profile web sites—including eBay, Buy.com, Amazon.com, ETrade Group and CNN.com—were knocked off the Net by millions of packets coming from thousands of far-flung computers.

But the stage was set for those high-profile attacks back in the summer of 1999. That's when university systems began finding software agents—tools planted by hackers to launch future denial-of-service attacks—hidden on unprotected machines inside their sprawling networks. In August of that year, a preliminary DDOS incident took down several hundred hosts at universities.

So it wasn't a huge surprise that, when the full-scale DDOS assault happened in February. Many attacks could be traced to "zombie" computers tucked away in research departments at Stanford University, the University of California at Santa Barbara, the University of Washington, Oregon State University and James Madison University, to name a few. "Why were universities so involved in these attacks? Because they're naked," said Stephen Northcutt, head of the SANS Institute's Global Incident Analysis Center in Bethesda, Maryland. "They're sitting out there on the Internet with no firewalls or anything."

"In many universities, there's really no way for IT staff to know what machines are out there, especially in the research areas," said Randy Marchany, coordinator of a computer security center for Virginia universities, which he operates out of Virginia Polytechnic Institute and State University (Virginia Tech) in Blacksburg, Virginia. And hackers have long considered university systems their playground, according to an East Coast hacker who goes by the handle "Yetzer-Ra." The research computers have the Internet access and processing power to do most anything hackers want them to do—and often they sit unsupervised and unused.

Typically, the computers themselves were obtained with grants from U.S. science agencies that are more interested in advanced research than computer security. "Many researchers are given money by the U.S. National Science Foundation and the National Institutes of Health to buy computers to conduct research. But they can't use that money for system administrators or security manpower. They can only use that grant money for equipment," explained Dave Dittrich, a senior security engineer at the University of Washington in Seattle. Dittrich was one of the first people to discover denial-of-service agents lurking in university networked systems.

And security experts are increasingly concerned that university systems may once again be used for massive denial-of-service attacks. The number of suspicious probes and scans designed to find vulnerable domain name servers on corporate networks shot up 280% in January 2001 and continue to climb, according to IT managers and a new survey conducted by a network security monitoring firm. A survey by Pilot Network Services found that suspected hackers made as many as 6,000 attempts—compared to approximately 2,200 in December 2000—to locate vulnerable domain name servers across corporate networks.

Pilot collected the information for the survey from its regional network operations centers, which monitor 70,000 corporate networks belonging to Pilot clients worldwide. The spike in the number of scans came as no surprise to many users and security experts, who said hackers are stepping up their efforts to uncover corporate systems that haven't been fixed for network vulnerabilities.

Meanwhile, other experts warned that hackers with track records of developing sophisticated automated hacking tools are already planning to cross-breed Internet worms, such as the recent Ramen worm, with other DNS exploits, thus creating the potential for widespread network problems.

"There are a couple of worms on the horizon that will probably be the next breaking story," said Amit Yoran, CEO of Riptech Inc., a network security firm in Alexandria, Virginia. "In literally a matter of hours, a very large number of zombie hosts can be created for planned distributed denial-of-service attacks, multiple hopping points to cover your tracks and other activities."

The cross-breeding of viruses and Internet worms to exploit security gaps represents a major shift in the way virus writers operate, said Chris Klaus, chief of technology officer at Internet Security Systems Inc. in Atlanta. "Now we're seeing an increase in the number of virus writers using the hacker mentality," Klaus said. Viruses are being designed that automatically search out compromised systems, he said. "If companies haven't thought of a way to routinely check their machines, they're sitting ducks."

Case Study Questions

1. What is the zombie role of many university computer systems in denial of service attacks?

2. What should universities do about this problem?

3. What should companies do to protect themselves from hacker attacks?

Source: Adapted from Deborah Radcliff, "University Computers Remain Hacker Havens," February 12, 2001, p. 17 and Dan Verton, "Suspicious Server Probes Multiply," *Computerworld*, February 19, 2001, pp. 1, 73.

E-Business, Security, Ethics, and Society

The use of information technologies in E-business systems has had major impacts on society, and thus raises ethical issues in the areas of crime, privacy, individuality, employment, health, and working conditions. See Figure 9.2.

However, you should also realize that information technology has had beneficial results as well as detrimental effects on society and people in each of these areas. For example, computerizing a manufacturing process may have the adverse effect of eliminating people's jobs, but also have the beneficial result of improving working conditions and producing products of higher quality at less cost. So your job as a manager or business professional should involve managing your work activities and those of others to minimize the detrimental effects of E-business systems and optimize their beneficial effects. That would represent an ethically responsible use of information technology.

Computer Crime in E-Business

Cyber crime is becoming one of the Net's growth businesses. Today, criminals are doing everything from stealing intellectual property and committing fraud to unleashing viruses and committing acts of cyber terrorism [36].

Computer crime is a growing threat to society caused by the criminal or irresponsible actions of individuals who are taking advantage of the widespread use and vulnerability of computers and the Internet and other networks. It thus presents a major challenge to the ethical use of information technologies. Computer crime poses serious threats to the integrity, safety, and survival of most E-business systems, and thus makes the development of effective security methods a top priority. See Figure 9.3.

Computer crime is defined by the Association of Information Technology Professionals (AITP) as including (1) the unauthorized use, access, modification, and destruction of hardware, software, data, or network resources; (2) the unauthorized release of information; (3) the unauthorized copying of software; (4) denying an end user access to his or her own hardware, software, data, or network resources; and (5) using or conspiring to use computer or network resources to illegally obtain information or tangible property. This definition was promoted by the AITP in a Model Computer Crime Act, and is reflected in many computer crime laws.

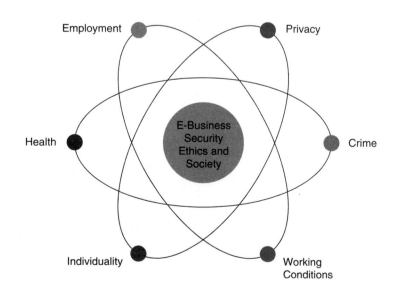

Figure 9.2

Important aspects of the security, ethical, and societal dimensions of E-business. Remember that information technologies can support both beneficial or detrimental effects on society in each of the areas shown.

Yahoo! and Others: Cyber Crime on the Internet	First it was Yahoo! Inc. The portal giant was shut down for three hours. Then retailer Buy.com Inc. was hit the next day, hours after going public. By that evening, eBay, Amazon.com, and CNN had gone dark. And in the morning, the mayhem continued with online broker E*Trade and others having traffic to their sites virtually choked off.

Gridlock. For all the sophisticated work on fire walls, intrusion-detection systems, encryption and computer security, E-businesses are at risk from *denial of service* (DOS) attacks, a relatively simple technique that's akin to dialing a telephone number repeatedly so that everyone else trying to get through will hear a busy signal.

Cyber crime on the Internet is on the rise. Consider just a quick smattering of recent events: In December, 1999, 300,000 credit-card numbers were snatched from online music retailer CD Universe. In March, the Melissa virus caused an estimated $80 million in damage when it swept around the world, paralyzing E-mail systems. That same month, hackers-for-hire pleaded guilty to breaking into phone giants AT&T, GTE, and Sprint, among others, for calling card numbers that eventually made their way to organized crime gangs in Italy. According to the FBI, the phone companies were hit for an estimated $2 million.

But one good thing: Such events are delivering a wake-up call to businesses that they need to spend as much time protecting their websites and networks as they do linking them with customers, suppliers, contractors—and you [36].

Hacking

Cyber thieves have at their fingertips a dozen dangerous tools, from "scans" that ferret out weaknesses in website software programs to "sniffers" that snatch passwords. All told, the FBI estimates U.S. computer losses at up to $10 billion a year [36].

Hacking, in computerese, is the obsessive use of computers, or the unauthorized access and use of networked computer systems. Illegal hackers (also called *crackers*) frequently assault the Internet and other networks to steal or damage data and programs. One of the issues in hacking is what to do about a hacker who commits only

Figure 9.3

The growth in electronic assaults and break-ins on business and government organizations via internal systems, the Internet, and other networks.

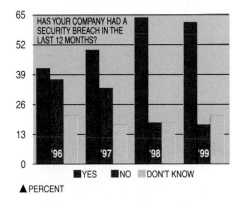

Computer security breaches are on the rise...

HAS YOUR COMPANY HAD A SECURITY BREACH IN THE LAST 12 MONTHS?

■ YES ■ NO ▨ DON'T KNOW

▲ PERCENT

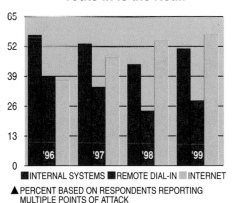

...And the most popular route in is the Net...

■ INTERNAL SYSTEMS ■ REMOTE DIAL-IN ▨ INTERNET

▲ PERCENT BASED ON RESPONDENTS REPORTING MULTIPLE POINTS OF ATTACK

DATA: FBI/COMPUTER SECURITY INSTITUTE.
SURVEY BASED ON APPROXIMATELY 500 RESPONSES FROM PRIVATE CORPORATIONS AND LARGE GOVERNMENT AGENCIES.

Source: Adapted from Ira Sager, Steve Hamm, Neil Gross, John Carey, and Robert Hoff, "Cyber Crime," *Business Week*, February 21, 2000, p. 39. Reprinted with special permission, copyright © 2000 by The McGraw-Hill Companies, Inc.

electronic breaking and entering; that is, gets access to a computer system, reads some files, but neither steals nor damages anything. This situation is common in computer crime cases that are prosecuted. In several states, courts have found that the typical computer crime statute language prohibiting malicious access to a computer system did apply to anyone gaining unauthorized access to another's computer networks. See Figure 9.4.

Hackers can monitor E-mail, Web server access, or file transfers to extract passwords or steal network files, or to plant data that will cause a system to welcome intruders. A hacker may also use remote services that allow one computer on a network to execute programs on another computer to gain privileged access within a network. Telnet, an Internet tool for interactive use of remote computers, can help hackers discover information to plan other attacks. Hackers have used Telnet to access a computer's E-mail port, for example, to monitor E-mail messages for passwords and other information about privileged user accounts and network resources. These are just some of the typical types of computer crimes that hackers commit on the Internet on a regular basis. That's why Internet security measures like encryption and fire walls, as discussed in the next section, are so vital to the success of electronic commerce and other E-business applications.

Figure 9.4

Examples of common hacking tactics to assault E-business enterprises and other organizations through the Internet and other networks.

Common Hacking Tactics

Denial of Service This is becoming a common networking prank. By hammering a website's equipment with too many requests for information, an attacker can effectively clog the system, slowing performance or even crashing the site. This method of overloading computers is sometimes used to cover up an attack.

Scans Widespread probes of the Internet to determine types of computers, services, and connections. That way the bad guys can take advantage of weaknesses in a particular make of computer or software program.

Sniffer Programs that covertly search individual packets of data as they pass through the Internet, capturing passwords or the entire contents.

Spoofing Faking an E-mail address or Web page to trick users into passing along critical information like passwords or credit card numbers.

Trojan Horse A program that, unknown to the user, contains instructions that exploit a known vulnerability in some software.

Back Doors In case the original entry point has been detected, having a few hidden ways back makes reentry easy—and difficult to detect.

Malicious Applets Tiny programs, sometimes written in the popular Java computer language, that misuse your computer's resources, modify files on the hard disk, send fake E-mail, or steal passwords.

War Dialing Programs that automatically dial thousands of telephone numbers in search of a way in through a modem connection.

Logic Bombs An instruction in a computer program that triggers a malicious act.

Buffer Overflow A technique for crashing or gaining control of a computer by sending too much data to the buffer in a computer's memory.

Password Crackers Software that can guess passwords.

Social Engineering A tactic used to gain access to computer systems by talking unsuspecting company employees out of valuable information such as passwords.

Dumpster Diving Sifting through a company's garbage to find information to help break into their computers. Sometimes the information is used to make a stab at social engineering more credible.

Source: Adapted from Ira Sager, Steve Hamm, Neil Gross, John Carey, and Robert Hoff, "Cyber Crime," *Business Week*, February 21, 2000, p. 40. Reprinted with special permission, copyright © 2000 by The McGraw-Hill Companies, Inc.

Cyber Theft

Many computer crimes involve the theft of money. In the majority of cases, they are "inside jobs" that involve unauthorized network entry and fraudulent alternation of computer databases to cover the tracks of the employees involved. Of course, more recent examples involve the use of the Internet, such as the widely publicized theft of $11 million from Citibank in late 1994. Russian hacker Vladimir Levin and his accomplices in St. Petersburg used the Internet to electronically break into Citibank's mainframe systems in New York. They then succeeded in transferring the funds from several Citibank accounts to their own accounts at banks in Finland, Israel, and California [34].

In most cases, the scope of such financial losses is much larger than the incidents reported. Most companies don't reveal that they have been targets or victims of computer crime. They fear scaring off customers and provoking complaints by shareholders. In fact, several British banks, including the Bank of London, paid hackers more than a half million dollars not to reveal information about electronic break-ins [34].

BuyDirect Inc.: Internet Credit Card Fraud

Fraud nearly vanquished San Francisco-based BuyDirect Inc. when it opened for business, said William Headapohl, president of the online software store. "Our fraud rate was unacceptably high and banks wanted to drop us. If we hadn't had strong financial backing and worked hard to reduce our fraud rates, we would have been put out of business pretty quickly." Using antifraud software and elaborate screening systems, the company reduced its fraud rate to under 1 percent. "The more it costs, the more someone will try to steal it," said Headapohl. "One of our first defenses was not to sell the really expensive products online."

Selling internationally is one of the key reasons for starting an electronic-commerce site, yet foreign sales are the riskiest of all. "Our international fraud rates were so bad in the beginning, we thought we were going to have to exclude overseas sales altogether," Headapohl said. "Companies like ours were routinely seeing fraud rates in excess of 20 percent."

Most successful Web merchants avoid fraud by outsourcing credit-card verification to third parties with sophisticated (and expensive) neural-net antifraud software. Or they develop their own antifraud systems. Another approach is to take verification procedures off-line and check cards manually [28].

Unauthorized Use at Work

The unauthorized use of computer systems and networks can be called *time and resource theft*. A common example is unauthorized use of company-owned computer networks by employees. This may range from doing private consulting or personal finances, or playing video games, to unauthorized use of the Internet on company networks. Network monitoring software, called *sniffers*, is frequently used to monitor network traffic to evaluate network capacity, as well as reveal evidence of improper use. See Figures 9.5 and 9.6.

According to one survey, 90 percent of U.S. workers admit to surfing recreational sites during office hours, and 84 percent say they send personal E-mail from work. So this kind of activity alone may not get you fired from your job. However, other Internet activities at work can bring instant dismissal. For example, *The New York Times* fired 23 workers in November of 1999 because they were distributing racist and sexually offensive jokes on the company's E-mail system [44].

Xerox Corporation fired more than 40 workers in 1999 for spending up to eight hours a day on pornography sites on the Web. Several employees even downloaded pornographic videos which took so much network bandwidth that it choked the company network and prevented co-workers from sending or receiving E-mail.

Figure 9.5

Online non-work-related employee activity and corporate policies.

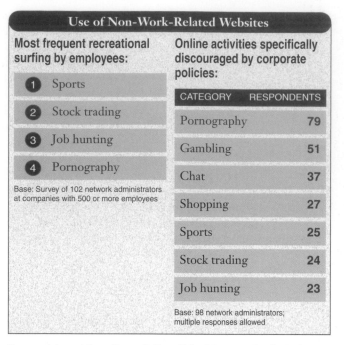

Source: Adapted from Stacy Collett, "Net Managers Battle Online Trading Boom," *Computerworld*, July 5, 1999, p. 24. Copyright 1999 by Computerworld, Inc., Framingham, MA 01701. Reprinted from *Computerworld*.

Figure 9.6

Network monitoring software (sniffers) like SurfWatch are used to monitor the use of the Internet by employees at work. SurfWatch can also block access to unauthorized websites.

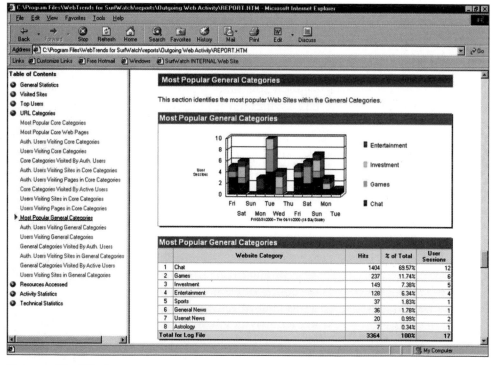

Courtesy of SurfWatch.com.

Xerox instituted an eight-member SWAT team on computer abuse that uses software to review every website its 40,000 computer users view each day. Other companies clamp down even harder, by installing software like SurfWatch, which enables them to block, as well as monitor access to off-limit websites [29].

American Fast Freight: Stealing Time and Resources	Pornography, check. Online auctions, check. Sports sites, check. MIS director Jeff LePage thought his company's network was insulated from the Internet sites that typically lure employees away from their work. Those activities are policed and in some cases blocked with monitoring software because the company policy at American Fast Freight Inc, in Seattle clearly states that any online activity "not specifically and exclusively work related" is prohibited.

So imagine LePage's surprise when a new culprit emerged: He recently discovered that one employee had visited a stock-monitoring website 186 times during a 12-day period. "We've been bitten by the online investing bug," LePage said. He isn't alone.

The stock market boom and the day-trading frenzy at websites such as E*TRADE.com and Schwab.com have created a form of recreational surfing that hits employers especially hard. The best time to trade is during business hours, and that means greater demands on a company's network bandwidth and resources, as well as a substantial productivity hit.

Experts said it's time for companies to drag out their Internet policy and specifically include a limit on personal investment activity. "If there's not a policy, there's going to be an argument," said Peter Kershaw, president of Content Technologies. Since the online trading incident at American Fast Freight, the company has amended its Internet usage policy to specifically prohibit use of online investing sites during work hours—except for lunchtime [6].

Software Piracy

Computer programs are valuable property and thus are the subject of theft from computer systems. However, unauthorized copying of software, or **software piracy,** is also a major form of software theft. Several major cases involving the unauthorized copying of software have been widely reported. These include lawsuits by the Software Publishers Association, an industry association of software developers, against major corporations that allowed unauthorized copying of their programs.

Unauthorized copying is illegal because software is intellectual property that is protected by copyright law and user licensing agreements. For example, in the United States, commercial software packages are protected by the Computer Software Piracy and Counterfeiting Amendment to the Federal Copyright Act. In most cases, the purchase of a commercial software package is really a payment to license its fair use by an individual end user. Therefore, many companies sign *site licenses* that allow them to legally make a certain number of copies for use by their employees at a particular location. Other alternatives are *shareware*, which allows you to make copies of software for others, and *public domain software*, which is not copyrighted.

Piracy of Intellectual Property

Software is not the only intellectual property subject to computer-based piracy. Other forms of copyrighted material, such as music, videos, images, articles, books and other written works are especially vulnerable to copyright infringement, which most courts have deemed illegal. Digitized versions can easily be captured by computer systems and made available for people to access or download at Internet websites, or can be readily disseminated by E-mail as file attachments. The development of peer-to-peer (P2P) networking technologies like the Napster and Gnutella models (discussed in Chapter 14) have made digital versions of copyrighted material even more vulnerable to unauthorized use. For example, Napster and other similar software enable direct MP3 audio file transfers of specified tracks of music between your PC and those of other users on the Internet. Thus, such software creates a *peer-to-peer network* of millions of Internet users who electronically trade digital versions of copyrighted or public domain music stored on their PC's hard drives. Let's look at the ongoing debate in this controversial area of intellectual property rights more closely with a real world example.

Napster: **Intellectual** **Property Battle-** **Ground**	The Recording Industry Association of America (RIAA) recently won its suit in U.S. courts against Napster, a San Mateo, California, dot-com, charging that Napster's primary function is to enable and encourage copyright violations. Nonsense, Napster had countered, we're just providing software. What Napster invented is Web software that makes downloading your favorite tunes incredibly simple and swift. The wrinkle: The music isn't actually traded through its site. Instead, Napster's software, which is free to anyone who wants to download it, allows you to zap a song from your computer via the Internet to another user's hard drive in under a minute. But RIAA execs feared Napster's burgeoning popularity would cut into CD sales. Moreover, the owners of the copyright on the downloaded music (typically held jointly by the record company's publishing subsidiary and the songwriter) don't get compensated. So the trade organization had sued, charging that Napster "has created and is operating a haven for music piracy on an unprecedented scale." Though that seems to be exactly what Napster was doing, two intellectual-property lawyers had argued that the law favored Napster. For one thing, Napster doesn't actually control any of the music—it never even passes through the website. "Napster is saying, 'We just put software out there,'" said John Lynch of Howrey Simon Arnold & White. "So the plaintiff has to prove Napster is inducing illegal activity. And inducing is not what they're really doing." What's more, the RIAA had to prove that Napster is used almost exclusively for illegal activity, argued Mark Lemley, a law professor at University of California at Berkeley. That would be difficult because Napster provides access to new, uncopyrighted artists as well. The company said it plans to allow other items, such as photos, to be sent, too. And Napster argued that it is essentially powerless to prevent users from trading copyrighted music and that it shouldn't be held responsible for their misconduct. RIAA general counsel Cary Sherman had emphatically dismissed that argument. "If you have knowledge that what you are doing is causing infringement," he says, "you're liable." Napster has since settled with German media giant Bertelsmann AG, and the two are working on deals with Bertelsmann's BMG label and CDNow online retailer, as well as a fee-based subscription service [23].

Computer Viruses

One of the most destructive examples of computer crime involves the creation of **computer viruses** or *worms. Virus* is the more popular term but, technically, a virus is a program code that cannot work without being inserted into another program. A worm is a distinct program that can run unaided. In either case, these programs copy annoying or destructive routines into the networked computer systems of anyone who accesses computers infected with the virus or who uses copies of magnetic disks taken from infected computers. Thus, a computer virus or worm can spread destruction among many users. Though they sometimes display only humorous messages, they more often destroy the contents of memory, hard disks, and other storage devices. Copy routines in the virus or worm spread the virus and destroy the data and software of many computer users. See Figure 9.7.

Facts about recent
computer viruses.

Computer Virus Facts

- **Melissa Virus**
  Type: Computer virus designed to attack files on a single PC.
  Replication method: Prompts Microsoft Outlook to send infected document to first 50 addresses in address book.
  Damage: Overwhelms corporate E-mail servers.
- **CIH, or Chernobyl Virus**
  Type: Data-triggered computer virus designed to attack files on a single PC.
  Replication method: Executes infected files sent via E-mail or on the Web.
  Damage: Erases entire hard drive and attempts to overwrite BIOS.
- **W32/Explorerzip.worm**
  Type: Internet worm designed to infect PCs on a network.
  Replication method: Sends infected E-mail attachment as response to incoming mail.
  Damage: Will delete .c, .cpp, .asm, .doc, .xls, and .ppt files from local hard drive.

Source: Adapted from Ann Harrison, "Internet Worm Destroys Data," *Computerworld*, June 14, 1999. Copyright 1999 by Computerworld, Inc., Framingham, MA 01701. Reprinted from *Computerworld*.

Computer viruses typically enter a computer system through E-mail and file attachments via the Internet and online services, or through illegal or borrowed copies of software. Copies of *shareware* software downloaded from the Internet can be another source of viruses. A virus usually copies itself into the files of a computer's operating system. Then the virus spreads to the main memory and copies itself onto the computer's hard disk and any inserted floppy disks. The virus spreads to other computers through E-mail, file transfers, other telecommunications activities, or floppy disks from infected computers. Thus, as a good practice, you should avoid using software from questionable sources without checking for viruses. You should also regularly *use antivirus programs* that can help diagnose and remove computer viruses from infected files on your hard disk.

Anatomy of a Virus: Melissa

If you receive an E-mail with the subject line "Important message from . . . ," be suspicious. If that message comes with a Word document attached called "List.Doc," you've likely been sent the Word/Melissa macro virus or worm. And if you open the document, it will send copies of itself to 50 E-mail addresses it gleans from your personal E-mail file. That gives it the ability to propagate very quickly—much quicker than the Happy99.exe worm, according to virus experts, which is why Melissa swept around the globe in a few days.

The document itself contains a list of 73 pornographic websites, along with user names and passwords for those sites. The virus can allow documents to be E-mailed to other people without warning, a potential security breach that should worry businesses and governments. About 60,000 users were infected at the company that made the first complaint, said Srivhes Sampath, general manager of McAfee Online. "It pretty much brings mail systems to a halt. . . . We've never seen anything spread like this" [41].

Privacy Issues

Information technology makes it technically and economically feasible to collect, store, integrate, interchange, and retrieve data and information quickly and easily. This characteristic has an important beneficial effect on the efficiency and effectiveness of computer-based information systems. However, the power of information technology to store and retrieve information can have a negative effect on the

right to privacy of every individual. For example, confidential E-mail messages by employees are monitored by many companies. Personal information is being collected about individuals every time they visit a site on the World Wide Web. Confidential information on individuals contained in centralized computer databases by credit bureaus, government agencies, and private business firms has been stolen or misused, resulting in the invasion of privacy, fraud, and other injustices. The unauthorized use of such information has seriously damaged the privacy of individuals. Errors in such databases could seriously hurt the credit standing or reputation of an individual.

Important privacy issues are being debated in business and government, as Internet technologies accelerate the ubiquity of global telecommunications connections in business and society. For example:

- Accessing individuals' private E-mail conversations and computer records, and collecting and sharing information about individuals gained from their visits to Internet websites and newsgroups (violation of privacy).
- Always knowing where a person is, especially as mobile and paging services become more closely associated with people rather than places (computer monitoring).
- Using customer information gained from many sources to market additional business services (computer matching).
- Collecting telephone numbers, E-mail addresses, credit card numbers, and other personal information to build individual customer profiles (unauthorized personal files).

Privacy on the Internet

If you don't take the proper precautions, any time you send an E-mail, access a website, post a message to a newsgroup, or use the Internet for banking and shopping . . . whether you're online for business or pleasure, you're vulnerable to anyone bent on collecting data about you without your knowledge. Fortunately, by using tools like encryption and anonymous remailers—and by being selective about the sites you visit and the information you provide—you can minimize, if not completely eliminate, the risk of your privacy being violated [35].

The Internet is notorious for giving its users a feeling of anonymity, when in actuality, they are highly visible and open to violations of their privacy. Most of the Internet and its World Wide Web, E-mail, chat, and newsgroups are still a wide open, unsecured electronic frontier, with no tough rules on what information is personal and private. Information about Internet users is captured legitimately and automatically each time you visit a website or newsgroup and recorded as a "cookie file" on your hard disk. Then the website owners, or online auditing services like WebTrack and Doubleclick, may sell the information from cookie files and other records of your Internet use to third parties. To make matters worse, much of the net and Web are easy targets for the interception or theft by hackers of private information furnished to websites by Internet users [29].

Of course, you can protect your privacy in several ways. For example, sensitive E-mail can be protected by encryption, if both E-mail parties use compatible encryption software built into their E-mail programs. Newsgroup postings can be made privately by sending them through *anonymous remailers* that protect your identity when you add your comments to a discussion. You can ask your Internet service provider not to sell your name and personal information to mailing list providers and other marketers. Finally, you can decline to reveal personal data and interests on online service and website user profiles to limit your exposure to electronic snooping [29].

RealNetworks Inc.: Privacy Violations	A security consultant discovered in late 1999 that RealJukebox software sent information about customers' listening habits back to RealNetworks without alerting users. The consultant, Richard Smith, charged that the company's RealPlayer product also collected user information. RealJukebox, which plays and organizes music from CDs and websites, has 13.5 million registered users. Users are asked to submit their names and E-mail addresses when they first download the product.
	RealNetworks has issued a patch that it said will disable the data collection functions. It also altered the privacy statement on its website to reflect the practice. It insisted that the data were meant to provide statistics on the aggregated use of RealJukebox, not data on individual users. Also, RealNetworks recently posted a new version of its player, RealPlayer 7, which it says doesn't report personal data [17].

Computer Matching

Computer profiling and mistakes in the **computer matching** of personal data are other controversial threats to privacy. Individuals have been mistakenly arrested and jailed, and people have been denied credit because their physical profiles or personal data have been used by profiling software to match them incorrectly or improperly with the wrong individuals. Another threat is the unauthorized matching of computerized information about you extracted from the databases of sales transaction processing systems, and sold to information brokers or other companies. A more recent threat is the unauthorized matching and sale of information about you collected from Internet websites and newsgroups you visit, as we discussed earlier. You are then subjected to a barrage of unsolicited promotional material and sales contacts as well as having your privacy violated [7, 35].

Privacy Laws

In the United States, the Federal Privacy Act strictly regulates the collection and use of personal data by governmental agencies (except for law enforcement investigative files, classified files, and civil service files). Other government **privacy laws** also attempt to enforce the privacy of computer-based files and communications. For example, in the United States, the Electronic Communications Privacy Act and the Computer Fraud and Abuse Act prohibit intercepting data communications messages, stealing or destroying data, or trespassing in federal-related computer systems. Since the Internet includes federal-related computer systems, privacy attorneys argue that the laws also require notifying employees if a company intends to monitor Internet usage. Another example is the Computer Matching and Privacy Act, which regulates the matching of data held in federal agency files to verify eligibility for federal programs.

Computer Libel and Censorship

The opposite side of the privacy debate is the right of people to know about matters others may want to keep private (freedom of information), the right of people to express their opinions about such matters (freedom of speech), and the right of people to publish those opinions (freedom of the press). Some of the biggest battlegrounds in the debate are the bulletin boards, E-mail boxes, and online files of the Internet and public information networks such as America Online and the Microsoft Network. The weapons being used in this battle include *spamming, flame mail*, libel laws, and censorship.

Spamming is the indiscriminate sending of unsolicited E-mail messages *(spam)* to many Internet users. Spamming is the favorite tactic of mass-mailers of unsolicited advertisements, or *junk E-mail*. Spamming has also been used by cyber criminals to spread computer viruses or infiltrate many computer systems.

Flaming is the practice of sending extremely critical, derogatory, and often vulgar E-mail messages *(flame mail)*, or newsgroup postings to other users on the Internet or online services. Flaming is especially prevalent on some of the Internet's special-interest newsgroups.

There have been many incidents of racist or defamatory messages on the Web that have led to calls for censorship and lawsuits for libel. In addition, the presence of sexually explicit material at many World Wide Web locations has triggered lawsuits and censorship actions by various groups and governments.

Other Challenges

Let's now explore some other important challenges that arise from the use of information technologies in E-business systems that were illustrated in Figure 9.2. These challenges include ethical and societal impacts of E-business in the areas of employment, individuality, working conditions, and health.

Employment Challenges

The impact of information technologies on **employment** is a major ethical concern and is directly related to the use of computers to achieve automation of work activities. There can be no doubt that the use of E-business technologies has created new jobs and increased productivity, while also causing a significant reduction in some types of job opportunities. For example, when computers are used for accounting systems or for the automated control of machine tools, they are accomplishing tasks formerly performed by many clerks and machinists. Also, jobs created by some E-business systems may require different types of skills and education than do the jobs that are eliminated. Therefore, individuals may become unemployed unless they can be retrained for new positions or new responsibilities.

However, there can be no doubt that E-business and E-commerce have created a host of new job opportunities. Many new jobs, including Internet webmasters, E-commerce directors, systems analysts, and user consultants, have been created in E-business organizations. New jobs have also been created in service industries that provide services to E-business firms. Additional jobs have been created because information technologies make possible the production of complex industrial and technical goods and services that would otherwise be impossible to produce. Thus, jobs have been created by activities that are heavily dependent on information technology, in such areas as space exploration, microelectronic technology, and telecommunications.

Computer Monitoring

One of the most explosive ethical issues concerning workplace privacy and the quality of working conditions in E-business is **computer monitoring.** That is, computers are being used to monitor the productivity and behavior of millions of employees while they work. Supposedly, computer monitoring is done so employers can collect productivity data about their employees to increase the efficiency and quality of service. However, computer monitoring has been criticized as unethical because it monitors individuals, not just work, and is done continually, thus violating workers' privacy and personal freedom. For example, when you call to make a reservation, an airline reservation agent may be timed on the exact number of seconds he or she took per caller, the time between calls, and the number and length of breaks taken. In addition, your conversation may also be monitored. See Figure 9.8.

Computer monitoring has been criticized as an invasion of the privacy of employees because, in many cases, they do not know that they are being monitored or don't know how the information is being used. Critics also say that an employee's right of due process may be harmed by the improper use of collected data to make personnel decisions. Since computer monitoring increases the stress on employees who must work under constant electronic surveillance, it has also been blamed for causing health problems among monitored workers. Finally, computer monitoring has

Figure 9.8

Computer monitoring can be used to record the productivity and behavior of people while they work.

Index Stock Imagery/Picture Quest.

been blamed for robbing workers of the dignity of their work. In effect, computer monitoring creates an "electronic sweatshop," where workers are forced to work at a hectic pace under poor working conditions.

Political pressure is building to outlaw or regulate computer monitoring in the workplace. For example, public advocacy groups, labor unions, and many legislators are pushing for action at the state and federal level in the United States. The proposed laws would regulate computer monitoring and protect the worker's right to know and right to privacy. In the meantime, lawsuits by monitored workers against employers are increasing. So computer monitoring of workers is one ethical issue in E-business that won't go away.

Challenges in Working Conditions

Information technology has eliminated monotonous or obnoxious tasks in the office and the factory that formerly had to be performed by people. For example, word processing and desktop publishing make producing office documents a lot easier to do, while robots have taken over repetitive welding and spray painting jobs in the automotive industry. In many instances, this allows people to concentrate on more challenging and interesting assignments, upgrades the skill level of the work to be performed, and creates challenging jobs requiring highly developed skills in the computer industry and within computer-using organizations. Thus, information technology can be said to upgrade the quality of work because it can upgrade the *quality of working conditions* and the content of work activities.

Of course, it must be remembered that some jobs in E-business systems—data entry, for example—are quite repetitive and routine. Also, to the extent that computers are utilized in some types of automation, IT must take some responsibility for the criticism of assembly-line operations that require the continual repetition of elementary tasks, thus forcing a worker to work like a machine instead of like a skilled craftsperson. Many automated operations are also criticized for relegating people to a "do-nothing" standby role, where workers spend most of their time waiting for infrequent opportunities to push some buttons. Such effects do have a detrimental effect on the quality of work, but they must be compared to the less burdensome and more creative jobs created by information technology.

Challenges to Individuality

A frequent criticism of E-business systems concerns their negative effect on the **individuality** of people. Computer-based systems are criticized as impersonal systems that dehumanize and depersonalize activities that have been computerized, since they eliminate the human relationships present in noncomputer systems.

Another aspect of the loss of individuality is the regimentation of the individual that seems to be required by some computer-based systems. These systems do not seem to possess any flexibility. They demand strict adherence to detailed procedures if the system is to work. The negative impact of IT on individuality is reinforced by horror stories that describe how inflexible and uncaring some organizations with computer-based processes are when it comes to rectifying their own mistakes. Many of us are familiar with stories of how computerized customer billing and accounting systems continued to demand payment and send warning notices to a customer whose account has already been paid, despite repeated attempts by the customer to have the error corrected.

However, many E-business systems have been designed to minimize depersonalization and regimentation. And many E-commerce systems are designed to stress personalization and community features to encourage repeated visits to E-commerce websites. Thus, the widespread use of personal computers and the Internet has dramatically improved the development of people-oriented and personalized information systems.

Health Issues

The use of information technology in the workplace raises a variety of **health issues.** Heavy use of computers is reportedly causing health problems like job stress, damaged arm and neck muscles, eye strain, radiation exposure, and even death by computer-caused accidents. For example, computer monitoring is blamed as a major cause of computer-related job stress. Workers, unions, and government officials criticize computer monitoring as putting so much stress on employees that it leads to health problems [9, 11].

People who sit at PC workstations or visual display terminals (VDTs) in fast-paced, repetitive keystroke jobs can suffer a variety of health problems known collectively as *cumulative trauma disorders* (CTDs). Their fingers, wrists, arms, necks, and backs may become so weak and painful that they cannot work. Many times strained muscles, back pain, and nerve damage may result. In particular, some computer workers may suffer from *carpal tunnel syndrome*, a painful, crippling ailment of the hand and wrist that typically requires surgery to cure.

Prolonged viewing of video displays causes eyestrain and other health problems in employees who must do this all day. Radiation caused by the cathode ray tubes (CRTs) that produce most video displays is another health concern. CRTs produce an electromagnetic field that may cause harmful radiation of employees who work too close for too long in front of video monitors. Some pregnant workers have reported miscarriages and fetal deformities due to prolonged exposure to CRTs at work. However, several studies have failed to find conclusive evidence concerning this problem. Still, several organizations recommend that female workers minimize their use of CRTs during pregnancy [9, 11].

Ergonomics

Solutions to some of these health problems are based on the science of **ergonomics,** sometimes called *human factors engineering*. The goal of ergonomics is to design healthy work environments that are safe, comfortable, and pleasant for people to work in, thus increasing employee morale and productivity. Ergonomics stresses the healthy design of the workplace, workstations, computers and other machines, and even software packages. Other health issues may require ergonomic solutions emphasizing job design, rather than workplace design. For example, this may require policies providing for work breaks from heavy VDT use every few hours, while

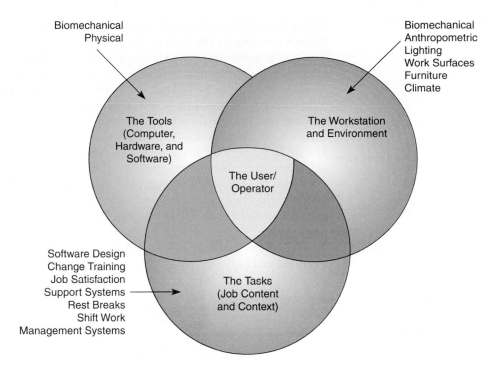

Figure 9.9

Ergonomic factors in the workplace. Note that good ergonomic design considers tools, tasks, the workstation, and environment.

Biomechanical
Physical

Biomechanical
Anthropometric
Lighting
Work Surfaces
Furniture
Climate

The Tools
(Computer,
Hardware, and
Software)

The Workstation
and Environment

The User/
Operator

Software Design
Change Training
Job Satisfaction
Support Systems
Rest Breaks
Shift Work
Management Systems

The Tasks
(Job Content
and Context)

limiting the CRT exposure of pregnant workers. Ergonomic job design can also provide more variety in job tasks for those workers who spend most of their workday at computer workstations. See Figure 9.9.

Societal Solutions

Computers and networks like the Internet and other information technologies can have many beneficial effects on society. We can use information technologies to solve human and social problems through **societal solutions** such as medical diagnosis, computer-assisted instruction, governmental program planning, environmental quality control, and law enforcement. For example, computers can help diagnose an illness, prescribe necessary treatment, and monitor the progress of hospital patients. Computer-assisted instruction (CAI) and computer-based training (CBT) enable interactive instruction tailored to the needs of students. Distance learning is supported by telecommunications networks, video conferencing, E-mail, and other technologies.

Information technologies can be used for crime control through various law enforcement applications. For example, computerized alarm systems allow police to identify and respond quickly to evidences of criminal activity. Computers have been used to monitor the level of pollution in the air and in bodies of water, to detect the sources of pollution, and to issue early warnings when dangerous levels are reached. Computers are also used for the program planning of many government agencies in such areas as urban planning, population density and land use studies, highway planning, and urban transit studies. Computers are being used in job placement systems to help match unemployed persons with available jobs. These and other applications illustrate that information technology can be used to help solve the problems of society.

You and Ethical Responsibility

As a business end user, you have a responsibility to promote ethical uses of information technology in the workplace. Whether you are a manager, business professional, or IS professional, you should accept the ethical responsibilities that come with your work activities. That includes properly performing your role as a vital human resource in the E-business systems you help develop and use in your organization. As a manager or business professional, it will be your responsibility to make decisions about business activities and the use of information technologies, which may have an ethical dimension that must be considered.

For example, should you electronically monitor your employees' work activities and electronic mail? Should you let employees use their work computers for private business or take home copies of software for their personal use? Should you electronically access your employees' personnel records or workstation files? Should you sell customer information extracted from transaction processing systems to other companies? These are a few examples of the types of decisions you will have to make that have a controversial ethical dimension. So let's take a closer look at several ethical foundations in business and information technology.

Ethical Foundations

People may use **ethical philosophies** or hold *ethical values* that guide them in ethical decision making. For example, four basic ethical philosophies are: egoism, natural law, utilitarianism, and respect for persons [9]. Briefly, these alternative ethical philosophies are:

- **Egoism.** What is best for a given individual is right.
- **Natural law.** Humans should promote their own health and life, propagate, pursue knowledge of the world and God, pursue close relationships with other people, and submit to legitimate authority.
- **Utilitarianism.** Those actions are right that produce the greatest good for the greatest number of people.
- **Respect for persons.** People should be treated as an end and not as a means to an end; and actions are right if everyone adopts the moral rule presupposed by the action.

Ethical values are more specific ethical concepts that people hold, and are heavily influenced by one's cultural background. For example, Figure 9.10 lists several Western and non-Western values. Notice that these values converge to support three basic ethical values that are common across many cultures today [10].

There are many **ethical models** of how humans apply their chosen ethical philosophies to the decisions and choices they have to make daily in work and other

---

Figure 9.10

Western and non-Western values and how they converge to support three common ethical values.

Non-Western	Western	Common Values
• *Kyosei* (Japanese): Living and working together for the common good.	• Individual liberty	• Respect for human dignity
• *Dharma* (Hindu): The fulfillment of inherited duty.	• Egalitarianism	• Respect for basic rights
• *Santutthi* (Buddhist): The importance of limited desires.	• Political participation	• Good citizenship
• *Zakat* (Muslim): The duty to give alms to the Muslim poor.	• Human rights	

Source: Adapted and reprinted by permission of *Harvard Business Review* from Thomas Donaldson, "Values in Tension: Ethics Away from Home," September–October 1996, p. 7. Copyright © 1996 by the President and Fellows of Harvard College; all rights reserved.

Figure 9.11

Figure 9.11

Ethical principles to help evaluate the potential harms or risks of the use of E-business technologies.

Principles of Technology Ethics
● **Proportionality.** The good achieved by the technology must outweigh the harm or risk. Moreover, there must be no alternative that achieves the same or comparable benefits with less harm or risk.
● **Informed Consent.** Those affected by the technology should understand and accept the risks.
● **Justice.** The benefits and burdens of the technology should be distributed fairly. Those who benefit should bear their fair share of the risks, and those who do not benefit should not suffer a significant increase in risk.
● **Minimized Risk.** Even if judged acceptable by the other three guidelines, the technology must be implemented so as to avoid all unnecessary risk.

areas of their lives. For example, some theories focus on people's decision-making processes and stress how various factors or our perceptions of them affect our ethical decision-making process. Thus, our personal, professional, and work environments and governmental/legal and social environments may affect our decision processes and lead to ethical or unethical behavior.

Another example is a *behavioral stage theory*, which says that people go through several stages of moral evolution before they settle on one level of ethical reasoning. In this model, if you reach the final stage of moral evolution, your actions are guided by self-chosen ethical principles, not by fear, guilt, social pressure, and so on.

A final dimension includes *ethical principles* that deal specifically with the ethics of the use of any form of technology. For example, Figure 9.11 lists four ethical principles that can serve as guidelines for the implementation of E-business systems and their technologies.

Business Ethics

Business ethics is concerned with the numerous ethical questions that managers must confront as part of their daily business decision making. For example, Figure 9.12 outlines some of the basic categories of ethical issues and specific business practices

Figure 9.12

Basic categories of ethical business issues. Information technology has caused ethical controversy in the areas of intellectual property rights, customer and employee privacy, security of company information, and workplace safety.

Equity	Rights	Honesty	Exercise of Corporate Power
Executive Salaries	Corporate Due Process	Employee Conflicts	Product Safety
Comparable Worth	Employee Health	of Interest	Environmental Issues
Product Pricing	Screening	**Security of Company**	Disinvestment
Intellectual	**Customer Privacy**	**Information**	Corporate Contributions
Property Rights	**Employee Privacy**	Inappropriate Gifts	Social Issues Raised by
Noncompetitive	Sexual Harassment	Advertising Content	Religious Organizations
Agreements	Affirmative Action	Government Contract	Plant/Facility Closures and
	Equal Employment	Issues	Downsizing
	Opportunity	Financial and Cash	Political Action Committees
	Shareholder Interests	Management Procedures	**Workplace Safety**
	Employment at Will	Questionable Business	
	Whistle-blowing	Practices in Foreign	
		Countries	

Source: Adapted from The Conference Board, "Defending Corporate Ethics," in Peter Madsen and Jay Shafritz, *Essentials of Business Ethics* (New York: Meridian, 1990), p. 18.

that have serious ethical consequences. Notice that the issues of employee privacy, security of company records, and workplace safety are highlighted because they have been major areas of ethical controversy in information technology.

How can managers make ethical decisions when confronted with business issues such as those listed in Figure 9.12? Several important alternatives based on theories of corporate social responsibility can be used [38, 39].

- **The stockholder theory** holds that managers are agents of the stockholders, and their only ethical responsibility is to increase the profits of the business without violating the law or engaging in fraudulent practices.

- **The social contract theory** states that companies have ethical responsibilities to all members of society, which allow corporations to exist based on a social contract. The first condition of the contract requires companies to enhance the economic satisfaction of consumers and employees. They must do that without polluting the environment or depleting natural resources, misusing political power, or subjecting their employees to dehumanizing working conditions. The second condition requires companies to avoid fraudulent practices, show respect for their employees as human beings, and avoid practices that systematically worsen the position of any group in society.

- **The stakeholder theory** maintains that managers have an ethical responsibility to manage a firm for the benefit of all its stakeholders, which are all individuals and groups that have a stake in or claim on a company. This usually includes the corporation's stockholders, employees, customers, suppliers, and the local community. Sometimes the term is broadened to include all groups who can affect or be affected by the corporation, such as competitors, government agencies, special interest groups, and the media. Balancing the claims of conflicting stakeholders is obviously not an easy task for managers.

Ethical Guidelines

We have now outlined several ethical principles that can serve as the basis for ethical conduct by managers, end users, and IS professionals. But what more specific guidelines might help your ethical use of information technology?

One way to answer this question is to examine statements of responsibilities contained in codes of professional conduct for IS professionals. A good example is the code of professional conduct of the Association of Information Technology Professionals (AITP), an organization of professionals in the computing field. Its code of conduct outlines the ethical considerations inherent in the major responsibilities of an IS professional. Figure 9.13 is a portion of the AITP code of conduct.

Business end users and IS professionals would live up to their ethical responsibilities by voluntarily following such guidelines. For example, you can be a **responsible end user** by (1) acting with integrity, (2) increasing your professional competence, (3) setting high standards of personal performance, (4) accepting responsibility for your work, and (5) advancing the health, privacy, and general welfare of the public. Then you would be demonstrating ethical conduct, avoiding computer crime, and increasing the security of any information system you develop or use.

As a business manager or professional, you should insist that the ethical and societal dimensions of information technology be considered when E-business and E-commerce systems are being developed and used. For example, a major design objective should be to develop systems that can be easily and effectively used by people. The objectives of the system must also include protection of the privacy of the individuals and the defense of the system against computer crime. The potential for misuse and malfunction of a proposed system must be analyzed and controlled to minimize such effects on its users. In that way, the security of people, hardware, software, networks, and data resources will be included in the systems design.

AITP Standards of Professional Conduct

In recognition of my obligation to my employer I shall:

- Avoid conflicts of interest and ensure that my employer is aware of any potential conflicts.
- Protect the privacy and confidentiality of all information entrusted to me.
- Not misrepresent or withhold information that is germane to the situation.
- Not attempt to use the resources of my employer for personal gain or for any purpose without proper approval.
- Not exploit the weakness of a computer system for personal gain or personal satisfaction.

In recognition of my obligation to society I shall:

- Use my skill and knowledge to inform the public in all areas of my expertise.
- To the best of my ability, ensure that the products of my work are used in a socially responsible way.
- Support, respect, and abide by the appropriate local, state, provincial, and federal laws.
- Never misrepresent or withhold information that is germane to a problem or a situation of public concern, nor will I allow any such known information to remain unchallenged.
- Not use knowledge of a confidential or personal nature in any unauthorized manner to achieve personal gain.

It should be obvious to you that many of the detrimental effects of information technology are caused by individuals or organizations that are not accepting the ethical responsibility for their actions. Like other powerful technologies, information technology possesses the potential for great harm or great good for all humankind. If managers, business professionals, and IS specialists accept their ethical responsibilities, then information technology can help make this world a better place for all of us.

Security Management of E-Business

E-Business Security

With Internet access proliferating rapidly, one might think that the biggest obstacle to electronic commerce would be bandwidth. But it's not; the number one problem is security. And part of the problem is that the Internet was developed for interoperability, not impenetrability [42].

As we saw in Section I, there are many significant threats to the security of E-business and E-commerce. That's why this section is dedicated to exploring the methods that E-business enterprises can use to manage their security. Business managers and professionals alike are responsible for the security, quality, and performance of the E-business systems in their business units. Like any other vital business assets, their information systems hardware, software, networks, and data resources need to be protected by a variety of security measures to ensure their quality and beneficial use. That's the business value of E-business security.

Analyzing the High-Tech Crime Network and eBSure

Read the Real World Case on the High-Tech Crime Network and eBSure on the next page. We can learn a lot from this case about the security challenges and security measures needed to protect corporate and E-commerce websites. See Figure 9.14.

Figure 9.14

John Lucich, international president of the High-Tech Crime Network, is a network security consultant to law-enforcement agencies and corporations.

Bernd Auers.

High-Tech Crime Network and eBSure: Outsourcing Firewalls and Network Security

Firewalls are security software guard dogs in a server box designed to resist brute-force attacks, foil hackers and generally police everything going in and out of networks. It's hard not to rely on them. But it's also easy to overestimate their importance in any enterprise security arsenal.

Firewalls can't go it alone. "What we do is a balancing act," says John Lucich, international president of the High-Tech Crime Network, a West Caldwell, New Jersey-based computerized network of law enforcement agencies from 15 countries. The amount of money spent on security products must be balanced against the worth of what's being protected, says Lucich.

Firewalls are part of a greater network and security infrastructure, which itself derives from a meticulous, well-documented security plan. Security experts are the guardians of that network, the kind of people who wake up at night in a cold sweat, wondering if the firewalls are blocking what they should. Their jobs require a lot of intense hours, because networks are constantly changing.

Security experts are scarce and expensive, so outsourcing provides an affordable way to benefit from such talent. Outsourcers also configure and maintain equipment and buy in bulk, saving their customers money. Finally, outsourced firewalls are often a good step to value-added monitoring services, which are also offered by outsourcers. Outsourcing companies can not only maintain firewalls and prevent attacks on corporate networks, but they can also see when those networks are being attacked and take the necessary steps to block the attackers.

Firewalls aren't network security silver bullets, however. Without a meticulous, well-documented security plan and a good overall infrastructure, firewalls merely provide the illusion of security. As an example of what not to do, Lucich says he was recently brought in to assess the security of a $2 billion company that had a $2,500-per-month contract with an Internet service provider to maintain a firewall on the company's network front door, which controlled everything that got in or out of the networks. But he found more than 12 backdoor vulnerabilities—things such as open ports and misconfigured routers. Anyone trying to break into a site typically goes for the unsecured parts first; hence, the firewall wasn't doing the company any good.

Kurt Ziegler, president of web monitoring software company eBSure Inc. in Dallas and former vice president of product security at Computer Associates International, says he opted for outsourcing network security a year ago because it made sense financially and didn't require hiring and training a security manager. In addition, he had to demonstrate exactly how secure his company was to clients who use his products to measure user behavior on their web sites. Logs of users' activities are sent back to eBSure, which analyzes them and passes the results on to clients. So enormous numbers of logs have to flow in past the firewalls, while malicious data must be blocked.

Ziegler evaluated both outsourced firewall and intrusion detection providers and selected Riptech Inc. in Alexandria, Virginia, to handle firewalls and provide full-time monitoring to determine in real time when his network is under attack. "They were extremely price competitive with any other alternative," he says.

Ziegler also hired an independent network penetration testing company to initially test eBSure's site and has the company recheck it about every six months. "I feel that's the only way I can really validate the security and that the company we're hiring is actually consistent with the skill level of the penetrators," he says. No company can really guarantee 100% security. "Anyone who guarantees that is a fool," says Ziegler, who acknowledges that eBSure has had "a couple of close ones" in the past year.

About six months ago, for instance, "some commercial software had gotten inside our house and was actually a Trojan horse sending data to somewhere else. And it was noticed by Riptech within four to five minutes of the time data was first going to a host other than ours," says Ziegler. The data was being sent to a server owned by Ashburn, Virginia-based UUNet Technologies Inc.: UUNet was unaware of what was going on. A phone call cleared up the problem and started an investigative trail that led to the apprehension of the hacker.

For Ziegler, the incident proved the value of having a lot of security experts watching his network. "Riptech detected the intrusion, and, immediately, we had a professional on the other end of the phone talking us through it," he says.

Case Study Questions

1. Why might a firewall fail to protect a company from hacker attacks?

2. What are several major security measures that a company should take to protect its networks and computer systems?

3. What are the benefits and limitations of outsourcing firewalls and other security measures?

Source: Adapted from Mathew Schwartz, "Trust But Verify," *Computerworld*, February 12, 2001, pp. 58–59.

John Lucich of the High-Tech Crime Network emphasizes both the importance and limitations of the use of firewalls to protect computer networks. He advises companies to have a complete E-business security plan and infrastructure, of which firewalls are only one important component. Lucich recounts an example of a $2 billion company that relied on a firewall but had over a dozen other security vulnerabilities that left them open to attack. Kurt Ziegler of eBSure outsources firewall protection and security monitoring to a security service provider as a lower cost but effective way to protect his E-commerce business. But he also hires a network penetration testing company to test his network security to assure that his security service is truly protecting his networks. Ziegler's security provider has also proven itself by detecting and tracing the source of a "Trojan horse" program that had been planted in their network by a hacker.

Security Management

The goal of **security management** is the accuracy, integrity, and safety of all E-business processes and resources. Thus, effective security management can minimize errors, fraud, and losses in the internetworked computer-based systems that interconnect today's E-business enterprises. As Figure 9.15 illustrates, security management is a complex task. As you can see, security managers must acquire and integrate a variety of security tools and methods to protect a company's E-business and E-commerce systems. We will discuss many of these security measures in this section.

Intel Corporation: Security Management Issues	"Protection of our information assets is paramount," explains Rich Cower, information security analyst at Intel Corp.'s Online Services Division. "But the difficulty is that this is a web of businesses. Intel has business connections all over the world to suppliers, contractors and others. Protecting your assets in an environment like this is especially tricky."

Figure 9.15

Examples of important security measures that are part of the security management of E-business systems.

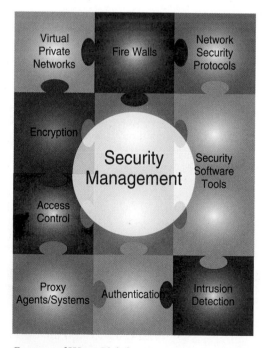

Courtesy of Wang Global.

That's why access controls are keys to security. Developers should access information related only to their products. Ditto for vendors, he says. Thus, Cower advises all high-tech companies to separate Internet, intranet, and extranet servers if necessary, especially those in research and development and other laboratories where free-sharing of information takes place. And, he says, install fire walls in all servers with connections to the outside and close off unused ports on corporate intranet and extranet servers. But with Intel's E-commerce activity growing, the company puts a lot of emphasis on employee awareness and collaboration with its vendor partners. So Intel, through employee orientation, newsletters, and spot checks, teaches its employees that "security is everyone's job," Cower adds [32].

Internetworked E-Business Defenses

Few professionals today face greater challenges than those IT managers who are developing Internet security policies for rapidly changing network infrastructures. How can they balance the need for Internet security and Internet access? Are the budgets for Internet security adequate? What impact will intranet, extranet and Web application development have on security architectures? How can they come up with best practices for developing Internet security policy? [42]

Thus, the security of today's internetworked E-business enterprises is a major management challenge. Many companies are still rushing to get fully connected to the Web and the Internet for E-commerce, and to reengineer their internal business processes with intranets, enterprise software, and extranet links to customers, suppliers, and other business partners. Vital network links and business flows need to be protected from external attack by cyber criminals or subversion by the criminal or irresponsible acts of insiders. This requires a variety of security tools and defensive measures, and a coordinated security management program. Let's take a look at some of these important security defenses.

Encryption

Encryption of data has become an important way to protect data and other computer network resources especially on the Internet, intranets, and extranets. Passwords, messages, files, and other data can be transmitted in scrambled form and unscrambled by computer systems for authorized users only. Encryption involves using special mathematical algorithms, or keys, to transform digital data into a scrambled code before they are transmitted, and to decode the data when they are received. The most widely used encryption method uses a pair of public and private keys unique to each individual. For example, E-mail could be scrambled and encoded using a unique *public key* for the recipient that is known to the sender. After the E-mail is transmitted, only the recipient's secret *private key* could unscramble the message. See Figure 9.16.

Encryption programs are sold as separate products or built into other software used for the encryption process. There are several competing software encryption standards, but the top two are RSA (by RSA Data Security) and PGP (pretty good privacy), a popular encryption program available on the Internet. Software products including Microsoft Windows NT, Novell Netware, Lotus Notes, and Netscape Communicator offer encryption features using RSA software.

Fire Walls

Another important method for control and security on the Internet and other networks is the use of **fire wall** computers and software. A network fire wall can be a communications processor, typically a *router*, or a dedicated server, along with fire wall software. A fire wall serves as a "gatekeeper" system that protects a company's intranets and other computer networks from intrusion by providing a filter and safe transfer point for access to and from the Internet and other networks. It screens all

Figure 9.16 How public key/private key encryption works.

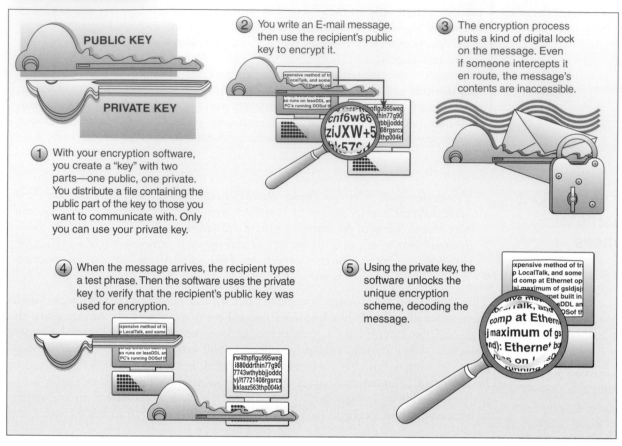

Source: Adapted from Jeffrey Rothfeder, "No Privacy on the Net," *PC World*, February 1997, pp. 224–25. Reprinted with the permission of *PC World* Communications, Inc.

network traffic for proper passwords or other security codes, and only allows authorized transmissions in and out of the network. Fire walls have become an essential component of organizations connecting to the Internet, because of its vulnerability and lack of security. Figure 9.17 illustrates an Internet/intranet fire wall system for a company.

Fire walls can deter, but not completely prevent, unauthorized access (hacking) into computer networks. In some cases, a fire wall may allow access only from trusted locations on the Internet to particular computers inside the fire wall. Or it may allow only "safe" information to pass. For example, a fire wall may permit users to read E-mail from remote locations but not to run certain programs. In other cases, it is impossible to distinguish safe use of a particular network service from unsafe use and so all requests must be blocked. The fire wall may then provide substitutes for some network services (such as E-mail or file transfer) that perform most of the same functions but are not as vulnerable to penetration.

Denial of Service Defenses

As attacks against major E-commerce players (described in Section I) have demonstrated, the Internet is extremely vulnerable to a variety of assaults by criminal hackers, especially **denial of service** (DOS) attacks. Figure 9.18 outlines the steps organizations can take to protect themselves from DOS attacks.

Denial of service assaults via the Internet depend on three layers of networked computer systems: (1) the victim's website, (2) the victim's Internet service provider

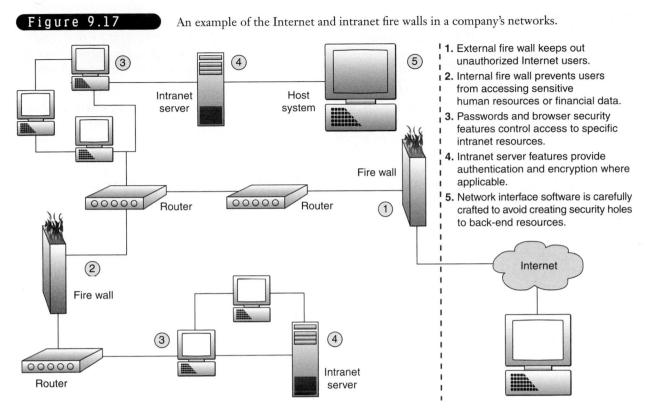

Figure 9.17   An example of the Internet and intranet fire walls in a company's networks.

1. External fire wall keeps out unauthorized Internet users.
2. Internal fire wall prevents users from accessing sensitive human resources or financial data.
3. Passwords and browser security features control access to specific intranet resources.
4. Intranet server features provide authentication and encryption where applicable.
5. Network interface software is carefully crafted to avoid creating security holes to back-end resources.

Source: Adapted from Lenny Liebman, "Are Intranets Safe?" *Communications Week*, August 5, 1996, p. 77.

(ISP), and (3) the sites of "zombie" or slave computers that were commandeered by the cyber criminals. For example, in the DOS attacks described in Section I, the hackers broke into hundreds of servers, mostly poorly protected servers at universities, and planted Trojan Horse .exe programs, which were then used to launch a barrage of service requests in a concerted attack at E-commerce websites like Yahoo! and eBay [31].

As Figure 9.18 shows, defensive measures and security precautions need to be taken at all three levels of the computer networks involved. These are the basic steps E-business companies and other organizations can take to protect their websites from denial of service and other hacking attacks.

Figure 9.18

How to defend against denial of service attacks.

Defending Against Denial of Service
● **At the zombie machines:** Set and enforce security policies. Scan regularly for Trojan Horse programs and vulnerabilities. Close unused ports. Remind users not to open .exe mail attachments.
● **At the ISP:** Monitor and block traffic spikes. Filter spoofed IP addresses. Coordinate security with network providers.
● **At the victim's website:** Create backup servers and network connections. Limit connections to each server. Install multiple intrusion-detection systems and multiple routers for incoming traffic to reduce choke points.

Source: Adapted from Deborah Radcliff, "Fighting the Flood," *Computerworld*, March 6, 2000, p. 66. Copyright 2000 by Computerworld, Inc., Framingham, MA 01701. Reprinted from *Computerworld*.

E-Mail Monitoring

Spot checks just aren't good enough anymore. The tide is turning toward systematic monitoring of corporate E-mail traffic using content-monitoring software that scans for troublesome words that might compromise corporate security. The reason: Users of monitoring software said they're concerned about protecting their intellectual property and guarding themselves against litigation [8].

As we mentioned in Section I, Internet and other online E-mail systems are one of the favorite avenues of attack by hackers for spreading computer viruses or breaking into networked computers. E-mail is also the battleground for attempts by companies to enforce policies against illegal, personal, or damaging messages by employees, and the demands of some employees and others, who see such policies as violations of privacy rights. Figure 9.19 highlights reasons why 75 surveyed companies are monitoring employees' E-mail, and outlines what statements should be in a company's E-mail monitoring policy [8].

American Fast Freight: Corporate E-Mail Monitoring

"I didn't really realize how much of a problem I had until I started using monitoring software," said Jeff LePage, director of MIS at American Fast Freight (AFF) in Kent, Washington. LePage is using MIME-sweeper software from Content Technologies to scan the content of E-mail on the company network. "Probably 30% of the E-mails going through our servers were not work-related," said LePage—an infraction of the company's E-mail usage policy.

At AFF, most of the problem was with joke mail, but there were also some inappropriate E-mail attachments. A year after putting monitoring software in place, the software is now capturing only two or three inappropriate E-mails per week from the company's 330 employees—requiring only a quick once-per-week check, LePage said. Although the monitoring software is fairly processor-intensive and can take several months to fine-tune, LePage said, "I'm very happy with the solution we've come up with" [8].

Virus Defenses

Is your PC protected from the latest viruses, worms, Trojan horses, and other malicious programs like Back Orifice that can wreak havoc on your PC? Chances are it is, if it's periodically linked to the corporate network. These days, corporate antivirus protection is a centralized function of information technology. Someone installs it for

Figure 9.19

Why companies monitor E-mail, and what a company's E-mail monitoring policy should contain.

Reasons for E-Mail Monitoring	E-Mail Monitoring Policy
57% Potential legal liability from information contained in E-mail	• A statement that computer systems are the company's property and are to be used for business purposes only.
51% Potential leaking of corporate secrets	• A clear definition of what is and isn't appropriate use of E-mail.
47% Use of E-mail for racial or sexual harassment	• A statement to employees that they can't expect E-mail to be private and that all E-mail may be monitored.
19% Complying with official regulations	• An explanation that violations can lead to disciplinary action, up to and including termination.
9% Personal (nonbusiness) use of E-mail	

Source: Adapted from Dominique Deckmyn, "More Managers Monitor E-Mail," *Computerworld*, October 18, 1999, pp. 1, 97. Copyright 1999 by Computerworld, Inc., Framingham, MA 01701. Reprinted from *Computerworld*.

you on your PC and notebook or, increasingly, distributes it over the network. The antivirus software runs in the background, popping up every so often to reassure you. The trend right now is to automate the process entirely [13].

Thus many companies are building defenses against the spread of viruses by centralizing the distribution and updating of antivirus software as a responsibility of their IS departments. Other companies are outsourcing the virus protection responsibility to their Internet service providers or to telecommunications or security management companies.

One reason for this trend is that the major antivirus software companies like Trend Micro (eDoctor and PC-cillin), McAfee (VirusScan), and Symantec (Norton Antivirus) have developed network versions of their programs which they are marketing to ISPs and others as a service they should offer to all their customers. The antivirus companies are also beginning to market *security suites* of software that integrate virus protection with fire walls, Web security, and content blocking features [18]. See Figure 9.20.

Sprint and US West: Antivirus Software Services	Trend Micro's eDoctor Global Network Internet antivirus software service builds malicious-code protection into service providers' networks, allowing customers to get virus scanning as a service from their Internet providers and managed service providers. This strategy delivers updated virus protection, around-the-clock support and faster virus response. Sprint Corp. in Kansas City, is licensing Trend Micro technology to provide corporate Internet gateway virus scanning as part of a suite of managed security applications for corporate customers. And US West Inc., the telecommunications company based in Denver, is using eDoctor to provide E-mail virus protection to its consumer and business Internet access subscribers. Breakwater Security Associates, a Seattle-based managed information security services provider, will also use the eDoctor technology, along with specialized training, to remotely manage network antivirus strategies for their customers [18].

Figure 9.20

An example of the display from an antivirus program to eliminate computer viruses.

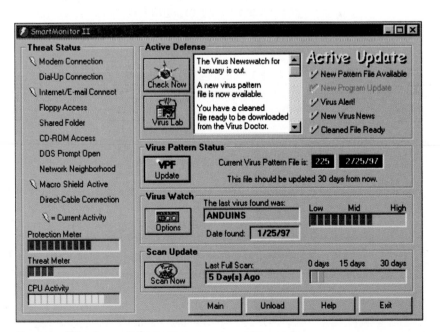

Courtesy of Touchstone Software.

Other Security Measures

Let's now briefly examine a variety of security measures that are commonly used to protect E-business systems and networks. These include both hardware and software tools like fault-tolerant computers and security monitors, and security policies and procedures like passwords and backup files. All of them are part of an integrated security management effort at many internetworked E-business enterprises today.

Security Codes

Typically, a multilevel **password** system is used for security management. First, an end user logs on to the computer system by entering his or her unique identification code, or user ID. The end user is then asked to enter a password in order to gain access into the system. (Passwords should be changed frequently and consist of unusual combinations of upper- and lowercase letters and numbers.) Next, to access an individual file, a unique file name must be entered. In some systems, the password to read the contents of a file is different from that required to write to a file (change its contents). This feature adds another level of protection to stored data resources. However, for even stricter security, passwords can be scrambled, or *encrypted*, to avoid their theft or improper use, as we will discuss shortly. In addition, *smart cards*, which contain microprocessors that generate random numbers to add to an end user's password, are used in some secure systems.

Backup Files

Backup files, which are duplicate files of data or programs, are another important security measure. Files can also be protected by *file retention* measures that involve storing copies of files from previous periods. If current files are destroyed, the files from previous periods can be used to reconstruct new current files. Sometimes, several generations of files are kept for control purposes. Thus, master files from several recent periods of processing (known as *child, parent, grandparent* files, etc.) may be kept for backup purposes. Such files may be stored off-premises, that is, in a location away from a company's data center, sometimes in special storage vaults in remote locations.

Security Monitors

Security of a network may be provided by specialized system software packages known as **system security monitors.** See Figure 9.21. System security monitors are programs that monitor the use of computer systems and networks and protect them from unauthorized use, fraud, and destruction. Such programs provide the security measures needed to allow only authorized users to access the networks. For example, identification codes and passwords are frequently used for this purpose. Security monitors also control the use of the hardware, software, and data resources of a computer system. For example, even authorized users may be restricted to the use of certain devices, programs, and data files. Additionally, security programs monitor the use of computer networks and collect statistics on any attempts at improper use. They then produce reports to assist in maintaining the security of the network.

Biometric Security

Biometric security is a fast-growing area of computer security. These are security measures provided by computer devices that measure physical traits that make each individual unique. This includes voice verification, fingerprints, hand geometry, signature dynamics, keystroke analysis, retina scanning, face recognition, and genetic pattern analysis. Biometric control devices use special-purpose sensors to measure and digitize a biometric profile of an individual's fingerprints, voice, or other physical trait. The digitized signal is processed and compared to a previously processed profile of the individual stored on magnetic disk. If the profiles match, the individual is allowed entry into a computer network and given access to secure system resources. See Figure 9.22.

Computer Failure Controls

Sorry, our computer systems are down is a well-known phrase to many end users. A variety of controls can prevent such computer failure or minimize its effects. Computer systems fail for several reasons—power failure, electronic circuitry malfunctions,

Figure 9.21

The eTrust security monitor manages a variety of security functions for major corporate networks, including monitoring the status of fire walls throughout a network.

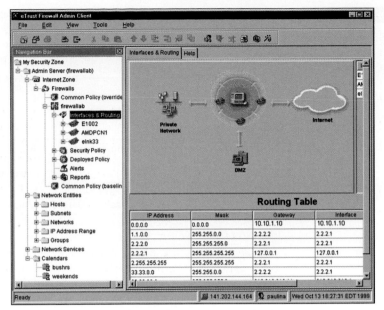

Computer Associates International, Inc.

telecommunications network problems, hidden programming errors, computer viruses, computer operator errors, and electronic vandalism. For example, computers are available with automatic and remote maintenance capabilities. Programs of preventive maintenance of hardware and management of software updates are commonplace. A backup computer system capability can be arranged with *disaster recovery* organizations. Major hardware or software changes are usually carefully scheduled and implemented to avoid problems. Finally, highly trained data center personnel and the use of performance and security management software help keep a company's computer system and networks working properly.

Fault Tolerant Systems

Many firms also use **fault tolerant** computer systems that have redundant processors, peripherals, and software that provide a *fail-over* capability to back up components in the event of system failure. This may provide a *fail-safe* capability where the computer system continues to operate at the same level even if there is a major hardware or software failure. However, many fault tolerant computer systems offer

Figure 9.22

An evaluation of common biometric security techniques based on user requirements, accuracy, and cost.

Evaluation of Biometric Techniques				
	USER CRITERIA		**SYSTEM CRITERIA**	
	INTRUSIVENESS	EFFORT	ACCURACY	COST
Dynamic signature verification	Excellent	Fair	Fair	Excellent
Face geometry	Good	Good	Fair	Good
Finger scan	Fair	Good	Good	Good
Hand geometry	Fair	Good	Fair	Fair
Passive iris scan	Poor	Excellent	Excellent	Poor
Retina scan	Poor	Poor	Very good	Fair
Voice print	Very good	Poor	Fair	Very good

Source: Adapted from Gary Anthes, "Biometrics," *Computerworld*, October 12, 1998, p. 30. Copyright 1998 by Computerworld, Inc., Framingham, MA 01701. Reprinted from *Computerworld*.

Figure 9.23

Methods of fault tolerance in computer-based information systems.

Layer	Threats	Fault Tolerant Methods
Applications	Environment, hardware and software faults	Application-specific redundancy and rollback to previous checkpoint
Systems	Outages	System isolation, data security, system integrity
Databases	Data errors	Separation of transactions and safe updates, complete transaction histories, backup files
Networks	Transmission errors	Reliable controllers; safe asynchrony and handshaking; alternative routing; error-detecting and error-correcting codes
Processes	Hardware and software faults	Alternative computations, rollback to checkpoints
Files	Media errors	Replication of critical data on different media and sites; archiving, backup, retrieval
Processors	Hardware faults	Instruction retry; error-correcting codes in memory and processing; replication; multiple processors and memories

Source: Adapted from Peter Neumann, *Computer-Related Risks* (New York: ACM Press, 1995), p. 231. Copyright © 1995, Association for Computing Machinery, Inc. By permission.

a *fail-soft* capability where the computer system can continue to operate at a reduced but acceptable level in the event of a major system failure. Figure 9.23 outlines some of the fault tolerant capabilities used in many computer systems and networks.

Disaster Recovery

Natural and man-made disasters do happen. Hurricanes, earthquakes, fires, floods, criminal and terrorist acts, and human error can all severely damage an organization's computing resources, and thus the health of the organization itself. Many companies, especially online E-commerce retailers and wholesalers, airlines, banks, and Internet service providers, for example, are crippled by losing even a few hours of computing power. Many firms could survive only a few days without computing facilities. That's why organizations develop **disaster recovery** procedures and formalize them in a *disaster recovery plan*. It specifies which employees will participate in disaster recovery and what their duties will be; what hardware, software, and facilities will be used; and the priority of applications that will be processed. Arrangements with other companies for use of alternative facilities as a disaster recovery site and offsite storage of an organization's databases are also part of an effective disaster recovery effort.

E-Business System Controls and Audits

Two final security management requirements that need to be mentioned are the development of information system controls and the accomplishment of E-business system audits. Let's take a brief look at these two security measures.

Information System Controls

Information system controls are methods and devices that attempt to ensure the accuracy, validity, and propriety of information system activities. Information system (IS) controls must be developed to ensure proper data entry, processing techniques, storage methods, and information output. Thus, IS controls are designed to monitor and maintain the quality and security of the input, processing, output, and storage activities of any information system. See Figure 9.24.

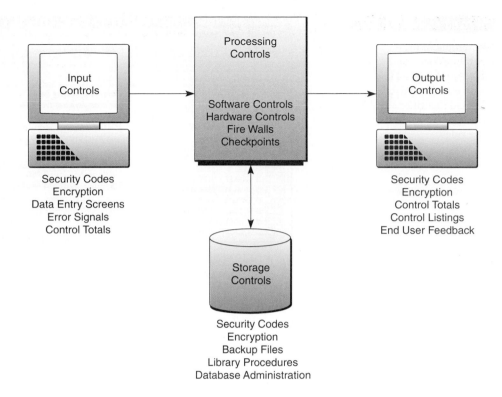

Figure 9.24

Examples of information system controls. Note that they are designed to monitor and maintain the quality and security of the input, processing, output, and storage activities of an information system.

For example, IS controls are needed to ensure the proper entry of data into an E-business system and thus avoid the garbage in, garbage out (GIGO) syndrome. Examples include passwords and other security codes, formatted data entry screens, and audible error signals. Computer software can include instructions to identify incorrect, invalid, or improper input data as it enters the computer system. For example, a data entry program can check for invalid codes, data fields, and transactions, and conduct "reasonableness checks" to determine if input data exceed specified limits or are out of sequence.

Auditing E-Business Systems

E-business systems should be periodically examined, or audited, by a company's internal auditing staff or external auditors from professional accounting firms. Such audits review and evaluate whether proper and adequate security measures and management policies have been developed and implemented. This typically involves verifying the accuracy and integrity of the E-business software used, as well as the input of data and output produced. Some firms employ special EDP auditors for this assignment. They may use special test data to test processing accuracy and the control procedures built into the software. The auditors may develop special test programs or use audit software packages. See Figure 9.25.

Another important objective of E-business system audits is testing the integrity of an application's *audit trail*. An **audit trail** can be defined as the presence of documentation that allows a transaction to be traced through all stages of its information processing. This journey may begin with a transaction's appearance on a source document and may end with its transformation into information on a final output document or report. The audit trail of manual information systems is quite visible and easy to trace. However, E-business systems have changed the form of the audit trail. Now auditors must know how to search electronically through disk and tape files of past activity to follow the audit trail of E-business systems.

Figure 9.25

An example of the capabilities of an audit software package. This package analyzes database rules and identifies any data records that deviate from those rules.

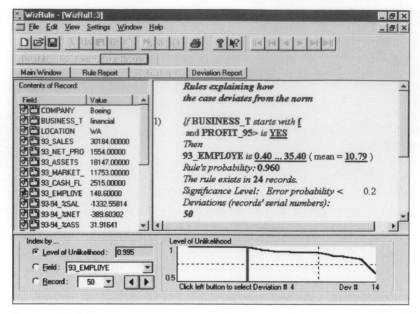

Courtesy WizSoft.

Many times, this *electronic audit trail* takes the form of *control logs* that automatically record all computer network activity on magnetic disk or tape devices. This audit feature can be found on many online transaction processing systems, performance and security monitors, operating systems, and network control programs. Software that records all network activity is also widely used on the Internet, especially the World Wide Web, as well as corporate intranets and extranets. Such an audit trail helps auditors check for errors or fraud, but also helps IS security specialists trace and evaluate the trail of hacker attacks on computer networks.

Figure 9.26 summarizes 10 security management steps you can take to protect your computer system resources from hacking and other forms of cyber crime.

Figure 9.26

How to protect yourself from cyber crime and other computer security threats.

Security Management for Internet Users

1. Use antivirus software and update it often to keep destructive programs off your computer.

2. Don't allow online merchants to store your credit card information for future purchases.

3. Use a hard-to-guess password that contains a mix of numbers and letters, and change it frequently.

4. Use different passwords for different websites and applications to keep hackers guessing.

5. Use the most up-to-date version of your Web browser, E-mail software and other programs.

6. Send credit card numbers only to secure sites; look for a padlock or key icon at the bottom of the browser.

7. Confirm the site you're doing business with. Watch your typing; it's amazon.com, not amazon.com.

8. Use a security program that gives you control over "cookies" that send information back to websites.

9. Install fire wall software to screen traffic if you use DSL or a cable modem to connect to the Net.

10. Don't open E-mail attachments unless you know the source of the incoming message.

Source: Adapted from Bill Joy, "Report from the Cyberfront," *Newsweek*, February 21, 2000, p. 44.

Summary

- **Ethical and Societal Dimensions of E-Business.** The vital role of E-business and E-commerce systems in society raises serious ethical and societal issues in terms of their impact on employment, individuality, working conditions, privacy, health, and computer crime. Managers, business professionals, and IS specialists can help solve the problems of improper use of IT by assuming their ethical responsibilities for the ergonomic design, beneficial use, and enlightened management of E-business technologies in our society. See Figure 9.2.

- **The Ethical Foundations of E-Business.** Business and IT activities involve many ethical considerations. Various ethical philosophies and models of ethical behavior may be used by people in forming ethical judgments. These serve as a foundation for ethical principles that can serve as guidelines for dealing with ethical business issues that may arise in E-business and E-commerce.

- **E-Business Security Management.** One of the most important responsibilities of the management of a company is to assure the security and quality of its E-business activities. Security management tools and policies can ensure the accuracy, integrity, and safety of the E-business systems and resources of a company, and thus minimize errors, fraud, and security losses in their E-commerce activities. See Figure 9.15.

Key Terms and Concepts

These are the key terms and concepts of this chapter. The page number of their first explanation is in parentheses.

1. Antivirus software (323)
2. Audit trail (345)
3. Auditing E-business systems (344)
4. Backup files (342)
5. Biometric security (342)
6. Business ethics (331)
7. Computer crime (316)
8. Computer matching (325)
9. Computer monitoring (326)
10. Computer virus (322)
11. Denial of service (338)
12. Disaster recovery (344)
13. Encryption (327)
14. Ergonomics (328)
15. Ethical and societal impacts of E-business (326)
    a. Employment (326)
    b. Health (328)
    c. Individuality (328)
    d. Societal solutions (329)
    e. Working conditions (327)
16. Ethical foundations (330)
17. Fault tolerant (343)
18. Fire wall (327)
19. Flaming (326)
20. Hacking (317)
21. Information system controls (344)
22. Intellectual property piracy (321)
23. Passwords (342)
24. Privacy issues (323)
25. Responsible end user (332)
26. Security management (326)
27. Software piracy (321)
28. Spamming (325)
29. System security monitor (342)
30. Unauthorized use (319)

Review Quiz

Match one of the key terms and concepts listed previously with one of the brief examples or definitions that follow. Try to find the best fit for the answers that seem to fit more than one term or concept. Defend your choices.

_____ 1. Ensuring the accuracy, integrity, and safety of E-business activities and resources.

_____ 2. Control totals, error signals, backup files, and security codes are examples.

_____ 3. Software that can control access and use of a computer system.

_____ 4. A computer system can continue to operate even after a major system failure if it has this capability.

_____ 5. A computer system that serves as a filter for access to and from other networks by a company's networked computers.

_____ 6. Periodically examine the accuracy and integrity of computer processing.

_____ 7. The presence of documentation that allows a transaction to be traced through all stages of information processing.

_____ 8. Using your voice or fingerprints to identify you electronically.

_____ 9. A plan to continue IS operations during an emergency.

_____ 10. Scrambling data during its transmission.

_____ 11. Ethical choices may result from decision-making processes, cultural values, or behavioral stages.

_____ 12. Managers must confront numerous ethical questions in their businesses.

_____ 13. Sending unsolicited E-mail indiscriminately.

_____ 14. Employees may have to retrain or transfer.

_____ 15. Computer-based systems may depersonalize human activities.

_____ 16. Constant long-term use of computers at work may cause health problems.

_____ 17. Computer-based monitoring of environmental quality is an example.

_____ 18. Tedious jobs are decreased and jobs are made more challenging.

_____ 19. Using computers to identify individuals that fit a certain profile.

_____ 20. Collecting information about you without your consent.

_____ 21. Using computers to monitor the activities of workers.

_____ 22. Overwhelming a website with requests for service from captive computers.

_____ 23. Using computers and networks to steal money, services, software, or data.

_____ 24. Using company computers to access the Internet during work hours for personal business.

_____ 25. Unauthorized copying of software.

_____ 26. Unauthorized copying of copyrighted material.

_____ 27. Electronic breaking and entering into a computer system.

_____ 28. A program makes copies of itself and destroys data and programs.

_____ 29. Finds and eliminates computer viruses.

_____ 30. Sending extremely critical, derogatory, and vulgar E-mail messages.

_____ 31. Designing computer hardware, software, and workstations that are safe, comfortable, and easy to use.

_____ 32. End users should act with integrity and competence in their use of information technology.

Discussion Questions

1. What can be done to improve E-commerce security on the Internet? Give several examples of security measures, and technologies you would use.

2. What potential security problems do you see in the increasing use of intranets and extranets in business? What might be done to solve such problems? Give several examples.

3. What artificial intelligence techniques can a business use to improve computer security and fight computer crime?

4. What are your major concerns about computer crime and privacy on the Internet? What can you do about it? Explain.

5. What is disaster recovery? How could it be implemented at your school or work?

6. Refer to the Real World Case on the University of Washington and Others in the chapter. What should be

done to fight the growth of hacker and virus attacks on business and consuemrs?

7. Is there an ethical crisis in E-business today? What role does information technology play in unethical business practices?

8. What are several business decisions that you will have to make as a manager that have both an ethical and IT dimension? Give examples to illustrate your answer.

9. Refer to the Real World Case on the High-Tech Crime Network and eBSure in the chapter. Should consumers install network firewalls and other security hardware and software products on their home systems? Why or why not?

10. What would be examples of one positive and one negative effect of the use of E-business technologies in each of the ethical and societal dimensions illustrated in Figure 9.2? Explain several of your choices.

Application Exercises

Complete the following exercises as individual or group projects that apply chapter concepts to real world business situations.

1. Internet Privacy and Anonymity:
An Ethical Dilemma

I recently came across some software that lets you cloak your identity on the Internet. It got me thinking about the whole issue of anonymity on the Net. Suppose a political activist in a country with limited civil rights sends an E-mail to an American human-rights group describing dreadful working conditions in a U.S.-owned factory. The plant's owners have to make changes—but not before local authorities, who monitor Internet traffic, throw the activist in jail. There, anonymity would have helped illuminate a problem.

Now suppose a child pornographer delivers his wares by E-mail. Authorities intercept the transmissions, but because the pornographer has successfully hidden his identity on the Net, they are unable to identify or find him. In that case, anonymity has protected a felon.

Whether you find these scenarios troubling will probably determine how you react to new software designed to allow people to send and receive E-mail, post messages to discussion groups, and participate in online chats in perfect anonymity. If, like me, you find both scenarios troubling, then what we have is an ethical dilemma.

I believe fervently in the right to free speech. I'm pleased that the Internet means that freedom of the press no longer is restricted, as A. J. Liebling once said, to the person who owns one. But I've also seen enough damage done by anonymous rumor and innuendo to recognize the danger that lurks in freedom without responsibility. I'm glad that such software for Internet anonymity will be available. But in the end, I hope that not many people will feel a need to use it.

a. Do you share the ethical misgivings of the author on this issue? Why or why not?

b. Should there be unrestricted use of software that provides anonymity on the Internet? Why or why not?

c. If you were able to decide this issue now, how would you decide for yourself? Your company? For society? Explain the reasons for your decisions.

Source: Adapted from Stephen Wildstrom, "A Big Boost for Net Privacy," *Business Week*, April 5, 1999, p. 23. Reprinted with special permission, copyright © 1999 by The McGraw-Hill Companies, Inc.

2. Your Internet Job Rights: Three Ethical Scenarios

Whether you're an employer or an employee, you should know what your rights are when it comes to Internet use in the workplace. Mark Grossman, a Florida attorney who specializes in computer and Internet law, gives answers to some basic questions.

Scenario 1

Nobody told you that your Internet use in the office was being monitored. Now you've been warned you'll be fired if you use the Internet for recreational surfing again. What are your rights?

Bottom line. When you're using your office computer, you have virtually no rights. You'd have a tough time convincing a court that the boss invaded your privacy by monitoring your use of the company PC on company time. You should probably be grateful you got a warning.

Scenario 2

Your employees are abusing their Internet privileges, but you don't have an Internet usage policy. What do you do?

Bottom line. Although the law isn't fully developed in this area, courts are taking a straightforward approach: If it's a company computer, the company can control the way it's used. You don't need an Internet usage policy to prevent inappropriate use of your company computers. To protect yourself in the future, distribute an Internet policy to your employees as soon as possible.

Scenario 3

Employee John Doe downloads adult material to his PC at work, and employee Jane Smith sees it. Smith then proceeds to sue the company for sexual harassment. As the employer, are you liable?

Bottom line. Whether it comes from the Internet or from a magazine, adult material simply has no place in the office. So Smith could certainly sue the company for making her work in a sexually hostile environment. The best defense is for the company to have an Internet usage policy that prohibits visits to adult sites. (Of course, you have to follow through. If someone is looking at adult material in the office, you must at least send the offending employee a written reprimand.) If the company lacks a strict Internet policy, though, Smith could prevail in court.

Ethical Questions

a. Do you agree with the advice of attorney Mark Grossman in each of the scenarios? Why or why not?

b. What would your advice be? Explain your positions.

c. Identify any ethical philosophies, values, or models you may be using in explaining your position in each of the scenarios.

Source: Adapted from James Martin. "You Are Being Watched," *PC World*, November 1997, p. 258. Reprinted with the permission of *PC World* Communications Inc.

3. Gantt Chart for an Intranet Development Project—Revisited

This project requires you to extend and modify the Gantt chart you created in *Application Exercise 3-1*. You should reread that exercise and retrieve the spreadsheet you created. If you were not assigned the Gantt chart exercise earlier complete part A of that assignment in order to create the initial Gantt chart that you will need to complete the exercise.

You should have noticed that there are some steps in this process that have no slack time—if they are delayed the whole project will be delayed, since there are successor steps that depend on them and are scheduled to begin as soon as the predecessor step is completed. Other steps do allow for some slack time—no successor steps begin immediately at their completion time, so that, if they are delayed a bit, the completion time of the project will not be affected. Tasks that have no slack time are called critical tasks and the set of tasks without slack time is called the critical path. Tasks on the critical path are tracked most closely to avoid delays—and they are usually given a different color on a Gantt chart.

a. Revise the Gantt chart from Chapter 3 by coloring tasks on the critical path in black and other tasks in light gray and print it out.

b. Suppose that the time to complete steps C, F, and D could each be reduced by one week by adding more workers to these tasks. Additional workers raise costs and are to be used only if time to complete the project will be reduced. On which steps would you add the additional workers? Add these changes to the spreadsheet and print out a copy.

One of the members of the team assigned to perform steps E and F has quit. The team estimates that, if she is not replaced, step E will now require 3 weeks and step F will require 4 weeks. Step F's completion time can be cut back to 3 weeks again by hiring another worker, but the team does not feel that task E can be shortened by adding a new worker.

c. Redraw the Gantt chart to show how completion of the project will be affected if this worker is not replaced and print out a copy of your chart.

d. Would you hire a replacement worker to work with the team on step F? Write a short report describing the modifications you have made to the original Gantt charts and your reasons for them.

4. Tracking Project Work at AAA Systems

You are responsible for managing information systems development projects at AAA Systems. To better track progress in completing projects you have decided to maintain a simple database table to track the time your employees spend on various tasks and the projects with which they are associated. It will also allow you to keep track of employee billable hours each week. A sample set of data for this table is shown below.

a. Build a database table to store the data shown below and enter the records shown as a set of sample data. (Note that this table has no natural unique identifier. A combination of the project name, task name, employee ID and production week is required to uniquely identify a row in this table.)

b. Create a query that will list the hours worked for all workers who worked more than 40 hours during production week 20.

c. Create a report grouped by project that will show the number of hours devoted to each task on the project and the total number of hours devoted to each project as well as a grand total of hours worked.

d. Create a report grouped by employee that will show their hours worked on each task and total hours worked. The user should be able to select a production week and have data for just that week presented in the report. (Be sure to keep a copy of your work for this project because it is used again in a later exercise.)

Project_Name	Task_Name	Employee_Id	Production_Week	Hours_worked
Fin-Goods-Inv	App. Devel.	456	21	40
Fin-Goods-Inv	DB Design	345	20	20
Fin-Goods-Inv	UI Design	234	20	16
HR	Analysis	234	21	24
HR	Analysis	456	20	48
HR	UI Design	123	20	8
HR	UI Design	123	21	40
HR	UI Design	234	21	32
Shipmt-Tracking	DB Design	345	20	24
Shipmt-Tracking	DB Design	345	21	16
Shipmt-Tracking	DB Development	345	21	20
Shipmt-Tracking	UI Design	123	20	32
Shipmt-Tracking	UI Design	234	20	24

The FBI and Recourse Technologies: Discovering Insider Security Threats

Ramon was an intellectual of sorts, highly educated, conservative in his politics, painfully introverted, somewhat arrogant and, according to some who knew him, kind of a geek. He was an expert programmer who preferred communicating with associates through e-mail rather than in person. He even hacked into his employer's computer system without permission to show management that there were serous security gaps that needed to be fixed.

But somewhere along the line, Ramon's career faltered, and he became frustrated and contemptuous of his employer. And since his arrest on February 18, 2001 for selling classified information, Ramon, also known as Robert Philip Hanssen, has been at the center of the worst insider spy case in FBI history.

However, the Hanssen case isn't unique to the government, say experts. Business and industry are at risk from similar perpetrators. And there are characteristics shared by disgruntled insiders that, combined with circumstances like pending layoffs, can send those with trusted access to the dark side of IT.

A study conducted by psychologists at Political Psychology Associates Ltd. In Bethesda, Maryland, found that most cases of insider abuse in business and government can be traced to individuals who are introverted, incapable of dealing with stress or conflict, and frustrated with their jobs, among other factors.

The behavioral research firm also pointed out, however, that many honest people in the workplace share these traits. Experts, therefore, recommend tight controls on sensitive information access, and monitoring tools that can catch insiders in the act.

"Often, there are feelings of betrayal and grudges," particularly during times of financial hardship at companies, said Eugene Schultz, an engineer at Lawrence Berkeley National Laboratory and an adjunct professor at the University of California, Berkeley. "There's no question that there is a link between insider activity and bad times at organizations."

For example, FBI agents at the New York field office had complained prior to Hanssen's arrival about the high cost of living, which led them to express concern about spying for financial gain. They may have been correct, as Hanssen is alleged to have asked his Russian handlers for diamonds to provide for his children's futures.

Schultz, who has written a study on the corporate use of "honey pots"—phony servers populated with false data designed to attract hackers—for Recourse Technologies Inc., a security software firm in Palo Alto, California, also said there's a clear link between job roles and insider activity. Surprisingly, systems administrators, network security personnel and senior executives are often the culprits.

Recourse Technologies CEO Frank Huera recently conducted a live demonstration of his company's Mantrap honey pot software during a sales call at a major computer manufacturer. Within 30 seconds, a member of the company's network security team attempted to hack the honey pot server.

In another case, a very large financial firm discovered it was losing money from its payroll systems. So it set up two dozen honey pots and gave each server an interesting name, such as "payroll server." The next morning, the company's chief operating officer was caught trying to jury-rig another executive's payroll account.

Eric Friedberg, formerly a computer and telecommunications crime coordinator at the U.S. Attorney's Office in New York, said companies should consider the new breed of software tools now emerging that could help detect unusual internal network activity. The new crop of tools includes Recourse's Manhunt suite and Raytheon Co.'s SilentRunner network discovery tools.

Had the FBI used such security products, it could have discovered that Hanssen was searching for his own name in FBI databases, according to Friedberg. Hanssen's searches for his name "would have been totally out of the ordinary. There's no legitimate reason for that," Friedberg said.

Case Study Questions

1. What psychological and business factors increase the risk of insider security threats?

2. Why do you think the FBI failed to discover Phillip Hanssen's illegal activity?

3. How can "honey pot" files and network security monitors help discover and deter illegal insider security threats?

Source: Adapted from Dan Verton, "Insider Monitoring Seen as Next Wave in IT Security," *Computerworld*, March 19, 2001, p. 33.

Visa, American Express, and GM: Managing E-Business Security Risk

Even with strong security, E-business risk is a fact of life in today's interconnected business world. But the fundamental problem with managing this new form of business risk, say IT managers, is that there are no metrics and no standards to measure the level of risk. Nevertheless, all business managers need to realize that those bits and bytes they call "just data" are really the corporation's lifeblood. And they must get their arms around the ultimate cost to the business if that data were lost, stolen or altered.

"We need to make a model where E-business risk is wrapped in the cost of doing business—like automobiles that transfer regulatory costs to the consumers," says Frank Reeder, who chairs both the computer system security and privacy advisory board at the U.S. Department of Commerce and the Center for Internet Security in Bethesda, Maryland.

Quantifying risk calls for statistics and benchmarks, things that are sorely lacking in this new era of E-business, says Paul Raines, head of global information risk management at Barclay's Capital, the investment division of Barclay's Group in London. "Most risk models so far have been qualitative: Define your assets by classifying your data sensitivity; define your risks for theft, disaster, hacking. Then you evaluate your site against these risks," Raines says.

But recently, the International Organization for Standardization approved a security standard that grew out of one used in Britain. This new standard includes a certification program in the areas of policy, asset classification, allocation of security resources and responsibilities, systems and network security, government compliance, physical security, employee training and awareness and access controls.

Now, Visa International and American Express are throwing their weight into security standards by making them mandatory for their electronic merchants. Their requirements are a little broader, encompassing mostly server-side credit card processing and storage, access controls and encryption. Analysts say these efforts will go a long way toward setting up future risk frameworks in the business-to-customer market.

"I consider the reach of Visa much stronger than any government agency or security company, because credit companies can say, 'If you don't follow our security policies, you can't process our cards,'" says Pete Lindstrom, an analyst at Boston-based Hurwitz Group.

The importance of E-business security standards to the audit community has been helpful in driving the message of E-business risk up to top company executives and boards of directors. For example, Jackie Wagner, general auditor at General Motors Corp. attended a security association meeting last April and brought along the chairman of GM's audit committee, Dennis Weatherstone, former CEO and chairman of J.P. Morgan & Co. When Weatherstone returned to GM, he brought the automaker's CIO into the boardroom to update the board of directors on system security.

"The audit committee and the board asked a lot of questions. All were about our level of risk and how we're addressing it," says Wagner (Specially, she notes, the board asked how GM drives accountability beyond the IT organization in managing exposure to risk.) Wagner says the board was happy with GM's security controls on its E-business systems.

The audit team hired Glenn Yauch, a Deloitte & Touche LLP consultant then stationed at GM, and placed him as director of GM's E-business. Yauch then launched a series of company-wide conferences about risk. "I pulled together resources from GM's audit services and mixed them with technical consultants. We put every risk we could think of on a board and created areas of risk," he says.

These areas include:

- E-business strategy: Alignment with existing strategy and marketing channels, marketplace and opportunity strengths; stakeholders (suppliers, customers, trading partners); and sponsorship.

- Business policy: regulations and customer data privacy.

- End-to-end process/transaction flow

- Data management: Integrity, availability and confidentiality of data stored in databases and in customer relationship management systems.

- Infrastructure: servers, firewalls, operating systems, routers and applications.

Yauch adds, "once we put this list together, we found this framework was flexible enough to evaluate e-business risk management issues in other business units as they rolled out E-business initiatives."

Case Study Questions

1. What should a business do about measuring and managing E-business risk?

2. Do you agree with what Visa and American Express are requiring of merchants that use their electronic credit card systems?   Why or why not?

3. How useful is GM's framework of areas of risk to any company's management of E-business risk? Explain.

Source: Adapted from Deborah Radcliff, "Calculating E-Risk," *Computerworld*, February 12, 2001, pp. 34–35.

Acxiom Inc.: Consumer Privacy Challenges in E-Business

What detail of you private life would you least like to see splashed across the Internet? Or added to a database, linked to your name and sold in a mailing list?

The privacy problem is simple. Companies need to glean information that will help target sales. Consumers want the convenience of secure E-commerce without worrying about having their identities stolen, being spammed, or having the aggregators of personal data knowing—and profiting from—every detail of their lives. As retailers and consumers force this issue, E-commerce could get squeezed in the process—particularly among companies that minimize the privacy concerns of their customers. Take Acxiom.

You may not know Acxiom. But the Conway, Arkansas, company probably knows you, having spent 30 years amassing a monster database of consumer information. It has dossiers on 160 million Americans—90 percent of U.S. households.

Acxiom has 20 million unlisted telephone numbers—gleaned mostly from those warranty cards you filled out when you bought that new coffee maker—that it sells to law enforcement agencies, lawyers, private investigators, debt collectors, and just about anybody else willing to pay its fee. Acxiom is often better at tracking down deadbeat dads than the police. That's because Acxiom combines the most extensive public records database ever gathered by a nongovernmental entity with consumer information it purchases from the private sector.

The company's biggest clients are data-hungry telemarketers, retailers, E-commerce companies, and direct mail marketers. Acxiom advises Wal-Mart on how to stock its shelves, while helping Citicorp decide the creditworthiness of potential customers.

"We are not a credit agency," sniffed Jerry Jones, Acxiom's legal and business-development leader, over an elaborate dinner recently at San Francisco's Ritz-Carlton. Mr. Jones and several of his colleagues were in the midst of a nationwide tour hawking their latest product—a data integration software system dubbed AbiliTec, which enables clients like Mercedes-Benz of America to access real-time detailed transaction information on shoppers, whether they are on the phone, at a dealership, or online. With something as simple as caller ID, a Mercedes-Benz operator can make a snap decision on whether or not a caller is a potential customer or a waste of time.

Mr. Jones says Acxiom is in the business of streamlining business. Maybe so, but Acxiom's power in advising clients on which customers to embrace and which to reject raises troubling privacy issues, argue privacy advocates like Deirdre Mulligan of The Center for Democracy and Technology.

Acxiom can help E-commerce clients "fraud score" web surfers. Using a combination of demographics, criminal background checks, and other factors, the company's clients can quickly prevent certain customers from purchasing items electronically. "It raises a whole bunch of troubling questions," Ms. Mulligan says.

Today, Acxiom bills itself as the largest data-mining company in the country. And it's hard to argue against that boast considering Acxiom has sales topping $1 billion annually and 5,600 employees worldwide. The company hopes its AbiliTec product will enable it to grow by 30 percent in 2001.

Some high-tech companies say increased privacy demands place an undue burden on their businesses. But critics like consumer rights groups and even some business advocates counter that the savvy ones will channel that resistance into a proactive approach. In other words, a privacy-friendly stance could win over more potential customers than the hard line would.

By making their practices compliant with whatever privacy standards are set and taking advantage of some innovative new tracking and encryption technologies, companies eventually could be able to offer consumers the protection they want without subtracting from their sales numbers. That could mean collecting the same data the companies always have, but not sharing it with others without first seeking permission, or assuring customers that sites that inevitably will track their web movements are held accountable for their practices.

Case Study Questions

1. What is the problem companies face when dealing with consumer privacy issues in E-business and E-commerce?

2. Are there any ethical issues in how Axciom uses its information on most American households? Why or why not?

3. What can companies do to proactively meet consumer privacy concerns, while capitalizing on the business value of their information?

Source: Adapted from Luc Hatlestad, "Privacy Matters," and Paul Elias, "Paid Informant," *Red Herring*, January 16, 2001, pp. 48–51, and Sami Lais, "No More Secrets," *Computerworld*, February 19, 2001, pp. 58–59.

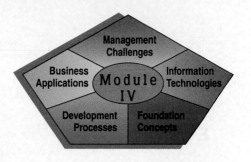

Management Challenges
Business Applications
Module IV
Information Technologies
Development Processes
Foundation Concepts

Chapter 10

Enterprise and Global Management of E-Business Technology

Chapter Highlights

Learning Objectives

After reading and studying this chapter, you should be able to:

1. Identify several ways that information technologies have affected the job of managers in E-business companies.

2. Explain how problems of information system performance can be reduced by the involvement of business managers in IS planning and management.

3. Identify the seven major dimensions of the E-business organization and explain how they affect the success of E-business companies.

4. Identify each of the three components of E-business technology management and use examples to illustrate how they might be implemented in an E-business enterprise.

5. Identify several cultural, political, and geoeconomic challenges that confront managers in the management of global E-business technologies.

6. Explain the effect on global E-business strategy of the trend toward a transnational business strategy by international business organizations.

7. Identify several considerations that affect the choice of IT applications, IT platforms, data access policies, and systems development methods by a global E-business enterprise.

Managing E-Business Technologies

E-Business and IT

The strategic and operational importance of information technology in E-business enterprises is no longer questioned.

Information technology is the bloodstream that feeds the business process.

So says Jacques Nasser, the hard-driving CEO of Ford Motor Company, who is intent on transforming Ford into a global E-business enterprise and a major player in global E-commerce [25]. Thus, there is a real need for business managers and professionals to understand how to manage this vital organizational function. In this section, we will explore how IT affects managers and E-business organizations, and stress the importance of a customer and business value focus for the management of E-business technologies. So whether you plan to be an entrepreneur and run your own business, a manager in a corporation, or a business professional, managing E-business systems and technologies will be one of your major responsibilities.

Analyzing Raytheon and Deere & Co.

Read the Real World Case on Raytheon and Deere & Co. on the next page. We can learn a lot about how companies evaluate E-business and E-commerce. See Figure 10.1.

Eric Singleton of Raytheon insists that a manager or business professional must find a way to measure E-business and E-commerce performance and business value. Raytheon uses a balanced scorecard approach that is required of all their E-businesses, and reported regularly to Singleton and monthly to the chairman of the company.

Figure 10.1

Eric Singleton is director of global E-business for Raytheon Co. and uses a balanced scorecard approach to evaluate the performance of Raytheon's E-business.

Furnald/Gray.

Raytheon and Deere & Co.: Metrics for E-Business Management

Many companies seem to be just doing E-business and not measuring at all. We worry about people just throwing up their hands and saying 'We can't measure this, and anyway, we have to do it," says Jim Bugnitz, managing director of the E-Business Forum. But metrics are crucial in E-business. "If you can't describe something in business numerically, you're not doing your job properly," says Eric Singleton, director of global E-business at Raytheon Co. in Lexington, Massachusetts. "How can you communicate success, failure or the gaps that need to be closed?"

Balanced Scorecard

Singleton learned the metrics mantra while steeped in the metrics-centric Six Sigma quality program at Allied Signal Inc. Now, as director of global E-business at Raytheon Co., he's managing the performance of all the company's E-businesses using a balanced-scorecard approach. Here's what it measures:

- *Innovation and flexibility:* Average time from concept to start; speed to match a rival's site; speed at which the competition will match your site; time between relaunches.

- *Customer loyalty:* Percentage who return within a year; time between visits; duration of visit; conversion rate; percentage who give personal information.

- *Transactional excellence:* Unique visitors each month; online sales abandoned; percentage of orders correct; time to respond to a customer; percentage of orders filled on time.

- *Customer information:* Percentage of E-mail addresses collected out of all traffic.

- *Infrastructure reliability:* Time to load a page; network uptime and scalability.

- *Supply-chain excellence:* Inventory levels; inventory turns; order confirmation time; percentage of products built to order.

- *Valuation and financial performance:* Return on invested capital; market capitalization migration (the changing value of the overall business)

- *Digital quotient:* For complementary E-business channels, percentage of total revenue generated online.

At Raytheon, these metrics are reported up the line regularly to Singleton, who reports monthly to the chairman on the state of every E-business. "The purpose is to manage the business, drive decision on whether to keep the business, add resources in areas where there's a gap and figure out how to capture successes and apply them to other E-businesses," he says. "It works for Raytheon; I don't see why it can't work for everyone."

Project Metrics

At Deere & Co. in Moline, Illinois, for example, Jim Harl looked at a bunch of E-business metrics to establish the value of an E-business supply chain project before Deere committed to it. "Everybody gets excited about doing E-business, but if you get caught up in it, you may put in some neat, great technology that doesn't touch your bottom line," says Harl, Deere's manager of E-business for supply management. "Don't lose site of the fact that it's a tool in the context of a larger business plan."

Deere spends $1.5 billion annually on indirect materials and services—from office supplies to drill bits to travel—that don't go into products. Harl's challenge was to use technology to manage that expense, and he felt that the Internet might be the tool to drive those procurement costs down.

He started by measuring the existing indirect materials procurement process. "We looked at everything you do—all the people, all the time on computers, putting [the purchase order] in an envelope—we mapped that out in excruciating detail," he says. Then he determined which steps would go away in an internet system and how that translated into driving down cycle time and costs.

The company estimated that a web-based system could save tens of millions of dollars. Only then did Deere purchase Ariba Buyer software, which it plans to implement with a select group of indirect material suppliers to execute that part of the supply chain more efficiently. "If it's done right, it should reduce the suppliers' costs, too," Harl says.

The pre-project metrics proved to Harl that there was business value in the Internet tool he envisioned. "It's not E-commerce for its own sake," he says. "It's how do I use these tools to bring greater value to our supply chain?" As the project moves forward, Deere will see whether expected savings materialize, Harls says, "and if not, why not."

Case Study Questions

1. Should E-commerce and E-business ventures be subject to the same business and financial metrics and standards as traditional business proposals? Why or why not?

2. How does Raytheon's balanced scorecard approach help them manage their E-commerce and E-business initiatives?

3. Should Deere's exhaustive evaluation of the case for an E-business procurement system be a model for evaluating every proposed E-business venture? Why or why not?

Source: Adapted from Kathleen Melymuka, "Measuring your On-line Profitability," *ComputerWorld ROI*, March/April 2001, pp. 19–23.

Jim Harl of Deere & Co. led an exhaustive study before Deere installed the new E-business, whose performance they will continue to evaluate after implementaton.

Managers and E-Business Technologies

Really difficult business problems always have many aspects. Often a major decision depends on an impromptu search for one or two key pieces of auxiliary information and a quick ad hoc analysis of several possible scenarios. You need software tools that easily combine and recombine data from many sources. You need Internet access for all kinds of research. Widely scattered people need to be able to collaborate and work the data in different ways [11].

So says Bill Gates, chairman of Microsoft Corporation, of his own and his management team's experience with the managerial effects of E-business technologies. Thus, as Figure 10.2 illustrates, the competitive pressures of today's E-business and technology environment are encouraging managers to rethink their use and management of information technology. Many business executives now see information technology as an enabling platform for electronic commerce, and for managing the cross-functional and interorganizational E-business processes of their business units. In addition, the Internet, intranets, extranets, and the Web are interconnecting individuals, teams, business units, and business partners in close business relationships that promote the communication, collaboration, and decision making needed in today's competitive global marketplace.

Thus, information technology has become a major force for precipitating or enabling organizational and managerial change. Thanks to Internet technologies and other dynamic hardware, software, data and network developments, computing power and information resources are now more readily available to more managers than ever before. In fact, these and other information technologies have already enabled innovative changes in managerial decision making, organizational structures, and managerial work activities [8, 16, 29].

Figure 10.2

Information technology must be managed to meet the challenges of today's internetworked E-business and technology environment, and the customer value and business value imperatives for success in the new economy.

E-Business Developments

Suppliers → Customers

Information Technology Developments

Customer Value Business Value

- E-business and E-commerce transformation of business strategies and processes
- Agility, flexibility, and time compression of development, manufacturing, and delivery supply chain cycles
- Reengineering and cross-functional integration of business processes using Internet technologies
- Competitive advantage, total quality, and customer value focus

- Use of the Internet, intranets, extranets, and the Web as the primary IT infrastructure
- Diffusion of technology to internetwork employees, customers and suppliers
- Global and enterprise computing, collaboration and decision support systems
- Integrated cross-functional enterprise software replaces legacy systems

- Give customers what they want, when and how they want it, at the lowest cost
- Interenterprise coordination of manufacturing and business processes
- Effective distribution and channel partnerships
- Responsiveness and accountability to customers

Source: Adapted in part from Ravi Kalakota and Marcia Robinson, *E-Business 2.0: Roadmap for Success* (Reading, MA: Addison-Wesley, 2001), pp. 273, 279. © 2001 Addison-Wesley Publishing Company, Inc. Reprinted by permission of Addison-Wesley Longman Inc.

For example, the decision support capabilities provided by Web-enabled decision support system technologies are changing the focus of managerial decision making. Managers freed from number-crunching chores must now face tougher strategic policy questions in order to develop realistic alternatives for today's dynamic E-business and E-commerce environment. In addition, many companies now use the Internet, intranets, and enterprise collaboration systems to coordinate their work activities and business processes. Middle managers no longer need to serve as conduits for the transmission of operations feedback or control directives between operational managers and teams, and top management. Thus, many companies have reduced the layers and numbers of middle management, and encouraged the growth of workgroups of task-focused teams. Let's take a look at a real world example given by Bill Gates of Microsoft.

Microsoft: The Impact of IT on District Sales Managers

At Microsoft, our information systems have changed the role of our district sales managers. When MS Sales (our intranet-based revenue measurement and decision support system) first came online, our Minneapolis general manager ran a variety of numbers for her district at a level of detail never possible before. She discovered that excellent sales among other customer segments were obscuring a poor showing among large customers in her district. In fact, the district was dead last among U.S. districts in that category. Finding that out was a shock but also a big motivator for the large-customer teams in the district. By the end of the year Minneapolis was the top-growing district for sales to large customers.

If you're a district manager at Microsoft today, you must be more than a good sales leader helping your team close the big deals, which has been the traditional district sales manager role. Now you can be a business thinker. You have numbers to help you run your business. Before, even if you were concerned about the retail store revenue in your area, you had no view whatsoever of those results. Now you can look at sales figures and evaluate where your business is strong, where your business is weak, and where your business has its greatest potential, product by product, relative to other districts. You can try out new programs and see their impact. You can talk to other managers about what they're doing to get strong results. Being a district sales manager in our organization is a much broader role than what it was five years ago because of the digital tools we've developed and their ease of use [11].

Poor IS Performance

The future arrived a little early for Hershey Foods. In July, to be exact, when a botched big-software project meant the chocolate maker literally couldn't deliver the goods. The failure jacked up product delivery times from five days to 12, increased inventory costs by 29% and kicked the props from under Hershey's third-quarter sales (a $150 million drop, or 12%) and profits (down almost $20 million, or 19%). After a catastrophe like that, could anybody still believe IT can't have a big impact on business? [14]

So, managing information technology is not an easy task. The information systems function has performance problems in many organizations. The promised benefits of information technology have not occurred in many documented cases. Studies by management consulting firms and university researchers have shown that many businesses have not been successful in managing their use of information technology. Figure 10.3 dramatizes the results of the failure of a large corporation to manage the development and implementation of a major ERP project to reengineer its business processes. Thus, it is evident that in many organizations, information technology is not being used effectively and efficiently. For example:

- Information technology is not being used *effectively* by companies that use IT primarily to computerize traditional business processes instead of using it for electronic commerce, Web-enabled decision support, and innovative E-business processes and products.

Figure 10.3

The perils of poor IS performance. Hershey suffered severe business losses after the failure of a major ERP implementation to reengineer its business processes.

The Results of Hershey's Big IT Failure

- A 19% drop in third-quarter profits and a 12% sales decline

- An inability to ship complete orders to some retail customers

- An increase in typical delivery times from 5 days to 12

- A 29% increase in year-to-year inventory costs

- Strained customer relations and major market-share losses

Source: Adapted from Craig Steadman, "Failed ERP Gamble Haunts Hershey," *Computerworld*, November 1, 1999, p. 1. Copyright 1999 by Computerworld, Inc., Framingham, MA 01701. Reprinted from *Computerworld*.

- Information technology is not being used *efficiently* by information systems that provide poor response times and frequent downtimes, or IS professionals and consultants who do not properly manage application development projects.

Let's look closer at Hershey Foods as a real world example.

Hershey Foods: Anatomy of a Disaster

A $112 million ERP project blew up in the face of Hershey Foods Corp. Now it is struggling to fix order-processing problems that are hampering its ability to ship candy and other products to retailers. Analysts and sources in the industry said the Hershey, Pennsylvania, manufacturer appears to have lost a gamble when it installed a wide swath of SAP AG's R/3 enterprise resource planning applications, plus companion packages from two other vendors, simultaneously during one of its busiest shipping seasons. The sources said Hershey squeezed what was originally envisioned as a four-year project into just 30 months before going live with the full ERP system in July of 1999. That's when retailers begin ordering large amounts of candy for back-to-school and Halloween sales.

Hershey wouldn't specify whether the problems stem from its configuration of the system or the software itself, which also includes planning and scheduling applications developed by Manugistics Group, and a pricing promotions package from Siebel Systems. Manugistics said it's working with Hershey and the other vendors on "business process improvements." A spokesman for IBM, the lead consultant on the project, said the new system required "enormous" changes in the way Hershey's workers do their jobs. Siebel officials weren't available for comment.

Hershey turned on some of SAP's finance applications, plus its purchasing, materials management, and warehousing modules, in January. The order-processing and billing portions of R/3 were added along with the Manugistics and Siebel packages in July. Jim Shepherd, an analyst at AMR Research, said most companies install ERP systems in a more staged manner, especially when applications from multiple vendors are involved. "These systems tie together in very intricate ways, and things that work fine in testing can turn out to be a disaster when you go live," Shepherd said. He added that the software Hershey turned on all at once in July was "a huge bite to take, given that processing orders is the lifeblood of their business" [31].

Management Involvement and Governance

What is the solution to problems of poor performance in the information systems function? There are no quick and easy answers. However, the experiences of successful organizations reveal that extensive and meaningful **managerial and end user involvement** is the key ingredient of high-quality information systems performance. Involving business managers in the governance of the IS function and business professionals in the development of IS applications should thus shape the response of management to the challenge of improving the business value of information technology [8, 16].

Involving managers in the management of IT (from the CEO to the managers of business units) requires the development of *governance structures* (such as executive councils and steering committees) that encourage their active participation in planning and controlling the business uses of IT. Thus, many organizations have policies that require managers to be involved in IT decisions that affect their business units. This helps managers avoid IS performance problems in their business units and development projects. Without this high degree of involvement, managers cannot hope to improve the strategic business value of information technology. Also, as we said in Chapter 7, the problems of employee resistance and poor user interface design can only be solved by direct end user participation in systems development projects.

The E-Business Organization

Just as the value chain has been disintermediated, so too has the traditional organization. The Digital Age organization is no longer a single corporate entity, but rather an extended network consisting of a streamlined global core, market-focused business units and shared support services [29].

E-business companies are reengineering (or *E-engineering*) their organizational structures and roles, as well as their business processes, as they strive to become agile, customer-focused, value-driven enterprises. One way to express this phenomenon is

Figure 10.4 Comparing the E-organization model of internetworked E-business enterprises to the pre-E-organization model used by many companies.

	Pre-E-Organization	E-Organization
Organization Structure	● Hierarchical ● Command-and-control	● Centerless, networked ● Flexible structure that is easily modified
Leadership	● Selected "stars" step above ● Leaders set the agenda ● Leaders force change	● Everyone is a leader ● Leaders create environment for success ● Leaders create capacity for change
People and Culture	● Long-term rewards ● Vertical decision making ● Individuals and small teams are rewarded	● "Own your own career" mentality ● Delegated authority ● Collaboration expected and rewarded
Coherence	● Hard-wired into processes ● Internal relevance	● Embedded vision in individuals ● Impact projected externally
Knowledge	● Focused on internal processes ● Individualistic	● Focused on customers ● Institutional
Alliances	● Complement current gaps ● Ally with distant partners	● Create new value and outsource uncompetitive services ● Ally with competitors, customers, and suppliers
Governance	● Internally focused ● Top-down	● Internal and external focus ● Distributed

Source: Adapted from Gary Neilson, Bruce Pasternack, and Albert Visco, "Up the E-Organization! A Seven-Dimensional Model of the Centerless Enterprise," *Strategy & Business*, First Quarter 2000, p. 53.

illustrated in Figure 10.4, which outlines several key dimensions of the new E-business organization, compared to the same dimensions of a pre-E-business organization model used by many companies. The seven dimensions of the *E-organization* model demonstrate that E-business and E-commerce appear to provide a major impetus for companies to make major changes to their organizational structures and roles. Let's look at a real world example that exemplifies and illustrates all seven dimensions of this new E-business organization model [29].

Cisco Systems: The Ultimate E-Organization

Cisco Systems Inc. may well be the best example of what we mean by an e.org. At present, Cisco does more business online than any other company, with electronic sales averaging more than $20 million a day. The clear market leader in the business-to-business networking hardware industry, it is the ultimate networked enterprise.

Organization Structure: Cisco maintains a strong web of strategic partnerships and systems integration with suppliers, contractors, and assemblers. This network of alliances provides a flexible structure that enables the "e-stended" Cisco enterprise to shift toward new market opportunities, and away from old ones. Although it outsources functions, including a large part of its manufacturing, it also leverages its innovative human resources and IT departments as shared services to the benefit of all its business units.

Leadership: John Chambers has proven to be a strong, visionary leader, but Cisco is led by more than just a single person. The company has made more than 40 acquisitions in its short history, and many acquired companies live on as autonomous Cisco business units. But Cisco does not install new leadership for those business units; managers of the acquired companies usually have the independence to run their business units. Even more telling, Cisco's senior management is filled with executives from acquired companies. These entrepreneurial managers are not pushed out of the company; their skills as leaders are valued at all levels of Cisco.

People and Culture: Cisco's culture is straight out of the e.org textbook, and extends all the way to the company's endless search for talent. Cisco has proven to be very effective at recruiting those whom the company calls "passive" job seekers—people who aren't actively looking for a new job. The company is a recruitment innovator in the competitive Silicon Valley marketplace. The company has a Web page, for example, to connect a potential hire with a Cisco employee who works in the same sort of position. The volunteer employee "friend," and not a trained recruiter, will then call the prospect to talk about life at Cisco. This inside view of the company is an important selling tool for recruitment; it also gives employees a voice in the continued growth of the company. And Cisco's human resources ability extends to the culture of the organization and its ability to retain talent. The result? Turnover is low, at 6.7 percent annually, compared to an industry average of 18 percent. And turnover of acquired-company staff at Cisco is even lower—just 2.1 percent, compared to an industry average of more than 20 percent. (Of course, a relentlessly increasing stock price doesn't hurt.)

Coherence: Cisco is almost religious when it comes to customer focus, and the customer focus goes right to the top. CEO John Chambers was reportedly late for his very first board meeting in 1994 because he was on the phone with an unhappy customer. The board excused him. Under Chambers, Cisco senior executives have their bonuses tied to customer satisfaction ratings, and the company has spared no expense developing its online service and support model to provide its customers with the industry's broadest range of hardware products, as well as related software and services. The customer focus permeates the entire organization—even to the engineering department, a group not traditionally thought of as customer oriented.

Knowledge: Cisco has leveraged the Internet to optimize every step in the value chain from sales to order-processing to customer service to manufacturing. The extent to which Cisco has tied its business partners together with shared knowledge is staggering. Web-based systems allow suppliers to tap directly into Cisco's manufacturing and order systems with real-time access to product logistics information and order flow. Cisco also shares demand forecasts, intellectual capital, electronic communication tools, and volume targets. The result? Suppliers' production processes are "pulled" by Cisco's customer demand. The company's knowledge-sharing goes even further, providing online service and support to end customers; 70 percent of technical support requests are now filed electronically, generating an average customer service rating of 4+ on a 5-point scale. Cisco has saved considerable money from this online migration—an estimated $500 million a year from improved supply chain management, online technical support, software distribution via downloads and other Internet-enabled processes.

Alliances: It's not just knowledge that Cisco distributes electronically with its network of partners. Cisco's alliance partners are an integral component of the company's ability to serve customers, and Cisco treats them as part of the company. Indeed, half of customer orders that come in over its website are routed electronically to a supplier who ships directly to the customer.

Governance: Cisco's ability to grow while managing its autonomous business units and bringing together its alliance partners is indicative of its internal and external governance policies. Perhaps this is best illustrated by Cisco's acquisitions ability. The company is well known for its rapid acquisitions process, and for its ability to integrate its acquisitions quickly into the Cisco family. The Cisco integration team has the acquisitions process down to a science.

Cisco has upped the ante and established the table stakes in the industry, not only for its competitors, but also for its suppliers, by utilizing the Internet to maximum advantage. Yet its primary product, networking hardware, is not even a product that lends itself to Internet distribution. These components are not only difficult to subdivide and describe for an E-commerce website, they are highly specialized. Still Cisco has been able to make the sales and buying experience very Web accessible and very lucrative [29].

Figure 10.5 provides an example of the E-organization structure of an E-business company. Notice that there is a global executive core, four market-focused business units, and two shared support services business units. However, all six business units are customer and market focused. Even the shared support services units must provide competitive services to the global core, other business units, and external customers, since uncompetitive services may be outsourced to external vendors [29].

E-Business Technology Management

Figure 10.6 illustrates a popular approach to managing information technology in an internetworked E-business enterprise. This managerial approach has three major components:

- Managing the joint development and implementation of E-business and IT strategies.
- Managing the development of E-business applications and the research and implementation of new information technologies.
- Managing the IT processes, professionals, and subunits within a company's IT organization and IS function.

Figure 10.5

An example of the organizational structure of an E-business enterprise.

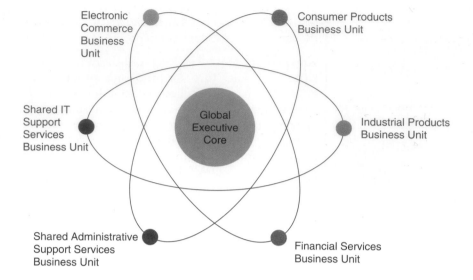

Figure 10.6

The major components of E-business technology management. Note the executives with primary responsibilities in each area.

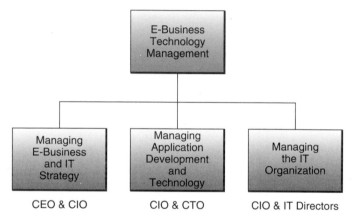

Source: Derived in part from Omar El Sawy, Arvind Malhotra, Sanjay Gosain, and Kerry Young, "IT-Intensive Value Innovation in the Electronic Economy: Insights from Marshall Industries," *MIS Quarterly*, September 1999, pp. 323–27. Reprinted with permission from the *MIS Quarterly*.

Let's look at a real world example.

Avnet Marshall: Managing IT

Figure 10.7 contrasts how Avnet Marshall's information technology management differs from conventional IT management. Notice that they use the model of E-business technology management illustrated in Figure 10.6. For example, in technology management, Avnet Marshall uses a best of breed approach that supports business needs, instead of enforcing a standardized and homogeneous choice of hardware, software, database, and networking technologies. In managing its IT organization, Avnet Marshall hires IS professionals who can integrate IT with business. These IS professionals are organized in work groups around E-business initiatives that focus on building E-commerce services for customers [8].

Managing the IS Function

A radical shift is occurring in corporate computing—think of it as the recentralization of management. It's a step back toward the 1970s, when a data-processing manager could sit at a console and track all the technology assets of the corporation. Then came

Figure 10.7

Comparing conventional and E-Business IT management approaches.

IT Management	Conventional Practices	Avnet Marshall's E-Business Practices
Technology management	• Approach to IT infrastructure may sacrifice match with business needs for vendor homogeneity and technology platform choices	• Best-of-breed approach to IT infrastructure in which effective match with business needs takes precedence over commitment to technology platforms choices and vender homogeneity
Managing the IT organization	• Hire "best by position" who can bring specific IT expertise • Departments organized around IT expertise with business liaisons and explicit delegation of tasks • IT projects have separable cost/value consideration. Funding typically allocated within constraints of yearly budget for IT function	• Hire "best athletes" IS professionals who can flexibly integrate new IT and business competencies • Evolving workgroups organized around emerging IT-intensive business initiatives with little explicit delegation of tasks • IT funding typically based on value proposition around business opportunity related to building services for customers. IT project inseparable part of business initiative

Source: Adapted from Omar El Sawy, Arvind Malhotra, Sanjay Gosain, and Kerry Young, "IT-Intensive Value Innovation in the Electronic Economy: Insights from Marshall Industries," *MIS Quarterly*, September 1999, p. 324. Reprinted with permission from the *MIS Quarterly*.

the 1980s and early 1990s. Departments got their own PCs and software; client/server networks sprang up all across companies.

Three things have happened in the past couple of years: The Internet boom inspired businesses to connect all those networks; companies put on their intranets essential applications without which their businesses could not function; and it became apparent that maintaining PCs on a network is very, very expensive. Such changes create an urgent need for centralization [21].

Organizing IT

In the early years of computing, the development of large mainframe computers and telecommunications networks and terminals caused a **centralization** of computer hardware and software, databases, and information specialists at the corporate level of organizations. Next, the development of minicomputers and microcomputers accelerated a **downsizing** trend, which prompted a move back toward **decentralization** by many business firms. Distributed client/server networks at the corporate, department, workgroup, and team levels came into being. This promoted a shift of databases and information specialists to some departments, and the creation of *information centers* to support end user and workgroup computing.

Lately, the trend is to establish more centralized control over the management of the IS resources of a company, while still serving the strategic needs of its business units, especially their E-business and E-commerce initiatives. This has resulted in the development of hybrid structures with both centralized and decentralized E-business-focused components. See Figure 10.8.

Some companies spin off their information systems function into IS *subsidiaries* that offer IS services to external organizations as well as to their parent company. Recently, large companies have created or spun off their E-commerce and Internet-related business units or IT groups into separate ".com" companies or business units. Figure 10.9 summarizes some of these E-business or E-commerce companies.

Many corporations **outsource,** that is, turn over all or parts of their IS operations to outside contractors known as *systems integrators*. In addition, many companies are outsourcing software procurement and support to *application service providers* (ASPs), who provide and support business application and other software via

Figure 10.8

The organizational structure of the IT function at Avnet Marshall.

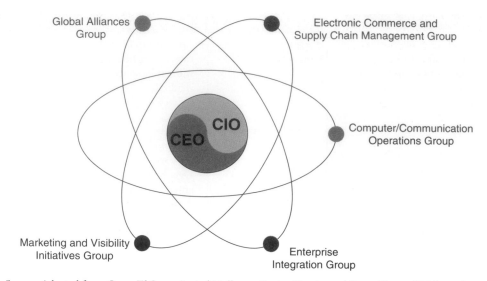

Source: Adapted from Omar El Sawy, Arvind Malhotra, Sanjay Gosain, and Kerry Young, "IT-Intensive Value Innovation in the Electronic Economy: Insights from Marshall Industries," *MIS Quarterly*, September 1999, p. 325. Reprinted with permission from the *MIS Quarterly*.

Internet and intranets to all of a company's employee workstations. See Figure 10.10. Let's look at some real world examples.

Premiere, Monsanto, and Fleetwood: Using ASPs	**Premiere Technologies, Inc.**

Premiere Technologies, Inc.
IT leader: Douglas B. Hadaway, vice president of finance
Goal: Rescue a failing PeopleSoft ERP project without compromising core business efforts.
ASP: TransChannel LLC, Atlanta
Solution: Premiere turned the whole project over to the ASP to manage.
Result: "We're saving about $3 million over five years by giving the work to TransChannel," Hadaway says.

Monsanto Co.
IT leader: Kathryn Kissam, director of corporate branding and identity
Goal: Centralize Monsanto's vast, very distributed library of logos, images, and branding specifications into a single library that employees can access worldwide —and do it quickly.
ASP: Imation Corp., Oakdale, Minn.
Solution: Imation created and maintains the Monsanto Image Gallery, an application that lets any company intranet user search, sort and use Monsanto's logos and images.
Result: "We save money because we don't have to commission new images with every new project or distribute new logo updates to every office in the world," Kissam says.

Fleetwood Retail Corp.
IT leader: Don Palmour, vice president of technology.
Goal: Deploy and manage an entire suite of Lotus Domino applications in Fleetwood's more than 200 mostly rural sales centers.
ASP: Interliant Inc., Purchase, N.Y.
Solution: Fleetwood bought the Domino licenses but turned everything else over to Interliant, which centrally manages the entire suite. Everything—including tape backup—is done in the ASP's central offices.
Result: "This was the only way we could ramp up that quickly. There's no question we get better service than we could provide ourselves," Palmour says. [27].

Figure 10.9

Examples of companies that have spun off Internet, E-commerce, and IT functions into separate dot-com companies or business units.

Company	E-Business Unit	Activities
General Motors Corp. Detroit	e-GM (www.gm.com)	Oversees all of GM's Internet-and E-commerce-related activities, including research and development, manufacturing, Web-based sales and financing
Amway Corp. Ada, Mich.	Quixtar (www.quixtar.com)	E-commerce—enables online ordering by independent Amway sellers
Barnes & Noble Inc. New York	barnesandnoble.com (www.bn.com)	Online book sales
Bank One Corp. Chicago	WingSpan Bank (www.wingspan.com)	Internet banking
Starbucks Corp. Seattle	Starbucks X (www.starbucks.com)	Online, direct-to-consumer sales of coffee and other merchandise
Eastman Chemical Co. Kingsport, Tenn.	CustomerFirst (www.eastman.com)	E-commerce and systems integration services

Source: Adapted from Julia King, "The Lure of Internet Spin-Offs," *Computerworld*, October 18, 1999, p. 20. Copyright 1999 by Computerworld, Inc., Framingham, MA 01701. Reprinted from *Computerworld*.

Managing Application Development

Application development management involves managing activities such as systems analysis and design, prototyping, applications programming, project management, quality assurance, and system maintenance for all major E-business/IT development projects. Managing application development requires managing the activities of teams of systems analysts, software developers, and other IS professionals working on a variety of information systems development projects. In addition, some systems development groups have established *development centers* staffed with IS professionals. Their role is to evaluate new application development tools and to help information systems specialists use them to improve their application development efforts.

Managing IS Operations

IS operations management is concerned with the use of hardware, software, network, and personnel resources in the corporate or business unit **data centers** (computer centers) of an organization. Operational activities that must be managed include computer system operations, network management, production control, and production support.

Figure 10.10

Comparing application service providers to other service providers. Many companies outsource some of their IT functions to such service providers.

Acronym	Definition	Description
ASP	Application service provider	An online channel for packaged software. Applications can vary by ASP but generally focus on high-end applications like databases, enterprise resource planning, and customer relationship management.
BSP	Business service provider	An Internet software developer that makes its applications available only via the Web. Generally, the software is specific in function or proprietary.
ISP	Internet service provider	A business that offers Internet access. Some, like AOL, offer it to millions of customers. Others, like Exodus, offer it to other SPs. Manages network infrastructure.
WSP	Wholesale service provider	A packager of applications for distribution online; not unlike a virtual value-added reseller.

Source: Adapted from Mark Hall, "Service Providers Give Users More IT Options," *Computerworld*, February 7, 2000, p. 40. Copyright 2000 by Computerworld, Inc., Framingham, MA 01701. Reprinted from *Computerworld*.

Most operations management activities are being automated by the use of software packages for computer system performance management. These **system performance monitors** monitor the processing of computer jobs, help develop a planned schedule of computer operations that can optimize computer system performance, and produce detailed statistics that are invaluable for effective planning and control of computing capacity. Such information evaluates computer system utilization, costs, and performance. This evaluation provides information for capacity planning, production planning and control, and hardware/software acquisition planning. It is also used in quality assurance programs, which stress quality of services to business end users. See Figure 10.11.

System performance monitors also supply information needed by **chargeback systems** that allocate costs to users based on the information services rendered. All costs incurred are recorded, reported, allocated, and charged back to specific end user business units, depending on their use of system resources. When companies use this arrangement, the information services department becomes a service center whose costs are charged directly to business units, rather than being lumped with other administrative service costs and treated as an overhead cost.

Many performance monitors also feature **process control** capabilities. Such packages not only monitor but automatically control computer operations at large data centers. Some use built-in expert system modules based on knowledge gleaned from experts in the operations of specific computer systems and operating systems. These performance monitors provide more efficient computer operations than human-operated systems. They also enable "lights out" data centers at some companies, where computer systems are operated unattended, especially after normal business hours.

Human Resource Management of IT

The success or failure of an information services organization rests primarily on the quality of its people. Many computer-using firms consider recruiting, training, and retaining qualified IS personnel as one of their greatest challenges. Managing information services functions involves the management of managerial, technical, and

---

Figure 10.11

A computer system performance monitor in action. The CA-Unicenter TNG package can monitor and manage a variety of computer systems and operating systems.

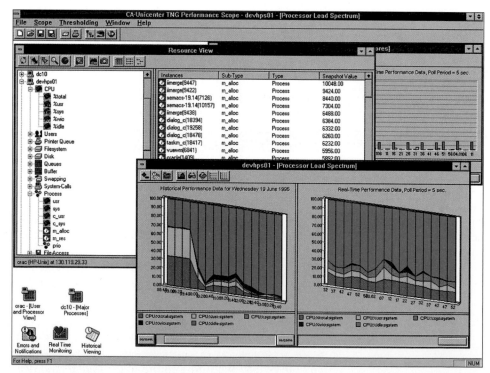

Courtesy of Computer Associates International, Inc.

clerical personnel. One of the most important jobs of information services managers is to recruit qualified personnel and to develop, organize, and direct the capabilities of existing personnel. Employees must be continually trained to keep up with the latest developments in a fast-moving and highly technical field. Employee job performance must be continually evaluated and outstanding performances rewarded with salary increases or promotions. Salary and wage levels must be set, and career paths must be designed so individuals can move to new jobs through promotion and transfer as they gain in seniority and expertise.

The CIO and Other IT Executives

The **chief information officer** (CIO) oversees all use of information technology in many companies, and brings them into alignment with strategic business goals. Thus, all traditional computer services, Internet technology, telecommunications network services, and other IS technology support services are the responsibility of this executive. Also, the CIO does not direct day-to-day information services activities. Instead, CIOs concentrate on business/IT planning and strategy. They also work with the CEO and other top executives to develop strategic uses of information technology in electronic business and commerce that help make the firm more competitive in the marketplace. Many companies have also filled the CIO position with executives from the business functions or units outside the IS field. Such CIOs emphasize that the chief role of information technology is to help a company meet its strategic business objectives.

Top IT Jobs: Requirements and Compensation

* **Chief technology officer**
Base salary range: $100,000 to $250,000-plus; varies by location
Bonus range: Up to 30% of salary
If you're second-in-command to the CIO or chief technology officer and you have years of applications development experience, your next move should be into the chief technology officer's spot. To land this job, you'll need to be a passionate problem-solver with a demonstrated record of reducing cycle time. "You have to talk in terms of 'Damn the torpedoes, let's get this straight into production,'" says Phil Schneider-meyer, an executive recruiter at Korn/Ferry International in Los Angeles.

* **E-commerce architect**
Base salary range: $120,000 to $200,000-plus; varies by location
Bonus range: Up to 20% of salary
If you know Java, Perl, C++, and Corba and have experience in systems architecture, deep-pocketed companies are dying to have you work on their E-commerce sites. "Architects who can design the Internet solution from concept through implementation are probably the hottest thing going," says Heinz Bartesch, a recruiter at Professional Consulting Network Inc. (PCN) in San Francisco.

* **Technical team leader**
Base salary range: $100,000 to $200,000-plus; varies by location
Bonus range: Up to 20% of salary
Senior technical team leaders with good communication, project management and leadership skills, as well as knowledge of Web languages and databases, are now worth their weight in gold.

* **Practice manager**
Base salary range: $80,000 to $200,000-plus; varies by location
Bonus range: Up to 20% of salary
If you've got a background in IT assessment and a pedigree in business development (MBA preferred), you can land a job as a point person for big projects. You'll need skills in IT operations and software assessment, as well as in marketing, staffing, budgeting, and building customer relationships [10].

Technology Management

The management of rapidly changing technology is important to any organization. Changes in information technology, like the rise of the PC, client/server networks, and the Internet and intranets, have come swiftly and dramatically and are expected to continue into the future. Developments in information systems technology have had, and will continue to have, a major impact on the operations, costs, management work environment, and competitive position of many organizations.

Thus, all information technologies must be managed as a technology platform for integrated E-business and E-commerce systems. Such technologies include the Internet, intranets, and a variety of electronic commerce and collaboration technologies, as well as integrated enterprise software for customer relationship management, enterprise resource planning, and supply chain management. In many companies, technology management is the primary responsibility of a *chief technology officer* (CTO) who is in charge of all information technology planning and deployment.

Managing User Services

Teams and workgroups of business professionals commonly use PC workstations, software packages, and the Internet, intranets, and other networks to develop and apply information technology to their work activities. Thus many companies have responded by creating **user services,** or *client services*, functions to support and manage end user and workgroup computing.

End user services provides both opportunities and problems for business unit managers. For example, some firms create an *information center* group staffed with user liaison specialists, or Web-enabled intranet help desks. IS specialists with titles such as user consultant, account executive, or business analyst may also be assigned to end user workgroups. These specialists perform a vital role by troubleshooting problems, gathering and communicating information, coordinating educational efforts, and helping business professionals with application development.

In addition to these measures, most organizations still establish and enforce policies for the acquisition of hardware and software by end users and business units. This ensures their compatibility with company standards for hardware, software, and network connectivity. See Figure 10.12. Also important is the development of applications with proper security and quality controls to promote correct performance and safeguard the integrity of corporate and departmental networks and databases.

Figure 10.12 The benefits derived from company IT standards.

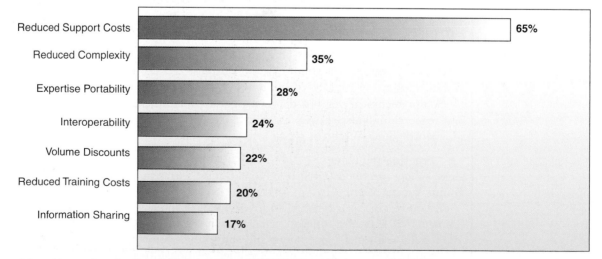

Source: Adapted in part from Jan Rowell, "Getting Control of TCO." Special Advertising Supplement, *ComputerWorld*, November 17, 1997.

Section II **Global E-Business Technology Management**

The International Dimension

Whether they are in Berlin or Bombay, Kuala Lumpur or Kansas, San Francisco or Seoul, companies around the globe are developing new models to operate competitively in a digital economy. These models are structured, yet agile; global, yet local; and they concentrate on maximizing the risk-adjusted return from both knowledge and technology assets [16].

Thus, international dimensions have become a vital part of managing an E-business enterprise in the internetworked global economies and markets of today. Whether you become a manager in a large corporation or the owner of a small business, you will be affected by international business developments, and deal in some way with people, products, or services whose origin is not from your home country.

Analyzing TRW, Toyota, and Cendant

Read the Real World Case on TRW, Toyota, and Cendant on the next page. We can learn a lot about the challenges and opportunities facing companies involved in global E-business and E-commerce. See Figure 10.13.

The companies in this case underscore the fact that global E-business technology management involves a variety of technical, logistical, cultural, and human resource issues. For example, Mostafa Mehrabani of TRW has formed a global system of quick-response teams to provide emergency support if major E-business system problems arise, and global centers of excellence to help with other problems and requirements. Barbra Cooper of Toyota is finding ways to blend some of the managerial characteristics from Japanese, American, and other cultures to better develop a new global IT architecture and alignment between global business and IT strategies. Finally, Lawrence Kinder of Cendant is working to meld the IT leaders from Canada, Europe, and the U.S. into a global E-business management team that helps him develop and improve global E-business strategies for Cendant.

Figure 10.13

Lawrence Kinder is executive vice president and CIO of Cendant Corporation, and brings together IT leaders from Canada, Europe, and the U.S. to participate in global E-business strategy development.

Katherine Lambert.

TRW, Toyota and Cendant: Global E-Business Management Issues

In the world of global IT operations, timing is everything. And so is knowing the ropes of the country you're in. Take, for example, Cleveland-based TRW Inc., a $17 billion technology, manufacturing and services company with operations in 35 countries. When TRW's plant in Poland experiences a problem with its enterprise resource planning system or its global wide area network, the first wave of support comes from the local IT team. If that group is unsuccessful in righting the situation, backup is called in from a second team and even a third in the same time zone in either the U.K. or Germany.

Speed is of the essence, and local support means faster access to end users and resources, such as service providers, telephone companies and equipment. This clustering of quick-response IT support teams by time zones and proximity is just one of the lessons learned by Mostafa Mehrabani, who has served as vice president and CIO at TRW for three years and for the past two years has developed the company's global IT operations.

"For awhile, we were trying to perform day-to-day support of LANs and IT development for our Asian operations from the U.S.," he says. "We came to the conclusion that while you can get someone on the phone, it isn't the same as being there and understanding the culture." So TRW developed centers of excellence, which are groups of subject-matter experts who assist employees throughout the company with their problems and requirements. "Often, we don't have the luxury of certain technical expertise in every part of the world, and we don't have the need for full-time experts in every region. Pooling resources to solve global IT issues is a major advantage," says Mehrabani.

For Barbra Cooper, group vice president and CIO at Toyota Motor sales U.S.A. in Torrance, California, it was knowing how to pluck the strengths from each culture to form a seamless IT operation. "You have to find the best blending of culture for balance and build a new management model," she says. The merging of Japanese and American cultures at Toyota, which has operations in 26 countries, has wedded the best traits of both groups, Cooper says. "The Japanese corporate culture brings more civility and less negativism throughout the informal corporate network," she says. "The Americans bring more risk-taking and the ability to adapt and be flexible."

You can't allow one culture to dominate another, adds Cooper. Instead, the challenge is to combine them. However, Toyota has only recently placed a few non-Japanese IT professionals in locations other than the U.S., and the company has just started to focus on moving away from a Japanese-dominated view and developing a global IT strategy and structure. It's important to guide the development of this global group, says Cooper, so she's helping form a global IT architecture committee that will create a business alignment strategy and link it to Toyota's global objectives.

Lawrence Kinder faced a different kind of global challenge. He is executive vice president and CIO with global responsibility for IT at Cendant Corp., which recently acquired Avis Group holdings. His company, a service and information provider for automotive transportation and vehicle management in Garden City, New York, grew internationally in 1999 by acquiring PHH Vehicle Management Services the world's second-largest vehicle leasing and fleet management company, and Wright Express LLC, the world's largest credit card and information services provider.

"We grew organically in North America and built a solid and stable IT foundation that we have been able to leverage in Europe," Kinder says. The key is to take the time to understand the day-to-day workings of each local IT group, he says, and to put strategic IT on the back burner until all groups can focus on leveraging their cultures and talents.

Kinder says he regularly brings together company leaders with similar roles from the U.S., Canada and Europe to "give each other a shot of adrenaline." He says developing and supporting global businesses is more demanding than supporting time to strategize. "Giving IT staff the opportunity to think more broadly about their applications and solve international business problems has created a true learning organization," he says.

Case Study Questions

1. What are the business benefits of TRW's use of quick-response teams and centers of excellence?

2. Do you agree with how Toyota is trying to blend managerial characteristics from several cultures in developing a new global IT architecture and IT/business alignment? Why or why not?

3. Do you approve of how Cendant is attempting to meld IT groups from several countries into a global organization? Why or why not?

Source: Adapted from Emily Leinfuss, "Blend It, Mix It, Unify It," *Computerworld*, March 26, 2001, p. 38–39

Global E-Business Technology Management

Figure 10.14 illustrates the major dimensions of the job of managing global information technology that we will cover in this section. Notice that all global IT activities must be adjusted to take into account the cultural, political, and geoeconomic challenges that exist in the international business community. Developing appropriate E-business and IT strategies for the global marketplace should be the first step in **global E-business technology management.** Once that is done, end user and IS managers can move on to developing the portfolio of applications needed to support E-business/IT strategies; the hardware, software, and Internet-based technology platforms to support those applications; the data resource management methods to provide necessary databases; and finally the systems development projects that will produce the global information systems required.

Cultural, Political, and Geoeconomic Challenges

"Business as usual" is not good enough in global business operations. The same holds true for global E-business technology management. There are too many cultural, political, and geoeconomic (geographic and economic) realities that must be confronted in order for a business to succeed in global markets. As we have just said, global E-business technology management must focus on developing global E-business IT strategies and managing global E-business application portfolios, Internet technologies, platforms, databases, and systems development projects. But managers must also accomplish that from a perspective and through methods that take into account the cultural, political, and geoeconomic differences that exist when doing business internationally.

For example, a major **political challenge** is that many countries have rules regulating or prohibiting transfer of data across their national boundaries (transborder data flows), especially personal information such as personnel records. Others severely restrict, tax, or prohibit imports of hardware and software. Still others have local content laws that specify the portion of the value of a product that must be added in that country if it is to be sold there. Other countries have reciprocal trade agreements that require a business to spend part of the revenue they earn in a country in that nation's economy [28].

Geoeconomic challenges in global business and IT refer to the effects of geography on the economic realities of international business activities. The sheer physical distances involved are still a major problem, even in this day of Internet telecommunications and jet travel. For example, it may still take too long to fly in specialists when IT problems occur in a remote site. It is still difficult to communicate in real time across the world's 24 time zones. It is still difficult to get good-quality telephone and telecommunications service in many countries. There are still problems finding the job skills required in some countries, or enticing specialists

The major dimensions of global E-business technology management.

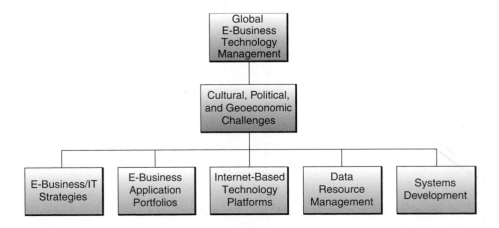

from other countries to live and work there. Finally, there are still problems (and opportunities) in the great differences in the cost of living and labor costs in various countries. All of these geoeconomic challenges must be addressed when developing a company's global business and IT strategies.

Cultural challenges facing global business and IT managers include differences in languages, cultural interests, religions, customs, social attitudes, and political philosophies. Obviously, global IT managers must be trained and sensitized to such cultural differences before they are sent abroad or brought into a corporation's home country. Other cultural challenges include differences in work styles and business relationships. For example, should one take one's time to avoid mistakes, or hurry to get something done early? Should one go it alone or work cooperatively? Should the most experienced person lead, or should leadership be shared? The answers to such questions depend on the culture you are in and highlight the cultural differences that might exist in the global workplace. Let's take a look at a real world example involving the Internet and electronic commerce.

Challenges in the European Union

The non-European student might imagine that the European Union (EU)—a highly sophisticated "single market" embracing 370 million citizens in 15 countries—is ideal ground for a fertile and orderly multinational marketplace in E-commerce. But most Europeans would greet that assumption with a cynical shrug.

The EU's worst-kept secret is that it is a continent of thinly disguised (and sometimes wholly undisguised) national protectionism; of no common language; of widely differing legal and consumer cultures and attitudes toward privacy, and of elaborate trade legislation arrived at by grindingly slow negotiation and imposed with varying degrees of vigor in different member states.

But it would be wrong to imply that there is no hope for a coordinated European E-commerce regime. In fact there is everything to play for, and the game has barely begun [34].

From Paris, Texas, to Paris, France, information technology experts believe that the European E-commerce market is set to blossom over the next five years. But is business ready for Europe's imminent E-revolution? European Internet use is growing at an annual rate of 99%, and companies will have to act quickly to satisfy the demand that will result from improved technologies and increased Internet access. European E-commerce will be further boosted over the next few years by the Euro.

However, Americans who want to lure European buyers to their websites will have to jump many hurdles they don't see in the United States. One hindrance is the tangle of cross-border regulations governing commerce. E-commerce legal specialist Holly Towle, a partner at Washington law firm Preston Gates & Ellis LLP, points out that many companies wrongly assume that EU directives are the equivalent of U.S. federal legislation. Towle cites the EU Distance Contract Directive as a case in point. "Under the EU rule, a company could deliver an absolutely perfect product after making full disclosure of all elements required by the rule, and still the EU customer could return it for any or no reason," she says. "That concept simply does not exist in the U.S. and should cause many sellers to refuse to incur the costs, delays, and risks of shipping products into the EU" [24].

Global E-Business Strategies

Figure 10.15 illustrates that many firms are moving toward **transnational strategies** in which they integrate their global E-business activities through close cooperation and interdependence among their international subsidiaries and their corporate headquarters. Businesses are moving away from (1) multinational strategies where foreign subsidiaries operate autonomously; (2) international strategies in

Figure 10.15

Companies operating internationally are moving toward transnational E-business strategies. Note some of the chief differences between international, global, and transnational business and IT strategies.

Comparing Global E-Business Strategies

International	**Global**	**Transnational**
• Autonomous operations.	• Global sourcing.	• Virtual E-business operations via global alliances.
• Region specific.	• Multiregional.	• World markets and mass customization.
• Vertical integration.	• Horizontal integration.	• Global E-commerce and customer service.
• Specific customers.	• Some transparency of customers and production.	• Transparent manufacturing.
• Captive manufacturing.	• Some cross regionalization.	• Global supply chain and logistics.
• Customer segmentation and dedication by region and plant.		• Dynamic resource management.

Information Technology Characteristics

International	**Global**	**Transnational**
• Stand-alone systems.	• Regional decentralization.	• Logically consolidated, physically distributed, Internet connected.
• Decentralized/no standards.	• Interface dependent.	• Common global data resources.
• Heavy reliance on interfaces.	• Some consolidation of applications and use of common systems.	• Integrated global enterprise systems.
• Multiple systems, high redundancy and duplication of services and operations.	• Reduced duplication of operations.	• Internet, intranet, extranet Web-based applications.
• Lack of common systems and data.	• Some worldwide IT standards.	• Transnational IT policies and standards.

Source: Adapted and reprinted from Michael Mische, "Transnational Architecture: A Reengineering Approach," *Information Systems Management* (New York: Auerbach Publications), Winter 1995, p. 18. © 1995 Research Institute of America. Used with permission; and Nicholas Vitalari and James Wetherbe, "Emerging Best Practices in Global Systems Development," in *Global Information Technology and Systems Management*, Prashant Palvia et al., editors (Marietta, GA: Ivy League Publishing, 1996), p. 336.

which foreign subsidiaries are autonomous but are dependent on headquarters for new processes, products, and ideas; or (3) global strategies, where a company's worldwide operations are closely managed by corporate headquarters [26].

In the transnational approach, a business depends heavily on its information systems and Internet technologies to help it integrate its global business activities. Instead of having independent IS units at its subsidiaries, or even a centralized IS operation directed from its headquarters, a transnational business tries to develop an integrated and cooperative worldwide hardware, software, and Internet based architecture for its IT platform. Figure 10.16 illustrates how transnational business and IT strategies were implemented by global companies [35].

Global E-Business Applications

The applications of information technology developed by global companies depend on their E-business and IT strategies and their expertise and experience in IT. However, their IT applications also depend on a variety of **global business drivers,** that is, business requirements caused by the nature of the industry and its competitive or environmental forces. One example would be companies like airlines or hotel chains that have global customers, that is, customers who travel widely or have global operations. Such companies will need global E-business capabilities for online transaction processing so they can provide fast, convenient service to their customers or face losing them to their competitors. The economies of scale provided by global E-business operations are another business driver that requires the support of global IT applications. Figure 10.17 summarizes some of the business requirements that make global E-business a competitive necessity [15].

Of course, many global IT applications, particularly finance, accounting, and office applications, have been in operation for many years. For example, most

Figure 10.16

Examples of how transnational business and IT strategies were implemented by global companies.

Tactic	Global Alliances	Global Sourcing and Logistics	Global Customer Service
Examples	British Airways / US Air KLM / Northwest Qantas / American	Benetton	American Express
IT Environment	Global network (online reservation system)	Global network, EPOS terminals in 4,000 stores, CAD/CAM in central manufacturing, robots and laser scanner in their automated warehouse	Global network linked from local branches and local merchants to the customer database and medical or legal referrals database
Results	• Coordination of schedules • Code sharing • Coordination of flights • Co-ownership	• Produce 2000 sweaters per hour using CAD/CAM • Quick response (in stores in 10 days) • Reduced inventories (just-in-time)	• Worldwide access to funds • "Global Assist" Hotline • Emergency credit card replacement • 24-hour customer service

Source: Adapted from Nicholas Vitalari and James Wetherbe, "Emerging Best Practices in Global System Development," in *Global Information Technology and Systems Management*, Prashant Palvia et al., editors (Marietta, GA: Ivy League Publishing, 1996), pp. 338–42.

multinational companies have global financial budgeting and cash management systems, and office automation applications such as fax and E-mail systems. However, as global operations expand and global competition heats up, there is increasing pressure for companies to install global E-commerce and E-business applications for their customers and suppliers. Examples include global E-commerce websites and customer service systems for customers and global supply chain management systems for suppliers. In the past, such systems relied almost exclusively on privately constructed or government-owned telecommunications networks. But the explosive business use of the Internet, intranets, and extranets for electronic commerce has made such applications much more feasible for global companies.

Figure 10.17

These are some of the business reasons driving global E-business applications.

Business Drivers for Global E-Business
• **Global customers.** Customers are people who may travel anywhere or companies with global operations. Global IT can help provide fast, convenient service.
• **Global products.** Products are the same throughout the world or are assembled by subsidiaries throughout the world. Global IT can help manage worldwide marketing and quality control.
• **Global operations.** Parts of a production or assembly process are assigned to subsidiaries based on changing economic or other conditions. Only global IT can support such geographic flexibility.
• **Global resources.** The use and cost of common equipment, facilities, and people are shared by subsidiaries of a global company. Global IT can keep track of such shared resources.
• **Global collaboration.** The knowledge and expertise of colleagues in a global company can be quickly accessed, shared, and organized to support individual or group efforts. Only global IT can support such enterprise collaboration.

Gillette and Nypro: Global ERP Issues	For a company like the Gillette Co. in Boston, consistency of product—and therefore consistency of operations—is of paramount importance. Gillette installed ERP applications from SAP AG and PeopleSoft Inc. because they automatically create reports in different languages. "We select vendors who can satisfy global needs," explains CIO Pat Zilvitis. Although development work is done in Boston, deployment and screen labeling is handled locally to overcome language barriers.

Other companies approach globalization strategies differently, allowing for more decentralized control where factories produce products for local customers. Nypro Inc., a plastics molding company based in Clinton, Massachusetts, operates in 12 countries and uses its global presence as a selling point. To meet the needs of global customers, Nypro runs an ERP system from Chicago-based System Software Associates called eBPCS.

Building plants in China and providing them with networked ERP systems is the latest project for Jay Leader, Nypro's director of application development. He points out that it's no more feasible for him to modify code written in Chinese than it is to have Chinese employees operate systems in English. He says he believes that Internet-based applications, with their capacity to personalize what each user sees, represent the best hope for localization of content, because one system can personalize content and data sources for each user. For ERP, localization is more difficult because the systems aren't meant to be flexible. Nypro, however, puts control over ERP data extraction and manipulation in local hands [30].

Global IT Platforms

The management of technology platforms (also called the technology infrastructure) is another major dimension of global IT management. That is, managing the hardware, software, data resources, Internet, intranet, extranet sites, and computing facilities that support global E-business operations. The management of a global IT platform is not only technically complex but also has major political and cultural implications.

For example, hardware choices are difficult in some countries because of high prices, high tariffs, import restrictions, long lead times for government approvals, lack of local service or spare parts, and lack of documentation tailored to local conditions. Software choices can also present unique problems. Software packages developed in Europe may be incompatible with American or Asian versions, even when purchased from the same hardware vendor. Well-known U.S. software packages may be unavailable because there is no local distributor, or because the software publisher refuses to supply markets that disregard software licensing and copyright agreements [15].

Establishing computing facilities internationally is another global challenge. Companies with global business operations usually establish or contract with systems integrators for additional data centers in their subsidiaries in other countries. These data centers meet local and regional computing needs, and even help balance global computing workloads through communications satellite links. However, offshore data centers can pose major problems in headquarter's support, hardware and software acquisition, maintenance, and security. That's why many global companies turn to application service providers or systems integrators like EDS or IBM to manage their overseas operations.

The Internet as a Global IT Platform

What makes the Internet and the World Wide Web so important for international business? This interconnected matrix of computers, information, and networks that reaches tens of millions of users in over one hundred countries is a business environment free of traditional boundaries and limits. Linking to an online global infrastructure offers companies unprecedented potential for expanding markets, reducing costs, and improving profit margins at a price that is typically a small percentage of the corporate communications budget. The Internet provides an interactive channel for direct communication and data exchange with customers, suppliers, distributors, manufacturers, product developers, financial backers, information providers—in fact, with all parties involved in a given business venture [6].

So the Internet and the World Wide Web have now become vital components in international business and commerce. Within a few years, the Internet, with its interconnected network of thousands of networks of computers and databases, has established itself as a technology platform free of many traditional international boundaries and limits. By connecting their businesses to this online global infrastructure, companies can expand their markets, reduce communications and distribution costs, and improve their profit margins without massive cost outlays for new telecommunications facilities. Figure 10.18 outlines key considerations for global E-commerce websites.

The Internet, along with its related intranet and extranet technologies, provides a low-cost interactive channel for communications and data exchange with employees, customers, suppliers, distributors, manufacturers, product developers, financial backers, information providers, and so on. In fact, all parties involved can use the Internet and other related networks to communicate and collaborate to bring a business venture to its successful completion [6]. However, as Figure 10.19 illustrates, much work needs to be done to bring secure Internet access and electronic commerce to more people in more countries. But the trend is clearly on continued expansion of the Internet as it becomes a pervasive IT platform for global business.

Global Data Access Issues

The British and European legislative framework for E-commerce is still in its infancy, and there are large areas yet to be tackled. These include the full gamut of data protection and privacy issues. Under the European Convention on Human Rights, for example, employees are entitled to E-mail privacy; yet employers are regarded in law as the publishers of their employees' E-mails, and—as test cases against companies such as Norwich Union P.L.C. and British Gas have established—can be held legally responsible for their content [34].

Global data access issues have been a subject of political controversy and technology barriers in global business operations for many years, but have become more visible with the growth of the Internet and the pressures of E-commerce. A major

Figure 10.18

Key questions for companies establishing global Internet websites.

Key Questions for Global Websites
● Will you have to develop a new navigational logic to accommodate cultural preferences?
● What content will you translate, and what content will you create from scratch to address regional competitors or products that differ from those in the United States?
● Should your multilingual effort be an adjunct to your main site, or will you make it a separate site, perhaps with a country-specific domain name?
● What kinds of traditional and new media advertising will you have to do in each country to draw traffic to your site?
● Will your site get so many hits that you'll need to set up a server in a local country?
● What are the legal ramifications of having your website targeted at a particular country, such as laws on competitive behavior, treatment of children, or privacy?

Source: Adapted from Alice Laplante, "Global Boundaries.com," Global Innovators Series, *Computerworld*, October 6, 1997, p. 17. Copyright 1997 by Computerworld, Inc., Framingham, MA 01701. Reprinted from *Computerworld*.

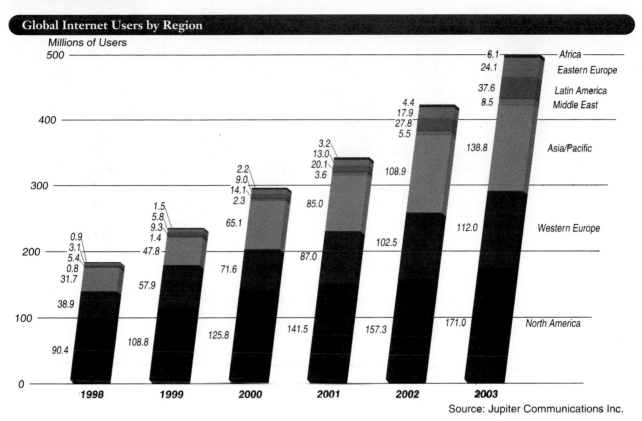

Figure 10.19 Current and projected numbers of Internet users by world region.

Source: Jupiter Communications Inc.

Source: Adapted from Martin VanderWeyer, "The World Debates," *Strategy & Business*, First Quarter 2000, p. 69.

example is the issue of **transborder data flows** (TDF), in which business data flow across international borders over the telecommunications networks of global information systems. Many countries view TDF as violating their national sovereignty because transborder data flows avoid customs duties and regulations for the import or export of goods and services. Others view transborder data flows as violating their laws to protect the local IT industry from competition, or their labor regulations for protecting local jobs. In many cases, the data flow business issues that seem especially politically sensitive are those that affect the movement out of a country of personal data in E-commerce and human resource applications.

Many countries, especially those in the European Union, may view transborder data flows as a violation of their privacy legislation since, in many cases, data about individuals are being moved out of the country without stringent privacy safeguards. For example, Figure 10.20 outlines the key provisions of a data privacy agreement between the U.S and the European Union. The agreement exempts U.S. companies engaging in international E-commerce from EU data privacy sanctions if they join a self-regulatory program that provides EU consumers with basic information about and control over how their personal data are used. Thus, the agreement is said to provide a "safe harbor" for such companies from the requirements of the EU's Data Privacy Directive, which bans the transfer of personal information on EU citizens to countries that do not have adequate data privacy protection [32].

iXL Enterprises: Global E-Commerce Data Issues

E-commerce applications are, by default, accessible to almost anyone in the world who has Internet access. Their extensive reach doesn't, however, automatically translate into global business. Victoria Bracewell-Short, who leads the globalization practice at E-commerce consultancy iXL Enterprises Inc. in Atlanta, says clients often ask her, "Isn't this just a translation or content management issue?" But companies that treat it as such can run into problems. Asking for information as basic as a name, a mailing address, or an E-mail address during initial registration can raise hackles in countries where citizens are nervous about giving out personal data.

"Americans take it for granted that when they log on a site, it recognizes and displays their preferences," says Bracewell-Short. But in Germany, she points out, there are much more stringent regulations governing how E-commerce sites gather customer data. For example, using cookies to collect customer preference data without telling the user is illegal there, so companies that hope to build online relationships with customers must adapt their technology plans accordingly [30].

Internet Access Issues

The Paris-based organization Reporters Without Borders (RSF) reports that there are 45 countries that "restrict their citizens' access to the Internet." At its most fundamental, the struggle between Internet censorship and openness at the national level revolves around three main means: controlling the conduits, filtering the flows, and punishing the purveyors. In countries such as Burma, Libya, North Korea, Syria, and the countries of Central Asia and the Caucasus, Internet access is either banned or subject to tight limitations through government-controlled ISPs, says the RSF [33].

Figure 10.21 outlines the restrictions to public Internet access by the governments of 20 countries deemed most restrictive by the Paris-based Reporters Without Borders (RSF). See their website at www.rsf.fr.

So the Internet has become a global battleground over public access to data and information at business and private sites on the World Wide Web. Of course this becomes a business issue because restrictive access policies severely inhibit the growth of E-commerce with such countries. Most of the rest of the world has decided that restricting Internet access is not a viable policy, and in fact, would hurt their countries' opportunities for economic growth and prosperity. Instead, national and international efforts are being made to rate and filter Internet content deemed inappropriate or criminal, such as websites for child pornography or terrorism. In any event, countries that significantly restrict Internet access are also choosing to restrict their participation in the growth of electronic commerce [33].

To RSF and others, these countries' rulers face a lose-lose struggle against the Information Age. By denying or limiting Internet access, they stymie a major engine of economic growth. But by easing access, they expose their citizenry to ideas potentially

Figure 10.20 Key data privacy provisions of the agreement to protect the privacy of consumers in E-commerce transactions between the U.S. and the European Union.

U.S. – EU Data Privacy Requirements
● Notice of purpose and use of data collected
● Ability to opt out of third-party distribution of data
● Access for consumers to their information
● Adequate security, data integrity and enforcement provisions

Source: Adapted from Patrick Thibodeau, "Europe and U.S. Agree on Data Rules," *Computerworld*, March 20, 2000, p. 6. Copyright 2000 by Computerworld, Inc., Framinghum, MA 01701. Reprinted from *Computerworld*.

Figure 10.21

Countries that restrict or forbid Internet access by their citizens.

Global Government Restrictions on Internet Access

- **High Government Access Fees**
  Kazakhstan, Kyrgyzstan
- **Government Monitored Access**
  China, Iran, Saudi Arabia, Azerbaijan, Uzbekistan
- **Government Filtered Access**
  Belarus, Cuba, Iraq, Tunisia, Sierra Leone, Tajikistan, Turkmenistan, Vietnam
- **No Public Access Allowed**
  Burma, Libya, North Korea, Sudan

Source: Data from Reporters Without Borders in Stewart Taggart, "Censor Census," *Business 2.0*, March 2000, pp. 358–59.

destabilizing to the status quo. Either way, many people will get access to the electronic information they want. "In Syria, for example, people go to Lebanon for the weekend to retrieve their E-mail," says Virginie Locussol, RSF's desk officer for the Middle East and North Africa [33].

Global Systems Development

Just imagine the challenges of developing efficient, effective, and responsive applications for business end users domestically. Then multiply that by the number of countries and cultures that may use a global E-business system. That's the challenge of managing global systems development. Naturally, there are conflicts over local versus global system requirements, and difficulties in agreeing on common system features such as multilingual user interfaces and flexible design standards. And all of this effort must take place in an environment that promotes involvement and "ownership" of a system by local end users. Thus, one IT manager estimates:

It takes 5 to 10 times more time to reach an understanding and agreement on system requirements and deliverables when the users and developers are in different countries. This is partially explained by travel requirements and language and cultural differences, but technical limitations also contribute to the problem [15].

Other systems development issues arise from disturbances caused by systems implementation and maintenance activities. For example: "An interruption during a third shift in New York City will present midday service interruptions in Tokyo." Another major development issue relates to the trade-offs between developing one system that can run on multiple computer and operating system platforms, or letting each local site customize the software for its own platform [15]. See Figure 10.22.

Other important global systems development issues are concerned with global standardization of data definitions. Common data definitions are necessary for sharing data among the parts of an international business. Differences in language, culture, and technology platforms can make global data standardization quite difficult. For example, a sale may be called "an 'order booked' in the United Kingdom, an 'order scheduled' in Germany, and an 'order produced' in France" [28]. However, businesses are moving ahead to standardize data definitions and structures. By moving their subsidiaries into data modeling and database design, they hope to develop a global data architecture that supports their global business objectives.

Systems Development Strategies

Several strategies can be used to solve some of the systems development problems that arise in global IT. First is transforming an application used by the home office into a global application. However, often the system used by a subsidiary that has the best version of an application will be chosen for global use. Another approach is setting up a *multinational development team* with key people from several subsidiaries to ensure that the system design meets the needs of local sites as well as corporate headquarters.

Figure 10.22

The global use of information technology depends on international systems development efforts.

Michael Yamishita/Corbis.

A third approach is called *parallel development*. That's because parts of the system are assigned to different subsidiaries and the home office to develop at the same time, based on the expertise and experience at each site. Another approach is the concept of *centers of excellence*. In this approach, an entire system may be assigned for development to a particular subsidiary based on their expertise in the business or technical dimensions needed for successful development. Obviously, all of these approaches require development team collaboration and managerial oversight to meet the global needs of a business. So, global systems development teams are making heavy use of the Internet, intranets, groupware, and other electronic collaboration technologies [15].

Guy Carpenter & Co: Global Systems Development	Guy Carpenter & Co., a $450 million New York reinsurance company, outsourced development of a Web-based insurance brokerage system to PRT Group Ltd., which operates out of Bridgetown, Barbados. "We have half the systems development team on site in New York, and half the people in Barbados," said John Gropper, CIO at Guy Carpenter. The two groups are connected via a high-speed communications link, and Barbados is a four-hour flight from New York. With this kind of project management and communication in place, "there's very little difference in executing a project on the other side of the world versus executing it on the other side of the street," says outsourcing consultant Chris Kizzier.

PRT Group is just a short stroll from a sun-drenched, white-sand Caribbean beach, housed in a 55,000-square-foot software development center, staffed by about 200 English-speaking IT workers from India, Jamaica, Malaysia, the United Kingdom, and elsewhere around the globe. They work on software development and maintenance projects for U.S. clients, including J.P. Morgan & Co. and Prudential Insurance Company of America, which have both invested in the company, and Travelers Corp. and Pfizer Inc.

Big factors contributing to the growth of global systems development team projects include the ever-increasing speed and reliability of communications technology and better project-management discipline. "With advancements in communications and the Internet, the world has shrunk down to the size of a pea, and the fact that you might be 9,000 miles away is irrelevant once you put the right project management disciplines in place," says Kizzier [18, 19].

Summary

- **Managers and IT.** E-business technologies are changing the distribution, relationships, resources, and responsibilities of managers. That is, IT is helping to eliminate layers of management, enabling more collaborative forms of management, providing managers with significant information technology resources, and confronting managers with major E-business and E-commerce challenges.

- **IS Performance.** Information systems are not being used effectively or efficiently by many organizations. The experiences of successful organizations reveal that the basic ingredient of high-quality information system performance is extensive and meaningful management and user involvement in the governance and development of IT applications. Thus, managers may serve on executive IT groups and create IS management functions within their business units.

- **The E-Business Organization.** The organizational structure and roles of E-business companies are undergoing major changes as they strive to become agile, customer focused, value-driven enterprises. Figure 10.4 summarizes the major characteristics of the E-business organization compared to the structure and roles of a previous organization model.

- **E-Business Technology Management.** Managing IT in an E-business company can be viewed as having three major components: (1) managing the joint development and implementation of E-business and IT strategies, (2) managing the development of E-business applications and the research and implementation of new information technologies, and (3) managing IT processes, professionals, and subunits within a company's IT organization and IS function. Refer to Figures 10.6, and 10.7, which illustrate components and examples of E-business technology management and strategic planning.

- **Managing Global IT.** The international dimensions of managing global E-business technologies include dealing with cultural, political, and geoeconomic challenges posed by various countries; developing appropriate business and IT strategies for the global marketplace; and developing a portfolio of global E-business and E-commerce applications and an Internet-based technology platform to support them. In addition, data access methods have to be developed and systems development projects managed to produce the global E-business applications that are required to compete successfully in the global marketplace.

- **Global E-Business and IT Strategies and Issues.** Many businesses are becoming global companies and moving toward transnational E-business strategies in which they integrate the global business activities of their subsidiaries and headquarters. This requires that they develop a global IT platform, that is, an integrated worldwide hardware, software, and Internet-based network architecture. Global companies are increasingly using the Internet and related technologies as a major component of this IT platform to develop and deliver global IT applications that meet their unique global business requirements. Global IT and end user managers must deal with limitations on the availability of hardware and software, restrictions on transborder data flows, Internet access, and movement of personal data, and difficulties with developing common data definitions and system requirements.

Key Terms and Concepts

These are the key terms and concepts of this chapter. The page number of their first explanation is in parentheses.

1. Application development management (367)
2. Centralization or decentralization of IT (365)
3. Chargeback systems (368)
4. Chief information officer (369)
5. Chief technology officer (369)
6. Cultural, political, and geoeconomic challenges (373)
7. Data center (367)
8. Downsizing (365)
9. E-business organization (358)
10. Global business drivers (375)
11. Global E-business technology management (373)

a. E-business applications (375)
b. E-business/IT strategies (374)
c. Data access issues (378)
d. IT platforms (377)
e. Systems development issues (381)
12. Human resource management of IT (368)
13. Information systems performance (376)
14. Internet access issues (380)
15. Internet as a global IT platform (377)
16. Management impact of E-business technologies (358)

17. Management involvement in IT (364)
18. Managing E-business technologies (363)
19. Managing the IS function (359)
20. Operations management (358)
21. Outsourcing IS operations (365)
22. Spinning off IT business units (366)
23. System performance monitor (368)
24. Technology management (370)
25. Transborder data flows (379)
26. Transnational strategy (374)
27. User services (370)

Review Quiz

Match one of the key terms and concepts listed previously with one of the brief examples or definitions that follow. Try to find the best fit for the answers that seem to fit more than one term or concept. Defend your choices.

_____ 1. Managers now have a lot of information processing power and responsibility for the use of E-business technologies.

_____ 2. Information systems have not been used efficiently or effectively.

_____ 3. An executive IT council is an example.

_____ 4. E-business and E-commerce processes affect organizational roles and structures.

_____ 5. Managing E-business/IT planning and the IS function within a company.

_____ 6. Managing application development, data center operations, and user services are examples.

_____ 7. Many IT organizations have centralized and decentralized units.

_____ 8. Managing the creation and implementation of new E-business applications.

_____ 9. End users need liaison, consulting, and training services.

_____ 10. Planning and controlling data center operations.

_____ 11. Corporate locations for computer system operations.

_____ 12. Rapidly changing technological developments must be anticipated, identified, and implemented.

_____ 13. Recruiting and developing IT professionals.

_____ 14. The executive responsible for strategic E-business/IT planning and management.

_____ 15. The executive in charge of researching and implementing new information technologies.

_____ 16. Software that helps monitor and control computer systems in a data center.

_____ 17. The cost of IS services may be allocated back to end users.

_____ 18. Many business firms are replacing their mainframe systems with networked PCs and servers.

_____ 19. Using outside contractors to provide and manage IS operations.

_____ 20. Companies may create independent IT or E-commerce business units.

_____ 21. Managing IT to support a company's international E-business operations.

_____ 22. Integrating global E-business activities through cooperation among international subsidiaries and corporate headquarters.

_____ 23. Differences in customs, governmental regulations, and the cost of living are examples.

_____ 24. Global customers, products, operations, resources, and collaboration.

_____ 25. Applying IT to global E-commerce systems is an example.

_____ 26. The goal of some organizations is to develop integrated Internet-based networks for global electronic commerce.

_____ 27. Transborder data flows and security of personal databases are top concerns.

_____ 28. Standardizing global use of computer systems, software packages, telecommunications networks, and computing facilities is an example.

_____ 29. The Internet is a natural global networking choice.

_____ 30. Global telecommunications networks like the Internet move data across national boundaries.

_____ 31. Some countries deny or limit Internet access.

_____ 32. Agreement is needed on common user interfaces and website design features in global IT.

Discussion Questions

1. What has been the impact of E-business technologies on the work relationships, activities, and resources of managers?

2. What can business unit managers do about performance problems in the use of information technology and the development and operation of information systems in their business units?

3. Refer to the Real World Case on Raytheon and Deere & Co. in the chapter. What are the benefits and limitations of the balanced scorecard approach to evaluating E-business and E-commerce projects?

4. How are Internet technologies affecting the structure and work roles of modern organizations? For example, will middle management wither away? Will companies consist primarily of self-directed project teams of knowledge workers? Explain your answers.

5. Should the IS function in a business be centralized or decentralized? What recent developments support your answer?

6. Refer to the Real World Case on TRW, Toyota, and Cendant in the chapter. What is the top global E-business management challenge today? Why?

7. How will the Internet, intranets, and extranets affect each of the components of global E-business technology management, as illustrated in Figure 10.15? Give several examples.

8. How might cultural, political, or geoeconomic challenges affect a global company's use of the Internet? Give several examples.

9. Will the increasing use of the Internet by firms with global E-business operations change their move toward a transnational business strategy? Explain.

10. How might the Internet, intranets, and extranets affect the business drivers or requirements responsible for a company's use of global IT, as shown in Figure 10.18? Give several examples to illustrate your answer.

Application Exercises

Complete the following exercises as individual or group projects that apply chapter concepts to real world business situations.

1. CEO Express: Top-Rated Website for Executives

Check out this top-rated site (www.ceoexpress.com) for busy executives. See Figure 10.23. Membership is free and open to students and professors, too. Great news from hundreds of links to top U.S. and international newspapers, business and technology magazines, and news services. Hundreds of links to business and technology research sources and references are provided, as well as to travel services, online shopping, and recreational websites.

a. Evaluate the CEO Express website as a source of useful links to business and technology news, analysis, and research sources for business executives and professionals.

b. Report on one item of business or IT news, analysis, or research that might have value for your present or future career in business.

2. The Worldly Investor: Global Business Issues

Check out worldlyinvestor.com (www.worldlyinvestor. com). See Figure 10.24. This easy-to-use website features concise commentary on global business, fi-

nance, and technology issues and emerging markets, as well as Q&As. For example, a commentator recently noted that Indian stocks were down and likely to take another hit from international index reshuffling. Other stories featured international auto industry analysis and commentary on several global E-commerce deals.

a. Evaluate the worldlyinvestor.com website as a source of useful global business and IT news and analysis for the business professional or investor.

b. Report on one item of global business or IT news or analysis that might have value for your present or future career in business.

Source: Adapted from "Net Finance," Technology Buyers Guide, *Fortune*, Winter 2000, p. 246. © 2000 Time Inc. All rights reserved.

3. Tracking Shopping Related Internet Use Across the United States

The U.S. Census Bureau has surveyed households concerning their use of the Internet in December of 1998 and in August of 2000. The sample records shown below illustrate the structure of a database table based on data from these surveys that has been extracted and is avail-

Figure 10.23

The CEO Express website.

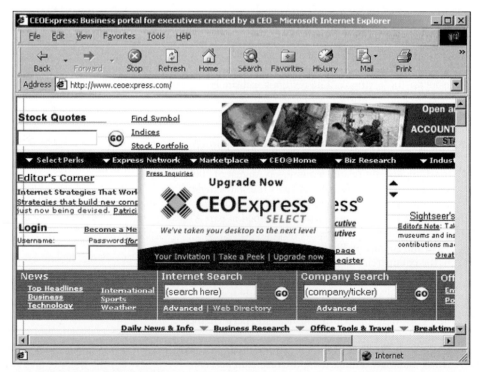

Courtesy of CEO Express, © 2000.

Figure 10.24

The Worldlyinvestor.com website.

Courtesy of The WorldlyInvestor, Inc., © 2000.

able on the website for this textbook. The Use98 column indicates the estimated number of individuals in each state who regularly used the Internet to shop, pay bills, or for some other commercial purpose in December of 1998. The No_Use98 column provides an estimate of the number not using the Internet for those purposes in December of 1998. The Use00 and No_Use00 columns provide the same type of data for August of 2000. These figures are based on survey data and may be subject to significant error, especially for less populous states, but they do allow you to assess the degree of state-to-state variation in E-Commerce related Internet use. Download the database file for this exercise from the website for this textbook. The textbook website is *www.mhhe.com/business/mis/obrien/obrien5e/index.html*. Click on downloads under the student resources section of that page.

a. Create and print a query that shows the proportion of the population in each state who used the Internet for shopping and related activities in August of 2000: Use00/(Use00/No_Use00) and sort the states in descending order by this usage proportion.

b. Calculate the usage proportion described in part A for the country as a whole for both December of 1998 and August of 2000 and determine the change in the commercial usage proportion between the two periods. Produce similar proportions for you home state and at least two adjacent states. (You may use database queries to find these proportions or you may copy the data to a spreadsheet and perform the calculations there)

c. Prepare a set of PowerPoint slides or similar presentation materials summarizing the results in parts A

and B and describing their implications for web-based marketing.

State	Use98	No_Use98	Use00	No_Use00
AL	183641	4107068	447023	4132225
AK	61261	533460	102968	481889
AZ	258602	4500880	528993	4417750
AR	53658	2448054	183010	2323339
CA	2036246	30804742	4475743	29460000

4. Worldwide Internet Users

Figure 10.19 provides a set of estimates and projections of the numbers of Internet users in various regions of the world. Record the data from that table into a spreadsheet for further analysis or copy it from the download file for this exercise in the website for this textbook at *www.mhhe.com/business/mis/obrien/obrien5e/index.html*. To download the file click on downloads under the student resources section of that page and find the file for this exercise.

a. Add a section to the spreadsheet showing the percentage growth from year to year for each region. Then create an appropriate chart of this data.

b. Add a section showing the absolute change in users each year for each region. For instance, the absolute change figures for North America would be 108.8 − 90.4 or 18.4 for 1999, 125.8 − 108.8 or 17 for 2000 and so on. Create Pie charts to show the distribution of projected Internet growth for the years 2002 and 2003.

c. Create a memorandum to your instructor summarizing your results and their implications. Include an assessment of how accurate you feel these projections are likely to be.

Rite Aid Corporation: Failure in E-Business Technology Management

Multimillion-dollar losses, allegations of software-based consumer fraud, computer problems at an advanced distribution center and a new CIO have put the IT group at Rite Aid Corp. through the wringer during the past two years.

Once known as innovative IT practitioners, the 500 members of Rite Aid's IT staff are now more cautious and money-conscious than ever. "They were past leading-edge," says Loren Foster, a project leader and systems engineer at Rite Aid from 1987 to 1996. "We loved it. You got to play with all the new toys," says Foster, now an independent contractor. But these days he says, "they don't have the luxury to experiment."

For example, Camp Hill, Pennsylvania-based Rite Aid in 1994 became one of the first pharmacy chains to use a nationwide satellite network, which allowed its customers to walk into any Rite Aide store in the U.S. and get prescriptions filled or refilled on the spot. But having lost $1.1 billion in fiscal 2000 and $461.5 million the year before, Rite Aid is no longer a high-tech playground. IT missteps, such as computer problems at an advanced distribution center, made matters worse.

With $14.7 billion in sales for fiscal 2000, Rite Aid is still one of the world's biggest pharmacy chains. But now it's more prudent about its IT spending, says Don Davis, who was named CIO last February as part of an executive shakeup to address Rite Aid's financial troubles.

"In the past, the company took more liberty [with IT spending]. We're more cautious about that now," Davis says, acknowledging that Rite Aid has seen an undisclosed number of IT people quit as a result. For example, before Davis took over IT, Rite Aid had staffed up for a major E-commerce drive. It planned to launch an Internet store front in 1999 to sell and refill prescriptions online. But then the company decided that buying 25% of Drugstore.com Inc. would be less expensive and more lucrative.

After a 10-year, $7.6 million deal with Drugstore.com was announced in June 1999, "the people associated with the old plan were disillusioned," Davis says.

Then in early 1999, Rite Aid suffered unexpected software problems at a new state-of-the-art distribution center in Perryman, Maryland. Inventory counts were routinely incorrect, and automated warehouse stocking machines misplaced products.

The glitches delayed the opening of the new warehouse while internal IT and logistics people worked on fixes. Meanwhile, an old center in Pennsylvania had to stay open for an extra five months. All of that meant that profit margins on Rite Aid's products shrank—from 26% in fiscal 1998 to 23% in fiscal 2000.

In response to its huge loses, Rite Aid has said it expects to spend more than $94 million to reassess and restate its financial results for 1998 and 1999. That includes rerunning mainframe-based accounting systems and paying IT people overtime to work with internal and external accountants and auditors during the process.

Still, Rite Aid doesn't plan to replace its combination homegrown/Geac Computer Corp. accounting system, though Davis had expected to do that when he took the job. "The basic capabilities are OK," he says. Instead, Davis says he plans to build a new decision-support application to refine financial reports that flow through the accounting departments. It will be a combination of an as-yet unselected package and internally built software.

One of the risks Rite Aid faces in spending less freely on IT is falling behind key rivals Walgreen Co. and CVS Corp., says Mark Husson, an analyst at Merrill Lynch & Co. A shortage of pharmacists in the U.S. has spurred both of those companies to try to automate pharmacy operations as much as possible and to cut the number of hours pharmacists are needed, Husson says.

If Rite Aid can't keep up, "then there is a big cost pressure from the increased need for pharmacists' hours, and a lesser chance of finding pharmacists who want to work there," he says.

Meanwhile, Rite Aid's troubles may provide an opening for competing pharmacy chains. "You pay close attention to what's happening to your neighbors and whether you can leapfrog ahead when you know the other guy is tied down at the moment," says the CIO of a competing chain who requested anonymity.

Still, Rite Aid must be careful not to cut IT spending—and experimentation—too deeply, says Paul R. Brown, chairman of the accounting department at New York University's Stern School of Business. The use of IT in product and inventory management is central to pharmacies, Brown says. "Rite Aid is still struggling and in an industry that's highly, highly competitive," he says. IT strategy "is one of the last areas where I'd be shooting for no room for error."

Case Study Questions

1. What are several possible causes of Rite Aid's IT troubles?

2. What should Rite Aid's strategies be concerning investments in information technologies?

3. What should Rite Aid's strategies be concerning E-business and E-commerce applications of IT?

Source: Adapted from Kim Nash, "Where Rite Aid Went Wrong," *Computerworld*, February 26, 2001, pp. 38–39.

Royal & Sun, Nypro, and Phillips Petroleum: Managing Global Disaster Recovery

So your organization has gone global, with mission-critical applications spanning time zones and national borders. You're more extended—and more vulnerable, relying on not only the glass house with mainframes down the hall, but also on an Internet service provider in Guatemala or a telecommunications company in Kazakhstan to get your fancy web-enabled applications to customers and suppliers.

Multinational companies have been running global applications for decades, of course. But in the past, they were often hosted on tightly controlled internal computer systems, accessed over expensive but reliable private networks and could tolerate an occasional 24-hour outage. Today's global applications are often a mishmash of custom and off-the-shelf applications running across the less-reliable web, and because they're important, they must be brought back up within hours or even minutes—not days—after a crash.

Global systems often involve not only multiple locations or divisions of a company but also systems controlled by suppliers or customers. "We have more than 300 E-commerce initiatives in our organization," says Julia Graham, group risk manager at London-based Royal & Sun Alliance Insurance Group PLC. "With a web-based business, you could have many joint venture partners and suppliers, and the plan becomes a matrix of different recovery needs based on the potential scenarios that might arise."

Different regions of the world differ widely in the quality of physical recovery sites and the quality of staff at those sites, say IT managers. And because these applications support vital business functions, they must often be brought back up immediately.

"It's not fun," says Jay Leader, director of application development at Nypro Inc. in Clinton, Massachusetts, a plastics molding company that operates 75 servers and has 4,000 users around the world. "It's hard enough…to do domestically, when everyone speaks the same language and is in the same time zone," he says, but it's even harder "to try to coordinate an IT vendor in Singapore and a vendor from China."

Agreeing on how to bring a failed system back up is both more important and more tricky in a multinational environment. People in different parts of the world work according to different schedules and cultural rules—not to mention the fact that they speak different languages and live in different time zones.

"Synchronization of the recovery is real key," says Marshall McGraw, manager of IT business services at Phillips Petroleum Co. in Bartlesville, Oklahoma. Say, for example, an outage that hits an enterprise resource planning system at midnight in Germany stops data flowing to and from a factory in Singapore. The factory will keep using parts and shipping products. But when the system in Germany is brought back up, the staffs in Singapore and Germany must synchronize the two databases not to the point when the German system went down but to the last backup on the German system.

Since synchronization is also required in day-to-day operations, some companies link disaster recovery planning to regular IT operations. That means linking the change management and version control done in the corporate data center to that done at a back-up site, says McGraw.

"Let's say we do an upgrade internally to SAP[R/3] that affects the data that needs to be recovered, or [we change] the configuration of the hardware on which R/3 runs," says McGraw. Unless the backup site knows about every such change, he says, "you spend a week trying to find all the changes you made since you last declared a disaster." Once the procedures are in place to keep the backup site in the loop, the ongoing effort to communicate those changes is minimal, he says.

Many multinational companies issue centrally mandated guidelines for business recovery, leaving local units substantial flexibility in how they reach the goal. Some keep the strictest rein on applications that gather and share information affecting the entire business, giving local units more autonomy on site-specific systems. Phillips Petroleum, for example, has centralized the operation and backup of its core SAP R/3 and Oracle applications, says McGraw. Every 24 hours, IT staff at headquarters ship backup tapes to a disaster recovery center. The central IT group also arranges for backup network links should the primary web connections go down. Remote sites are free to make their own arrangements for hot sites, data backup and backup network links, assuming they follow common recovery procedures.

Something as expensive and unglamorous as disaster planning won't happen unless senior executives demand and corporate auditors check to make sure it's done. Management backing makes disaster recovery an easier sell at Phillips, says McGraw. "We in IT aren't going out there trying to beat on people or begging people to have these things in place," he says. "Our board expects business recovery plans to be in place."

Case Study Questions

1. What challenges in global IT management are revealed in this case?

2. What global IT management solutions are being implemented by the companies in this case?

3. Julia Graham of Royal-Sun says that global E-commerce applications present new challenges in IT disaster recovery. How would you meet such challenges? Give several examples.

Source: Adapted from Robert Scheier, "Averting Disaster," *Computerworld*, January 15, 2001, pp. 46–47.

Shutterfly, FedEx, and AltaVista: Global Outsourcing of Customer Support

Faced with a shortage of talent and real estate in Silicon Valley, Mike Lambreth, customer service manager at Shutterfly Inc., recently outsourced some customer support functions. But representatives who answer questions via e-mail about digital photography from Shutterfly customers aren't just a state away. They sit in a 65,000-square foot facility in Bangalore, India, halfway around the world from the firm's headquarters in Redwood City, California.

The thought of overseas customer support may have seemed far-fetched just a short time ago because of logistical problems such as high telecommunications costs and language and cultural barriers. But Shutterfly is among a growing list of firms that are not only turning to third parties to manage customer support but are also relying on workers from foreign shores.

"Finding qualified people for core business operations, is difficult enough in this area without having to run a huge e-mail operation," said Lambreth. He added that Shutterfly receives as many as 600 customer e-mails per day. Los Gatos, California-based 24/7 Customer.com manages Shutterfly's service center in Bangalore.

Yet Shutterfly is far from unique. General Electric Co., American Express Co., British Airways PLC, FedEx Corp. and Citibank, a unit of Citigroup Inc. all have overseas customer support operations.

Two of the driving factors behind the growing interest in offshore call centers are declining telecommunications costs and maturing Internet technologies. Bandwidth costs, for instance, are dropping at a rate of about 60% per year, said Jay Patel, an analyst at the Yankee Group. In addition, he said, many clients are even beginning to outsource their call center operations and their web-based support overseas.

FedEx has operated overseas call centers for more than a decade, and now the company is thinking about outsourcing some of those operations, according to Sheila Harrell, vice president of strategic analysis and planning at the Memphis-based package transport firm. Improvements in telecommunications and customer relationship management software have made outsourcing a viable business alternative, she said.

And although FedEx's 40 overseas call centers mostly handle queries from the U.S., Harrell said the company is planning to network its call centers so support staffers have the customer information they need to handle worldwide calls. "Our goal is to operate 24/7 around the world and offer customers traveling abroad consistency in how their data is handled," she said.

But setting up offshore call centers isn't without its challenges. Even if outsourcers select countries with well-educated, English-speaking populations, many find that they need to provide training to familiarize the foreign staff with American culture. Another obstacle is the high price of calling overseas. To help combat the problem 24/7 Customer.com uses voice over IP phone systems, which send voice over data networks, instead of relying on costly traditional phone lines. Voice over IP can yield a potential savings of as much as 35% vs. traditional Centrex service or private branch exchange systems

A number of Fortune 500 companies, mostly in the financial services and telecommunications industries, have already outsourced some of their call center operations but are reluctant to disclose that information. "A lot of companies don't want to let you know that some other business has their customer data," said Brian Bingham, a senior analyst at IDC. The problem, Bingham explained, is that some clients believe that turning over business to a company that's "outside your domain" will cause firms to lose touch with their customers.

But Elizabeth Herrell, research director at Giga Information Group, estimates that about one in five call centers are outsourced, either in the U.S. or overseas, and she expects that figure to double by 2005. Part of the reason is that call centers are attractive business opportunities in English-speaking third-world countries. For example, Monrovia, California-based Etelecare International, another call center outsourcer, boasts on its web site that it operates a 300-seat facility in Manila in an "economic development zone near major universities."

Jeff Ferro, customer care manager at AltaVista in Palo Alto, California, said that when he decided to outsource some E-mail support to 24/7 Customer last summer, he thought it would "involve a lot of micromanaging." But, he said, he was pleasantly surprised. It required only one trip by a staff member to the overseas facility to make sure everything was in place. The decision to use 24/7 Customer.com paid off, said Ferro, who added that by switching to an overseas outsourcer, Alta Vista wound up slashing customer support costs by 25%.

Case Study Questions

1. What are the business benefits of establishing or outsourcing customer support centers overseas?

2. What business challenges and limitations are involved?

3. How would you manage overseas customer support so your company would not "lose touch with their customers"?

Source: Adapted from Julekha Dash, "Customer Support Moves Overseas," *Computerworld*, March 19, 2001, p. 18.

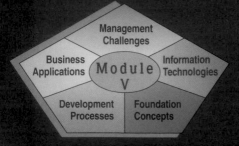

Management
Challenges

Business
Applications

Module
V

Information
Technologies

Development
Processes

Foundation
Concepts

Module V

Review of Information

Technologies

What challenges do information system technologies pose for business professionals? What basic knowledge should you possess about information technology? The four chapters of this module give you an overview of some of the major technologies used in E-business systems and their implications for business managers and professionals.

At the option of your instructor, you may be assigned one or more of the following chapters to review before covering other chapters in the text:

- **Chapter 11: Computer Hardware,** reviews trends and developments in microcomputer, midrange, and mainframe computer systems; basic computer system concepts; and the major types of technologies used in peripheral devices for computer input, output, and storage.

- **Chapter 12: Computer Software,** reviews the basic features and trends in the major types of application software and system software used to support enterprise and end user computing.

- **Chapter 13: Data Resource Management,** emphasizes management of the data resources of computer-using organizations. This chapter reviews key database management concepts and applications in business information systems.

- **Chapter 14: Telecommunications and Networks,** presents an overview of telecommunications networks, applications, and trends, and reviews technical telecommunications alternatives.

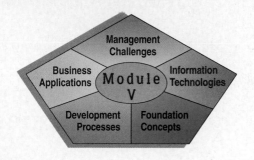

Management Challenges

Business Applications

Module V

Information Technologies

Development Processes

Foundation Concepts

Computer Hardware

Chapter Outline

Section I

Computer Systems: End User and Enterprise Computing

Real World Case: BTG, NEC Electronics, and Biogen: The Business Case for Server Compute Farms

Trends in Computer Systems

Microcomputer Systems

Midrange Computer Systems

Mainframe Computer Systems

Technical Note: The Computer System Concept

Section II

Computer Peripherals: Input, Output, and Storage Technologies

Real World Case: Longs Drugs and Textron: Desktop Versus Network Computing

Peripherals

Input Technology Trends

Pointing Devices

Pen-Based Computing

Speech Recognition Systems

Optical Scanning

Other Input Technologies

Output Technologies and Trends

Video Output

Printed Output

Storage Trends and Trade-Offs

Semiconductor Memory

Magnetic Disk Storage

Magnetic Tape Storage

Optical Disk Storage

Learning Objectives

After reading and studying this chapter, you should be able to:

1. Identify the major types, trends, and uses of microcomputer, midrange, and mainframe computer systems.

2. Outline the major technologies and uses of computer peripherals for input, output, and storage.

3. Identify and give examples of the components and functions of a computer system.

4. Identify the computer systems and peripherals you would acquire or recommend for a business of your choice, and explain the reasons for your selections.

Section I

Computer Systems: End User and Enterprise Computing

All computers are systems of input, processing, output, storage, and control components. In this section, we will discuss the trends, applications, and some basic concepts of the many types of computer systems in use today. In Section II, we will cover the changing technologies for input, output, and storage that are provided by the peripheral devices that are part of modern computer systems.

Analyzing BTG, NEC Electronics, and Biogen

Read the Real World Case BTG, NEC Electronics, and Biogen on the next page. We can learn a lot about the use of networked computer systems in business from this case. See Figure 11.1.

NEC Electronics and Biogen require a lot of computing power for compute-intensive applications like computer chip design and human genome research. They could have chosen to use a supercomputer, powerful mainframe computer systems, or large server farms filled with high-powered servers (typically used for high-volume transaction processing) to provide the peak computing power they needed. Instead, they turned to compute farms of servers networked for high-performance computing. BTG's load-sharing technology combines the memory capacity and processing power of a large group of servers into a single, large, virtual-computing resource optimized to handle compute-intensive jobs. Compute farms can thus approach the computing power of mainframes and supercomputers without the major costs and system changes that would require. Thus, BTG makes a strong case for using compute farms for a variety of other applications in business and industry, such as financial-risk modeling and oil and gas exploration.

Figure 11.1

Kanti Purohit, COO (left), and CEO Ron Ranauro of Blackstone Technology Group have helped expand the use of compute farms in business.

Webb Chapell.

BTG, NEC Electronics, and Biogen: The Business Case for Server Compute Farms

Christa Schidzik's job as manager of systems administration at the NEC Electronics chip design facility in Dusseldorf, Germany, is often more a resource management challenge than a technology challenge. Engineers who design CPUs and application-specific integrated circuits must develop their complex designs and simulate the chips' program code—compute-intensive tasks that create fluctuating demands for mainframe-class power.

"Before, we had big servers for every department, and normally, it was never enough," Schidzik recalls. Then she heard about compute farms: servers pooled to create a single computing resource optimized for CPU and memory-intensive applications. After trying to configure a farm on its own, NEC called Blackstone Technology Group (BTG) in Worcester, Massachusetts. Using BTG's ComputeFarm Advantage consulting service and software, Schidzik says, NEC had 50 users accessing a farm within a week. Server utilization has since doubled, but the need for new hardware has been mitigated, and spikes in demand are more easily accommodated. "I'm quite sure we couldn't have survived without the farm," Schidzik concludes.

BTG started 1996 as a distributor of electronic design automation (EDA) tools before relaunching with its compute-farm services in 1999. "We started to see a bigger and bigger opportunity" in offering compute farms to customers, says Kanti Purohit, BTG's chief operating officer. BTG's offerings range from construction of compute farms from the ground up to reconfiguration and management. It also offers software that lets companies function as application service providers to sell compute power over intranets or the Internet.

The company has signed on biotech heavyweights such as Biogen Inc. and Celera Genomics Group. Biogen threw the switch on its farm, built on 200 Intel-based Linux servers and a Sun Microsystems portal node in December 2000. It will use the new capacity mostly for data analysis to look for pharmaceutical "targets" in the human genome. Biogen selected ComputeFarm Advantage over more generic offerings from Compaq Computer and Silicon Graphics, according to Rainer Fuchs, director of research informatics.

Compute farms approach the computing power of mainframes by aggregating servers into one large, virtual resource that's accessible by workstations and optimized to run large jobs that may take minutes or hours. They differ from server farms, which process large numbers of short bursts of transactions. BTG claims that its expertise is in knowing how to configure a company's networked PCs and outfit them with special management, scheduling and performance—monitoring software. Its staff has expertise in compute-intensive scientific specialties like bioinformatics.

BTG says compute farms cost a fraction of what centralized big iron systems cost because they harness the computing resources of cheaper hardware. Decentralization across networked PCs produces additional benefits such as improved scalability (since capacity can grow in smaller increments than with mainframes) and reliability (because power failures and other hardware glitches won't bring down the whole system). Compute farms also let users retain the convenience and power of their desktop workstations rather than forcing them to access a mainframe.

CEO Ron Ranauro says BTG wants to expand into other compute-intensive markets, starting with financial risk modeling, digital content creation, oil and gas exploration and mechanical design automation. BTG competes with mainframe and supercomputer vendors, as well as other compute-farm vendors such as Compaq and Sun, with whom it also has partnerships. These and other firms, such as Microsoft, also offer related clustering technology for aggregating computing resources. One—Linux Networx in Sandy, Utah—assembles Linux clusters for some of the same industries as BTG, including EDA, bioinformatics and oil and gas.

Purohit says the early going was tough because few people understood the compute-farm concept. Making money on load sharing—essentially a commodity—was another problem, as was "coming up with a business model that is going to be sustainable in an environment where the major platform vendors are going to be a player," Ranauro says. BTG's expertise and technology have won the respect of customers and partners. "They are a powerful emerging player in a space that I don't think has gotten a lot of attention and likely will going forward," says Jilani Zeribi, an analyst at Current Analysis in Sterling, Virginia.

"Blackstone's competitors, in my opinion, are people using dedicated high-powered computers to solve compute-intensive problems. Blackstone's argument—and I think it's really compelling—is that's a lot of money to throw at a problem that you're not dealing with all the time. They've made a compelling business case. Throwing compute power at something is only going to get more and more difficult to justify and harder for companies to do."

Case Study Questions

1. What is the purpose of compute farms compared to server farms?

2. How do the companies in this case use compute farms? What other business applications are possible?

3. What are the business benefits and challenges of compute farms compared to other systems?

Source: Adapted from David Essex, "Compute Farms Bring Power to the PC," *Computerworld*, January 22, 2001, p. 70.

Trends in Computer Systems

Today's computer systems come in a variety of sizes, shapes, and computing capabilities. Rapid hardware and software developments and changing end-user needs continue to drive the emergence of new models of computers, from the smallest hand-held *personal digital assistant* for end users, to the largest multiple-CPU mainframe for the enterprise.

Categories such as *mainframe, midrange computers,* and *microcomputers* are still used to help us express the relative processing power and number of end users that can be supported by different types of computers. But as Figure 11.2 illustrates, these are not precise classifications, and they do overlap each other. Thus, other names are commonly given to highlight the major uses of particular types of computers. Examples include personal computers, network servers, network computers, and technical workstations.

In addition, experts continue to predict the merging or disappearance of several computer categories. They feel, for example, that many midrange and mainframe systems have been made obsolete by the power and versatility of *client/server* networks of end user microcomputers and servers. Most recently, some industry experts have predicted that the emergence of network computers and *information appliances* for applications on the Internet and corporate intranets will replace many personal computers, especially in large organizations and in the home computer market. Only time will tell whether such predictions will equal the expectations of industry forecasters.

Computer Generations

It is important to realize that major changes and trends in computer systems have occurred during the major stages—or **generations**—of computing, and will continue into the future. The first generation of computers developed in the early 1950s, the second generation blossomed during the late 1960s, the third generation took

Figure 11.2

Examples of computer system categories.

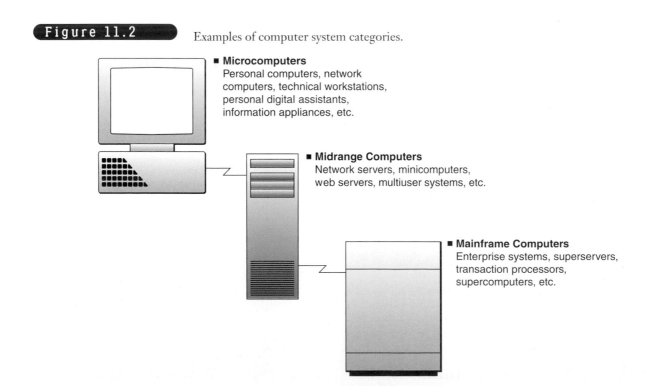

■ **Microcomputers**
Personal computers, network computers, technical workstations, personal digital assistants, information appliances, etc.

■ **Midrange Computers**
Network servers, minicomputers, web servers, multiuser systems, etc.

■ **Mainframe Computers**
Enterprise systems, superservers, transaction processors, supercomputers, etc.

computing into the 1970s, and the fourth generation has been the computer technology of the 1980s and 1990s. A fifth generation of computing systems and devices that accelerates the trends of the previous generations is expected to evolve in the early 21st century. Figure 11.3 highlights trends in the characteristics and capabilities of computers. Notice that computers continue to become smaller, faster, more reliable, less costly to purchase and maintain, and more interconnected within computer networks.

Whether we are moving into a *fifth generation* of computing is a subject of debate since the concept of generations may no longer fit the continual, rapid changes occurring in computer hardware, software, data, and networking technologies. But in any case, we can be sure that progress in computing will continue to accelerate, and that the development of Internet-based technologies and applications will be one of the major forces driving computing in the 21st century.

Microcomputer Systems

The entire center of gravity in computing has shifted. For millions of consumers and business users, the main function of desktop PCs is as a window to the Internet. Computers are now communications devices, and consumers want them to be as cheap as possible [5].

Microcomputers are the most important category of computer systems for businesspeople and consumers. Though usually called a *personal computer,* or PC, a

Figure 11.3   Major trends in computer system capabilities.

	First Generation	Second Generation	Third Generation	Fourth Generation	Fifth Generation?
SIZE (Typical computers)	Room Size Mainframe	Closet Size Mainframe	Desk-Size Minicomputer	Desktop and Laptop Microcomputers	Networked Computers of all sizes
NETWORKING	None	Mainframe-Based Networks of Video Terminals	Mainframe and Minicomputer– Based Networks	Local Area and Client/Server Networks	The Internet, Intranets, and Extranets
CIRCUITRY	Vacuum Tubes	Transistors	Integrated Semi-conductor Circuits	Large-Scale Inte-grated (LSI) Semi-conductor Circuits	Very-Large-Scale Integrated (VLSI) Semiconductor Circuits
DENSITY (Circuits per component)	One	Hundreds	Thousands	Hundreds of Thousands	Millions
SPEED (Instructions/second)	Hundreds	Thousands	Millions	Tens of Millions	Billions
RELIABILITY (Failure of circuits)	Hours	Days	Weeks	Months	Years
MEMORY (Capacity in characters)	Thousands	Tens of Thousands	Hundreds of Thousands	Millions	Billions
COST (Per million instructions)	$10	$1.00	$.10	$.001	$.0001

microcomputer is much more than a small computer for use by an individual. The computing power of microcomputers now exceeds that of the mainframes of previous computer generations at a fraction of their cost. Thus, they have become powerful networked *professional workstations* for business professionals.

Microcomputers come in a variety of sizes and shapes for a variety of purposes, as Figure 11.4 illustrates. For example, PCs are available as hand-held, notebook, laptop, portable, desktop, and floor-standing models. Or, based on their use, they include home, personal, professional, workstation, and multiuser systems. Most microcomputers are *desktops* designed to fit on an office desk, or *laptops* for those who want a small, portable PC for their work activities. Figure 11.5 offers advice on some of the key features you should consider in acquiring a high-end workstation, multimedia PC, or beginner's system. This should give you some idea of the range of features available in today's microcomputers.

Some microcomputers are powerful **workstation computers** (technical workstations) that support applications with heavy mathematical computing and graphics

Figure 11.4   Examples of microcomputer systems.

a. A notebook microcomputer.
Stone.

b. The microcomputer as a professional workstation.
Mug Shots-The Stock Market.

c. The microcomputer as a technical workstation.
Andy Sacks/Stone.

Figure 11.5 Recommended features for the three types of PC users.

Financial Pro	Multimedia Heavy	Newcomer
To track the market's every tremor, you'll need more than just a fast machine:	Media pros and dedicated amateurs will want a Mac G4 or a 750 MHz Intel chip, and:	Save money with a Celeron processor in the 500 MHz range. Also look for:
• 1 Gigahertz processor • 128MB or 256MB RAM • Cable-modem or DSL Internet connection • 18-inch flat-panel display • CD-RW drive for backup	• 20 GB hard drive or more • 18-inch or larger flat-screen CRT or flat-panel LCD • High-end color printer • DVD-RAM or CD-RW drive • Deluxe speaker system	• 64MB RAM • 10 GB hard drive • Internal 56K modem • 24X CD-ROM drive • Basic inkjet printer

Source: Adapted from "Rev Up for the Web," Technology Buyers Guide, *Fortune*, Summer 2000, p. 106.

display demands such as computer-aided design (CAD) in engineering, or investment and portfolio analysis in the securities industry. Other microcomputers are used as **network servers.** They are usually more powerful microcomputers that coordinate telecommunications and resource sharing in small local area networks (LANs), and Internet and intranet websites.

Network Computers

Network computers (NCs) are emerging as a serious business computing platform. NCs are known as *thin clients*, as compared to traditional *fat client* full-featured PCs. Somewhere in between are stripped-down PCs known as **NetPCs** or *legacy-free PCs*, designed for the Internet and a limited range of applications within a company. Examples are Compaq's iPaq, HP's e-PC, and eMachine's eOne. See Figure 11.6.

Figure 11.6

Comparing the network computer to the NetPC and the network terminal.

Network computer
• Operating system, application software, and data storage are provided by Internet, intranet, or extranet servers
• Uses a web browser and can process Java-enabled software applications called *applets*
• Managed remotely and centrally by network servers
• Generally has no hard disk drive

NetPC (Legacy-free PC)
• Works like a PC, with its own software
• Has a hard drive, but may have no floppy drive or CD-ROM
• Box may have no expansion slots or serial or parallel ports
• Operating system and applications are managed centrally by network servers

Network terminal
• An inexpensive terminal-like device without its own disk storage
• Depends on the servers in a network for most of its processing power
• Multiuser version of Windows 2000, Linux, or Unix as the server operating system
• Microsoft Office or Sun StarOffice–like multiuser software on the Internet or intranet Web server

Network computers are a microcomputer category designed primarily for use with the Internet and corporate intranets by clerical workers, operational employees, and knowledge workers with specialized or limited computing applications. NCs are low-cost, sealed, networked microcomputers with no or minimal disk storage. Users of NCs depend primarily on Internet and intranet servers for their operating system and Web browser, Java-enabled application software, and data access and storage. Examples include the Sun Ray 1, IBM Network Station, and the NCD Explora network computers. See Figure 11.7.

One of the main attractions of network computers is their lower cost of purchase, upgrades, maintenance, and support compared to full-featured PCs. Other benefits to business include ease of software distribution and licensing, computing platform standardization, reduced end user support requirements, and improved manageability through centralized management and enterprisewide control of computer network resources [4].

Information Appliances

PCs aren't the only option: A host of smart gadgets and information appliances—from cellular phones and pagers to handheld PCs and Web-based game machines—promise Internet access and the ability to perform basic computational chores [5].

Hand-held microcomputer devices known as **personal digital assistants** (PDAs) are one of the most popular devices in the **information appliance** category. PDAs use touch screens, pen-based handwriting recognition, or keypads so mobile workers can send and receive E-mail, access the Web, and exchange information such as appointments, to-do lists, and sales contacts with their desktop PCs or Web servers.

Information appliances may also take the form of *set-top boxes* and video-game consoles that connect to your home TV set. These devices enable you to surf the World Wide Web or send and receive E-mail and watch TV programs or play video games at the same time. An example is the Sony or Phillips WebTV Plus Receiver, which uses Microsoft's WebTV network service. Other information appliances

Figure 11.7   Examples of a network computer, the Sun Ray 1 enterprise appliance (left), and an information appliance, the Netpliance i-opener.

Sun Microsystems.

Netpliance.

include wireless PDAs and cellular and PCS phones and wired telephone-based home appliances that can send and receive E-mail and access the Web.

Computer Terminals

Computer terminals are undergoing a major conversion to networked computer devices. *Dumb terminals*, which are keyboard/video monitor devices with limited processing capabilities, are being replaced by *intelligent terminals*, which are modified networked PCs, network computers, or other thin clients. Also included are **network terminals,** which may be *Windows terminals*, that are dependent on network servers for Windows software, processing power, and storage, or *Internet terminals*, which depend on Internet or intranet website servers for their operating systems and application software.

Intelligent terminals take many forms and can perform data entry and some information processing tasks independently. This includes the widespread use of **transaction terminals** in banks, retail stores, factories, and other work sites. Examples are automated teller machines (ATMs), factory production recorders, and retail point-of-sale (POS) terminals. These intelligent terminals use keypads, touch screens, and other input methods to capture data and interact with end users during a transaction, while relying on servers or other computers in the network for further transaction processing.

Midrange Computer Systems

Midrange computers, including high-end network servers and minicomputers are multiuser systems that can manage networks of PCs and terminals. Though not as powerful as mainframe computers, they are less costly to buy, operate, and maintain than mainframe systems, and thus meet the computing needs of many organizations. See Figure 11.8.

> *Burgeoning data warehouses and related applications such as data mining and online analytical processing are forcing IT shops into higher and higher levels of server configurations. Similarly, Internet-based applications, such as Web servers and electronic commerce, are forcing IT managers to push the envelope of processing speed and storage capacity and other [business] applications, fueling the growth of high-end servers* [17].

Figure 11.8

Hundreds of rack-mounted servers help power a Sun Microsystems iForce Center Internet hosting facility.

Sun Microsystems.

Midrange computers have become popular as powerful **network servers** to help manage large Internet websites, corporate intranets and extranets, and client/server networks. Electronic commerce and other business uses of the Internet are popular high-end server applications, as are integrated enterprisewide manufacturing, distribution, and financial applications. Other applications, like data warehouse management, data mining, and online analytical processing (which we discuss in Chapters 6 and 13), are contributing to the growth of high-end servers and other midrange systems [17].

Midrange computers first became popular as **minicomputers** for scientific research, instrumentation systems, engineering analysis, and industrial process monitoring and control. Minicomputers could easily handle such uses because these applications are narrow in scope and do not demand the processing versatility of mainframe systems. Thus, midrange computers serve as industrial process-control and manufacturing plant computers, and they still play a major role in computer-aided manufacturing (CAM). They can also take the form of powerful technical workstations for computer-aided design (CAD) and other computation and graphics-intensive applications. Midrange computers are also used as *front-end computers* to assist mainframe computers in telecommunications processing and network management.

Mainframe Computer Systems

Several years after dire pronouncements that the mainframe was dead, quite the opposite is true: Mainframe usage is actually on the rise. And it's not just a short-term blip. One factor that's been driving mainframe sales is cost reductions [of 35 percent or more]. Price reductions aren't the only factor fueling mainframe acquisitions. IS organizations are teaching the old dog new tricks by putting mainframes at the center stage of emerging applications such as data mining and warehousing, decision support, and a variety of Internet-based applications, most notably electronic commerce [17].

Mainframe computers are large, fast, and powerful computer systems. For example, mainframes can process hundreds of million instructions per second (MIPS). Mainframes also have large primary storage capacities. Their main memory capacity can range from hundreds of megabytes to many gigabytes of primary storage. And mainframes have slimmed down drastically in the last few years, dramatically reducing their air-conditioning needs, electrical power consumption, and floor space requirements, and thus their acquisition and operating costs. Most of these improvements are the result of a move from water-cooled mainframes to a newer air-cooled technology for mainframe systems [15]. See Figures 11.9 and 11.10.

Thus, mainframe computers continue to handle the information processing needs of major corporations and government agencies with high transaction processing volumes or complex computational problems. For example, major international banks, airlines, oil companies, and other large corporations process millions of sales transactions and customer inquiries each day with the help of large mainframe systems. Mainframes are still used for computation-intensive applications such as analyzing seismic data from oil field explorations or simulating flight conditions in designing aircraft. Mainframes are also widely used as *superservers* for the large client/server networks and high-volume Internet websites of large companies. And as previously mentioned, mainframes are becoming a popular business computing platform for data mining and warehousing, and electronic commerce applications [15]. See Figure 11.11.

Supercomputer Systems

Supercomputers have now become "scalable servers" at the top end of the product lines that start with desktop workstations. Market-driven companies, like Silicon Graphics, Hewlett-Packard, and IBM, have a much broader focus than just building the world's fastest computer, and the software of the desktop computer has a much greater overlap with that of the supercomputer than it used to, because both are built from the same cache-based microprocessors [12].

This new IBM eServer z900 mainframe computer processes up to 2.5 billion instructions per second.

IBM Corporation.

The term **supercomputer** describes a category of extremely powerful computer systems specifically designed for scientific, engineering, and business applications requiring extremely high speeds for massive numeric computations. The market for supercomputers includes government research agencies, large universities, and major corporations. They use supercomputers for applications such as global weather forecasting, military defense systems, computational cosmology and astronomy, microprocessor research and design, large-scale data mining, and so on.

Supercomputers use *parallel processing* architectures of interconnected microprocessors (which can execute many instructions at the same time in parallel). They can perform arithmetic calculations at speeds of billions of floating-point operations per second (*gigaflops*). Teraflop (1 trillion floating-point operations per second) supercomputers, which use advanced massively parallel processing (MPP) designs of thousands of interconnected microprocessors, are becoming available. Purchase prices for large supercomputers are in the $5 million to $50 million range.

Comparing a traditional water-cooled mainframe with a comparable air-cooled system.

IBM	ES/3090 Model 600E (water cooled)	S/390 Ry4 (air cooled)
Processors	6-way	10-way
Processing power	390 MIPS	400 MIPS
Electrical needs	138.8 KVA	5 KVA
Floor space	974 sq. ft.	52 sq. ft.
Weight	31,590 pounds	2,057 pounds

Figure 11.11

Why companies are using mainframes as servers for electronic commerce.

Mainframes as E-Commerce Servers
● Most critical business data may already be stored on the mainframe.
● Mainframe scalability can handle growing Internet traffic.
● Mainframe applications were designed to work with thin clients such as network computers and terminals.
● Built-in mainframe security can be combined with new cryptographic coprocessors and fire wall capabilities.
● Data are safer on the mainframe than on many servers.
● Internet tools are integrated right into the mainframe's OS/390 operating system.
● New mainframes offer huge savings in size, energy, and maintenance.

However, the use of symmetric multiprocessing (SMP) and distributed shared memory (DSM) designs of smaller numbers of interconnected microprocessors has spawned a breed of *minisupercomputers* with prices that start in the hundreds of thousands of dollars. For example IBM's RS/6000 SP starts at $150,000 for a one-processing-node SMP computer. However, it can be expanded to hundreds of processing nodes, which drives its price into the tens of millions of dollars. For example, an IBM RS/6000 SP with 152 processing nodes and a total of 2,048 Power3+ microprocessors was installed at the Lawrence Berkeley National Laboratory during 2000. The system cost $33 million and has a peak processing capacity of over 3 teraflops [6]. Thus, supercomputers continue to advance the state of the art for the entire computer industry. See Figure 11.12.

Figure 11.12

This Blue Horizon IBM RS/6000 SP at the University of California at San Diego Supercomputer Center, is one of the most powerful supercomputers in the world.

UCSDSC.

Technical Note: The Computer System Concept

As a business professional, you do not need a detailed technical knowledge of computers. However, you do need to understand some basic concepts about computer systems. This should help you be an informed and productive user of computer system resources.

A computer is more than a high-powered collection of electronic devices performing a variety of information processing chores. A computer is a *system*, an interrelated combination of components that performs the basic system functions of input, processing, output, storage, and control, thus providing end users with a powerful information processing tool. Understanding the computer as a **computer system** is vital to the effective use and management of computers. You should be able to visualize any computer this way, from the smallest microcomputer device, to a large computer network whose components are interconnected by telecommunications network links throughout a building complex or geographic area.

Figure 11.13 illustrates that a computer is a system of hardware devices organized according to the following system functions:

- **Input.** The input devices of a computer system include keyboards, touch screens, pens, electronic mouses, optical scanners, and so on. They convert data into electronic form for direct entry or through a telecommunications network into a computer system.

- **Processing.** The **central processing unit** (CPU) is the main processing component of a computer system. (In microcomputers, it is the **main microprocessor.** See Figure 11.14.) Conceptually, the circuitry of a CPU can be subdivided into two major subunits: the arithmetic-logic unit and the control unit. It is the electronic circuits of the **arithmetic-logic** unit that perform the arithmetic and logic functions required to execute software instructions. The CPU also includes circuitry for devices such as *registers* and *cache memory* for high-speed, temporary storage of instruction and data elements, as well as various subsidiary processors.

Figure 11.13 The computer system concept. A computer is a system of hardware components and functions.

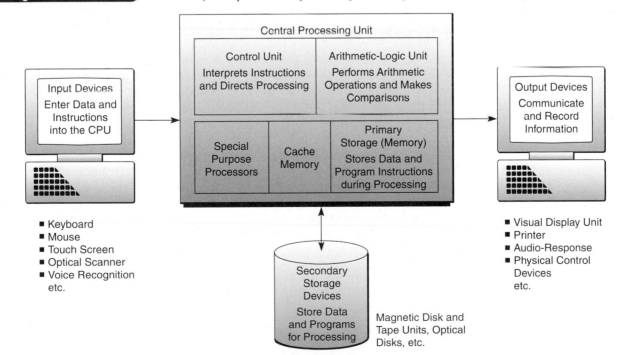

Figure 11.14

This Intel Pentium 4 microprocessor operates at 1.5 GHz clock speeds, and features 256K of cache memory and a Rapid Execution Engine with dual arithmetic-logic units that execute basic instructions at twice the clock speed of the core processor.

Intel Corporation.

- **Output.** The output devices of a computer system include video display units, printers, audio response units, and so on. They convert electronic information produced by the computer system into human-intelligible form for presentation to end users.

- **Storage.** The storage function of a computer system takes place in the storage circuits of the computer's **primary storage unit,** or *memory,* supported by **secondary storage** devices such as magnetic disk and optical disk drives. These devices store data and software instructions needed for processing.

- **Control.** The **control unit** of a CPU is the control component of a computer system. Its circuits interpret software instructions and transmit directions to the other components of the computer system.

Computer Processing Speeds

How fast are computer systems? Early computer operating speeds were measured in **milliseconds** (thousandths of a second) and **microseconds** (millionths of a second). Now computers operate in the **nanosecond** (billionth of a second) range, with **picosecond** (trillionth of a second) speed being attained by some computers. Such speeds seem almost incomprehensible. For example, an average person taking one step each nansecond would circle the earth about 20 times in one second!

We have already mentioned the *teraflop* speeds of some supercomputers. However, most computers can now process program instructions at *million instructions per second* (MIPS) speeds. Another measure of processing speed is *megahertz* (MHz), or millions of cycles per second, and *gigahertz* (GHz), or billions of cycles per second. This rating is commonly called the *clock speed* of a microprocessor, since it is used to rate microprocessors by the speed of their timing circuits or internal clock.

However, such ratings can be misleading indicators of the effective processing speed of microprocessors. That's because processing speed depends on a variety of factors including the size of circuitry paths, or *buses* that interconnect microprocessor components; the capacity of instruction processing *registers*; the use of high-speed *memory-caches*; and the use of specialized microprocessors such as a math co-processor to do arithmetic calculations faster.

Section II Computer Peripherals: Input, Output, and Storage Technologies

The right peripherals can make all the difference in your computing experience. A top-quality monitor will be easier on your eyes—and may change the way you work. A scanner can edge you closer to that ever-elusive goal—the paperless office. Backup-storage systems can offer bank-vault security against losing your work. CD-ROM drives can be essential for education and entertainment. Memory cards, 3-D graphics, and other devices will help you configure your computer to meet your needs. Some may be the digital equivalent of chrome bumpers and tailfins, but the right choice of peripherals can make a big difference [10].

Analyzing Longs Drugs and Textron

Read the Real World Case Longs Drugs and Textron on the next page. We can learn a lot about the tradeoffs between desktop computing and network computing from this case. See Figure 11.15.

The Internet is driving changes to the desktop computing model where the networked PC is king. The reach of Internet-based computing is extending out to wireless devices with Internet access like cell phones and PDAs, other home and office information appliances, and network computers. Companies like Longs and Textron no longer see the need to finance, maintain, and manage corporate networks of fat client PCs with their own disk drives and software packages for most users. They prefer the network computing model which uses the Internet, intranets, and other networks to share server-based software, databases, and application processing with network computers and other thin clients throughout the company. Technologies like smart cards enable any thin client on the network to provide instant access to a user's applications and databases. However, the lack of an adequate Java-based office software suite for network computing is a major impediment to corporate-wide deployment of network

Figure 11.15

Brian Kilcourse is Senior Vice-President and CIO of Longs Drugs, and leads their drive toward network computing.

Longs Drugs Corp./Photo Composite by Paul Hava.

Longs Drugs and Textron: Desktop Versus Network Computing

The disruption to the centralized desktop computing model has been building for years and is now coming to a head. And it's being driven by none other than the Internet. With the proliferation of distributed networks, companies like Oracle, Sun Microsystems, and IBM see an opportunity to make inroads into Microsoft's desktop dominance. "The desktop is no longer the domain of Windows," says Mark Jarvis, senior vice president and chief marketing officer with Oracle. "It's been extended to other devices like cell phones, PDAs, and other appliances."

Make no mistake, the PC is still the dominant computing device. But with an increasing number of non-PC devices being used to access the Internet, even Microsoft is adjusting to this development. Experts contend the desktop is being reordered into two separate categories: the "edge," or networked devices, which are used to access information; and the "enterprise," or servers, where all the heavy-duty computing is done. Big retailer Longs Drugs and giant conglomerate Textron Corporation are good examples of the battle going on.

Longs Drug Stores

In 1997, ahead of most large networked companies, Longs Drug Stores Corp. ripped out its client/server networks and went all Internet protocol networks. Today, the pharmacy chain is big into thin clients, Java applications and—soon—wireless technology. So even though $4 billion Longs isn't the biggest firm in the U.S. corporate food chain, "there's a lot more interesting complexity in the technology arena here than you'd normally find in a company our size," says Brian Kilcourse, senior vice president and CIO at the Walnut Creek, California–based company.

IT at Longs has always been decentralized—a tough position to defend in the late 1980s and early 1990s when predominant IT thinking called for centralization. But it had to be that way. Longs' distributed, "the network is the computer" IT philosophy reflects the company's general approach to business. Regional managers, and those at Longs' 425 stores, have wide decision-making power. A know-it-all central IT base would be rejected, says Kilcourse, and it is these key players whose decision power is behind Longs' choice of a fat server/thin client network computing model.

Textron Corporation

Phyllis Michaelides, Textron's new chief technology officer, is fighting a war to rid the company almost entirely of "fat clients." She wants to vanquish every computer that has its own hard drive and its own software. "They don't make sense," she says, speaking of PC's with hard drives and Textron's reliance on them. "Every time we want to do a software upgrade we've got to send out all these IT guys. It costs a lot of money and time to do that. We want to create a system where all the software anyone will ever need will be on the network, and they can access it anywhere in the world. That way we just upgrade everything once, and you use whatever you want whenever you want."

But how? "Follow me," Michaelides says, and marches into the office of Mike Skibo, her first lieutenant in this war. "Show him the Sun Ray," Michaelides says, and Skibo pops a card into a gray $399 Sun Microsystems Sun Ray appliance. Skibo's monitor instantly pops to life as he explains how the streamlined system's smart card allows the network to identify him and then displays whatever documents he was working on. "Now try mine." Michaelides says, inserting another smart card, and instantly the computer shows the documents that were just on the machine in her office.

If Michaelides and Skibo succeed in their project it will mean that colleagues who are working together won't need to schlep around laptops to collaborate. "That's not all it means," Michaelides says. "Laptops cost about $3,000 a piece, and you always have to upgrade them, but these things are cheap. If they break we can literally just throw them away. The units themselves never have to have their software individually upgraded because we do the upgrades on the network." By the end of the year Michaelides expects a full trial run of the system to be in effect on at least one Textron shop floor, but she won't divulge specifics.

The major impediment is that an all-out shift would mean leaving Textron's Windows-based systems for a Java platform, and at the moment Java office applications for word processing, spreadsheet, and presentation programs are not adequate. "Those are coming though," she says. "This is an evolutionary process, and it's not all going to happen at once. Some users, like heavy spreadsheet users, will probably always be on PCs with Windows, but for most people this will be much easier."

Case Study Questions

1. Why do companies like Longs and Textron want to get rid of their "fat client" PCs with their disk drives and individual software packages?

2. Do you approve of the use of this network computing model as a standard for corporate computer networks? Why or why not?

3. Does the rapid growth of web-enabled cell phones, PDAs, and other information appliances support the network computing, Windows PC, or some other model of computing? Defend your position.

Source: Adapted from John Galvin, "Manufacturing the Future," *Smart Business*, March 2001, p. 90, Om Malik, "Dueling Desktops," *Red Herring*, March 6, 2001, p. 94, and Kim Nash, "Keeping the Wheels Turning," *Computerworld*, March 26, 2001, p. 24.

computers at companies like Textron. Thus, the networked PC with its own software and disk drives continues to dominate the office desktop at most companies.

Peripherals

A computer is just a high-powered "processing box" without peripherals. **Peripherals** is the generic name given to all input, output, and secondary storage devices that are part of a computer system. Peripherals depend on direct connections or telecommunications links to the central processing unit of a computer system. Thus, all peripherals are **online** devices; that is, they are separate from, but can be electronically connected to and controlled by a CPU. (This is the opposite of **offline** devices that are separate from and not under the control of the CPU.) The major types of peripherals and media that can be part of a computer system are discussed in this section. See Figure 11.16.

Input Technology Trends

Figure 11.17 emphasizes that there has been a major trend toward the increased use of input technologies that provide a more **natural user interface** for computer users. You can now enter data and commands directly and easily into a computer system through pointing devices like electronic mice and touch pads, and technologies like optical scanning, handwriting recognition, and voice recognition. These developments have made it unnecessary to always record data on paper *source documents* (such as sales order forms, for example) and then keyboard the data into a computer in an additional data entry step. Further improvements in voice recognition and other technologies should enable an even more natural user interface in the future.

Pointing Devices

Keyboards are still the most widely used devices for entering data and text into computer systems. However, **pointing devices** are a better alternative for issuing commands, making choices, and responding to prompts displayed on your video screen. They work with your operating system's **graphical user interface** (GUI), which presents you with icons, menus, windows, buttons, bars, and so on, for your selection. For example, pointing devices such as electronic mouses and touchpads allow you to easily choose from menu selections and icon displays using point-and-click or point-and-drag methods. See Figure 11.18.

Figure 11.16

Some advice about peripherals for a business PC.

Peripherals Checklist
● **Monitors.** Bigger is better for computer screens. Consider a 19-inch or 21-inch CRT monitor, or a 15-inch LCD flat panel display. That gives you much more room to display spreadsheets, Web pages, lines of text, open windows, etc. The clarity of a monitor's image is important, too. Look for models with at least an XGA resolution of 1024 ×768 pixels.
● **Printers.** Your choice is between laser printers or color inkjet printers. Lasers are better suited for high-volume business use. Moderately priced color inkjets provide high-quality images and are well-suited for reproducing photographs. Per-page costs are higher than for laser printers.
● **Scanners.** You'll have to decide between a compact, sheet-fed scanner or a flatbed model. Sheet-fed scanners will save desktop space, while bulkier flat-bed models provide higher speed and resolution. Resolution is a key measure of quality; you'll want at least 300 dpi.
● **Hard Disk Drives.** Bigger is better; as with closet space, you can always use the extra capacity. So go 5 to 10 gigabytes at the minimum, 20 gigabytes at the max.
● **CD-ROM and DVD Drives.** CD-ROM and DVD drives are becoming a necessity for software installation and multimedia applications. Consider a high-speed variable-speed model (20X to 32X) for faster, smoother presentations.
● **Backup Systems.** Essential. Don't compute without them. Removable mag disk cartridges (like the Iomega Zip and Jazz drives) are convenient and versatile, and fast too.

Figure 11.17 Input technology trends. Note the trend toward input methods that provide a more natural user interface.

	First Generation	Second Generation	Third Generation	Fourth Generation	Fifth Generation?
INPUT MEDIA/ METHOD	Punched Cards Paper Tape	Punched Cards	Key to Tape/Disk	Keyboard Data Entry Pointing Devices Optical Scanning	Voice Recognition Touch Devices Handwriting Recognition

TREND: Toward Direct Input Devices That Are More Natural and Easy to Use. ⟶

The **electronic mouse** is the most popular pointing device used to move the cursor on the screen, as well as to issue commands and make icon and menu selections. By moving the mouse on a desktop or pad, you can move the cursor onto an icon displayed on the screen. Pressing buttons on the mouse activates various activities represented by the icon selected.

The trackball, pointing stick, and touchpad are other pointing devices most often used in place of the mouse. A **trackball** is a stationary device related to the mouse. You turn a roller ball with only its top exposed outside its case to move the cursor on the screen. A **pointing stick** (also called a *trackpoint*) is a small button-like device, sometimes likened to the eraserhead of a pencil. It is usually centered one row above the space bar of a keyboard. The cursor moves in the direction of the pressure you place on the stick. The **touchpad** is a small rectangular touch-sensitive surface usually placed below the keyboard. The cursor moves in the direction your finger moves on the pad. Trackballs, pointing sticks, and touchpads are easier to use than a mouse for portable computer users and are thus built into most notebook computer keyboards.

Figure 11.18

This IBM ThinkPad laptop microcomputer features a large LCD screen, built-in CD-ROM, floppy disk drives, stereo speakers, and a trackpoint pointing device.

IBM Corporation.

Touch screens are devices that allow you to use a computer by touching the surface of its video display screen. Some touch screens emit a grid of infrared beams, sound waves, or a slight electric current that is broken when the screen is touched. The computer senses the point in the grid where the break occurs and responds with an appropriate action. For example, you can indicate your selection on a menu display by just touching the screen next to that menu item.

Pen-Based Computing

Handwriting-recognition systems convert script into text quickly and are friendly to shaky hands as well as those of block-printing draftsmen. The pen is more powerful than the keyboard in many vertical markets, as evidenced by the popularity of pen-based devices in the utilities, service, and medical trades [10].

Pen-based computing technologies are being used in many hand-held computers and personal digital assistants. These small PCs and PDAs contain fast processors and software that recognizes and digitizes handwriting, handprinting, and hand drawing. They have a pressure-sensitive layer like a graphics pad under their slatelike liquid crystal display (LCD) screen. So instead of writing on a paper form fastened to a clipboard or using a keyboard device, you can use a pen to make selections, send E-mail, and enter handwritten data directly into a computer. See Figure 11.19.

A variety of other penlike devices are available. One example is the *digitizer pen* and *graphics tablet*. You can use the digitizer pen as a pointing device, or use it to draw or write on the pressure-sensitive surface of the graphics tablet. Your handwriting or drawing is digitized by the computer, accepted as input, displayed on its video screen, and entered into your application.

Figure 11.19

Using a personal digital assistant (PDA) that accepts pen-based input for sales transaction processing.

Jeff Sciortino.

Speech Recognition Systems

Speech recognition is gaining popularity in the corporate world among nontypists, people with disabilities, and business travelers, and is most frequently used for dictation, screen navigation, and Web browsing [3].

Speech recognition promises to be the easiest method for data entry, word processing, and conversational computing, since speech is the easiest, most natural means of human communication. Speech input has now become technologically and economically feasible for a variety of applications. Early speech recognition products used *discrete speech recognition*, where you had to pause between each spoken word. New *continuous speech recognition* (CSR) software recognizes continuous, conversationally paced speech. See Figure 11.20.

Speech recognition systems digitize, analyze, and classify your speech and its sound patterns. The software compares your speech patterns to a database of sound patterns in its vocabulary and passes recognized words to your application software. Typically, speech recognition systems require training the computer to recognize your voice and its unique sound patterns in order to achieve a high degree of accuracy. Training such systems involves repeating a variety of words and phrases in a training session, as well as using the system extensively.

Examples of continuous speech recognition software are NaturallySpeaking by Dragon Systems, ViaVoice by IBM, VoiceXpress by Lernout & Hauspie, and FreeSpeech by Phillips. Most products have 30,000-word vocabularies expandable to 60,000 words, and sell for less than $200. Training to 95 percent accuracy may take several hours. Longer use, faster processors, and more memory make 99 percent accuracy possible [3].

Speech recognition devices in work situations allow operators to perform data entry without using their hands to key in data or instructions and to provide faster

Figure 11.20

Peter Corrales, owner of Barocco To Go in Greenwich Village, New York, ignores his PC keyboard and mouse to check inventory with voice recognition technology.

IBM Corporation.

and more accurate input. For example, manufacturers use speech recognition systems for the inspection, inventory, and quality control of a variety of products; and airlines and parcel delivery companies use them for voice-directed sorting of baggage and parcels. Speech recognition can also help you operate your computer's operating systems and software packages through voice input of data and commands. For example, such software can be voice-enabled so you can send E-mail and surf the World Wide Web.

Speaker-independent voice recognition systems, which allow a computer to understand a few words from a voice it has never heard before, are being built into products and used in a growing number of applications. Examples include *voice-messaging computers*, which use speech recognition and voice response software to verbally guide an end user through the steps of a task in many kinds of activities. Typically, they enable computers to respond to verbal and Touch-Tone input over the telephone. Examples of applications include computerized telephone call switching, telemarketing surveys, bank pay-by-phone bill-paying services, stock quotations services, university registration systems, and customer credit and account balance inquiries.

Optical Scanning

Few people understand how much scanners can improve a computer system and make your work easier. Their function is to get documents into your computer with a minimum of time and hassle, transforming just about anything on paper—a letter, a logo, or a photograph—into the digital format that your PC can make sense of. Scanners can be a big help in getting loads of paper off your desk and into your PC [10].

Optical scanning devices read text or graphics and convert them into digital input for your computer. Thus, optical scanning enables the direct entry of data from source documents into a computer system. For example, you can use a compact desktop scanner to scan pages of text and graphics into your computer for desktop publishing and Web publishing applications. Or you can scan documents of all kinds into your system and organize them into folders as part of a *document management* library system for easy reference or retrieval.

There are many types of optical scanners, but they all employ photoelectric devices to scan the characters being read. Reflected light patterns of the data are converted into electronic impulses that are then accepted as input into the computer system. Compact desktop scanners have become very popular due to their low cost and ease of use with personal computer systems. However, larger, more expensive *flatbed scanners* are faster and provide higher resolution color scanning. See Figure 11.21.

Another optical scanning technology is called **optical character recognition** (OCR). OCR scanners can read the OCR characters and codes on merchandise tags, product labels, credit card receipts, utility bills, insurance premiums, airline tickets, and other documents. OCR scanners are also used to automatically sort mail, score tests, and process a wide variety of forms in business and government.

Devices such as hand-held optical scanning **wands** are frequently used to read OCR coding on merchandise tags, product labels, and other media. Many business applications involve reading *bar coding*, a code that utilizes bars to represent characters. One common example is the Universal Product Code (UPC) bar coding that you see on product labels, product packaging, and merchandise tags. For example, the automated checkout scanners found in supermarkets read UPC bar coding. Supermarket scanners emit laser beams that are reflected off a UPC bar code. The reflected image is converted to electronic impulses that are sent to the in-store computer, where they are matched with pricing information. Pricing information is returned to the terminal, visually displayed, and printed on a receipt for the customer. See Figure 11.22.

Figure 11.21

Using a flatbed scanner for desktop publishing.

Melissa Farlow.

Other Input Technologies

Magnetic stripe technology is a familiar form of data entry that helps computers read credit cards. The iron oxide coating of the magnetic stripe on the back of such cards can hold about 200 bytes of information. Customer account numbers can be recorded on the mag stripe so it can be read by bank ATMs, credit card authorization terminals, and many other types of magnetic stripe readers.

Smart cards that embed a microprocessor chip and several kilobytes of memory into debit, credit, and other cards are popular in Europe, and becoming available in the United States. One example is Holland, where over 8 million smart debit cards have been issued by Dutch banks. Smart debit cards enable you to store a cash balance on the card and electronically transfer some of it to others to pay

Figure 11.22

Using an optical scanning wand to read bar coding of inventory data.

Image Bank.

for small items and services. The balance on the card can be replenished in ATMs or other terminals.

The smart debit cards used in Holland feature a microprocessor and either 8 or 16 kilobytes of memory, plus the usual magnetic stripe. The smart cards are widely used to make payments in parking meters, vending machines, newsstands, pay telephones, and retail stores [9].

Digital cameras represent another fast-growing set of input technologies. Digital still cameras and digital video cameras (digital camcorders) enable you to shoot, store, and download still photos or full motion video with audio into your PC. Then you can use image-editing software to edit and enhance the digitized images and include them in newsletters, reports, multimedia presentations, and Web pages [8].

The computer systems of the banking industry can magnetically read checks and deposit slips using **magnetic ink character recognition** (MICR) technology. Computers can thus sort and post checks to the proper checking accounts. Such processing is possible because the identification numbers of the bank and the customer's account are preprinted on the bottom of the checks with an iron oxide-based ink. The first bank receiving a check after it has been written must encode the amount of the check in magnetic ink on the check's lower right-hand corner. The MICR system uses 14 characters (the 10 decimal digits and 4 special symbols) of a standardized design. Equipment known as *reader-sorters* read a check by first magnetizing the magnetic ink characters and then sensing the signal induced by each character as it passes a reading head. In this way, data are electronically captured by the bank's computer systems.

Output Technologies and Trends

Computers provide information to you in a variety of forms. Figure 11.23 shows you the trends in output media and methods that have developed over the generations of computing. As you can see, video displays and printed documents have been, and still are, the most common forms of output from computer systems. But other natural and attractive output technologies such as **voice response** systems and multimedia output are increasingly found along with video displays in business applications.

For example, you have probably experienced the voice and audio output generated by speech and audio microprocessors in a variety of consumer products. Voice messaging software enables PCs and servers in voice mail and messaging systems to interact with you through voice responses. And of course, multimedia output is common on the websites of the Internet and corporate intranets.

Video Output

Of all the peripherals you can purchase for your system, a [video] monitor is the one addition that can make the biggest difference. Forget about faster processors, bigger hard drives, and the like. The fact is, the monitor is the part of your system you spend the most time interacting with . . . Invest in a quality monitor, and you'll be thankful every time you turn on your computer [10].

Figure 11.23

Output technology trends. Note the trend from paper documents to more natural forms of video, audio, and multimedia output.

	First Generation	Second Generation	Third Generation	Fourth Generation	Fifth Generation?
OUTPUT MEDIA/ METHOD	Punched Cards Printed Reports and Documents	Punched Cards Printed Reports and Documents	Printed Reports and Documents Video Displays	Video Displays Audio Responses Printed Reports and Documents	Video Displays Voice Responses Hyperlinked Multimedia Documents
TREND: Toward Direct Output Methods That Communicate Naturally, Quickly, and Clearly.					

Video displays are the most common type of computer output. Most desktop computers rely on **video monitors** that use a *cathode ray tube* (CRT) technology similar to the picture tubes used in home TV sets. Usually, the clarity of the video display depends on the type of video monitor you use and the graphics circuit board installed in your computer. These can provide a variety of graphics modes of increasing capability. A high-resolution, flicker-free monitor is especially important if you spend a lot of time viewing multimedia on CDs or the Web, or the complex graphical displays of many software packages.

The biggest use of **liquid crystal displays** (LCDs) is to provide a visual display capability for portable microcomputers and PDAs, though the use of "flat panel" LCD video monitors for desktop PC systems is growing. LCD displays need significantly less electric current and provide a thin, flat display. Advances in technology such as *active matrix* and *dual scan* capabilities have improved the color and clarity of LCD displays. See Figure 11.24.

Printed Output

Printing information on paper is still the most common form of output after video displays. Thus, most personal computer systems rely on an inkjet or laser printer to produce permanent (hard copy) output in high-quality printed form. Printed output is still a common form of business communications, and is frequently required for legal documentation. Thus, computers can produce printed reports and correspondence, documents such as sales invoices, payroll checks, bank statements, and printed versions of graphic displays.

Inkjet printers, which spray ink onto a page one line at a time, have become the most popular, low-cost printers for microcomputer systems. They are quiet, produce several pages per minute of high-quality output, and can print both black-and-

Figure 11.24

Using a flat panel LCD video monitor for a desktop PC system.

Toshiba Image Bank.

white and high-quality color graphics. **Laser printers** use an electrostatic process similar to a photocopying machine to produce many pages per minute of high-quality black-and-white output. More expensive color laser printers and multifunction inkjet and laser models that print, fax, scan, and copy are other popular choices for business offices. See Figure 11.25.

Storage Trends and Trade-Offs

Data and information must be stored until needed using a variety of storage methods. For example, many people and organizations still rely on paper documents stored in filing cabinets as a major form of storage media. However, you and other computer users are more likely to depend on the memory circuits and secondary storage devices of computer systems to meet your storage requirements. Figure 11.26 illustrates major trends in primary and secondary storage methods. Progress in very-large-scale integration (VLSI), which packs millions of memory circuit elements on tiny semiconductor memory chips, is responsible for continuing increases in the main-memory capacity of computers. Secondary storage capacities are also escalating into the billions and trillions of characters, due to advances in magnetic and optical media.

There are many types of storage media and devices. Figure 11.27 illustrates the speed, capacity, and cost relationships of several alternative primary and secondary storage media. Note the cost/speed/capacity trade-offs as one moves from semiconductor memories to magnetic disks, to optical disks, and to magnetic tape. High-speed storage media cost more per byte and provide lower capacities. Large-capacity storage media cost less per byte but are slower. This is why we have different kinds of storage media.

However, all storage media, especially memory chips and magnetic disks, continue to increase in speed and capacity and decrease in cost. Developments like automated high-speed cartridge assemblies have given faster access times to magnetic tape, and the speed of optical disk drives continues to increase.

Corbis.

Figure 11.26   Major trends in primary and secondary storage media.

	First Generation	Second Generation	Third Generation	Fourth Generation	Fifth Generation?
PRIMARY STORAGE	Magnetic Drum	Magnetic Core	Magnetic Core	LSI Semiconductor Memory Chips	VLSI Semiconductor Memory Chips
TREND: Toward Large Capacities Using Smaller Microelectronic Circuits.					
SECONDARY STORAGE	Magnetic Tape Magnetic Drum	Magnetic Tape Magnetic Disk	Magnetic Disk Magnetic Tape	Magnetic Disk Optical Disk Magnetic Tape	Optical Disk Magnetic Disk
TREND: Toward Massive Capacities Using Magnetic and Optical Media.					

Note in Figure 11.27 that semiconductor memories are used mainly for primary storage, though they are sometimes used as high-speed secondary storage devices. Magnetic disk and tape and optical disk devices, on the other hand, are used as secondary storage devices to greatly enlarge the storage capacity of computer systems. Also, since most primary storage circuits use RAM (random access memory) chips, which lose their contents when electrical power is interrupted, secondary storage devices provide a more permanent type of storage media.

Computer Storage Fundamentals

Data are processed and stored in a computer system through the presence or absence of electronic or magnetic signals in the computer's circuitry or in the media it uses. This is called a "two-state" or **binary representation** of data, since the computer and the media can exhibit only two possible states or conditions. For example, transistors and other semiconductor circuits are either in a conducting or nonconducting state. Media such as magnetic disks and tapes indicate these two states by having magnetized spots whose magnetic fields have one of two different directions, or polarities. This binary characteristic of computer circuitry and media is what makes the binary number system the basis for representing data in computers. Thus, for electronic circuits, the conducting (ON) state represents the number one, while the nonconducting (OFF) state represents the number zero. For magnetic media, the magnetic field of a magnetized spot in one direction represents a one, while magnetism in the other direction represents a zero.

Figure 11.27

Storage media cost, speed, and capacity trade-offs. Note how cost increases with faster access speeds, but decreases with the increased capacity of storage media.

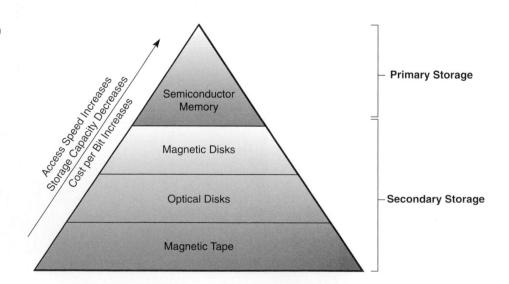

The smallest element of data is called a **bit**, or binary digit, which can have a value of either zero or one. The capacity of memory chips is usually expressed in terms of bits. A **byte** is a basic grouping of bits that the computer operates as a single unit. Typically, it consists of eight bits and represents one character of data in most computer coding schemes. Thus, the capacity of a computer's memory and secondary storage devices is usually expressed in terms of bytes. Computer codes such as ASCII (American Standard Code for Information Interchange) use various arrangements of bits to form bytes that represent the numbers zero through nine, the letters of the alphabet, and many other characters. See Figure 11.28.

Storage capacities are frequently measured in **kilobytes** (KB), **megabytes** (MB), **gigabytes** (GB), or **terabytes** (TB). Although kilo means 1,000 in the metric system, the computer industry uses K to represent 1,024 (or 2^{10}) storage positions. Therefore, a capacity of 10 megabytes, for example, is really 10,485,760 storage positions, rather than 10 million positions. However, such differences are frequently disregarded in order to simplify descriptions of storage capacity. Thus, a megabyte is roughly 1 million bytes of storage, a gigabyte is roughly 1 billion bytes and a terabyte represents about 1 trillion bytes, while a **petabyte** is over 1 quadrillion bytes!

Direct and Sequential Access

Primary storage media such as semiconductor memory chips are called **direct access** or random access memories (RAM). Magnetic disk devices are frequently called direct access storage devices (DASDs). On the other hand, media such as magnetic tape cartridges are known as **sequential access** devices.

The terms *direct access* and *random access* describe the same concept. They mean that an element of data or instructions (such as a byte or word) can be directly stored and retrieved by selecting and using any of the locations on the storage media. They also mean that each storage position (1) has a unique address and (2) can be individually accessed in approximately the same length of time without having to search through other storage positions. For example, each memory cell on a microelectronic semiconductor RAM chip can be individually sensed or changed in the same length of time. Also any data record stored on a magnetic or optical disk can be accessed directly in approximately the same time period. See Figure 11.29.

Sequential access storage media such as magnetic tape do not have unique storage addresses that can be directly addressed. Instead, data must be stored and retrieved using a sequential or serial process. Data are recorded one after another in a predetermined sequence (such as in numeric order) on a storage medium.

Figure 11.28

Examples of ASCII computer code.

Character	ASCII Code	Character	ASCII Code	Character	ASCII Code
0	00110000	A	01000001	N	01001110
1	00110001	B	01000010	O	01001111
2	00110010	C	01000011	P	01010000
3	00110011	D	01000100	Q	01010001
4	00110100	E	01000101	R	01010010
5	00110101	F	01000110	S	01010011
6	00110110	G	01000111	T	01010100
7	00110111	H	01001000	U	01010101
8	00111000	I	01001001	V	01010110
9	00111001	J	01001010	W	01010111
		K	01001011	X	01011000
		L	01001100	Y	01011001
		M	01001101	Z	01011010

Figure 11.29

Sequential versus direct access storage. Magnetic tape is a typical sequential access medium. Magnetic disks are typical direct access storage devices.

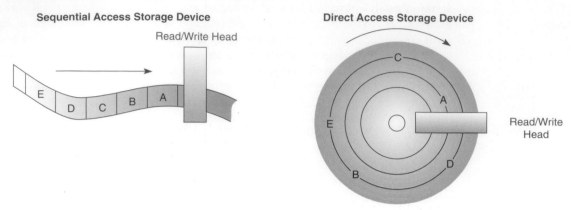

Locating an individual item of data requires searching the recorded data on the tape until the desired item is located.

Semiconductor Memory

Memory is the coalman to the CPU's locomotive: For maximum PC performance, it must keep the processor constantly stoked with instructions. Faster CPUs call for larger and faster memories, both in the cache where data and instructions are stored temporarily, and in the main memory [10].

The primary storage (main memory) of your computer consists of microelectronic **semiconductor memory** chips. It provides you with the working storage your computer needs to process your applications. Plug-in memory circuit boards containing 32 megabytes or more of memory chips can be added to your PC to increase its memory capacity. Specialized memory can help improve your computer's performance. Examples include external cache memory of 512 kilobytes to help your microprocessor work faster, or a video graphics accelerator card with 16 megabytes of RAM for faster and clearer video performance. Removable credit-card-size and smaller "flash memory" RAM cards can also provide several megabytes of erasable direct access storage for PDAs or hand-held PCs.

Some of the major attractions of semiconductor memory are its small size, great speed, and shock and temperature resistance. One major disadvantage of most semiconductor memory is its **volatility.** Uninterrupted electric power must be supplied or the contents of memory will be lost. Therefore, emergency transfer to other devices or standby electrical power (through battery packs or emergency generators) is required if data are to be saved. Another alternative is to permanently "burn in" the contents of semiconductor devices so that they cannot be erased by a loss of power.

Thus, there are two basic types of semiconductor memory: random access memory (RAM) and read only memory (ROM).

- **RAM: random access memory.** These memory chips are the most widely used primary storage medium. Each memory position can be both sensed (read) and changed (written), so it is also called read/write memory. This is a volatile memory.

- **ROM: read only memory.** Nonvolatile random access memory chips are used for permanent storage. ROM can be read but not erased or overwritten. Frequently used control instructions in the control unit and programs in primary storage (such as parts of the operating system) can be permanently burned in to the storage cells during manufacture. This is sometimes called *firmware.*

Variations include PROM (programmable read only memory) and EPROM (erasable programmable read only memory), which can be permanently or temporarily programmed after manufacture.

Magnetic Disk Storage

Multi-gigabyte magnetic disk drives aren't extravagant, considering that full-motion video files, sound tracks, and photo-quality images can consume colossal amounts of disk space in a blink [10].

Magnetic disks are the most common form of secondary storage for your computer system. That's because they provide fast access and high storage capacities at a reasonable cost. Magnetic disk drives contain metal disks that are coated on both sides with an iron oxide recording material. Several disks are mounted together on a vertical shaft, which typically rotates the disks at speeds of 3,600 to 7,600 revolutions per minute (rpm). Electromagnetic read/write heads are positioned by access arms between the slightly separated disks to read and write data on concentric, circular tracks. Data are recorded on tracks in the form of tiny magnetized spots to form the binary digits of common computer codes. Thousands of bytes can be recorded on each track, and there are several hundred data tracks on each disk surface, thus providing you with billions of storage positions for your software and data. See Figure 11.30.

Types of Magnetic Disks

There are several types of magnetic disk arrangements, including removable disk cartridges as well as fixed disk units. Removable disk devices are popular because they are transportable and can be used to store backup copies of your data offline for convenience and security.

- **Floppy disks,** or magnetic diskettes, consist of polyester film disks covered with an iron oxide compound. A single disk is mounted and rotates freely inside a protective flexible or hard plastic jacket, which has access openings to accommodate the read/write head of a disk drive unit. The 3 1/2-inch floppy disk, with capacities of 1.44 megabytes, is the most widely used version, with a newer Superdisk technology offering 120 megabytes of storage.

- **Hard disk drives** combine magnetic disks, access arms, and read/write heads into a sealed module. This allows higher speeds, greater data recording densities, and closer tolerances within a sealed, more stable environment. Fixed or removable disk cartridge versions are available. Capacities of hard drives range from several hundred megabytes to many gigabytes of storage.

Figure 11.30 Magnetic disk media: A hard magnetic disk drive and a 3 1/2-inch floppy disk.

Quantum.

Eric Kamp/Index Stock Photography.

RAID Storage

RAID computer storage equipment—big, refrigerator-size boxes full of dozens of inter-linked magnetic disk drives that can store the equivalent of 100 million tax returns—hardly gets the blood rushing. But it should. Just as speedy and reliable networking opened the floodgates to cyberspace and E-commerce, ever-more-turbocharged data storage is a key building block of the Internet [11].

Disk arrays of interconnected microcomputer hard disk drives have replaced large-capacity mainframe disk drives to provide many gigabytes of online storage. Known as **RAID** (redundant arrays of independent disks), they combine from 6 to more than 100 small hard disk drives and their control microprocessors into a single unit. RAID units provide large capacities with high access speeds since data are accessed in parallel over multiple paths from many disks. RAID units also provide a *fault tolerant* capacity, since their redundant design offers multiple copies of data on several disks. If one disk fails, data can be recovered from backup copies automatically stored on other disks. *Storage area networks* (SANs) are high-speed *fiber channel* local area networks that can interconnect many RAID units and thus share their combined capacity through network servers with many users.

Magnetic Tape Storage

Tape storage is moving beyond backup. Disk subsystems provide the fastest response time for mission-critical data. But the sheer amount of data users need to access these days as part of huge enterprise applications, such as data warehouses, requires affordable [magnetic tape] storage [16].

Magnetic tape is still being used as a secondary storage medium in business applications. The read/write heads of magnetic tape drives record data in the form of magnetized spots on the iron oxide coating of the plastic tape. Magnetic tape devices include tape reels and cartridges in mainframes and midrange systems, and small cassettes or cartridges for PCs. Magnetic tape cartridges have replaced tape reels in many applications and can hold over 200 megabytes.

One growing business application of magnetic tape involves the use of high-speed 36-track magnetic tape cartridges in robotic automated drive assemblies that can directly access hundreds of cartridges. These devices provide lower-cost storage to supplement magnetic disks to meet massive data warehouse and other online business storage requirements. Other major applications for magnetic tape include long-term *archival* storage and backup storage for PCs and other systems [16].

Optical Disk Storage

CD-ROM technology has become a necessity. Most software companies have stopped distributing their elephantine programs on floppies altogether. Many corporations are now rolling their own CDs to distribute product and corporate information that once filled bookshelves [10].

Optical disks are a fast-growing storage medium. One version for use with microcomputers is called **CD-ROM** (compact disk-read only memory). CD-ROM technology uses 12-centimeter (4.7 inch) compact disks (CDs) similar to those used in stereo music systems. Each disk can store more than 600 megabytes. That's the equivalent of over 400 1.44 megabyte floppy disks or more than 300,000 double-spaced pages of text. A laser records data by burning permanent microscopic pits in a spiral track on a master disk from which compact disks can be mass produced. Then CD-ROM disk drives use a laser device to read the binary codes formed by those pits.

CD-R (compact disk-recordable) is a popular optical disk technology. CD-R drives or *CD burners* are commonly used to permanently record digital music tracks or digital photo images on CDs. The major limitation of CD-ROM and CD-R disks is that recorded data cannot be erased. However, **CD-RW** (CD-rewritable) drives have now become available that record and erase data by using a laser to heat a microscopic point on the disk's surface. In CD-RW versions using magneto-optical technology, a magnetic coil changes the spot's reflective properties from one direction to another, thus recording a binary one or zero. A laser device can then read the binary codes on the disk by sensing the direction of reflected light.

Optical disk capacities and capabilities have increased dramatically with the emergence of an optical disk technology called **DVD** (digital video disk or digital versatile disk). DVDs can hold from 3.0 to 8.5 gigabytes of multimedia data on each side of a compact disk. The large capacities and high quality images and sound of DVD technology are expected to eventually replace CD-ROM and CD-RW technologies for data storage, and promise to accelerate the use of DVD drives for multimedia products that can be used in both computers and home entertainment systems. Thus, **DVD-ROM** is beginning to replace magnetic tape videocassettes for movies and other multimedia products, while **DVD-RAM** is being used for backup and archival storage of large data and multimedia files. See Figure 11.31.

Business Applications

One of the major uses of optical disks in mainframe and midrange systems is in **image processing,** where long-term archival storage of historical files of document images must be maintained. Mainframe and midrange computer versions of optical disks use 12-inch plastic disks with capacities of several gigabytes, with up to 20 disks held in jukebox drive units. Financial institutions, among others, are using optical scanners to capture digitized document images and store them on **WORM** (write once, read many) versions of such optical disks as an alternative to microfilm media.

One of the major business uses of CD-ROM disks for personal computers is to provide a publishing medium for fast access to reference materials in a convenient, compact form. This includes catalogs, directories, manuals, periodical abstracts, part listings, and statistical databases of business and economic activity. Interactive multimedia applications in business, education, and entertainment are another major use of CD-ROM and DVD disks. The large storage capacities of CD-ROM and DVD are a natural choice for computer video games, educational videos, multimedia encyclopedias, and advertising presentations.

Thus, optical disks have become a popular storage medium for image processing and multimedia business applications, and they appear to be a promising alternative to magnetic disks and tape for very large *mass storage* capabilities for enterprise computing systems. However, rewritable optical technologies are still maturing, and most optical disk devices are significantly slower and more expensive (per byte of storage) than magnetic disk devices. So optical disk systems are not expected to displace magnetic disk technology in the near future for many business applications.

Figure 11.31

Optical disk storage includes CD and DVD technologies.

PhotoDisc, Inc.

Summary

- **Computer Systems.** Major types and trends in computer systems are summarized in Figures 11.2 and 11.3. A computer is a system of information processing components that perform input, processing, output, storage, and control functions. Its hardware components include input and output devices, a central processing unit (CPU), and primary and secondary storage devices. The major functions and hardware in a computer system are summarized in Figure 11.13.

- **Microcomputer Systems.** Microcomputers are used as personal computers, network computers, personal digital assistants, technical workstations, and information appliances. Like most computer systems today, microcomputers are interconnected in a variety of telecommunications networks. This typically includes local area networks, client/server networks, intranets and extranets, and the Internet.

- **Other Computer Systems.** Midrange computers are increasingly used as powerful network servers, and for many multiuser business data processing and scientific applications. Mainframe computers are larger and more powerful than most midsize computers. They are usually faster, have more memory capacity, and can support more network users and peripheral devices. They are designed to handle the information processing needs of large organizations with high volumes of transaction processing, or with complex computational problems. Supercomputers are a special category of extremely powerful mainframe computer systems designed for massive computational assignments.

- **Peripheral Devices.** Refer to Figures 11.16, 11.17, 11.23, 11.26, and 11.27 to review the important trends and capabilities of peripheral devices for input, output, and storage discussed in this chapter.

Key Terms and Concepts

These are the key terms and concepts of this chapter. The page number of their first explanation is given in parentheses.

1. Binary representation (416)
2. Central processing unit (403)
3. Computer system (403)
4. Computer terminal (399)
5. Digital cameras (413)
6. Direct access (417)
7. Generations of computing (394)
8. Information appliance (398)
9. Laptop computer (396)
10. Liquid crystal displays (414)
11. Magnetic disk storage (419)
    a. Floppy disk (419)
    b. Hard disk (419)
    c. RAID (420)
12. Magnetic ink character recognition (413)
13. Magnetic stripe (412)
14. Magnetic tape (420)
15. Mainframe computer (400)
16. Microcomputer (400)
17. Microprocessor (403)
18. Midrange computer (399)
19. Minicomputer (395)
20. Network computer (397)
21. NetPC (397)
22. Network server (397)
23. Network terminal (399)
24. Offline (407)
25. Online (407)
26. Optical character recognition (411)
27. Optical disk storage (420)
    a. CD-ROM (420)
    b. CD-R (420)
    c. CD-RW (420)
    d. DVD (421)
    e. WORM disks (421)
28. Optical scanning (411)
29. Pen-based computing (409)
30. Peripheral devices (407)
31. Personal digital assistant (398)
32. Pointing devices (407)
    a. Electronic mouse (408)
    b. Pointing stick (408)
    c. Touchpad (408)
    d. Trackball (408)
33. Primary storage (404)
34. Printers (414)

35. Secondary storage (416)
36. Semiconductor memory (418)
    a. RAM (418)
    b. ROM (418)
37. Sequential access (417)
38. Smart cards (412)
39. Speech recognition (410)
40. Storage capacity elements (416)
    a. Bit (417)
    b. Byte (417)
    c. Kilobyte (417)
    d. Megabyte (417)
    e. Gigabyte (417)
    f. Terabyte (417)
41. Storage media trade-offs (415)
42. Supercomputer (400)
43. Time elements (404)
    a. Millisecond (404)
    b. Microsecond (404)
    c. Nanosecond (404)
    d. Picosecond (404)
44. Touch-sensitive screen (409)
45. Trends in computers (394)
46. Video output (413)
47. Volatility (418)
48. Wand (411)
49. Workstation (396)

Review Quiz

Match one of the previous key terms and concepts with one of the following brief examples or definitions. Try to find the best fit for answers that seem to fit more than one term or concept. Defend your choices.

1. Computers will become smaller, faster, more reliable, easier to use, and less costly.
2. Major stages in the development of computing.
3. A computer is a combination of components that perform input, processing, output, storage, and control functions.
4. The main processing component of a computer system.
5. A small, portable PC.
6. Devices for consumers to access the Internet.
7. The memory of a computer.
8. Magnetic disks and tape and optical disks perform this function.
9. Input/output and secondary storage devices for a computer system.
10. Connected to and controlled by a CPU.
11. Separate from and not controlled by a CPU.
12. Results from the presence or absence or change in direction of electric current, magnetic fields, or light rays in computer circuits and media.
13. The central processing unit of a microcomputer.
14. Can be a desktop/laptop, or hand-held computer.
15. A computer category between microcomputers and mainframes.
16. A computer that can handle the information processing needs of large organizations.
17. Hand-held microcomputers for communications and personal information management.
18. Low-cost microcomputers for use with the Internet and corporate intranets.
19. Low-cost network-enabled PCs with reduced features.
20. A terminal that depends on network servers for its software and processing power.
21. A computer that manages network communications and resources.
22. The most powerful type of computer.
23. A magnetic tape technology for credit cards.
24. One billionth of a second.
25. Roughly one billion characters of storage.
26. Includes electronic mouses, trackballs, pointing sticks, and touchpads.
27. You can write on the pressure-sensitive LCD screen of hand-held microcomputers with a pen.
28. Moving this along your desktop moves the cursor on the screen.
29. You can communicate with a computer by touching its display.
30. Produces hard copy output such as paper documents and reports.
31. Promises to be the easiest, most natural way to communicate with computers.
32. Capturing data by processing light reflected from images.
33. Optical scanning of bar codes and other characters.

34. Bank check processing uses this technology.

35. A debit card with an embedded microprocessor and memory is an example.

36. A device with a keyboard and a video display networked to a computer is a typical example.

37. Photos or video can be captured and downloaded to your PC for image processing.

38. A video output technology.

39. A hand-held device that reads bar coding.

40. Storage media cost, speed, and capacity differences.

41. You cannot erase the contents of these storage circuits.

42. The memory of most computers consists of these storage circuits.

43. The property that determines whether data are lost or retained when power fails.

44. Each position of storage can be accessed in approximately the same time.

45. Each position of storage can be accessed according to a predetermined order.

46. Microelectronic storage circuits on silicon chips.

47. Uses magnetic spots on metal or plastic disks.

48. Uses magnetic spots on plastic tape.

49. Uses a laser to read microscopic points on plastic disks.

50. Vastly increases the storage capacity and image and sound quality of optical disk technology.

Discussion Questions

1. Do you agree with the statement: "The network is the computer"? Why or why not?

2. What trends are occurring in the development and use of the major types of computer systems?

3. Refer to the Real World Case on BTG, NEC Electronics, and Biogen in the chapter. Will compute-farms make traditional mainframes and supercomputers obsolete? Why or why not?

4. Do you think that network computers (NCs) will replace personal computers (PCs) in business applications? Explain.

5. Are networks of PCs and servers making mainframe computers obsolete? Explain.

6. Refer to the Real World Case on Longs Drugs and Textron in the chapter. Is there a role for network computing in business other than replacing office desktop PC systems? Discuss.

7. What are several trends that are occurring in the development and use of peripheral devices? Why are these trends occurring?

8. When would you recommend the use of each of the following: (1) network computers, (2) NetPCs, (3) network terminals, or (4) information appliances in business applications?

9. What processor, memory, magnetic disk storage, and video display capabilities would you require for a personal computer that you would use for business purposes? Explain your choices.

10. What other peripheral devices and capabilities would you want to have for your business PC? Explain your choices.

Application Exercises

1. Input Alternatives
Which method of input would you recommend for the following activities? Explain your choices.
a. Entering data from printed questionnaires.
b. Entering data from telephone surveys.
c. Entering data from bank checks.
d. Entering data from merchandise tags.
e. Entering data from business documents.

2. Output Alternatives
Which method of output would you recommend for the following information products? Explain your choices.
a. Visual displays for portable microcomputers.
b. Legal documents.
c. Color photographs.
d. Financial results for top executives.
e. Responses for telephone transactions.

3. Purchasing Computer Systems for Your Workgroup
You have been asked to get pricing information for a potential purchase of 5 PCs for the members of your work group. Go to the Internet to get prices for these units from at least two prominent PC suppliers.

The list below shows the specifications for the basic system you have been asked to price and potential upgrades to each feature. You will want to get a price for the basic system described below and a separate price for each of the upgrades shown.

	Basic Unit	Upgrade
CPU (gigahertz)	1.3	1.5
Hard Drive (gigbytes)	40	80
RAM (megabytes)	256	512
CD-ROM	48 speed	8 Speed DVD
Monitor (inches)	17	21

Network cards and modems will not be purchased with these systems. These features will be added from stock already owned by the company. Take the standard warranty and servicing coverage offered by each supplier, but be sure to note any differences in coverage.
a. Prepare a spreadsheet summarizing this pricing information and showing the cost, from each supplier, of the following options: a. 5 units with the basic con-figuration, b. 3 units with the basic configuration and 2 units with all of the upgrades, c. 3 units with the basic configuration plus the monitor upgrade and 2 units with all upgrades, and d. all 5 units fully upgraded.
b. Prepare a set of power point slides or similar presentation materials summarizing your results. Include a discussion of the warranty and servicing contract options available form each supplier.

4. Price and Performance Trends for Computer Hardware
The table below shows a set of price and capacity figures for common components of personal computers. Typical prices for Microprocessors, Random Access Memory (RAM), and Hard Disk storage prices are shown. The performance of typical components has increased substantially over time, so the speed (for the microprocessor) or the capacity (for the storage devices) is also listed. Although there have been improvements in these components that are not reflected in these capacity measures, it is interesting to examine trends in these measurable characteristics.
a. Create a spreadsheet based on the figures below and including a new column for each component showing the price per unit of capacity. (Cost per megahertz of speed for microprocessors, and cost per megabyte of storage for RAM and hard disk devices.)
b. Create a set of graphs highlighting your results and illustrating trends in price per unit of performance (speed) or capacity.
c. Write a short paper discussing the trends you found. How long do you expect these trends to continue? Why?

	1991	1993	1995	1997	1999	2001
Microprocessor						
Speed (Megahertz)	25	33	100	125	350	1,000
Cost	$180	$125	$275	$250	$300	$251
RAM Chip						
Megabytes per chip	1	4	4	16	64	256
Cost	$55	$140	$120	$97	$125	$90
Hard Disk Device						
Megabytes per Disk	105	250	540	2,000	8,000	40,000
Cost	$480	$375	$220	$250	$220	$138

Office Depot and NetByTel: Web-Enabled Voice Recognition Systems

Call it E-commerce without the browser. Shoppers who want to buy office supplies from Office Depot's web site can simply dial a toll-free number and place orders using an interactive voice-response system that does the web browsing for them. Office Depot's application, built and hosted by NetByTel Inc. in Boca Raton, Florida, uses voice synthesis and recognition technologies to let shoppers find and purchase goods from the retailer's online catalog.

Ken Jackowitz, Office Depot's vice president of business systems, says NetByTel's technology, which understands and interprets natural language phrases, offers a user-friendly alternative to interactive voice response—the typical "press 1 for . . ." telephone application. With the new voice technology, spoken commands are sent to a speech server that recognizes the spoken word and sends the results to a VoiceXML server. VoiceXML software processes the request and formulates a response, which is then sent back over the phone using synthesized speech.

With the NetByTel system, customers provide the necessary information by responding verbally to prompts instead of punching buttons. If NetByTel needs information from Office Depot—a product description, for example—it retrieves it by initiating an XML-based client session with the Office Depot web site in Delray Beach, Florida. Jackowitz says no burden was placed on his IT team because the system leveraged Office Depot's existing infrastructure to provide the data interface, and NetByTel developed and hosted the applications.

The new system accounts for 5% of all of Office Depot's retail catalog orders, Jackowitz says. Orders handled by NetByTel cost 88% less to process than orders placed through a human operator, he estimates, and orders that come through the system average more items than the average six items per order placed through human operators.

Because NetByTel develops and hosts the applications for each customer and charges a flat per-transaction fee, Office Depot's up-front cost for voice recognition technology was low. That pay-as-you-go business model, says Jackie Fenn, an analyst at Gartner Group Inc., means that NetByTel has a solid financial proposition for most of its customers.

But NetByTel's approach may not make sense for companies where speech recognition is a key component of the business model, Fenn says. Companies that want to build multiple voice-based applications may find it more economical in the long run to buy the necessary technology and train internal people to use it. A large organization, like Fidelity Investments, which has extensive voice-based customer self-service applications, wouldn't be a good customer, she says.

However, NetByTel's CEO and co-founder, Neal Bernstein, says he doesn't see many companies taking the applications in-house. The secret to a successful voice-based application, he says, isn't just the technology, but also the human factors, such as knowing when and how long to pause for responses, how to differentiate among ambiguous answers and how to design a script so that customers feel comfortable with the system.

Bernstein says the firm's immediate plans are to improve the naturalness of the product's speaking voice. Long-term goals include improving the software's understanding of natural-language commands. NetByTel also plans to expand the types of applications it builds, says Bernstein. Right now, the vendor focuses on voice-recognition ordering systems for web-based E-commerce sites. But NetByTel could also support applications like expense reporting and delivery-status updates, he says.

There's already an example of such an application at Office Depot. NetByTel's order entry application was so successful, says Jackowitz, that Office Depot commissioned a voice-based system for the company's delivery drivers to report problems. As a result, more up-to-date information has been available to service representatives who handle order-status inquiries, he says.

Case Study Questions

1. What is the business purpose and value of Office Depot's web-enabled voice recognition system?

2. What other E-commerce and E-business applications might benefit from this technology? Give several examples.

3. Should a company attempt to buy this technology and develop applications itself, or let providers like NetByTel develop and host such applications? Why or why not?

Source: Adapted from Amy Johnson, "Helping Web Sites Take Phone Calls," *Computerworld*, February 5, 2001, p. 65, and Robert Poe, "Now You're Talking," *Business 2.0*, February 6, 2001, pp. 52–53.

Staples, Ames, Best Buy and REI: Using In-Store Web Kiosks

In a bid to boost sales and services through its E-commerce website, office products retailer Staples Inc. last week announced that it has equipped each of its 954 U.S. stores with interactive Internet kiosks that customers can use to order items from the company's online catalog.

Framingham, Massachusetts–based Staples, which previously tested the kiosks at 20 stores, said it's installing up to four of the systems at each retail location. The kiosks will pave the way for the company to expand the number of items that can be ordered in its stores from 7,500 to 45,000, plus more than 100,000 software packages and dozens of business services.

The idea of in-store Internet kiosks isn't new. Barnes & Noble Inc., Best Buy Co. and Kmart Corp. have all installed microcomputer-based networked kiosk systems for online Web catalog browsing and buying in an attempt to make it possible for shoppers to buy items that can't be crammed onto the shelves. But the success of interactive systems that let shoppers browse through web-based catalogs depends heavily on the makeup of a retailer's customer base and whether the technology goes beyond what can be bought in a store, said Barrett Ladd, an analyst at Gomez Advisors.

For example, Ames Department Stores, based in Rocky Hill, Connecticut, installed kiosks in 10 of its stores in 1999 so customers could view products from vendors, said corporate spokeswoman Amy Romano. The experiment lasted only about six months; the discount retailer's customer base—harried mothers with children in tow—simply didn't have time to browse a website, Romano said. She also agreed with Ladd that at least some of the disinterest in the kiosks had to do with Ames' customers being less computer-savvy than shoppers at higher-end stores.

Minneapolis-based Best Buy has seen great success with two types of kiosks it installed in 412 stores: one on which customers can buy laptop and desktop computers, and another for shopping at the store's online site, Bestbuy.com. A spokeswoman said that in December, more than one-third of Best Buy's computer sales came from in-store kiosk orders.

REI sees the web as a way of expanding its retail floor space. From the website, customers can order items that the store may not have in stock—and there are bound to be a few because the site stocks 78,000 items, tens of thousands more than a typical store or catalog. Store employees can also order items from the website via their cash registers, which have been Internet-enabled since 1999.

Kiosks, which started showing up in REI stores in 1997, are not just for order-taking. Customers and employees can print out background information from REI's website related to the products in the store—say, a price list for all canoes or a list of the kinds of clothes and gear needed on a cold-weather kayak trip. Seema Williams, a senior analyst with Forrester Research, notes that REI could be more creative with its kiosks. Rather that just offering access to the website, kiosks could offer access to special applications designed to help customers make a decision about a product in the store. However, REI is quick to point out that its in-store kiosks have been a hit with their customers for several years now, with revenues from all kiosks equaling the average revenue of a traditional store.

A study on the success of Internet kiosks that was conducted by Summit Research Associates found that three out of 10 projects failed because the machines weren't sufficiently maintained or didn't function properly from the start. But Francie Mendelsohn, the research firm's president, doesn't think Staples is likely to join the list of the failures. Staples is "a very smart . . . retailer," she said.

Case Study Questions

1. What are several reasons why providing in-store Web kiosks can be a successful E-business initiative?

2. What are several reasons why installing such kiosks can be an E-business failure?

3. What other applications could be supported by in-store Web kiosks besides online catalog shopping? Give several examples.

Source: Adapted from Lucas Mearian, "Staples Joins Kiosk Retailers," *Computerworld*, February 5, 2001, p. 12, and Sari Kalin, "E-Business as Usual," *Darwin*, February 2001, p. 51.

Grede Foundries and IBM: Mainframes for Linux and Web Applications

"Linux is bringing a lot more flexibility to the mainframe than ever before," said Rich Smrcina, a data center manager at Milwaukee-based Grede Foundries Inc. The company currently has two website software servers running the Linux open-source operating system on its IBM mainframe, in addition to other Linux server software used for e-mail and network monitoring. The Linux systems have been in place for more than a year and have "been great so far" from a performance and reliability standpoint, Smrcina said.

As part of an effort to tap users such as Grede, IBM said it plans to roll out a series of Linux initiatives aimed at delivering education, certification, co-marketing, incentives and technical support for its business partners. And Big Blue is putting big money behind its words. IBM chairman Lou Gerstner vowed to invest $1 billion in expanding support for all Linux applications in 2001. IBM obviously sees a great business opportunity in supporting Linux for a wide variety of business and scientific applications, as well as the open-source community that supports it.

IBM is betting that its increased support for Linux applications on mainframes, combined with the ability of those systems to simultaneously run multiple workloads, will help drive big-iron machines into new kinds of applications. The computer maker is predicting that at least half of its mainframe sales will go into new E-business application areas such as enterprise resource planning, E-commerce, customer relationship management and server consolidations, said Dan Colby, IBM's general manager of enterprise servers.

The performance, reliability and enormous scalability of mainframes continue to make them a natural fit for those applications, Colby said. He added that IBM is hoping to attract users through mainframes such as its new zSeries 900, which are able to run virtually thousands of Linux server applications within a single box. IBM also plans to attract users with the increasing availability of Linux-enabled mainframe tools and software.

IBM is also strengthening efforts to keep business users from migrating off its mainframes. For example, users who are contemplating switching from IBM's older mainframes to other computer systems will be able to get financial incentives, greater discounts, bundled software deals and migration services if they remain with IBM. Also, users of IBM's Generation 3 and Generation 4 mainframes will automatically be upgraded to a Generation 5 system when they buy a Linux mainframe software engine for $250,000.

In addition, IBM has developed a line of small mainframes using Intel microprocessors in a multiprocessor design, and is aiming these mainframe servers at lower-end customers that typically require 30 MIPS of performance or less. For example, IBM has just introduced a 64-processor mainframe server with up to 64 gigabytes of memory to service this market.

IBM's mainframe forecasts are consistent with the 40% to 45% growth in demand for mainframe MIPs that's expected in 2001, said David Floyer, an analyst at ITCentrix. Much of the expected growth will come from users trying to extend their mainframe environments to new applications, he said. "Many of IBM's customers have their core data and applications on their mainframes. They want to web-enable those applications and provide access to that data for other applications," Floyer explained.

IBM is also hoping to make some incremental sales by winning back customers who are currently using plug-compatible mainframes from former big-iron vendors Hitachi Data Systems and Amdahl Corp. Both companies abandoned the mainframe business in 2000, leaving IBM as the world's sole supplier of mainframe computer systems.

Case Study Questions

1. What does this case reveal about the future of the mainframe as a viable category of computer systems?

2. Why is IBM choosing support for Linux as a strategy for expanding the use of mainframes?

3. Do you think that IBM will be successful in expanding the use of mainframe computer systems? Why or why not?

Source: Adapted from Jaikumar Vijayan, "IBM: Linux Apps Will Drive Big-Iron Usage," *Computerworld*, March 5, 2001, p. 10, and Todd Weiss, "IBM Adds Supercomputer Features to Linux Servers," *Computerworld*, March 26, 2001, p.14.

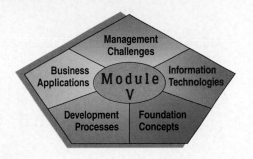

Management
Challenges

Business
Applications

Module
V

Information
Technologies

Development
Processes

Foundation
Concepts

Chapter 12

Computer Software

Chapter Highlights

Learning Objectives

After reading and studying this chapter, you should be able to:

1. Describe several important trends occurring in computer software.

2. Give examples of several major types of application and system software.

3. Explain the purpose of several popular software packages for end user productivity and collaborative computing.

4. Outline the functions of an operating system.

5. Describe the main uses of high-level, fourth-generation, object-oriented, and Web-oriented programming languages and tools.

Section I

Application Software: End User Applications

Introduction to Software

This chapter presents an overview of the major types of software you depend on as you work with computers and access computer networks. It discusses their characteristics and purposes and gives examples of their uses. Before we begin, let's look at an example of the changing world of software in business.

Analyzing Hershey Direct and Norm Thompson

Read the Real World Case on on Hershey Direct and Norm Thompson on the next page. We can learn a lot about the business impact of offering software as online services from this example. See Figure 12.1

The software world is changing, as the Internet drives changes in other information technologies and applications. One of the latest developments is for software companies (like Intuit, for example), to make software available online to consumers and businesses to use for a fee on a per use basis, rather than purchasing and downloading software products. The other related development is from companies called application services providers (ASPs), who offer to completely handle the processing of selected business applications for a company as an online service. Hershey Direct is an example of a company E-commerce division which contracted with an ASP called Usinternetworking to set up and handle the applications needed to run their website so they could concentrate on the business aspects of their E-commerce intiative. Norm Thompson is an example of a company that evaluated and rejected the ASP model as being significantly more expensive than doing everything themselves. But the big software companies like Oracle, SAP, and Peoplesoft are entering the ASP and online software services business, seeing it as a major new source of revenue for their products.

Software Trends

Let's begin our analysis of software by looking at an overview of the major types and functions of **application software** and **system software** available to computer users, shown in Figure 12.2. This figure summarizes the major categories of system

Figure 12.1

Tim Chou, President of Oracle Business OnLine, says that software companies must offer software as services to survive.

Robert Holmgren.

Hershey Direct and Norm Thompson: Evaluating Online Software Services

The rules of the software game have changed over the past five years. Today's consumers are less inclined to spend money on desktop software applications. Most applications come bundled with their PCs, personal digital assistants (PDAs), MP3 players or video cameras. Or are given away like Microsoft's Explorer or Netscape's Navigator browsers. Even Sun Microsystems gives away its productivity suite, Star Office, as a free download.

Now, plenty of people believe that the wave of the future is offering software as a service that's delivered over the Web. Corporations have been complaining for years about the expense and trouble of computing systems. They have to pay millions of dollars for hardware and software, then more each year to maintain and update them. But with application service providers handling these tasks, they could concentrate on running their businesses—and simply pay the ASP a monthly fee.

For example, Carey Eisenhower, Internet marketing manager for the Hershey Direct Division of Hershey Foods Corp., says he's saving at least 20% per year on software management costs because he's a customer of ASP pioneer USinternetworking. There is an added plus: "We didn't have the expertise to build an E-commerce site. USi did," says Eisenhower.

The notion of software as a service could turn the traditional packaged software world upside down. USi's innovation was to offer the full array of corporate applications—from accounting to materials planning—as services delivered via the Web. IDC dubbed this an application service provider (ASP).

For a while, the computing world was nuts about ASPs. But just as quickly they fell out of favor. So what went wrong? The biggest obstacle has been inertia. It's just plain hard to persuade people to try something new. Corporate IT departments are reluctant to give up control over their computing systems. And CEOs are worried about net security and fret about handing important business data over to another company.

Even among customers who get satisfactory service, there's a tendency to move cautiously. At Hershey, for example, just one tiny portion of the company, an E-commerce site called Hershey Direct, has gone online with an ASP. The rest of the company's computing systems are run through a separate computing division that sticks to running software the old-fashioned way.

For some, the numbers simply don't add up. "I just don't see the benefit," says Matthew Abraham, vice president of information systems at Norm Thompson, an apparel catalog company in Portland, Oregon. Abraham took a hard look at the ASP services of both USi and Corio because he didn't want to invest in the equipment and personnel to run new human resources software from PeopleSoft. His conclusion: He would have actually spent 20% more per year with an ASP than if he handled everything himself. The ASPs claim they would have been cheaper partly because they believe Abraham underestimates the cost of building and operating fail-safe computing systems like the ones they provide.

The big software companies are quickly becoming forces to reckon with. The furthest along: Intuit Corp., the $1 billion maker of financial and tax software for small businesses and consumers. Already, Intuit is reaping more than 20% of its revenues from online services. Every piece of packaged Intuit software, from the QuickBooks accounting program to TurboTax, has an online counterpart.

While Intuit has the jump on its brethren, other major software makers vow to excel at delivering their software as services. Software heavyweights such SAP, Oracle, and PeopleSoft have a distinct advantage over the first generation ASPs when it comes to profit margins. They don't have to buy somebody else's software—they make it themselves. In the past year, Oracle doubled, to 100, the number of customers using its finance, manufacturing, and customer-service applications online. With SAP, 16 ASPs are hosting its applications for 150 companies, and now it has begun selling services directly to customers.

However, software giant Microsoft is going at this market a bit differently. While it offers its Office desktop applications to customers through a handful of online hosting services, its main goal is to provide a new Web-oriented platform of software products for corporations and ASPs to build upon—the so-called .Net technology.

But Oracle's Tim Chou, President of Oracle Business OnLine is adamant: "If software companies don't do this maybe not today, but somewhere down the line—they are going to die."

Case Study Questions

1. Do you agree that "the rules of the software game have changed"? Why or why not?

2. What are the advantages and disadvantages to a business of using software as a service provided by an ASP or software company?

3. Should consumers switch to using software as a service, instead of buying software packages? Why or why not?

Source: Adapted from Om Malik, "Dueling Desktops," *Red Herring*, March 6, 2001, pp. 94–96, and Jim Kerstetter, "Software Shakeout," *Business Week*, March 5, 2001, pp. 72–80.

and application software we will discuss in this chapter. Of course, this is a conceptual illustration. The types of software you will encounter depend primarily on the types of computers and networks you use, and on what specific tasks you want to accomplish.

Figure 12.3 emphasizes several major **software trends.** First, there has been a major trend away from custom-designed programs developed by the professional programmers of an organization. Instead, the trend is toward the use of off-the-shelf software packages acquired by end users from software vendors. This trend dramatically increased with the development of relatively inexpensive and easy-to-use application software packages and multipurpose *software suites* for microcomputers. The trend has accelerated recently, as software packages are designed with Web-enabled networking capabilities and collaboration features that optimize their usefulness for end users and workgroups on the Internet and corporate intranets and extranets. Also, many software packages can now be downloaded, updated, managed, and rented or leased from software companies or *application service providers* (ASPs) over the Internet and corporate intranets.

Second, there has been a steady trend away from (1) technical, machine-specific programming languages using binary-based or symbolic codes, or (2) *procedural languages*, which use brief statements and mathematical expressions to specify the sequence of instructions a computer must perform. Instead, the trend is toward the use of a visual graphic interface for object-oriented programming, or toward non-procedural *natural languages* for programming that are closer to human conversation. This trend accelerated with the creation of easy-to-use, nonprocedural *fourth-generation languages* (4GLs). It continues to grow as developments in object technology, graphics, and artificial intelligence produce natural language and graph-

Figure 12.2

An overview of computer software. Note the major types and examples of application and system software.

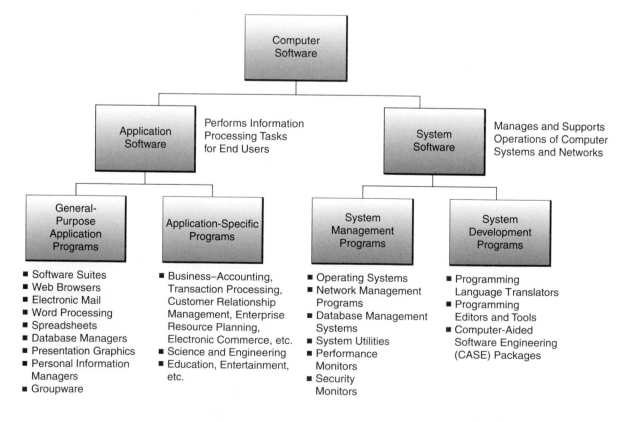

Figure 12.3   Trends in computer software. The trend in software is toward multipurpose, Web-enabled, expert-assisted packages with natural language and graphical user interfaces.

	FIRST GENERATION	SECOND GENERATION	THIRD GENERATION	FOURTH GENERATION	FIFTH GENERATION?
	Trend: Toward Easy-to-Use Multipurpose Web–Enabled Application Packages for Productivity and Collaboration				
Software Trends	User-Written Programs Machine Languages	Packaged Programs Symbolic Languages	Operating Systems High-Level Languages	Database Management Systems Fourth-Generation Languages Microcomputer Packages	Natural and Object-Oriented Languages Multipurpose Graphic-Interface Network-Enabled Expert-Assisted Packages
	Trend: Toward Visual or Conversational Programming Languages and Tools				

ical user interfaces that make both programming tools and software packages easier to use.

In addition, artificial intelligence features are built into many types of software packages. For example, software suites provide intelligent help features called *wizards* that help you perform common software functions like graphing parts of a spreadsheet or generating reports from a database. Other software packages use capabilities called *intelligent agents* to perform activities based on instructions from a user. For example, some electronic mail packages can use an intelligent agent capability to organize, send, and screen E-mail messages for you.

These major trends seem to be converging to produce a fifth generation of powerful, multipurpose, expert-assisted, and Web-enabled software packages with natural language and graphical interfaces to support the productivity and collaboration of both end users and IS professionals.

Application Software for End Users

Figure 12.2 showed that application software includes a variety of programs that can be subdivided into general-purpose and application-specific categories. Thousands of **application-specific** software packages are available to support specific applications of end users in business and other fields. For example, application-specific packages in business support managerial, professional, and business uses such as transaction processing, decision support, accounting, sales management, investment analysis, and electronic commerce. Application-specific software for science and engineering plays a major role in the research and development programs of industry and the design of efficient production processes for high-quality products. Other software packages help end users with personal finance and home management, or provide a wide variety of entertainment and educational products.

General-purpose application programs are programs that perform common information processing jobs for end users. For example, word processing programs, spreadsheet programs, database management programs, and graphics programs are popular with microcomputer users for home, education, business, scientific, and many other purposes. Because they significantly increase the productivity of end users, they are sometimes known as *productivity packages*. Other examples include Web browsers, electronic mail, and *groupware*, which help support communication and collaboration among workgroups and teams.

Software Suites and Integrated Packages

Let's begin our discussion of popular general-purpose application software by looking at **software suites.** That's because the most widely used productivity packages come bundled together as software suites such as Microsoft Office, Lotus Smart-Suite, Corel WordPerfect Office, and Sun's StarOffice. Examining their components gives us an overview of the important software tools that you can use to increase your productivity.

Figure 12.4 compares the basic programs that make up the top four software suites. Notice that each suite integrates software packages for word processing, spreadsheets, presentation graphics, database management, and personal information management. Microsoft, Lotus, Corel, and Sun bundle several other programs in each suite, depending on the version you select. Examples include programs for Internet access, E-mail, Web publishing, desktop publishing, voice recognition, financial management, electronic encyclopedias, and so on.

A software suite costs a lot less than the total cost of buying its individual packages separately. Another advantage is that all programs use a similar **graphical user interface** (GUI) of icons, tool and status bars, menus, and so on, which gives them the same look and feel, and makes them easier to learn and use. Software suites also share common tools, such as spell checkers and help wizards to increase their efficiency. Another big advantage of suites is that their programs are designed to work together seamlessly and import each other's files easily, no matter which program you are using at the time. These capabilities make them more efficient and easier to use than using a variety of individual package versions.

Of course, putting so many programs and features together in one super-size package does have some disadvantages. Industry critics argue that many software suite features are never used by most end users. The suites take up a lot of disk space, from over 100 megabytes to over 150 megabytes, depending on which version or functions you install. So such software is sometimes derisively called *bloatware* by its critics. The cost of suites can vary from as low as $100 for a competitive upgrade to over $700 for a full version of some editions of the suites.

These drawbacks are one reason for the continued use of **integrated packages** like Microsoft Works, Lotus eSuite WorkPlace, AppleWorks, and so on. Integrated packages combine some of the functions of several programs—word processing, spreadsheets, presentation graphics, database management, and so on—into one software package. See Figure 12.5.

Because Works programs leave out many features and functions that are in individual packages and software suites, they cannot do as much as those packages do. However, they use a lot less disk space (less than 10 megabytes), cost less than a hundred dollars, and are frequently pre-installed on many low-end microcomputer sys-

Figure 12.4

The basic program components of the top four software suites. Other programs may be included, depending on the suite edition selected.

Programs	Microsoft Office	Lotus SmartSuite	Corel WordPerfect Office	Sun StarOffice
Word Processor	Word	WordPro	WordPerfect	StarWriter
Spreadsheet	Excel	1-2-3	Quattro Pro	StarCalc
Presentation Graphics	PowerPoint	Freelance	Presentations	StarImpress
Database Manager	Access	Approach	Paradox	StarBase
Personal Information Manager	Outlook	Organizer	Corel Central	StarSchedule

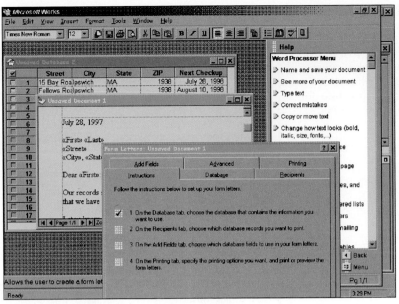

Figure 12.5

Using the Microsoft Works integrated package. It provides word processing, spreadsheet, file management, telecommunications, and graphics capabilites in one package.

D. Moskowitz/Warm Boot.

tems. So integrated packages have proven that they offer enough functions and features for many computer users, while providing some of the advantages of software suites in a smaller package.

Web Browsers and More

The most important software component for many computer users today is the once simple and limited, but now powerful and feature-rich, **Web browser.** A browser like Netscape Navigator or Microsoft Explorer is the key software interface you use to point and click your way through the hyperlinked resources of the World Wide Web and the rest of the Internet, as well as corporate intranets and extranets. Once limited to surfing the Web, browsers are becoming the universal software platform on which end users launch into information searches, E-mail, multimedia file transfer, discussion groups, and many other Internet, intranet, and extranet applications. See Figure 12.6.

Industry experts are predicting that the Web browser will be the model for how most people will use networked computers in the future. So now, whether you want to watch a video, make a phone call, download some software, hold a videoconference, check your E-mail, or work on a spreadsheet of your team's business plan, you can use your browser to launch and host such applications. That's why browsers are being called the *universal client*, that is, the software component installed on the workstations of all the clients (users) in client/server networks throughout an enterprise.

Electronic Mail

The first thing many people do at work all over the world is check their E-mail. **Electronic mail** has changed the way people work and communicate. Millions of end users now depend on E-mail software to communicate with each other by sending and receiving electronic messages via the Internet or their organizations' intranets or extranets. E-mail is stored on network servers until you are ready. Whenever you want to, you can read your E-mail by displaying it on your workstations. So, with only a few minutes of effort (and a few microseconds or minutes of transmission time), a message to one or many individuals can be composed, sent, and received. See Figure 12.7.

Figure 12.6

You can use a Web browser like Netscape Navigator to access the Quicken.com website and link to the Charles Schwab website for investment information.

Courtesy of Quicken.com.

As we mentioned earlier, E-mail software is now a component of top software suites and Web browsers. Free E-mail packages like Microsoft HotMail and Netscape WebMail are available to Internet users from online services and Internet service providers. Full-featured E-mail software like Microsoft Exchange E-Mail or Netscape Messenger can route messages to multiple end users based on predefined mailing lists and provide password security, automatic message forwarding, and remote user access. They also allow you to store messages in folders with provisions for adding attachments to message files. E-mail packages may also enable you to edit and send graphics and multimedia as well as text, and provide bulletin board and computer conferencing capabilities. Finally, your E-mail software may automatically filter and sort incoming messages (even news items from online services) and route them to appropriate user mailboxes and folders.

Word Processing and Desktop Publishing

Software for **word processing** has transformed the process of writing. Word processing packages computerize the creation, editing, revision, and printing of *documents* (such as letters, memos, and reports) by electronically processing your *text data* (words, phrases, sentences, and paragraphs). Top word processing packages like Microsoft Word, Lotus WordPro, and Corel WordPerfect can provide a wide variety of attractively printed documents with their desktop publishing capabilities. These packages can also convert all documents to HTML format for publication as Web pages on corporate intranets or the World Wide Web.

Word processing packages also provide advanced features. For example, a spelling checker capability can identify and correct spelling errors, and a thesaurus feature helps you find a better choice of words to express ideas. You can also identify and correct grammar and punctuation errors, as well as suggest possible improvements in your writing style, with grammar and style checker functions. Another text productivity tool is an idea processor or outliner function. It helps you organize and outline your thoughts before you prepare a document or develop a presentation.

Figure 12.7

Using the Microsoft
Outlook E-mail package.

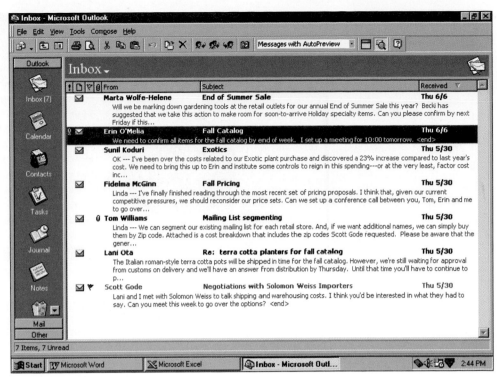

Courtesy of Microsoft Corporation.

Besides converting documents to HTML format, you can also use the top packages to design and create Web pages from scratch for an Internet or intranet website. See Figure 12.8.

End users and organizations can use **desktop publishing** (DTP) software to produce their own printed materials that look professionally published. That is, they can design and print their own newsletters, brochures, manuals, and books with several type styles, graphics, photos, and colors on each page. Word processing packages and desktop publishing packages like Adobe PageMaker and QuarkXPress are used to do desktop publishing. Typically, text material and graphics can be generated by word processing and graphics packages and imported as text and graphics files. Optical scanners may be used to input text and graphics from printed material. You can also use files of *clip art*, which are predrawn graphic illustrations provided by the software package or available from other sources.

The heart of desktop publishing is a page design process called *page makeup* or *page composition*. Your video screen becomes an electronic pasteup board with rulers, column guides, and other page design aids. Text material and illustrations are then merged into the page format you design. The software will automatically move excess text to another column or page and help size and place illustrations and headings. Most DTP packages provide WYSIWYG (What You See Is What You Get) displays so you can see exactly what the finished document will look like before it is printed.

Electronic Spreadsheets

Electronic spreadsheet packages like Lotus 1-2-3, Microsoft Excel, and Corel QuattroPro are used for business analysis, planning, and modeling. They help you develop an *electronic spreadsheet*, which is a worksheet of rows and columns that can be stored on your PC or a network server, or converted to HTML format and stored as a Web page or *websheet* on the World Wide Web. Developing a

Figure 12.8

Using the Microsoft Word word processing package. Note the insertion of clip art.

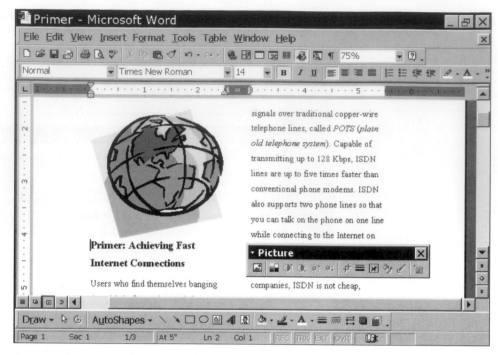

Courtesy of Microsoft Corporation.

spreadsheet involves designing its format and developing the relationships (formulas) that will be used in the worksheet. In response to your input, the computer performs necessary calculations based on the formulas you defined in the spreadsheet, and displays results immediately, whether at your workstation or website. Most packages also help you develop graphic displays of spreadsheet results. See Figure 12.9.

Figure 12.9

Using an electronic spreadsheet package, Microsoft Excel. Note the use of graphics.

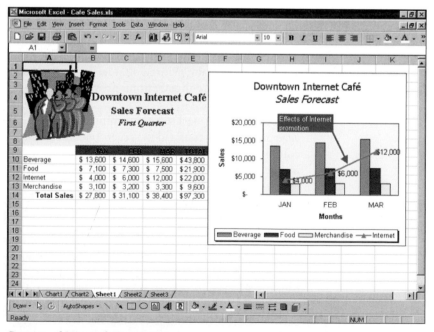

Courtesy of Microsoft Corporation.

For example, you could develop a spreadsheet to record and analyze past and present advertising performance for a business. You could also develop hyperlinks to a similar websheet at your marketing team's intranet website. Now you have a decision support tool to help you answer *what-if questions* you may have about advertising. For example, "What would happen to market share if advertising expense increased by 10 percent?" To answer this question, you would simply change the advertising expense formula on the advertising performance worksheet you developed. The computer would recalculate the affected figures, producing new market share figures and graphics. You would then have a better insight on the effect of advertising decisions on market share. Then you could share this insight with a note on the websheet at your team's intranet website.

Database Management

Microcomputer versions of **database management** programs have become so popular that they are now viewed as general-purpose application software packages like word processing and spreadsheet packages. Database management packages such as Microsoft Access, Lotus Approach, or Corel Paradox allow you to set up and manage databases on your PC, network server, or the World Wide Web. See Figure 12.10. Most database managers can perform four primary tasks, which we will discuss further in Chapter 13.

- **Database development.** Define and organize the content, relationships, and structure of the data needed to build a database, including any hyperlinks to data on Web pages.
- **Database interrogation.** Access the data in a database to display information in a variety of formats. End users can selectively retrieve and display information and produce forms, reports, and other documents, including Web pages.
- **Database maintenance.** Add, delete, update, and correct the data in a database, including hyperlinked data on Web pages.
- **Application development.** Develop prototypes of Web pages, queries, forms, reports, and labels for a proposed business application. Use a built-in 4GL or application generator to program the application.

Figure 12.10

Using a database management package. Note how Microsoft Access lets you select and preview a variety of database files.

Courtesy of Microsoft Corporation.

Presentation Graphics and Multimedia

Which type of display would you rather see: columns or rows of numbers, or a graphics display of the same information? **Presentation graphics** packages help you convert numeric data into graphics displays such as line charts, bar graphs, pie charts, and many other types of graphics. Most of the top packages also help you prepare multimedia presentations of graphics, photos, animation, and video clips, including publishing to the World Wide Web. Not only are graphics and multimedia displays easier to comprehend and communicate than numeric data but multiple-color and multiple-media displays also can more easily emphasize key points, strategic differences, and important trends in the data. Presentation graphics has proved to be much more effective than tabular presentations of numeric data for reporting and communicating in advertising media, management reports, or other business presentations.

Presentation graphics software packages like Microsoft PowerPoint, Lotus Freelance, or Corel Presentations give you many easy-to-use capabilities that encourage the use of graphics presentations. For example, most packages help you design and manage computer-generated and -orchestrated *slide shows* containing many integrated graphics and multimedia displays. Or you can select from a variety of predesigned *templates* of business presentations, prepare and edit the outline and notes for a presentation, and manage the use of multimedia files of graphics, photos, sounds, and video clips. And of course, the top packages help you tailor your graphics and multimedia presentation for transfer in HTML format to websites on corporate intranets or the World Wide Web. See Figure 12.11.

Multimedia Software Technologies

Hypertext and hypermedia are software technologies for multimedia presentations. By definition, hypertext contains only text and a limited amount of graphics. Hypermedia are electronic documents that contain multiple forms of media, including text, graphics, video, and so on. Key topics and other presentations in hypertext or hypermedia documents are indexed by software links so that they can be quickly searched by the reader. For example, if you click your mouse button on an underlined term on a hypermedia document, your computer may instantly bring up another display

Figure 12.11

Using a presentation graphics package, Microsoft PowerPoint.

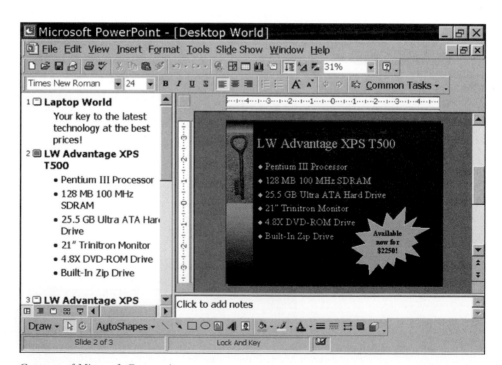

Courtesy of Microsoft Corporation.

using text, graphics, and sound related to that term. Once you finish viewing that presentation, you can return to what you were reading originally, or jump to another part of the document.

Hypertext and hypermedia are developed by using software packages that rely on specialized programming languages like Java and the Hypertext Markup Language (HTML), which create hyperlinks to other parts of a document or to other documents and multimedia files. Hypertext and hypermedia documents can thus be programmed to let a reader navigate through a multimedia database by following a chain of hyperlinks through various multimedia files. The websites on the World Wide Web of the Internet are a popular example of this technology. Thus, the use of hypertext and hypermedia software in Web browsers and other programs provides an environment for online interactive multimedia presentations. See Figure 12.12.

Personal Information Managers

The **personal information manager** (PIM) is a popular software package for end user productivity and collaboration, and is a popular application for personal digital assistant (PDA) hand-held devices. PIMs such as Lotus Organizer and Microsoft Outlook help end users store, organize, and retrieve information about customers, clients, and prospects, or schedule and manage appointments, meetings, and tasks. The PIM package will organize data you enter and retrieve information in a variety of forms, depending on the style and structure of the PIM and the information you want. For example, information can be retrieved as an electronic calendar or list of appointments, meetings, or other things to do; the timetable for a project; or a display of key facts and financial data about customers, clients, or sales prospects. See Figure 12.13.

Figure 12.12

Examples of software technologies for multimedia productions and presentations available on the World Wide Web.

Online Multimedia Technologies
● **Liquid Audio www.liquidaudio.com** Liquid Audio's Liquid Player is a program you can download for free to play Web-based audio tracks. MP3 and Liquid Audio compressed files are reproduced with CD-quality sound. The program lets you view album art and lyrics while you listen, set up custom play lists, and purchase a copy of the music from the publisher.
● **Macromedia Shockwave and Flash www.macromedia.com** Macromedia makes some of the most popular software for jazzing up Web pages with sound and animation. If your browser doesn't have the Shockwave and Flash player plug-ins, you can download them for free here. Check out the ShockRave website (www.shockrave.com) for a sampling of what's out there.
● **MP3.com www.mp3.com** The granddaddy of MP3 sites, MP3.com provides an open marketplace for thousands of artists and their fans. Listen to free sample tracks, then buy the whole album if it appeals to you. A new radio station, mp3radio.com, features streaming MP3s and links to purchase CDs.
● **RealNetworks www.real.com** RealNetworks software, RealPlayer G2, provides a slick user interface and much improved transmission of compressed audio and video. G2 is free, but for $29.95 you can download a copy of RealPlayer Plus G2, which offers several advanced features: an audio equalizer, fine-tuning for video, the ability to save media clips to your hard drive, phone support, a manual and CD-ROM, and one-click searches for broadcasts on the Web.
● **Winamp www.winamp.com** For Windows users, Winamp is a great shareware program—they ask for $10 to $20 if you keep using it—for playing back nearly every type of digital audio file you find online. Along with its virtual graphic equalizers, Winamp's SHOUTcast plug-in enables you to broadcast or listen to streaming MP3 radio.

Source: Adapted from "Tune In," Technology Buyers Guide, *Fortune*, Winter 2000, pp. 268–72, and "Changing the Channels," Technology Buyers Guide, *Fortune*, Winter 2001, pp. 266–70.

Figure 12.13

Using a personal
information manager
(PIM): Microsoft Outlook.

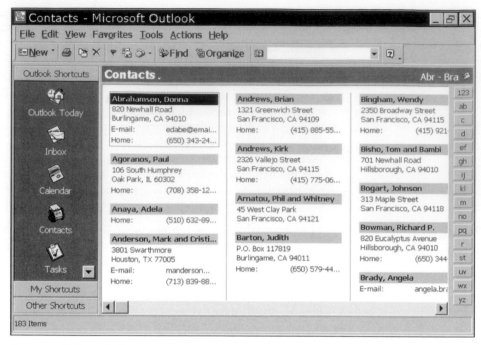

Courtesy of Microsoft Corporation.

Personal information managers are sold as independent programs or are included in software suites, and vary widely in their style, structure, and features. For example, Lotus Organizer uses a notebook with tabs format, while Microsoft Outlook organizes data about people as a continuous A-to-Z list. Most PIMs emphasize the maintenance of *contact lists*, that is, customers, clients, or prospects. Scheduling appointments and meetings and task management are other top PIM applications. PIMs are now changing to include the ability to access the World Wide Web and provide E-mail capability. Also, some PIMs use Internet and E-mail features to support team collaboration by sharing information such as contact lists, task lists, and schedules with other networked PIM users.

Groupware

Groupware is *collaboration software*, that is, software that helps workgroups and teams work together to accomplish group assignments. Groupware is a fast-growing category of general-purpose application software that combines a variety of software features and functions to facilitate collaboration. For example, groupware products like Lotus Notes, Novell GroupWise, Microsoft Exchange, and Netscape Communicator support collaboration through electronic mail, discussion groups and databases, scheduling, task management, data, audio and videoconferencing, and so on. See Figure 12.14.

Groupware products are changing in several ways to meet the demand for better tools for collaboration. Groupware is now designed to use the Internet and corporate intranets and extranets to make collaboration possible on a global scale by *virtual teams* located anywhere in the world. For example, team members might use the Internet for global E-mail, project discussion forums, and joint Web page development. Or they might use corporate intranets to publish project news and progress reports, and work jointly on documents stored on Web servers.

Collaborative capabilities are also being added to other software to give them groupware features. For example, in the Microsoft Office software suite, Microsoft Word keeps track of who made revisions to each document, Excel tracks all changes made to a spreadsheet, and Outlook lets you keep track of tasks you delegate to other team members.

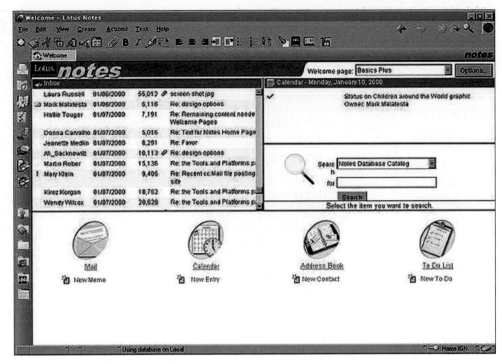

Figure 12.14

Lotus Notes is the leading corporate groupware package.

Courtesy of Lotus Development Corporation.

Other Business Software

As we mentioned earlier, there are many other types of application software used in business today. Application software packages support managerial and operational uses such as accounting, transaction processing, customer relationship management, enterprise resource planning, data warehousing and data mining, and electronic commerce, to name a few.

For example, data warehousing and data mining are discussed in Chapters 6 and 13; accounting, marketing, manufacturing, human resource management, and financial management applications are covered in Chapter 4, along with customer relationship management, enterprise resource planning, supply chain management, and electronic commerce. Decision support and data analysis applications are explored in Chapter 6. Figure 12.15 illustrates some of these major application software categories.

Figure 12.15

Some of the major application software categories in an E-business enterprise.

Source: Adapted from Ravi Kalakota and Marcia Robinson, *E-business: Roadmap for Success* (Reading, MA: Addison-Wesley, 2001), p. 243. © 2001 Addison-Wesley Publishing Company, Inc. Reprinted by permission of Addison-Wesley Longman Inc.

System Software: Computer System Management

System Software Overview

Analyzing TravelNow and BEA Systems

System software consists of programs that manage and support a computer system and its information processing activities. For example, operating systems and network management programs serve as a vital *software interface* between computer networks and hardware and the application programs of end users.

Read the Real World Case on TravelNow and BEA Systems on the next page. We can learn a lot about the business value of new developments in system software from this example. See Figure 12.16.

Like many companies, TravelNow has discovered that system software called application servers can dramatically improve the transaction processing capacity and capabilities of their E-commerce website. Application servers act as "middleware" between a website's application software and its computer operating systems. They not only significantly increase the processing efficiency of a site, but make changes and additions in web applications and functions a lot easier to implement. For example, instead of having to add more networked computer servers to handle a big increase in workload, TravelNow paid $90,000 for industry leader BEA System's WebLogic application server, and was able to reduce its website servers from twenty two to only three. However, they also had to pay over $500,000 in consultant's fees to rewrite all of their web applications in Java to work with WebLogic. But TravelNow's web applications can now be modified much more easily, and TravelNow is convinced that their old system would not have been able to handle the big increase in demands on their website.

Overview

Figure 12.17 shows that we can group system software into two major categories:

- **System management programs.** Programs that manage the hardware, software, network, and data resources of the computer system during its execution of the various information processing jobs of users. Examples of important system management programs are operating systems, network management programs, database management systems, and system utilities.

Bill Coleman, CEO of BEA Systems, leads the development of WebLogic Server, the industry's leading application server.

Darryl Estrine.

TravelNow and BEA Systems: The Business Case for Application Servers

When Chris Kuhn became the new chief information officer at TravelNow in July 1999, he realized that the online travel agency's website was headed for expensive trouble. Hotel and airline bookings had grown 220 percent during the previous year, and since there were no signs of slowing, he knew the site would start crashing if he didn't expand its capacity. Until recently that would have meant buying additional Web server hardware, networking those machines together, and hiring more employees to manage it all. But Kuhn decided to try another, potentially far less costly route: an application server, a new software technology that promised to greatly expand the site's capacity—without buying any new machines or enlarging the staff—and add lots of flexibility in the bargain.

Application servers essentially make a website's important work—running search engines, verifying a user's credit-card number, serving up news articles, and so forth—much faster and more efficient. An application server amounts to a layer of software inserted between a server's operating system (Windows, Linux, Sun Microsystems's Solaris, or another) and all those search engines and credit-card verifiers. It handles the heavy demands of serving up webpages, accessing databases, and hooking into back-office servers. Think of it as a kind of automatic transmission for your E-business; a super agile intermediary between your website's applications and the raw power of the server's CPU and operating system.

Another nice thing about an application server is that it greatly simplifies the procedure for adding new functions to your website. Most application servers use Sun's Java programming language, and unlike older programs written for a specific set of hardware and software, Java programs can work unchanged on almost any system. So if you suddenly realize that your website needs a function that, say, allows customers to see their previous purchases, adding that function is a matter of simply dropping in a bit of code.

Off-the-shelf applications written in Java—content management software and personalization routines, for example—can easily be added to the collection of software on your application server. And most of these servers run on multiple hardware and software configurations, so moving from low-end Windows or Linux machines to higher powered Unix servers doesn't require a painful process of "porting," or rewriting, all of your code.

It's hard to argue with benefits like those, and sure enough, the market for application servers is exploding. The current industry leader is BEA Systems, whose market capitalization, now nearly $20 billion, has risen 20-fold in the past two years. Giga Research estimates that BEA will end the year in a tie with IBM's WebSphere server for the greatest market share, at 24 percent each, with Art Technology Group's Dynamo server coming in third at 10 percent.

And where, you ask, is Microsoft? Off in its own proprietary world. Microsoft does offer application server features embedded within its super-heavy-duty versions of Windows 2000, but it is not written in Java and is tightly bound to Microsoft software and Intel-compatible hardware.

If you've never heard of BEA, you're not alone. You are, however, missing out on one of the biggest stories in the software industry. In the six years since Bill Coleman, Ed Scott, and Alfred Chuang founded BEA—christening it with each of their first initials—the San Jose–based company has become the leading supplier of application servers. More importantly, the application server is rapidly becoming a key component of E-business. By being the first to market and by staying one technological step ahead of the competition, BEA has poised itself to pull in more than $1 billion in revenues in 2001. And CEO Coleman has already proclaimed victory for BEA's technology.

So it should come as no surprise that TravelNow's Kuhn eventually settled on BEA's WebLogic Server, which cost about $90,000 in 1999 but allowed him to reduce his hardware from 22 servers to just three. There was a catch: It took almost six months to rewrite the site's applications in Java, with consulting fees of more than $500,000. But now that his programmers can add new functions and rewrite old ones much more easily than before, Kuhn doesn't expect to go through another rewrite anytime soon. He's glad he made the switch to an application server. "Our growth rate has been faster and harder than all the other years combined," he says. "There's no way the old system could have handled it."

Case Study Questions

1. What is the purpose of an application server?

2. What are some of the benefits and limitations of application servers for a business?

3. Why do you think Microsoft is not offering similar application server products? Is this a good business strategy? Why or why not?

Source: Adapted from Owen Thomas, "Websites Made Easier," *eCompany*, January/February 2001, and Ian Mount, "Bill Coleman Is Leading the Number one Software Company in a Niche That's About to Explode!" *eCompany*, March 2001, p. 106.

Figure 12.17

The system and application software interface between end users and computer hardware.

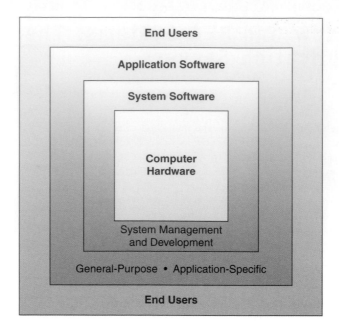

* **System development programs.** Programs that help users develop information system programs and procedures and prepare user programs for computer processing. Major development programs are programming language translators and editors, other programming tools, and CASE (computer-aided software engineering) packages.

Operating Systems

The most important system software package for any computer is its operating system. An **operating system** is an integrated system of programs that manages the operations of the CPU, controls the input/output and storage resources and activities of the computer system, and provides various support services as the computer executes the application programs of users.

The primary purpose of an operating system is to maximize the productivity of a computer system by operating it in the most efficient manner. An operating system minimizes the amount of human intervention required during processing. It helps your application programs perform common operations such as accessing a network, entering data, saving and retrieving files, and printing or displaying output. If you have any hands-on experience on a computer, you know that the operating system must be loaded and activated before you can accomplish other tasks. This emphasizes the fact that operating systems are the most indispensable components of the software interface between users and the hardware of their computer systems.

Operating System Functions

An operating system performs five basic functions in the operation of a computer system: providing a user interface, resource management, task management, file management, and utilities and support services. See Figure 12.18.

The User Interface. The **user interface** is the part of the operating system that allows you to communicate with it so you can load programs, access files, and accomplish other tasks. Three main types of user interfaces are the *command-driven*, *menu-driven*, and *graphical user interfaces*. The trend in user interfaces for operating systems and other software is moving away from the entry of brief end user commands, or even the selection of choices from menus of options. Instead, most software provides

Figure 12.18

The basic functions of an operating system include a user interface, resource management, task management, file management, and utilities and other functions.

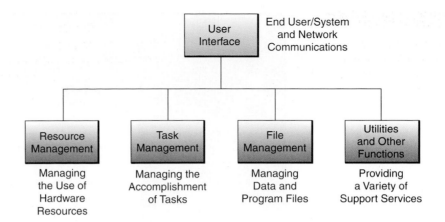

an easy-to-use **graphical user interface** (GUI) that uses icons, bars, buttons, boxes, and other images. GUIs rely on pointing devices like the electronic mouse or touch-pad to make selections that help you get things done. See Figure 12.19.

Resource Management. An operating system uses a variety of **resource management** programs to manage the hardware and networking resources of a computer system, including its CPU, memory, secondary storage devices, telecommunications processors, and input/output peripherals. For example, memory management programs keep track of where data and programs are stored. They may also subdivide memory into a number of sections and swap parts of programs and data between memory and magnetic disks or other secondary storage devices. This can provide a computer system with a **virtual memory** capability that is significantly larger than the real memory capacity of its primary storage circuits. So, a computer with a virtual memory capability can process large programs and greater amounts of data than the capacity of its memory chips would normally allow.

File Management. An operating system contains **file management** programs that control the creation, deletion, and access of files of data and programs. File management also involves keeping track of the physical location of files on magnetic disks and other secondary storage devices. So operating systems maintain directories of information about the location and characteristics of files stored on a computer system's secondary storage devices.

Task Management. The **task management** programs of an operating system manage the accomplishment of the computing tasks of end users. They give each task a slice of a CPU's time and interrupt the CPU operations to substitute other tasks. Task management may involve a **multitasking** capability where several computing tasks can occur at the same time. Multitasking may take the form of *multiprogramming*, where the CPU can process the tasks of several programs at the same time, or *timesharing*, where the computing tasks of several users can be processed at the same time. The efficiency of multitasking operations depends on the processing power of a CPU and the virtual memory and multitasking capabilities of the operating system it uses.

Most microcomputer, midrange, and mainframe operating systems provide a multitasking capability. With multitasking, end users can do two or more operations (e.g., keyboarding and printing) or applications (e.g., word processing and financial analysis) concurrently, that is, at the same time. Multitasking on microcomputers has also been made possible by the development of more powerful microprocessors and their ability to directly address much larger memory capacities (up to 4 gigabytes).

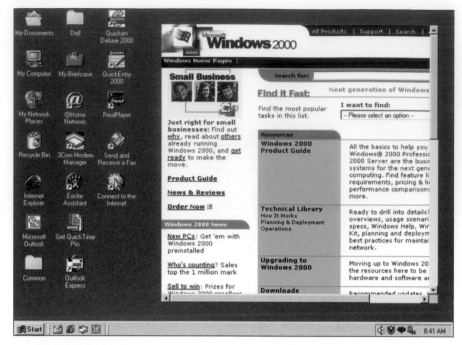

Figure 12.19

The graphical user interface of Microsoft's Windows 2000 operating system.

Courtesy of Microsoft Corporation.

This allows an operating system to subdivide primary storage into several large partitions, each of which can be used by a different application program.

In effect, a single computer can act as if it were several computers, or *virtual machines*, since each application program is running independently at the same time. The number of programs that can be run concurrently depends on the amount of memory that is available and the amount of processing each job demands. That's because a microprocessor (or CPU) can become overloaded with too many jobs and provide unacceptably slow response times. However, if memory and processing capacities are adequate, multitasking allows end users to easily switch from one application to another, share data files among applications, and process some applications in a *background* mode. Typically, background tasks include large printing jobs, extensive mathematical computation, or unattended telecommunications sessions.

Popular Operating Systems

Figure 12.20 compares the four top operating systems today. For many years, MS-DOS (Microsoft Disk Operating System) was the most widely used microcomputer operating system. It is a single-user, single-tasking operating system, but was given a graphical user interface and limited multitasking capabilities by combining it with Microsoft Windows. Microsoft began replacing its DOS/Windows combination in 1995 with the Windows 95 operating system, featuring a graphical user interface, true multitasking, networking, multimedia, and many other capabilities. Microsoft introduced an enhanced Windows 98 version during 1998, and a Windows Me (Millennium Edition) consumer PC system in 2000, with a Windows XP version due in 2001.

Microsoft introduced its **Windows NT** (New Technology) operating system in 1995. Windows NT is a powerful, multitasking, multiuser operating system that is installed on many network servers to manage client/server networks and on PCs with high-performance computing requirements. New Server and Workstation versions were introduced in 1997. Microsoft merged its Windows 98 and Windows NT products into the **Windows 2000** operating system during the year 2000.

Figure 12.20   A comparison of popular operating systems.

Windows 2000 — *Microsoft*	Solaris 8 UNIX — *Sun Microsystems*
What's New Improvements in reliability and the ability to manage computer networks less expensively. Handles some of the more demanding computing jobs, such as managing major websites.	**What's New** Solaris handles servers with as many as 64 microprocessors—compared with 32 for Windows 2000. Also, eight computers can be clustered together to work as one, compared with four for Windows 2000.
Strengths It is inexpensive. Used with servers based on Intel microprocessors, it's about one-third as expensive as UNIX-based combos from the likes of Sun.	**Strengths** Solaris has emerged as the server operating system of choice for large websites. It's super-reliable and handles the most demanding tasks.
Weaknesses It still can't run on most powerful servers, and many computer systems administrators don't trust it for complex computing tasks.	**Weaknesses** It is more expensive than Windows 2000 systems, though Sun is now offering Solaris free on low-end Sun servers.
Netware 5.1 — *Novell*	**Linux 6.1 — *Red Hat Software***
What's New Novell's directory software now runs on Windows 2000, Solaris, and Linux servers as well as NetWare, making it easier for companies to manage complex networks.	**What's New** It's easier to install than it used to be. Also, customers can now cluster up to eight servers—which means better reliability.
Strengths The directory software for keeping track of computers, programs, and people on a network has proved vital to companies such as Ford and Wal-Mart, and this update keeps it ahead.	**Strengths** Red Hat taps into tens of thousands of volunteer programmers who help out with improvements to the open-source Linux operating system. Plus, Red Hat's server package is nearly free: $149.
Weaknesses NetWare is primarily a networking system—not able to run general applications such as databases or accounting.	**Weaknesses** Linux is good for serving up Web pages, but isn't as effective as Windows 2000 at handling more complex jobs.

Source: Adapted from Steve Hamm, Peter Burrows, and Andy Reinhardt, "Is Windows Ready to Run E-Business?" *Business Week*, January 24, 2000, pp. 154–60. Reprinted with special permission, copyright © 2000 by The McGraw-Hill Companies, Inc.

Windows 2000 has four versions, including:

- *Professional:* a full-featured operating system for PC desktops and laptops.
- *Server:* a multipurpose operating system for network servers and Web servers in smaller networks.
- *Advanced Server:* a network operating system to manage large networks and websites powered by *server farms* of many servers.
- *Datacenter Server:* a high-performance network operating system for large-scale business applications, such as online transaction processing and data warehousing.

Originally developed by AT&T, **UNIX** now is also offered by other vendors, including Solaris by Sun Microsystems and AIX by IBM. UNIX is a multitasking, multiuser, network-managing operating system whose portability allows it to run on mainframes, midrange computers, and microcomputers. UNIX is a popular choice for Web and other network servers.

Linux is a low-cost, powerful, and reliable UNIX-like operating system that is rapidly gaining market share as a high-performance operating system for network servers and Web servers in both small and large networks. Linux was developed as free or low-cost *shareware* or *open-source software* over the Internet in the 1990s by Linus Torvald of Finland and millions of programmers around the world. Linux is still being enhanced in this way, but is sold with extra features and support services by software vendors such as Red Hat, Caldera, and VA Linux. PC versions are also available, which support office software suites, Web browsers, and other application software.

The **Mac OS X** is the latest operating system from Apple for the iMac and other Macintosh microcomputers. The Mac OS X has a new graphical user interface as well as advanced multitasking and multimedia capabilities, along with a new suite of Internet services called iTools [9].

Network Management Programs

Today's information systems rely heavily on the Internet, intranets, extranets, local area networks, and other telecommunications networks to interconnect end user workstations, network servers, and other computer systems. This requires a variety of system software for **network management,** including **network operating systems,** network performance monitors, telecommunications monitors, and so on. These programs are used by network servers and other computers in a network to manage network performance. Network management programs perform such functions as automatically checking client PCs and video terminals for input/output activity, assigning priorities to data communications requests from clients and terminals, and detecting and correcting transmission errors and other network problems. In addition, some network management programs function as *middleware* to help diverse networks communicate with each other. See Figure 12.21.

Examples of network management programs include Novell NetWare, the most widely used network operating system for complex interconnected local area networks. Microsoft's Windows NT Server and its new Windows 2000 server versions are other popular network operating systems. IBM's telecommunications monitor CICS (Customer Identification and Control System) is an example of a widely used *telecommunications monitor* for mainframe-based wide area networks. IBM's NetView and Hewlett-Packard's OpenView are examples of network management programs for managing several mainframe-based or midrange-based computer networks.

Database Management Systems

In Section I, we discussed microcomputer database management programs like Microsoft Access, Lotus Approach, and Corel Paradox. In mainframe and midrange computer systems, a **database management system** (DBMS) is considered an important system software package that controls the development, use, and maintenance of the databases of computer-using organizations. A DBMS program helps organizations use their integrated collections of data records and files known

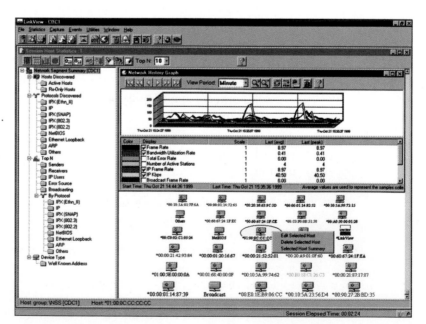

Courtesy of Tinwald Corporation.

as databases. It allows different user application programs to easily access the same database. For example, a DBMS makes it easy for an employee database to be accessed by payroll, employee benefits, and other human resource programs. A DBMS also simplifies the process of retrieving information from databases in the form of displays and reports. Instead of having to write computer programs to extract information, end users can ask simple questions in a *query language*. Thus, many DBMS packages provide *fourth-generation languages* (4GLs) and other application development features. Examples of popular mainframe and midrange packages are IBM's DB2 Universal Database and Oracle 9i by Oracle Corporation. We will discuss database management software in more detail in Chapter 13.

Other System Management Programs

Several other types of system management software are marketed as separate programs or are included as part of an operating system. Utility programs, or **utilities,** are an important example. Programs like Norton Utilities perform miscellaneous housekeeping and file conversion functions. Examples include data backup, data recovery, virus protection, data compression, and file defragmentation. Most operating systems also provide many utilities that perform a variety of helpful chores for computer users. See Figure 12.22.

Other examples of system support programs include performance monitors and security monitors. **Performance monitors** are programs that monitor and adjust the performance and usage of one or more computer systems to keep them running efficiently. **Security monitors** are packages that monitor and control the use of computer systems and provide warning messages and record evidence of unauthorized use of computer resources. A recent trend is to merge both types of programs into operating systems like Microsoft's Windows 2000 Datacenter Server, or into system management software like Computer Associates' CA-Unicenter, which can manage both mainframe systems and servers in a data center.

Programming Languages

To understand computer software, you need a basic knowledge of the role that programming languages play in the development of computer programs. A **programming language** allows a programmer to develop the sets of instructions that constitute a computer program. Many different programming languages have been developed, each with its own unique vocabulary, grammar, and uses.

Figure 12.22

The Diskeeper utility is a top-rated defragmentation program that dynamically eliminates fragmented file storage (as shown here), which dramatically improves hard drive performance.

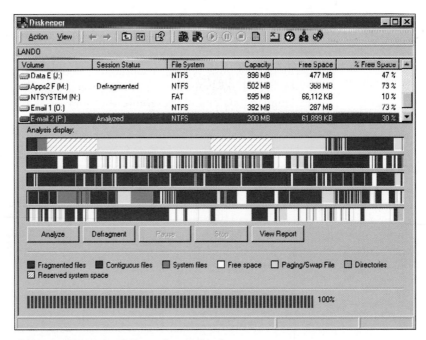

Courtesy of Executive Software International.

Machine Languages

Machine languages (or *first-generation languages*) are the most basic level of programming languages. In the early stages of computer development, all program instructions had to be written using binary codes unique to each computer. This type of programming involves the difficult task of writing instructions in the form of strings of binary digits (ones and zeros) or other number systems. Programmers must have a detailed knowledge of the internal operations of the specific type of CPU they are using. They must write long series of detailed instructions to accomplish even simple processing tasks. Programming in machine language requires specifying the storage locations for every instruction and item of data used. Instructions must be included for every switch and indicator used by the program. These requirements make machine language programming a difficult and error-prone task. A machine language program to add two numbers together in the CPU of a specific computer and store the result might take the form shown in Figure 12.23.

Assembler Languages

Assembler languages (or *second-generation languages*) are the next level of programming languages. They were developed to reduce the difficulties in writing machine language programs. The use of assembler languages requires language translator programs called *assemblers* that allow a computer to convert the instructions of such language into machine instructions. Assembler languages are frequently called symbolic languages because symbols are used to represent operation codes and storage locations. Convenient alphabetic abbreviations called *mnemonics* (memory aids) and other symbols represent operation codes, storage locations, and data elements. For example, the computation X = Y + Z in an assembler language might take the form shown in Figure 12.23.

Assembler languages are still used as a method of programming a computer in a machine-oriented language. Most computer manufacturers provide an assembler language that reflects the unique machine language instruction set of a particular line of computers. This feature is particularly desirable to *system programmers*, who program system software (as opposed to application programmers, who program application software), since it provides them with greater control and flexibility in designing a program for a particular computer. They can then produce more efficient software, that is, programs that require a minimum of instructions, storage, and CPU time to perform a specific processing assignment.

High-Level Languages

High-level languages (or *third-generation languages*) use instructions, which are called *statements*, that use brief statements or arithmetic expressions. Individual high-level language statements are actually *macroinstructions;* that is, each individual statement generates several machine instructions when translated into machine language by high-level language translator programs called *compilers* or *interpreters*. High-level language statements resemble the phrases or mathematical expressions required to

Figure 12.23

Examples of four levels of programming languages. These programming language instructions might be used to compute the sum of two numbers as expressed by the formula X = Y + Z.

● **Machine Languages:** Use binary coded instructions 1010 11001 1011 11010 1100 11011	● **High-Level Languages:** Use brief statements or arithmetic notations BASIC: X = Y + Z COBOL: COMPUTE X = Y + Z
● **Assembler Languages:** Use symbolic coded instructions LOD Y ADD Z STR X	● **Fourth-Generation Languages:** Use natural and nonprocedural statements SUM THE FOLLOWING NUMBERS

express the problem or procedure being programmed. The *syntax* (vocabulary, punctuation, and grammatical rules) and the *semantics* (meanings) of such statements do not reflect the internal code of any particular computer. For example, the computation $X = Y + Z$ would be programmed in the high-level languages of BASIC and COBOL as shown in Figure 12.23.

A high-level language is easier to learn and program than an assembler language, since it has less-rigid rules, forms, and syntaxes. However, high-level language programs are usually less efficient than assembler language programs and require a greater amount of computer time for translation into machine instructions. Since most high-level languages are machine independent, programs written in a high-level language do not have to be reprogrammed when a new computer is installed, and programmers do not have to learn a different language for each type of computer. Figure 12.24 highlights some of the major high-level languages still being used in some form today.

Fourth-Generation Languages

The term **fourth-generation language** describes a variety of programming languages that are more nonprocedural and conversational than prior languages. These languages are called fourth-generation languages (4GLs) to differentiate them from machine languages (first generation), assembler languages (second generation), and high-level languages (third generation).

Most fourth-generation languages are **nonprocedural languages** that encourage users and programmers to specify the results they want, while the computer determines the sequence of instructions that will accomplish those results. Thus, fourth-generation languages have helped simplify the programming process. **Natural languages** are 4GLs that are very close to English or other human languages. Research and development activity in artificial intelligence (AI) is developing programming languages that are as easy to use as ordinary conversation in one's native tongue. For example, INTELLECT, a natural language 4GL, would use a statement like, "What are the average exam scores in MIS 200?" to program a simple average exam score task.

The ease of use of 4GLs is gained at the expense of some loss in flexibility. It is frequently difficult to override some of the prespecified formats or procedures of 4GLs. Also, the machine language code generated by a program developed by a 4GL is frequently much less efficient (in terms of processing speed and amount of storage capacity needed) than a program written in a language like COBOL. Thus, some large transaction processing applications programmed in a 4GL have not provided reasonable response times when faced with a large amount of real-time transaction processing and end user inquiries. However, 4GLs have shown great success in business applications that do not have a high volume of transaction processing.

Figure 12.24

Highlights of several important high-level languages.

Ada: Named after Augusta Ada Byron, considered the world's first computer programmer. Developed for the U.S. Department of Defense as a standard "high-order language" to replace COBOL and FORTRAN.
BASIC: (Beginner's All-Purpose Symbolic Instruction Code). A simple procedure-oriented language designed for end user programming.
C: A mid-level structured language developed as part of the UNIX operating system. It resembles a machine-independent assembler language.
COBOL: (COmmon Business Oriented Language). An Englishlike language widely used for programming business applications.
FORTRAN: (FORmula TRANslation). A high-level language designed for scientific and engineering applications.
Pascal: Named after Blaise Pascal. Developed specifically to incorporate structured programming concepts.

Object-Oriented Languages

Object-oriented programming (OOP) languages like Visual Basic, C++, and Java have become major tools of software development. Briefly, while most other programming languages separate data elements from the procedures or actions that will be performed upon them, OOP languages tie them together into **objects.** Thus, an object consists of data and the actions that can be performed on the data. For example, an object could be a set of data about a bank customer's savings account, and the operations (such as interest calculations) that might be performed upon the data. Or an object could be data in graphic form such as a video display window, plus the display actions that might be used upon it. See Figure 12.25.

In procedural languages, a program consists of procedures to perform actions on each data element. However, in object-oriented systems, objects tell other objects to perform actions on themselves. For example, to open a window on a computer video display, a beginning menu object could send a window object a message to open and a window will appear on the screen. That's because the window object contains the program code for opening itself.

Object-oriented languages are easier to use and more efficient for programming the graphics-oriented user interfaces required by many applications. Also, once objects are programmed, they are reusable. Therefore, reusability of objects is a major benefit of object-oriented programming. For example, programmers can construct a user interface for a new program by assembling standard objects such as windows, bars, boxes, buttons, and icons. Therefore, most object-oriented programming packages provide a GUI that supports a "point and click," "drag and drop" visual assembly of objects known as *visual programming*. Figure 12.26 shows a display of the Visual Basic object-oriented programming environment. Object-oriented technology is discussed further in the coverage of object-oriented databases in Chapter 13.

HTML, XML, and Java

HTML, XML, and Java are three programming languages that are important tools for building multimedia Web pages, websites, and Web-based applications.

HTML (Hypertext Markup Language) is a page description language that creates hypertext or hypermedia documents. HTML inserts control codes within a document at points you can specify that create links (*hyperlinks*) to other parts of the document or to other documents anywhere on the World Wide Web. HTML embeds control codes in the ASCII text of a document that designate titles, headings, graphics, and multimedia components, as well as hyperlinks within the document.

Figure 12.25

An example of a bank savings account object. This object consists of data about a customer's account balance and the basic operations that can be performed on those data.

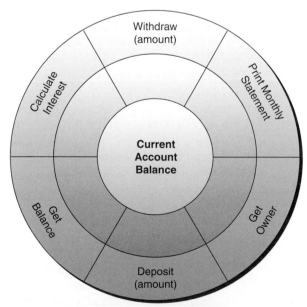

Savings Account Object

Figure 12.26   The Visual Basic object-oriented programming environment.

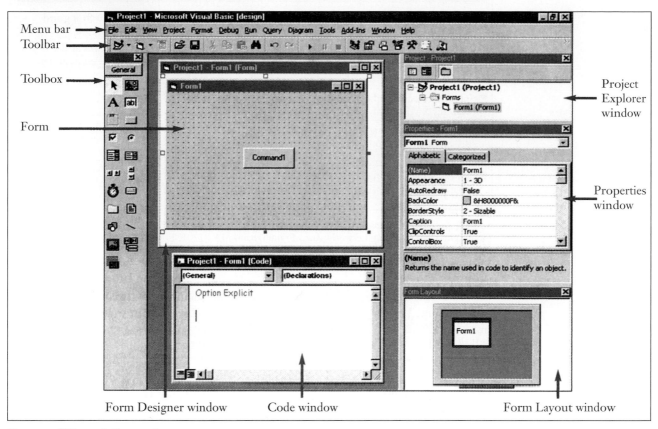

Menu bar
Toolbar
Toolbox
Form
Project Explorer window
Properties window
Form Designer window   Code window   Form Layout window

Courtesy of Microsoft Corporation.

As we mentioned earlier, several of the programs in the top software suites will automatically convert documents into HTML formats. These include Web browsers, word processing and spreadsheet programs, database managers, and presentation graphics packages. These and other specialized *Web publishing* programs like Microsoft FrontPage and Lotus FastSite provide a range of features to help you design and create multimedia Web pages without formal HTML programming.

XML (eXtensible Markup Language) is not a Web page format description language like HTML. Instead, XML describes the contents of Web pages by applying identifying tags or *contextual labels* to the data in Web documents. For example, a travel agency Web page with airline names and flight times would use hidden XML tags like "airline name" and "flight time" to categorize each of the airline flight times on that page. Or product inventory data available at a website could be labeled with tags like "brand," "price," and "size." By classifying data in this way, XML makes website information a lot more searchable, sortable, and easier to analyze.

For example, XML-enabled search software could easily find the exact product you specify if the product data at a website had been labeled with identifying XML tags. And a website that used XML could more easily determine what Web page features its customers used and what products they investigated. Thus XML promises to make electronic commerce a lot easier and more efficient by supporting the automatic electronic exchange of business data between companies and their customers, suppliers, and other business partners. Figure 12.27 outlines some of the pros and cons of XML [5, 6].

Java is an object-oriented programming language created by Sun Microsystems that is revolutionizing the programming of applications for the World Wide Web and corporate intranets and extranets. Java is related to the C++ and Objective C

Figure 12.27

The benefits and limitations of XML.

Pros and Cons of XML	
Why XML is a good idea:	**Why XML may not be such a good idea:**
• Its self-describing tags identify what your content is all about	• Majority of online browsers still see only HTML; you will need to add an XML-to-HTML translator
• Data is easily repurposed via tags	• Performance is still slower than equivalent HTML documents
• Creating, using and reusing tags is easy, making XML highly extensible	• The XML-tagged document is still rare; you will likely be doing a lot of conversion of older data
• XML data types map easily among different applications, so it's very interoperable	• Standard tag sets for different applications and industries aren't in widespread use yet
• It makes transferring data easy; simply give it XML tags	

Source: Amy Helen Johnson, "XML Xtends Its Reach." *Computerworld*, October 18, 1999, p. 80. Copyright 1999 by Computerworld, Inc., Framingham, MA 01701. Reprinted from *Computerworld*.

programming languages, but is much simpler and secure, and is computing platform independent. Java is also specifically designed for real-time, interactive, Web-based network applications. So Java applications consisting of small application programs, called **applets,** can be executed by any computer and any operating system anywhere in a network.

The ease of creating Java applets and distributing them from network servers to client PCs and network computers is a major reason for Java's popularity. Applets can be small special-purpose application programs or small modules of larger application programs. Applets can reside at websites on a network server until needed by client systems, and are easy to distribute over the Internet or intranets and extranets. Applets are platform independent too—they can run on Windows, UNIX, and Macintosh systems without modification. Java continues to improve its speed of execution (which has been a major limitation), and thus is becoming the alternative to Microsoft's Active X language for many organizations intent on capitalizing on the business potential of the Internet, as well as their own intranets and extranets [10].

Programming Software

A variety of software packages are available to help programmers develop computer programs. For example, *programming language translators* are programs that translate other programs into machine language instruction codes that computers can execute. Other software packages, such as programming language editors, are called *programming tools* because they help programmers write programs by providing a variety of program creation and editing capabilities. See Figure 12.28.

Language Translator Programs

Computer programs consist of sets of instructions written in programming languages that must be translated by a **language translator** into the computer's own machine language before they can be processed, or executed, by the CPU. Programming language translator programs (or *language processors*) are known by a variety of names. An **assembler** translates the symbolic instruction codes of programs written in an assembler language into machine language instructions, while a **compiler** translates high-level language statements.

An **interpreter** is a special type of compiler that translates and executes each statement in a program one at a time, instead of first producing a complete machine language program, as compilers and assemblers do. Java is an example of an interpreted language. Thus, the program instructions in Java applets are interpreted and executed *on-the-fly* as the applet is being executed by a client PC.

Figure 12.28

Using the graphical
programming interface of
Visual Café, a Java
programming tool.

Courtesy of Symantec.

Programming Tools

Software development and the computer programming process have been enhanced by adding *graphical programming interfaces* and a variety of built-in development capabilities. Language translators have always provided some editing and diagnostic capabilities to identify programming errors or *bugs*. However, most software development programs now include powerful graphics-oriented *programming editors* and *debuggers*. These programming tools help programmers identify and minimize errors while they are programming. Such programming tools provide a computer-aided programming *environment* or *workbench*. This decreases the drudgery of programming while increasing the efficiency and productivity of software developers. Other programming tools include diagramming packages, code generators, libraries of reusable objects and program code, and prototyping tools. Many of these same tools are part of the toolkit provided by *computer-aided software engineering* (CASE) packages.

Summary

- **Software.** Computer software consists of two major types of programs: (1) application software that directs the performance of a particular use, or application, of computers to meet the information processing needs of users, and (2) system software that controls and supports the operations of a computer system as it performs various information processing tasks. Refer to Figure 12.2 for an overview of the major types of software.

- **Application Software.** Application software includes a variety of programs that can be segregated into general-purpose and application-specific categories. General-purpose application programs perform common information processing jobs for end users. Examples are word processing, electronic spreadsheet, database management, telecommunications, and presentation graphics programs. Application-specific programs accomplish information processing tasks that support specific business functions or processes, scientific or engineering applications, and other computer applications in society.

- **System Software.** System software can be subdivided into system management programs and system development programs. System management programs manage the hardware, software, network, and data resources of a computer system during its execution of information processing jobs. Examples of system management programs are operating systems, network management programs, database management systems, system utilities, performance monitors, and security monitors. Network management programs support and manage telecommunications activities and network performance telecommunications networks. Database management systems control the development, integration, and

maintenance of databases. Utilities are programs that perform routine computing functions, such as backing up data or copying files, as part of an operating system or as a separate package. System development programs help IS specialists and end users develop computer programs and information system procedures. Major development programs are language translators, programming editors and other programming tools.

- **Operating Systems.** An operating system is an integrated system of programs that supervises the operation of the CPU, controls the input/output storage functions of the computer system, and provides various support services. An operating system performs five basic functions: (1) a user interface for system and network communications with users, (2) resource management for managing the hardware resources of a computer system, (3) file management for managing files of data and programs, (4) task management for managing the tasks a computer must accomplish, and (5) utilities and other functions that provide miscellaneous support services.

- **Programming Languages.** Programming languages are a major category of system software. They require the use of a variety of programming packages to help programmers develop computer programs, and language translator programs to convert programming language instructions into machine language instruction codes. The five major levels of programming languages are machine languages, assembler languages, high-level languages, fourth-generation languages, and object-oriented languages. Object-oriented languages like Java and special-purpose languages like HTML and XML are being widely used for Web-based business applications.

Key Terms and Concepts

These are the key terms and concepts of this chapter. The page number of their first explanation is given in parentheses.

Review Quiz

Match one of the previous key terms and concepts with one of the brief examples or definitions that follow. Try to find the best fit for answers that seem to fit more than one term or concept. Defend your choices.

_____ 1. Programs that manage and support the operations of computers.

_____ 2. Programs that direct the performance of a specific use of computers.

_____ 3. A system of programs that manages the operations of a computer system.

_____ 4. Managing the processing of tasks in a computer system.

_____ 5. Managing the use of CPU time, primary and secondary storage, telecommunications processors, and input/output devices.

_____ 6. Managing the input/output, storage, and retrieval of files.

_____ 7. The function that provides a means of communication between end users and an operating system.

_____ 8. The use of icons, bars, buttons, and other image displays to help you get things done.

_____ 9. Provides a greater memory capability than a computer's actual memory capacity.

_____ 10. Programs that manage and support the performance of networks.

_____ 11. Software that manages telecommunications in complex local area networks.

_____ 12. Manages and supports the maintenance and retrieval of data stored in databases.

_____ 13. Translates high-level instructions into machine language instructions.

_____ 14. Performs housekeeping chores for a computer system.

_____ 15. A category of application software that performs common information processing tasks for end users.

_____ 16. Software available for the specific applications of end users in business, science, and other fields.

_____ 17. Helps you surf the Web.

_____ 18. Use your networked computer to send and receive messages.

_____ 19. Creates and displays a worksheet for analysis.

_____ 20. Allows you to create and edit documents.

_____ 21. You can produce your own brochures and newsletters.

_____ 22. Helps you keep track of appointments and tasks.

_____ 23. A program that performs several general-purpose applications.

_____ 24. A combination of individual general-purpose application packages that work easily together.

_____ 25. Software to support the collaboration of teams and work groups.

_____ 26. Uses instructions in the form of coded strings of ones and zeros.

_____ 27. Uses instructions consisting of symbols representing operation codes and storage locations.

_____ 28. Uses instructions in the form of brief statements or the standard notation of mathematics.

_____ 29. Might take the form of query languages and report generators.

_____ 30. Languages that tie together data and the actions that will be performed upon the data.

_____ 31. You don't have to tell the computer how to do something, just what result you want.

_____ 32. As easy to use as one's native tongue.

_____ 33. Includes programming editors, debuggers, and code generators.

_____ 34. Produces hyperlinked multimedia documents for the Web.

_____ 35. A popular object-oriented language for Web-based applications.

_____ 36. A small application program distributed from a Web server.

_____ 37. Toward powerful, integrated, network-enabled, expert-assisted packages with easy-to-use graphic and natural language interfaces for productivity and collaboration.

Discussion Questions

1. What major trends are occurring in software? What capabilities do you expect to see in future software packages?

2. How do the different roles of system software and application software affect you as a business end user? How do you see this changing in the future?

3. Refer to the Real World Case on Hershey Direct and Norm Thompson in the chapter. Why are middleware-like application servers necessary in today's computing environment?

4. Why is an operating system necessary? That is, why can't an end user just load an application program in a computer and start computing?

5. Should a Web browser be integrated into an operating system? Why or why not?

6. Refer to the Real World Case on TravelNow and BEA Systems in the chapter. Why do software companies think people will pay to use their software on a per use basis? Do you agree? Why or why not?

7. Are software suites, Web browsers, and groupware merging together? What are the implications for a business and its end users?

8. How are HTML, XML, and Java affecting business applications on the Web?

9. Do you think Windows 2000 and Linux will surpass Unix and Netware as operating systems for network and Web servers? Why or why not?

10. Which application software packages are the most important for a business end user to know how to use? Explain the reasons for your choices.

Application Exercises

Complete the following exercises as individual or group projects that apply chapter concepts to real world business situations.

1. ABC Department Stores: Software Selection

ABC Department Stores would like to acquire software to do the following tasks. Identify what software packages they need.

a. Surf the Web and their intranets and extranets.

b. Send messages to each others' computer workstations.

c. Help employees work together in teams.

d. Use a group of productivity packages that work together easily.

e. Help sales reps keep track of meetings and sales calls.

f. Type correspondence and reports.

g. Analyze rows and columns of sales figures.

h. Develop a variety of graphical presentations.

2. Evaluating Software Packages

Which of the software packages mentioned in this chapter have you used?

a. Briefly describe the advantages and disadvantages of one of these packages.

b. How would such a package help you in a present or future job situation?

c. How would you improve the package you used?

3. Tracking Employee Software Training

You have the responsibility for managing software training for Sales, Accounting, and Operations De-

partment Workers in your organization. The data below presents summary information about training sessions held in the last quarter. You want to record this information in a database table and use that table to record information about all future training sessions as they occur.

a. Create a database table to store this information and enter the ten records shown below. Session ID can serve as the primary key. Print out a listing of your table.

b. Create and print the results of queries showing: a. Average attendance at Database Fundamentals Classes, b. the total number of hours of spreadsheet, SS, class attendance by workers in each department, and c. the average attendance for each course (Title).

c. Generate a report Grouped by Category and showing the number of sessions, average attendance and total hours of training provided for each course title. Your report should include subtotal and grand total figures as well.

d. If the number of hours and category for a particular course title are always the same, e.g., the Spreadsheet Fundamentals class is always 16 hours long and in the SS Category, can you see any problems caused by recording the hours and category as an attribute of this table? (Be sure to keep a copy of your work for this project because it is used again in a later exercise.)

Session ID	Hours	Title	Category	Sales Attendees	Accounting Attendees	Operations Attendees
100	16	Spreadsheet Fundamentals	SS	5	3	8
101	24	Database Fundamentals	DB	4	6	4
102	12	Using Presentation Graphics	PR	9	2	3
103	16	Advanced Spreadsheet	SS	1	9	6
104	24	Database Fundamentals	DB	3	8	4
105	12	Using Presentation Graphics	PR	10	1	3
106	16	Advanced Database Features	DB	0	8	4
107	8	Enliven Your Presentations	PR	9	0	2
108	16	Spreadsheet Fundamentals	SS	2	7	7
109	16	Advanced Spreadsheet	SS	1	6	4

4. Matching Training to Software Use

As in the previous exercise, You have responsibility for managing software training for Sales, Accounting, and Operations Department Workers in your organization. You have surveyed the workers to get a feel for the amount of time spent using various packages and the results are shown below. The values shown are the total number of workers in each department and the total weekly hours of use of each type of package. You have been asked to prepare a spreadsheet summarizing this data and comparing the use of the various packages across departments, and relating these data to the training data from the previous exercise.

Department	Employees	Spreadsheet	Database	Presentation
Sales	225	410	1100	650
Operations	195	820	520	110
Accounting	235	1050	1225	190

a. Create a spreadsheet that will emphasize the average use and training per worker of each type of package and make it easy to compare the usage across departments. To do this you will first enter the data shown above. Next perform a query on the data of the previous application exercise to determine the total hours of training on each type of package for each department and add these results to your spreadsheet. Be sure to add overall use and training categories to show overall use and training across packages. Compute the average weekly use per worker by dividing hours by the number of workers in the department. Compute a similar figure for training hours by dividing by the number of workers and then dividing by 13 to convert the quarterly data to a weekly basis.

b. Create a set of graphs summarizing your results. Be sure to include a graph comparing training hours per package and usage hours per package in some way.

c. A committee has been formed to schedule future software training classes at your company. You have been asked to present the results of your analysis as a starting point for this committee's work. Using presentation software, produce a brief summary highlighting key results and including related spreadsheet pages and graphs needed to support your findings.

FreeMarkets Inc.: Converting to Windows 2000 Servers

Executives at online auction provider FreeMarkets Inc. had a problem. Explosive growth was creating demand for higher scalability and uptime from their data center, but the Windows NT Server infrastructure—a web server farm with database systems built on top of Microsoft's SQL Server—was running out of gas. With IT systems at the core of FreeMarkets' business, it was a problem that could strangle growth.

The Pittsburgh-based company helps business users set up and manage online auctions for industrial parts and other commodities using FreeMarkets' FullSource and DirectSource services and FreeMarkets Desktop and end-user applications. Sales have grown fast. In the first half of 2000 alone, the company exceeded the $3 billion in trades it had executed the previous year.

To support that growth, says Tony Bernard, FreeMarkets' director of technical architecture, the company needed "five nines" availability (99.999% uptime) and a more scalable infrastructure than its NT-based systems offered. "We would reboot our servers once a month," he says. FreeMarkets also wanted to implement QuickSource, a major upgrade of its do-it-yourself auction service. The company had to pull this off without affecting the availability of its applications.

In late 1999, FreeMarkets made the initial decision to migrate the data center to the yet-to-be-released Windows 2000 operating system and to overhaul the company's production servers "to have a more scalable and reliable architecture for our application environment," recalls John Benzinger, FreeMarkets' vice president of IT.

Windows 2000 was promising the scalability and reliability FreeMarkets needed. But it wasn't a shoe-in: With a large number of its key applications written in Java, the company seriously considered using Linux. "The drawback was that in most cases, it was going to mean a forklift upgrade for our data center and complete retraining," Bernard says. The company determined that going exclusively with Microsoft development tools and architecture would help simplify product development in ways not possible with a more Java-centric approach, he says. "There were too many vendors, too many components, too many pieces of the puzzle," Bernard says of Java.

By early 2000, a plan was put in place to migrate web servers and QuickSource database servers in a "guinea pig" phase for the migration project. By early spring, a team of Benzinger's operations experts had tested some auction components on Windows 2000 servers. "We kind of knew how that application performed on NT," Bernard recalls. "We ran it on the new environment and we saw a noticeable improvement."

The team created an architecture running on new Compaq ProLiant multi-CPU servers that includes:

- a QuickSource database application server cluster running Windows 2000 Datacenter Server and SQL Server 2000

- an enterprise application server cluster running Windows 2000 Advanced Servers that handle interactions with suppliers

- a nonclustered web server farm running Windows 2000 Advanced Server serves QuickSource pages and handles incoming requests

- dual-clustered back office application servers running Windows 2000 Datacenter Server and OneWorld enterprise resource planning (ERP) software from J. D. Edwards & Co., which handles accounting and billing.

Last September, FreeMarkets rolled out QuickSource, the first production application, on its new architecture. Some of the company's databases and basic auction components had also been moved onto the Windows 2000 servers, according to Benzinger. "We have a lot of supplier information that is part of all of our products, and those databases were migrated over. We didn't have any issues I would even classify as significant," he says.

Uptime across the new system improved noticeably. Monthly reboots, common with NT became a thing of the past. But each reboot took 30 minutes longer when it was needed. Performance also improved; web pages, for example, seem to load in about half the time. The new multiprocessor Compaq servers account for part of that difference, but "Windows 2000 itself is a faster operating system," Bernard says, "and SQL Server 2000 seems to perform better."

Both Bernard and Benzinger say they're impressed with the new system's reliability. But FreeMarkets remains focused on the ongoing data center migration. "Our goal is to build a highly available Datacenter Server cluster running SQL Server 2000 and consolidate all of our databases," Bernard says. So far, the results have been promising. FreeMarkets says maintenance costs have declined by 20% and auction capacity has risen 70% since the migration began in late 1999.

Case Study Questions

1. What problems were FreeMarkets hoping to solve by installing Windows 2000 Servers?

2. What benefits have resulted?

3. Do networked multiprocessor servers running Windows Datacenter Server and other Windows Servers make mainframes obsolete? Why or why not?

Source: Adapted from David Essex, "Betting on Win 2K," *ComputerWorld*, February 26, 2001, pp. 56–57.

Transcentric and Aircast: Evaluating XML Versus EDI

For years, enterprises have relied on traditional electronic data interchange (EDI) to simplify and speed up their transactions with customers, suppliers and other partners. Now, along comes the document-tagging language XML, with the potential to reach new markets, simplify access, populate web pages and serve as an Esperanto format for transactions of all kinds. Should companies stay with EDI? Should they move to XML? Should they try to get EDI and XML to interoperate? Many are finding that they can do all of the above—if they use the right tools in the right ways.

Many enterprises embracing both EDI and XML started out in the EDI arena years or decades ago. For instance, St. Louis–based Transentric, which began life as the technology arm of the Union Pacific Corp. rail conglomerate, has been using EDI for more than 20 years. It currently handles more than a million transactions per day with some 8,000 partners on its value-added network (VAN).

Aircast Inc. in Summit, New Jersey, is another example. The maker of orthopedic braces and other medical products began establishing EDI connections with very large distributors of its products when it was unusual for small businesses to get involved with EDI. Aircast's motivation was simple: To expand the market for its products, it had to adopt the preferred connection method of the larger companies, namely EDI. That investment paid off: Approximately 40% of Aircast's business moves over EDI.

Enterprises have a variety of motivations for wanting to get involved with XML. Many are desperate to get involved in E-commerce but have no idea how to get started, given their current technology. In industries that already have on-line marketplaces and portals springing into existence, XML is often the required admission ticket. Many firms view the advent of XML as the golden opportunity to automate processes from beginning to end, with the XML format as the central touchstone. "We have a goal to eliminate manual processes entirely," says Susan McKay, vice president of customer and information systems at Aircast.

For EDI companies, the motivations emerge from some of the drawbacks to EDI itself. Most EDI traffic flows over private networks, which can be expensive. The open and free Internet beckons, and while EDI over the Internet is possible, it's not fun. In contrast, XML is a child of the Internet and seems a more natural format to use. EDI is also primarily a one-to-one technology, while web-based marketplaces allow many-to-one connectivity. "One goal for exploring XML is to broaden our group of trading partners to include those who—for whatever reason—don't use EDI," says Ken Olsen, assistant vice president of marketing at Transentric. In addition, Transentric aims to use its combined EDI and XML prowess to give such increased access to partners as part of its value-added message-management offering.

As with the original adoption of EDI, one draw of XML is the fact that your potential business partners may be using it. "Many of our large clients—including automotive and chemical vertical industries—are moving into the growing XML user community," says Randy Morin, director of E-business solutions at Transentric. That's because it's advantageous to have data in XML format for supporting e-commerce and portal sites.

But XML's dark secret is that it's slower than EDI. The messages must be larger—as much as 10 times larger—requiring greater band width and more cycles to move and process. For those merely seeking any-to-any connectivity, this isn't a major barrier. But when you start thinking about handling enterprise-level volumes of transactions, you clearly have to explore the ramifications of moving to XML.

Will XML supplant EDI as the format of choice for electronic transactions? That depends on whom you ask. "XML is going to replace EDI," McKay asserts simply. Certainly there are many people who say they believe—or hope—that's true. They view the current emergence of XML as simply one phase in the inevitable transition. The next stage might then be to the proposed electronic business XML (ebXML) standard, which promises even better E-commerce application development capabilities.

Others view EDI as coexisting with XML indefinitely, not because they are ignoring the merits of XML, but because they acknowledge the merits and existing base of EDI. "For two companies exchanging a high volume of transactions, you don't need XML—and XML may well impede their connections," says Olson. For well-defined, repetitive and high-volume situations, leaving EDI to do its work makes the most sense for the present. "Especially for large organizations, it makes sense to continue their existing EDI connections," he says.

Case Study Questions

1. Why are companies like Transentric and Aircast beginning to use XML?

2. Why are companies like Transentric continuing to use EDI?

3. Will XML eventually replace EDI for E-business and E-commerce applications? Why or why not?

Source: Adapted from Edmund DeJesus, "XML? EDI? Or Both?" *Computerworld*, January 8, 2001, pp. 54–56, and Michael Meehan, "B2B Standard Ready for Scrutiny," *Computerworld*, March 26, 2001, pp. 1, 16.

Zagat Survey and Royal & Sun Alliance: Evaluating Microsoft.net

Every couple of years, Microsoft Corp. hoists a flag to rally the troops. Win32, ActiveX and Windows DNA would, we were told, revolutionize the business of creating and employing software. Because these campaigns addressed important issues, they were greeted with a measure of enthusiasm. Because they entailed risk, uncertainty and retraining, they were greeted with an equal measure of weary skepticism.

So it is for the new campaign, which is called .Net, but this time, enthusiasts appear to outweigh skeptics. Everyone agrees that business applications and network services are becoming the same thing. IT has learned, and will never forget, the lessons of the first-generation Web: open standards, universal access, rapid development, continuous deployment.

Now the second-generation web is being constructed, and Microsoft is determined to be one of its architects. Chastened by its failure to catch the first wave and challenged by the thriving open-source and Java communities, it's put together a compelling strategy. Microsoft aims, as usual, to deliver tools and environments that take care of software plumbing, so the majority of developers can focus on creating the applications they're hired to build, using XML interfaces, object-oriented programming languages, and component object models.

Some aspects have been known for a while. XML interfaces to Web services similar to .Net's standards such as Simple Object Access Protocol (SOAP), have been in use for several years. One early adopter of the XML interfaces strategy was New York–based Zagat Survey LLC, whose website delivers reviews of thousands of restaurants in dozens of cities. Zagat's content flows to Web browsers and Wireless Application Protocol (WAP) mobile devices like PDAs. The two presentations share a common XML layer, according to Chief Technology Officer Steve Forte. "Our wireless app calls all the same stuff, on the same server, as does our HTML app," he says.

Zagat has very specific plans for its first SOAP implementation. Today, Zagat links from its pages to a partner site, OpenTable, which offers a dining reservation service. This works, but Zagat would rather keep customers on Zagat.com and connect them to OpenTable behind the scenes. Again, this is entirely feasible today. OpenTable need not wait for .Net in order to produce an XML interface to its reservation service, and Zagat need not wait for .Net in order to use that interface.

Domenick Branciforte, enterprise architecture manager at Royal & Sun Alliance Insurance Company of Canada in Toronto, is another .Net evaluator who's excited by the prospect of pervasive Web services. For example, employees use an intranet portal to access corporate information services. They go to Yahoo's or Fidelity Investments' sites to access external services. "Portals bring information together," says Branciforte. "But then we have a proliferation of portals, so what did that solve?"

Branciforte says he wants to create direct business-to-business connections between his company and partners such as the Department of Motor Vehicles. To the extent that services are available through conventional portals, this is possible today. "But when you find yourself doing HTML screen-scraping, it's a warning sign, a symptom of a bigger problem that you should solve," Branciforte says.

He says it's significant that in Visual Studio.Net, the creation and use of Web services is "a cornerstone, a given." This isn't rocket science, he points out. Like the Internet's core protocols, SOAP is pretty simple, and that's good. "This wasn't the time for Microsoft to get fancy," he adds. "It was time for Microsoft to get simple."

At Royal & Sun Alliance, Branciforte's team has been preparing for .Net by shoring up the Windows infrastructure. That means upgrading from Windows NT to Windows 2000, and ensuring that Internet Information Server is "in place, optimized and understood." Its first .Net pilot project will probably be a business-to-business web service.

Zagat.com has aggressive plans to launch a new hotel-rating site, based on .Net in 2001. Forte says early indications are promising, but a .Net depoyment will be contingent on stress-testing that hasn't yet been done. "If .Net explodes and shoots off sparks," the main site will be unaffected, and the new site could fall back to conventional Visual Basic, says Forte.

So if you're already a 100% pure Microsoft company, .Net is the way to go. Otherwise, you'll want to watch and wait for the open-source and Java communities to rise to the challenge. The second-generation Web will emerge in many forms. All of them, though, will likely be influenced by the .Net blueprint, which is remarkably clear and complete.

Case Study Questions

1. What are Microsoft's technical and business purposes in developing the .Net technology?

2. How are Zagat and Royal & Sun hoping to benefit from using .Net technologies?

3. What are some potential benefits and limitations of .Net for business?

Source: Adapted from Jon Udell, "Developing for .Net," *Computerworld*, March 5, 2001, pp. 46–48.

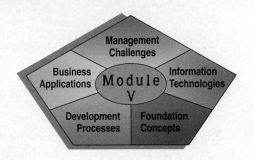

Management Challenges
Business Applications
Module V
Information Technologies
Development Processes
Foundation Concepts

Chapter 13

Data Resource Management

Chapter Highlights

Learning Objectives

After reading and studying this chapter, you should be able to:

1. Explain the importance of implementing data resource management processes and technologies in an organization.

2. Outline the advantages of a database management approach to managing the data resources of a business.

3. Explain how database management software helps business professionals and supports the operations and management of a business.

4. Provide examples to illustrate each of the following concepts:
   a. Major types of databases.
   b. Data warehouses and data mining.
   c. Logical data elements.
   d. Fundamental database structures.
   e. Database access methods.
   f. Database development.

Managing Data Resources

Data Resource Management

Data are a vital organizational resource that need to be managed like other important business assets. Today's E-business enterprises cannot survive or succeed without quality data about their internal operations and external environment.

> *With each online mouse click, either a fresh bit of data is created or already-stored data are retrieved from all those E-commerce websites, filled with data-rich photos, stock graphs, and music videos. And the thousands of new web pages created each day need a safe, stable managed environment to hang out. All that's on top of the heavy demand for industrial-strength data storage already in use by scores of big corporations. What's driving the growth is a crushing imperative for corporations to analyze every bit of information they can extract from their huge data warehouses for competitive advantage. That has turned the data storage and management function into a key strategic role of the information age [9].*

That's why organizations and their managers need to practice **data resource management,** a managerial activity that applies information systems technologies like *database management, data warehousing,* and other data management tools to the task of managing an organization's data resources to meet the information needs of their business stakeholders. This chapter will show you the managerial implications of using data resource management technologies and methods to manage an organization's data assets to meet the information requirements of E-business companies.

Analyzing Shop At Home and Others

Read the Real World Case on Shop At Home and Others the next page. We can learn a lot from this case about how companies are using a variety of data resource management techniques to provide business intelligence to decision makers for competitive advantage. See Figure 13.1.

Raoul Benavides.

Shop At Home and Others: Data Resource Management for Business Intelligence

Shop At Home Inc. in Newport, Tennessee, is deluged with customer information. Not only does it sell collectibles, gemstones and other items through its 24-hour television broadcast, but it also has a companion web site—Collectibles.com—that lets customers order items or chat live with the show's hosts.

"We have so many channels that a person can come through that we have to understand the demographics and the program mix," says Lee Martin, vice president of systems development at the company. For example, he says do customers order on the Web or on television, or is there a mix? Do more products sell on the Web vs. television?

Even more important to the broadcast and E-commerce company is balancing its average price point with its volume of combined phone and online orders. Right now, its price point is just less than $200 to attract higher-end jewelry buyers. But if it goes too high, call volume suffers. "We have to look at our product mix from a strategic standpoint to best achieve profitability," Martin says. "And the only way we can find out the type of information as quickly as we need to is a business intelligence system."

Simply put, business intelligence systems quickly and cost-effectively supply users with information to make strategic business decisions. Such systems encompass a range of software, starting with the extraction, transformation and loading data mining tools that pull data from transaction systems and either prepare it for analysis or feed it into data marts or warehouses.

Data modeling is also involved, whether you plan to use a proprietary multidimensional database or a relational database. The business intelligence tools themselves range from complex query/analysis to simple reporting tools. They display information graphically so business users can quickly recognize key trends.

"There are a lot of business intelligence tools out there," says Sharon Sibigtroth, managing director of strategic data management at New York-based AXA Financial Inc., a member of Paris-based AXA Group, one of the world's largest providers of insurance and financial services. "The issue becomes, 'Do you have the right data, and have you used good design principles behind the database that the tools are going against?'"

AXA is currently breaking up its large DB2-based data warehouse into data marts focused on functional areas so users can take advantage of business intelligence tools from the likes of Cognos Inc. in Ottawa, Canada. With as many as 4.5 million customers, AXA is trying to provide employees with an in-depth understanding of its customers from profitability, retention and cross-selling perspectives.

Sibigtroth says it's important to hire database designers and data modelers with a solid understanding of multidimensional and relational databases. "If they start to use the tool and don't understand the architectural fundamentals, their cubes or reports won't perform very well," she says.

"Combine business skills with a solid footing in databases and queries, and you have a great mix for business intelligence systems. But it doesn't all have to come from one person. Shop At Home Network as created a team of three senior developers for its Oracle-based business intelligence system. One team member is responsible for creating the end user's view into the data. Another is a business analyst and project lead who finds out what types of queries are needed and how users want to see information summarized to create the best system design. The third, a database administrator, is responsible for the physical structure of the warehouse itself and making sure it gets loaded correctly so users get the right information.

In order to get top recognition as a business intelligence guru, it's best to take a renewed interest in how your business works. After all, the point of business intelligence is to give users near-instantaneous access to new information and enable them to make midcourse corrections on a regular basis.

For example, Ken Buchanan, vice president of information reporting at Health Risk Management (HRM) Inc., relies on his team of database administrators, software engineers, quality-assurance professionals and data modelers in order to be able to use the most sophisticated capabilities in the company's business intelligence system from MicroStrategy Inc. But, he says, he also relies on professionals who are "somewhere between technicians and content experts," some of whom are businesspeople with an aptitude for technology.

Minneapolis-based Health Risk Management provides health plan management and information services to managed-care and insurance companies. The system from MicroStrategy enables HRM to build reports for a variety of users and allows these users to receive the reports in the format they choose. The business intelligence system even provides parameters for users themselves to customize the reports they want to see to better meet their informational needs.

Case Study Questions

1. How does Shop At Home manage and capitalize on their data resources for business intelligence?

2. How will data marts help AXA's users get better business intelligence from their data warehouse?

3. What else could data resource management specialists do to help Health Resource Management provide better decision support tools for its business users?

Source: Adapted from Mary Brandell, "Masters of Business Intelligence," *Computerworld*, February 26, 2001, p. 61.

Business intelligence systems are decision support systems that rely heavily on data mining, data warehousing, and a variety of other data resource management techniques to provide strategic information to decision makers. For example, Shop At Home uses their business intelligence systems to continually analyze their customer demographics, program, product, and order mix, and average price point, so they can make adjustments to these factors to achieve optimum profitability. The AXA Group is moving from a central data warehouse approach to functional area data marts so its business users can take advantage of new business intelligence software tools. Health Risk Management relies on a team of data resource management and business professionals to develop customized business intelligence reports for a variety of business users. All three companies emphasize that they rely on professionals who combine business and data resource management skills to maintain high quality data resources and business intelligence tools that provide strategic information products to business decision makers.

Foundation Data Concepts

Before we go any further, let's review some fundamental concepts about how data are organized in information systems. As we first mentioned in Chapter 1, a hierarchy of several levels of data has been devised that differentiates between different groupings, or elements, of data. Thus, data may be logically organized into characters, fields, records, files, and databases, just as writing can be organized in letters, words, sentences, paragraphs, and documents. Examples of these logical data elements are shown in Figure 13.2.

Character

The most basic logical data element is the **character,** which consists of a single alphabetic, numeric, or other symbol. One might argue that the bit or byte is a more elementary data element, but remember that those terms refer to the physical storage elements provided by the computer hardware, discussed in Chapter 11. From a user's point of view (that is, from a *logical* as opposed to a physical or hardware view of data), a character is the most basic element of data that can be observed and manipulated.

Field

The next higher level of data is the **field,** or data item. A field consists of a grouping of characters. For example, the grouping of alphabetic characters in a person's name forms a name field, and the grouping of numbers in a sales amount forms a sales amount

Figure 13.2

Examples of the logical data elements in information systems. Note especially the examples of how data fields, records, files, and databases are related.

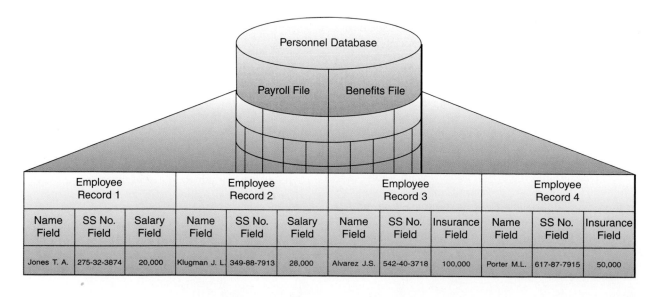

field. Specifically, a data field represents an **attribute** (a characteristic or quality) of some **entity** (object, person, place, or event). For example, an employee's salary is an attribute that is a typical data field used to describe an entity who is an employee of a business.

Record

Related fields of data are grouped to form a **record.** Thus, a record represents a collection of *attributes* that describe an *entity*. An example is the payroll record for a person, which consists of data fields describing attributes such as the person's name, Social Security number, and rate of pay. *Fixed-length* records contain a fixed number of fixed-length data fields. *Variable-length* records contain a variable number of fields and field lengths.

File

A group of related records is a data **file,** or *table.* Thus, an employee file would contain the records of the employees of a firm. Files are frequently classified by the application for which they are primarily used, such as a *payroll file* or an *inventory file,* or the type of data they contain, such as a *document file* or a *graphical image file.* Files are also classified by their permanence, for example, a payroll *master file* versus a payroll weekly *transaction file.* A transaction file, therefore, would contain records of all transactions occurring during a period and might be used periodically to update the permanent records contained in a master file. A *history file* is an obsolete transaction or master file retained for backup purposes or for long-term historical storage called *archival storage.*

Database

A **database** is an integrated collection of logically related records or *objects.* As we explained in Chapter 12, an object consists of data values describing the attributes of an *entity,* plus the operations that can be performed upon the data. We will explain object-oriented databases in Section II.

A database consolidates records previously stored in separate files into a common pool of data records that provides data for many applications. The data stored in a database are independent of the application programs using them and of the type of secondary storage devices on which they are stored. For example, a personnel database consolidates data formerly segregated in separate files such as payroll files, personnel action files, and employee skills files. See Figure 13.3.

Figure 13.3

A personnel database consolidates data formerly kept in separate files.

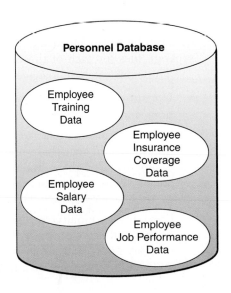

Figure 13.4

An example of a database management approach in a banking information system. Note how the savings, checking, and installment loan programs use a database management system to share a customer database. Note also that the DBMS allows a user to make a direct, ad hoc interrogation of the database without using application programs.

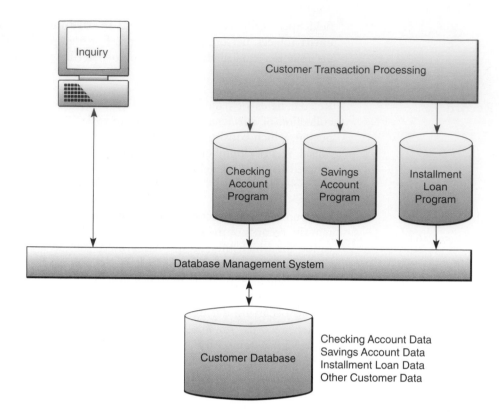

The Database Management Approach

The development of databases and database management software is the foundation of modern methods of managing organizational data. The **database management approach** consolidates data records and objects into databases that can be accessed by many different application programs. In addition, an important software package called a *database management system* (DBMS) serves as a software interface between users and databases. This helps users easily access the records in a database. Thus, database management involves the use of database management software to control how databases are created, interrogated, and maintained to provide information needed by end users and their organizations.

For example, customer records and other common types of data are needed for several different applications in banking, such as check processing, automated teller systems, bank credit cards, savings accounts, and installment loan accounting. These data can be consolidated into a common *customer database*, rather than being kept in separate files for each of those applications. See Figure 13.4.

Thus, the database management approach involves three basic activities:

- Updating and maintaining common databases to reflect new business transactions and other events requiring changes to an organization's records.

- Providing information needed for each end user's application by using application programs that share the data in common databases. This sharing of data is supported by the common software interface provided by a database management system package. Thus, end users and programmers do not have to know where or how data are physically stored.

- Providing an inquiry/response and reporting capability through DBMS software so that end users can use Web browsers and the Internet or corporate intranets to easily interrogate databases, generate reports, and receive quick responses to their ad hoc requests for information. Let's look at a real world example.

**Borders.com:
Website
Database
Management**

Borders' online store, located at www.borders.com, offers more than 10 million books, audio books, CDs, cassettes, and videos—all available to ship from stock to any home or business. Borders.com is driven by the IBM Net Commerce suite of E-business software and IBM's popular DB2 database management system.

If you want to find a particular book, CD, audio-cassette, or video, a search engine based on a DB2 module rapidly returns the results you want in a format most conducive to making a purchasing decision. As simple as they may seem, these searches are no trivial feat for a database management system. Just searching for a specific title takes three queries to three different database tables, each of which has about 20 million rows. But thanks to Border's unique database design of which has about 20 million rows. But thanks to Border's unique database design and DB2's fast indexing scheme, the Borders search engine can return results for most searches in about four-tenths of a second.

DB2 manages a huge database that stores information on all of the items offered on the site, as well as customer registration, order, inventory, shipping, and other information required to manage the online store. Net Data Web and database connectivity software enable Net Commerce software to provide access to the Borders.com database from any Web browser [5].

Using Database Management Software

Let's take a closer look at the capabilities provided by database management software. A **database management system** (DBMS) is a set of computer programs that controls the creation, maintenance, and use of the databases of an organization and its end users. As we said in Chapter 12, database management packages are available for micro, midrange, and mainframe computer systems. The four major uses of a DBMS are illustrated in Figure 13.5; common DBMS software components and functions are summarized in Figure 13.6.

Database Development

Database management packages like Microsoft Access or Lotus Approach allow end users to easily develop the databases they need. However, large organizations with client/server or mainframe-based systems usually place control of enterprisewide database development in the hands of **database administrators** (DBAs) and other database specialists. This improves the integrity and security of organizational databases. Database developers use the *data definition language* (DDL) in database management systems like Oracle 9i or IBM's DB2 to develop and specify the data contents, relationships, and structure of each database, and to modify these database specifications when necessary. Such information is cataloged and stored in a database of data defi-

Figure 13.5

The four major uses of a DBMS package are database development, database interrogation, database maintenance, and application development.

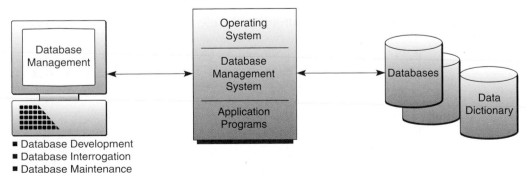

- Database Development
- Database Interrogation
- Database Maintenance
- Application Development

Figure 13.6   Common software components and functions of a database management system.

Common DBMS Software Components
● **Database definition.** Language and graphical tools to define entities, relationships, integrity constraints, and authorization rights
● **Nonprocedural access.** Language and graphical tools to access data without complicated coding
● **Application development.** Graphical tools to develop menus, data entry forms, and reports
● **Procedural language interface.** Language that combines nonprocedural access with full capabilities of a programming language
● **Transaction processing.** Control mechanisms to prevent interference from simultaneous users and recover lost data after a failure
● **Database tuning.** Tools to monitor and improve database performance

Source: Adapted from Michael V. Mannino, *Database Application Development and Design*. Burr Ridge, IL: McGraw-Hill Irwin, 2001, p. 7.

nitions and specifications called a *data dictionary*, which is maintained by the DBA. We will discuss database development further in Section II of this chapter.

The Data Dictionary. Data dictionaries are another tool of database administration. A data dictionary is a computer-based catalog or directory containing **metadata,** that is, data about data. A data dictionary includes a software component to manage a database of data definitions, that is, metadata about the structure, data elements, and other characteristics of an organization's databases. For example, it contains the names and descriptions of all types of data records and their interrelationships, as well as information outlining requirements for end users' access use of application programs, and database maintenance and security.

Data dictionaries can be queried by the database administrator to report the status of any aspect of a firm's metadata. The administrator can then make changes to the definitions of selected data elements. Some *active* (versus *passive*) data dictionaries automatically enforce standard data element definitions whenever end users and application programs use a DBMS to access an organization's databases. For example, an active data dictionary would not allow a data entry program to use a nonstandard definition of a customer record, nor would it allow an employee to enter a name of a customer that exceeded the defined size of that data element.

Database Interrogation

The database interrogation capability is a major benefit of a database management system. End users can use a DBMS by asking for information from a database using a *query language* or a *report generator*. They can receive an immediate response in the form of video displays or printed reports. No difficult programming is required. The **query language** feature lets you easily obtain immediate responses to ad hoc data requests: You merely key in a few short inquiries. The **report generator** feature allows you to quickly specify a report format for information you want presented as a report. Figure 13.7 illustrates the use of a DBMS report generator.

SQL Queries. SQL, or Structured Query Language, is a query language found in many database management packages. The basic form of an SQL query is:

SELECT . . . FROM . . . WHERE . . .

After SELECT you list the data fields you want retrieved. After FROM you list the files or tables from which the data must be retrieved. After WHERE you specify conditions that limit the search to only those data records in which you are interested. Figure 13.8 compares an SQL query to a natural language query for information on customer orders.

Figure 13.7

Using the report generator of Microsoft Access.

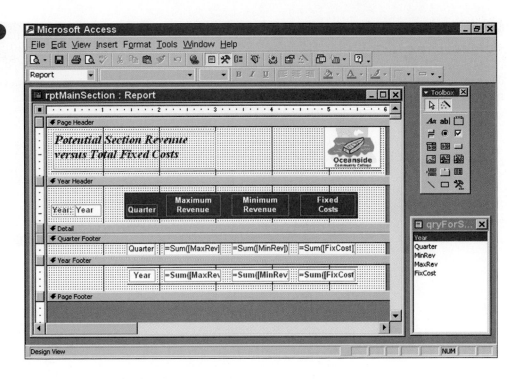

Graphical and Natural Queries. Many end users (and IS professionals) have difficulty correctly phrasing SQL and other database language queries. So most end user database management packages offer GUI (graphical user interface) point-and click methods, which are easier to use and are translated by the software into SQL commands. See Figure 13.9. Other packages are available that use *natural language* query statements similar to conversational English (or other languages), as was illustrated in Figure 13.8.

Database Maintenance

The databases of an organization need to be updated continually to reflect new business transactions and other events. Other miscellaneous changes must also be made to ensure accuracy of the data in the databases. This **database maintenance** process is accomplished by transaction processing programs and other end user application packages, with the support of the DBMS. End users and information specialists can also employ various utilities provided by a DBMS for database maintenance.

Application Development

DBMS packages play a major role in **application development.** End users, systems analysts, and other application developers can use the internal 4GL programming language and built-in software development tools provided by many DBMS

Figure 13.8

Comparing a natural language query with an SQL query.

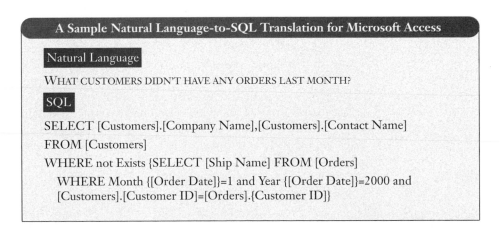

A Sample Natural Language-to-SQL Translation for Microsoft Access

Natural Language

WHAT CUSTOMERS DIDN'T HAVE ANY ORDERS LAST MONTH?

SQL

SELECT [Customers].[Company Name],[Customers].[Contact Name]

FROM [Customers]

WHERE not Exists {SELECT [Ship Name] FROM [Orders]
    WHERE Month {[Order Date]}=1 and Year {[Order Date]}=2000 and
    [Customers].[Customer ID]=[Orders].{Customer ID]}

Figure 13.9

Using the Query Wizard of the Microsoft Access database management package to develop a query.

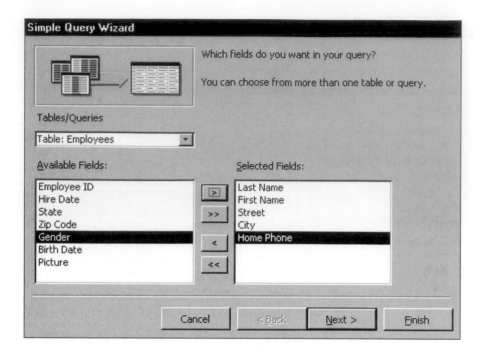

packages to develop custom application programs. For example, you can use a DBMS to easily develop the data entry screens, forms, reports, or Web pages of a business application. A DBMS also makes the job of application programmers easier, since they do not have to develop detailed data-handling procedures using a conventional programming language every time they write a program. Instead, they can include *data manipulation language* (DML) statements in their programs that call on the DBMS to perform necessary data-handling activities.

Types of Databases

Continuing developments in information technology and its business applications have resulted in the evolution of several major types of databases. Figure 13.10 illustrates several major conceptual categories of databases that may be found in many organizations.

Operational Databases

These databases store detailed data needed to support the business processes and operations of the E-business enterprise. They are also called *subject area databases* (SADB), *transaction databases*, and *production databases*. Examples are a customer database, human resource database, inventory database, and other databases containing data generated by business operations. This includes databases of Internet and electronic commerce activity, such as *click stream data* describing the online behavior of customers or visitors to a company's website.

Distributed Databases

Many organizations replicate and distribute copies or parts of databases to network servers at a variety of sites. These distributed databases can reside on network servers on the World Wide Web, on corporate intranets or extranets, or on other company networks. Distributed databases may be copies of operational or analytical databases, hypermedia or discussion databases, or any other type of database. Replication and distribution of databases is done to improve database performance and security. Ensuring that all of the data in an organization's distributed databases are consistently and concurrently updated is a major challenge of distributed database management.

External Databases

Access to a wealth of information from external databases is available for a fee from commercial online services, and with or without charge from many sources on the Internet, especially the World Wide Web. Websites provide an endless variety of

Figure 13.10   Examples of the major types of databases used by organizations and end users.

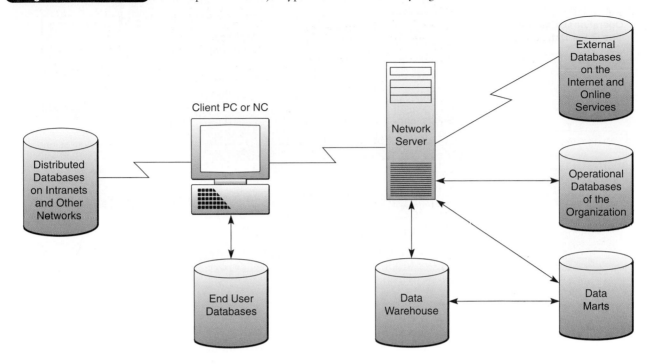

hyperlinked pages of multimedia documents in *hypermedia databases* for you to access. Data are available in the form of statistics on economic and demographic activity from *statistical* data banks. Or you can view or download abstracts or complete copies of hundreds of newspapers, magazines, newsletters, research papers, and other published material and other periodicals from *bibliographic* and *full text* databases.

Data Warehouses and Data Mining

A **data warehouse** stores data that have been extracted from the various operational, external, and other databases of an organization. It is a central source of data that have been cleaned, transformed, and cataloged so they can be used by managers and other business professionals for data mining, online analytical processing, and other forms of business analysis, market research, and decision support. Data warehouses may be subdivided into **data marts,** which hold subsets of data from the warehouse that focus on specific aspects of a company, such as a department or a business process.

Figure 13.11 illustrates the components of a complete data warehouse system. Notice how data from various operational and external databases are captured, cleaned, and transformed into data that can be better used for analysis. This acquisition process might include activities like consolidating data from several sources, filtering out unwanted data, correcting incorrect data, converting data to new data elements, and aggregating data into new data subsets.

This data is then stored in the enterprise data warehouse, from where it can be moved into data marts or to an *analytical data store* that holds data in a more useful form for certain types of analysis. Metadata that defines the data in the data warehouse is stored in a metadata repository and cataloged by a metadata directory. Finally, a variety of analytical software tools can be provided to query, report, mine, and analyze the data for delivery to business end users via Internet and intranet Web systems or other networks.

The components of a complete data warehouse system.

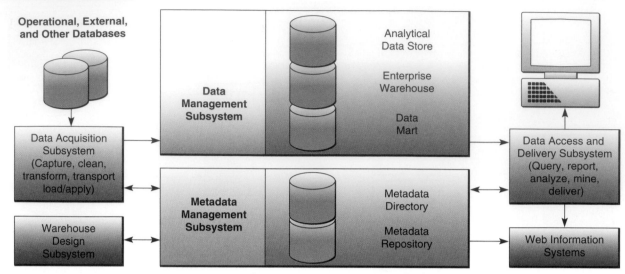

Adapted courtesy of Hewlett-Packard.

Data Mining

Data mining is a major use of data warehouse databases. In data mining, the data in a data warehouse are analyzed to reveal hidden patterns and trends in historical business activity. This can be used to help managers make decisions about strategic changes in business operations to gain competitive advantages in the marketplace. See Figure 13.12.

Data mining can discover new correlations, patterns, and trends in vast amounts of business data (frequently several terabytes of data), stored in data warehouses. Data mining software uses advanced pattern recognition algorithms, as well as a variety of mathematical and statistical techniques to sift through mountains of data to extract previously unknown strategic business information. We discuss data mining, online analytical processing (OLAP), and other technologies that analyze the data in databases and data warehouses to provide vital support for business decisions in Chapter 6. Let's look at a real world example.

Bank of America: Mining a Data Warehouse

The Bank of America (BofA) is using a data warehouse and data mining software to develop more accuracy in marketing and pricing financial products, such as home equity loans. BofA's data warehouse is so large—for some customers, there are 300 data points—that traditional analytic approaches are overwhelmed. For each market, BofA can offer a variety of tailored product packages by adjusting fees, interest rates, and features. The result is a staggering number of potential strategies for reaching profitable customers. Sifting through the vast number of combinations requires the ability to identify very fine opportunity segments.

Data extracted from the data warehouse were analyzed by data mining software to discover hidden patterns. For example, the software discovered that a certain set of customers were 15 times more likely to purchase a high-margin lending product. The bank also wanted to determine the sequence of events leading to purchasing. They fed the parameters to the Discovery software from HYPERparallel and built a model for finding other customers. This model proved to be so accurate that it discovered people already in the process of applying and being approved for the lending product. Using this profile, a final list of quality prospects for solicitation was prepared. The resulting direct marketing response rates have dramatically exceeded past results [14].

Figure 13.12 How data mining extracts business knowledge from a data warehouse.

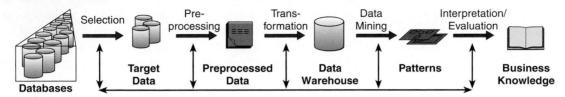

Source: Adapted from Usama Fayyad, Gregory Piatetsky-Shapiro, and Padhraic Smith, "The KDD Process for Extracting Useful Knowledge from Volumes of Data,"*Communications of the ACM*, November 1996, p. 29. Copyright © 1996, Association of Computing Machinery. Used by permission.

Hypermedia Databases on the Web

The most compelling business driver today is the Internet. Because so much of the information flying across the Internet is [multimedia], companies need databases that can store, retrieve, and manage other data types, particularly documents, video, and sound [17].

The rapid growth of websites on the Internet and corporate intranets and extranets has dramatically increased the use of databases of hypertext and hypermedia documents. A website stores such information in a **hypermedia database** consisting of hyperlinked pages of multimedia (text, graphic and photographic images, video clips, audio segments, and so on). That is, from a database management point of view, the set of interconnected multimedia pages at a website is a database of interrelated hypermedia pages, rather than interrelated data records [3].

Figure 13.13 shows how you might use a Web browser on your client PC to connect with a Web network server. This server runs Web server software to access and transfer the Web pages you request. The website illustrated in Figure 13.13 uses a hypermedia database consisting of HTML (Hypertext Markup Language) pages, image files, video files, and audio. The Web server software acts as a database management system to manage the transfer of hypermedia files for downloading by the multimedia plug ins of your Web browser.

Implementing Data Resource Management

Propelled by the Internet, intranets, a flood of multimedia information, and applications such as data warehousing and data mining, data storage at most companies is growing faster than ever. That has information technology managers in the most information-intensive industries wondering if technology can keep up with the surging tide—and, if it can, whether they can manage it [2].

Figure 13.13 The components of a Web-based information system include Web browsers, servers, and hypermedia databases.

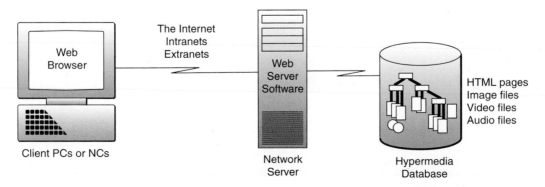

Managers and business professionals need to view data as an important resource that they must manage properly to ensure the success and survival of their organizations. But this is easier said than done. For example, database management is an important application of information technologies to the management of a firm's data resources. However, other major data resource management efforts are needed in order to supplement the solutions provided by a database management approach. Those are (1) database administration, (2) data planning, and (3) data administration. See Figure 13.14.

Database administration is an important data resource management function responsible for the proper use of database management technology. Database administration includes responsibility for developing and maintaining the organization's data dictionary, designing and monitoring the performance of databases, and enforcing standards for database use and security. Database administrators and analysts work with systems developers and end users to provide their expertise to major systems development projects.

Data planning is a corporate planning and analysis function that focuses on data resource management. It includes the responsibility for developing an overall data architecture for the firm's data resources that ties in with the firm's strategic mission and plans, and the objectives and processes of its business units. Data planning is done by organizations that have made a formal commitment to long-range planning for the strategic use and management of their data resources.

Data administration is another vital data resource management function. It involves administering the collection, storage, and dissemination of all types of data in such a way that data become a standardized resource available to all end users in the organization. The focus of data administration is the support of an organization's business processes and strategic business objectives. Data administration may also include responsibility for developing policies and setting standards for corporate database design, processing, and security arrangements.

Figure 13.14   Data resource management includes database administration, data planning, and data administration activities.

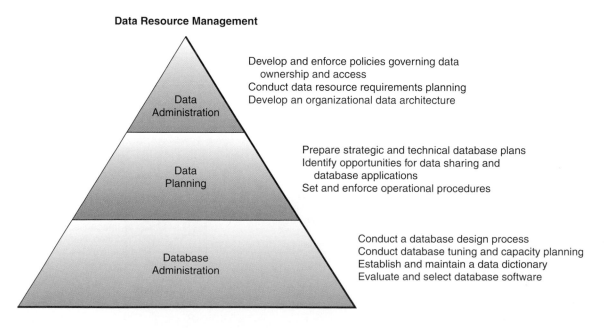

Challenges of Data Resource Management

The data resource management approach provides business managers and professionals with several important benefits. Database management reduces the duplication of data and integrates data so that they can be accessed by multiple programs and users. Software is not dependent on the format of the data or the type of secondary storage hardware being used. Business professionals can use inquiry/response and reporting capabilities to easily obtain information they need from databases, data warehouses, or data marts, without complex programming. Software development is simplified, because programs are not dependent on either the logical format of the data or their physical storage location. Finally, the integrity and security of data is increased, since access to data and modification of data are controlled by data management software, data dictionaries, and a data administration function.

The challenge of data resource management arises from its technological complexity and the vast amounts of business data that need to be managed. Developing large databases of complex data types and installing data warehouses can be difficult and expensive. More hardware capability is required, since storage requirements for the organization's data, overhead control data, and the database management or data warehouse software are greater. Longer processing times may result from this additional data and software complexity. Finally, if an organization relies on centralized databases, its vulnerability to errors, fraud, and failures is increased. Yet problems of inconsistency of data can arise if a distributed database approach is used. Therefore, supporting the security and integrity of their databases and data warehouses is a major objective of data resource management for E-business enterprises.

Section II

Technical Foundations of Database Management

Database Management

Just imagine how difficult it would be to get any information from an information system if data were stored in an unorganized way, or if there was no systematic way to retrieve it. Therefore, in all information systems, data resources must be organized and structured in some logical manner so that they can be accessed easily, processed efficiently, retrieved quickly, and managed effectively. Thus, data structures and access methods ranging from simple to complex have been devised to efficiently organize and access data stored by information systems. In this section, we will explore these concepts, as well as more technical concepts of database management.

Analyzing Payless Shoe Source

Read the Real World Case on Payless Shoe Source on the next page. We can learn a lot about storage management software, functions, and strategies that are an important part of data resource management from this case. See Figure 13.15.

Companies are being flooded with data captured by their E-commerce and E-business systems, so their demand for storage capacity is increasing rapidly. Many companies are using storage management software tools to help them manage their diverse systems of storage resources, instead of just buying more disk and tape storage hardware. For example, Dick Gorman of Payless Shoe Source is using storage management tools to administer over 6 terabytes of storage capacity. The tools allow him to easily reallocate storage capacity among competing applications as their storage needs change, and perform the other storage management functions listed in the case. Payless is also considering moving to a storage area network (SAN) environment to help consolidate and integrate their storage systems. Choosing a SAN storage architecture would be one of several ways companies like Payless could implement storage management strategies aimed at consolidating and standardizing their storage systems to make them easier to manage and more adaptable to changing business needs.

Database Structures

The relationships among the many individual records stored in databases are based on one of several logical data structures, or models. Database management system packages are designed to use a specific data structure to provide end users with quick, easy

Figure 13.15

Dick Gorman is senior storage administrator for Payless Shoe Source, and allocates storage capacity among competing applications.

Steve Curtis.

Payless Shoe Source: The Challenges of Storage Management

As demand for storage for E-commerce and E-business applications at many companies doubles or grows even more each year, IT managers may find it easier to add more storage than to better manage the amount they already have. But ineffective management means they buy more storage than they need, driving up administrative costs and increasing storage problems.

Managing storage capacity isn't simple. Systems typically include mainframe devices, JBOD (just a bunch of disks) setups, server-attached storage, network-attached storage (NAS) and storage-area networks (SAN). "There is no grand framework. The management tools are all different, unique to each device," notes Scott Robinson, chief technology officer at Minneapolis-based Datalink Corp.

Proponents of storage-area networks argue that they are ideal for consolidating and managing storage. SANs put storage on a separate network, where it can be centrally managed and accessed by multiple servers. By themselves, though, SANs don't solve the problem of heterogeneous storage management—not yet. As a result, "SANs give you a framework for storage management, but the SAN doesn't make storage management inherently easy, Robinson says. To the contrary, SANs add management complexity because you have to manage the SAN with its disk arrays, switches and hosts bus adapters from multiple vendors, as well as a Fibre Channel network, which introduces a new set of management headaches.

"Storage is so cheap that some managers feel it's smarter to buy more than to spend money to manage it," says Dick Gorman, senior storage administrator at Payless ShoeSource Inc. in Topeka, Kansas. Although this strategy may work for the short term, "people are always demanding more storage; there's no end to it," he says. Sooner or later, every organization has to apply some management controls, and practice storage management functions such as:

- **Backup management:** Overseeing regular operational backup procedures
- **Problem management:** Identifying and troubleshooting storage problems
- **Change management:** Configuring storage devices and tracking configuration changes
- **Dynamic allocation:** Changing and reconfiguring storage volumes on the fly
- **Capacity planning:** Analyzing storage usage trends to predict future needs
- **Storage performance tuning:** Tweaking application, server, network and device parameters to improve storage performance
- **Data retention and archiving:** Where infrequently needed data is stored for regulatory or historical purposes.

Payless ShoeSource turned to CA's CA-Vantage storage management software to manage its mainframe, Windows NT and AIX server storage, encompassing five different Symmetrix storage arrays from EMC Corp. From a single workstation console, Gorman can perform a variety of storage management functions for Payless' systems. These include utilization trend analysis, usage forecasting and monitoring of the tape backup system. Payless also uses Tivoli Storage Manager to back up its NT and AIX servers and storage array to the mainframe, which transfers it to backup tapes. Using CA-Vantage, Gorman can place data sets into specific pools and allocate the pools to different storage devices based on performance and growth considerations. He can also establish categories and track usage trends for each category of storage and storage pool, and can monitor capacity and constraints, set thresholds and generate alerts.

Storage at Payless amounts to 6TB today. Gorman administers it all, which is possible only because of CA-Vantage, he says. "If I didn't have CA-Vantage, I'd have to go out to check on the storage every day, and I don't have that kind of time," he says. The company would have to hire at least one more storage administrator, maybe more, he says.

Storage management also saves Payless money by enabling Gorman to easily reallocate capacity among different applications. This allows the company to delay additional storage purchases. Payless is considering purchasing a SAN, which Gorman believes would make the allocation of storage capacity even easier.

The ultimate goal of enterprise wide heterogeneous storage tools is to manage all the diverse, distributed storage in the enterprise as a single virtual storage pool. "It would be nice to see the entire farm and just point and click to add, delete or move storage," Gorman notes. In the meantime, companies like his are concentrating on implementing storage management strategies such as:

- **Establish** a storage architecture
- **Standardize** to reduce diversity of storage systems
- **Consolidate** servers and storage devices
- **Define** your storage management needs
- **Implement** storage management tools.

Case Study Questions

1. What is storage management? Why has it become a necessary part of IT management?
2. How does a SAN affect storage management?
3. How do software tools help companies like Payless manage their storage resources?

Source: Adapted from Alan Radding "Mix and Match Storage," *Computerworld*, March 19, 2001, pp. 62–63.

access to information stored in databases. Five fundamental database structures are the hierarchical, network, relational, object-oriented, and multidimensional models. Simplified illustrations of the first three database structures are shown in Figure 13.16.

Hierarchical Structure

Early mainframe DBMS packages used the **hierarchical structure,** in which the relationships between records form a hierarchy or treelike structure. In the traditional hierarchical model, all records are dependent and arranged in multilevel structures, consisting of one *root* record and any number of subordinate levels. Thus, all of the relationships among records are *one-to-many*, since each data element is related to only one element above it. The data element or record at the highest level of the hierarchy (the department data element in this illustration) is called the root ele-

Figure 13.16

Example of three fundamental database structures. They represent three basic ways to develop and express the relationships among the data elements in a database.

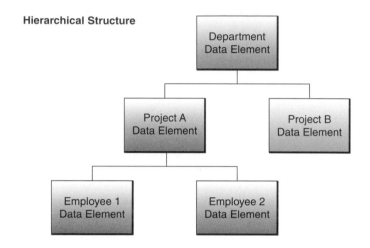

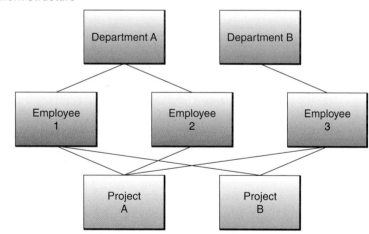

Relational Structure

Department Table

Deptno	Dname	Dloc	Dmgr
Dept A			
Dept B			
Dept C			

Employee Table

Empno	Ename	Etitle	Esalary	Deptno
Emp 1				Dept A
Emp 2				Dept A
Emp 3				Dept B
Emp 4				Dept B
Emp 5				Dept C
Emp 6				Dept B

ment. Any data element can be accessed by moving progressively downward from a root and along the branches of the tree until the desired record (for example, the employee data element) is located.

Network Structure

The **network structure** can represent more complex logical relationships, and is still used by some mainframe DBMS packages. It allows *many-to-many* relationships among records; that is, the network model can access a data element by following one of several paths, because any data element or record can be related to any number of other data elements. For example, in Figure 13.16, departmental records can be related to more than one employee record, and employee records can be related to more than one project record. Thus, one could locate all employee records for a particular department, or all project records related to a particular employee.

Relational Structure

The **relational model** has become the most popular of the three database structures. It is used by most microcomputer DBMS packages, as well as by most midrange and mainframe systems. In the relational model, all data elements within the database are viewed as being stored in the form of simple **tables.** Figure 13.16 illustrates the relational database model with two tables representing some of the relationships among departmental and employee records. Other tables, or **relations,** for this organization's database might represent the data element relationships among projects, divisions, product lines, and so on. Database management system packages based on the relational model can link data elements from various tables to provide information to users. For example, a DBMS package could retrieve and display an employee's name and salary from the employee table in Figure 13.16, and the name of the employee's department from the department table, by using their common department number field (Deptno) to link or join the two tables.

Multidimensional Structure

The multidimensional database structure is a variation of the relational model that uses multidimensional structures to organize data and express the relationships between data. You can visualize multidimensional structures as cubes of data and cubes within cubes of data. Each side of the cube is considered a dimension of the data. Figure 13.17 is an example that shows that each dimension can represent a different category, such as product type, region, sales channel, and time [7].

Each cell within a multidimensional structure contains aggregated data related to elements along each of its dimensions. For example, a single cell may contain the total sales for a product in a region for a specific sales channel in a single month. A major benefit of multidimensional databases is that they are a compact and easy-to-understand way to visualize and manipulate data elements that have many interrelationships. So multidimensional databases have become the most popular database structure for the analytical databases that support *online analytical processing* (OLAP) applications, in which fast answers to complex business queries are expected. We discuss OLAP applications in Chapter 6.

Object-Oriented Structure

The **object-oriented** database model is considered to be one of the key technologies of a new generation of multimedia Web-based applications. We introduced the concept of objects when we discussed object-oriented programming in Chapter 12. As Figure 13.18 illustrates, an **object** consists of data values describing the attributes of an entity, plus the operations that can be performed upon the data. This *encapsulation* capability allows the object-oriented model to better handle more complex types of data (graphics, pictures, voice, text) than other database structures.

The object-oriented model also supports *inheritance;* that is, new objects can be automatically created by replicating some or all of the characteristics of one or more *parent* objects. Thus, in Figure 13.18, the checking and savings account objects can both inherit the common attributes and operations of the parent bank account object. Such capabilities have made *object-oriented database management systems*

Figure 13.17   An example of the different dimensions of a multidimensional database.

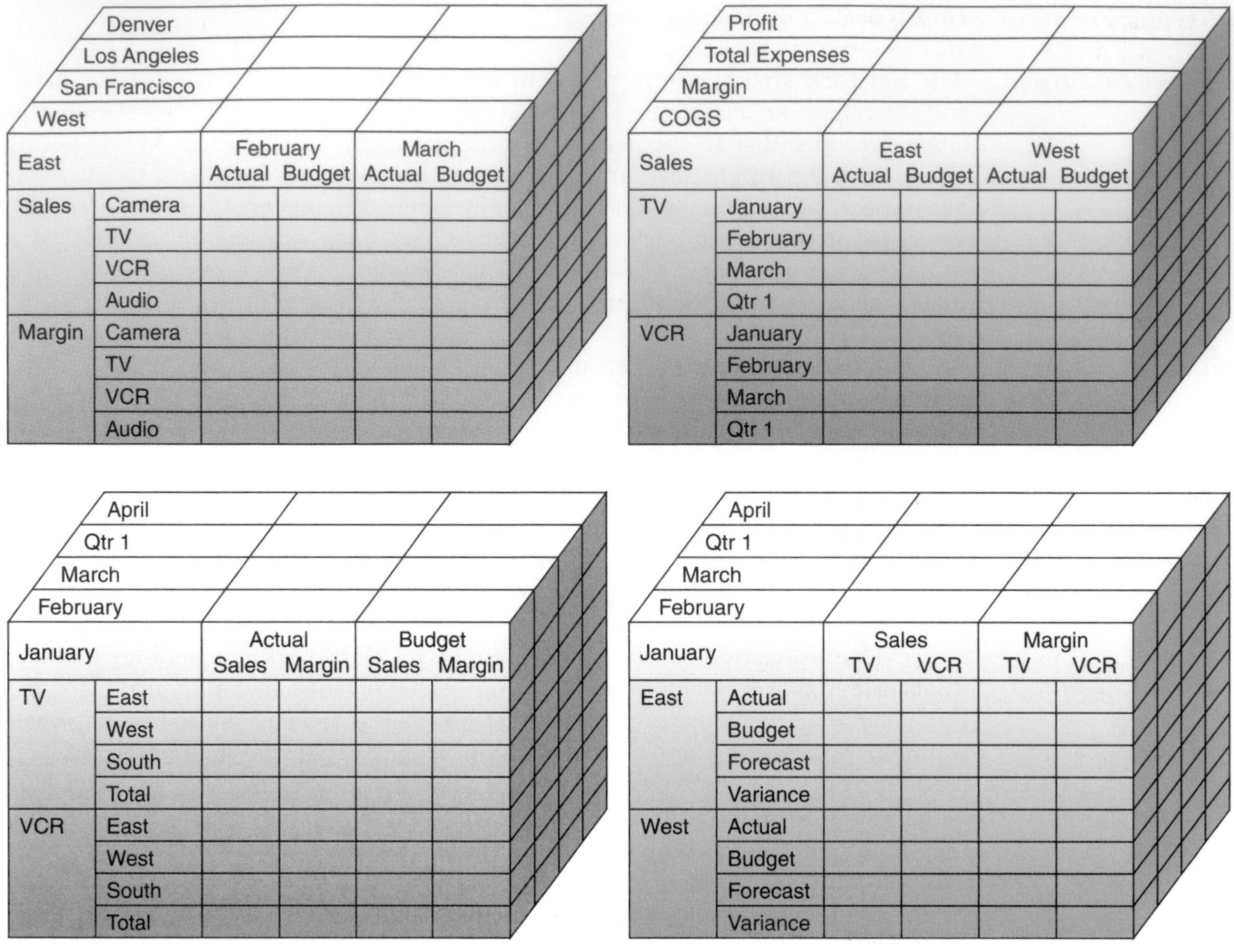

(OODBMS) popular in computer-aided design (CAD) and in a growing number of applications. For example, object technology allows designers to develop product designs, store them as objects in an object-oriented database, and replicate and modify them to create new product designs. In addition, multimedia Web-based applications for the Internet and corporate intranets and extranets have become a major application area for object technology, as we will discuss shortly.

Evaluation of Database Structures

The hierarchical data structure was a natural model for the databases used for the structured, routine types of transaction processing that was a characteristic of many business operations. Data for these operations can easily be represented by groups of records in a hierarchical relationship. However, there are many cases where information is needed about records that do not have hierarchical relationships. For example, it is obvious that, in some organizations, employees from more than one department can work on more than one project (refer back to Figure 13.16). A network data structure could easily handle this many-to-many relationship. It is thus more flexible than the hierarchical structure in support of databases for many types of business operations. However, like the hierarchical structure, because its relationships must be specified in advance, the network model cannot easily handle ad hoc requests for information.

Relational databases, on the other hand, allow an end user to easily receive information in response to ad hoc requests. That's because not all of the relationships

Figure 13.18

The checking and savings
account objects can inherit
common attributes and
operations from the bank
account object.

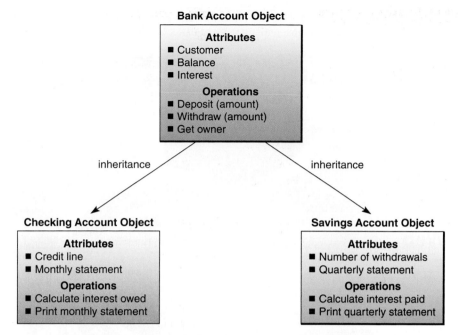

Source: Adapted from Ivar Jacobsen, Maria Ericsson, and Ageneta Jacobsen, *The Object Advantage: Business Process Reengineering with Object Technology* (New York: ACM Press, 1995), p. 65. Copyright © 1995, Association for Computing Machinery. By permission.

between the data elements in a relationally organized database need to be specified when the database is created. Database management software (such as Oracle 8, DB2, Access, and Approach) creates new tables of data relationships using parts of the data from several tables. Thus, relational databases are easier for programmers to work with and easier to maintain than the hierarchical and network models.

The major limitation of the relational model is that relational database management systems cannot process large amounts of business transactions as quickly and efficiently as those based on the hierarchical and network models, or complex, high-volume applications as well as the object-oriented model. This performance gap has narrowed with the development of advanced relational DBMS software with object-oriented extensions. The use of database management software based on the object-oriented and multidimensional models is growing steadily, as these technologies are playing a greater role for OLAP and Web-based applications.

Object Technology and the Web

Object-oriented database software is finding increasing use in managing the hypermedia databases and Java applets on the World Wide Web and corporate intranets and extranets. Industry proponents predict that object-oriented database management systems will become the key software component that manages the hyperlinked multimedia pages and other types of data that support corporate websites. That's because an OODBMS can easily manage the access and storage of objects such as document and graphic images, video clips, audio segments, and other subsets of Web pages.

Object technology proponents argue that an object-oriented DBMS can work with such *complex data types* and the Java applets that use them much more efficiently than relational database management systems. However, major relational DBMS vendors have countered by adding object-oriented modules to their relational software. Examples include multimedia object extensions to IBM's DB2, Informix's DataBlades for their Universal Server, and Oracle's object-based "cartridges" for their Universal Server and Oracle 9i. See Figure 13.19. Let's look at another real world example.

Figure 13.19 Oracle's Universal Server is an example of a hybrid relational/object-oriented DBMS that can manage many types of data.

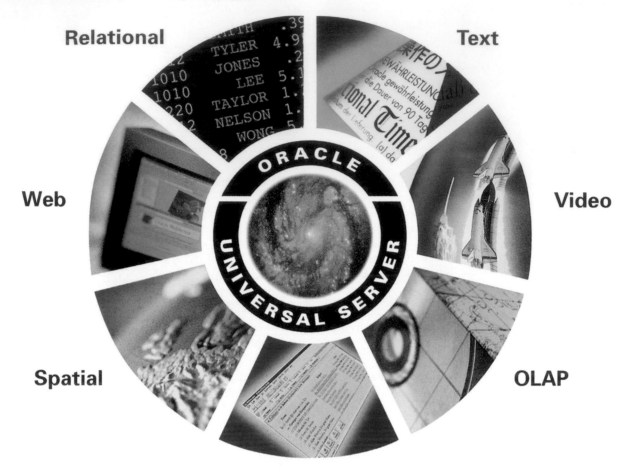

Courtesy of Oracle Corporation.

Enron Energy Services: Object Versus Relational	Houston-based Enron Energy Services, a unit of Enron Corp., found that its Oracle relational database billing application was running out of gas. Depending on local contracts and regulations in more than 100 markets nationwide, Enron may act as an energy wholesaler or energy retailer. Different customer types are charged different rates, pay different taxes, or get billing information in different formats.

Enron originally wrote its billing application to access an Oracle relational database that contained three dozen tables for billing alone. But performance was unacceptable. Asking the relational DBMS to perform the complex queries necessary to produce the customized bills "was like assembling an automobile from scratch" tens of thousands of times per day, according to senior developer Tom Dahl.

Enron didn't replace Oracle but instead added an ObjectStore database management system to create an object database that serves as a buffer. The daily joins are performed in Oracle, but the results are stored in an ObjectStore database, which produces the data needed to create the actual bill. Performance is faster and maintenance is easier with the new relational/object approach. Enron estimates that the new system can handle tens of thousands of transactions per day [4].

Accessing Databases

Efficient access to data is important. In database maintenance, records or objects have to be continually added, deleted, or updated to reflect business transactions. Data must also be accessed rapidly so information can be produced in response to end user requests.

Key Fields

That's why all data records usually contain one or more identification fields, or *keys*, that identify the record so it can be located. For example, the Social Security number of a person is often used as a *primary* **key field** that uniquely identifies the data records of individuals in student, employee, and customer files and databases. Other methods also identify and link data records stored in several different database files. For example, hierarchical and network databases may use *pointer fields*. These are fields within a record that indicate (point to) the location of another record that is related to it in the same file, or in another file. Hierarchical and network database management systems use this method to link records so they can retrieve information from several different database files.

Relational database management packages use primary keys to link records. Each table (file) in a relational database must contain a primary key. This field (or fields) uniquely identifies each record in a file and must also be found in other related files. For example, in Figure 13.16, department number (Deptno) is the primary key in the Department table and is also a field in the Employee table. As we mentioned earlier, a relational database management package could easily provide you with information from both tables by joining the tables and retrieving the information you want. See Figure 13.20.

Sequential Access

One of the original and basic ways to access data is by **sequential access.** This method uses a *sequential organization*, in which records are physically stored in a specified order according to a key field in each record. For example, payroll records could be placed in a payroll file in a numerical order based on employee Social Security numbers. Sequential access is fast and efficient when dealing with large volumes of data that need to be processed periodically. However, it requires that all new transactions be sorted into the proper sequence for sequential access processing. Also, most of the database or file may have to be searched to locate, store, or modify even a small number of data records. Thus, this method is too slow to handle applications requiring immediate updating or responses.

Direct Access

When using **direct access** methods, records do not have to be arranged in any particular sequence on storage media. However, the computer must keep track of the storage location of each record using a variety of *direct organization* methods so that data can be retrieved when needed. New transactions data do not have to be sorted, and processing that requires immediate responses or updating is easily handled. There are a number of ways to directly access records in the direct organization method. Let's take a brief look at three widely used methods to accomplish such direct access processing.

Figure 13.20

Joining the Employee and Department tables in a relational database enables you to selectively access data in both tables at the same time.

Department Table

Deptno	Dname	Dloc	Dmgr
Dept A			
Dept B			
Dept C			

Employee Table

Empno	Ename	Etitle	Esalary	Deptno
Emp 1				Dept A
Emp 2				Dept A
Emp 3				Dept B
Emp 4				Dept B
Emp 5				Dept C
Emp 6				Dept B

One common technique of direct access is **key transformation.** This method performs an arithmetic computation on a key field of record (such as a product number or Social Security number) and uses the number that results from that calculation as an address to store and access that record. Thus, the process is called key transformation because an arithmetic operation is applied to a key field to transform it into the storage location address of a record. Another direct access method used to store and locate records involves the use of an **index** of record keys and related storage addresses. A new data record is stored at the next available location, and its key and address are placed in an index. The computer uses this index whenever it must access a record.

In the **indexed sequential access method** (ISAM), records are stored in a sequential order on a magnetic disk or other direct access storage device based on the key field of each record. In addition, each database contains an index that references one or more key fields of each data record to its storage location address. Thus, an individual record can be directly located by using its key fields to search and locate its address in the database index, just as you can locate key topics in this book by looking them up in its index. As a result, if a few records must be processed quickly, the index is used to directly access the record needed. However, when large numbers of records must be processed periodically, the sequential organization provided by this method is used. For example, processing the weekly payroll for employees or producing monthly statements for customers could be done using sequential access processing of the records in the database.

Database Development

Developing small, personal databases is relatively easy using microcomputer database management packages. See Figure 13.21. However, developing a large database of complex data types can be a complex task. In many companies, developing and managing large corporate databases are the primary responsibility of the database administrator and database design analysts. They work with end users and systems analysts to model business processes and the data they require. Then they determine (1) what data definitions should be included in the database and (2) what structure or relationships should exist among the data elements.

Data Planning and Database Design

As Figure 13.22 illustrates, database development may start with a top-down **data planning process.** Database administrators and designers work with corporate and end user management to develop an *enterprise model* that defines the basic business

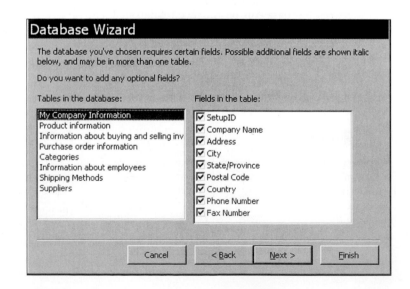

Figure 13.22

Database development involves data planning and database design activities. Data models that support business processes are used to develop databases that meet the information needs of users.

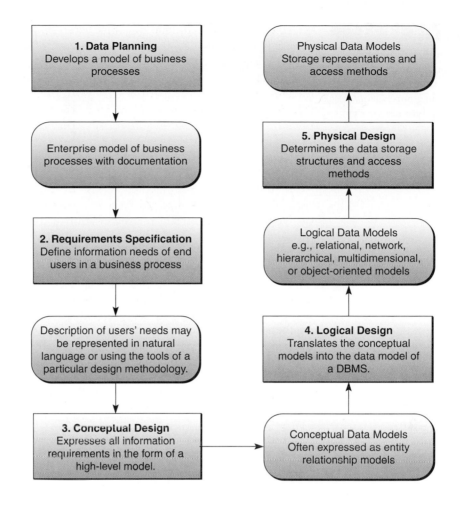

process of the enterprise. Then they define the information needs of end users in a business process, such as the purchasing/receiving process that all businesses have [18].

Next, end users must identify the key data elements that are needed to perform their specific business activities. This frequently involves developing *entity relationship diagrams* (ERDs) that model the relationships among the many entities involved in business processes. For example, Figure 13.23 illustrates some of the relationships in a purchasing/receiving process. End users and database designers could use ERD models to identify what supplier and product data are required to automate their purchasing/receiving and other business processes using enterprise resource management (ERP) or supply chain management (SCM) software.

Such user views are a major part of a **data modeling** process where the relationships between data elements are identified. Each data model defines the logical relationships among the data elements needed to support a basic business process. For example, can a supplier provide more than one type of product to us? Can a customer have more than one type of account with us? Can an employee have several pay rates or be assigned to several project workgroups?

Answering such questions will identify data relationships that have to be represented in a data model that supports a business process. These data models then serve as logical frameworks (called *schemas and subschemas*) on which to base the *physical design* of databases and the development of application programs to support the business processes of the organization. A schema is an overall logical view of the relationships among the data elements in a database, while the subschema is a

Figure 13.23

This entity relationship diagram illustrates some of the relationships among entities in a purchasing/receiving business process.

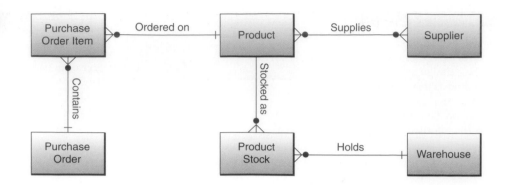

logical view of the data relationships needed to support specific end user application programs that will access that database.

Remember that data models represent *logical views* of the data and relationships of the database. Physical database design takes a *physical view* of the data (also called the internal view) that describes how data are to be physically stored and accessed on the storage devices of a computer system. For example, Figure 13.24 illustrates these different database views and the software interface of a bank database processing system. In this example, checking, savings, and installment lending are the business processes whose data models are part of a banking services data model that serves as a logical data framework for all bank services.

Figure 13.24

Examples of the logical and physical database views and the software interface of a banking services information system.

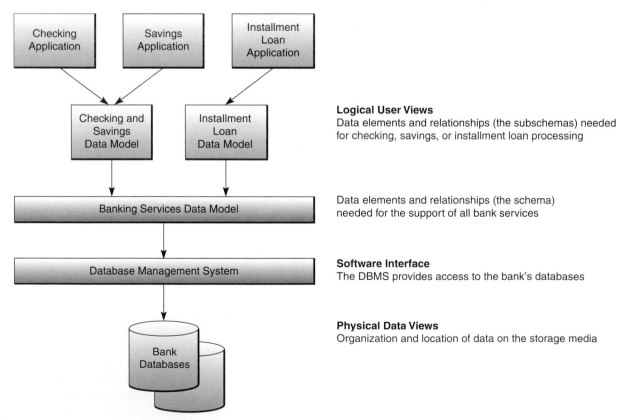

Summary

- **Data Resource Management.** Data resource management is a managerial activity that applies information systems technology and management tools to the task of managing an organization's data resources. It includes the database administration function that focuses on developing and maintaining standards and controls for an organization's databases. Data administration, however, focuses on the planning and control of data to support business functions and strategic organizational objectives. This includes a data planning effort that focuses on developing an overall data architecture for a firm's data resources.

- **Database Management.** The database management approach affects the storage and processing of data. The data needed by different applications are consolidated and integrated into several common databases, instead of being stored in many independent data files. Also, the database management approach emphasizes updating and maintaining common databases, having users' application programs share the data in the database, and providing a reporting and an inquiry/response capability so end users can easily receive reports and quick responses to requests for information.

- **Database Software.** Database management systems are software packages that simplify the creation, use, and maintenance of databases. They provide software tools so end users, programmers, and database administrators can create and modify databases, interrogate a database, generate reports, do application development, and perform database maintenance.

- **Types of Databases.** Several types of databases are used by business organizations, including operational, distributed, and external databases. Data warehouses are a central source of data from other databases that have been cleaned, transformed and cataloged for business analysis and decision support applications. That includes data mining, which attempts to find hidden patterns and trends in the warehouse data. Hypermedia databases on the World Wide Web and corporate intranets and extranets store hyperlinked multimedia pages at a website. Web server software can manage such databases for quick access and maintenance of the Web database.

- **Database Development.** The development of databases can be easily accomplished using microcomputer database management packages for small end user applications. However, the development of large corporate databases requires a top-down data planning effort. This may involve developing enterprise and entity relationship models, subject area databases, and data models that reflect the logical data elements and relationships needed to support the operation and management of the basic business processes of the organization.

- **Data Access.** Data must be organized in some logical manner on physical storage devices so that they can be efficiently processed. For this reason, data are commonly organized into logical data elements such as characters, fields, records, files, and databases. Database structures, such as the hierarchical, network, relational, and object-oriented models, are used to organize the relationships among the data records stored in databases. Databases and files can be organized in either a sequential or direct manner and can be accessed and maintained by either sequential access or direct access processing methods.

Key Terms and Concepts

These are the key terms and concepts of this chapter. The page number of their first explanation is in parentheses.

1. Data dictionary (472)
2. Data mining (476)
3. Data modeling (489)
4. Data planning (478)
5. Data resource management (466)
6. Database administration (478)
7. Database administrator (471)
8. Database access (487)
   a. Direct (487)
   b. Sequential (487)
9. Database management approach (470)
10. Database management system (471)
11. Database structures (480)

   a. Hierarchical (482)
   b. Multidimensional (483)
   c. Network (483)
   d. Object-oriented (483)
   e. Relational (483)
12. DBMS uses (471)
   a. Application development (473)
   b. Database development (471)
   c. Database interrogation (472)
   d. Database maintenance (473)
13. Key field (487)
14. Logical data elements (468)
   a. Character (468)

   b. Field (468)
   c. Record (469)
   d. File (469)
   e. Database (469)
15. Metadata (472)
16. Query language (472)
17. Report generator (472)
18. Types of databases (474)
   a. Data warehouse (475)
   b. Distributed (474)
   c. External (474)
   d. Hypermedia (477)
   e. Operational (474)

Review Quiz

Match one of the key terms and concepts listed previously with one of the brief examples or definitions that follow. Try to find the best fit for answers that seem to fit more than one term or concept. Defend your choices.

_____ 1. The use of integrated collections of data records and files for data storage and processing.

_____ 2. A DBMS allows you to create, interrogate, and maintain a database, create reports, and develop application programs.

_____ 3. A specialist in charge of the databases of an organization.

_____ 4. This DBMS feature allows users to easily interrogate a database.

_____ 5. Defines and catalogs the data elements and data relationships in an organization's database.

_____ 6. Helps you specify and produce reports from a database.

_____ 7. The main software package that supports a database management approach.

_____ 8. Databases are dispersed to the Internet and corporate intranets and extranets.

_____ 9. Databases that organize and store data as objects.

_____ 10. Databases of hyperlinked multimedia documents on the Web.

_____ 11. The management of all the data resources of an organization.

_____ 12. Developing databases and maintaining standards and controls for an organization's databases.

_____ 13. Processing data in a data warehouse to discover key business factors and trends.

_____ 14. Enterprise planning that ties database development to the support of basic business processes.

_____ 15. Developing conceptual views of the relationships among data in a database.

_____ 16. A customer's name.

_____ 17. A customer's name, address, and account balance.

_____ 18. The names, addresses, and account balances of all of your customers.

_____ 19. An integrated collection of all of the data about your customers.

_____ 20. An identification field in a record.

_____ 21. A treelike structure of records in a database.

_____ 22. A tabular structure of records in a database.

_____ 23. Records are organized as cubes within cubes in a database.

_____ 24. Transactions are sorted in ascending order by Social Security number before processing.

_____ 25. Unsorted transactions can be used to immediately update a database.

_____ 26. Databases that support the major business processes of an organization.

_____ 27. A centralized and integrated database of current and historical data about an organization.

_____ 28. Databases available on the Internet or provided by commercial information services.

Discussion Questions

1. How should an E-business enterprise store, access, and distribute data and information about their internal operations and external environment?

2. What roles do database management, data administration, and data planning play in managing data as a business resource?

3. What are the advantages of a database management approach to organizing, accessing, and managing an organization's data resources? Give examples to illustrate your answer.

4. Refer to the Real World Case on Shop At Home and others in the chapter. What key capabilities of data resource management are needed to support a useful business intelligence system?

5. What is the role of a database management system in an E-business information system?

6. Databases of information about a firm's internal operations were formerly the only databases that were considered to be important to a business. What other kinds of databases are important for a business today?

7. Refer to the Real World Case on Payless Shoe Source in the chapter. How could a company's storage management strategies support its use of IT for competitive advantage?

8. What are the benefits and limitations of the relational database model for business applications today?

9. Why is the object-oriented database model gaining acceptance for developing applications and managing the hypermedia databases at business websites?

10. How have the Internet, intranets, extranets, and the World Wide Web affected the types and uses of data resources available to business end users?

Application Exercises

Complete the following exercises as individual or group projects that apply chapter concepts to real world business situations.

1. Calculating Training Costs

Database systems typically involve multiple tables that are related to each other and can be combined on the basis of their logical relationship. In this exercise, we will take the database file in **Application Exercise 12-1**, modify it, and add a second related table containing information about courses.

The data below describe a set of training classes that are available to workers in the Sales, Accounting, and Operations departments. For each course there is a title which can be used to identify it (Title), the duration of the class in hours (Hours), the fixed costs of an instructor and room for the class (Fixed Cost) and a per student cost for materials (Unit Cost).

Title	Category	Hours	Fixed_ Cost	Unit_ Cost
Advanced Database Features	DB	16	$3,250.00	$120.00
Advanced Spreadsheet	SS	16	$3,000.00	$90.00
Database Fundamentals	SS	24	$4,000.00	$100.00
Enliven Your Presentations	PR	8	$1,000.00	$30.00
Spreadsheet Fundamentals	SS	16	$2,500.00	$65.00
Using Presentation Graphics	PR	12	$1,500.00	$40.00

a. If you have not completed **Application Exercise 12-1** complete part A of that exercise now. For this exercise, we will delete the Hours and Category columns from the existing table because they are characteristics of the course and not a particular session, so delete those columns now. Next create a course table with the structure and data shown in the example above. Make sure that the Title column in this new table has exactly the same data type and length that you used for the Title column on the previous table. Create and print a listing of a query that joins the two tables based on the common Title column and displays all columns of both tables.

b. Create a report that could be used to bill the costs of each session to the appropriate departments. Each de-partment will be billed only for Unit Costs, so join the tables and multiply unit cost by the number of attendees from each department to get the billing for that department. Include a total to be billed to each department across all training sessions that have been held.

c. Create a report grouped by Course and Category that shows the total cost of each session (Fixed cost + unit Cost * total attendees) and cost per attendee (the above divided by total attendees).

Tracking Project Work at AAA Systems 2

Database systems typically involve multiple tables that are related to each other and can be combined on the basis of their logical relationship. In this exercise, we will take the database file created in **Application Exercise 9-2**, modify it, and add a second related table containing information about Employees.

The data for the Employee Table is quite simple and consist only of the Employee ID, the Employee Name, and the Billing rate used when charging the employee's work against a project task. The Employee ID is used to identify the employee and to link this data to the project hours data in the existing table.

Employee_Id	Employee_Name	Billing_Rate
123	C. Davis	$70.00
234	J. Jones	$90.00
345	B. Bates	$110.00
456	B. Smith	$80.00

a. If you have not completed **Application Exercise 9-2** complete part A of that exercise now. Open up the database file you created for **Application Exercise 9-2**. Next create an employee table with the structure and data shown in the example above. Make sure that the Employee Id column in this new table has exactly the same data type and length that you used for the Employee Id column on the previous table. Create and print a listing of a query that joins the two tables based on the common Employee ID column and displays all columns of both tables.

b. Create a report grouped by employee that lists their Id and Name and then shows the production week, hours worked that week and amount billed (hours worked times billing rate) for that week.

c. Create a report grouped project name that shows the total amount billed for each task within each project.

Liquid Audio and Others: The Promise of Storage Area Networks

It seemed to come out of nowhere. IT and business professionals used to talk about storage the same way people used to drink coffee before Starbucks came along: need it, got it, but not that interesting. Today, though, the storage market is hot. With $13.5 billion in sales in 2000, and an eye-popping 35 percent increase year-over-year, a lot of folks are paying attention.

Storage area networks (SANs) represent half that market and all the growth. But it's not just about the numbers; it's about the SAN revolution—a network-based architecture that separates servers from storage and provides tremendous performance and flexibility around data management that not even mainframes could supply in the old world. It came just in time, too. The Meta Group predicts that by 2004, companies will be managing ten times as much data as they do today.

E-business and E-commerce have emerged as the driving forces behind this data explosion. Whether it's server logs of web-site usage or critical customer transaction history, data has begotten data. And business applications that use data effectively have led to significant competitive advantages for enterprises. Data has become a critical asset for E-businesses. Think about it: as data becomes more central to an enterprise, more individuals and groups need access to that data, adding layer upon layer of complexity as applications and integration efforts try to make the system work. The problems surrounding the sharing of storage are huge. Large storage suppliers have developed methods for administrators to share computers, but not ways for them truly to share storage.

This is where SANs have defined and will continue to define the storage market. Storage networks provide the flexibility and scalability businesses need to handle all those new disk drives and all that data. Many web-centric companies like AltaVista have racks full of servers to handle web applications on the front end and racks full of servers to handle database applications on the back end. Even older companies like J.P. Morgan, which have well-established data centers, are seeing more servers stacked in racks to handle growing application demands. A distributed, network-based architecture like SAN gives businesses and applications the ability to have multisource access, collaboration, and sharing of that data.

Despite early performance challenges, however, early adopters of SANs have reaped huge benefits for their businesses in terms of cost and customer service. One company that has benefited is Liquid Audio, an E-commerce company that recently installed a Fibre Channel SAN and server-clustering environment for its worldwide business-to-business music delivery application. It considers its data-center infrastructure to be a significant competitive advantages because it enables continuous application availability that yields uninterrupted service to customers.

Another example is Itis Services, a company founded by former EMC sales executives. The demand for application-driven data-center networks is keeping new service providers like Itis extremely busy. The company focuses strictly on storage-networking consulting and integration at Fortune 500 companies. Service-level agreements requiring the highest levels of application availability make it necessary for Itis to use innovations in its data-center proposals for clients. For example, it is incorporating intelligent controllers from Troika Networks to take advantage of automatic failover and failback features for continuous application availability. Itis can't hire people fast enough to keep up with new business demands from clients like large financial institutions, publishing houses, and industrial manufacturers.

It is still early in the SAN game. Companies continue to innovate next-generation systems as companies like EMC, Sun, and Network Appliance work with vendors like Troika and Brocade to deliver the high-performance, fail-safe systems that data centers will continue to need as they build out their storage area and server-to-server networks.

Storage has become more about application management than the storage connectivity. What was once a simple (and dull) story about storage has emerged as a more interesting one about a critical application network for the data center, connecting all of the servers and data storage elements necessary to run business-critical applications.

It's really the business application that matters. As more sophisticated and innovative technologies enhance data-intensive applications, winning companies will put the power of those data-driven applications into use to become even more competitive in the dynamic global marketplace.

Case Study Questions

1. Why has storage technology become such a critical factor in today's business world?

2. What is a storage area network? What are its benefits and challenges to a business like Liquid Audio?

3. Why has "storage management become more about application management than about storage connectivity" for companies like Itis Services?

Source: Adapted from Jennifer Fonstad, "Storage: Big Demands, But Bid Advances Too," *Red Herring*, January 16, 2001, p. 42, and Lucas Mearian, "EMC Begins Targeting Multivendor SANs", *Computerworld*, Februrary 26, 2001, p. 23.

UPMC Health, First Union and Vencor: Storage Management Alternatives

Managing overflowing company data resources is a major challenge in today's E-business environment. Bringing in enterprise-class—and often single-vendor—storage subsystems helps bring order and manageability to growing storage requirements, IT managers say. But while the management software sold with these systems serves many key functions well, key tools may be lacking, and no tools are yet available that provide truly centralized control across all enterprise storage resources.

UPMC Health

When UPMC Health Systems wanted to better manage storage and backups for a diverse array of computer systems across the company, the Pittsburgh-based health care provider decided to consolidate by building storage-area networks (SAN). The SAN arrays and Storage Works management software from Compaq Computer Corp. have helped ease management headaches, says Joe Furmanski, UPMC's manager of systems and planning. But in a multi-vendor-systems environment, the new Compaq management tools still can't do it all.

The health care company originally introduced Storage Works Management software five or six years ago, says Furmanski, who oversees 55 mixed-vendor Unix servers and several minicomputers and workstations, as well as 240 Compaq ProLiant servers, most of which still use direct-attached RAID storage.

The new SANs also play a role in managing backups. Two data centers in Pittsburgh hold 30TB of data between them, and UPMC uses 300 digital tape drives attached to the SAN to fill nearly 8,000 tapes. The data center staffs (about 20 people in total) spend 40% of their time on storage management issues. "Most of the things we do are 24/7, so there aren't a lot of backup windows," says Furmanski.

First Union

First Union Corp., the nation's sixth-largest bank, took a different approach to solving its storage management problems but faces similar issues. The Charlotte, North Carolina-based firm saw its storage needs skyrocket because of increased internal use of data warehousing tools and a move into E-commerce that added nearly 400 servers. First Union now stores 120TB of data in its Charlotte and Jacksonville, Florida data centers, and a planned custom-build check-imaging system will add to the total later this year. "It's been at least a 200% growth, from a storage perspective, every year," says Gary Fox, First Union's vice president of IT.

First Union considered using SANs, which off-load storage systems to dedicated high-speed networks controlled by Fibre Channel switches. It instead went with network-attached storage (NAS), putting dedicated storage devices directly on the company's production network. The network-attached storage technology involves attaching lower-cost application-specific disk storage devices (for example, a server and disk array dedicated to caching Web content), directly to a company's corporate network, instead of more costly mainframe-class RAID storage boxes or SANs.

Fox maintains approximately 1,000 NT and 1,000 Unix servers attached to 67 storage systems supplied by EMC Corp. The Control Center software that comes with the EMC hardware is Fox's primary management tool, and he says the amount of time and effort required to support the Unix server storage has decreased. But management across all enterprise storage systems is still lacking. "We will use this approach until we find a tool that will globally manage it," says Fox.

Vencor

A desire to consolidate disparate storage and server systems—some inherited in acquisitions—while implementing disaster recovery plans was the main reason behind a new storage area network at Louisville, Kentucky-based Vencor Inc., a provider of long-term health care services. "We've been in the process of trying to standardize," says Charles Wardrip, Vencor's director of IS operations and telecommunications. The company built what Wardrip describes as a mainframelike storage model.

"Everything that used to be distributed was now brought into the data center," including 28TB of data on 700 NT and Unix servers, Wardrip says. "We were concerned about interoperability. We felt like if we went with a single vendor, then they had some responsibility for what they sold. Our goal was really to have a single vendor who has some skin in the game."

Seven people manage Vencor's SAN, which is built around EMC Symmetrix disk arrays. Tivoli's TSM software is the primary management tool—the cornerstone of the new backup and recovery system. But Wardrip says he sees a need for broader control. "We need better storage management tools, because utilization and long-range capacity planning are big issues for us," Wardrip emphasizes.

Case Study Questions

1. How does converting to storage area networks help companies like UPMC and Vencor better manage their storage resources?

2. What are the advantages of network-attached storage technology to companies like First Union?

3. What system management software capabilities are still needed, according to the companies in this case?

Source: Adapted from David Essex, "Managing the Data Store," Computerworld, January 22, 2001, pp. 66–67.

National City Bank and Staples: The Roles and Requirements of Data Mining

When Greg James decided to develop a five-year career plan in the early 1990's, he took out a blank sheet of paper. On it, he wrote down his background, which included large-scale database systems, enterprise system architectures, strategic planning and artificial intelligence. He began drawing lines between the experiences that related to one another, "and data mining was what popped out at me," he says.

That exercise underscores the interdisciplinary value of data mining and was the start of a successful career for James, who's now serving as vice president of information marketing at National City Bank in Cleveland.

Data mining involves extracting hidden predictive information from databases to solve business problems. In some cases, analysts mine data for interesting patterns within a segment of the customer base. Then they look for something that might describe why those patterns are happening, James says.

In other projects, such as a direct-marketing campaign, the analysts know upfront the variety of potential results they're trying to predict. Then they develop predictive models to identify likely customers. Either way, James says, data mining requires a varied background. "It's not just a computer science or marketing or statistics discipline," he says.

On any given data mining project, James says, you would want a staff that has a familiarity with statistical concepts; a thorough understanding of the business objectives; project management skills, especially in rapid development or research and development; and experience in large databases, data warehouses, online analytical processing and business intelligence systems. Other requisite skills include fluency with database access tools such as SQL, and programming experience with a data mining tool. National City Bank uses several such tools, including SPSS's Clementine, SAS Institute's Enterprise Miner and Group 1 Software's Model 1.

But of all the skills that data miners should have the most important ones are data analysis and business knowledge. "You really are flying blind if you don't know what you're trying to achieve for the business," James says.

Win Fuller, director of marketing analysis at Framingham, Massachusetts-based Staples Inc., a leading office superstore chain, agrees. "You need to know data mining techniques and how to use the tools," he says. "But it's more important to be able to distill that information into something that management can use."

Fuller, who has a doctorate in econometrics and seven years' management consulting experience, works with a system that contains purchase histories for 15 million customers. Another nontechnical part of the job, he says, is translating general requests from business managers into productive information, using his knowledge of the data available and mining techniques.

"Most people in upper management don't have a clue how you work," Fuller says. "Sometimes, you have to push back and diplomatically say, 'Yes, we can do that, but it will take 10 years,' or 'It doesn't make sense to do that.'"

It's also crucial to acquire experience with processing large amounts of information, Fuller says. "You need to handle data sets that are hundreds of millions of records, detect glitches in that data and know which statistical tools to apply," he says.

New data mining software tools that are appearing on the market require less knowledge of statistics and programming. "More and more, data mining technologies are becoming embedded in vertical applications," says Judson Groshong, vice president of marketing at Accrue Software. "We have hidden the details of the actual algorithms so that the only things users see are the business parameters," says Groshong. The applications are simple enough for a businessperson to use, but a technologist still needs to prepare the data and ensure its accuracy, he says.

But that won't endanger a data miner's job. "The thing that makes good data miners better than mediocre ones is something that is hard to teach and impossible to automate; a good intuition for what variables are likely to be useful and a feel for how to coax information out of data," Fuller says. For example, although tools can automate the model-building process, "only a human knows to replace a ZIP code with characteristics of that ZIP code, such as median income and ratio of renters to owners."

Case Study Questions

1. How does data mining support business decision making? Give an example to illustrate your answer.

2. What capabilities can skilled data mining professionals use to support business decision making?

3. What are the benefits and limitations of date mining software tools for business professionals and data mining specialists?

Source: Adapted from Mary Brandel, "Spinning Data into Gold," *Computerworld*, March 26, 2001, p. 67.

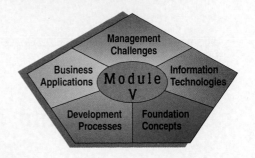

Management
Challenges

Business
Applications

Module
V

Information
Technologies

Development
Processes

Foundation
Concepts

Telecommunications and Networks

Chapter Highlights

Learning Objectives

After reading and studying this chapter; you should be able to:

1. Identify several major developments and trends in the industries, technologies, and applications of telecommunications and networks.

2. Identify the basic components, functions, and types of telecommunications networks used in business.

3. Explain the functions of major types of telecommunications network hardware, software, media, and services.

Overview of Telecommunications and Networks

Internetworking the Enterprise

When computers are networked, two industries—computing and communications—converge, and the result is vastly more than the sum of the parts. Suddenly, computing applications become available for business-to-business coordination and commerce, and for small as well as large organizations. The global Internet creates a public place without geographic boundaries—cyberspace—where ordinary citizens can interact, publish their ideas, and engage in the purchase of goods and services. In short, the impact of both computing and communications on our society and organizational structures is greatly magnified [11].

Thus, telecommunications and network technologies are internetworking and revolutionizing business and society. The Internet, the Web, and intranets and extranets are networking business processes and employees together, and connecting them to their customers, suppliers, and other business stakeholders. This chapter presents the telecommunications and network foundations for these developments.

Analyzing WebLinc and Others

Read the Real World Case on WebLinc and Others on the next page. We can learn a lot about the role that wireless telecommunications technologies can play in business. See Figure 14.1.

Wireless LANs have been around for a long time, but are growing in popularity in business since new technologies like WiFi have significantly improved their speed and performance, and reduced their cost. Companies like WebLinc, SuretyBond.com, and Blueprint Ventures have found that the conveniences and flexibility of wireless LANs promotes better collaboration and increased productivity among their employees. Though the initial cost of wireless-enabled laptops typically exceeds the costs of desktop PCs, wireless users say that the cost of the hardware to operate a wireless LAN is much less than that needed to implement a wire-based LAN for the same number of users. Thus, the use of wireless LANs is expected to continue to increase in the business workplace.

Figure 14.1

SuretyBond.com employees take advantage of a wireless-enabled laptop and their wireless LAN in a business meeting.

Evan Kafka.

WebLinc and Others: The Business Case for Wireless LANs

Mike Bouissey works on the top floor of a seven-story building in Philadelphia's Center City. But on warm, sunny days, he slips his notebook computer under his arm and heads up one more flight. Whenever weather permits, Bouissey, a project manager for web-design company WebLinc, works on the building's flat, asphalt-topped roof. He's never out of touch. He forwards calls from his desk to his cell phone, and —although there's not a cord or a cable in sight—he remains logged on to the company's local area network (LAN), using radio waves rather than wires. He can send and receive e-mail, build web pages, track his team's progress, and do anything else he'd do downstairs in the office, all while sitting on a blanket in the sun. His only limitation: he must stick close to one of three domed skylights so that his computer can stay in touch with the network's base station downstairs. Beyond that, he's set—at least as long as his 2.5 pound Sony PictureBook's batteries last.

But working without wires isn't just a warm-weather perk for outdoor enthusiasts like Bouissey. About two-thirds of WebLinc's 45 staffers use wireless laptop computers full time inside the company's 12,000-square-foot headquarters. So do most of the eight employees at financial-insurance company SuretyBond.com, that subleases part of WebLinc's office space and shares its LAN. The payoff, according to devotees at both companies; true in-house mobility. People can work almost anyplace they want—not just where the wires are.

Whether they're at their desks or gathered around conference tables, both companies' wireless users are always on-line—either on WebLinc's in-house network or on the Web. There's no running back and forth to desktop computers, no logging off one machine and on to another, no hunting around for an available phone jack. From anywhere on (or in Bouissey's case, above) the seventh floor, users just open their computers and sign on once. They then can access files, print documents, write reports, create or run presentations, check e-mail, chat in real time, do research and in some cases, even update their customers' web sites. They can also access the network with wireless handheld computers or web-enabled phones.

Bouissey says that going mobile makes sense for fluid, fast-growing companies like his own, which has grown to nearly 50 employees today. As WebLinc—whose customers include Crayola and Urban Outfitters—expands, it's easy to get new employees up and running: they just sit somewhere, turn on their newly issued notebooks, and get to work. "We don't have to run any new wires; all you need is an outlet," he explains. WebLinc, like many other companies, often shuffles people around as it expands. From a technology standpoint, moving is no big deal with a wireless network: workers can just pack up their computers and go. Finally, if a machine needs service, the owner can just carry it over to the closest information-systems staffer and swap it for a new one.

Another wireless convert is Blueprint Ventures in San Francisco, where all ten employees switched to a wireless LAN last year. General partner Bart Schachter credits the change with streamlining the venture-capital firm's meetings. "We can pick up and go to a conference room, and it's like we never left our desks. You don't know until you have wireless access how often somebody says 'Oh, what's the answer to this question?' and you can look it up right there," says Schachter, whose company has invested in MobileStar and other wireless technologies. "You can take notes right there. You don't have to go back to your office and type them in. Productivity goes up 1,000%.

If you're thinking about switching to a wireless network, you need to know about Wi-Fi. Also known as the less friendly designation IEEE 802.1lb, Wi-Fi—for wireless fidelity—refers to the newest technical standard for wireless networking. The standard boosts networking speed from sluggish—2Mb, or 2 million bits of information per second—to supercharged at 11Mb per second. That allows wireless networks to run faster than traditional Ethernet networks, which top out at 10Mb. And that's why suddenly businesses everywhere are interested in Wi-Fi.

While everybody mentions the system's mobility first, pioneers insist that their wire-free LANs save money, too. True, laptop computers often cost more up front than their deskbound counterparts. But other no-wire network hardware costs far less. And like all true believers, executives in wire-free workplaces seem convinced they're just the first of many. "In 5 to 10 years I think the world will be wireless," says Schachter, pointing out that other countries already lead U.S. business in widespread adoption of wireless technology. "We don't have to dream the future," he says. "The future is happening."

Case Study Questions

1. What is the business value of wireless LANs for the companies in this case?

2. What are some disadvantages and limitations of wireless LANs?

3. Would you prefer a wireless laptop to a networked PC in your business workplace? Why or why not?

Source: Adapted from Anne Stuart, "Cutting the Cord," *Inc. Tech*, 2001, No. 1, pp. 78–82.

Major trends in business
telecommunications.

Industry trends — Toward more competitive vendors, carriers, alliances and network services, accelerated by deregulation and the growth of the Internet and the World Wide Web.

Technology trends — Toward extensive use of Internet, digital fiber-optic, and wireless technologies to create high-speed local and global internetworks for voice, data, images, audio, and videocommunications.

Application trends — Toward the pervasive use of the Internet, enterprise intranets, and interorganizational extranets to support electronic business and commerce, enterprise collaboration, and strategic advantage in local and global markets.

Trends in Telecommunications

Telecommunications is the exchange of information in any form (voice, data, text, images, audio, video) over computer-based networks. Major trends occurring in the field of telecommunications have a significant impact on management decisions in this area. You should thus be aware of major trends in telecommunications industries, technologies, and applications that significantly increase the decision alternatives confronting business managers and professionals. See Figure 14.2.

Industry Trends

The competitive arena for telecommunications service has changed dramatically in many countries in recent years. The telecommunications industry has changed from government-regulated monopolies to a deregulated market with fiercely competitive suppliers of telecommunications services. Numerous companies now offer businesses and consumers a choice of everything from local and global telephone services to communications satellite channels, mobile radio, cable TV, cellular phone services, and Internet access. See Figure 14.3.

The explosive growth of the Internet and the World Wide Web has spawned a host of new telecommunications products, services, and providers. Driving and responding to this growth, business firms have dramatically increased their use of the Internet and the Web for electronic commerce and collaboration. Thus, the service and vendor options available to meet a company's telecommunications needs have increased significantly, as have a business manager's decision-making alternatives.

Technology Trends

Open systems with unrestricted connectivity, using **Internet networking technologies** as their technology platform, are today's primary telecommunications technology drivers. Web browser suites, HTML Web page editors, Internet and intranet servers and network management software, TCP/IP Internet networking products, and network security fire walls are just a few examples. These technologies are being applied in Internet, intranet, and extranet applications, especially those for electronic commerce and collaboration. This trend has reinforced previous industry and technical moves toward building client/server networks based on an open systems architecture.

Open systems are information systems that use common standards for hardware, software, applications, and networking. Open systems, like the Internet and corporate intranets and extranets, create a computing environment that is open to

Figure 14.3

The spectrum of telecommunications-based services available today.

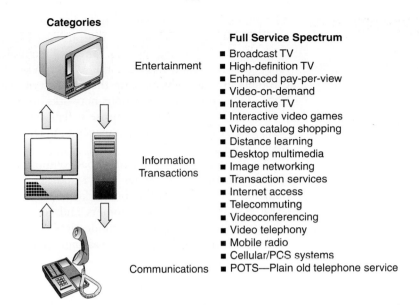

Categories

Entertainment

Information Transactions

Communications

Full Service Spectrum

- Broadcast TV
- High-definition TV
- Enhanced pay-per-view
- Video-on-demand
- Interactive TV
- Interactive video games
- Video catalog shopping
- Distance learning
- Desktop multimedia
- Image networking
- Transaction services
- Internet access
- Telecommuting
- Videoconferencing
- Video telephony
- Mobile radio
- Cellular/PCS systems
- POTS—Plain old telephone service

Source: Adapted from Samir Chatterjee, "Requirements for Success in Gigabit Networking," *Communications of the ACM*, July 1997, p. 64. Copyright © 1997, Association of Computing Machinery. By permission.

easy access by end users and their networked computer systems. Open systems provide greater **connectivity,** that is, the ability of networked computers and other devices to easily access and communicate with each other and share information. Any open systems architecture also provides a high degree of network **interoperability.** That is, open systems enable the many different applications of end users to be accomplished using the different varieties of computer systems, software packages, and databases provided by a variety of interconnected networks. Frequently, software known as *middleware* may be used to help diverse systems work together.

Telecommunications is also being revolutionized by the rapid change from analog to **digital network technologies.** Telecommunication systems have always depended on voice-oriented analog transmission systems designed to transmit the variable electrical frequencies generated by the sound waves of the human voice. However, local and global telecommunications networks are rapidly converting to digital transmission technologies that transmit information in the form of discrete pulses, as computers do. This provides (1) significantly higher transmission speeds, (2) the movement of larger amounts of information, (3) greater economy, and (4) much lower error rates than analog systems. In addition, digital technologies allow telecommunications networks to carry multiple types of communications (data, voice, video) on the same circuits.

Another major trend in telecommunications technology is a change from reliance on copper wire-based media and land-based microwave relay systems to fiber-optic lines and cellular, PCS, communications satellite, and other wireless technologies. Fiber-optic transmission, which uses pulses of laser-generated light, offers significant advantages in terms of reduced size and installation effort, vastly greater communication capacity, much faster transmission speeds, and freedom from electrical interference. Satellite transmission offers significant advantages for organizations that need to transmit massive quantities of data, audio, and video over global networks, especially to isolated areas. Cellular, PCS, mobile radio, and other wireless systems are connecting cellular and PCS phones, PDAs, and other wireless appliances to the Internet and corporate networks.

Business Application Trends

The changes in telecommunications industries and technologies just mentioned are causing a significant change in the business use of telecommunications. The trend toward more vendors, services, Internet technologies, and open systems, and the rapid growth of the Internet, the World Wide Web, and corporate intranets and extranets dramatically increase the number of feasible telecommunications applications. Thus, telecommunications networks are now playing vital and pervasive roles in electronic commerce, enterprise collaboration, and internal business applications that support the operations, management, and strategic objectives of both large and small companies.

An organization's local and global computer networks can dramatically cut costs, shorten business lead times and response times, support electronic commerce, improve the collaboration of workgroups, develop online operational processes, share resources, lock in customers and suppliers, and develop new products and services. This makes telecommunications a more complex and important decision area for businesses that must increasingly find new ways to compete in both domestic and global markets.

The Business Value of Telecommunications

What *business value* is created by the trends in business applications of telecommunications we have identified? A good way to summarize the answer to this question is shown in Figure 14.4. Information technology, especially in telecommunications-based business applications, helps a company overcome geographic, time, cost, and structural barriers to business success. Figure 14.4 outlines examples of the business value of these four strategic capabilities of telecommunications and other information technologies. This figure emphasizes how several applications of electronic commerce can help a firm capture and provide information quickly to end users at remote geographic locations at reduced costs, as well as supporting its strategic organizational objectives.

For example, traveling salespeople and those at regional sales offices can use the Internet, extranets, and other networks to transmit customer orders from their laptop or desktop PCs, thus breaking geographic barriers. Point-of-sale terminals and an online sales transaction processing network can break time barriers by supporting immediate credit authorization and sales processing. Teleconferencing can be

Figure 14.4 Examples of the business value of electronic commerce applications of telecommunications.

Strategic Capabilities	EC Examples	Business Value
Overcome geographic barriers: Capture information about business transactions from remote locations	Use the Internet and extranets to transmit customer orders from traveling salespeople to a corporate data center for order processing and inventory control	Provides better customer service by reducing delay in filling orders and improves cash flow by speeding up the billing of customers
Overcome time barriers: Provide information to remote locations immediately after it is requested	Credit authorization at the point of sale using online POS networks	Credit inquiries can be made and answered in seconds
Overcome cost barriers: Reduce the cost of more traditional means of communication	Desktop videoconferencing between a company and its business partners using the Internet, intranets, and extranets	Reduces expensive business trips; allows customers, suppliers, and employees to collaborate, thus improving the quality of decisions reached
Overcome structural barriers: Support linkages for competitive advantage	Business-to-business electronic commerce websites for transactions with suppliers and customers using the Internet and extranets	Fast, convenient services lock in customers and suppliers

used to cut costs by reducing the need for expensive business trips since it allows customers, suppliers, and employees to participate in meetings and collaborate on joint projects. Finally, business-to-business electronic commerce websites are used by the business to establish strategic relationships with their customers and suppliers by making business transactions fast, convenient, and tailored to the needs of the business partners involved.

The Internet Revolution

Suddenly it seems that the Internet is everywhere. After two decades of relative obscurity as a government and research network, the Internet burst upon the 1990s to penetrate the public consciousness, capturing headlines and attracting millions of users around the world. Every indication points to even faster growth in the 21st century [2].

The explosive growth of the **Internet** is a revolutionary phenomenon in computing and telecommunications. The Internet has become the largest and most important network of networks today, and has evolved into a global *information superhighway*. The Internet is constantly expanding, as more and more businesses and other organizations and their users, computers, and networks join its global web. Thousands of business, educational, and research networks now connect millions of computer systems and users in more than 200 countries to each other. The Internet has also become a key platform for a rapidly expanding list of information and entertainment services and business applications, including enterprise collaboration and electronic commerce systems.

The Internet evolved from a research and development network (ARPANET) established in 1969 by the U.S. Defense Department to enable corporate, academic, and government researchers to communicate with E-mail and share data and computing resources. The Net doesn't have a central computer system or telecommunications center. Instead, each message sent has a unique address code so any Internet server in the network can forward it to its destination. Also, the Internet does not have a headquarters or governing body. The Internet Society in Reston, Virginia, is one of several volunteer groups of individual and corporate members who promote use of the Internet and the development of new communications standards. These common standards are the key to the free flow of messages among the widely different computers and networks of the many organizations and *Internet service providers* (ISPs) in the system.

The Internet is growing rapidly. For example, the Internet grew from over 70 million to over 110 million host computers from early 2000 to early 2001. Figure 14.5 gives you a good idea of the dramatic growth of the Internet.

Internet Applications

The most popular Internet applications are E-mail, browsing the sites on the World Wide Web, and participating in *newsgroups* and *chat rooms*. Internet E-mail messages usually arrive in seconds or a few minutes anywhere in the world, and can take the form of data, text, fax, and video files. Internet browser software like Netscape Navigator and Microsoft Explorer enables millions of users to *surf* the World Wide Web by clicking their way to the multimedia information resources stored on the hyperlinked pages of businesses, government, and other websites. Websites offer information and entertainment, and are the launch sites for electronic commerce transactions between businesses and their suppliers and customers. As discussed in Chapter 5, E-commerce websites offer all manner of products and services via online retailers, wholesalers, service providers, and online auctions.

The Internet provides electronic discussion forums and bulletin board systems formed and managed by thousands of special-interest newsgroups. You can participate in discussions or post messages on thousands of topics for other users with the same interests to read and respond to. Other popular applications include downloading software and information files and accessing databases provided by thousands

Figure 14.5   The rapid growth of the Internet.

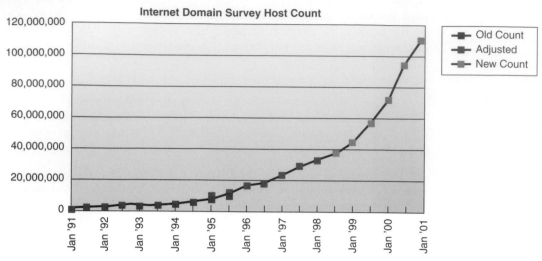

Source: Internet Software Consortium (www.isc.org).

of business, government, and other organizations. You can make online searches for information at websites in a variety of ways, using search sites and search engines such as Yahoo!, Google, and Fast Search. Logging on to other computers on the Internet and holding real-time conversations with other Internet users in *chat rooms* are also popular uses of the Internet. See Figure 14.6.

A Telecommunications Network Model

Before we get any further in our discussion of telecommunications, we should understand the basic components of a **telecommunications network.** Generally, a *communications network* is any arrangement where a *sender* transmits a message to a *receiver* over a *channel* consisting of some type of *medium.* Figure 14.7 illustrates a simple conceptual model of a telecommunications network, which shows that it consists of five basic categories of components:

- **Terminals,** such as networked personal computers, network computers, or information appliances. Any input/output device that uses telecommunications

Figure 14.6

Popular uses of the Internet.

● **Surf.** Point and click your way to thousands of hyperlinked websites and resources for multimedia information, entertainment, or electronic commerce.
● **E-mail.** Exchange electronic mail with millions of Internet users.
● **Discuss.** Participate in discussion forums or post messages on bulletin board systems formed by thousands of special-interest newsgroups.
● **Chat.** Hold real-time text conversations in website chat rooms with Internet users around the world.
● **Buy and Sell.** You can buy and sell practically anything via E-commerce retailers, wholesalers, service providers, and online auctions.
● **Download.** Transfer data files, software, reports, articles, pictures, music, videos, and other types of files to your computer system.
● **Compute.** Log on to and use thousands of Internet computer systems around the world.
● **Other Uses:** Make long-distance phone calls, hold desktop videoconferences, listen to radio programs, watch television, play video games, explore virtual worlds, etc.

Figure 14.7

The five basic components in a telecommunications network: (1) terminals, (2) telecommunications processors, (3) telecommunications channels, (4) computers, and (5) telecommunications software.

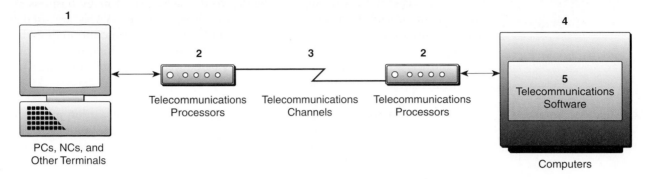

networks to transmit or receive data is a terminal, including telephones and the various computer terminals discussed in Chapter 11.

- **Telecommunications processors,** which support data transmission and reception between terminals and computers. These devices, such as modems, switches, and routers, perform a variety of control and support functions in a telecommunications network. For example, they convert data from digital to analog and back, code and decode data, and control the speed, accuracy, and efficiency of the communications flow between computers and terminals in a network.

- **Telecommunications channels** over which data are transmitted and received. Telecommunications channels may use combinations of **media,** such as copper wires, coaxial cables, or fiber-optic cables, or use wireless systems like microwave, communications satellite, radio, and cellular systems to interconnect the other components of a telecommunications network.

- **Computers** of all sizes and types are interconnected by telecommunications networks so that they can carry out their information processing assignments. For example, a mainframe computer may serve as a *host computer* for a large network, assisted by a midrange computer serving as a *front-end processor*, while a microcomputer may act as a *network server* in a small network.

- **Telecommunications control software** consists of programs that control telecommunications activities and manage the functions of telecommunications networks. Examples include network management programs of all kinds, such as *telecommunications monitors* for mainframe host computers, *network operating systems* for network servers, and *Web browsers* for microcomputers.

No matter how large and complex real world telecommunications networks may appear to be, these five basic categories of network components must be at work to support an organization's telecommunications activities. This is the conceptual framework you can use to help you understand the various types of telecommunications networks in use today.

Types of Telecommunications Networks

There are many different types of telecommunications networks. However, from an end user's point of view, there are only a few basic types, such as wide area and local area networks and interconnected networks like the Internet, intranets, and extranets, as well as client/server and interenterprise networks.

Wide Area Networks

Telecommunications networks covering a large geographic area are called **wide area networks** (WANs). Networks that cover a large city or metropolitan area *(metropolitan area networks)* can also be included in this category. Such large networks have become a necessity for carrying out the day-to-day activities of many business and government organizations and their end users. For example, WANs are used by many multinational companies to transmit and receive information among their employees, customers, suppliers, and other organizations across cities, regions, countries, and the world. Figure 14.8 illustrates an example of a global wide area network for a major multinational corporation.

Local Area Networks

Local area networks (LANs) connect computers and other information processing devices within a limited physical area, such as an office, classroom, building, manufacturing plant, or other work site. LANs have become commonplace in many organizations for providing telecommunications network capabilities that link end users in offices, departments, and other workgroups.

LANs use a variety of telecommunications media, such as ordinary telephone wiring, coaxial cable, or even wireless radio and infrared systems, to interconnect microcomputer workstations and computer peripherals. To communicate over the network, each PC usually has a circuit board called a *network interface card*. Most LANs use a more powerful microcomputer having a large hard disk capacity, called a *file server* or **network server,** that contains a **network operating system** program that controls telecommunications and the use and sharing of network resources. For example, it distributes copies of common data files and software packages to the other microcomputers in the network and controls access to shared laser printers and other network peripherals. See Figure 14.9.

Intranets and Extranets

Intranets are designed to be open, but secure, internal networks whose Web browsing software provides easy point-and-click access by end users to multimedia infor-

Figure 14.8   A global wide area network (WAN): The Chevron MPI (Multi-Protocol Internetwork).

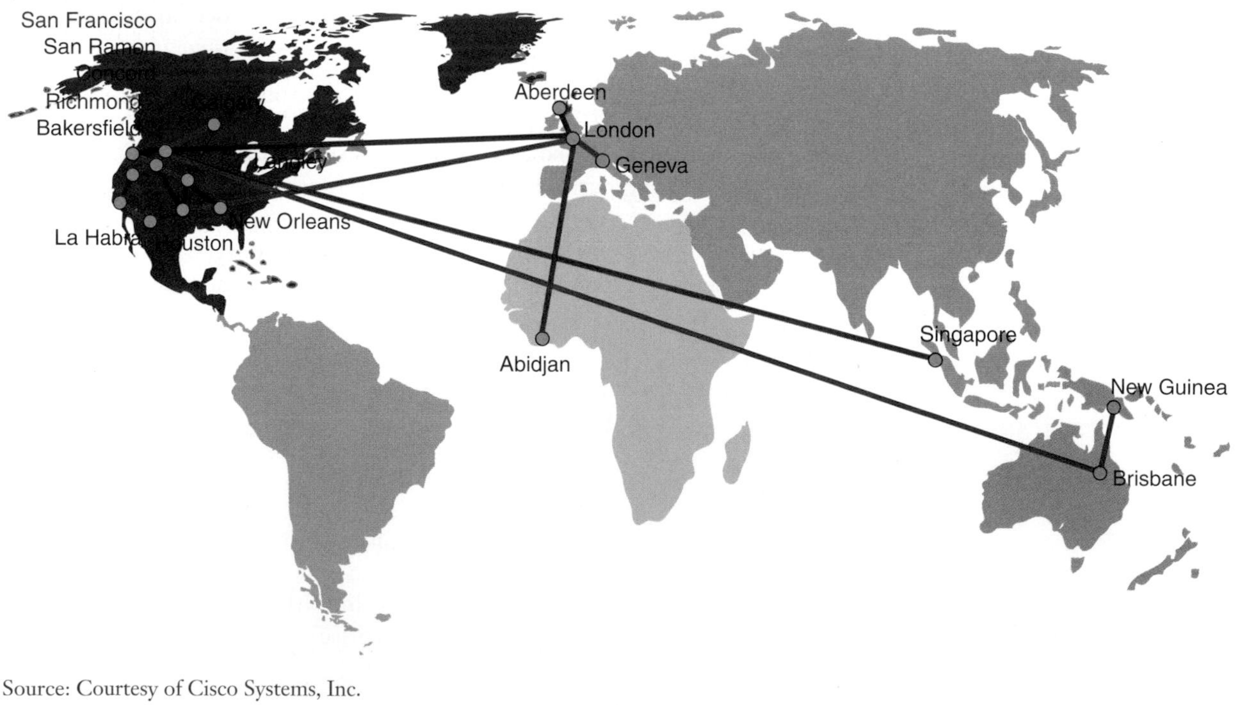

Source: Courtesy of Cisco Systems, Inc.

Figure 14.9

A local area network (LAN). Note how the LAN allows users to share hardware, software, and data resources.

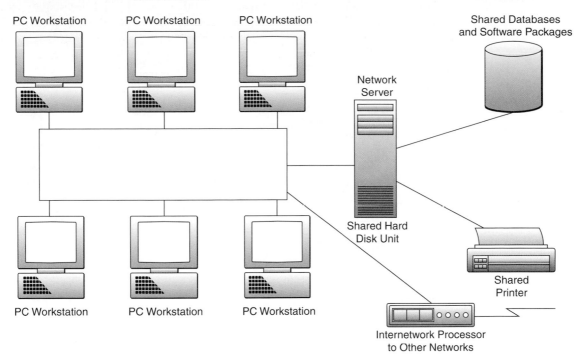

mation on internal websites. Intranet websites may be established on internal Web servers by a company, its business units, departments, and workgroups. For example, a human resources department may establish an intranet website so employees can easily access up-to-the-minute information on the status of their benefits accounts, as well as the latest information on company benefits options. One of the attractions of corporate intranets is that their Internet-like technology makes them more adaptable, as well as easier and cheaper to develop and use than either traditional client/server or mainframe-based legacy systems. See Figure 14.10.

Extranets are networks that link some of the intranet resources of a company with other organizations and individuals. For example, extranets enable customers, suppliers, subcontractors, consultants, and others to access selected intranet websites and other company databases. Organizations can establish private extranets among themselves, or use the Internet as part of the network connections between them.

Many organizations use *virtual private networks* (VPNs) to establish secure intranets and extranets. A **virtual private network** is a secure network that uses the Internet as its main *backbone network*, but relies on the fire walls and other security features of its Internet and intranet connections and those of participating organizations. Thus, for example, VPNs would enable a company to use the Internet to establish secure intranets between its distant branch offices and manufacturing plants, and secure extranets between itself and its customers and suppliers. Let's look at a real world example.

Figure 14.10

An example of intranets and extranets.

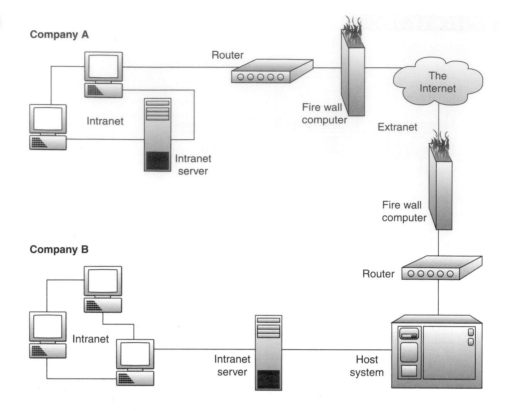

On Command Corporation: Benefits of a VPN

On Command Corporation has replaced its low-speed private-line network with a quicker virtual private network (VPN) so it can provide faster customer service to hotels worldwide that have bought its in-room TV. The VPN service is managed by Internet service provider Concentrick Networks Corporation. The virtual network has slashed the time it takes agents to access data from customer support systems from several minutes to just seconds. The virtual net links 12 far-flung regional offices with the $225 million firm's San Jose, California, headquarters.

Because VPN links are much cheaper than dedicated connections, On Command was able to afford much higher bandwidth—24 times the bandwidth of its 56K bit/sec. private-line network—for about the same price: $1,200 per site per month. The 1.544M bit/sec. lines that On Command now use give its agents access to technical data, information on trouble tickets, and contracts to handle customer inquiries faster. Before the virtual network, agents had to take information from customers, hang up, wait several minutes for the data to arrive, and then call customers back to answer their questions. Now the data arrives in a matter of seconds [16].

Client/Server Networks

Client/server networks have become the predominant information architecture of enterprisewide computing. In a client/server network, end user PC or NC workstations are the **clients.** They are interconnected by local area networks and share application processing with network **servers,** which also manage the networks. (This arrangement of clients and servers is sometimes called a *two-tier* client/server architecture.) Local area networks are also interconnected to other LANs and wide area networks of client workstations and servers. Figure 14.11 illustrates the functions of the computer systems that may be in client/server networks, including optional host systems and superservers.

Figure 14.11

The functions of the computer systems in client/server networks.

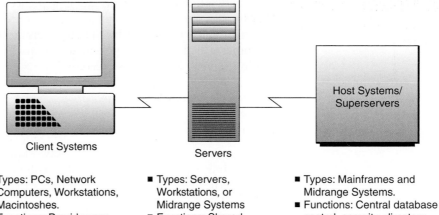

Client Systems

Servers

Host Systems/ Superservers

- Types: PCs, Network Computers, Workstations, Macintoshes.
- Functions: Provide user interface, perform some/most processing on an application.

- Types: Servers, Workstations, or Midrange Systems
- Functions: Shared computation, application control, distributed databases.

- Types: Mainframes and Midrange Systems.
- Functions: Central database control, security, directory management, heavy-duty processing.

A continuing trend is the **downsizing** of larger computer systems by replacing them with client/server networks. For example, a client/server network of several interconnected local area networks may replace a large mainframe-based network with many end user terminals. This typically involves a complex and costly effort to install new application software that replaces the software of older, traditional mainframe-based business information systems, now called **legacy systems.** Client/server networks are seen as more economical and flexible than legacy systems in meeting end user, workgroup, and business unit needs, and more adaptable in adjusting to a diverse range of computing workloads.

Network Computing

The growing reliance on the computer hardware, software, and data resources of the Internet, intranets, extranets, and other networks has emphasized that for many users, "the network is the computer." This **network computing** or *network-centric* concept views networks as the central computing resource of any computing environment.

Figure 14.12 illustrates that in network computing, **network computers** and other *thin clients* provide a browser-based user interface for processing small application programs called **applets.** Thin clients include network computers, Net PCs, and other

Figure 14.12

The functions of the computer systems in network computing.

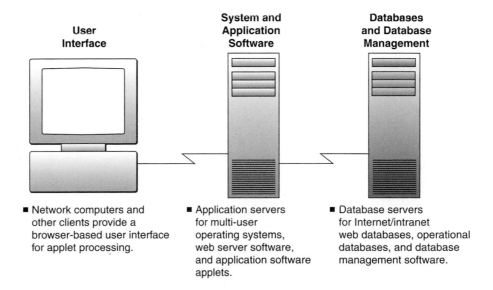

User Interface

System and Application Software

Databases and Database Management

- Network computers and other clients provide a browser-based user interface for applet processing.

- Application servers for multi-user operating systems, web server software, and application software applets.

- Database servers for Internet/intranet web databases, operational databases, and database management software.

low-cost network devices or information appliances. Application and database servers provide the operating system, application software, applets, databases, and database management software needed by the end users in the network. Network computing is sometimes called a *three-tier* client/server model, since it consists of thin clients, application servers, and database servers.

Peer-to-Peer Networks

Peer-to-peer networking is a civilization-altering event for the media industry. Every consumer now is a producer, distributor, and marketer . . . of intellectual property and information content . . . a "human node" with vast new powers [1].

The emergence of peer-to-peer (P2P) networking technologies and applications is being hailed as a development that will revolutionize E-business and E-commerce and the Internet itself. Whatever the merits of such claims, it is clear that peer-to-peer networks are a powerful telecommunications networking tool for many business applications.

Figure 14.13 illustrates two major models of **peer-to-peer networking** technology. In the Napster architecture, P2P file-sharing software connects your PC to a central server that contains a directory of all of the other users *(peers)* in the network. When you request a file, the software searches the directory for any other users who have that file and are online at that moment. It then sends you a list of user names that are active links to all such users. Clicking on one of these user names prompts the software to connect your PC to their PC (making a *peer-to-peer* connection) and automatically transfers the file you want from their hard drive to yours.

The Gnutella architecture is a *pure* peer-to-peer network, since there is no central directory or server. First, the file-sharing software in a Gnutella-style P2P network connects your PC with one of the online users in the network. Then an active link to

Figure 14.13

The two major forms of peer-to-peer networks.

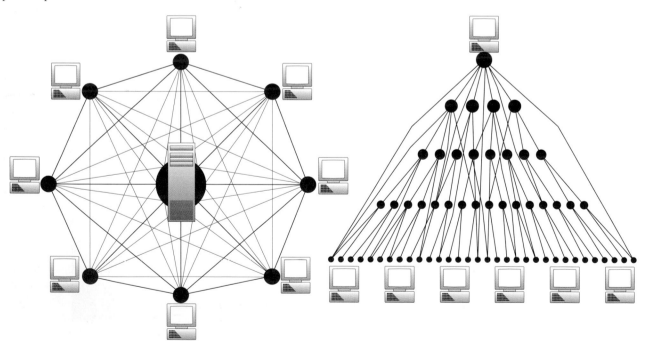

■ A peer-to-peer network with a directory of all peers on a central server: the Napster architecture.

■ A pure peer-to-peer network with no central directory server: the Gnutella architecture.

your user name is transmitted from peer to peer to all the online users in the network that the first user (and the other online users) encountered in previous sessions. In this way, active links to more and more peers spread throughout the network the more it is used. When you request a file, the software searches every online user and sends you a list of active file names related to your request. Clicking on one of these automatically transfers the file from their hard drive to yours.

One of the major advantages and limitations of the Napster architecture is its reliance on a central directory and server. The directory server can be slowed or overwhelmed by too many users or technical problems. However, it also provides the network with a platform that can better protect the integrity and security of the content and users of the network. Some applications of Gnutella P2P networks, on the other hand, have been plagued by slow response times and bogus and corrupted files containing viruses, junk, static, and empty code [1, 8].

Napster.com: Challenges and Promises	Napster is an Internet-based business in San Mateo, Calif., founded by then 19-year-old Shawn Fanning and 20-year-old Sean Parker in September, 1999. Napster developed software that lets people trade music files over the Internet with astonishing ease and at an unbeatable price—free. Since then Napster managed to turn the music industry inside out, igniting an ugly legal battle with the Recording Industry Association of America, which is fighting to keep people from making copies of songs without paying for them. Napster lost a crucial court decision and is trying to develop payment-based services to stay in business.

But Napster's import goes far beyond the balance of power in the music business. Napster represents a new idea, a peer-to-peer architecture for exchanging information. No one can say yet how important the idea will become or how it will change things. It could, for instance, change the way the Internet works, lessening its role as a repository of information and making it a conduit that lets any PC owner reach into any other wired hard drive in the world. Napster-like services could emerge as the next killer app, creating a hunger for greater band-width and ever more powerful PCs. The invasive nature of these services could force us to rethink our attitude toward privacy in a wired world too [8].

Interenterprise Networks	Many business applications of telecommunications involve the use of the Internet, extranets, and other networks to form **interenterprise networks.** Such networks link a company's headquarters and other locations to the networks of its customers, suppliers, and other organizations. For example, you can think of a customer account inquiry system that provides intranet access by employees and extranet access by customers as an example of an interenterprise network. So is the use of electronic data interchange (EDI) systems that link the computers of a company with those of its suppliers and customers for the electronic exchange of business documents. Of course, electronic commerce marketplaces for buying and selling products and services on the World Wide Web typically depend on Internet and extranet interenterprise networks established among businesses, customers, and suppliers.

Thus, the business use of telecommunications networks has moved beyond the boundaries of the enterprise. Now many business firms are using the Internet and other networks to extend their information systems to their customers and suppliers, both domestically and internationally. As we saw in Chapter 2, such interenterprise systems build strategic business relationships and alliances with those stakeholders in an attempt to increase and lock in their business, while locking out competitors. Also, transaction processing costs are frequently reduced, and the quality of service to customers and suppliers improves significantly. See Figure 14.14.

Figure 14.14

GE Global eXchange Services is an example of an interenterprise network. It provides Web-based marketplace services to help businesses engage in electronic commerce.

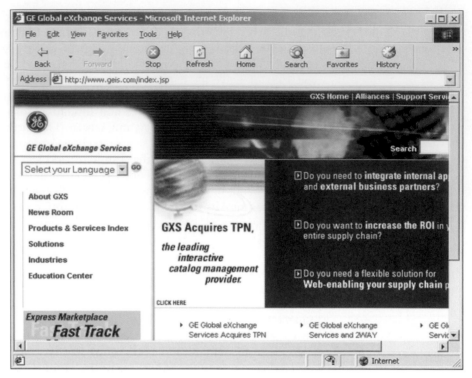

Courtesy of GE Global eXchange Services.

Section II Technical Telecommunications Alternatives

Telecom- munications Alternatives

Telecommunications is a highly technical, rapidly changing field of information systems technology. Most business professionals do not need a detailed knowledge of its technical characteristics. However, it is necessary that you understand some of the important characteristics of the basic components of telecommunications networks. This understanding will help you participate effectively in decision making regarding telecommunications alternatives.

Analyzing Piasecki Steel, Lguide, and CyberTrain

Read the Real World Case on Piasecki Steel, Lguide, and CyberTrain on the next page. We can learn a lot about the business impact of Internet-based telecommunications alternatives from this case. See Figure 14.15.

The demand for some forms of broadband access to the Internet across the U.S. by businesses and consumers exceeds the present capability of telecommunications companies, who are also reluctant to extend service to less populated areas. Some companies, like Piasecki Steel, must settle for older and slower technologies like ISDN. But other businesses, such as Lguide.com and CyberTrain, are able to install broadband alternatives like DSL and fixed wireless, and a few companies now have cable modem access. Lguide.com is one of the many who have experienced poor support from telecom companies who have failed to live up to their promised ability to extend DSL service in some areas of the country. CyberTrain is enjoying the benefits of its fixed wireless service, and is not affected by that alternative's slower uploading speeds. While few companies have cable modem access, the business use of that alternative is growing as cable and telecom companies extend their reach and new technologies continue to improve the quality of cable modem's performance.

Figure 14.16 outlines key telecommunications components and alternatives. Remember, a basic understanding and appreciation, not a detailed knowledge, are sufficient for most business end users.

Figure 14.15

Chris Hedrick, CEO of Lguide.com, continues to depend on DSL service despite previous problems with poor support from his former Internet service provider.

Courtesy Rex Rystedt.

Piasecki Steel, Lguide.com and CyberTrain: Evaluating Broadband Alternatives

Welcome to most of America, a maddening patchwork of high-speed and low-speed Internet access areas. Despite the incessant drone of Internet service providers promising high-speed web surfing, one-third of small businesses can't tap into the newer services. Why? Reaching every nook and cranny of the country is expensive, and service providers are hesitant to install expensive equipment in sparsely populated regions where they might not turn a profit.

"We find it a little frustrating," says Debra Milstein, office manager of Piasecki Steel Construction Co. in Schodack, New York. Like a lot of construction companies that seek municipal work in New York State, Piasecki Steel is required to download bidding information over the Web. Unfortunately, Piasecki Steel can't get high-speed Internet service and risks losing out to rivals who can. So, reluctantly, it has placed an order for ISDN (integrated service digital network), an older technology that offers a 128 kbps connection at best. To make matters more frustrating, Piasecki Steel employees who live just miles away, in places such as Kinderhook, can get 256 Kbps DSL service in their own homes.

Which broadband technology is best for your small company? It depends on your business, your budget, and your location.

DSL

The most common form of DSL, known as "asymmetrical," or ADSL, allows users to download as much as 7 Mbps of data from the Web and upload as much as 640 Kbps. For that, businesses can expect to pay about $200 a month, plus $150 for the modem. But ISPS that offer DSL have been besieged by complaints of poor customer service and slow deployment.

Problems with DSL providers go back for years. Chris Hedrick, founder and CEO of Lguide.com, an online computer-training business with offices in Tacoma and Olympia, Washington, closed his Olympia site after getting fed up with U.S. West Inc., now part of Qwest Communications International. "It took 42 different calls to get our DSL connected to Olympia, and I knew the CEO," says Hedrick, who until 1999 served as technology policy advisor to Washington State Governor Gary Locke. Last June, Hedrick consolidated his entire operation in Tacoma, and now gets DSL from Tacoma's city-owned ISP, Click!Network.

Fixed Wireless

Wireless is one of the best bets for small businesses. At least for now. This medium—typically called fixed wireless because data are sent between a user's computer and a stationary antenna—is the easiest and most cost-effective for both ISPS and users to install. While not as powerful as DSL, fixed wireless services are likely to show up first in many regions. For Lauran James, owner of CyberTrain, a tiny computer-training business on the outskirts of Memphis, WorldCom's fixed wireless service was just right. "I didn't realize how slow my 56K connection was until I tried this," says James. Since November, CyberTrain has paid $150 a month to connect her four full-time employees and as many as ten students to the Internet.

Another good thing about fixed wireless: While it could take months to get your DSL hookup, it'll take just a day or two to get your fixed wireless installed and activated. Expect to spend $500 to $800 for business installations and equipment, plus an additional $150 to $200 in monthly charges.

Fixed wireless does have its drawbacks, however. To work, there must be a relatively clear "line of sight" between the antenna mounted on the user's rooftop and the service provider's antenna, sometimes located as far as 35 miles away. Also, while users can download web pages at a respectable 1 million bits per second (Mbps), uploading data is much slower—512 Kbps, or less. "If you're strictly looking at high speed—for non-transaction-based information—fixed wireless is a great opportunity," says Curt Williams, broadband services products manager at Sprint Corp. "If you're a small business that needs to connect to suppliers, I would lean more toward DSL."

Cable Modems

A high-speed cable connection offers a compelling alternative, if you can get it. Of the 3.8 million cable modems now installed nationwide, fewer than 380,000 are installed in businesses. For example, Time Warner Cable of Maine, one of the cable operator's most prolific cable modem installers, has installed 23,000 cable modems—just 2,000 of those in businesses, including 1,600 with 50 or less employees.

Cable providers typically charge $80 to $225 a month for standard business connections (1.5 Mbps or less). Premium services—for example, a dedicated line that provides 2 Mbps uploading and downloading—can run as high as $1,000 a month. While cable is oft-criticized for being less reliable and more vulnerable to hackers than DSL, some industry analysts say cable is now superior because of recent advances in technology.

Case Study Questions

1. What are the benefits and limitations of : (a) DSL, (b) fixed wireless, and (c) cable modems?

2. Which technology would you recommend for: (a) a small business, and (b) home use. Why?

3. What other Internet access technologies would you consider for small business or home use? Why?

Source: Adapted from Kevin Ferguson "Broadband or Bust," *Business Week Frontier*, March 5, 2001, F21–F24.

Figure 14.16

Key telecommunications network components and alternatives.

Network Component	Examples of Alternatives
Media	Twisted-pair wire, coaxial cable, fiber optics, microwave radio, communications satellites, cellular and PCS systems, wireless mobile and LAN systems
Processors	Modems, multiplexers, switches, routers, hubs, gateways, front-end processors, private branch exchanges
Software	Network operating systems, telecommunications monitors, Web browsers, middleware
Channels	Analog/digital, switched/nonswitched, circuit/message/packet/cell switching, bandwidth alternatives
Topology/architecture	Star, ring and bus topologies, OSI, and TCP/IP architectures

Telecommunications Media

Telecommunications channels make use of a variety of **telecommunications media.** These include twisted-pair wire, coaxial cables, and fiber-optic cables, all of which physically link the devices in a network. Also included are terrestrial microwave, communications satellites, cellular phone systems, and packet and LAN radio, all of which use microwave and other radio waves. In addition, there are infrared systems, which use infrared light to transmit and receive data. See Figure 14.17.

Twisted-Pair Wire

Ordinary telephone wire, consisting of copper wire twisted into pairs (**twisted-pair wire**), is the most widely used medium for telecommunications. These lines are used in established communications networks throughout the world for both voice and data transmission. Thus, twisted-pair wiring is used extensively in home and office telephone systems and many local area networks and wide area networks.

Coaxial Cable

Coaxial cable consists of a sturdy copper or aluminum wire wrapped with spacers to insulate and protect it. The cable's cover and insulation minimize interference and distortion of the signals the cable carries. Groups of coaxial cables may be bundled together in a big cable for ease of installation. These high-quality lines can be placed underground and laid on the floors of lakes and oceans. They allow high-speed data transmission and are used instead of twisted-pair wire lines in high-service metropolitan areas, for cable TV systems, and for short-distance connection of

Figure 14.17

Telecommunications wire and cable alternatives.

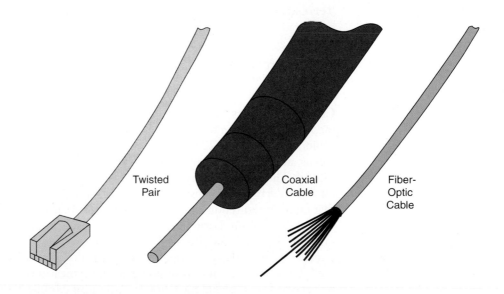

Twisted Pair   Coaxial Cable   Fiber-Optic Cable

computers and peripheral devices. Coaxial cables are also used in many office buildings and other work sites for local area networks.

Fiber Optics

Fiber optics uses cables consisting of one or more hair-thin filaments of glass fiber wrapped in a protective jacket. They can conduct pulses of visible light elements (*photons*) generated by lasers at transmission rates as high as 320 billion bits per second. This is about 640 times greater than coaxial cable and 32,000 times better than twisted-pair wire lines. Fiber-optic cables provide substantial size and weight reductions as well as increased speed and greater carrying capacity. A half-inch-diameter fiber-optic cable can carry over 500,000 channels, compared to about 5,500 channels for a standard coaxial cable.

Fiber-optic cables are not affected by and do not generate electromagnetic radiation; therefore, multiple fibers can be placed in the same cable. Fiber-optic cables have less need for repeaters for signal retransmissions than copper wire media. Fiber optics also has a much lower data error rate than other media and is harder to tap than electrical wire and cable. Fiber-optic cables have already been installed in many parts of the world, and they are expected to replace other communications media in many applications.

New optical technologies such as *dense wave division multiplexing* (DWDM) can split a strand of glass fiber into 40 channels, which enables each strand to carry 5 million calls. In the future, DWDM technology is expected to split each fiber into 1,000 channels, enabling each strand to carry up to 122 million calls. In addition, newly developed *optical routers* will be able to send optical signals up to 2,500 miles without needing regeneration, thus eliminating the need for repeaters every 370 miles to regenerate signals [13, 15].

Wireless Technologies

Wireless telecommunications technologies rely on radio wave, microwave, infrared, and visible light pulses to transport digital communications without wires between communications devices. Wireless technologies include terrestrial microwave, communications satellites, cellular and PCS telephone and pager systems, mobile data radio, wireless LANs, and various wireless Internet technologies. Each technology utilizes specific ranges (in megahertz) of electromagnetic frequencies that are specified by national regulatory agencies to minimize interference and encourage efficient telecommunications. Let's briefly review some of these major wireless communications technologies.

Terrestrial Microwave

Terrestrial microwave involves earthbound microwave systems that transmit high-speed radio signals in a line-of-sight path between relay stations spaced approximately 30 miles apart. Microwave antennas are usually placed on top of buildings, towers, hills, and mountain peaks, and they are a familiar sight in many sections of the country. They are still a popular medium for both long-distance and metropolitan area networks.

Communications Satellites

Communications satellites also use microwave radio as their telecommunications medium. Many communications satellites are placed in stationary geosynchronous orbits approximately 22,000 miles above the equator. Satellites are powered by solar panels and can transmit microwave signals at a rate of several hundred million bits per second. They serve as relay stations for communications signals transmitted from earth stations. Earth stations use dish antennas to beam microwave signals to the satellites that amplify and retransmit the signals to other earth stations thousands of miles away.

While communications satellites were used initially for voice and video transmission, they are now also used for high-speed transmission of large volumes of data. Because of time delays caused by the great distances involved, they are not suitable for interactive, real-time processing. Communications satellite systems are operated by several firms, including Comsat, American Mobile Satellite, and Intellsat.

A variety of other satellite technologies are being implemented to improve global business communications. For example, many companies use networks of small satellite dish antennas known as VSAT (very-small-aperture terminal) to connect their stores and distant work sites via satellite. Other satellite networks use many low-earth orbit (LEO) satellites orbiting at an altitude of only 500 miles above the earth. Companies like Globalstar offer cellular phone, paging, and messaging services to users anywhere on the globe.

Cellular and PCS Systems

Cellular and PCS telephone and pager systems use several radio communications technologies. However, all of them divide a geographic area into small areas, or *cells*, typically from one to several square miles in area. Each cell has its own low-power transmitter or radio relay antenna device to relay calls from one cell to another. Computers and other communications processors coordinate and control the transmissions to and from mobile users as they move from one area to another.

Cellular phone systems have long used analog communications technologies operating at frequencies in the 800 to 900 MHz cellular band. Newer cellular systems use digital technologies, which provide greater capacity and security, and additional services such as voice mail, paging, messaging, and caller ID. These capabilities are also available with the new PCS (Personal Communications Services) phone systems. PCS operates at 1,900 MHz frequencies using digital technologies that are related to digital cellular. However, PCS phone systems cost substantially less to operate and use than cellular systems and have lower power consumption requirements [14].

The Wireless Web

Wireless access to the Internet, intranets, and extranets is growing as more Web-enabled information appliances proliferate. Smart telephones, pagers, PDAs, and other portable communications devices have become *very thin clients* in wireless networks. Agreement on a standard *wireless application protocol* (WAP) has encouraged the development of many wireless Web applications and services. The telecommunications industry continues to work on *third generation* (3G) wireless technologies whose goal is to raise wireless transmission speeds to enable streaming video and multimedia applications on mobile devices.

For example, the Palm VII PDA can send and receive E-mail and provides Web access via a "Web clipping" technology that generates custom-designed Web pages from many popular financial, securities, travel, sport, entertainment, and E-commerce websites. Another example is the Sprint PCS Wireless Web phone, which delivers similar Web content and E-mail services via a Web-enabled PCS phone [3]. See Figure 14.18.

Figure 14.18

The Palm VII PDA gives users Internet access for E-mail and website services.

Fisher/Thatcher/Stone.

Figure 14.19 illustrates the wireless application protocol that is the foundation of wireless mobile Internet and Web applications. The WAP standard specifies how Web pages in HTML or XML are translated into a *wireless markup language* (WML) by *filter* software and preprocessed by *proxy* software to prepare the Web pages for wireless transmission from a Web server to a Web-enabled wireless device [11].

Telecommunications Processors

Telecommunications processors such as modems, multiplexers, switches, and routers perform a variety of support functions between the computers and other devices in a telecommunications network. Let's take a look at some of these processors and their functions. See Figure 14.20.

Modems

Modems are the most common type of communications processor. They convert the digital signals from a computer or transmission terminal at one end of a communications link into analog frequencies that can be transmitted over ordinary telephone lines. A modem at the other end of the communications line converts the transmitted data back into digital form at a receiving terminal. This process is known as *modulation* and *demodulation*, and the word *modem* is a combined abbreviation of those two words. Modems come in several forms, including small stand-alone units, plug-in circuit boards, and removable modem cards for laptop PCs. Most modems also support a variety of telecommunications functions, such as transmission error control, automatic dialing and answering, and a faxing capability.

Modems are used because ordinary telephone networks were first designed to handle continuous analog signals (electromagnetic frequencies), such as those generated by the human voice over the telephone. Since data from computers are in digital form (voltage pulses), devices are necessary to convert digital signals into appropriate analog transmission frequencies and vice versa. However, digital communications networks that use only digital signals and do not need analog/digital conversion are becoming commonplace. Since most modems also perform a variety of telecommunications support functions, devices called digital modems are still used in digital networks. Figure 14.21 compares several new modem and telecommunications technologies for access to the Internet and other networks by home and business users [12].

Figure 14.19

The wireless application protocol (WAP) architecture for wireless Internet services to mobile information appliances.

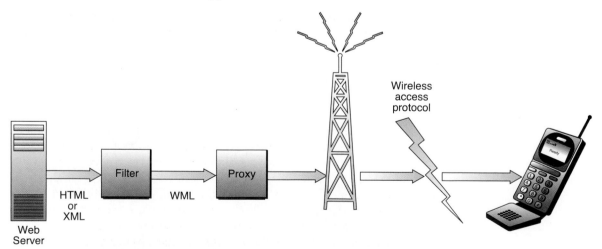

Source: Adapted from David G. Messerschmitt, *Network Applications: A Guide to the New Computing Infrastructure* (San Francisco: Morgan Kaufmann Publishers, 1999), p. 350.

Figure 14.20

The communications processors involved in a typical Internet connection.

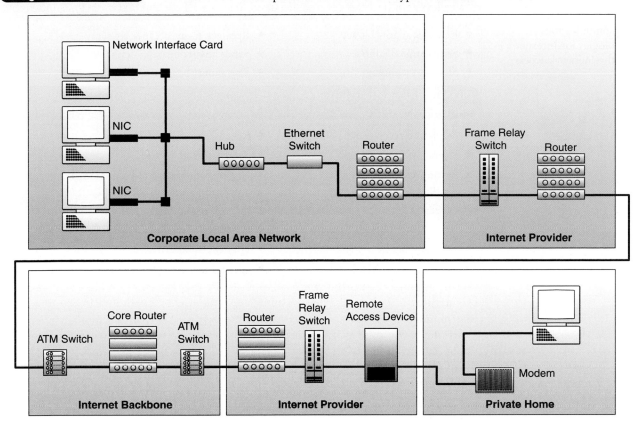

Multiplexers

A **multiplexer** is a communications processor that allows a single communications channel to carry simultaneous data transmissions from many terminals. Thus, a single communications line can be shared by several terminals. Typically, a multiplexer merges the transmissions of several terminals at one end of a communications channel, while a similar unit separates the individual transmissions at the receiving end.

This is accomplished in two basic ways. In *frequency division multiplexing* (FDM), a multiplexer effectively divides a high-speed channel into multiple slow-speed channels. In *time division multiplexing* (TDM), the multiplexer divides the time each terminal can use the high-speed line into very short time slots, or time frames. The most advanced and popular type of multiplexer is the *statistical time division multiplexer*, most commonly referred to as a statistical multiplexer. Instead of giving all terminals equal time slots, it dynamically allocates time slots only to active terminals according to priorities assigned by a telecommunications manager.

Internetwork Processors

Telecommunications networks are interconnected by special-purpose communications processors called **internetwork processors** such as switches, routers, hubs, and gateways. A *switch* is a communications processor that makes connections between telecommunications circuits in a network so a telecommunications message can reach its intended destination. A *router* is a more intelligent communications processor that interconnects networks based on different rules or *protocols*, so a telecommunications message can be routed to its destination. A *hub* is a port switching communications processor. Advanced versions of hubs provide automatic switching among connections called *ports* for shared access to a network's resources. Workstations, servers, printers, and other network resources are connected to ports, as are switches and routers

Figure 14.21

Comparing modem and telecommunications technologies for Internet and other network access.

Modem (56K bit/sec)	DSL (Digital Subscriber Line) Modem
• Receives at 56K bit/sec.	• Receives at up to 256K bit/sec.
• Sends at 28.8K bit/sec.	• Sends at 64K bit/sec.
• Slowest technology	• Users must be near switching centers
ISDN (Integrated Services Digital Network)	**Cable Modem**
• Sends and receives at 128K bit/sec.	• Receives at 1.5 to 3M bit/sec.
• Users need extra lines	• Sends at 128K bit/sec.
• Becoming obsolete	• Cable systems need to be upgraded
Home Satellite	**Local Microwave**
• Receives at 400K bit/sec.	• Sends and receives at 512K to 1.4M bit/sec.
• Sends via phone modem	• Higher cost alternative
• Slow sending, higher cost	• May require line of sight to base antenna

provided by the hub to other networks. Networks that use different communications architectures are interconnected by using a communications processor called a *gateway*. All these devices are essential to providing connectivity and easy access between the multiple LANs and wide area networks that are part of the intranets and client/server networks in many organizations.

Telecom-munications Software

Software is a vital component of all telecommunications networks. In Chapter 12, we discussed telecommunications and network management software, which may reside in PCs, servers, mainframes, and communications processors like multiplexers and routers. For example, mainframe-based wide area networks frequently use *telecommunications monitors or teleprocessing* (TP) monitors. CICS (Customer Identification Control System) for IBM mainframes is a typical example. Servers in local area networks frequently rely on Novell NetWare, Sun's Solaris, UNIX, Linux, or Microsoft Windows 2000 Servers.

Corporate intranets use network management software like the iPlanet Portal Server, which is one of several programs for network management, electronic commerce, and application development in Sun Microsystems and Netscape's iPlanet software servers for the Internet, intranets, and extranets. Many software vendors offer telecommunications software known as *middleware*, which can help diverse networks communicate with each other. A variety of communications software packages are available for microcomputers, especially Internet Web browsers like Netscape Navigator and Microsoft Explorer. See Figure 14.22.

Telecommunications software packages provide a variety of communications support services. For example, they work with a communications processor (such as a modem) to connect and disconnect communications links and establish communications parameters such as transmission speed, mode, and direction.

Network management packages such as LAN network operating systems and WAN telecommunications monitors determine transmission priorities, route (switch) messages, poll terminals in the network, and form waiting lines (queues) of transmission requests. They also detect and correct transmission errors, log statistics of network activity, and protect network resources from unauthorized access.

Figure 14.22

This website management software monitors and evaluates website usage and resources.

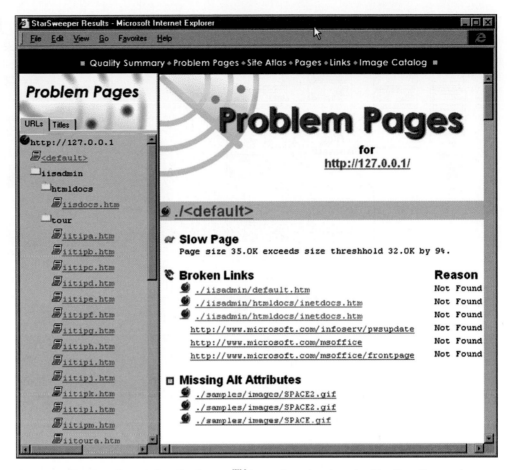

Courtesy of StarBase Corporation. StarSweeper™ is a registered trademark of StarBase Corporation.

Network Topologies

There are several basic types of network *topologies*, or structures, in telecommunications networks. Figure 14.23 illustrates three basic topologies used in wide area and local area telecommunications networks. A *star* network ties end user computers to a central computer. A *ring* network ties local computer processors together in a ring on a more equal basis. A *bus* network is a network in which local processors share the same bus, or communications channel. A variation of the ring network is the *mesh* network. It uses direct communications lines to connect some or all of the computers in the ring to each other. Another variation is the *tree* network, which joins several bus networks together.

Client/server networks may use a combination of star, ring, and bus approaches. Obviously, the star network is more centralized, while ring and bus networks have a more decentralized approach. However, this is not always the case. For example, the central computer in a star configuration may be acting only as a *switch*, or message-switching computer, that handles the data communications between autonomous local computers. Star, ring, and bus networks differ in their performances, reliabilities, and costs. A pure star network is considered less reliable than a ring network, since the other computers in the star are heavily dependent on the central host computer. If it fails, there is no backup processing and communications capability, and the local computers are cut off from each other. Therefore, it is essential that the host computer be highly reliable. Having some type of multiprocessor architecture to provide a fault tolerant capability is a common solution.

Ring and bus networks are most common in local area networks. Ring networks are considered more reliable and less costly for the type of communications in such

Figure 14.23 The ring, star, and bus network topologies.

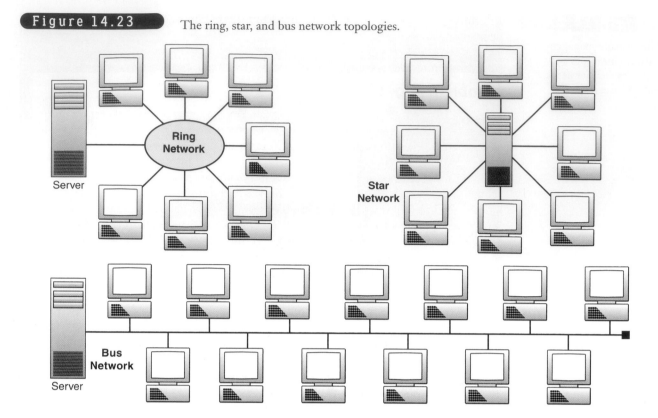

networks. If one computer in the ring goes down, the other computers can continue to process their own work as well as to communicate with each other.

Network Architectures and Protocols

Until quite recently, there was a lack of sufficient standards for the interfaces between the hardware, software, and communications channels of telecommunications networks. This situation hampered the use of telecommunications, increased its costs, and reduced its efficiency and effectiveness. In response, telecommunications manufacturers and national and international organizations have developed standards called *protocols* and master plans called *network architectures* to support the development of advanced data communications networks.

Protocols. A **protocol** is a standard set of rules and procedures for the control of communications in a network. However, these standards may be limited to just one manufacturer's equipment, or to just one type of data communications. Part of the goal of communications network architectures is to create more standardization and compatibility among communications protocols. One example of a protocol is a standard for the physical characteristics of the cables and connectors between terminals, computers, modems, and communications lines. Other examples are the protocols that establish the communications control information needed for *handshaking*, which is the process of exchanging predetermined signals and characters to establish a telecommunications session between terminals and computers. Other protocols deal with control of data transmission reception in a network, switching techniques, internetwork connections, and so on.

Network Architectures. The goal of network architectures is to promote an open, simple, flexible, and efficient telecommunications environment. This is accomplished by the use of standard protocols, standard communications hardware and software interfaces, and the design of a standard multilevel interface between end users and computer systems.

The OSI Model

The International Standards Organization (ISO) has developed a seven-layer Open Systems Interconnection (OSI) model to serve as a standard model for network architectures. Dividing data communications functions into seven distinct layers promotes the development of modular network architectures, which assists the development, operation, and maintenance of complex telecommunications networks. Figure 14.24 illustrates the functions of the seven layers of the OSI model architecture.

The Internet's TCP/IP

The Internet uses a system of telecommunications protocols that has become so widely used that it is equivalent to a network architecture. The Internet's protocol suite is called Transmission Control Protocol/Internet Protocol and is known as TCP/IP. As Figure 14.24 shows, TCP/IP consists of five layers of protocols that can be related to the seven layers of the OSI architecture. TCP/IP is used by the Internet and by all intranets and extranets. Many companies and other organizations are thus converting their client/server networks to TCP/IP technology, which are now commonly called IP networks.

Bandwidth Alternatives

The communications speed and capacity of telecommunications networks can be classified by **bandwidth.** This is the frequency range of a telecommunications channel; it determines the channel's maximum transmission rate. The speed and capacity of data transmission rates are typically measured in bits per second (BPS). This is sometimes referred to as the *baud* rate, though baud is more correctly a measure of signal changes in a transmission line.

Figure 14.24

The seven layers of the OSI communications network architecture, and the five layers of the Internet's TCP/IP protocol suite.

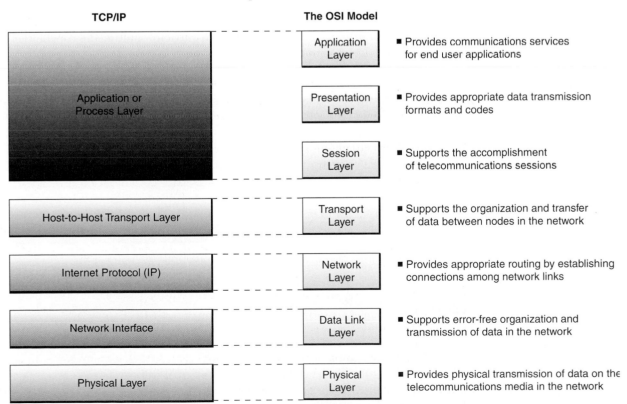

Narrow-band channels typically provide low-speed transmission rates up to 64K BPS, but can now handle up to 2 million BPS. They are usually unshielded twisted-pair lines commonly used for telephone voice communications, and for data communications by the modems of PCs and other devices. Medium-speed channels (*medium-band*) use shielded twisted-pair lines for transmission speeds up to 100 MBPS.

Broadband channels provide high-speed transmission rates at intervals from 256,000 BPS to several billion BPS. Typically, they use microwave, fiber optics, or satellite transmission. Examples are 1.54 million BPS for T1 and 45M BPS for T3 communications channels, up to 100 MBPS for communications satellite channels, and between 52 MBPS and 10 GBPS for fiber-optic lines. See Figures 14.25 and 14.26.

Switching Alternatives

Regular telephone service relies on *circuit switching*, in which a switch opens a circuit to establish a link between a sender and receiver; it remains open until the communication session is completed. In message switching, a message is transmitted a block at a time from one switching device to another.

Packet switching involves subdividing communications messages into fixed or variable groups called packets. For example, in the X.25 protocol, packets are 128 characters long, while they are of variable length in the *frame relay* technology. Packet switching networks are frequently operated by *value-added carriers* who use computers and other communications processors to control the packet switching process and transmit the packets of various users over their networks.

Early packet switching networks were X.25 networks. The X.25 protocol is an international set of standards governing the operations of widely used, but relatively slow, packet switching networks. *Frame relay* is another popular packet switching protocol, and is used by many large companies for their wide area networks. Frame relay is considerably faster than X.25, and is better able to handle the heavy telecommunications traffic of interconnected local area networks within a company's wide area client/server network. ATM (*asynchronous transfer mode*) is an emerging high-capacity *cell switching* technology. An ATM switch breaks voice, video, and other data into fixed cells of 53 bytes (48 bytes of data and 5 bytes of control information) and routes them to their next destination in the network. ATM networks are being developed by many companies needing its fast, high-capacity multimedia capabilities for voice, video, and data communications.

Figure 14.25

Examples of telecommunications transmission speeds by type of media and network technology.

Type of Media	Maximum BPS
Twisted pair—unshielded/shielded	2M/100M
Coaxial cable—baseband/broadband	264M/550M
Satellite/terrestrial microwave	200M
Wireless LAN radio	3.3M
Infrared LAN	4M
Fiber-optic cable	320G

Network Technologies	Typical-Maximum BPS
Standard Ethernet or token ring	10–16M
High-speed Ethernet	100M–1G
FDDI: fiber distributed data interface	100M
DDN: digital data network	2.4K–2M
PSN: packet switching network	2.4K–64K
Frame relay network	1.5M–45M
ISDN: integrated services digital network	64K/128K–2M
ATM: asynchronous transfer mode	25/155M–2.4G
OC: Optical Carrier	52M–10G

KBPS = thousand BPS or kilobits per second.   GBPS = billion BPS or gigabits per second.
MBPS = million BPS or megabits per second.

Figure 14.26

Why four large retail chains chose different network technologies to connect their stores.

Company	Technology	Why
Sears	Frame relay	Reliable, inexpensive and accommodates mainframe and Internet protocols
Rack Room	VSAT	Very inexpensive way to reach small markets and shared satellite dishes at malls
Hannaford	ATM	Very high bandwidth; combines voice, video, and data
7-Eleven	ISDN	Can use multiple channels to partition traffic among different uses

Source: Adapted from David Orenstein, "Price, Speed, Location All Part of Broadband Choice," *Computerworld*, July 26, 1999, p. 62. Copyright 1999 by Computerworld, Inc., Framingham, MA 01701. Reprinted from *Computerworld*.

Summary

- **Telecommunications Trends.** Organizations are becoming internetworked enterprises that use the Internet, intranets, and other telecommunications networks to support E-business operations and collaboration within the enterprise, and with their customers, suppliers, and other business partners. Telecommunications has entered a deregulated and fiercely competitive environment with many vendors, carriers, and services. Telecommunications technology is moving toward open, internetworked digital networks for voice, data, video, and multimedia. A major trend is the pervasive use of the Internet and its technologies to build interconnected enterprise and global networks, like intranets and extranets, to support enterprise collaboration, electronic commerce, and other E-business applications.

- **The Internet Revolution.** The explosive growth of the Internet and the use of its enabling technologies have revolutionized computing and telecommunications. The Internet has become the key platform for a rapidly expanding list of information and entertainment services and business applications, including enterprise collaboration and electronic commerce systems. Open systems with unrestricted connectivity using Internet technologies are the primary telecommunications technology drivers in E-business systems. Their primary goal is to promote easy and secure access by business professionals and consumers to the resources of the Internet, enterprise intranets, and interorganizational extranets.

- **Telecommunications Networks.** The major generic components of any telecommunications network are (1) terminals, (2) telecommunications processors, (3) communications channels, (4) computers, and (5) telecommunications software. There are several basic types of telecommunications networks, including wide area networks (WANs) and local area networks (LANs). Most WANs and LANs use client/server, network computing, and Internet technologies to form intranets, extranets, and other interorganizational networks.

- **Network Alternatives.** Key telecommunications network alternatives and components are summarized in Figure 14.16 for telecommunications media, processors, software, channels, and network architectures. A basic understanding of these major alternatives will help business end users participate effectively in decisions involving telecommunications issues. Telecommunications processors include modems, multiplexers, internetwork processors, and various devices to help interconnect and enhance the capacity and efficiency of telecommunications channels. Telecommunications channels use such media as twisted-pair wire, coaxial cables, fiber-optic cables, terrestrial microwave, communications satellites, cellular and PCS systems, and other wireless technologies. Telecommunications software, such as network operating systems, telecommunications monitors, and Web browsers, controls and supports the communications activity in a telecommunications network.

Key Terms and Concepts

These are the key terms and concepts of this chapter. The page number of their first explanation is in parentheses.

1. Bandwidth alternatives (523)
2. Business value of telecommunications (502)
3. Cellular phone systems (517)
4. Client/server networks (508)
5. Coaxial cable (515)
6. Communications satellites (516)
7. Downsizing (509)
8. Extranets (507)
9. Fiber-optics (516)
10. The Internet (503)
11. Internet revolution (503)
12. Internet technologies (500)
13. Internetwork processors (519)
14. Interenterprise networks (511)
15. Intranets (506)
16. Legacy systems (509)
17. Local area network (506)
18. Modem (518)
19. Multiplexer (519)
20. Network architectures (522)
    a. OSI (523)
    b. TCP/IP (523)
21. Network computing (509)
22. Network operating system (506)
23. Network server (506)
24. Network topologies (521)
25. Open systems (500)
26. Peer-to-peer networks (510)
27. Switching alternatives (524)
28. Telecommunications channels (505)
29. Telecommunications media (515)
30. Telecommunications network components (504)
31. Telecommunications processors (505)
32. Telecommunications software (520)
33. Trends in telecommunications (500)
34. Virtual private network (507)
35. Wide area network (506)
36. Wireless technologies (516)

Review Quiz

Match one of the key terms and concepts listed previously with one of the brief examples or definitions that follow. Try to find the best fit for answers that seem to fit more than one term or concept. Defend your choices.

_____ 1. Fundamental changes have occurred in the competitive environment, the technology, and the application of telecommunications.

_____ 2. Telecommunications networks help companies overcome geographic, time, cost, and structural barriers to business success.

_____ 3. Includes terminals, telecommunications processors, channels, computers, and control software.

_____ 4. A communications network covering a large geographic area.

_____ 5. A communications network in an office, a building, or other work site.

_____ 6. Communications data move in these paths using various media in a network.

_____ 7. Coaxial cable, microwave, and fiber optics are examples.

_____ 8. A communications medium that uses pulses of laser light in glass fibers.

_____ 9. A wireless mobile telephone technology.

_____ 10. Includes modems, multiplexers, and internetwork processors.

_____ 11. Includes programs such as network operating systems and Web browsers.

_____ 12. A common communications processor for microcomputers.

_____ 13. Helps a communications channel carry simultaneous data transmissions from many terminals.

_____ 14. Star, ring, and bus networks are examples.

_____ 15. Cellular and PCS systems can connect mobile information appliances to the Internet.

_____ 16. A computer that handles resource sharing and network management in a local area network.

_____ 17. Intranets and extranets can use their network fire walls and other security features to establish secure Internet links within an enterprise or with its trading partners.

_____ 18. The software that manages a local area network.

_____ 19. An international standard, multilevel set of protocols to promote compatibility among telecommunications networks.

_____ 20. The standard suite of protocols used by the Internet, intranets, extranets, and some other networks.

_____ 21. End user computers connect directly with each other.

_____ 22. Information systems with common hardware, software, and network standards that provide easy access for end users and their networked computer systems.

_____ 23. Interconnected networks need communications processors such as switches, routers, hubs, and gateways.

_____ 24. A global network of millions of business, government, educational, and research networks; computer systems; databases; and end users.

_____ 25. The rapid growth in the business and consumer use of the Internet, and the use of its technologies in internetworking organizations.

_____ 26. Websites, Web browsers, HTML documents, hypermedia databases, and TCP/IP networks are examples.

_____ 27. Networks where end user PCs are tied to network servers to share resources and application processing.

_____ 28. Network computers provide a browser-based interface for software and databases provided by servers.

_____ 29. Replacing mainframe-based systems with client/server networks.

_____ 30. Older, traditional mainframe-based business information systems.

_____ 31. Telecommunications networks come in a wide range of speed and capacity capabilities.

_____ 32. Examples are packet switching using frame relay and cell switching using ATM technologies.

_____ 33. Telecommunications networks frequently interconnect an organization with its customers and suppliers.

_____ 34. Internet-like networks between a company and its business partners.

_____ 35. Internet-like networks within an enterprise.

Discussion Questions

1. The Internet is the driving force behind developments in telecommunications, networks, and other information technologies. Do you agree or disagree? Why?

2. How is the trend toward open systems, connectivity, and interoperability related to business use of the Internet, intranets, and extranets?

3. Refer to the Real World Case on WebLinc and Others in the chapter. Should businesses go all wireless, or are there still advantages to wire-based networking?

4. How will wireless information appliances and services affect the business use of the Internet and the Web? Explain.

5. What are the business benefits and management problems of client/server networks?

6. What examples can you give showing that trends in telecommunications include more telecommunications alliances and providers, and a greater variety of telecommunications services?

7. Why are companies expanding their use of interenterprise networks?

8. Refer to the Real World Case on Piasecki Steel, Lguide, and CyberTrain in the chapter. What can telecom companies and Internet service providers do to improve their Internet access services?

9. The explosive growth of the Internet and the use of its enabling technologies will continue in the 2000s. Do you agree or disagree? Why?

10. The insatiable demand for everything wireless, video, and Web-enabled everywhere will be the driving force behind developments in telecommunications, networking, and computing technologies for the forseeable future. Do you agree or disagree? Why?

Application Exercises

Complete the following exercises as individual or group projects that apply chapter concepts to real world business situations.

1. Evaluating Online Trading Websites

It's as voyeuristic as Internet sex sites, more addictive than video games, and a lot easier to play—and you can win (or lose) big money! It's online investing, one of the hottest destinations in cyberspace. Once the preserve of a few computer-literate plungers, online trading could one day account for much of the hundreds of millions in securities transactions each year. See Figure 14.27.
Some top sites:
- **Charles Schwab & Co.** (www.schwab.com). The one to beat. Leverages its huge customer base to gain the lead on the Web.
- **E*Trade** (www.etrade.com). A brash upstart whose ad push and emphasis on low prices catapulted it into the top players.
- **Datek Online** (www.datek.com). Active daytraders' paradise. Real-time quotes and trades. Refund if order not completed in a minute.

a. Surf to the online trading sites shown above. Evaluate and rank them based on ease of use, speed, cost, and quality of investment research and help provided.

b. Write up the results of your evaluations in a one- or two-page report. Which is your favorite online trading site? Why? Your least favorite? Explain.

Source: Adapted from Nelson D. Schwartz, "Can't Keep a Good Day Trader Down," *Fortune*, February 19, 2001, p. 146–150. © 2001 Time Warner Inc. All rights reserved.

2. Evaluating Online Banking Websites

On the Web, banking has been less popular than stock trading, mainly because of some limitations of the technology. You can't withdraw cash using a PC. But some of the biggest players want your business, and options for managing your accounts and paying bills have improved.

American Express
(www.americanexpres.com/banking).
Why leave home? Amex offers very attractive interest rates on deposits, lots of personal finance information, and links to online trading.

Bank of America
(www.bankofamerica.com).
Sleek, no-nonsense design is pitched to retail and business customers alike. Interesting advertising of international business services in Asia on the home page during the Olympics in Sydney.

CompuBank
(www.compubank.com).
All Net, all the time. CompuBank's Website gets kudos for detailed account information and security. Ranks among the low-price leaders in fees, while paying among the highest rates on deposits.

My Citi
(www.myciti.com).
Citigroup wants to help you round up all your financial activity and park it here. The site updates your finances to include your latest credit card bill, for instance. Security is top-notch.

Wells Fargo
(www.wellsfargo.com).
This West Coast innovator has taken its act national. Good design aimed at both consumers and commercial accounts. Color scheme looks odd unless you're a San Francisco 49ers fan.

Figure 14.27

Datek is one of the top online investment Websites.

Wingspan
(www.wingspanbank.com).
After a recent overhaul, Wingspan's site makes online banking relatively painless. A good comeback for the online unit of troubled BankOne's First USA subsidiary.

a. Check out several of these online banking sites. Evaluate and rank them based on ease of use, speed, banking fees and other costs, and the amount and quality of their online banking services.

b. Write up the results of your evaluations in a one-or two-page report. Which is your favorite banking site? Why? Your least favorite? Explain.

c. How would you improve the sites you visited? Include your recommendations in your report.

Source: Adapted from "Stake Your Claim to Wealth," Technology Buyers Guide, *Fortune*, Winter 2001, p. 252.

3. MNO Incorporated Communications Network

MNO Incorporated is considering acquiring its own leased lines to handle its voice and data communications between its 14 distribution sites in three regions around the country. The peak load of communications for each site is expected to be a function of the number of phone lines and the number of computers at that site. You have been asked to gather this information, as shown below, and place it in a database file.

a. Create a database table with an appropriate structure to store the data above. Site Location can serve as the primary key for this table. Enter the records shown above and get a printed listing of your table.

b. Survey results suggest that the peak traffic to and form a site will be approximately 2 kilobits per second for each phone line plus 10 kilobits per second for each computer. Create a report showing the estimated peak demand for the telecommunications system at each site in kilobits. Create a second report grouped by region and showing regional subtotals and a total for the system as a whole.

Site Location	Region	Phone Lines	Computers
Boston	East	228	95
New York	East	468	205
Richmond	East	189	84
Atlanta	East	192	88
Detroit	East	243	97
Cincinnati	East	156	62
New Orleans	Central	217	58
Chicago	Central	383	160
Saint Louis	Central	212	91
Houston	Central	238	88
Denver	West	202	77
Los Angeles	West	364	132
San Francisco	West	222	101
Seattle	West	144	54

4. Prioritizing Calls to Service Centers

ABC Products International has over 100 offices worldwide and has 12 service centers worldwide which handle computer related problems of the company's employees. Each center is open only about 10 hours a day and calls can be placed to other centers around the globe to provide 24-hour service. You are assigned to the New Orleans office and have been asked to develop a database that will list all available service centers at a particular time of day and sort them so that the center with the lowest communications cost appears first.

The table below summarizes this information with the hours shown reflecting local New Orleans time.

a. Create a database table structure to store the data shown above, and enter the set of records above. (Use the short time format and a 24-hour clock for the Opening Hour and Closing Hour figures.) Print out a listing of this table.

b. Create a query that will allow the user to enter the current time and will Display a list of the locations and phone numbers of service centers that are open, sorted so that the location with the lowest communication cost per minute is listed first. Test your query to be sure that it works across all hours of the day. Print out results for 3:00, 10:00, 18:00, and 23:00. (Note that centers open through Midnight have a closing hour that is earlier than their opening hour and require different treatment. Hint: Centers that open after 14:00 close at times earlier than their opening time. Literal time values can be entered in Access by placing # around the values, e.g. #14:00#.)

Site Location	Phone No	Opening Hour	Closing Hour	Comm. Cost Per Minute
Berlin	49 348281723	15:00	1:00	$0.24
Boston	617 6792814	9:00	19:00	$0.12
Cairo	20 33721894	16:00	2:00	$0.30
Honolulu	808 373-1925	4:00	14:00	$0.18
London	44 4622649172	14:00	0:00	$0.20
Mexico City	52 273127901	8:00	18:00	$0.25
New Delhi	91 7432631952	19:00	5:00	$0.32
Rio De Janeiro	55 8202131485	11:00	21:00	$0.32
San Francisco	650 212-9047	6:00	16:00	$0.13
Seoul	82 164195023	22:00	8:00	$0.28
St. Petersburg	7 4837619103	16:00	2:00	$0.30
Sydney	61 934816120	0:00	10:00	$0.27

Northeast Utilities and Guaranteed Overnight Delivery: Challenges of Mobile Wireless Applications

What a difference five years makes in the fast-changing wireless world. From a failed mobile wireless project in the mid-1990's, Andy Kasznay learned how to get payback from a current inspection-reporting application. The mobile wireless project launched in 1995 by Northeast Utilities Inc. in Berlin, Connecticut, failed at a cost of $1 million, says Kasznay, a software engineer at the utility, which has 1.2 million customers.

"It was a year and half of time lost, with a year trying to make it work and half a year realizing it wouldn't work," he says in reflection. "I considered it a huge loss, but we learned a lot." In fact, the lessons learned from a wireless failure could make your next endeavor a success. What Kasznay and Northeast learned helped the utility build another mobile wireless application two years ago that's still working well, Kasznay says.

With the current application, 15 field inspectors carry rugged laptops equipped with wireless modems. They connect to an enterprise database to track spills of hazardous materials such as polychlorinated biphenyls, also known as PCBs, which are used to insulate electricity transformers. The application lets chemists and people who monitor government environmental filings get up-to-the minute reports. It also saves time, because all the information is entered directly into the proper fields without having to be transcribed.

"It's definitely paying for itself over the paper-based system," Kasznay says. "In fact, we have better information everywhere in the organization and a reduction in the things that have fallen through the cracks." He says each rugged Panasonic CF27 laptop costs $6,000, and each month of airtime per user costs approximately $30.

Kasznay's wireless failure-to-success experience isn't uncommon and provides lessons for how firms should deploy mobile wireless projects. The best advice is to start small and work up to bigger projects. At Northeast, for example, the success of the spill-reporting application has given IT workers the confidence to consider sending power-outage reports to executives via smart phones and wireless information to crews repairing streetlights, Kasznay says.

He says the 1995 failure spurred Northeast to build a reliable mobile wireless infrastructure. Because even the best wireless networks have gaps in service. Northeast also built in the ability for inspectors to download data to a laptop on a reported spill and keep inputting data even if they hit a dead coverage zone. What they report is then automatically cached until a wireless connection is reestablished.

At Guaranteed Overnight Delivery in Newark, New Jersey, the organizational learning curve has been steep. But a mobile wireless package delivery application that's cost-effective and increases productivity has been found, says Heath Snow, director of technology. Guaranteed believes that a fast, reliable wireless network and inexpensive off-the-shelf hardware have made a big difference in the latest application, according to Snow. "It's been a grueling path to go through," he says. "But our current application has reached return on investment in a year."

Guaranteed has equipped its drivers in the northeastern U.S. with about 300 Blackberry wireless handhelds from Research in Motion Ltd. (RIM) in Waterloo, Ontario, for the past 12 months, Snow says. By using the devices to get delivery information wirelessly from a dispatcher, drivers now make as many as 20 deliveries per day with as many as 10 pickups, compared with 115 deliveries and five pickups before the handhelds were used.

Cingular Wireless in Atlanta, formerly Bell-South Wireless Data LP, provides "fantastic" network coverage and response times of 56K bit/sec. for short-message connections, Snow says. If a driver moves out of the coverage area, the system keeps repeating a message until he's back in range. The RIM handhelds, each of which costs about $350, have replaced two previous ruggedized handhelds that cost as much as $3,000 apiece, Snow says. But Guaranteed has a long-term deal with Cingular that allows it to get updated hardware when it comes on the market. The cost of airtime is up to $40 per month, Snow says.

He attributes the increase in driver efficiency to a more reliable network. Drivers and dispatchers get a confirmation when a message is sent, which saves them from having to find a phone to double-check. With the new mobile wireless system, drivers don't even carry cell phones, which would only increase costs, Snow says.

Case Study Questions

1. What did Northeast Utilities learn from its mobile wireless project failure?

2. What are the business benefits of Northeast's new mobile wireless system?

3. What are the business costs and benefits of Guaranteed's new wireless application?

Source: Adapted from Matt Hamblen, "Get Payback on Wireless," *Computerworld*, January 1, 2001, p. S44–45.

Genuine Parts and Equity Residential: Evaluating Virtual Private Networks

Connecting thousands of retail stores to central data centers can cost a bundle. That spurs some firms, such as Genuine Parts Co. in Norcross, Georgia, to run away from expensive frame relay and toward less-costly virtual private networks (VPN) that use the Internet. Officials at Genuine said last week that the company was in the process of deploying a VPN from Bethesda, Maryland-based Lockheed Martin Telecommunications. By the end of the year, the VPN will connect 750 of Genuine's company-owned NAPA Auto Parts retail stores to data centers in Norcross, Georgia and Dallas.

According to Thomas Braswell, senior vice president of IT at Genuine, the network will eventually hook up an additional 5,000 NAPA franchise operations. Braswell said he decided to consider frame relay or a VPN to connect stores because the existing dial-up system that polled his stores twice a day for parts orders and receipts, was no longer able to handle the transaction volumes, response times, Internet access, and interactivity needed in today's E-business environment.

Braswell wanted a network that would link NAPA stores to his central ordering database at the company's data centers around the clock, which would enable stores to share information on stock status. He also wanted to give NAPA stores e-mail access and applications that would allow customers to order parts over the Internet.

Conventional wisdom would suggest using frame relay," Braswell said, because it's a proven phone company technology that corporations have been using for years to connect network end points over dedicated circuits. Unlike a VPN, which amounts to using the Internet as a wide-area network, frame-relay connections use a private infrastructure.

But Braswell said frame relay has a drawback: its cost. He discovered that the monthly fee to run the network over a VPN through an outsourcer would be approximately 50% less than the cost of a frame-relay system. Security and performance remained a concern, however.

Although a VPN, by definition, is an encrypted, end-to-end private tunnel through the Internet. Braswell said he wanted assurance from the five network outsourcers he was considering using that they could provide security and guarantee a level of availability and performance that he could live with.

Braswell said he made sure performance of the VPN connection was comparable to frame relay by setting up several stores with dual connections. He then elected to go with Lockheed Martin as the network outsourcer. "Lockheed Martin uses Data Encryption Standard encryption on the VPN, which gives us the level of security we need," Braswell said.

Another reason many companies are turning to VPNs is that telecom equipment manufacturers and software companies are developing network management software tools that make corporate VPNs easier to deploy, update and monitor.

The idea of a VPN that securely tunnels through the public Internet to connect offices and remote workers seems straight-forward enough. But network managers who have taken VPNs beyond the pilot stage and into full deployment know firsthand that managing VPN encryption, maintaining data tunnel integrity and validating software on hundreds of thousands of client computers and office firewalls can be a formidable job.

John Shelest, a senior network engineer at Equity Residential Properties Trust, a real estate investment trust that owns and manages more than 1,100 properties throughout the U.S., said his Check Point VPN has enabled his company to securely connect its remote offices to its Chicago headquarters.

It isn't easy to keep VPN client software updated for 1,100 users and to validate those changes in addition to changes on the company's eight firewalls, said Shelest. He has been testing Check Point's Next Generation (NG) infrastructure management software and said NG resolves many of the complexities of managing a Check Point VPN. NG lets him push software changes out to remote PCs without end-user intervention, Shelest explained. He added that he also likes the NG graphical user interface, which makes it easier to define user security polices and lets him turn over firewall management to less-experienced staffers.

Case Study Questions

1. Why did Genuine Parts choose a VPN over a frame relay network?

2. Why did Genuine Parts outsource their VPN to Lockheed Martin? What issues were involved and resolved?

3. How do new VPN software tools help Equity Residential manage its own VPN?

Source: Adapted from James Cope, "NAPA Stores, Data Centers to Link Via VPN," *Computerworld*, January 29, 2001, p. 12, and "New Tools Aimed at VPN Management," *Computerworld*, March 12, 2001, p. 12.

American Honda and Ford: Wireless Supply Chain Networks

American Honda

Honda Motor Co., like all carmakers, was pretty much helpless when it came to responding quickly to fickle consumer demand. The company essentially guessed, for example, how many black V-6 Accord sedans people wanted, made a bunch of them, shipped them to dealers, and hoped for the best. Dealers, meanwhile, had no real say in the cars they received, and had to wait at least four months for orders. The months-long lag between the time a vehicle was manufactured and the time a new owner drove it off the lot was just a frustrating fact of life in the car business.

Even if this gap can't be eliminated, it can at least be reduced significantly—which is precisely what Honda's U.S. distributor, has done. In 1996, Dan Bonawitz, a vice president at American Honda, based in Torrance, California, launched a computerized assault on the lag time. With the help of a core team of 10 techies from Syncata, an E-business consultancy in El Segundo, California, Bonawitz's people created a networked supply chain that has transformed the automaker into one of the most fleet-footed in the business. The goal of Honda's Market Oriented Vehicle Environment (MOVE) project was to build a network that would let everyone involved—from headquarters to plants to dealers—collaborate to improve production flow. All of American Honda's 1,300 dealerships would be able to place their orders directly with Honda headquarters and get updates on order-shipment status.

Here's how the system works: Dealers are connected to Honda corporate via a virtual private network and log on through PCs using a simple, Windows-like interface. Once a month, they view suggested orders created by Honda's sales and production group and can change those orders based on current demand—for example, ask for more silver Honda Accords with automatic transmissions. This up-to-the-minute market data allows Honda to generate production orders that are then sent to seven plants, with MOVE software calculating the most efficient way to distribute the production load.

Fully completed in October 2000, the MOVE system is a hit with dealers—and with Honda headquarters. Lead time on orders has dropped from 120 days to between 30 and 60, and the company says it matches 95 percent of dealers' requests for cars. American Honda won't disclose costs or any specific financials related to the MOVE project, but it claims that the new automated ordering system has allowed it to reduce inventories at factories and dealerships by approximately 50 percent.

For any company selling 100,000 vehicles or more per month, 50 percent reductions in wholesale and retail inventories result in substantial cost savings in areas ranging from storage fees to finance costs," says American Honda spokesman Stephen Keeney. "Plus, the increased efficiency of being able to distribute particular vehicles to the points where the greatest demand exists for those models provides a definite competitive advantage."

Ford Motor Co.

Citing poor coordination between its production lines and its extensive supply chain, Ford Motor Co. last week outlined the business drivers for overhauling its manufacturing plants with wireless networks that should allow workers to call in automotive parts orders from the shop floor. "We're trying to clean up our production lines," said Jim Buczkowski, director of manufacturing and supply-chain systems at the Dearborn, Michigan-based auto giant. "If you pile up inventory all over the place, it's more difficult to control what's going on." Controlling line movement and reducing inventory levels are top strategic initiatives for the nation's No. 2 automaker, said Buczkowski.

But perhaps more important, Ford's wireless overhaul is the first step in a broader technology drive that's aimed at enabling build-to-order systems through which vehicle manufacturing gets initiated by actual customer orders instead of by forecasting, he said.

During the past two years, Ford has been implementing a wireless network called e-Smart in 25 plants in the U.S., Spain and Belgium. e-Smart synchronizes in-plant parts replenishment activities on Ford's production lines and inventory bays, and with its suppliers.

When an inventory bin on one of Ford's production lines reaches a minimum level, a line operator simply pushes a call button that's located on either a piece of equipment or a nearby wall. This action sends a 2.4 GHz wireless signal that triggers a request to the parts maker for materials such as a fender or ball-bearing supplier, and to the plant's internal inventory center. The system also sends periodic wireless updates to the network to help synchronize parts deliveries to both the plan and the assembly line.

Case Study Questions

1. What are the business benefits of Honda American's MOVE system over their previous supply chain systems?

2. What are the business benefits to Ford of converting its factories to the wireless e-Smart network?

3. Does Honda's MOVE system and Ford's e-Smart system give them a competitive advantage? Why or why not?

Source: Adapted from Lee Gladwin, "Automaker Drives Wireless in Plants," *Computerworld*, February 19, 2001, p.14.

Real World

Case Studies

Introduction

This appendix contains the following five case studies:

These real world cases describe the problems and opportunities in the business use of information technology confronted by a variety of E-business enterprises. They are based on real situations faced by actual organizations and are all designed to give you an opportunity to (1) integrate your knowledge of major information system concepts gained from reading and studying the text material, and (2) apply your knowledge to situations faced by real world business firms and other organizations.

Solving Case Studies

Several approaches can be used in analyzing cases. The simplest approach is to read the case and then try to find the answers to the questions at the end of each case study. This should give you a good exposure to the business and information system situations contained in the case. A more formal methodology is outlined in Figure A.1. Use this methodology to help you analyze a case study, develop an information system solution, and write up your results. Of course, you must first read the case, highlighting phrases or making notes that identify problems, opportunities, or other facts that may have a major bearing on your solution of the case.

Solution Constraints

The analysis you perform and the solution you develop with the methodology outlined in Figure A.1 will be limited by several major constraints. Being aware of these constraints will help you use this methodology more effectively. These constraints are:

- **Information.** The amount of data and information you can gather in a situation or find in case study material. Remember that in the real world, decisions usually have to be based on incomplete information.

- **Assumptions.** The number of assumptions you make or are allowed to make. Good, rational assumptions are a key ingredient in good solutions, since there

A systems solution
methodology. Use this
methodology to help you
analyze an actual or case
study situation, develop
a solution, and write up
your results.

A Systems Solution Methodology
1. Identification of problems, opportunities, and symptoms. Separate major problems or opportunities from their symptoms. Identify the major components of systems you feel are most involved in the problems or opportunities that you discover.
2. Statement of the problem. Briefly state the major problems or opportunities facing the organization.
3. Summary of alternative solutions. Briefly identify several alternative solutions to the problems you have identified.
4. Evaluation of alternative solutions. Evaluate the alternative solutions using evaluation criteria that reveal their advantages and disadvantages.
5. Rationale for the selected solution. Select the solution that best meets the evaluation criteria, and briefly explain the reasons for its selection.
6. Information system design proposal. Propose a design for any new or improved information systems required by the selected solution. Use one or more tools of analysis and design to illustrate your design proposal.
7. Implementation plan. Propose an implementation plan for the selected solution.

is never enough information available in either real world situations or case studies. You should identify and explain the reasons for any major assumptions you make.

- **Knowledge.** The amount of knowledge about business and information systems you possess. Hopefully, this will increase as you cover more of this textbook and as you progress in your business education and career. For now, do the best you can with the knowledge you have.

- **Time.** The amount of time you spend on the analysis of the problem. Obviously, the more time you have, the more information you can gather, and the more analysis you can perform. Of course, time constraints are typical in the real world, so make judicious use of the time you have.

Textron Corporation:

The E-Business

Transformation Process

The Chief Innovation Officer

Ken Bohlen is chief innovation officer (yes, innovation officer) of the massive $12.8 billion multi-industry conglomerate Textron. At the moment, he is trying to explain what this old industrial behemoth needs to overhaul itself into a new, streamlined behemoth for the age of digital commerce by telling a story about Albert Einstein:

"The father of modern physics is teaching a second-year physics class and the students are understandably thrilled to be there. On the last day of class Einstein hands out the final exam. There's a lot of shuffling and hushed talk and finally a student speaks up. 'Dr. Einstein,' the student says, 'this is the same test as last year.'

" 'Ahhh, yes,' Einstein says, 'But this year...the *answers* are different.' "

Like that test, Textron has to both evolve and stay the same, Bohlen explains. "We have to change this company," he says, "but we are still Textron. We still make our money with industrial and financial products, and that isn't going to change. What's going to change is the way we answer questions and the way we do those same things."

Figure A.2

Ken Bohlen is Chief Innovation Officer and Leader of Textron's E-Business Change Process.

James Smolka.

What, specifically, does that mean? "Here's an easy one," he says. "Why do expense reports have to be signed by three accountants? Why not just one? Nobody knows, it's just the way it was done last year. That type of thinking has to change. A lot of what we are talking about is just cultural. The Internet part is easy.

"Change is difficult," he continues. "I can't just walk into a division and say, 'From now on all expense reports will be done online, period.' They'll look at me and say, 'Who the hell are you? We've been doing it like this for five years and it's work fine.'" Yet if the problems were limited to expense reports, Bohlen's job wouldn't be so daunting.

He speaks of the Internet as an enabler of innovation. Yes, he wants the company to take advantage of the Internet, but he also wants its people to act like the Internet, constantly exchanging information and ideas. The impact of this concept should not be underestimated: It's fundamentally not part of Textron's traditional corporate culture to share ideas across division, and that's part of what Bohlen hopes the Internet can bring as a tool and as a model. "The Internet is going to allow us to innovate," he says, sounding like he's had to repeat that line far too many times. "If we don't, we aren't going to be around in five years." See Figure A.2.

The Trouble with Conglomerates

Just what is Textron? The easier question, perhaps is what isn't Textron? The company has 70,992 employees working in four definitively old-economy businesses including aviation, automotive, industrial, and finance—all of them profitable.

The aircraft division includes Bell Helicopter, which controls more than one-third of the global commercial market, as well as Cessna Aircraft, which controls over 50 percent of the corporate jet market and brought in $2.2 billion in 1999. The automotive division reaped $2.9 billion in revenues in 1999 by supplying the car industry with everything from airbag doors to "blow-molded modular fluid systems." The industrial division brought in $4.4 billion in 1999, selling it all—from polymer pumps to power transmissions. Textron is also the world leader in the wholly unglamorous business of fasteners, essentially the screws that bind two manufactured elements together. Need a loan or a lease for any of the high-ticket Textron items, say, an $18.5 million Cessna Citation X? Textron Financial will arrange it for you.

So, what's with the changespeak, the Einstein parables, the talk of extinction? Textron has a record of 44 consecutive quarters of earnings growth, which every employee in its Providence, Rhode Island, headquarters will point out in conversation. Over the past decade earnings per share have grown annually at 19 percent, while total return to shareholders has averaged 23 percent compared with 18 percent for the rest of the Standard & Poor's Index. Not a bad record.

The problem is that Textron is run like a classic conglomerate, and Lewis B. Campbell, the company's chairman, realized in 1999 that the future isn't going to look like the past for old-style conglomerates. The Internet has changed everything (as worn as that shibboleth sounds), and it will ultimately enable Textron's smaller competitors to act more quickly and service their customers better. Textron needs to be just as responsive.

To illustrate the situation, and perhaps because it reminds him of his Iowa homeland, Bohlen draws four silos on a yellow pad, representing Textron's four major industries. "That's how Textron looks now. Four groups acting independently," he says.

Traditionally Textron was run like a holding company, bolting new acquisitions onto the mothership, but letting its managers have near-total autonomy in running their shops as long as profit increased. Now the company is betting that by getting managers to share ideas, it can unlock innovation.

And it's not only in the realm of new ideas that effort is being duplicated. The different divisions have separate *everything*, from human resources to accounting to information technology, and Bohlen thinks the Internet can get rid of all the excess.

He begins drawing lines that cut across the four silos, linking them all together. "Now," he says, "we need to act like an operating company."

Let the Transformation Begin

Bohlen had been on the job just 75 days when he began making the case to the management committee that nothing less than an E-business baptismal was needed for Textron. He wanted to take some of the company's top managers and indoctrinate them. "They said, 'What do you need, three days? No problem,'" Bohlen recalls. "I said, 'No, I'm talking about four weeks.'"

With that, 33 of Textron's managers converged on the Chicago O'Hare Marriott for four weeks, Monday noon to Friday noon each week. Cambridge Technology Partners, which was hired to help with the baptismal, brought in a 34-year-old South African named Graham Allen to speak to the group. Allen worked for Timken, an Ohio company that makes bearings for everything from disk drives to drilling rigs. This was a company the Textron executives could relate to.

Allen told the assembled about an online company Timken formed by the name of Handpiece Headquarters. Handpieces are electric dental drills. When the bearings in the drills break down, Timken does the warranty and repair work. Allen's group automated what was a labor-intensive, paperwork-driven process so customers (dentist's offices) could now do everything online. If Timken's handpieces could be given digital sex appeal, then there was no stopping Textron's Chesivale TSL2 phone line simulators.

By week two, the so-called E-business council broke into groups to brainstorm ideas. By week three Textron chairman Campbell and John Janitz, the company's president, flew out for a report as the council honed in on seven ideas. The first idea was to leverage Textron's size in purchasing by creating an E-procurement system for all of the sundry products a company with over 70,000 employees uses.

The second and third ideas were to create web-based marketplaces; these projects are currently in development. The fourth concept, which is also in the design phase, was to use the Internet to enhance Textron's supply-chain management. The fifth concept was integration of all the various divisions' information technology. The sixth plan, also still in development, is to share human resources services, centrally integrating benefits information, hiring practices, and resumes on the Web.

Finally, the seventh idea was to develop an E-business SWAT team that would work as an in-house consultant to every division. To head this effort, the Chicago group and Bohlen approached Timken's Allen, who had just finished talking about handpieces. See Figure A.3.

The Process of Progress

It's 8:30 a.m. on a winter Wednesday, and Ken Bohlen's staff is gathered for its monthly meeting. It's been almost a year since Bohlen joined Textron, and the work that needs to be done seems monumental. A few minutes earlier he sat in his office saying, "This is still very much a work in progress, but you've to realize there are limited resources, and this sort of thing doesn't happen instantly. This also costs money, and we've got a tradition of earnings, which we are very proud of, and so we've got to balance that with the need for change. What you are seeing is Textron in transformation, warts and all."

This is the central stress point at Textron: paying for the change while continuing to manage earnings growth in an economy that is shifting into a lower gear, especially in areas like automotive where Textron has a lot of exposure. Chrysler, for example, announced a $1.25 billion loss in the fourth quarter of 2000, due in part to a consumer slowdown, and 42 percent of Textron's automotive sales go directly to Chrysler. Fewer car purchases at Chrysler translate into fewer Textron dashboard systems.

If Textron expects to continue earnings growth, the other divisions will have to make up the difference, and costly plans, like ramping up Textron's Internet ability,

Textron's E-Business Approach

1. Establish an e-procurement system. Textron factories used to purchase their supplies independently, precluding the potential for cost savings that comes with bulk buying. Textron enlisted the help of Ariba and is automating all purchasing. Soon all product catalogs and forms will be online, streamlining the process and allowing Textron to save an estimated total of $150 million by 2002.

2. Create web-based marketplaces. Textron's profitable aviation division could serve as a place to launch a web store. This idea is still on the runway.

3. Manage the supply chain. Textron could use the Internet to better manage its own supply chain. This project is also still largely on the drawing board, but the idea is simple. Produce only the products that customers want, exactly when they want them.

4. Integrate the technology infrastructure. Textron's different units purchase their technology separately as well. To change that, the company hired Bob Ratcliff from Allied Signal. At press time he was in the process of signing a $59 million deal with AT&T to be the sole Internet provider for Textron. Soon Ratcliff expects that all Textron's divisions will link into one monster network as opposed to having different divisions link into several separate networks.

5. Streamline human resources. Like purchasing and IT, Textron's different units all have their own human resources departments, and the Chicago group hypothesized that the Internet could help consolidate their work. For example, benefits information could all be placed online, and the corporation could share an online database of resumes across all the divisions instead of having them work separately and potentially miss good candidates.

6. Create an E-business SWAT team. Textron developed a small, dedicated team to parachute into different divisions and work as an in-house E-business consultant. Graham Allen heads up the five-person team. The digital strategy team, as the group is called, is working on a portal that will create an all-purpose, ready-to-go E-commerce site that could then be rolled out across all of Textron's business units.

will have to proceed more slowly. "Sure, give me $60 million right now and we will make a lot of things happen right away," Bohlen says. "But that's not going to happen right now, so what we have to do is go out there and show the different groups that this stuff really matters. It's a process."

Bob Ratcliff, group director, advanced technology and enterprise solutions, gets up to speak about a long-term $59 million companywide contract with AT&T that will create one service provider for the entire Textron system. Phyllis Michaeledes, Textron's new chief technology officer, gives an update on switching the entire computer system to a network format in which no one will need a personal hard drive.

Allen, the former Timken exec, introduces the latest member of his five-person digital SWAT team. Also from Timken, Tom Henricks is a former NASA astronaut and space shuttle commander who will likely spend a lot of time with the aviation group's E-business efforts. The two talk briefly about their portal strategy, which is to develop the building blocks of an E-commerce web site that can be rolled out system wide to Textron's four divisions and scores of sub-businesses.

Bohlen, the classic optimist, takes the floor again and tells his group that they are making progress, even if it is incremental. As part of the plan to get the company to act like an Internet and not just use it, Bohlen talks about the evolution of Textron's permanent E-business council in which managers from across the company meet regularly to share information and concepts.

To show that this isn't lip service, Textron chairman Campbell has decreed that starting this year, half of managers' pay and promotion will be tied to how they perform in the council, not just how their specific business unit performs, In other words, if business was great, but managers did nothing to contribute to the E-business council, then they should expect half their normal bonus and salary increase.

Measure by Measure

At the end of the day Bohlen is back in his office taking stock of what he's done. By every measure most of the change is yet to come, but the company has, in less than a year, made marked progress. Textron now has 50 web sites up and running. Some, like www.greenlee.textron.com, for now primarily offer online brochures of electronic- and cable-testing equipment. But in other areas Textron's web sites have already transformed a line of business. Take the company's so-called asset disposition business, in which a dedicated group of analysts and marketers find buyers for assets the company no longer needs. Textron took the business to the Web last year under the name Assetcontrol.com, and it has already listed $33 million in assets and sold $12 million worth of inventory, a 388 percent increase over previous years.

Textron Financial, which handles $1 billion in financing for other Textron products, can now take online applications for 50 percent of its business. It's also created online-only financing companies like Flyancing.com, which lends money for jet purchases. The company's E-procurement initiative, also less than a year old, has already saved millions.

"We're getting there," Bohlen says.

Case Study Questions

1. **Transformation and the Internet**
   a. Should a profitable conglomerate like Textron change because of the Internet? Why or why not?
   b. How does CIO Ken Bohlen think Textron should change because of the Internet? Do you agree? Why or why not?
   c. What are the barriers to change at Textron? What would you propose to help overcome the barriers to change and innovation at Textron?

2. **The Process of E-Business Transformation**
   a. Do you approve of how Textron initiated its E-business transformation process? Why or why not?
   b. Evaluate each of the proposals of Textron's first E-business council. How well do they support Textron's E-business transformation process?

   c. What else might you have proposed if you had been on that council? Why?

3. **The Status of E-Business Transformation**
   a. Has Textron made enough progress in E-business transformation since they began the process? Why or why not?
   b. Is E-business transformation being sufficiently supported and encouraged at Textron? Why or why not?
   c. What else would you propose to encourage and implement E-business changes at Textron? Explain the reasons for your recommendations.

Source: Adapted from John Galvin, "Manufacturing the Future," *Smart Business*, March 2001, pp. 87–95.

Recreational Equipment Inc.:

Climbing to Success in Retail

E-Commerce

Clicks and Bricks United

When outdoor gear purveyor Recreational Equipment Inc. (REI) outgrew its head-quarters in a Seattle suburb last fall, the Web team had to take a hike. Just to another cement building on the same half-block-long campus, mind you—not much of a trek for the climbers, runners, cyclists and other super-fit nature-lovers who make up REI's workforce. Yet it was far enough for REI's Web chief to justify buying a new corporate fleet: 24 trendy scooters, anodized the same pine green as REI's woodsy logo.

REI execs didn't want to separate the web-heads from their offline coworkers. But since there wasn't room to keep all employees in one building, investing in hip inter-building transportation seemed the next best thing. The scooters also reflected a corporate mind-set that has driven REI's online efforts for the past five years: Keep the website connected to the rest of the business.

REI bet on a click-and-mortar strategy back when conventional wisdom said that agile dotcoms—unencumbered by the bureaucracy and costly storefronts of brick-and-mortar dinosaurs—would win. Today, it appears that REI bet right. In 1999, it drew in $41 million of its $621 million in sales via the Web, and at press time was on track to double Web sales in 2000. Many pundits now believe that companies like REI that do business online and offline will triumph over those that operate only in one realm or the other. Customers want to shop wherever and whenever they want, so companies need to be able to meet customers' needs in any sales channel—in REI's case, that means stores, catalogs and websites—and make it easy for patrons to move seamlessly among channels.

Some of REI's success can be traced to its pre-web attributes. But much of it stems from crucial choices REI made during its earliest days of forming its online strategy—choices that any one trying to fashion a click-and-mortar strategy, retail or otherwise can still learn from today.

A Natural Evolution

Long before anyone had ever conceived of the Internet as a venue for commerce (or even conceived of the Internet itself), REI had some built-in advantages for doing business online. The company has decades of experience in shipping orders directly to customers; it started running a catalog operation not long after it was founded in 1938 by a Seattle mountaineer. Companies with well-established, direct-to-consumer sales capability offline have an edge when they move online, since they already have fulfillment systems in place, says Andrew Bartels, a senior research analyst at Giga Information Group. He contends that's why companies like L.L. Bean, Lands' End, Southwest Airlines and Computer Discount Warehouse have been successful online.

What's more, REI is a member-owned cooperative, and its 1.7 million active members represent about 85 percent of its in-store customers. Members share in REI profits, based on how much money they spend. That means REI has long needed to have a single view of its customers and their buying history across all of its distribution channels. It's a useful capability if you're trying to figure out whether your website is bringing in new business or just cannibalizing your existing business.

The E-commerce Leaders

In early 1996, REI's then COO and Executive Vice President Dennis Madsen began to explore the possibilities for web commerce. Madsen, an avid sportsman who likes to conduct "working runs"—jogging meetings on the running trail near REI's campus—during his lunch hour, doesn't consider himself a techie. But he could see the Web as the natural evolution of direct-to-customer catalog sales—that is, as another way to extend REI's reach beyond the four walls of its stores. At the time, there was no clear road map for brick-and-mortar companies to follow when they went online. Many companies with established offline brands just ignored the Web, figuring that online sales wouldn't amount to much anytime soon. But Madsen believed that the Internet was an opportunity for REI to better serve its customers. In 1997, a customer survey backed Madsen's instincts: REI found that 85 percent of its customers had access to the Internet at home or at work. Madsen's foresight abut the Web paid off professionally too; REI's board appointed him CEO early in 2001, saying his role as E-commerce champion demonstrated his drive to find new ways for REI to grow. See Figure A.4.

Madsen put together a team to get an E-commerce website up and running, and he made a crucial management pick: He appointed Matt Hyde, a lanky, energetic REI insider, to run the online group, rather than searching for some hotshot web

Figure A.4

Dennis Madsen is CEO of REI, and led the company to E-commerce success.

Mark Robert Halper.

guru from the outside. Hyde had started at REI as a part-timer (a geologist by training, he had moved to Seattle in the late '80's to be closer to great climbing, and he needed a way to pay the bills). He had risen quickly through the retail ranks, and he had a real affinity for the newfangeled web technology. But more important, he had a deep knowledge of REI's customers.

"This business isn't about technology," says Madsen, a 34-year REI veteran who started working on the retail store floor when he was just a teenager. "It's about understanding the customer and translating that understanding into strategies and tactics that will take care of his need and expectations."

A Surefooted Approach

Unlike many companies at the time, REI didn't treat the Web effort like a pilot project or an experiment. From the start, Hyde says, the company regarded it as a real business and held it to specific service and financial goals. Given that the Web was seen as a core part of REI's business, Hyde decided it was crucial to do all site development in-house. Many brick-and-mortar companies back then chose to outsource development to get a site up and running quickly, and even today, some analysts see outsourcing as a best practice. Hyde, however, still believes REI needed to have web development skills as a core comptency.

It's also been common for businesses rushing to establish a web presence to cut corners by limiting—or even skipping—integration with legacy systems. But for Hyde, there was never any question that REI's site would integrate with its legacy systems and existing fulfillment operation: Co-op members needed to be able to get credit for whatever orders they placed, wherever they placed them. And it would have been crazy to not take advantage of REI's new distribution center with its six miles of conveyor belts; it had already been designed to handle both store and catalog fulfillment out of the same inventory.

Website growth drove REI to build a 145,000-square-foot mezzanine in its distribution center in 2000; the new level holds 25,000 more products. To be able to fulfill web orders with the same-day speed that online shoppers demand, REI now bar codes all packages. Overhead scanners record the weight of each package on the conveyor belt and calculate postage. A new order routing process lets REI pick and process orders based on customer type and the speed of delivery requested. See Figure A.5.

Early on, REI made another key decision: It would spend heavily to launch and market its website, and it would accept losses in the early years. In 1996, when REI launched the retail site, and in 1997, the site did not make a profit—not unusual in online retailing. (Amazon.com has yet to operate in the black since it went public.) Madsen wasn't happy about the red ink and neither was REI's board. But at the time—the height of the dotcom-funding frenzy—Madsen felt he had little choice. "The Internet pure-plays had such deep pockets that they weren't spending their money appropriately, and they were creating hardships for themselves and for established retailers like REI," Madsen says. "We felt compelled to play the game the way the rest of the retailers were playing it."

REI's online group turned a profit in 1998 and 1999. But it dipped slightly into the red in 2000—planned losses to pay for improvements such as expanding the website overseas and adding functionality, according to a spokeswoman. Even though dotcom retailers are struggling, that doesn't mean the pressure is off REI; it still must invest in the future. "Every year we have to do things a little bit better to stay ahead of customers' expectations," Madsen says. The same holds true for the company overall. Its profits have dropped slightly each year since 1997, in part because of web investments and in part because of other initiatives aimed at growth, such as construction of its new superstore in Denver and expansion into Japan.

Figure A.5

REI's newly expanded distribution center supports web, catalog, and in-store sales.

Mark Robert Halper.

No Spinoff

Other brick-and-mortar companies faced with early competition from then well-funded dotcoms chose the spinoff route to raise capital for their web efforts. Barnes & Noble, for example, spun off its web business and took it public, spurning integration between the two channels—and later got criticized for its click-and-mortar gap. In October 2000, the company decided to take a radical turn in its strategy, announcing plans to install Internet service counters in Barnes & Noble superstores and to let online customers return items to stores. It is also starting a loyalty program that will encompass both online and in-store purchases.

The spinoff strategy still appeals to some retailers, although perhaps less so now that the market for dotcom retail IPOs has tanked. Last year, Wal-Mart turned to Accel Partners to help turn around its much-criticized website and launched a separate dotcom group based in Silicon Valley. Still, Madsen believes he made the right choice in not carving off the website from the rest of the business. "When customers think of REI, they don't think of us as a dotcom business or a catalog business or a brick-and-mortar business," he says. "They think of our brand as encompassing all of those channels of distribution. And the expectations they have of us are identical no matter how they shop from us."

Blazing New Retail Trails

Visit any of REI's stores, and you'll see its click-and-mortar strategy in action. It's not the kind of action you'll find on the two-story climbing walls that have become a regular feature at REI's new stores. But amidst the tents, portable cookstoves, hiking boots, Baby Joggers, beef jerky and other outdoorsy gear, you'll find kiosks that let customers surf REI's website. Unlike some brick-and-mortars that have built anemic websites for fear of eating into offline sales, REI sees the web as a natural extension of the retail sales floor. So customers can use the kiosks to order any of the 78,000 REI items that may not be in stock in a particular store—as can store employees with their Internet—enabled cash registers. And kiosks revenues add up: Total revenues across all kiosks equal the revenues of an average REI store, Hyde says.

REI strives to give consumers the same message across its website, stores and catalog. Customers can buy products online or via the catalog and return them in stores, if they wish. Even as REI strives for harmony across its channels, it has not shied away from using the website to see whether there's a market for new products before it rolls them out in its retail stores. Last year, it debuted two new departments—fitness and fly-fishing—on the Web. After they proved to be successful online, REI started introducing them in a few of its stores. REI even launched a fully translated Japanese-language website months before it opened its first store in Japan—albeit, with prices at first quoted in dollars and fulfillment handled through its Seattle distribution center. (Prices are now in yen, and REI opened a distribution center and customer support center in the Yokohama area in April 2000.)

The Next Ascent

There's room for REI to improve the integration between its stores and its website. While the website offers real-time information about whether a product is in stock at REI's distribution center, it doesn't let customers view inventory availability in a particular store, nor does it let them order items online and pick them up in the store. An REI spokeswoman says that members have never asked for this functionality, so the company has no immediate plans to offer it. But some analysts believe that such integration will give click-and-mortar companies a huge advantage over dotcom companies if they can pull it off. Circuit City is one of the rare brick-and-mortars to do so.

Still, REI's current click-and-mortar efforts appear to be paying off quite nicely: 50 percent of REI's website customers are newcomers to REI—that is, they are non-members. And REI's existing customers haven't just shifted their spending from bricks to clicks, Hyde says. A survey showed that customers who shopped in REI's stores in 1998 and then also started shopping on its website in 1999 spent 22 percent more money in REI's stores in 1999. "The value of integrating multiple channels is pretty remarkable," Forrester's Williams says. "REI is one of the few retailers that has demonstrated it."

Bartels, the Giga analyst, believes that in the long term, when every company has a presence online and offline, REI will see more channel shift—that is, people will move their spending from offline to online, rather than spending more overall with REI. "But in the near term, companies that do support different channels will gain incremental sales over those that don't," he says. "There are people who like to primarily buy online, and then there are people who like to do research online but still buy in the store. A pure Internet company can capture the first type of customers, but a click-and-mortar company can capture both."

REI intends to keep serving both kinds of customers—and maintain tight ties between its website and its stores. "We want to do everything in our power to keep these two lines of business integrated fully and with a common face to the customer," Madsen says.

Case Study Questions

1. Bricks and Clicks Strategies

a. Was a bricks and clicks strategy a natural evolution for REI? Explain your position.

b. Why does a bricks and clicks strategy now seem to be the best E-commerce strategy for retailers like REI?

c. Will this advantage continue into the future? Why or why not?

2. E-commerce Development Strategies

a. Do you approve of how REI developed and integrated its E-commerce website into its business? Why or why not?

b. Did REI finance and market its E-commerce website properly? Why or why not?

c. Should REI have carved out its E-commerce website from the rest of the business like Wal-Mart and others are doing even now? Explain your position.

3. E-commerce Retailing Strategies

a. Are in-store Web kiosks a good E-commerce investment for REI? Why or why not?

b. Is using the REA Web site to test market new products before introducing them into their stores a good business idea? Explain your answer.

c. What else should REI do to improve its E-commerce performance and profitability? Outline the reasons for your proposals.

Source: Adapted from Sari Kalin, "E-Business as Usual," *Darwin*, February 2001, pp. 46–52.

Virgin Group Ltd.: Building an E-Commerce Megaportal

The Virgin King

In the world of E-commerce, speed plays kingmaker. Richard C.N. Branson, the charismatic founder and chairman of London-based Virgin Group Ltd., has placed a tardy bid for this throne. Branson acknowledged in the winter of 1998 that his company had been an Internet laggard, a candid admission from such a high-profile CEO. Branson is just as open these days about the hundreds of millions of dollars he is spending to make virgin.com one of the top E-commerce megaportals of the United Kingdom, and then the rest of Europe and the world. Branson bankrolled his E-commerce venture by selling a 49 percent stake in his Singapore Airlines for $979 million. Then he hired San Francisco-based Internet services company iXL to craft the look and feel of the virgin.com portal. But to take the portal global, Branson, who only started mapping an Internet strategy in the Fall of 1999, has his work cut out for him, analysts say.

But Branson has made a career of confounding his critics. The Virgin Group spans 170 businesses, from airlines and railroads to music stores and condoms. So when the British tycoon moves online, one shouldn't expect just digital music and virtual airline reservations. Try some 5,500 London households paying gas and electric bills online through Virgin's web site since July 2000. An additional 2,000 Brits tooling around in cars they bought on the Net, thanks to a new Virgin service launched a month earlier. Then there are the nearly 2 million people in the country booking train tickets through Virgin—and 1 million using the Web to tap Virgin's help in managing $4 billion in assets, including insurance, mortgage, and investment funds. And don't forget the $58,000 worth of wine they're buying online from Branson each week.

The irony here is that Britain's most colorful and controversial entrepreneur is no big fan of technology. "I'm not that interested in the Net, personally," says Virgin's 50-year old owner, who doesn't use a computer and instead keeps copious notes in leather-bound notebooks. What Branson does like is the ability to use the Net to bring order to his unwieldy conglomerate. "A lot of people never thought Virgin was very logical because we didn't specialize in any one area," says Branson, comfortably seated in the London townhouse that doubles as his office. "But then the Internet comes along, and I'm able to pretend that it was a carefully crafted plan," he jokes. See Figure A.6.

A Web Megastore

Carefully crafted or not, virgin.com is a digital giant in the making. Still in its first year, the web site is attracting 1.9 million visitors a month and ranks as the 12th most popular web destination in Britain, according to market researcher MMXI Europe. Now, Branson is trying to build virgin.com into one of the world's top portals. He has spent more than $225 million to develop net businesses and services, ranging from a global mobile phone company to radiofreevirgin.com, a sister site offering software to turn a PC into a digital radio. Branson believes the Virgin name, known for its hip, consumer-friendly image and exceptional service, will translate well across a rash of web businesses. "Virgin.com isn't a company, it's a brand," says Will White-horn, a Virgin director, who oversees the company's e-commerce activities.

The stellar red-and-white Virgin logo is a big draw for partners, too. They like the fact that Branson splashes the Virgin logo and its web address across everything from shopping bags in the Virgin Megastores, to the sides of trains and the tails of planes, saving a fortune in advertising. "Virgin's approach to the Net has been very clever," says Simon Knox, professor of brand marketing at the Cranfield University School of Management in Bedford. "Each launch of a new business builds upon the one before, rather than developing isolated branded businesses."

And then there's the way Branson is using the Web to streamline operations inside his empire. His Virgin Atlantic Airways Ltd. and record stores now order inventory online as needed, instead of having to keep huge stashes of CDs and parts close by. The privately held company estimates that the Internet will boost efficiencies and shave 15% off its overall costs this year, although it declines to provide specific figures.

Branson is betting that such E-business efficiencies will grow as virgin.com becomes an E-commerce conglomerate. By putting all of Virgin's businesses on one easily accessible site, he can cross-promote the company's seemingly limitless offerings. For instance, users might log on to the Web site to buy an airline ticket on Virgin Atlantic and then check out a mortgage or order a case of wine. "I normally use Virgin's web site for entertainment listings, but I was surprised by the amount of stuff they offer," says London web designer Steven Scott, who logged on recently to check out airfares and ended up buying CDs.

Now Brits can find another online service from Virgin. In December 2000, Branson launched an online auction business available through virgin.com. To kick off the service, nine Virgin companies auctioned flights, cars, wine, and mobile phones.

Figure A.6

Richard Branson, Virgin's chairman and founder, is leading Virgin's charge into E-commerce.

Ockenfels 3/Corbis Outline.

For the first two weeks, consumers were able to name their price—since all bidding began at $1.50. Now the range of goods and services offered changes weekly. "Considering the brand recognition that Virgin has wherever it operates, they've got the right strategy in place: an online marketplace for offline products," says Jamie Wood, head of European equity research at J.P. Morgan & Co. "The Web works best when a brand aggregates a variety of services into one place with a guaranteed level of service." See Figure A.7.

Late to the Web Game

Despite all its nifty Net services, Virgin is late to the Web. So far most of the ventures behind virgin.com are available only in Britain. The company's online sales total a puny $216 million. That's just a fraction of Virgin's overall sales of $5.2 billion. And it's way behind the $500 million in e-commerce and advertising revenues that rival American Online Inc. generated for the fiscal year 2000 ended June 30. Critics also question whether plastering Virgin's logo over such a disparate range of businesses undermines the clarity or integrity of the brand.

The Virgin brand hasn't gained much traction among Net shoppers in the U.S. That's why Virgin announced in December of 1999 that it was temporarily pulling back from online music sales in the U.S. through its Virgin Megastore site. Virgin says the level of U.S. sales has not been sufficient to justify maintaining a full-service E-commerce operation. Virgin Megastore now plans to focus its online efforts on providing music-related content while expanding the number of stores in the U.S.

Figure A.7

A sample of Virgin E-commerce sites available via the virgin.com Web portal.

Virgin E-Commerce Businesses

- **Virgin Atlantic Airways.** This is Virgin's biggest online moneymaker. The airline uses the Net to sell tickets and to cut inventory costs by ordering spare parts as needed over the Web instead of stocking them in a warehouse.
- **Virgin Cars.** A virtual showroom where consumers can compare models before buying online at prices 17% cheaper than traditional dealerships. Buyers get maintenance thrown in and can arrange financing, as well as sell their existing car on the site.
- **Virgin Direct.** Along with partners, Virgin sells insurance, mortgages, and investment funds. It has more than 1 million customers and $4 billion in assets.
- **Virgin Energy.** The Internet-based gas and electricity supplier went live in July 2000. The venture, 25% owned by London Electricity, has attracted 5,500 consumers and plans to roll out across Europe. Customers who haven't saved money after switching will receive a refund of the difference plus 20%.
- **Virgin Mobile.** The joint venture with Deutsche Telekom's cellular company, One 2 One, was launched in November 1999. Virgin Mobile has 548,000 customers in Britain and is expanding to Australia and Southeast Asia. Customers get mobile-phone service, e-mail, and online services such as dining tips.
- **Virgin Money.** The financial service, launched in June 2000, is similar to Charles Schwab. Besides online trading users get financial info and can compare every financial product available on the market—not just Virgin's.
- **Virgintravelstore.com.** The online travel agency launched in December 2000. Net shoppers can book everything from airline flights to hotel rooms to guided tours from a wide selection of travel companies, including Virgin.
- **Thetrainline.com.** Started in February, 1999, as a joint venture with British transport company Stagecoach. The site sells tickets for Britain's 23 train operators, has 1.8 million users, and is adding 55,000 new ones each week.
- **Virginwines.com.** The site for British wine connoisseurs was launched in 2000. It uses software to analyze buyers' purchase patterns to help guide them through a list of 17,500 wines. Sales are averaging $58,000 per week.
- **Radiofreevirgin.com.** The free digital radio tuner, when downloaded to a PC, gives listeners CD-quality music from 50 net channels. Launched in the U.S. in February 2000, the site boasts 500,000 users and hopes to go global.

from 19 to about 40 by 2005. Because the U.S. is still a small share of Virgin Megastore's overall sales, the company hopes that increasing its presence in America will eventually strengthen its position online.

Branson also faces tough competition from such global net players as AOL and Yahoo!, which already have well established portals offering almost the same fare. "Everyone wants to be a leading portal these days," says analyst Mikael Arnbjerg of market researcher IDC in Copenhagen. "Virgin can leverage its brand in certain market sectors, but that's not enough to become a major player."

Branson doesn't deny any of these challenges. But he insists that Virgin's strength is that the brand isn't inextricably linked to just one business or product, Unlike other cell phone operators, Virgin can cross-sell a variety of products and services to its mobile phone customers. And because brick-and-mortar retailers tend to specialize in one area of the market, Virgin believes its diverse offerings will be a major advantage. Virgin is betting that selling its own merchandise, something neither AOL nor Yahoo does, will give it an edge over the big online players. "Being completely virtual and simply selling other people's products is a zero-sum game," says Whitehorn.

Wireless M-Commerce

Where Branson's strategy has the potential to pay off handsomely is via mobile E-commerce on the wireless Web. Virgin already sells mobile phones and offers Virgin Mobile, a wireless network that is a joint venture with Deutsche Telekom's cellular company, One 2 One. By 2005, mobile phones are expected to account for more than 40% of the estimated $20 billion in European e-commerce transactions, according to London-based market research company Mintel. "Branson realizes the considerable potential for mobile phones as a M-commerce distribution channel, and any of his businesses can benefit from this," says Peter Richardson, principal analyst at the Gartner Group, a consultancy in Egham, Surrey.

How? Virgin Mobile gives Branson a direct line to customers without incurring extra marketing costs. Using short text messages, Virgin can offer targeted promotions for any of its products and services. Today, some 20% of Virgin Mobile's revenue is e-mail and other data communications, but Branson estimates that nearly 50% of the wireless network's revenues will come from non-voice traffic by 2005. By then, Branson believes most of the transactions on virgin.com will be made through cell phones instead of PCs. Branson envisions a day when Virgin Mobile users will be able to reserve a seat on Virgin Trains while waiting on the platform, simply by pressing a button on their phones. Once aboard, Virgin Mobile users can check their investments through the Virgin Direct financial services site, book a vacation through Virgin Holidays Ltd., or listen to the top-selling tracks at the Virgin Megastores over radiofreevirgin.com.

The day when people use their phones to buy tickets for the train is coming soon—thanks to Branson. Skeptics doubted he would be able to make a business out of booking tickets online. After all, buying via the Web requires planning—something people who purchase their tickets at the station are not used to doing. But TheTrainLine.com, a joint venture with British transportation company Stagecoach Holdings PSC, is doing a brisk trade. The site sells tickets for Britain's 23 train operators, including Virgin's train line. Some 2 million people use the service, and 55,000 new customers visit the site each week. Revenue for the operation was expected to hit $144 million by year-end 2000, and Virgin expects to break even by the end of 2001.

What could give Branson a bigger boost on the Web is Virgin's reputation for super service. In June 2000, the company launched Virgin Cars, an online site where British consumers can buy a broad range of makes and models at an average discount of 17% from those sold in dealerships. Virgin can offer lower prices by buying cars from European dealerships, where the vehicles are far cheaper than in

Britain due to the strength of the pound. That advantage won't last forever. So Branson is building a reputation for quality and white-glove treatment by offering a service package that includes warranty, roadside assistance, and pickup-and-delivery maintenance, including a clean car when it's returned.

E-Business Efficiency

Branson doesn't view the Web as a tool simply to boost the top line. Virgin is using the Internet to streamline its far-flung operations. Virgin Atlantic Airways, for instance, is tapping into the Net to improve the efficiency of its supply chain. The airline now buys most of its new and used parts online. Whenever mechanics need a part, they log on and place their order—instead of Virgin having to stock a complete array of plane parts. This E-business just-in-time approach, says Whitehorn, has helped the carrier achieve great savings by reducing the amount of inventory it needs to warehouse. If a plane is stranded on the tarmac or in the hangar because of a faulty part, Virgin Atlantic can check the Web for a local supplier that stocks that part, and it is sent to the runway in a matter of hours, something that would have been impossible three years ago.

Using the Net, Branson has even resuscitated his money-losing V Shop retail chains. The British chain, known until recently as Our Price, is a miniature version of the Virgin Megastore, where customers can buy music, videos, entertainment gear, software, and mobile phones, In September 2000, the stores were renamed V Shops. Instead of stocking massive amounts of CDs, videos, and games, V Shops now keep only the most popular products on its shelves. The rest are held at a fulfillment house contracted by Virgin. Customers who want to buy something other than what the store has in stock can choose from an additional 110,000 products available via in-store kiosks hooked to the Net. Currently, 10% of all sales are through their in-store Web kiosks.

The impact on the bottom line is considerable. By slashing its in-store inventory in half, Virgin is saving around $300,000 a year at each of the 150 V Shops. Monthly sales are up an average of 40%, and Virgin anticipates all of the retooled V Shops will be profitable in their first year. "Technology has enabled us to put a dying business back on its feet and make a small store big," says Virgin Entertainment Group CEO Simon Wright.

Case Study Questions

1. Late to the Web Game
   a. Why do you think Virgin was late launching into E-commerce?
   b. Is Virgin too late to achieve great success in global E-commerce? Why or why not?
   c. Is Virgin's late charge into E-commerce being properly developed, financed, and marketed? Outline the reasons for your answer.

2. Building the Web Megastore
   a. Is the virgin.com E-commerce megaportal concept a good business idea? Why or why not?
   b. Do the new Web businesses included in virgin.com have sound E-commerce prospects? Outline your evaluation of each virgin.com business listed in Figure A.7.
   c. Is the Virgin brand capable of attracting sufficient E-commerce traffic to assure a profitable level of

revenue for all virgin.com companies? Explain your reasoning.

3. Expanding the Web Megaportal
   a. Will Virgin be able to successfully capitalize on wireless M-commerce as a major E-commerce channel for virgin.com companies? Why or why not?
   b. How do Virgin's new E-business capabilities contribute to the success and expansion of its traditional and E-commerce businesses?
   c. What business proposals could you present to Richard Branson to help improve the chances for the success of virgin.com? Outline the reasons for your proposals.

Source: Adapted from Kim Gerard, "Unlike a Virgin," *Business 2.0*, June 13, 2000, pp.240–42, and Kerry Capell, "Virgin Takes E-Wing," *Business Week eBiz*, January 22, 2001, pp. EB 30–34.

Enron Corporation: Creating and Dominating Electronic Markets

The Multitasking Trader

Inside Enron's gleaming, gray, 50-story headquarters in downtown Houston, a 26-year-old trader named John Arnold sits at his desk, from which he trades well north of $1 billion worth of energy futures every day. *Multitasking* doesn't begin to describe what Arnold does: Five flat-screen computer monitors bombard him with a constant stream of news, national weather data, and prices for natural gas futures (contracts for a specified amount of gas at a specified future date); a headset pumps more prices into his right ear, a regular phone dedicated to customers is cradled to his left; and a squawk box links him to traders at other desks. Meanwhile his colleagues within earshot are also shouting orders at him. It is amazing he doesn't overload. Yet Arnold, Enron's top trader, never seems to lose his cool.

"Before," he says, "we would price a structured trade 30 to 50 times a day. Now, we price trades 30 times a minute." That's "before" as in before the Internet. Enron is one of the world's largest traders of energy products: natural gas, oil, electricity, and other commodities. But until a year ago, Arnold was still doing all his trading by phone, and he was lucky to bring in a third of the trades he does today. Since then, the company has launched EnronOnline, which has vastly increased the amount of information Arnold can process as well as multiplied the uses to which that information can be put. See Figure A.8.

The Impact of EnronOnline

To get a sense of the Web's impact on Enron, consider the volume of trades flowing through EnronOnline. Roughly 60 percent of Enron's transactions pass through the website; since it went live on November 29, 1999, Arnold and his colleagues have used it to buy and sell more than $300 billion in commodities. In the third quarter of 2000, Enron traded 86 percent more natural gas and 52 percent more electricity than in the third quarter of 1999, before EnronOnline was up and running

Of course, the past year's volatility in energy prices played a role in that increase, but the company would have been hard-pressed to handle it without the Web. During the first nine months of 2000, Enron's profits rose 45 percent to $919 million, on revenues that doubled to $60 billion. (The company does engage in other operations, such as building power plants and operating gas pipelines, but 90 percent of its revenues come from wholesale trading.)

Enron is, in other words, the biggest, baddest B2B E-commerce company on the planet, and its experience belies the idea that innovation is impossible in large organizations. The premise of Enron's business hasn't changed much over the last decade: It trades commodities, and—as with traders of pork bellies, soy beans, or any commodity—its ability to make money depends on the quality of its information. The

Web, by its very nature, makes information more fungible, transparent, easy to access. And Enron has taken full advantage of it to interact and trade with companies more than ever before.

It's not just about trading gas and electricity: Enron executives are united in the belief that damn near anything can be traded as a commodity so they are hell-bent on identifying new markets where this model can be applied. "We have made a commitment to Wall Street to grow at a 15 percent compound annual rate," says Ken Rice, the CEO of a division that trades fiber-optic capacity, "so we have to find new markets to grow into." Enron has gradually expanded the range of commodities it sells to include paper products, plastics, metals, bandwidth, pollution emission credits, weather derivatives, and commercial credit. The Web has become its testing ground, a cheap way to see where its market-making skills can best be brought to bear.

The Case Against B2B Exchanges

Given how much of Enron's activity is fueled by the Web, it's surprising that E-commerce came as a revelation to president and CEO Jeff Skilling. "If you had told me in October 1999 that the total volume we would transact in 2000 over the Web would be even $10 billion, I would have said, 'No way,'" he says. Back in that Paleolithic time, B2B exchanges were all the rage: Startups were popping up to create online marketplaces where companies in different industries could post offers to buy and sell goods.

But Skilling wasn't buying the B2B exchange concept. He saw the exchanges as little more than bulletin boards where transactions might or might not occur, rather than a trading system like Enron's that guarantees to fill orders at a quoted price, with Enron acting as the principal. Altra Energy Technologies, for instance, one of the most successful B2B exchanges, also trades gas and power. However, depending on the commodity, only 10 to 50 percent of the orders posted on Altra ever get

Figure A.8

A glimpse at Enron's massive trading operations.

Paul Howell/The Liaison Agency.

filled. The value of all of Altra's web-auction transactions in the first three quarters of 2000 was $16 billion, roughly equal to a single week's worth of trades on EnronOnline.

"I had made it known throughout the organization that I did not believe in these B2B exchanges," says Skilling. So well known, in fact, that his minions didn't even tell him about EnronOnline until they had built it and brought it to him just before the launch. Sitting in his mahogany-paneled office the size of a handball court, Skilling is now a devout E-business convert. He describes how the Web fits perfectly with Enron's business. His explanation is, at times as abstract as the Miro hanging beside him, but it boils down to the fact that Enron is good at creating markets where none existed and the Web makes it easier to do that.

The Case for Online Markets

"The age-old economic trade-off in designing a business has been the value of specialization vs the cost of interaction," says Skilling, who was a McKinsey consultant before joining Enron in 1990. "We want to create markets to replace those vertically integrated linkages." Which is to say, large firms traditionally tended to be vertically integrated because the costs of finding reliable suppliers and of completing a transaction (the interaction costs) outweighed the cost of doing everything in-house. Over the past few decades, the trend has been away from verticality and toward outsourcing. Skilling suggests that online trading will hasten that movement. "The Web," he says, "is the next stage of massively knocking down the interaction costs."

To better understand what he means, consider the role Enron plays in the natural gas industry. In the past, gas was gas—you just bought it. Then in the 1980s, with deregulation setting in and prices fluctuating wildly, Enron created a market in natural gas and related financial products. By building a large portfolio, and by using its own pipeline network to connect to transporters and producers, Enron was able to match supply and demand. It could, say, promise two months of gas at a fixed price to a buyer, then find the cheapest producer and transporter. By breaking the transaction in to pieces and buying each piece at the lowest possible price, Enron reduced the interaction costs between producers, transporters, and customers—and still found enough left over to charge a spread. Score one for the power of markets.

All markets are actually big information-processing machines that can take thousands of millions of inputs in the form of demand and supply signals and spit out judgments of relative worth in the form of prices. With the Web, however, Enron can match supply and demand more quickly and efficiently. In the pre-web days, as John Arnold, the hyperwired trader, remembers it, "We used to benefit by knowing the relative value of gas better than anybody else. The lack of price transparency was a benefit to us—that was how we made money. Now we have destroyed that business model, and we make money through increased volumes and very clear price transparency."

The Market Operating System

The more Enron trades a commodity, the more easily it can package that commodity into unique, higher-margin products. Enron's first long-term gas contract in1989 required nine-months of calls and meetings and 400 to 500 deals with about 150 different producers. That was one contract for one customer. It was worth the trouble—such complex deals come with a 20 to 75 percent profit margin, compared with 5 to 7 percent for a simple energy futures contract—but it was still an arduous process. By the late 90s, Enron's portfolio of gas contracts was so large that similar deals took only two weeks to assemble, and its traders were doing two or three a week. Today, with EnronOnline and a larger portfolio, Enron's traders strike about five such deals a day, each in less than a second.

"Like Microsoft created DOS," explains management strategist Gary Hamel, who counts Enron as a client, "Enron is creating MOS: the market operation system. And they can apply it everywhere." By learning to identify and exploit certain universal features of commodities transactions, Enron is replicating its business model and extending it across the economy, both to existing markets and some new ones. Nowhere is this prospect juicier than in the trading and packaging of Internet bandwidth, a market that may ultimately prove even larger than energy.

Its bandwidth business, Enron Broadband Services, aims to become the world's largest trader of bandwidth, and Wall Street analysts are so bullish about the two-year-old unit's prospects that they attribute to it a full 20 to 25 percent of Enron's stock value. Such optimism may have something to do with the fact that Ken Rice, the division's CEO, previously headed up Enron's energy-trading business.

The Blockbuster Deal

It was Rice who oversaw a deal, announced last summer, in which Blockbuster Video agreed to partner with Enron to provide video-on-demand to Blockbuster's customers over the next 20 years. That deal prompted some to ask: What is Enron doing in the movie-rental business? Simple: It is testing its MOS, seeing if the process that worked for gas can work for bandwidth. Rice's plan is for Enron to build a portfolio of contracts from suppliers and customers, and then offer bandwidth-on-demand and other services by matching different parts of that portfolio. His traders might buy a fiber-optic line for a year at a fixed price from AT&T, and then sell parts of its capacity to corporations looking to use it for only a month at a time. Since the growth of the Internet is creating a vast array of bandwidth needs, Rice hopes that demand will increase not just for simple bandwidth trades, but for bundled, high-margin instruments as well.

That's were David Cox comes in. When Rice started the broadband unit two years ago, Cox, a master developer, was the first person he asked to come with him. As vice president for content management, Cox hunts for companies with content they need to put online. Blockbuster CEO John Antioco had long been trying to find a way to do video-on-demand. But whenever he talked to fiber-network companies about creating a nationwide-video-on-demand service, they told him it would cost $3 billion to $4 billion. Worse, he'd have to pay up front for a big pipe that would lie in the ground, empty, until he figured out how to fill it. It was too costly and too risky.

Last summer, Cox convinced Antioco that Enron's market-base approach was the way to go. He explained how Enron would buy bandwidth as needed, and that Blockbuster wouldn't have to provide any cash up front. Instead, Enron would share the proceeds from every Blockbuster movie rental over the Internet—for the next 20 years. During this period, the deal could bring in a total of $5 billion in revenues to Enron—and help Enron establish itself as the most important go-between in a growing bandwidth market.

The Case Against Bandwidth Trading

All of that assumes that the concept actually works. Quite apart from technical issues such as bringing broadband to the homes of Blockbuster customers, and guaranteeing the data speeds necessary for video, Enron must overcome some deep-seated skepticism among its potential clientele. For instance, Stan Woodward, an executive at Yahoo Broadcast, which streams more video over the Internet than anyone, doesn't believe bandwidth trading is even possible. "We don't think it works," he says bluntly. "We've heard the pitch. We asked questions. We didn't get any answers."

Woodward would love to sell his unused bandwidth, but says he can't because the high-capacity lines he leases are specifically tuned to Yahoo's particular hardware. He adds that bandwidth trading would add a step to the flow of data, which could lower the quality of the connection. Also, in many cases, the rates a company pays to a telecom provider, as well as the level of service it is guaranteed, are details it is contractually forbidden to discuss, much less trade on for profit. If companies could sell their unused bandwidth, they'd be competing against their own bandwidth providers. No wonder Woodward is dubious. "A barrel of oil equals a barrel of oil," he says, "but a megabit of bandwidth does not equal a megabit of bandwidth."

The Case for Bandwidth Trading

But Rice has heard these arguments before. And it turns out that a barrel of oil does *not* equal a barrel of oil. Back when Enron began trading oil futures, critics said it couldn't be done because oil from Texas was not the same as oil from, say, Saudi Arabia—the two vary in viscosity and sulfur content. So, for oil to become a tradable commodity, Enron and others defined benchmarks against which any oil could be measured. The same thing had to be done in every other market Enron operates in.

Rice plans to do the same with bandwidth. Despite the skepticism of Yahoo and others, bandwidth does show signs of being a commodity-in-the-making: Like the energy markets of the mid-1980's, there are many buyers and sellers (every big corporation and many retail consumers want to buy bandwidth, and every telecom, ISP, cable, and fiber-optics company wants to sell it); prices are set at inflexible but ever-changing rates; and carriers typically sell capacity only for long periods.

Moreover, most companies use only a fraction of the bandwidth they pay for, which means plenty of it is available at any given time. As for those secret agreements, one Enron executive notes that there are ways to get around the confidentiality clauses of most bandwidth service contracts. Enron obviously has a lot of educating to do, but it has already proven itself in similar scenarios; the stock market, at least, seems to be betting it will once again come out a winner.

In fact, Enron is already trading links between New York and Los Angeles. And while most of these lines are for plain old voice calls, 15 to 20 percent are for data traffic. The data portion should grow as Enron learns how to create contracts that specify reference standards such as allowable error rates. If history is any guide, more complicated deals should become possible as those standards are defined. So Enron might one day be able to, say, purchase bandwidth from a telecom, then sell it to corporations for daytime usage and to Blockbuster customers in the evenings and on weekends. (Enron's bandwidth unit isn't profitable yet, but it went from practically zero revenues in 1999 to $345 million in the first three quarters of 2000—growth that goes a long way toward answering Rice's critics.)

There's another factor in Enron's bandwidth scheme that makes it even more compelling: Enron is building its own 15,000-mile fiber-optic network—just as earlier it laid 32,000 miles of gas and oil pipelines—so it can honor its commitments and ensure the easy transfer of bandwidth from one carrier's network to another. This network will cost Enron $1.5 billion, but because it will serve as the connective tissue between other existing fiber networks, Enron will be able to piggyback on the tens of billions of dollars already invested by other providers. These kinds of figures make Altra Energy and other pure-play exchanges look pretty anemic.

Enron's Startup Markets

When it became obvious in the Spring of 2000 that EnronOnline was going to become a huge success, the executives who created it were dispatched to sprinkle E-commerce pixie dust all over the company. The result was a new division called Enron Net Works, designed to help spawn internal startups from EnronOnline. Enron is using these new companies—which now include ClickPaper.com, Commodity Logic, DealBench.com, EnronCredit.com, and EnronMetals.com—to test its business model in non-energy related markets. See Figure A.9.

Paper products, for instance, used to be traded on EnronOnline, but they got lost in the sea of energy products also traded there. Since Net Works created Click-Paper in June 2000, 1 million tons of paper, pulp, and wood—valued at $670 million—have been traded through the site. In contrast, independent business-to-business marketplace PaperExchange has traded only 50,000 tons of paper products since it went live in mid-1999.

Figure A.9

What Enron is trading online and building on the ground.

Enron's Online Markets

- **Wholesale Energy** Enron still makes most of its money trading energy. Its earnings from sales to utilities and other wholesale customers should grow at a 35% to 40% annual pace for at least several years, it says. However, the company is also branching out into entirely new markets.
- **Retail Energy** Enron signed new contracts worth $16 billion in 2000 to manage energy needs for big business customers.
- **Broadband** It projects a $450 billion worldwide market for communications bandwidth trading and services by 2005. It has begun distributing video-on-demand and other content over its own high-speed fiber network to customers like Blockbuster.
- **Paper, Pulp, and Lumber** Enron launched a specialized web site, Clickpaper.com, tailored to the $330 billion wood products market and bought newsprint maker Garden State Paper Co. for $72 million in October 2000 to ensure access to supplies.
- **Media** The plan is to create a market for trading advertising time and space in TV, radio, and print. That includes offering advertisers, TV networks, and publishers ways to hedge risks, such as long-term, fixed-price contracts.
- **Steel** The company's first target is a $22 billion segment of the commodity steel business. Enron plans to lease a network of regional distribution centers to ensure reliable deliveries.

Source: Adapted from Wendy Zellner, Christopher Palmeri, Peter Coy, and Laura Cohn, "Power Play," *Business Week*, February 12, 2001, p. 74.

Net Works may also spin off Commodity Logic, which will bottle up Enron's own back-office systems (for settlements and for scheduling transportation and warehousing) into web-based software that others can use for themselves. Another one of Net Work's companies is DealBench which provides web-based project management software. Enron has already used DealBench's collaborative software to manage a $3.3 billion bank-loan syndication and take bids on construction materials for its new office tower in Houston (Enron ended up saving 35 percent on 100,000 square feet of carpet). DealBench chief Harry Arora says that being a startup inside a large corporation like Enron has distinct advantages—access to customers and capital, to name two. His competitors at stand-alone startups, on the other hand, "are spending the majority of their time trying to raise money."

And then there is EnronCredit, founded to trade bankruptcy swaps. These swaps protect companies that have extended credit to other corporations, in the event that the latter go belly-up and cannot meet their trade obligations. "Nobody ever saw trade credit before," points out Enron CEO Jeff Skilling. "It used to stay on the balance sheet." By creating a market for it, Enron is allowing companies to sell off that credit risk and transfer it onto somebody else's books. EnronCredit is, in effect, helping companies turn themselves inside out, which in a way is what all of Enron's startups aim to do.

Online Markets Risks and Rewards

As Skilling extends his MOS to new markets—chemicals, steel, data storage, financial settlements, even trucking—there is always the danger that Enron will misjudge which industries are ready for its market-making. For example, the separately traded stock for Azurix, Enron's water spin-off, is down about 60 percent from last year's IPO price because Azurix underestimated, among other things, the political barriers to trading water rights.

But this is a company that learns from experience. If Enron can extend its trading model into other areas—and prove that bandwidth and other goods and services are as fungible as oil or gas—it will succeed in transforming its ancient form of trade into a powerful lubricant of the economy. As corporations flatten, they must concentrate more than ever on what they do best and outsource everything else. Where verticality once ruled business, complexity is now king. By commoditizing products and services, Enron's markets help companies cope with that complexity by making it easier for them either to outsource or to cherry-pick what they need from other companies.

"This is the essence of what the Internet is doing," says Skilling, "rebuilding and reworking what used to be internal processes." Enron hopes to insert itself into this gap between what companies do best and what they leave to others. That's a tricky place to set up shop, but it could be one of the sweetest spots in the economy. To get there, Enron needs to keep experimenting, and the Web is the cheapest lab around.

Case Study Questions

1. The Impact of Enron Online
   a. How has Enron's business mix and model changed because of Enron Online?
   b. What role does Enron Online now play in Enron's business?
   c. What has been the impact of Enron Online on Enron's trading profits and performance?

2. Enron's Online Markets Revolution
   a. Enron thinks the Web now makes it possible to create electronic markets for trading practically anything online. Do you agree or disagree? Why?
   b. Enron says that the Internet has dramatically changed the economic tradeoffs concerning which processes a business feels it must perform internally, and those it can now outsource to other companies via online markets. Do you agree or disagree? Why?
   c. Do you agree with Enron that its Enron Online business model is superior to those of most online B2B exchanges? Why or why not?

3. The Bandwidth Trading Battle
   a. Do you think that Enron's agreement with Blockbuster Video is a sound business deal? Why or why not?

   b. Do you agree or disagree with the arguments against the feasibility of trading broadband contracts? Why?
   c. Do you think Enron will be successful in its bandwidth trading business? Why or why not?

4. The Risks and Rewards of Online Markets
   a. Do the startup companies Enron created to develop new online markets listed in Figure A.9 have good prospects for E-commerce success? Defend your evaluations.
   b. Enron views the Web as a testing ground for online trading markets. What is the possible risk to Enron of failures like its Azurex spinoff? Explain.
   c. What are Enron's prospects for long term business success in its chosen online markets trading role? Explain your reasoning.

Source: Adapted from Erick Schonfeld, "The Power Brokers," *eCompany*, January/February 2001, pp. 116–124.

Convisint LLC: Challenges of an Industry-Led Global Electronic Marketplace

When Enemies Meet

There will always be drama when enemies convene. Especially when it's nighttime and the enemies are alone, and especially when they've never met. So it was on one evening in February 2000 at Detroit's upper-crust Townsend Hotel, when Harold Kutner and Brian Kelley, senior executives from General Motors and Ford Motor, came together for the first time—in secret—at the suggestion of a mutual major parts supplier.

The big supplier had placed a couple of calls a few weeks earlier, to lodge a complaint of sorts, first with Kutner, GM's worldwide purchasing czar, then with Kelley, president of Ford's company-wide E-commerce initiatives. Look, he told the executives, as a supplier to both of you, I'm being forced to get up to speed on your two new, different, and highly complex online purchasing systems. That's doubling my effort; isn't there some way GM and Ford can do this together?

Kutner, 60, recounts the tale. His smile might be boyish, but his voice is newsreel emphatic. "My answer," he booms, remembering the phone call, "was...*No.*" But Kutner's eventual evening with Kelley at the Townsend was enough to encourage second thoughts. The men, it turned out, had rapport. And the auto industry, they agreed—mired in a four-year price slump and plagued with so many costly inefficiencies in its supply structure—had a now-or-never opportunity staring it down.

That is, build one vast electronic tent under which thousands of auto parts and equipment companies that feed Big Auto's supply chain could talk and do business together. Create a web-based, easy to access platform across which tens of thousands of businesses can buy and sell supplies, exchange information regarding forecasts, inventory, billing, shipment, and product design—in real time. Then, you'll not only gut costs, you'll turn the auto business upside-down.

Less than a month after Kutner and Kelley's meeting, Ford and GM fired the shot hear round the B-to-B world: They would abandon their separate efforts to build online empires out of their own camps of suppliers and manufacturers, and instead join hands to launch a single system that would form the world's biggest online industry marketplace. If DaimlerChrysler signed on as well, the new entity would command $240 billion per year in purchasing power through 90,000 member companies worldwide, generate an estimated $3 billion a year in short-term transaction revenue, and—if you trust some analysts' math—eventually lop off $3,000 from the production cost of your average 21st century car. That same day, the German-American hybrid that is DaimlerChrysler, dumped its own E-commerce plans to announce that it wanted in, too. Within weeks, Nissan of Japan and Renault of France joined the group, making Covisint a huge global marketplace in waiting. See Figure A.10.

Brian Kelley, Ford's president of E-commerce initiatives, was a key player with GM's Harold Kutner in creating the Covisint global exchange.

Derek Blagg.

The Demise of the B2B Independents

Back in early 2000, E-marketplace mavericks such as VerticalNet and Ventro and more than 1,000 other new electronic business markets were considered serous threats to the back-end business of big corporate dinosaurs such as GM and Ford and so many others. But by early 2001, Ventro, the company spun from the now-defunct chemical exchange, Chemdex—which had a first-quarter 2000 market capitalization of $11 billion—was in need of a lifeline to stay in business as a software vendor. VerticalNet, another original B-to-B bellwether, is similarly mired in a profitless valuation nose dive, and its all-star CEO, Joe Galli, left in January 2001.

Unable to generate the critical mass of transaction volume that the independent E-marketplaces promised, and clearly underestimating the needs and clout of old-line business, the independents have become an endangered species in 2001. Fewer than 100, some analysts predict, will be left by the end of the year. To put it bluntly, they've been displaced by $3.5 billion in corporate funding, driving the launch of dozens of new industry-backed exchanges: Covisint in auto, Transora in packaged goods, MyAircraft.com in aerospace, GlobalNet Exchange in retail.

Covisint's Slow Start

But it's Covisint that big business will have its eyes on most. Never before has an industry so large and complex—and in many ways, incorrigibly slow—attempted to do so much, so fast. Over a year out of the gate, having secured an estimated $240 million in corporate funding, more than 200 employees chipped in by the partners, and the U.S. and German government agencies' seal of competitive approval, the performance sheet looks quite meager.

By mid-January 2001, the mega-exchange had signed up just 20 suppliers. It had conducted 80 supply auctions for seven clients, and managed to get 100 supplier catalogs up and running on servers. While basic purchasing functions have been in place since October 2000, company officials haven't yet chosen a tech vendor for the much-hyped supply-chain management features; meanwhile, analysts are wondering whether the fragile detente between Covisint's two competing software partners—Oracle and Commerce One—will endure as Covisint ramps up. Perhaps most telling of the challenges ahead, the new year passed without an announcement of a long-sought chief executive—one who will be flanked by business partners who, for most of the 20th century, served as vicious combatants.

Regardless, Covisint's success will begin—or end—with its biggest suppliers, such as $13 billion Dana, which delivers a rolling chassis to GM every 108 minutes, and Johnson Controls, the $17 billion maker of instrument panels. And at least for the moment, ambivalence, rather than startup enthusiasm, seems to prevail. "There are about 250 middleware companies calling us weekly," says Mike Suman, a group vice president at Johnson Controls. "They say, 'Hello, my name is X and I'm your E-solutions provider,' and you go, 'Oh really?'" Suman shrugs: "We haven't heard Covisint's business model yet."

An Industry Stuck in Reverse

Among other reasons, big business will be watching Covisint to see just how up to the task the B-to-B exchange model really is. The automotive industry, after all, is one of grave complexity: Where a computer comprises about 30 components or SKUs, a car or light truck is made up of about 5,000. GM coordinates production at 29 different far-flung plants, yet the whole system has got to move faster.

Small wonder, then, that in auto's first century, breakthroughs in truly universal connectivity have been few and far between. While ambitious executives such as Kutner aim to follow Dell Computer's example of radically streamlining communication from the customer to the plant, others balk at the analogy.

Auto industry analyst Maryann Keller, who left her post recently as head of Priceline.com's auto services, screeches at the mention of it: "Give Michael Dell a thousand parts to deliver and tell him to open a plant in Mexico. Come on! The parts he needs for a year could probably fit in a single 747. The Dell model does not apply to the auto industry!" And for that matter, it doesn't apply to most other industries now taking aim at the mention at the electronic exchange model; Dell's supply structures simply aren't as complex.

But eventually, something has to give. For four years, despite flush economic times in other industries, the prices of cars and trucks have remained flat; by some measure they've dropped. And parts suppliers have watched their own prices fall even between 2 and 3 percent. While SUVs have grown bigger, their makers' margins have shrunk, as an entire industry has watched its forecasters bumble and its products melt down into commodities.

Costly glitches abound in the business of car making. Vehicles no one wants sit on dealers' lots, unused raw materials sit in suppliers' warehouses, and an estimated $230 billon worth of excess inventory piles up yearly, largely to cover for scanty information about what consumers want and what carmakers will need to build it. It takes an average of 53 days to get a car built and delivered to its customer today, while only one or two of those days are actually spent on assembly; a full 36 days go by, according to a June 2000 report by Roland Berger, creating a schedule for production, processing orders for materials, and purchasing from suppliers.

Then comes the paper. Ninety-five percent of the companies in the automotive sector still communicate and transact via snail mail, fax, and telephone. The remaining 5 percent rely on *Electronic Data Interchange (EDI)* systems, originally developed in the 1960s, but still used only by the bigger companies that can afford them. The result? Higher costs across the board. Where flush Ford might link up with its big-money, Tier 1 chassis supplier, the hose maker down the line works only by fax and phone. The administrative costs alone of procuring materials for a car amount to about $95—multiply that by the 17 million vehicles a year made in North America.

The Lure of Covisint

Attacking each of these problems, plus others plaguing the processes of designing new models each year, underscores Covisint's proposition to the industry. The pay-off: a reduction of $2,000 to $3,000 off production costs for every $19,000 car that lands in the lot, according to Gary Lapidus, an auto industry analyst for Goldman Sachs. And even if such figures are wishful—Michael Heidingsfelder at Roland Berger estimates savings closer to $1,200, and most others agree—it still adds up enough to draw investors.

Which is one reason why, in the name of Covisint, age-old enemies such as DaimlerChrysler and Ford began getting chummy a year ago; it's why this young company, not yet even settled in a permanent location, has continued to promise an IPO in 2001; it's why bankers got away with closing an equity deal between Covisint and Commerce One that valued the former, still short a CEO and a single paying customer, at $59 billion. See Figure A.11.

What Covisint Promises

Ask most anyone in the auto industry what the Internet will do to change his or her business, and the answer will be broken into three parts: procurement, product development, and supply-chain management.

Procurement promises savings of two types. One is in the actual sticker price. Finding the best sources of a material, pushing down its price, and arriving at amounts and conditions that result in the cheapest deals—these are benefits Covisint offers

Figure A.11

The status of the Covisint global online marketplace.

Facts About Covisint

- **Covisint LLC**: www.covisint.com
  Founded: February 2000
  Temporary HQ: Southfield, Michigan
  Acting CEO: Rico Digirolamo of GM
  Partners: Ford Motor, General Motors, DaimlerChrysler, Renault, Nissan, Commerce One, Oracle
  Employees: 200
  Valuation: $59 billion
- **Key participants**: The founding automakers promise to work with more than 90,000 global suppliers, but so far Covisint will confirm that only 20 have signed on. Most are Tier 1 suppliers such as Dana, Lear, and Freudenberg-NOK, which sell completed components such as axles, brake systems, seats, instrument panels, and engine gaskets.
- **Key services**:
  - Procurement tools for automakers to buy completed parts, and parts suppliers to purchase their own raw materials, through online catalogs and auctions.
  - Virtual product design and development. A collaborative product design system that will allow all parties—car designers and engineers, parts manufacturers, and materials suppliers—to share documents, CAD illustrations, and schedules, and automatically send updates and changes to the entire development team.
  - Supply chain management tools that link automakers with the entire supply chain, from Tier 1 suppliers to raw-materials providers. Covisint promises online, global, instant communication among all suppliers for demand forecasting, capacity planning, transactions, and logistics to ultimately create the "build-to-order" automobile.
- **The big promise**: Save automakers anywhere from $2,000 to $3,000 per $19,000 vehicle; reduce the vehicle development cycle from 42 months to 12 to 18 months.
- **Key victory**: Cleared of antitrust concerns by the U.S. Federal Trade Commission and the German antitrust agency the Bundeskartellamt in September 2000.
- **Key competitors**: Volkswagen, IBM, Ariba, and i2 announced last year they would build their own exchange for the European market. In the U.S., online marketplace FreeMarkets hosts material auctions for more than 15 auto industry customers.
- **Key challenges**: Naming a CEO, winning the confidence of Tier 1 suppliers; launching supply chain services that promise bigger long-term returns.

buyers who use its site. Through the Covisint interface, buyers can search supply catalogs and run reverse auctions (or regular auctions if they're sellers); they can announce auctions weeks in advance; and adjust deals.

The second potential savings from purchasing will come from the basic costs of processing transactions. If suppliers are not comfortable striking a deal for $500,000 worth of instrument panels online, they can certainly process the paperwork at the site once the deal is done. If a company spends about $80 billion each year on supplies (typical of a Ford or GM), it's not unreasonable, says the Roland Berger report, to imagine saving $150 million simply by streamlining slow and costly processing.

Design Collaboration

Where Covisint's services get less familiar, and where greater potential revenue lies, is in moving product development and demand-forecasting functions online. Today, product development takes two to four years. A single design change, in the world of automotive engineers, takes about five weeks to filter through layers of engineers and managers.

Plus, internal design collaboration is one thing—engineers have to ensure all the right people have signed off, for instance, and that no one is confused about what the latest version is. But from supplier to supplier to original equipment manufacturer (OEM), that communication is especially unwieldy. "You have to put drawings on a disk," says Andy Simpson, a consultant at Cap Gemini Ernst & Young, who has been working with Covisint since last August, "FedEx those to your counterpart, and hope they can translate what you sent to their CAD software. Either that, or you get on a plane and have a meeting.

Covisint promises to fix that. "The idea is collaboration," says Suman of Johnson Controls, "where our designers in Japan and Germany and Michigan can search a database and find a sun visor that we already have tooled. "We're going away from episodic events where teams meet every week, flying in from all around the world, to where they never meet and a design launch is virtual."

This is the vision of Covisint's Virtual Project Workplace, a shared platform for anyone with a stake in, say, how big the handle on a hatchback is or what shape the grip of the stick shift is. Designers can look at pictures; measure parts; consider new specifications; argue about specs; alert colleagues of their tasks; keep out snoops; store every picture or bit of conversation generated; link them to spreadsheets or Word documents; and route serial tasks from person to person. Files from any of the CAD programs used in the industry can be translated through a one- or two-step process, with all the 3-D viewing functions available and networked, so everyone at the same time can watch a shock absorber somersaulting.

So far, 40 top suppliers have looked at the design demo. Six are actually using the tools, though only in-house. But the goal is that Ford engineers will collaborate not just internally but with—just imagine—Firestone tire engineers, as well as with Firestone's rubber supplier.

A Realtime Supply Chain

Last of the big Covisint promises—and where, for many of these mammoth exchange models, the rubber must eventually meet the road—is to deliver supply chain-speeding tools and services. Software platforms such as Commerce One's will serve as Covisint's primary purchasing engine for parts and help generate one-third of the expected cost savings to the automakers. The other two-thirds (which for Covisint, will be a source of long-term income), must come from more complex back-end services, such as features that allow Tier 1 companies to know where a part is and when it is expected to arrive, or enable participants to do simultaneous online demand forecasting, up and down the chain. That's where auto business analysts begin to wax truly visionary, picturing a massive upheaval in the industry that starts with made-to-order cars (exactly the way you want them within 10 days of your order) and ends with whole new kinds of factories creating whole new mix-and-match modules.

The operating principle: The more inventory you create that is *not* to a customer's liking (whether that customer be a Saturn soccer mom or a transmission-maker buying gaskets), the more money you lose—on dropped prices, marketing efforts, anything that'll get the unwanted gaskets off the shelf.

Covisint's grandest business proposition is to make all orders and forecasts immediately and securely available to all the links in the chain, so that participating builders of a car or a part can respond to a need simultaneously. Today, if dealers are asking for more four-wheel drives, the folks at GM will eventually hear about it; but what about Dana, which makes axles? It waits for GM to analyze its needs and send out a release asking for a shipment. By making the same demand data available to the multiple tiers all at once, automakers crunch crucial days and wring dollars out of the cycle.

Says Kutner passionately, "We've got to get our supply base *sensing* what our needs are—not waiting for a release saying on October 1, we need 1,200 parts."

Winning Over the Suppliers

Another significant challenge on the road ahead: winning over the industry's Tier 1 suppliers, who are likely to reap the greatest benefit of switching to an exchange, among all the players in the supply chain. But their needs are in some ways as complex as the auto makers, and Covisint, they feel, probably won't be able to serve them all. Suman of Johnson Controls, one of the largest plastic and steel users in the world, puts it vividly: "If you buy 150 tons of steel, it's very hard to find someone that happens to have that available. For us, using Covisint won't always make sense."

Early on, the pervasive concern in this sector of the industry was that the goal of Covisint was to put a fatal squeeze on suppliers, especially small ones. But through the institution of a customer council and aggressive pitching, Covisint has won the willingness of at least its biggest trading partners. "One thing this company has done a good job at," says Prouty of AMR, "is getting the Tier 1 suppliers on board." Neil De Koker, who represents the supplier community at the Original Equipment Suppliers Association, seconds that. "Attitudes are completely different from what they were in March 2000," he says.

But for many suppliers, it's still hang-back-and-see. Dana, for example, is not only playing choosy with Covisint, its getting itself out ahead by creating its own E-marketplace. Back when Covisint was just a press release, Dana ($13 billion in sales, 82,000 employees) was already running transactions over its own exchange. And it was doing it with a couple of the Covisint founders' fiercest Internet rivals, FreeMarkets and Ariba. "The strategy for most in Tier 1," says Doug Grimm, vice president of Global Strategic Sourcing at Dana, "is to have a dual or triple strategy. We're using some E-commerce systems already, with or without Covisint."

For the smaller suppliers, it's a different story; unlikely to see a significant boost in their bottom lines if they submit to reverse auctions, they will most likely take their cues from the bigger customers above them. Thus Covisint has spent none of its resources wooing these potential players. Says one industry insider: "Among the smaller companies, Covisint wasn't contacting anyone and wasn't responsive to those that were trying to get involved." "It's the typical auto industry approach of, 'I'll squeeze profits out of the suppliers down the line,'" adds one auto industry consultant. "I talk to a lot of first-, second- and third-tier suppliers. They're saying the automakers just want to take profits away from them. It's not negotiating at arm's length, it's holding them by the throat at arm's length."

Questioning the Business Model

Once you've fathomed the scope of Covisint's promises, you still have to consider its business model. For all its services—auctions, design tools, inventory shrinkage—ready and not yet ready to launch, as of January 2001, no prices had been set for any of them. AMR estimates that it will take anywhere from $250 million to $400 million to build Covisint to its desired specs. Meanwhile, what Covisint *will* say about its business prospects is simply hard to believe. GM's Kutner calls Covisint "potentially the biggest Internet company in the world" and claims it will draw "you know, maybe a trillion dollars in revenue."

A *trillion*?

Were Covisint to charge the 0.5 or 1.5 percent the typical E-marketplaces charge for transactions, and were the industry to direct every last dollar of its purchases through the system, that would still leave them about $980 billion shy of Kutner's mark. Forrester's Garretson puts it at $3 billion annually, based on 1 percent of transactions and chuckles at Kutner's trillion.

Regardless, most important to Covisint's stability are the formal "claw-back" commitments the five auto founders have made to guarantee transaction volume—the coveted critical mass that eluded so many of the independent net marketplaces. Kutner says GM alone will contribute $85 billion in business annually into the exchange; Ford and DaimlerChrysler say they will funnel somewhat lower levels, and Renault and Nissan even less. If any partner fails to comply, it faces a penalty: The founding auto companies' equity is tied to their compliance and claw-backs. "If I don't put my $85 billion through this exchange," says Kutner, "I'm going to lose part of my equity ownership."

But consider the underpinnings of those claw-back arrangements. The partners lose equity if their participation falls short. But equity in what? In a company that hasn't decided where its headquarters will be? In a company that hasn't set prices yet? How difficult would that be to walk away from?

Praying for Success

So of course, many around Covisint are praying these days. The lower-tier suppliers are praying for mercy as they anticipate competing for business online; dealers are praying for the holy reduction in inventory; the founding partners are praying for critical mass at a marketplace pitted against other new exchanges; and everyone's praying for an end to an industry-wide slump.

But back in Detroit, GM CEO Richard Wagner assures the troops there is no retreat: "We did roar into this Covisint, and it is the right thing to do....We're not turning back." Wagner says he firmly believes that Covisint will capture a significant piece of the $300 billion in purchases made annually by its current automotive members.

And Kutner shows no sign of caving in to recession-spun conservatism. "We're going to be connected to 100,000 companies," he asserts without a blink. "The revenue potential is so large that most of the average minds in the banking community cannot even visualize it."

Well, neither can anyone else.

Case Study Questions

1. **The Problems of the Auto Industry**
   a. What are some of the major supply chain problems within the auto industry?
   b. What are some major business problems that are caused by the auto industry's supply chain inefficiencies?
   c. What are some of the major information systems problems and limitations within the present supply chains of the auto industry?

2. **The Promises of Covisint**
   a. How does Covisint promise to improve the auto industry's procurement process? What business benefits are supposed to result?
   b. How does Covisint promise to improve the auto industry's supply chain process? What business benefits are supposed to result?
   c. How does Covisint promise to improve the product development process of the auto industry? What business benefits are supposed to result?

3. **The Problems of Covisint**
   a. Does Covisint have a sound business model? Explain why or why not.

   b. How should Covisint encourage the participation and cooperation of more of the auto industry's suppliers in its exchange?
   c. What other problems with Covisint do you recognize? What should be done about them?

4. **The Future of Covisint**
   a. What should be done to accellerate the development and use of Covisint in the auto industry?
   b. Do the survival problems of the independent B2B E-commerce exchanges have a bearing on what Covisint should do to survive and succeed? Explain the reasons for your answer.
   c. If you were named the new CEO of Covisint, what might be a few of your first major business decisions or proposals to assure the success of Covisint? Outline the reasons for these actions.

Source: Adapted from Martha Baer and Jeffrey Davis, "Some Assembly Required," *Business 2.0*, February 20, 2001, pp. 76–85, and Michael Meehan, "Confidence In B2B Sinks To Major Low," *Computerworld*, April 9, 2001, pp. 1, 73.

Review Quiz Answers

Chapter 1

Foundations of Information Systems in Business

1. 21	7. 26c	13. 11	19. 4	25. 27a	31. 17d	37. 29
2. 22	8. 16	14. 28	20. 18	26. 27b	32. 17e	38. 20
3. 19	9. 1	15. 13	21. 14	27. 25	33. 30	39. 12
4. 26	10. 10	16. 2	22. 14a	28. 17a	34. 30c	40. 23a
5. 26a	11. 7	17. 3	23. 14b	29. 17b	35. 30b	41. 23
6. 26b	12. 9	18. 15	24. 27	30. 17c	36. 30a	42. 8

Competing with Information Technology

1. 3	4. 11	7. 6	10. 14	13. 1	16. 8	18. 16
2. 4	5. 5	8. 18	11. 2	14. 19	17. 9	19. 7
3. 12	6. 13	9. 10	12. 17	15. 15		

The Internetworked E-Business Enterprise

1. 24	7. 25	13. 5	19. 31	24. 16	29. 23	34. 34
2. 13	8. 21	14. 7	20. 11	25. 17	30. 27	35. 32
3. 3	9. 26	15. 8	21. 30	26. 18	31. 28	36. 38
4. 6	10. 2	16. 9	22. 12	27. 19	32. 29	37. 35
5. 14	11. 1	17. 10	23. 15	28. 22	33. 33	38. 37
6. 20	12. 4	18. 36				

Electronic Business Systems

1. 10	7. 22	13. 6	18. 16	23. 18	28. 13	33. 4
2. 8	8. 17	14. 5	19. 24	24. 3	29. 25	34. 30
3. 14	9. 32	15. 29	20. 1	25. 2	30. 20	35. 26
4. 10a	10. 9	16. 19	21. 23	26. 28	31. 35	36. 33
5. 11	11. 21	17. 31	22. 27	27. 15	32. 36	37. 34
6. 12	12. 7					

Electronic Commerce Systems

1. 5	5. 4	9. 8d	13. 9	17. 2c	20. 7	23. 1
2. 5b	6. 8	10. 8i	14. 2	18. 2b	21. 8e	24. 3
3. 5a	7. 8a	11. 8f	15. 2d	19. 6	22. 10	25. 11
4. 5c	8. 8g	12. 8c	16. 2a			

Chapter 6

E-Business Decision Support

1. 10	7. 29	13. 1c	19. 4	24. 30	29. 13b	34. 21
2. 9	8. 7	14. 1a	20. 11	25. 31	30. 20	35. 27
3. 23	9. 6	15. 1b	21. 22	26. 17	31. 18	36. 15
4. 5	10. 26	16. 12	22. 2	27. 13	32. 14	37. 19
5. 25	11. 1	17. 28	23. 2a	28. 13a	33. 13d	38. 16
6. 24	12. 1d	18. 3				

Chapter 7

Developing E-Business Strategies

1. 8	3. 7	5. 10	7. 11	9. 6	11. 3
2. 2b	4. 9	6. 2a	8. 5	10. 4	12. 1

Chapter 8

Developing E-Business Solutions

1. 19	6. 11b	11. 8	16. 18	21. 22	26. 6	31. 2
2. 27	7. 28a	12. 5	17. 9	22. 24	27. 10	32. 26
3. 15	8. 11a	13. 29	18. 20	23. 1	28. 7a	33. 4
4. 3	9. 21	14. 12	19. 30	24. 16	29. 7c	34. 24
5. 28b	10. 23	15. 14	20. 25	25. 17	30. 7b	

Chapter 9

Security and Ethical Challenges of E-Business

1. 26	6. 3	11. 16	16. 15b	21. 9	25. 27	29. 1
2. 21	7. 2	12. 6	17. 15d	22. 11	26. 22	30. 19
3. 29	8. 5	13. 28	18. 15e	23. 7	27. 20	31. 14
4. 17	9. 12	14. 15a	19. 8	24. 30	28. 10	32. 25
5. 18	10. 13	15. 15c	20. 24			

Chapter 10

Enterprise and Global Management of E-Business Technology

1. 16	6. 19	11. 7	16. 23	21. 11	25. 11a	29. 15
2. 13	7. 2	12. 24	17. 3	22. 26	26. 11b	30. 25
3. 17	8. 1	13. 12	18. 8	23. 6	27. 11c	31. 14
4. 9	9. 27	14. 4	19. 21	24. 10	28. 11d	32. 11e
5. 18	10. 20	15. 5	20. 22			

Chapter 11

Computer Hardware

1. 45	9. 30	16. 15	23. 13	30. 36	37. 5	44. 6
2. 7	10. 25	17. 31	24. 43c	31. 39	38. 10	45. 37
3. 3	11. 24	18. 20	25. 40e	32. 28	39. 48	46. 36
4. 2	12. 1	19. 21	26. 32	33. 26	40. 41	47. 11
5. 9	13. 17	20. 23	27. 29	34. 12	41. 36b	48. 14
6. 8	14. 16	21. 22	28. 32a	35. 38	42. 36a	49. 27
7. 33	15. 18	22. 42	29. 44	36. 4	43. 47	50. 27d
8. 35						

Chapter 12

Computer Software

1. 33	7. 36	13. 18	18. 7	23. 16	28. 14	33. 29
2. 2	8. 12	14. 37	19. 8	24. 31	29. 10	34. 15
3. 26	9. 38	15. 11	20. 40	25. 13	30. 25	35. 17
4. 34	10. 22	16. 3	21. 6	26. 19	31. 24	36. 1
5. 30	11. 23	17. 39	22. 27	27. 4	32. 21	37. 35
6. 9	12. 5					

Chapter 13

Data Resource Management

1. 9	5. 1	9. 11d	13. 2	17. 14c	21. 11a	25. 8a
2. 12	6. 17	10. 18d	14. 4	18. 14d	22. 11e	26. 18e
3. 7	7. 10	11. 5	15. 3	19. 14e	23. 11b	27. 18a
4. 16	8. 18b	12. 6	16. 14b	20. 13	24. 8b	28. 18c

Chapter 14

Telecommunications and Networks

1. 33	6. 28	11. 32	16. 23	21. 26	26. 12	31. 1
2. 2	7. 29	12. 18	17. 34	22. 25	27. 17	32. 27
3. 30	8. 9	13. 19	18. 22	23. 13	28. 21	33. 14
4. 35	9. 3	14. 24	19. 20a	24. 10	29. 7	34. 8
5. 17	10. 31	15. 36	20. 20b	25. 11	30. 16	35. 15

Selected References

Chapter 1—Foundations of Information Systems in Business

1. Emigh, Jacquiline. "E-Commerce Strategies." *Computerworld*, August 16, 1999.

2. Ewusi-Mensah, Kewku. "Critical Issues in Abandoned Information Systems Development Projects." *Communications of the ACM*, September 1997.

3. Fingar, Peter; Harsha Kumar; and Tarun Sharma. *Enterprise E-Commerce*. Tampa, FL: Meghan-Kiffer Press, 2000.

4. Haylock, Christina Ford, and Len Muscarella. *Net Success*. Holbrook, MA: Adams Media Corporation, 1999.

5. Hills, Mellanie. *Intranet Business Strategies*. New York: John Wiley & Sons, 1997.

6. Iansiti, Marco, and Alan MacCormick. "Developing Products on Internet Time." *Harvard Business Review*, September–October 1997.

7. Kalakota, Ravi, and Marcia Robinson. *E-Business: Roadmap for Success*. Reading, MA: Addison-Wesley, 1999.

8. Kalakota, Ravi, and Andrew Whinston. *Electronic Commerce: A Manager's Guide*. Reading, MA: Addison-Wesley, 1997.

9. Lee, Allen. "Inaugural Editor's Comments." *MIS Quarterly*, March 1999.

10. Leinfuss, Emily. "Making the Cut." *Computerworld*, September 20, 1999.

11. Marion, Larry. "Snap, Crackle, Pop, and Crash—Go the Income Statements." *Datamation* (www.datamation. com), February 1999.

12. Norris, Grant; James Hurley; Kenneth Hartley; John Dunleavy; and John Balls. *E-Business and ERP: Transforming the Enterprise*. New York: John Wiley & Sons, 2000.

13. Radcliff, Deborah. "Aligning Marriott." *Computerworld*, April 20, 2000.

14. Seybold, Patricia. *Customers.com: How to Create a Profitable Business Strategy for the Internet and Beyond*. New York: Times Business, 1998.

15. Shapiro, Carl, and Hal Varian. *Information Rules: A Strategic Guide to the New Economy*. Boston, MA: Harvard Business School Press, 1999.

16. Silver, Mark; M. Lynn Markus; and Cynthia Mathis Beath. "The Information Technology Interaction Model: A Foundation for the MBA Core Course." *MIS Quarterly*, September 1995.

17. Steadman, Craig. "ERP Pioneers." *Computerworld*, January 18, 1999.

18. Wagner, Mitch. "Firms Spell Out Appropriate Internet Use for Employees." *Computerworld*, February 5, 1996.

Chapter 2—Competing with Information Technology

1. Applegate, Lynda; F. Warren McFarlan; and James McKenney. *Corporate Information Systems Management: Text and Cases*. Burr Ridge, IL: Irwin/McGraw-Hill, 1999.

2. Bowles, Jerry. "Best Practices for Global Competitiveness." Special Advertising Section. *Fortune*, November 24, 1997.

3. Caron, J. Raymond; Sirkka Jarvenpaa; and Donna Stoddard. "Business Reengineering at CIGNA Corporation: Experiences and Lessons from the First Five Years." *MIS Quarterly*, September 1994.

4. Cash, James I., Jr.; Robert G. Eccles; Nitin Nohria; and Richard L. Nolan. *Building the Information-Age Organization: Structure, Control, and Information Technologies*. Burr Ridge, IL: Richard D. Irwin, 1994.

5. Christensen, Clayton. *The Innovators Dilemma: When New Technologies Cause Great Firms to Fail*. Boston: Harvard Business School Press, 1997.

6. Clemons, Eric, and Michael Row. "Sustaining IT Advantage: The Role of Structural Differences." *MIS Quarterly*, September 1991.

7. Collett, Stacy. "Spun-off Sabre to Sell Software to AMR Rivals." *Computerworld*, December 20, 1999.

8. Cronin, Mary. *Doing More Business on the Internet*. 2nd ed. New York: Van Nostrand Reinhold, 1995.

9. Cronin, Mary. *The Internet Strategy Handbook*. Boston: Harvard Business School Press, 1996.

10. Davenport, Thomas H. *Process Innovation: Reengineering Work through Information Technology*. Boston: Harvard Business School Press, 1993.

11. Deckmyn, Dominique. "Product Data Management Moves Toward Mainstream." *Computerworld*, November 8, 1999.

12. El Sawy, Omar, and Gene Bowles. "Redesigning the Customer Support Process for the Electronic Economy: Insights from Storage Dimensions." *MIS Quarterly*, December 1997.

13. El Sawy, Omar; Arvind Malhotra; Sanjay Gosain; and Kerry Young. "IT-Intensive Value Innovation in the Electronic Economy: Insights from Marshall Industries." *MIS Quarterly*, September 1999.

14. Emigh, Jacquiline. "E-Commerce Strategies." *Computerworld*, August 16, 1999.

15. Evans, Phillip, and Thomas Wurster. "Strategy and the New Economics of Information." *Harvard Business Review*, September–October 1997.

16. Frye, Colleen. "Imaging Proves Catalyst for Reengineering." *Client/Server Computing*, November 1994.

17. Garner, Rochelle. "Please Don't Call IT Knowledge Management!" *Computerworld*, August 9, 1999.

18. Garvin, David. "Building a Learning Organization." *Harvard Business Review*, July–August 1995.

19. Goldman, Steven; Roger Nagel; and Kenneth Preis. *Agile Competitors and Virtual Organizations: Strategies for Enriching the Customer*. New York: Van Nostrand Reinhold, 1995.

20. Grover, Varun, and Pradipkumar Ramanlal. "Six Myths of Information and Markets: Information Technology Networks, Electronic Commerce, and the Battle for Consumer Surplus." *MIS Quarterly*, December 1999.

21. Hamm, Steve, and Marcia Stepaneck. "From Reengineering to E-Engineering." *Business Week e.biz*, March 22, 1999.

22. Hibbard, Justin. "Spreading Knowledge." *Computerworld*, April 7, 1997.

23. Kalakota, Ravi, and Marcia Robinson. *E-Business: Roadmap For Success*. Reading, MA: Addison-Wesley, 1999.

24. Kerwin, Kathleen; Marcia Stepanek; and David Welch. "At Ford, E-Commerce is Job1." *Business Week*, February 28, 2000.

25. Kettinger, William; Varun Grover; Subashish Guha; and Albert Segars. "Strategic Information Systems Revisited: A Study in Sustainability and Performance." *MIS Quarterly*, March 1994.

26. Kettinger, William; Varun Grover; and Albert Segars. "Do Strategic Systems Really Pay Off? An Analysis of Classic Strategic IT Cases." *Information Systems Management*, Winter 1995.

27. Kettinger, William; James Teng; and Subashish Guha. "Business Process Change: A Study of Methodologies, Techniques, and Tools." *MIS Quarterly*, March 1997.

28. Kover, Amy. "Schwab Makes a Grand Play for the Rich." *Fortune*, February 7, 2000.

29. Melymuka, Kathleen. "GE's Quality Gamble," *Computerworld*, June 8, 1998, p. 64.

30. Mooney, John; Vijay Gurbaxani; and Kenneth Kramer. "A Process Oriented Framework for Assessing the Business Value of Information Technology." *The DATA BASE for Advances in Information Systems*, Spring 1996.

31. Neumann, Seev. *Strategic Information Systems: Competition through Information Technologies*. New York: Macmillan College Publishing Co., 1994.

32. Nonaka, Ikujiro. "The Knowledge Creating Company." *Harvard Business Review*, November–December 1991.

33. Pegels, C. Carl. *Total Quality Management: A Survey of Its Important Aspects*. Danvers, MA: boyd & fraser publishing co., 1995.

34. Porter, Michael, and Victor Millar. "How Information Gives You Competitive Advantage." *Harvard Business Review*, July–August 1985.

35. Prokcsch, Steven. "Unleashing the Power of Learning: An Interview with British Petroleum's John Browne." *Harvard Business Review*, September–October 1997.

36. Resnick, Rosalind. "The Virtual Corporation." *PC Today*, February 1995.

37. Seybold, Patricia. *Customers.com: How to Create a Profitable Business Strategy for the Internet and Beyond*. New York: Times Books, 1998.

38. Shapiro, Carl, and Hal Varian. *Information Rules: A Strategic Guide to the Network Economy*. Boston: Harvard Business School Press, 1999.

39. Siekman, Philip. "Why Infotech Loves Its Giant Job Shops." *Fortune*, May 12, 1997.

40. Wallace, Bob. "Ford Suppliers Get Call to Design." *Computerworld*, March 8, 1999.

Chapter 3—The Internetworked E-Business Enterprise

1. Anderson, Heidi. "The Rise of the Extranet." *PC Today*, February 1997.

2. Andreessen, Marc. "The Networked Enterprise: Netscape Enterprise Vision and Product Roadmap." White Paper, Netscape Communications Corporation, 1997.

3. Barksdale, Jim. "The Next Step: Extranets." *Netscape Columns: The Main Thing*, December 3, 1996.

4. Bly, Bob. "Workflow: The Key to Increasing Business Productivity." Special Advertising Section, *Fortune*, March 17, 1997.

5. Bowles, Jerry. "The Web Within: The Next Generation Intranet." *Fortune*, April 14, 1997.

6. Burden, Kevin. "Coming into Focus." *Computerworld*, January 11, 1999.

7. Campbell, Ian. "The Intranet: Slashing the Cost of Doing Business." Research Report, International Data Corporation, 1996.

8. Cole-Gomolski, Barb. "Chat Rooms Move into Board Rooms." *Computerworld*, November 3, 1997.

9. "Conversation Piece." In Technology Buyers Guide. *Fortune*, Winter 1998.

10. Cronin, Mary. *Doing More Business on the Internet.* New York: Van Nostrand Reinhold, 1995.

11. Cronin, Mary. *Global Advantage on the Internet.* New York: Van Nostrand Reinhold, 1996.

12. El Sawy, Omar; Arvind Malhotra; SavJay Gosain; and Kerry Young. "IT-Intensive Value Innovation in the Electronic Economy: Insights from Marshall Industries." *MIS Quarterly*, September 1999.

13. Gates, Bill. *Business @ the Speed of Thought.* New York: Warner Books, 1999.

14. "Get It Together." Technology Guide. *Fortune*, Winter 2000.

15. Gow, Kathleen. "Risk vs. Opportunity." The Premier 100 Supplement to *Computerworld*, February 24, 1997.

16. Hills, Mellanie. *Intranet as Groupware.* New York: Wiley, 1997.

17. Hills, Mellanie. *Intranet Business Strategies.* New York: Wiley, 1997.

18. Kalakota, Ravi, and Marcia Robinson. *E-Business: Roadmap for Success.* Reading, MA: Addison-Wesley, 1999.

19. King, Nelson. "E-Mail Reinvents Itself." *Internet World*, November 1997.

20. Ladbe, Dave. "Global Village Helps US West Improve Customer Service." *Netscape Columns: Intranet Executive*, November 1, 1996.

21. Machlis, Sharon. "Web Site Serves the Little Guys." *Computerworld*, January 18, 1999.

22. Maglitta, Joseph. "Net Gain, Net Pain." *Computerworld Intranets*, June 24, 1996.

23. Messerschmitt, David. *Networked Applications: A Guide to the New Computing Infrastructure.* San Francisco: Morgan Kaufman Publishers, 1999.

24. Murray, Gerry. "Making Connections with Enterprise Knowledge Portals." White Paper. *Computerworld*, September 6, 1999.

25. O'Brien, Atiye. "Friday Intranet Focus." *Upside.com: Hot Private Companies*, Upside Publishing Company, 1996.

26. Orenstein, David. "Corporate Portals." *Computerworld*, June 28, 1999.

27. Ouellette, Tim. "Opening Your Own Portal." *Computerworld*, August 9, 1999.

28. Papows, Jeff. "Endquotes." *NetReady Adviser*, Winter 1997.

29. Phelps, Alan. "Knowledge Is Power." *Smart Computing*, February 2000.

30. Reichard, Kevin. "Hosting Your Own Chat." *Internet World*, October 1997.

Chapter 4—Electronic Business Systems

1. Armor, Daniel. *The E-Business (R)Evolution: Living and Working in an Interconnected World.* Upper Saddle River, NJ: Prentice Hall, 2000.

2. Ashbrand, Deborah. "Squeeze Out Excess Costs with Supply Chain Solutions." *Datamation*, March 1997.

3. "Davenport, Thomas. *Process Innovation: Reengineering Work Through Information Technology.* Boston: Harvard Business School Press, 1993.

4. Diese, Martin; Conrad Nowikow; Patrick King; and Amy Wright. *Executives Guide to E-Business: From Tactics to Strategy.* New York: John Wiley & Sons, 2000.

5. Donahue, Sean. "Supply Traffic Control." *Business 2.0.* February 2000.

6. El Sawy, Omar Arvind Malhotra; Sanjay Gosain and Kerry Young. "IT-Intensive Value Innovation in the Electronic Economy: Insights from Marshal Industries." *MIS Quarterly*, September 1999.

7. El Sawy, Omar. *Redesigning Enterprise Processes for E-Business.* New York: McGraw-Hill Irwin, 2001.

8. Essex, David. "Enterprise Application Integration." *Computerworld*, October 4, 1999.

9. Essex, David. "Get into Web Portals." *Computerworld*, March 15, 1999.

10. Fellenstein, Craig, and Ron Wood. *Exploring E-Commerce, Global E-Business, and E-Societies.* Upper Saddle River, NJ: Prentice Hall, 2000.

11. Gates, Bill. *Business @ the Speed of Thought.* New York: Warner Books, 1999.

12. Geoff, Leslie. "CRM: The Cutting Edge of Serving Customers." *Computerworld*, February 28, 2000.

13. Hamel, Gary, and Jeff Sandler. "The E-Corporation." *Fortune*, December 7, 1998.

14. Hamm, Steve, and Robert Hoff. "An Eagle Eye on Customers." *Business Week*, February 21, 2000.

15. Hodges, Judy. "The Rise of the Self Service Employee." *Computerworld HR Online*, September 8, 1997.

16. Johnson, Amy. "CRM Rises to the Top." *Computerworld*, August 16, 1999.

17. Kalakota, Ravi, and Marcia Robinson. *E-Business: Roadmap for Success.* Reading, MA: Addison-Wesley, 1999.

18. Keen, Peter, and Craigg Balance. *Online Profits: A Manager's Guide to Electronic Commerce.* Boston: Harvard Business School Press, 1997.

19. McCann, Stefanie. "Career Opportunities in Enterprise Resource Planning." *Computerworld,* February 7, 2000.

20. McCarthy, Vance. "ERP Gets Down to E-Business." *HP World,* January 2000.

21. Norris, Grant; James Hurley; Kenneth Hartley; John Dunleavy; and John Balls. *E-Business and ERP: Transforming the Enterprise.* New York: John Wiley & Sons, 2000.

22. Orenstein, David. "Enterprise Application Integration." *Computerworld,* October 4, 1999.

23. Papows, Jeff. *Enterprise.com: Market Leadership in the Information Age.* Reading, MA: Perseus Books, 1998.

24. Ranadive, Vivek. *The Power of Now.* New York: McGraw-Hill, 1999.

25. Steadman, Craig. "ERP Guide: Vendor Strategies, Future Plans." *Computerworld,* July 19, 1999.

26. Tapscott, Don; David Ticoll; and Alex Lowy. *Digital Capital: Harnessing the Power of Business Webs.* Boston: Harvard Business School Press, 2000.

27. Tucker, Jay. "The New Money: Transactions Pour Across the Web." *Datamation,* April 1997.

28. "Your Body, Your Job." Technology Buyer's Guide. *Fortune,* Winter 2000.

Chapter 5—Electronic Commerce Systems

1. Anthes, Gary. "Cha Aims Big with Micropayment Service." *Computerworld,* July 26, 1999.

2. Armor, Daniel. *The E-Business (R)Evolution: Living and Working in an Interconnected World.* Upper Saddle River, NJ: Prentice Hall, 2000.

3. "Click Here to Shop." Technology Buyers Guide. *Fortune,* Winter 2000.

4. Collett, Stacy. "Sun, Newscape Develop Bill Payment Software." *Computerworld,* December 13, 1999.

5. Cross, Kim. "Need Options? Go Configure." *Business 2.0,* February 2000.

6. Davis, Jeffrey. "How IT Works." *Business 2.0,* February 2000.

7. Davis, Jeffrey. "Mall Rats." *Business 2.0,* January 1999.

8. Diese, Martin; Conrad Nowikow; Patrick King; and Amy Wright. *Executives Guide to E-Business: From Tactics to Strategy.* New York: John Wiley & Sons, 2000.

9. El Sawy, Omar Arvind Malhotra; Sanjay Gosain and Kerry Young. "IT-Intensive Value Innovation in the Electronic Economy: Insights from Marshal Industries." *MIS Quarterly,* September 1999.

10. Fellenstein, Craig, and Ron Wood. *Exploring E-Commerce, Global E-Business, and E-Societies.* Upper Saddle River, NJ: Prentice Hall, 2000.

11. Fingar, Peter; Harsha Kumar; and Tarun Sharma. *Enterprise E-Commerce.* Meghan-Kiffer Press: Tampa, FL, 2000.

12. Gates, Bill. *Business @ the Speed of Thought.* New York: Warner Books, 1999.

13. Gulati, Ranjay, and Jason Garino. "Get the Right Mix of Clicks and Bricks." *Harvard Business Review,* May–June 2000.

14. Haylock, Christina, and Len Muscarella. *Net Success.* Holbrook, MA: Adams Media Corporation, 1999.

15. Hoque, Faisal. *E-Enterprise: Business Models, Architecture and Components.* Cambridge, UK: Cambridge University Press, 2000.

16. Kalakota, Ravi, and Marcia Robinson. *E-Business: Roadmap for Success.* Reading, MA: Addison-Wesley, 1999.

17. Kalakota, Ravi, and Andrew Whinston. *Electronic Commerce: A Manager's Guide.* Reading, MA: Addison-Wesley, 1997.

18. Kalakota, Ravi, and Andrew Whinston. *Frontiers of Electronic Commerce.* Reading, MA: Addison-Wesley, 1996.

19. Kastner, Peter, and Christopher Stevens. "Electronic Commerce: A True Challenge for IT Managers." In "Enterprise Solutions: Electronic Commerce." Special Advertising Supplement to *Computerworld,* January 13, 1997.

20. Keen, Peter, and Craigg Balance. *Online Profits: A Manager's Guide to Electronic Commerce.* Boston: Harvard Business School Press, 1997.

21. "Keep the 0010001 Happy." Technology Buyers Guide. *Fortune,* Summer 2000.

22. Korper, Steffano, and Juanita Ellis. *The E-Commerce Book: Building the E-Empire.* San Diego: Academic Press, 2000.

23. Leon, Mark. "Trading Spaces." *Business 2.0,* February 2000.

24. Loshin, Peter. "The Electronic Marketplace." *PC Today,* July 1996.

25. Machlis, Sharon. "Portals Link Buyers, Sellers." *Computerworld,* January 25, 1999.

26. Machlis, Sharon. "Web Retailers Try to Keep Their Hits Up." *Computerworld,* February 8, 1999.

27. Martin, Chuck. *The Digital Estate: Strategies for Competing, Surviving, and Thriving in an Internetworked World.* New York: McGraw-Hill, 1997.

28. Morgan, Cynthia. "Dead Set Against SET?" *Computerworld*, March 29, 1999.

29. Robinson, Edward. "Battle to the Bitter End(-to-End)." *Business 2.0*, July 25, 2000.

30. Rosenoer, Jonathan; Douglas Armstrong; and J. Russell Gates. *The Clickable Corporation: Successful Strategies for Capturing the Internet Advantage*. New York: The Free Press, 1999.

31. Schwartz, Evan. *Digital Darwinism*. New York: Broadway Books, 1999.

32. Schwartz, Evan. *Webonomics*. New York: Broadway Books, 1997.

33. Senn, James. "Electronic Data Interchange: Elements of Implementation." *Information Systems Management*, Winter 1992.

34. "Servers with a Smile." Technology Buyers Guide. *Fortune*, Summer 2000.

35. Seybold, Patricia, with Ronnie Marshak. *Customers Com: How to Create a Profitable Business Strategy for the Internet and Beyond*. New York: Times Business, 1998.

36. Shapiro, Carl, and Hal Varian. *Information Rules: A Strategic Guide to the Network Economy*. Boston: Harvard Business School Press, 1999.

37. Sliwa, Carol. "Users Cling to EDI for Critical Transactions." *Computerworld*, March 15, 1999.

38. Tapscott, Don; David Ticoll; and Alex Lowy. *Digital Capital: Harnessing the Power of Business Webs*. Boston: Harvard Business School Press, 2000.

39. "Telefónica Servicios Avanzados De Informació Leads Spain's Retail Industry into Global Electronic Commerce." At www.netscape.com/solutions/business/profiles, March 1999.

40. Trombly, Marcia. "Electronic Billing Merger Should Benefit Billers, Banks." *Computerworld*, February 21, 2000.

41. Tully, Shawn. "The B2B Tool That Is Really Changing the World." *Fortune*, March 20, 2000.

Chapter 6—E-Business Decision Support

1. Allen, Bradley. "Case-Based Reasoning: Business Applications." *Communications of the ACM*, March 1994.

2. Ashline, Peter, and Vincent Lai. "Virtual Reality: An Emerging User-Interface Technology." *Information Systems Management*, Winter 1995.

3. Begley, Sharon. "Software au Naturel." *Newsweek*, May 8, 1995.

4. Belcher, Lloyd, and Hugh Watson. "Assessing the Value of Conoco's EIS." *MIS Quarterly*, September 1993.

5. Blackburn, David; Rik Henderson; and Gary Welz. "VRML Evolution: State of the Art Advances." *Internet World*, December 1996.

6. Blattberg, Robert C.; Rashi Glazer; and John D. C. Little. *The Marketing Information Revolution*. Boston: The Harvard Business School Press, 1994.

7. Bose, Ranjit, and Vijayan Sugumaran. "Application of Intelligent Agent Technology for Managerial Data Analysis and Mining." *The Data Base for Advances in Information Systems*, Winter 1999.

8. Botchner, Ed. "Data Mining: Plumbing the Depths of Corporate Databases." Special Advertising Supplement. *Computerworld*, April 21, 1997.

9. Buta, Paul. "Mining for Financial Knowledge with CBR." *AI Expert*, February 1994.

10. Bylinsky, Gene. "To Create Products, Go into a CAVE." *Fortune*, February 5, 1996.

11. Cox, Earl. "Relational Database Queries Using Fuzzy Logic." *AI Expert*, January 1995.

12. Cronin, Mary. "Using the Web to Push Key Data to Decision Makers." *Fortune*, September 29, 1997.

13. Darling, Charles. "Ease Implementation Woes with Packaged Datamarts." *Datamation*, March 1997.

14. "Dayton Hudson Knows What's in Store for Their Customers." Advertising Section. *Intelligent Enterprise*, January 5, 1999.

15. Deck, Stewart. "Data Visualization." *Computerworld*, October 11, 1999.

16. Deck, Stewart. "Data Warehouse Project Starts Simply." *Computerworld*, February 15, 1999.

17. Deck, Stewart. "Early Users Give Nod to Analysis Package." *Computerworld*, February 22, 1999.

18. Deck, Stewart. "Mining Your Business." *Computerworld*, May 17, 1999.

19. Egan, Richard. "The Expert Within." *PC Today*, January 1995.

20. Finkelstein, Richard. *Understanding the Need for Online Analytical Servers*. Ann Arbor, MI: Comshare, 1994.

21. Finkelstein, Richard. "When OLAP Does Not Relate." *Computerworld*, December 12, 1994.

22. Freeman, Eva. "Birth of a Terabyte Data Warehouse." *Datamation*, April 1997.

23. Freeman, Eva. "Desktop Reporting Tools." *Datamation*, June 1997.

24. Gantz, John. "The New World of Enterprise Reporting Is Here." *Computerworld*, February 1, 1999.

25. Gates, Bill. *Business @ the Speed of Thought*. New York: Warner Books, 1999.

26. Goldberg, David. "Genetic and Evolutionary Algorithms Come of Age." *Communications of the ACM*, March 1994.

27. Gorry, G. Anthony, and Michael Scott Morton. "A Framework for Management Information Systems." *Sloan Management Review*, Fall 1971; republished Spring 1989.

28. Hall, Mark. "Supercomputing: From R&D to P&L." *Computerworld*, December 13, 1999.

29. "Helping Customers Help Themselves." Advertising Section. *Intelligent Enterprise*, January 5, 1999.

30. Higgins, Kelly. "Your Agent Is Calling." *Communications Week*, August 5, 1996.

31. Jablonowski, Mark. "Fuzzy Risk Analysis: Using AI Systems." *AI Expert*, December 1994.

32. Kalakota, Ravi, and Marcia Robinson. *E-Business: Roadmap for Success*. Reading, MA: Addison-Wesley, 1999.

33. Kalakota, Ravi, and Andrew Whinston. *Electronic Commerce: A Manager's Guide*. Reading, MA: Addison-Wesley, 1997.

34. King, James. "Intelligent Agents: Bringing Good Things to Life." *AI Expert*, February 1995.

35. King, Julia. "Infomediaries." *Computerworld*, November 1, 1999.

36. King, Julia. "Sharing GIS Talent with the World." *Computerworld*, October 6, 1997.

37. Kurszweil, Raymond. *The Age of Intelligent Machines*. Cambridge, MA: The MIT Press, 1992.

38. Lais, Sami. "CA Advances Neural Network System." *Computerworld*, December 13, 1999.

39. Lundquist, Christopher. "Personalization in E-Commerce." *Computerworld*, March 22, 1999.

40. Machlis, Sharon. "Agent Technology." *Computerworld*, March 22, 1999.

41. Mailoux, Jacquiline. "New Menu at PepsiCo." *Computerworld*, May 6, 1996.

42. McNeill, F. Martin, and Ellen Thro. *Fuzzy Logic: A Practical Approach*. Boston: AP Professional, 1994.

43. Murray, Gerry. "Making Connections with Enterprise Knowledge Portals." White Paper. *Computerworld*, September 6, 1999.

44. Orenstein, David. "Application Keeps Merchandise Moving." *Computerworld*, February 22, 1999.

45. Ouellette, Tim. "Opening Your Own Portal." *Computerworld*, August 9, 1999.

46. Papows, Jeff. *Enterprise.com: Market Leadership in the Information Age*. Reading, MA: Perseus Books, 1998.

47. Phelps, Alan. "Knowledge Is Power." *Smart Computing*, February 2000.

48. Pimentel, Ken, and Kevin Teixeira. *Virtual Reality Through the New Looking Glass*. 2nd ed. New York: Intel/McGraw-Hill, 1995.

49. Scheir, Robert. "Will Push Pan Out?" *Computerworld*, February 17, 1997.

50. Turban, Efraim, and Jay Aronson. *Decision Support Systems and Intelligent Systems*. Upper Saddle River, NJ: Prentice Hall, 1998.

51. Vandenbosch, Betty, and Sid Huff. "Searching and Scanning: How Executives Obtain Information from Executive Information Systems." *MIS Quarterly*, March 1997.

52. Wagner, Mitch. "Engine Links Ads to Searches." *Computerworld*, June 2, 1997.

53. Wagner, Mitch. "Reality Check." *Computerworld*, February 26, 1997.

54. Watson, Hugh, and John Satzinger. "Guidelines for Designing EIS Interfaces." *Information Systems Management*, Fall 1994.

55. Watterson, Karen. "Parallel Tracks." *Datamation*, May 1997.

56. Winston, Patrick. "Rethinking Artificial Intelligence." Program Announcement, Massachusetts Institute of Technology, September 1997.

57. Wreden, Nick. "Enterprise Portals: Integrating Information to Drive Productivity." *Beyond Computing*, March 2000.

Chapter 7—Developing E-Business Strategies

1. Bowles, Jerry. "Best Practices for Global Effectiveness." Special Advertising Section, *Fortune*, November 24, 1997.

2. Clark, Charles; Nancy Cavanaugh; Carol Brown; and V. Sambamurthy. "Building Change-Readiness Capabilities in the IS Organization: Insights from the Bell Atlantic Experience." *MIS Quarterly*, December 1997.

3. Cole-Gomolski, Barb. "Users Loath to Share Their Know-How." *Computerworld*, November 17, 1997.

4. Collette, Stacy. "SWOT Analysis." *Computerworld*, July 19, 1999.

5. Cronin, Mary. *The Internet Strategy Handbook*. Boston: Harvard Business School Press, 1996.

6. Cross, John; Michael Earl; and Jeffrey Sampler. "Transformation of the IT Function at British Petroleum." *MIS Quarterly*, December 1997.

7. Das, Sidhartha; Shaker Zahra; and Merrill Warkentin."Integrating the Content and Process of Strategic MIS Planning with Competitive Strategy." *Decision Sciences Journal*, November/December 1991.

8. De Geus, Arie. "Planning as Learning." *Harvard Business Review*, March–April 1988.

9. De Geus, Arie. "The Living Company." *Harvard Business Review*, March–April 1997.

10. Deise, Martin; Conrad Nowikow; Patrick King; and Amy Wright. *Executive's Guide to E-Business: From Tactics to Strategy*. New York: John Wiley & Sons, 2000.

11. Earl, Michael. "Experiences in Strategic Information Systems Planning." *MIS Quarterly*, March 1993.

12. El Sawy, Omar; Arvind Malhotra; Sanjay Gosain; and Kerry Young. "IT Intensive Value Innovation in the Electronic Economy: Insights from Marshall Industries." *MIS Quarterly*, September 1999.

13. El Sawy, Omar, and Gene Bowles. "Redesigning the Customer Support Process for the Electronic Economy: Insights from Storage Dimensions." *MIS Quarterly*, December 1997.

14. Fingar, Peter; Harsha Kumar; and Tarun Sharma. *Enterprise E-Commerce: The Software Component Breakthrough for Business to Business Commerce*. Tampa, FL: Meghan-Kiffer Press, 2000.

15. Grover, Varun; James Teng; and Kirk Fiedler. "IS Investment Priorities in Contemporary Organizations." *Communications of the ACM*, February 1998.

16. Hawson, James, and Jesse Beeler. "Effects of User Participation in Systems Development: A Longitudinal Field Experiment." *MIS Quarterly*, December 1997.

17. Hills, Melanie. *Intranet Business Strategies*. New York: John Wiley & Sons, 1997.

18. Kalakota, Ravi, and Marcia Robinson. *E-Business: Roadmap for Success*, Reading, MA: Addison-Wesley, 1999.

19. Keen, Peter G. W. *Shaping the Future: Business Design through Information Technology*. Boston: Harvard Business School, 1991.

20. Kettinger, William; James Teng; and Subashish Guha. "Business Process Change: A Study of Methodologies, Techniques, and Tools." *MIS Quarterly*, March 1997.

21. Koudsi, Suzanne. "Actually, It Is Like Brain Surgery." *Fortune*, March 20, 2000.

22. La Plante, Alice. "Eyes on the Customer." *Computerworld*, March 15, 1999.

23. Maglitta, Joseph. "Rocks in the Gears: Reengineering the Workplace." *Computerworld*, October 3, 1994.

24. Norris, Grant; James Hurley; Kenneth Hartley; John Dunleavy; and John Balls. *E-Business and ERP: Transforming the Enterprise*. New York: John Wiley & Sons, 2000.

25. Prokesch, Steven. "Unleasing the Power of Learning: An Interview with British Petroleum's John Browne." *Harvard Business Review*, September–October 1997.

26. Senge, Peter. *The Fifth Discipline: The Art and Practice of the Learning Organization*. New York: Currency Doubleday, 1994.

Chapter 8—Developing E-Business Solutions

1. Anthes, Gary. "The Quest for E-Quality." *Computerworld*, December 13, 1999.

2. Burden, Kevin. "IBM Waxes, Others Wane." *Computerworld*, March 15, 1999.

3. Clark, Charles; Nancy Cavanaugh; Carol Brown; and V. Sambamurthy. "Building Change-Readiness Capabilities in the IS Organization: Insights from the Bell Atlantic Experience." *MIS Quarterly*, December 1997.

4. Cole-Gomolski, Barbara. "Companies Turn to Web for ERP Training." *Computerworld*, February 8, 1999.

5. Cole-Gomolski, Barbara. "Users Loath to Share Their Know-How." *Computerworld*, November 17, 1997.

6. Cronin, Mary. *The Internet Strategy Handbook*. Boston: Harvard Business School Press, 1996.

7. Cross, John; Michael Earl; and Jeffrey Sampler. "Transformation of the IT Function at British Petroleum." *MIS Quarterly*, December 1997.

8. El Sawy, Omar, and Gene Bowles. "Redesigning the Customer Support Process for the Electronic Economy: Insights from Storage Dimensions." *MIS Quarterly*, December 1997.

9. El Sawy, Omar; Arvind Malhotra; Sanjay Gosain; and Kerry Young. "IT Intensive Value Innovation in the Electronic Economy: Insights from Marshall Industries." *MIS Quarterly*, September 1999.

10. Fogarty, Kevin. "Net Manners Matter: How Top Sites Rank in Social Behavior." *Computerworld*, October 18, 1999.

11. Grover, Varun; James Teng; and Kirk Fiedler. "IS Investment Priorities in Contemporary Organizations." *Communications of the ACM*, February 1998.

12. Haskin, David. "If I Had a Cyberhammer." *Business Week Enterprise*, March 29, 1999.

13. Hawson, James, and Jesse Beeler. "Effects of User Participation in Systems Development: A Longitudinal Field Experiment." *MIS Quarterly*, December 1997.

14. Hills, Melanie. *Intranet Business Strategies*. New York: John Wiley & Sons, 1997.

15. Holtz, Shel. *PCWeek: The Intranet Advantage*. Emeryville, CA: Ziff-Davis Press, 1996.

16. Iansiti, Marco, and Alan MacCormack. "Developing Products on Internet Time." *Harvard Business Review*, September–October 1997.

17. Kalakota, Ravi, and Marcia Robinson. *E-Business: Roadmap for Success*. Reading, MA: Addison-Wesley, 1999.

18. Keen, Peter G. W. *Shaping the Future: Business Design through Information Technology*. Boston: Harvard Business School, 1991.

19. Kettinger, William; James Teng; and Subashish Guha. "Business Process Change: A Study of Methodologies, Techniques, and Tools." *MIS Quarterly*, March 1997.

20. LaPlante, Alice. "Eyes on the Customer." *Computerworld*, March 15, 1999.

21. Machlis, Sharon. "Web Retailers Retool for Mainstream Users." *Computerworld*, March 22, 1999.

22. Maglitta, Joseph. "Rocks in the Gears: Reengineering the Workplace." *Computerworld*, October 3, 1994.

23. Martin, Chuck. *The Digital Estate: Strategies for Competing, Surviving, and Thriving in an Internet-Worked World*. New York: McGraw-Hill, 1997.

24. Millard, Elizabeth, "Big Company Weakened." *Business 2.0*, January 2000.

25. Morgan, James N. *Application Cases in MIS*. 3rd ed. New York: Irwin/McGraw-Hill, 1999.

26. Nielsen, Jakob. "Jakob Nielsen on www.panasonic.com." *Red Herring*, February 2000.

27. Orenstein, David. "Software Is Too Hard to Use." *Computerworld*, August 23, 1999.

28. Ouellette, Tim. "Giving Users the Key to Their Web Content." *Computerworld*, July 26, 1999.

29. Ouellette, Tim. "Opening Your Own Portal." *Computerworld*, August 9, 1999.

30. Pereira, Rex Eugene. "Resource View of SAP as a Source of Competitive Advantage for Firms." *The Database for Advances in Information Systems*, Winter 1999.

31. Schwartz, Matthew. "Tweak This!" *Computerworld*, January 31, 2000.

32. Senge, Peter. *The Fifth Discipline: The Art and Practice of the Learning Organization*. New York: Currency Doubleday, 1994.

33. Sliwa, Carol. "E-Commerce Solutions: How Real?" *Computerworld*, February 28, 2000.

34. Steadman, Craig. "ERP Flops Point to Users' Plans." *Computerworld*, November 15, 1999.

35. Whitten Jeffrey, and Lonnie Bentley. *Systems Analysis and Design Methods*. 4th ed. New York: Irwin/McGraw-Hill, 1998.

36. Wreden, Nick. "Enterprise Portals: Integrating Information to Drive Productivity." *Beyond Computing*, March 2000.

Chapter 9—Security and Ethical Challenges of E-Business

1. Anthes, Gary. "Biometrics." *Computerworld*, October 12, 1998.

2. Anthes, Gary. "Lotsa Talk, Little Walk." In "Managing." *Computerworld*, September 21, 1998.

3. Bahar, Richard. "Who's Reading Your E-Mail?" *Fortune*, February 3, 1997.

4. Bloom, Paul; Robert Adler; and George Milne. "Identifying the Legal and Ethical Risks and Costs of Using New Information Technologies to Support Marketing Programs." In *The Marketing Information Revolution*, ed. Robert C. Blattberg, Rashi Glazer, and John D. C. Little. Boston: Harvard Business School Press, 1994.

5. Cole-Gomolski, Barb. "Quick Fixes Are of Limited Use in Deterring Force Diet of Spam." *Computerworld*, October 20, 1997.

6. Collett, Stacy. "Net Managers Battle Online Trading Boom." *Computerworld*, July 5, 1999.

7. Culnane, Mary. "How Did They Get My Name? An Exploratory Investigation of Consumer Attitudes Toward Secondary Information Use." *MIS Quarterly*, September 1993.

8. Deckmyn, Dominique. "More Managers Monitor E-Mail." *Computerworld*, October 18, 1999.

9. Dejoie, Roy; George Fowler; and David Paradice, eds. *Ethical Issues in Information Systems*. Boston: Boyd & Fraser, 1991.

10. Donaldson, Thomas. "Values in Tension: Ethics Away from Home." *Harvard Business Review*, September–October 1996.

11. Dunlop, Charles, and Rob Kling, eds. *Computerization and Controversy: Value Conflicts and Social Choices.* San Diego: Academic Press, 1991.

12. Duvall, Mel. "Protecting Against Viruses." *Inter@ctive Week,* February 28, 2000.

13. Essex, David. "Stop Desktop Virus Gremlins." *Computerworld,* December 6, 1999.

14. Ganesan, Ravi, and Ravi Sandhu, guest editors. "Security in Cyberspace." Special Section, *Communications of the ACM,* November 1994.

15. Harrison, Ann. "FBI Issues Software to Help Detect Web Attacks." *Computerworld,* February 14, 2000.

16. Harrison, Ann. "Internet Worm Destroys Data." *Computerworld,* June 14, 1999.

17. Harrison, Ann. "RealNetworks Slapped With Privacy Lawsuits." *Computerworld,* November 15, 1999.

18. Harrison, Ann. "Virus Scanning Moving to ISPs." *Computerworld,* September 20, 1999.

19. Joy, Bill. "Report From the Cyberfront." *Newsweek,* February 21, 2000.

20. Johnson, Deborah. "Ethics Online." *Communications of the ACM,* January 1997.

21. Kalakota, Ravi, and Andrew Whinston. *Electronic Commerce: A Manager's Guide.* Reading, MA: Addison-Wesley, 1997.

22. Kallman, Earnest, and John Grillo. *Ethical Decision Making and Information Technology: An Introduction with Cases.* New York: Mitchel McGraw-Hill, 1993.

23. Kover, Amy. "Who's Afraid of This Kid?" *Fortune,* March 20, 2000.

24. Levy, Stephen, and Brad Stone. "Hunting the Hackers." *Newsweek,* February 21, 2000.

25. Martin, James. "You Are Being Watched." *PC World,* November 1997.

26. McCarthy, Michael. "Keystroke Cops." *The Wall Street Journal,* March 7, 2000.

27. McFarland, Michael. "Ethics and the Safety of Computer Systems." *Computer,* February 1991.

28. Morgan, Cynthia. "Web Merchants Stung by Fraud." *Computerworld,* March 8, 1999.

29. Naughton, Keith. "CyberSlacking," *Newsweek,* November 29, 1999.

30. Neumann, Peter. *Computer-Related Risks.* New York: ACM Press, 1995.

31. Radcliff, Deborah. "Fighting the Flood." *Computerworld,* March 6, 2000.

32. Radcliff, Deborah. "Three Industries: Three Security Needs." *Computerworld,* November 29, 1999.

33. Robinson, Lori. "How It Works: Viruses." *Smart Computing,* March 2000.

34. Rothfeder, Jeffrey. "Hacked! Are Your Company Files Safe?" *PC World,* November 1996.

35. Rothfeder, Jeffrey. "No Privacy on the Net." *PC World,* February 1997.

36. Sager, Ira; Steve Hamm; Neil Gross; John Carey; and Robert Hoff. "Cyber Crime." *Business Week,* February 21, 2000.

37. Sandberg, Jared. "Holes in the Net." *Newsweek,* February 21, 2000.

38. Smith, H. Jefferson, and John Hasnas. "Debating the Stakeholder Theory." *Beyond Computing,* March–April 1994.

39. Smith, H. Jefferson, and John Hasnas. "Establishing an Ethical Framework," *Beyond Computing,* January–February 1994.

40. Stark, Andrew. "What's the Matter with Business Ethics?" *Harvard Business Review,* May–June 1993.

41. Sullivan, Bob. "Melissa Macro Worms Around Web." MSNBC.com, March 27, 1999.

42. Tate, Priscilla. "Internet Security: Can Best Practices Overcome Worst Perils?" White Paper. *Computerworld,* May 4, 1998.

43. Willard, Nancy. *The Cyberethics Reader.* Burr Ridge, IL: Irwin/McGraw-Hill, 1997.

44. York, Thomas. "Invasion of Privacy? E-Mail Monitoring Is on the Rise." *Information Week Online,* February 21, 2000.

Chapter 10—Enterprise and Global Management of E-Business Technology

1. Alter, Allan. "Harmonic Convergence." In "The Premier 100." *Computerworld,* November 16, 1998.

2. Brandel, Mary. "Think Global, Act Local." *Computerworld Global Innovators,* Special Section, March 10, 1997.

3. Bryan, Lowell; Jane Fraser; Jeremy Oppenheim; and Wilhelm Rall. *Race for the World: Strategies to Build a Great Global Firm.* Boston: Harvard Business School Press, 1999.

4. Christensen, Clayton. *The Innovators Dilemma: When New Technologies Cause Great Firms to Fail.* Boston: Harvard Business School Press, 1997.

5. Corbett, Michael. "Outsourcing: Creating Competitive Advantage Through Specialization, Alliances, and Innovation." *Fortune*, Special Advertising Section, October 14, 1996.

6. Cronin, Mary. *Global Advantage on the Internet*. New York: Van Nostrand Reinhold, 1996.

7. DeGeus, Arie. "The Living Company." *Harvard Business Review*, March–April, 1997.

8. El Sawy, Omar; Arvind Malhotra; Sanjay Gosain; and Kerry Young. "IT Intensive Value Innovation in the Electronic Economy: Insights from Marshall Industries." *MIS Quarterly*, September 1999.

9. El Sawy, Omar, and Gene Bowles. "Redesigning the Customer Support Process for the Electronic Economy: Insights from Storage Dimensions." *MIS Quarterly*, December 1997.

10. Fryer, Bronwyn. "Payroll Busters." *Computerworld*, March 6, 2000.

11. Gates, Bill. *Business @ the Speed of Thought*. New York: Warner Books, 1999.

12. Grover, Varun; James Teng; and Kirk Fiedler. "IS Investment Opportunities in Contemporary Organizations." *Communications of the ACM*, February 1998.

13. Hall, Mark. "Service Providers Give Users More IT Options." *Computerworld*, February 7, 2000.

14. Hayes, Frank. "The Main Event." *Computerworld*, November 8, 1999.

15. Ives, Blake, and Sirkka Jarvenpaa. "Applications of Global Information Technology: Key Issues for Management." *MIS Quarterly*, March 1991.

16. Kalakota, Ravi, and Marcia Robinson. *E-Business: Roadmap for Success*. Reading, MA: Addison-Wesley, 1999.

17. Kalin, Sari. "The Importance of Being Multiculturally Correct." Global Innovators Series, *Computerworld*, October 6, 1997.

18. King, Julia. "Exporting Jobs Saves IT Money." *Computerworld*, March 15, 1999.

19. King, Julia. "Sun and Pay Lures Coders to Barbados Outsourcer." *Computerworld*, March 15, 1999.

20. King, Julia. "The Lure of Internet Spin-Offs." *Computerworld*, October 18, 1999.

21. Kirkpatrick, David. "Back to the Future with Centralized Computing." *Fortune*, November 10, 1997.

22. LaPlante, Alice. "Global Boundaries.com." Global Innovators Series, *Computerworld*, October 6, 1997.

23. Luftman, Jerry. "Align in the Sand." Leadership Series. *Computerworld*, February 17, 1997.

24. McGrath, Dermot. "When 'E' Stands for Europe." *Computerworld*, September 6, 1999.

25. Melymuka, Kathleen. "Ford's Driving Force." *Computerworld*, August 30, 1999.

26. Mische, Michael. "Transnational Architecture: A Reengineering Approach." *Information Systems Management*, Winter 1995.

27. Morgan, Cynthia. "ASPs Speak the Corporate Language." *Computerworld*, October 25, 1999.

28. Palvia, Prashant; Shailendra Palvia; and Edward Roche, eds. *Global Information Technology and Systems Management*. Marietta, GA: Ivy League Publishing, 1996.

29. Neilson, Gary; Bruce Pasternack; and Albert Visco. "Up the E-Organization! A Seven-Dimensional Model of the Centerless Enterprise." *Strategy & Business*, First Quarter 2000.

30. Shand, Dawne. "All Information Is Local." *Computerworld*, April 10, 2000.

31. Steadman, Craig. "Failed ERP Gamble Haunts Hershey." *Computerworld*, November 1, 1999.

32. Thibodeau, Patrick. "Europe and U.S. Agree on Data Rules." *Computerworld*, March 20, 2000.

33. Taggart, Stewart. "Censor Census." *Business 2.0*, March 2000.

34. Vander Weyer, Martin. "The World Debates." *Strategy & Business*, First Quarter 2000.

35. Vitalari, Nicholas, and James Wetherbe. "Emerging Best Practices in Global Systems Development." In *Global Information Technology and Systems Management*, ed. Prashant Palvia et al. Marietta, GA: Ivy League Publishing, 1996.

Chapter 11—Computer Hardware

1. *Computerworld*, *PC Week*, *PC Magazine*, and *PC World* are just a few examples of many good magazines for current information on computer systems hardware and its use in end user and enterprise applications.

2. The World Wide Web sites of computer manufacturers such as Apple Computer, Dell Computer, Gateway, IBM, Hewlett-Packard, Compaq, and Sun Microsystems are good sources of information on computer hardware developments.

3. Alexander, Steve. "Speech Recognition." *Computerworld*, November 8, 1999.

4. Collette, Stacy. "Thin Client Devices Shipments Soar." *Computerworld*, September 20, 1999.

5. "Computing in the New Millenium." *Technology Buyers Guide*, *Fortune*, Winter 2000.

6. Crothers, Brooke. "IBM Wins Big on Supercomputer Deal." CNETNews.com, April 28, 1999.

7. Deckmyn, Dominique. "Dell Joins the Legacy-Free PC Movement." *Computerworld*, December 6, 1999.

8. "Desktop Power." In Technology Buyer's Guide. *Fortune*, Winter 1999.

9. Guyon, Janet. "Smart Plastic." *Fortune*, October 13, 1997.

10. "Hardware." In Technology Buyer's Guide. *Fortune*, Winter 1999.

11. Judge, Paul. "High Tech Star." *Business Week*, March 15, 1999.

12. Kennedy, Ken, and others. "A Nationwide Parallel Computing Environment." *Communications of the ACM*, November 1997.

13. Messerschmitt, David. *Networked Applications: A Guide to the New Computing Infrastructure.* San Francisco: Morgan Kaufmann Publishers, 1999.

14. Morgan, Cynthia. "Speech Recognition." *Computerworld*, September 27, 1998.

15. Ouellette, Tim. "Goodbye to the Glass House." *Computerworld*, May 26, 1997.

16. Ouellette, Tim. "Tape Storage Put to New Enterprise Uses." *Computerworld*, November 10, 1997.

17. Simpson, David. "The Datamation 100." *Datamation*, July 1997.

18. Sliwa, Carol. "Net Reliability Hinges on Web Site Architecture." *Computerworld*, August 30, 1999.

Chapter 12—Computer Software

1. Examples of many good magazines for current information and reviews of computer software for business applications can be found at ZD Net, the website for ZD Publications (www.zdnet.com), including *PC Magazine, PC Week, PC Computing, Macworld, Inter@ctive Week,* and *Computer Shopper.*

2. The World Wide Web sites of computer manufacturers and software companies like Microsoft, Sun Microsystems, Lotus, IBM, Apple Computer, Oracle, and Netscape Communications are good sources of information on computer software developments.

3. Hamm, Steve; Peter Burrows; and Andy Reinhardt. "Is Windows Ready to Run E-Business?" *Business Week*, January 24, 2000.

4. Jacobsen, Ivar; Maria Ericcson; and Ageneta Jacobsen. *The Object Advantage: Business Process Reengineering with Object Technology.* New York: ACM Press, 1995.

5. Johnson, Amy Helen. "XML Xtends Its Reach." *Computerworld*, October 18, 1999.

6. Kalish, David. "Computer Language Consensus Sought." Associated Press Online, www.marketwatch.com, February 1, 2000.

7. Nance, Barry. "Linux in a 3-Piece Suit?" *Computerworld*, September 6, 1999.

8. Satran, Dick. "Sun's Shooting Star." *Business 2.0*, February 2000.

9. Schlender, Brent. "Steve Jobs' Apple Gets Way Cooler." *Fortune*, January 24, 2000.

10. "Suite Deals," Technology Buyer's Guide, *Fortune*, Winter 2000.

11. Udell, John. "Java: The Actions on the Server." *Computerworld*, July 5, 1999.

Chapter 13—Data Resource Management

1. Ahrens, Judith, and Chetan Sankar. "Tailoring Database Training for End Users." *MIS Quarterly*, December 1993.

2. Anthes, Gary. "Minding the Storage." *Computerworld*. March 22, 1999.

3. Atwood, Thomas. "Object Databases Come of Age," *OBJECT Magazine*, July 1996.

4. Baer, Tony. "Object Databases." *Computerworld*, January 18, 1999.

5. "Borders Knows No Bounds in E-Business." From www.software.ibm/eb/borders, March 1999.

6. Bose, Ranjit, and Vijayan Sugumaran. "Application of Intelligent Agent Technology for Managerial Data Analysis and Mining." *The Data Base for Advances in Information Systems*, Winter 1999.

7. Finkelstein, Richard. *Understanding the Need for On-Line Analytical Servers.* Ann Arbor, MI: Arbor Software Corporation, 1994.

8. Jacobsen, Ivar; Maria Ericsson; and Ageneta Jacobsen. *The Object Advantage: Business Process Reengineering with Object Technology.* New York: ACM Press, 1995.

9. Judge, Paul. "High-Tech Star." *Business Week*, March 15, 1999.

10. Kalakota, Ravi, and Marcia Robinson. *E-Business: Roadmap for Success.* Reading, MA: Addison-Wesley, 1999.

11. Morgan, Cynthia. "Data Is King." *Computerworld*, March 27, 2000.

12. Lorents, Alden, and James Morgan. *Database Systems: Concepts, Management and Applications.* Fort Worth: The Dryden Press, 1998.

13. Mannino, Michael. *Database Application Development and Design*. Burr Ridge, IL: McGraw-Hill Irwin, 2001.

14. "Shedding Light on Data Warehousing for More Informed Business Solutions." Special Advertising Supplement. *Computerworld*, February 13, 1995.

15. Smith, Heather A., and James D. McKeen. "Object-Oriented Technology: Getting Beyond the Hype." *The Data Base for Advances in Information Systems*, Spring 1996.

16. Spiegler, Israel. "Toward a Unified View of Data: Bridging Data Structure and Content." *Information Systems Management*, Spring 1995.

17. Stedman, Craig. "Databases Grab Hold of Objects, Multimedia on the Web." *Computerworld*, October 21, 1996.

18. Storey, Veda, and Robert Goldstein. "Knowledge-Based Approaches to Database Design." *MIS Quarterly*, March 1993.

19. Ta Check, James. "IBM: Not by Databases Alone." *ZD Net*, February 3, 2000.

20. White, Colin, "Data Warehousing: Choosing the Right Tools." *Computerworld*, Special Advertising Supplement, March 2, 1998.

Chapter 14—Telecommunications and Networks

1. Blum, Jonathan. "Peering into the Future." *Red Herring*, November 13, 2000.

2. Cronin, Mary. *Global Advantage on the Internet*. New York: Van Nostrand Reinhold, 1996.

3. "Dialing for Data." In Technology Buyer's Guide, *Fortune*, Winter 2000.

4. Fernandez, Tony. "Beyond the Browser." *NetWorker*, March/April 1997.

5. Harler, Curt, and Donell Short. "Building Broadband Networks." Special advertising section, *Business Week*, July 12, 1999.

6. Housel, Thomas, and Eric Skopec. *Global Telecommunications Revolution: The Business Perspective*. Burr Ridge, IL: McGraw-Hill Irwin, 2001.

7. Kalakota, Ravi, and Marcia Robinson. *E-Business: Roadmap for Success*. Reading, MA: Addison-Wesley, 1999.

8. Kover, Amy. "Napster: Hot Idea of the Year." *Fortune*, June 26, 2000.

9. "Life on the Web." In Technology Buyer's Guide, *Fortune*, Winter 1999.

10. Martin, Chuck. *The Digital Estate: Strategies for Competing, Surviving, and Thriving in an Internetworked World*. New York: McGraw-Hill, 1997.

11. Messerschmitt, David. *Network Applications: A Guide to the New Computing Infrastructure*. San Francisco: Morgan Kaufmann Publishers, 1999.

12. Murphy, Kate. "Cruising the Net in Hyperdrive." *Business Week*, January 24, 2000.

13. Nee, Eric. "The Upstarts are Rocking Telecom." *Fortune*, January 24, 2000.

14. "Phones to Go." In Technology Buyer's Guide. *Fortune*, Winter 1999.

15. Rosenbush, Steve. "Charge of the Light Brigade," *Business Week*, January 31, 2000.

16. Wallace, Bob. "Hotels See Service From Virtual Net." *Computerworld*, February 9, 1998.

Accounting Information Systems
Information systems that record and report business transactions, the flow of funds through an organization, and produce financial statements. This provides information for the planning and control of business operations, as well as for legal and historical record-keeping.

Active Data Dictionary
A data dictionary that automatically enforces standard data element definitions whenever end users and application programs use a DBMS to access an organization's databases.

Ad Hoc Inquiries
Unique, unscheduled, situation-specific information requests.

Ada
A programming language named after Augusta Ada Byron, considered the world's first computer programmer. Developed for the U.S. Department of Defense as a standard high-order language.

Agile Competition
The ability of a company to profitably operate in a competitive environment of continual and unpredictable changes in customer preferences, market conditions, and business opportunities.

Algorithm
A set of well-defined rules or processes for the solution of a problem in a finite number of steps.

Analog Computer
A computer that operates on data by measuring changes in continuous physical variables such as voltage, resistance, and rotation. Contrast with Digital Computer.

Analytical Database
A database of data extracted from operational and external databases to provide data tailored to online analytical processing, decision support, and executive information systems.

Analytical Modeling
Interactive use of computer-based mathematical models to explore decision alternatives using what-if analysis, sensitivity analysis, goal-seeking analysis, and optimization analysis.

Applet
A small limited-purpose application program, or small independent module of a larger application program.

Application Development
See Systems Development.

Application Generator
A software package that supports the development of an application through an interactive terminal dialogue, where the programmer/analyst defines screens, reports, computations, and data structures.

Application Portfolio
A planning tool used to evaluate present and proposed information systems applications in terms of the amount of revenue or assets invested in information systems that support major business functions.

Application Software
Programs that specify the information processing activities required for the completion of specific tasks of computer users. Examples are electronic spreadsheet and word processing programs or inventory or payroll programs.

Application-Specific Programs
Application software packages that support specific applications of end users in business, science and engineering, and other areas.

Arithmetic-Logic Unit (ALU)
The unit of a computing system containing the circuits that perform arithmetic and logical operations.

Artificial Intelligence (AI)
A science and technology whose goal is to develop computers that can think, as well as see, hear, walk, talk, and feel. A major thrust is the development of computer functions normally associated with human intelligence, for example, reasoning, inference, learning, and problem solving.

ASCII: American Standard Code for Information Interchange
A standard code used for information interchange among data processing systems, communication systems, and associated equipment.

Assembler
A computer program that translates an assembler language into machine language.

Assembler Language
A programming language that utilizes symbols to represent operation codes and storage locations.

Asynchronous
Involving a sequence of operations without a regular or predictable time relationship. Thus operations do not happen at regular timed intervals, but an operation will begin only after a previous operation is completed. In data transmission, involves the use of start and stop bits with each character to indicate the beginning and end of the character being transmitted. Contrast with Synchronous.

Audit Trail
The presence of media and procedures that allow a transaction to be traced through all stages of information processing, beginning with its appearance on a source document and ending with its transformation into information on a final output document.

Automated Teller Machine (ATM)
A special-purpose transaction terminal used to provide remote banking services.

Automation
The automatic transfer and positioning of work by machines or the automatic operation and control of a work process by machines, that is, without significant human intervention or operation.

Back-End Processor
Typically, a smaller general-purpose computer that is dedicated to database processing using a database management system (DBMS). Also called a database machine or server.

Background Processing
The automatic execution of lower-priority computer programs when higher-priority programs are not using the resources of the computer system. Contrast with Foreground Processing.

Backward-Chaining
An inference process that justifies a proposed conclusion by determining if it will result when rules are applied to the facts in a given situation.

Bandwidth
The frequency range of a telecommunications channel, which determines its maximum transmission rate. The speed and capacity of transmission rates are typically measured in bits per second (BPS). Bandwidth is a function of the telecommunications hardware, software, and media used by the telecommunications channel.

Bar Codes
Vertical marks or bars placed on merchandise tags or packaging that can be sensed and read by optical character-reading devices. The width and combination of vertical lines are used to represent data.

Barriers to Entry
Technological, financial, or legal requirements that deter firms from entering an industry.

BASIC: Beginner's All-Purpose Symbolic Instruction Code
A programming language developed at Dartmouth College that is popular for microcomputer and time-sharing systems.

Batch Processing
A category of data processing in which data are accumulated into batches and processed periodically. Contrast with Real-Time Processing.

Baud
A unit of measurement used to specify data transmission speeds. It is a unit of signaling speed equal to the number of discrete conditions or signal events per second. In many data communications applications it represents one bit per second.

Binary
Pertaining to a characteristic or property involving a selection, choice, or condition in which there are two possibilities, or pertaining to the number system that utilizes a base of 2.

Biometric Controls
Computer-based security methods that measure physical traits and characteristics such as fingerprints, voice prints, retina scans, and so on.

Bit
A contraction of "binary digit." It can have the value of either 0 or 1.

Block
A grouping of contiguous data records or other data elements that are handled as a unit.

Branch
A transfer of control from one instruction to another in a computer program that is not part of the normal sequential execution of the instructions of the program.

Browser
See Web Browser.

Buffer
Temporary storage used to compensate for a difference in rate of flow of data or time of occurrence of events, when transmitting data from one device to another.

Bug
A mistake or malfunction.

Bulletin Board System (BBS)
A service of online computer networks in which electronic messages, data files, or programs can be stored for other subscribers to read or copy.

Bundling
The inclusion of software, maintenance, training, and other products or services in the price of a computer system.

Bus
A set of conducting paths for movement of data and instructions that interconnects the various components of the CPU.

Business Ethics
An area of philosophy concerned with developing ethical principles and promoting ethical behavior and practices in the accomplishment of business tasks and decision making.

Business Process Reengineering (BPR)
Restructuring and transforming a business process by a fundamental rethinking and redesign to achieve dramatic improvements in cost, quality, speed, and so on.

Byte
A sequence of adjacent binary digits operated on as a unit and usually shorter than a computer word. In many computer systems, a byte is a grouping of eight bits that can represent one alphabetic or special character or can be packed with two decimal digits.

C
A low-level structured programming language that resembles a machine-independent assembler language.

C++
An object-oriented version of C that is widely used for software package development.

Cache Memory
A high-speed temporary storage area in the CPU for storing parts of a program or data during processing.

Calendaring and Scheduling
Using electronic calendars and other groupware features to automatically schedule, notify, and remind the computer networked members of teams and workgroups of meetings, appointments, and other events.

Capacity Management
The use of planning and control methods to forecast and control information processing job loads, hardware and software usage, and other computer system resource requirements.

Case-Based Reasoning
Representing knowledge in an expert system's knowledge base in the form of cases, that is, examples of past performance, occurrences, and experiences.

Cathode Ray Tube (CRT)
An electronic vacuum tube (television picture tube) that displays the output of a computer system.

CD-ROM
An optical disk technology for microcomputers featuring compact disks with a storage capacity of over 500 megabytes.

Cellular Phone Systems
A radio communications technology that divides a metropolitan area into a honeycomb of cells to greatly increase the number of frequencies and thus the users that can take advantage of mobile phone service.

Central Processing Unit (CPU)
The unit of a computer system that includes the circuits that control the interpretation and execution of instructions. In many computer systems, the

CPU includes the arithmetic-logic unit, the control unit, and the primary storage unit.

Change Management
Managing the process of implementing major changes in information technology, business processes, organizational structures, and job assignments to reduce the risks and costs of change, and optimize its benefits.

Channel
(1) A path along which signals can be sent. (2) A small special-purpose processor that controls the movement of data between the CPU and input/output devices.

Chargeback Systems
Methods of allocating costs to end user departments based on the information services rendered and information system resources utilized.

Chat Systems
Software that enables two or more users at networked PCs to carry on on-line, real-time text conversations.

Check Bit
A binary check digit; for example, a parity bit.

Check Digit
A digit in a data field that is utilized to check for errors or loss of characters in the data field as a result of data transfer operations.

Checkpoint
A place in a program where a check or a recording of data for restart purposes is performed.

Chief Information Officer
A senior management position that oversees all information technology for a firm concentrating on long-range information system planning and strategy.

Client
(1) An end user. (2) The end user's networked microcomputer in client/server networks. (3) The version of a software package designed to run on an end user's networked microcomputer, such as a Web browser client, a groupware client, and so on.

Client/Server Network
A computer network where end user workstations (clients) are connected via telecommunications links to network servers and possibly to mainframe superservers.

Clock
A device that generates periodic signals utilized to control the timing of a computer. Also, a register whose contents change at regular intervals in such a way as to measure time.

Coaxial Cable
A sturdy copper or aluminum wire wrapped with spacers to insulate and protect it. Groups of coaxial cables may also be bundled together in a bigger cable for ease of installation.

COBOL: COmmon Business Oriented Language
A widely used business data processing programming language.

Code
Computer instructions.

Cognitive Science
An area of artificial intelligence that focuses on researching how the human brain works and how humans think and learn, in order to apply such findings to the design of computer-based systems.

Cognitive Styles
Basic patterns in how people handle information and confront problems.

Cognitive Theory
Theories about how the human brain works and how humans think and learn.

Collaborative Work Management Tools
Software that helps people accomplish or manage joint work activities.

Common Carrier
An organization that supplies communications services to other organizations and to the public as authorized by government agencies.

Communications Satellite
Earth satellites placed in stationary orbits above the equator that serve as relay stations for communications signals transmitted from earth stations.

Competitive Advantage
Developing products, services, processes, or capabilities that give a company a superior business position relative to its competitors and other competitive forces.

Competitive Forces
A firm must confront (1) rivalry of competitors within its industry, (2) threats of new entrants, (3) threats of substitutes, (4) the bargaining power of customers, and (5) the bargaining power of suppliers.

Competitive Strategies
A firm can develop cost leadership, product differentiation, and business innovation strategies to confront its competitive forces.

Compiler
A program that translates a high-level programming language into a machine-language program.

Computer
A device that has the ability to accept data; internally store and execute a program of instructions; perform mathematical, logical, and manipulative operations on data; and report the results.

Computer-Aided Design (CAD)
The use of computers and advanced graphics hardware and software to provide interactive design assistance for engineering and architectural design.

Computer-Aided Engineering (CAE)
The use of computers to simulate, analyze, and evaluate models of product designs and production processes developed using computer-aided design methods.

Computer-Aided Manufacturing (CAM)
The use of computers to automate the production process and operations of a manufacturing plant. Also called factory automation.

Computer-Aided Planning (CAP)
The use of software packages as tools to support the planning process.

Computer-Aided Software Engineering (CASE)
Same as Computer-Aided Systems Engineering, but emphasizing the importance of software development.

Computer-Aided Systems Engineering (CASE)
Using software packages to accomplish and automate many of the activities of information systems development, including software development or programming.

Computer Application
The use of a computer to solve a specific problem or to accomplish a particular job for an end user. For example, common business computer applications include sales order processing, inventory control, and payroll.

Computer-Assisted Instruction (CAI)
The use of computers to provide drills, practice exercises, and tutorial sequences to students.

Computer-Based Information System
An information system that uses computer hardware and software to perform its information processing activities.

Computer Crime
Criminal actions accomplished through the use of computer systems, especially with intent to defraud, destroy, or make unauthorized use of computer system resources.

Computer Ethics
A system of principles governing the legal, professional, social, and moral responsibilities of computer specialists and end users.

Computer Generations
Major stages in the historical development of computing.

Computer Graphics
Using computer-generated images to analyze and interpret data, present information, and do computer-aided design and art.

Computer Industry
The industry composed of firms that supply computer hardware, software, and services.

Computer-Integrated Manufacturing (CIM)
An overall concept that stresses that the goals of computer use in factory automation should be to simplify, automate, and integrate production processes and other aspects of manufacturing.

Computer Matching
Using computers to screen and match data about individual characteristics provided by a variety of computer-based information systems and databases in order to identify individuals for business, government, or other purposes.

Computer Monitoring
Using computers to monitor the behavior and productivity of workers on the job and in the workplace.

Computer Program
A series of instructions or statements, in a form acceptable to a computer, prepared in order to achieve a certain result.

Computer System
Computer hardware as a system of input, processing, output, storage, and control components. Thus a computer system consists of input and output devices, primary and secondary storage devices, the central processing unit, the control unit within the CPU, and other peripheral devices.

Computer Terminal
Any input/output device connected by telecommunications links to a computer.

Computer Virus or Worm
Program code that copies its destructive program routines into the computer systems of anyone who accesses computer systems that have used the program, or anyone who uses copies of data or programs taken from such computers. This spreads the destruction of

data and programs among many computer users. Technically, a virus will not run unaided, but must be inserted into another program, while a worm is a distinct program that can run unaided.

Concurrent Processing
The generic term for the capability of computers to work on several tasks at the same time, that is, concurrently. This may involve specific capabilities such as overlapped processing, multiprocessing, multiprogramming, multitasking, parallel processing, and so on.

Connectivity
The degree to which hardware, software, and databases can be easily linked together in a telecommunications network.

Context Diagram
The highest level data flow diagram. It defines the boundaries of a system by showing a single major process and the data inputs and outputs and external entities involved.

Control
(1) The systems component that evaluates feedback to determine whether the system is moving toward the achievement of its goal and then makes any necessary adjustments to the input and processing components of the system to ensure that proper output is produced. (2) A management function that involves observing and measuring organizational performance and environmental activities and modifying the plans and activities of the organization when necessary.

Control Listing
A detailed report that describes each transaction occurring during a period.

Control Totals
Accumulating totals of data at multiple points in an information system to ensure correct information processing.

Control Unit
A subunit of the central processing unit that controls and directs the operations of the computer system. The control unit retrieves computer instructions in proper sequence, interprets each instruction, and then directs the other parts of the computer system in their implementation.

Conversion
The process in which the hardware, software, people, network, and data resources of an old information system must be converted to the requirements of a new information system. This usually involves a parallel, phased, pilot, or plunge conversion process from the old to the new system.

Cooperative Processing
Information processing that allows the computers in a distributed processing network to share the processing of parts of an end user's application.

Cost/Benefit Analysis
Identifying the advantages or benefits and the disadvantages or costs of a proposed solution.

Critical Success Factors
A small number of key factors that executives consider critical to the success of the enterprise. These are key areas where successful performance will assure the success of the organization and attainment of its goals.

Cross-Functional Information Systems
Information systems that are integrated combinations of business information systems, thus sharing information resources across the functional units of an organization.

Cursor
A movable point of light displayed on most video display screens to assist the user in the input of data.

Customer Relationship Management (CRM)
A cross-functional E-business application that integrates and automates many customer serving processes in sales, direct marketing, account and order management, and customer service and support.

Cybernetic System
A system that uses feedback and control components to achieve a self-regulating capability.

Cylinder
An imaginary vertical cylinder consisting of the vertical alignment of tracks on each surface of magnetic disks that are accessed simultaneously by the read/write heads of a disk drive.

Data
Facts or observations about physical phenomena or business transactions. More specifically, data are objective measurements of the attributes (characteristics) of entities such as people, places, things, and events.

Data Administration
A data resource management function that involves the establishment and enforcement of policies and procedures for managing data as a strategic corporate resource.

Database
A collection of logically related records or files. A database consolidates many

records previously stored in separate files so that a common pool of data serves many applications.

Database Administration
A data resource management function that includes responsibility for developing and maintaining the organization's data dictionary, designing and monitoring the performance of databases, and enforcing standards for database use and security.

Database Administrator
A specialist responsible for maintaining standards for the development, maintenance, and security of an organization's databases.

Database Maintenance
The activity of keeping a database up-to-date by adding, changing, or deleting data.

Database Management Approach
An approach to the storage and processing of data in which independent files are consolidated into a common pool, or database, of records available to different application programs and end users for processing and data retrieval.

Database Management System (DBMS)
A set of computer programs that controls the creation, maintenance, and utilization of the databases of an organization.

Database Processing
Utilizing a database for data processing activities such as maintenance, information retrieval, or report generation.

Data Center
An organizational unit that uses centralized computing resources to perform information processing activities for an organization. Also known as a computer center.

Data Conferencing
Users at networked PCs can view, mark up, revise, and save changes to a shared whiteboard of drawings, documents, and other material.

Data Design
The design of the logical structure of databases and files to be used by a proposed information system. This produces detailed descriptions of the entities, relationships, data elements, and integrity rules for system files and databases.

Data Dictionary
A software module and database containing descriptions and definitions concerning the structure, data elements, interrelationships, and other characteristics of a database.

Data Entry
The process of converting data into a form suitable for entry into a computer system. Also called data capture or input preparation.

Data Flow Diagram
A graphic diagramming tool that uses a few simple symbols to illustrate the flow of data among external entities, processing activities, and data storage elements.

Data Management
Control program functions that provide access to data sets, enforce data storage conventions, and regulate the use of input/output devices.

Data Mining
Using special-purpose software to analyze data from a data warehouse to find hidden patterns and trends.

Data Model
A conceptual framework that defines the logical relationships among the data elements needed to support a basic business or other process.

Data Modeling
A process where the relationships between data elements are identified and defined to develop data models.

Data Planning
A corporate planning and analysis function that focuses on data resource management. It includes the responsibility for developing an overall information policy and data architecture for the firm's data resources.

Data Processing
The execution of a systematic sequence of operations performed upon data to transform it into information.

Data Resource Management
A managerial activity that applies information systems technology and management tools to the task of managing an organization's data resources. Its three major components are database administration, data administration, and data planning.

Data Warehouse
An integrated collection of data extracted from operational, historical, and external databases, and cleaned, transformed, and cataloged for retrieval and analysis (*data mining*), to provide business intelligence for business decision making.

Debug
To detect, locate, and remove errors from a program or malfunctions from a computer.

Decision-Making Process
A process of intelligence, design, and choice activities that result in the selection of a particular course of action.

Decision Support System (DSS)
An information system that utilizes decision models, a database, and a decision maker's own insights in an ad hoc, interactive analytical modeling process to reach a specific decision by a specific decision maker.

Demand Reports and Responses
Information provided whenever a manager or end user demands it.

Desktop Publishing
The use of microcomputers, laser printers, and page-makeup software to produce a variety of printed materials, formerly done only by professional printers.

Desktop Videoconferencing
The use of end user computer workstations to conduct two-way interactive video conferences.

Development Centers
Systems development consultant groups formed to serve as consultants to the professional programmers and systems analysts of an organization to improve their application development efforts.

Digital Computer
A computer that operates on digital data by performing arithmetic and logical operations on the data. Contrast with Analog Computer.

Digitizer
A device that is used to convert drawings and other graphic images on paper or other materials into digital data that are entered into a computer system.

Direct Access
A method of storage where each storage position has a unique address and can be individually accessed in approximately the same period of time without having to search through other storage positions. Same as Random Access. Contrast with Sequential Access.

Direct Access Storage Device (DASD)
A storage device that can directly access data to be stored or retrieved, for example, a magnetic disk unit.

Direct Data Organization
A method of data organization in which logical data elements are distributed randomly on or within the physical data medium. For example, logical data records distributed randomly on the surfaces of a magnetic disk file. Also called direct organization.

Direct Input/Output
Methods such as keyboard entry, voice input/output, and video displays that allow data to be input into or output from a computer system without the use of machine-readable media.

Disaster Recovery
Methods for ensuring that an organization recovers from natural and human-caused disasters that affect its computer-based operations.

Discussion Forum
An online network discussion platform to encourage and manage online text discussions over a period of time among members of special interest groups or project teams.

Distributed Databases
The concept of distributing databases or portions of a database at remote sites where the data are most frequently referenced. Sharing of data is made possible through a network that interconnects the distributed databases.

Distributed Processing
A form of decentralization of information processing made possible by a network of computers dispersed throughout an organization. Processing of user applications is accomplished by several computers interconnected by a telecommunications network, rather than relying on one large centralized computer facility or on the decentralized operation of several independent computers.

Document
(1) A medium on which data have been recorded for human use, such as a report or invoice. (2) In word processing, a generic term for text material such as letters, memos, reports, and so on.

Documentation
A collection of documents or information that describes a computer program, information system, or required data processing operations.

Downsizing
Moving to smaller computing platforms, such as from mainframe systems to networks of personal computers and servers.

Downtime
The time interval during which a device is malfunctioning or inoperative.

DSS Generator
A software package for a decision support system that contains modules for database, model, and dialogue management.

Duplex
In communications, pertaining to a simultaneous two-way independent transmission in both directions.

EBCDIC: Extended Binary Coded Decimal Interchange Code
An eight-bit code that is widely used by mainframe computers.

E-Business Decision Support
The use of Web-enabled DSS software tools by managers, employees, customers, suppliers, and other business partners of an internetworked E-business enterprise for customer relationship management, supply chain management, and other E-business applications.

E-Business Organization
An internetworked E-business enterprise whose organizational structure and roles have been reengineered to help it become a flexible, agile, customer-focused, value driven leader in E-commerce.

E-Business Planning
The process of developing a company's E-business vision, strategies, and goals, and how they will be supported by the company's information technology architecture and implemented by its E-business application development process.

E-Business Technology Management
Managing information technologies in an E-business enterprise by (1) the joint development and implementation of E-business and IT strategies by business and IT executives, (2) managing the research and implementation of new information technologies and the development of E-business applications, and (3) managing IT processes, professionals, and subunits within a company's IT organization and IS function.

Echo Check
A method of checking the accuracy of transmission of data in which the received data are returned to the sending device for comparison with the original data.

E-Commerce Marketplaces
Internet, intranet, and extranet websites and portals hosted by individual companies, consortiums of organizations, or third-party intermediaries providing electronic catalog, exchange, and auction markets to unite buyers and sellers to accomplish E-commerce transactions.

Economic Feasibility
Whether expected cost savings, increased revenue, increased profits, and reductions in required investment exceed the costs of developing and operating a proposed system.

EDI: Electronic Data Interchange
The automatic electronic exchange of business documents between the computers of different organizations.

Edit
To modify the form or format of data. For example: to insert or delete characters such as page numbers or decimal points.

Edit Report
A report that describes errors detected during processing.

EFT: Electronic Funds Transfer
The development of banking and payment systems that transfer funds electronically instead of using cash or paper documents such as checks.

Electronic Business (E-Business)
The use of Internet technologies to internetwork and empower business processes, electronic commerce, and enterprise communications and collaboration within a company and with its customers, suppliers, and other business stakeholders.

Electronic Commerce (E-Commerce)
The buying and selling, marketing and servicing, and delivery and payment of products, services, and information over the Internet, intranets, extranets, and other networks, between an internetworked enterprise and its prospects, customers, suppliers, and other business partners. Includes business-to-consumer (B2C), business-to-business (B2B), and consumer-to-consumer (C2C) E-commerce.

Electronic Communications Tools
Software that helps you communicate and collaborate with others by electronically sending messages, documents, and files in data, text, voice, or multimedia over the Internet, intranets, extranets, and other computer networks.

Electronic Conferencing Tools
Software that helps networked computer users share information and collaborate while working together on joint assignments, no matter where they are located.

Electronic Data Processing (EDP)
The use of electronic computers to process data automatically.

Electronic Document Management
An image processing technology in which an electronic document may consist of digitized voice notes and electronic graphics images, as well as digitized images of traditional documents.

Electronic Mail
Sending and receiving text messages between networked PCs over telecommunications networks. E-mail can also include data files, software, and multi-

media messages and documents as attachments.

Electronic Meeting Systems (EMS)
Using a meeting room with networked PCs, a large-screen projector, and EMS software to facilitate communication, collaboration, and group decision making in business meetings.

Electronic Payment Systems
Alternative cash or credit payment methods using various electronic technologies to pay for products and services in electronic commerce.

Electronic Spreadsheet Package
An application program used as a computerized tool for analysis, planning, and modeling that allows users to enter and manipulate data into an electronic worksheet of rows and columns.

Emulation
To imitate one system with another so that the imitating system accepts the same data, executes the same programs, and achieves the same results as the imitated system.

Encryption
To scramble data or convert it, prior to transmission, to a secret code that masks the meaning of the data to unauthorized recipients. Similar to enciphering.

End User
Anyone who uses an information system or the information it produces.

End User Computing Systems
Computer-based information systems that directly support both the operational and managerial applications of end users.

Enterprise Application Integration (EAI)
A cross-functional E-business application that integrates front-office applications like customer relationship management with back-office applications like enterprise resource management.

Enterprise Collaboration Systems
The use of groupware tools and the Internet, intranets, extranets, and other computer networks to support and enhance communication, coordination, collaboration, and resource sharing among teams and workgroups in an internetworked enterprise.

Enterprise Information Portal
A customized and personalized Web-based interface for corporate intranets that gives qualified users access to a variety of internal and external E-business and E-commerce applications, databases, software tools, and services.

Enterprise Model
A conceptual framework that defines the structures and relationships of business processes and data elements, as well as other planning structures, such as critical success factors, and organizational units.

Enterprise Resource Planning (ERP)
Integrated cross-functional software that reengineers manufacturing, distribution, finance, human resources and other basic business processes of a company to improve its efficiency, agility, and profitability.

Entity Relationship Diagram (ERD)
A data planning and systems development diagramming tool that models the relationships among the entities in a business process.

Entropy
The tendency of a system to lose a relatively stable state of equilibrium.

Ergonomics
The science and technology emphasizing the safety, comfort, and ease of use of human-operated machines such as computers. The goal of ergonomics is to produce systems that are user-friendly: safe, comfortable, and easy to use. Ergonomics is also called human factors engineering.

Exception Reports
Reports produced only when exceptional conditions occur, or reports produced periodically that contain information only about exceptional conditions.

Executive Information Systems (EIS)
An information system that provides strategic information tailored to the needs of executives and other decision makers.

Executive Support System (ESS)
An executive information system with additional capabilities, including data analysis, decision support, electronic mail, and personal productivity tools.

Expert System (ES)
A computer-based information system that uses its knowledge about a specific complex application area to act as an expert consultant to users. The system consists of a knowledge base and software modules that perform inferences on the knowledge and communicate answers to a user's questions.

Extranet
A network that links selected resources of a company with its customers, suppliers, and other business partners, using the Internet or private networks to link the organizations' intranets.

Facilities Management
The use of an external service organization to operate and manage the information processing facilities of an organization.

Fault Tolerant Systems
Computers that have multiple central processors, peripherals, and system software and that are able to continue operations even if there is a major hardware or software failure.

Faxing (Facsimile)
Transmitting and receiving images of documents over the telephone or computer networks using PCs or fax machines.

Feasibility Study
A preliminary study that investigates the information needs of end users and the objectives, constraints, basic resource requirements, cost/benefits, and feasibility of proposed projects.

Feedback
(1) Data or information concerning the components and operations of a system. (2) The use of part of the output of a system as input to the system.

Fiber Optics
The technology that uses cables consisting of very thin filaments of glass fibers that can conduct the light generated by lasers for high-speed telecommunications.

Field
A data element that consists of a grouping of characters that describe a particular attribute of an entity. For example: the name field or salary field of an employee.

Fifth Generation
The next generation of computing, which will provide computers that will be able to see, hear, talk, and think. This would depend on major advances in parallel processing, user input/output methods, and artificial intelligence.

File
A collection of related data records treated as a unit. Sometimes called a data set.

File Management
Controlling the creation, deletion, access, and use of files of data and programs.

Financial Management Systems
Information systems that support financial managers in the financing of a business and the allocation and control of financial resources. Include cash and securities management, capital budgeting, financial forecasting, and financial planning.

Fire Wall Computer
Computers, communications processors, and software that protect computer networks from intrusion by screening all network traffic and serving as a safe transfer point for access to and from other networks.

Firmware
The use of microprogrammed read-only memory circuits in place of hardwired logic circuitry. See also Microprogramming.

Floating Point
Pertaining to a number representation system in which each number is represented by two sets of digits. One set represents the significant digits or fixed-point "base" of the number, while the other set of digits represents the "exponent," which indicates the precision of the number.

Floppy Disk
A small plastic disk coated with iron oxide that resembles a small phonograph record enclosed in a protective envelope. It is a widely used form of magnetic disk media that provides a direct access storage capability for microcomputer systems.

Flowchart
A graphical representation in which symbols are used to represent operations, data, flow, logic, equipment, and so on. A program flowchart illustrates the structure and sequence of operations of a program, while a system flowchart illustrates the components and flows of information systems.

Foreground Processing
The automatic execution of the computer programs that have been designed to preempt the use of computing facilities. Contrast with Background Processing.

Format
The arrangement of data on a medium.

FORTRAN: FORmula TRANslation
A high-level programming language widely utilized to develop computer programs that perform mathematical computations for scientific, engineering, and selected business applications.

Forward Chaining
An inference strategy that reaches a conclusion by applying rules to facts to determine if any facts satisfy a rule's conditions in a particular situation.

Fourth-Generation Languages (4GL)
Programming languages that are easier to use than high-level languages like BASIC, COBOL, or FORTRAN. They are also known as nonprocedural, natural, or very-high-level languages.

Frame
A collection of knowledge about an entity or other concept consisting of a complex package of slots, that is, data values describing the characteristics or attributes of an entity.

Frame-Based Knowledge
Knowledge represented in the form of a hierarchy or network of frames.

Front-End Processor
Typically a smaller, general-purpose computer that is dedicated to handling data communications control functions in a communications network, thus relieving the host computer of these functions.

Functional Business Systems
Information systems within a business organization that support one of the traditional functions of business such as marketing, finance, or production. Functional business systems can be either operations or management information systems.

Functional Requirements
The information system capabilities required to meet the information needs of end users. Also called system requirements.

Fuzzy Logic Systems
Computer-based systems that can process data that are incomplete or only partially correct, that is, fuzzy data. Such systems can solve unstructured problems with incomplete knowledge, as humans do.

General-Purpose Application Programs
Programs that can perform information processing jobs for users from all application areas. For example, word processing programs, electronic spreadsheet programs, and graphics programs can be used by individuals for home, education, business, scientific, and many other purposes.

General-Purpose Computer
A computer that is designed to handle a wide variety of problems. Contrast with Special-Purpose Computer.

Generate
To produce a machine-language program for performing a specific data processing task based on parameters supplied by a programmer or user.

Genetic Algorithm
An application of artificial intelligence software that uses Darwinian (survival of the fittest) randomizing and other functions to simulate an evolutionary process that can yield increasingly better solutions to a problem.

Gigabyte
One billion bytes. More accurately, 2 to the 30th power, or 1,073,741,824 in decimal notation.

GIGO
A contraction of "Garbage In, Garbage Out," which emphasizes that information systems will produce erroneous and invalid output when provided with erroneous and invalid input data or instructions.

Global Company
A business that is driven by a global strategy so that all of its activities are planned and implemented in the context of a whole-world system.

Global E-Business Technology Management
Managing information technologies in a global E-business enterprise, amid the cultural, political, and geoeconomic challenges involved in developing E-business/IT strategies, global E-business and E-commerce applications portfolios, Internet-based technology platforms, and global data resource management policies.

Global Information Technology
The use of computer-based information systems and telecommunications networks using a variety of information technologics to support global business operations and management.

Globalization
Becoming a global enterprise by expanding into global markets, using global production facilities, forming alliances with global partners, and so on.

Goal-Seeking Analysis
Making repeated changes to selected variables until a chosen variable reaches a target value.

Graphical User Interface
A software interface that relies on icons, bars, buttons, boxes, and other images to initiate computer-based tasks for users.

Graphics
Pertaining to symbolic input or output from a computer system, such as lines, curves, and geometric shapes, using video display units or graphics plotters and printers.

Graphics Pen and Tablet
A device that allows an end user to draw or write on a pressure-sensitive tablet and have the handwriting or graphics digitized by the computer and accepted as input.

Graphics Software
A program that helps users generate graphics displays.

Group Decision Making
Decisions made by groups of people coming to an agreement on a particular issue.

Group Decision Support System (GDSS)
A decision support system that provides support for decision making by groups of people.

Group Support Systems (GSS)
An information system that enhances communication, coordination, collaboration, decision making, and group work activities of teams and workgroups.

Groupware
Software to support and enhance the communication, coordination, and collaboration among networked teams and workgroups, including software tools for electronic communications, electronic conferencing, and cooperative work management.

Hacking
(1) Obsessive use of a computer.
(2) The unauthorized access and use of computer systems.

Handshaking
Exchange of predetermined signals when a connection is established between two communications terminals.

Hard Copy
A data medium or data record that has a degree of permanence and that can be read by people or machines.

Hardware
(1) Machines and media. (2) Physical equipment, as opposed to computer programs or methods of use. (3) Mechanical, magnetic, electrical, electronic, or optical devices. Contrast with Software.

Hash Total
The sum of numbers in a data field that are not normally added, such as account numbers or other identification numbers. It is utilized as a control total, especially during input/output operations of batch processing systems.

Header Label
A machine-readable record at the beginning of a file containing data for file identification and control.

Heuristic
Pertaining to exploratory methods of problem solving in which solutions are discovered by evaluation of the progress made toward the final result. It is an exploratory trial-and-error approach guided by rules of thumb. Opposite of algorithmic.

Hierarchical Data Structure
A logical data structure in which the relationships between records form a hierarchy or tree structure. The relationships among records are one to many, since each data element is related only to one element above it.

High-Level Language
A programming language that utilizes macro instructions and statements that closely resemble human language or mathematical notation to describe the problem to be solved or the procedure to be used. Also called a compiler language.

Homeostasis
A relatively stable state of equilibrium of a system.

Host Computer
Typically a larger central computer that performs the major data processing tasks in a computer network.

Human Factors
Hardware and software capabilities that can affect the comfort, safety, ease of use, and user customization of computer-based information systems.

Human Information Processing
A conceptual framework about the human cognitive process that uses an information processing context to explain how humans capture, process, and use information.

Human Resource Information Systems (HRIS)
Information systems that support human resource management activities such as recruitment, selection and hiring, job placement and performance appraisals, and training and development.

Hybrid AI Systems
Systems that integrate several AI technologies, such as expert systems and neural networks.

Hypermedia
Documents containing multiple forms of media, including text, graphics, video, and sound, that can be interactively searched, like Hypertext.

Hypertext
Text in electronic form that has been indexed and linked (hyperlinks) by software in a variety of ways so that it can be randomly and interactively searched by a user.

Hypertext Markup Language (HTML)
A popular page description language for creating hypertext and hypermedia documents for World Wide Web and intranet websites.

Icon
A small figure on a video display that looks like a familiar office or other device such as a file folder (for storing a file) or a wastebasket (for deleting a file).

Image Processing
A computer-based technology that allows end users to electronically capture, store, process, and retrieve images that may include numeric data, text, handwriting, graphics, documents, and photographs. Image processing makes heavy use of optical scanning and optical disk technologies.

Impact Printers
Printers that form images on paper through the pressing of a printing element and an inked ribbon or roller against the face of a sheet of paper.

Index
An ordered reference list of the contents of a file or document together with keys or reference notations for identification or location of those contents.

Index Sequential
A method of data organization in which records are organized in sequential order and also referenced by an index. When utilized with direct access file devices, it is known as index sequential access method, or ISAM.

Inference Engine
The software component of an expert system, which processes the rules and facts related to a specific problem and makes associations and inferences resulting in recommended courses of action.

Infomediaries
Third-party market-maker companies who serve as intermediaries to bring buyers and sellers together by developing and hosting electronic catalog, exchange, and auction markets to accomplish E-commerce transactions.

Information
Information is data placed in a meaningful and useful context for an end user.

Information Appliance
Small Web-enabled microcomputer devices with specialized functions, such as hand-held PDAs, TV set-top boxes, game consoles, cellular and PCS phones, wired telephone appliances, and other Web-enabled home appliances.

Information Architecture
A conceptual framework that defines the basic structure, content, and relationships of the organizational databases that provide the data needed to support the basic business processes of an organization.

Information Center
A support facility for the end users of an organization. It allows users to learn to develop their own application programs and to accomplish their own information processing tasks. End users are provided with hardware support, software support, and people support (trained user consultants).

Information Float
The time when a document is in transit between the sender and receiver, and thus unavailable for any action or response.

Information Processing
A concept that covers both the traditional concept of processing numeric and alphabetic data, and the processing of text, images, and voices. It emphasizes that the production of information products for users should be the focus of processing activities.

Information Quality
The degree to which information has content, form, and time characteristics that give it value to specific end users.

Information Resource Management (IRM)
A management concept that views data, information, and computer resources (computer hardware, software, networks, and personnel) as valuable organizational resources that should be efficiently, economically, and effectively managed for the benefit of the entire organization.

Information Retrieval
The methods and procedures for recovering specific information from stored data.

Information Superhighway
An advanced high-speed Internet-like network that connects individuals, households, businesses, government agencies, libraries, schools, universities, and other institutions with interactive voice, video, data, and multimedia communications.

Information System
(1) A set of people, procedures, and resources that collects, transforms, and disseminates information in an organization. (2) A system that accepts data resources as input and processes them into information products as output.

Information System Model
A conceptual framework that views an information system as a system that uses the resources of hardware (machines and media), software (programs and procedures), people (users and specialists), and networks (communications media and network support) to perform input, processing, output, storage, and control activities that transform data resources (databases and knowledge bases) into information products.

Information System Specialist
A person whose occupation is related to the providing of information system services. For example: a systems analyst, programmer, or computer operator.

Information Systems Development
See Systems Development.

Information Technology (IT)
Hardware, software, telecommunications, database management, and other information processing technologies used in computer-based information systems.

Information Technology Architecture
A conceptual blueprint that specifies the components and interrelationships of a company's technology infrastructure, data resources, applications architecture, and IT organization.

Information Theory
The branch of learning concerned with the likelihood of accurate transmission or communication of messages subject to transmission failure, distortion, and noise.

Input
Pertaining to a device, process, or channel involved in the insertion of data into a data processing system. Opposite of Output.

Input/Output (I/O)
Pertaining to either input or output, or both.

Input/Output Interface Hardware
Devices such as I/O ports, I/O buses, buffers, channels, and input/output control units, which assist the CPU in its input/output assignments. These devices make it possible for modern computer systems to perform input, output, and processing functions simultaneously.

Inquiry Processing
Computer processing that supports the real-time interrogation of online files and databases by end users.

Instruction
A grouping of characters that specifies the computer operation to be performed.

Intangible Benefits and Costs
The nonquantifiable benefits and costs of a proposed solution or system.

Integrated Circuit
A complex microelectronic circuit consisting of interconnected circuit elements that cannot be disassembled because they are placed on or within a "continuous substrate" such as a silicon chip.

Integrated Packages
Software that combines the ability to do several general-purpose applications (such as word processing, electronic spreadsheet, and graphics) into one program.

Intelligent Agent
A special-purpose knowledge-based system that serves as a software surrogate to accomplish specific tasks for end users.

Intelligent Terminal
A terminal with the capabilities of a microcomputer that can thus perform many data processing and other functions without accessing a larger computer.

Interactive Marketing
A dynamic collaborative process of creating, purchasing, and improving products and services that builds close relationships between a business and its customers, using a variety of services on the Internet, intranets, and extranets.

Interactive Processing
A type of real-time processing in which users can interact with a computer on a real-time basis.

Interactive Video
Computer-based systems that integrate image processing with text, audio, and video processing technologies, which makes interactive multimedia presentations possible.

Interface
A shared boundary, such as the boundary between two systems. For example, the boundary between a computer and its peripheral devices.

Internet
The Internet is a rapidly growing network of thousands of business, educational, and research networks connecting millions of computers and their users in over 100 countries.

Internetwork Processor
Communications processors used by local area networks to interconnect them with other local area and wide area networks. Examples include switches, routers, hubs, and gateways.

Internetworked E-Business Enterprise
A business that uses the Internet, intranets, extranets, and other computer networks to support electronic commerce and other electronic business processes, decision making, and team and workgroup collaboration within the enterprise and among its customers, suppliers, and other business partners.

Internetworks
Interconnected local area and wide area networks.

Interoperability
Being able to accomplish end user applications using different types of computer systems, operating systems, and application software, interconnected by different types of local and wide area networks.

Interorganizational Information Systems
Information systems that interconnect an organization with other organizations, such as a business and its customers and suppliers.

Interpreter
A computer program that translates and executes each source language statement before translating and executing the next one.

Interrupt
A condition that causes an interruption in a processing operation during which another task is performed. At the conclusion of this new assignment, control may be transferred back to the point where the original processing operation was interrupted or to other tasks with a higher priority.

Intranet
An Internet-like network within an organization. Web browser software provides easy access to internal websites established by business units, teams, and individuals, and other network resources and applications.

Inverted File
A file that references entities by their attributes.

IT Architecture
A conceptual design for the implementation of information technology in an organization, including its hardware, software, and network technology platforms, data resources, application portfolio, and IS organization.

Iterative
Pertaining to the repeated execution of a series of steps.

Java
An object-oriented programming language designed for programming real-time, interactive Web-based applications in the form of applets for use on clients and servers on the Internet, intranets, and extranets.

Job
A specified group of tasks prescribed as a unit of work for a computer.

Job Control Language (JCL)
A language for communicating with the operating system of a computer to identify a job and describe its requirements.

Joystick
A small lever set in a box used to move the cursor on the computer's display screen.

K
An abbreviation for the prefix kilo-, which is 1,000 in decimal notation. When referring to storage capacity it is equivalent to 2 to the 10th power, or 1,024 in decimal notation.

Key
One or more fields within a data record that are used to identify it or control its use.

Keyboarding
Using the keyboard of a microcomputer or computer terminal.

Knowledge Base
A computer-accessible collection of knowledge about a subject in a variety of forms, such as facts and rules of inference, frames, and objects.

Knowledge-Based Information System
An information system that adds a knowledge base to the database and other components found in other types of computer-based information systems.

Knowledge Engineer
A specialist who works with experts to capture the knowledge they possess in order to develop a knowledge base for expert systems and other knowledge-based systems.

Knowledge Management
Organizing and sharing the diverse forms of business information created within an organization. Includes managing project and enterprise document libraries, discussion databases, intranet website databases, and other types of knowledge bases.

Knowledge Workers
People whose primary work activities include creating, using, and distributing information.

Language Translator Program
A program that converts the programming language instructions in a computer program into machine language code. Major types include assemblers, compilers, and interpreters.

Large-Scale Integration (LSI)
A method of constructing electronic circuits in which thousands of circuits can be placed on a single semiconductor chip.

Legacy Systems
The older, traditional mainframe-based business information systems of an organization.

Light Pen
A photoelectronic device that allows data to be entered or altered on the face of a video display terminal.

Liquid Crystal Displays (LCDs)
Electronic visual displays that form characters by applying an electrical charge to selected silicon crystals.

List Organization
A method of data organization that uses indexes and pointers to allow for nonsequential retrieval.

List Processing
A method of processing data in the form of lists.

Local Area Network (LAN)
A communications network that typically connects computers, terminals, and other computerized devices within a limited physical area such as an office, building, manufacturing plant, or other work site.

Locking in Customers and Suppliers
Building valuable relationships with customers and suppliers that deter them from abandoning a firm for its competitors or intimidating it into accepting less-profitable relationships.

Logical Data Elements
Data elements that are independent of the physical data media on which they are recorded.

Logical System Design
Developing general specifications for how basic information systems activities can meet end user requirements.

Loop
A sequence of instructions in a computer program that is executed repeatedly until a terminal condition prevails.

Machine Cycle
The timing of a basic CPU operation as determined by a fixed number of electrical pulses emitted by the CPU's timing circuitry or internal clock.

Machine Language
A programming language where instructions are expressed in the binary code of the computer.

Macro Instruction
An instruction in a source language that is equivalent to a specified sequence of machine instructions.

Mag Stripe Card
A plastic wallet-size card with a strip of magnetic tape on one surface; widely used for credit/debit cards.

Magnetic Disk
A flat circular plate with a magnetic surface on which data can be stored by selective magnetization of portions of the curved surface.

Magnetic Ink
An ink that contains particles of iron oxide that can be magnetized and detected by magnetic sensors.

Magnetic Ink Character Recognition (MICR)
The machine recognition of characters printed with magnetic ink. Primarily used for check processing by the banking industry.

Magnetic Tape
A plastic tape with a magnetic surface on which data can be stored by selective magnetization of portions of the surface.

Mainframe
A larger-size computer system, typically with a separate central processing unit, as distinguished from microcomputer and minicomputer systems.

Management Information System (MIS)
A management support system that produces prespecified reports, displays, and responses on a periodic, exception, demand, or push reporting basis.

Management Support System (MSS)
An information system that provides information to support managerial decision making. More specifically, an information-reporting system, executive information system, or decision support system.

Managerial End User
A manager, entrepreneur, or managerial-level professional who personally uses information systems. Also, the manager of the department or other organizational unit that relies on information systems.

Managerial Roles
Management as the performance of a variety of interpersonal, information, and decision roles.

Manual Data Processing
Data processing that requires continual human operation and intervention and that utilizes simple data processing tools such as paper forms, pencils, and filing cabinets.

Manufacturing Information Systems
Information systems that support the planning, control, and accomplishment of manufacturing processes. This includes concepts such as computer-integrated manufacturing (CIM) and technologies such as computer-aided manufacturing (CAM) or computer-aided design (CAD).

Marketing Information Systems
Information systems that support the planning, control, and transaction processing required for the accomplishment of marketing activities, such as sales management, advertising, and promotion.

Mass Storage
Secondary storage devices with extra-large storage capacities such as magnetic or optical disks.

Master File
A data file containing relatively permanent information that is utilized as an authoritative reference and is usually updated periodically. Contrast with Transaction File.

Mathematical Model
A mathematical representation of a process, device, or concept.

Media
All tangible objects on which data are recorded.

Megabyte
One million bytes. More accurately, 2 to the 20th power, or 1,048,576 in decimal notation.

Memory
Same as Primary Storage.

Menu
A displayed list of items (usually the names of alternative applications, files, or activities) from which an end user makes a selection.

Menu Driven
A characteristic of interactive computing systems that provides menu displays and operator prompting to assist an end user in performing a particular job.

Metadata
Data about data; data describing the structure, data elements, interrelationships, and other characteristics of a database.

Microcomputer
A very small computer, ranging in size from a "computer on a chip" to hand-held, laptop, and desktop units, and servers.

Micrographics
The use of microfilm, microfiche, and other microforms to record data in greatly reduced form.

Microprocessor
A microcomputer central processing unit (CPU) on a chip. Without input/output or primary storage capabilities in most types.

Microprogram
A small set of elementary control instructions called microinstructions or microcode.

Microprogramming
The use of special software (microprograms) to perform the functions of special hardware (electronic control circuitry). Microprograms stored in a read-only storage module of the control unit interpret the machine language instructions of a computer program and decode them into elementary microinstructions, which are then executed.

Microsecond
A millionth of a second.

Middleware
Software that helps diverse networked computer systems work together, thus promoting their interoperability.

Midrange Computer
A computer category between microcomputers and mainframes. Examples include minicomputers, network servers, and technical workstations.

Millisecond
A thousandth of a second.

Minicomputer
A type of midrange computer.

Model Base
An organized software collection of conceptual, mathematical, and logical models that express business relationships, computational routines, or analytical techniques.

Modem
(MOdulator-DEModulator) A device that converts the digital signals from input/output devices into appropriate frequencies at a transmission terminal and converts them back into digital signals at a receiving terminal.

Monitor
Software or hardware that observes, supervises, controls, or verifies the operations of a system.

Mouse
A small device that is electronically connected to a computer and is moved by hand on a flat surface in order to move the cursor on a video screen in the same direction. Buttons on the mouse allow users to issue commands and make responses or selections.

Multidimensional Structure
A database model that uses multidimensional structures (such as cubes or

cubes within cubes) to store data and relationships between data.

Multimedia Presentations
Providing information using a variety of media, including text and graphics displays, voice and other audio, photographs, and video segments.

Multiplex
To interleave or simultaneously transmit two or more messages on a single channel.

Multiplexer
An electronic device that allows a single communications channel to carry simultaneous data transmissions from many terminals.

Multiprocessing
Pertaining to the simultaneous execution of two or more instructions by a computer or computer network.

Multiprocessor Computer Systems
Computer systems that use a multiprocessor architecture in the design of their central processing units. This includes the use of support microprocessors and multiple instruction processors, including parallel processor designs.

Multiprogramming
Pertaining to the concurrent execution of two or more programs by a computer by interleaving their execution.

Multitasking
The concurrent use of the same computer to accomplish several different information processing tasks. Each task may require the use of a different program, or the concurrent use of the same copy of a program by several users.

Nanosecond
One billionth of a second.

Natural Language
A programming language that is very close to human language. Also called very-high-level language.

Network
An interconnected system of computers, terminals, and communications channels and devices.

Network Architecture
A master plan designed to promote an open, simple, flexible, and efficient telecommunications environment through the use of standard protocols, standard communications hardware and software interfaces, and the design of a standard multilevel telecommunications interface between end users and computer systems.

Network Computer
A low-cost networked microcomputer with no or minimal disk storage, which depends on Internet or intranet servers for its operating system and Web browser, Java-enabled application software, and data access and storage.

Network Computing
A network-centric view of computing in which "the network is the computer," that is, the view that computer networks are the central computing resource of any computing environment.

Network Data Structure
A logical data structure that allows many-to-many relationships among data records. It allows entry into a database at multiple points, because any data element or record can be related to many other data elements.

Neural Networks
Computer processors or software whose architecture is based on the human brain's meshlike neuron structure. Neural networks can process many pieces of information simultaneously and can learn to recognize patterns and programs themselves to solve related problems on their own.

Node
A terminal point in a communications network.

Nonprocedural Languages
Programming languages that allow users and professional programmers to specify the results they want without specifying how to solve the problem.

Numerical Control
Automatic control of a machine process by a computer that makes use of numerical data, generally introduced as the operation is in process. Also called machine control.

Object
A data element that includes both data and the methods or processes that act on those data.

Object-Based Knowledge
Knowledge represented as a network of objects.

Object-Oriented Language
An object-oriented programming (OOP) language used to develop programs that create and use objects to perform information processing tasks.

Object Program
A compiled or assembled program composed of executable machine instructions. Contrast with Source Program.

OEM: Original Equipment Manufacturer
A firm that manufactures and sells computers by assembling components produced by other hardware manufacturers.

Office Automation (OA)
The use of computer-based information systems that collect, process, store, and transmit electronic messages, documents, and other forms of office communications among individuals, workgroups, and organizations.

Offline
Pertaining to equipment or devices not under control of the central processing unit.

Online
Pertaining to equipment or devices under control of the central processing unit.

Online Analytical Processing (OLAP)
A capability of some management, decision support, and executive information systems that supports interactive examination and manipulation of large amounts of data from many perspectives.

Online Transaction Processing (OLTP)
A real-time transaction processing system.

Open Systems
Information systems that use common standards for hardware, software, applications, and networking to create a computing environment that allows easy access by end users and their networked computer systems.

Operand
That which is operated upon. That part of a computer instruction that is identified by the address part of the instruction.

Operating Environment
Software packages or modules that add a graphics-based interface between end users, the operating system, and their application programs, and that may also provide a multitasking capability.

Operating System
The main control program of a computer system. It is a system of programs that controls the execution of computer programs and may provide scheduling, debugging, input/output control, system accounting, compilation, storage assignment, data management, and related services.

Operation Code
A code that represents specific operations to be performed upon the operands in a computer instruction.

Operational Feasibility
The willingness and ability of management, employees, customers, and suppliers to operate, use, and support a proposed system.

Operations Support System (OSS)
An information system that collects, processes, and stores data generated by the operations systems of an organization and produces data and information for input into a management information system or for the control of an operations system.

Operations System
A basic subsystem of the business firm that constitutes its input, processing, and output components. Also called a physical system.

Opportunity
A basic condition that presents the potential for desirable results in an organization or other system.

Optical Character Recognition (OCR)
The machine identification of printed characters through the use of light-sensitive devices.

Optical Disks
A secondary storage medium using CD (compact disk) and DVD (digital versatile disk) technologies to read tiny spots on plastic disks. The disks are currently capable of storing billions of characters of information.

Optical Scanner
A device that optically scans characters or images and generates their digital representations.

Optimization Analysis
Finding an optimum value for selected variables in a mathematical model, given certain constraints.

Organizational Feasibility
How well a proposed information system supports the objectives of an organization's strategic plan for information systems.

Output
Pertaining to a device, process, or channel involved with the transfer of data or information out of an information processing system. Opposite of Input.

Outsourcing
Turning over all or part of an organization's information systems operation to outside contractors, known as systems integrators or service providers.

Packet
A group of data and control information in a specified format that is transmitted as an entity.

Packet Switching
A data transmission process that transmits addressed packets such that a channel is occupied only for the duration of transmission of the packet.

Page
A segment of a program or data, usually of fixed length.

Paging
A process that automatically and continually transfers pages of programs and data between primary storage and direct access storage devices. It provides computers with multiprogramming and virtual memory capabilities.

Parallel Processing
Executing many instructions at the same time, that is, in parallel. Performed by advanced computers using many instruction processors organized in clusters or networks.

Parity Bit
A check bit appended to an array of binary digits to make the sum of all the binary digits, including the check bit, always odd or always even.

Pascal
A high-level, general-purpose, structured programming language named after Blaise Pascal. It was developed by Niklaus Wirth of Zurich in 1968.

Pattern Recognition
The identification of shapes, forms, or configurations by automatic means.

PCM: Plug-Compatible Manufacturer
A firm that manufactures computer equipment that can be plugged into existing computer systems without requiring additional hardware or software interfaces.

Peer-To-Peer Network (P2P)
A computing environment where end user computers connect, communicate, and collaborate directly with each other via the Internet or other telecommunications network links.

Pen-Based Computers
Tablet-style microcomputers that recognize handwriting and hand drawing done by a pen-shaped device on their pressure-sensitive display screens.

Performance Monitor
A software package that monitors the processing of computer system jobs, helps develop a planned schedule of computer operations that can optimize computer system performance, and produces detailed statistics that are used for computer system capacity planning and control.

Periodic Reports
Providing information to managers using a prespecified format designed to provide information on a regularly scheduled basis.

Peripheral Devices
In a computer system, any unit of equipment, distinct from the central processing unit, that provides the system with input, output, or storage capabilities.

Personal Digital Assistant (PDA)
Hand-held microcomputer devices that enable you to manage information such as appointments, to-do lists, and sales contacts, send and receive E-mail, access the Web, and exchange such information with your desktop PC or network server.

Personal Information Manager (PIM)
A software package that helps end users store, organize, and retrieve text and numerical data in the form of notes, lists, memos, and a variety of other forms.

Physical System Design
Design of the user interface methods and products, database structures, and processing and control procedures for a proposed information system, including hardware, software, and personnel specifications.

Picosecond
One trillionth of a second.

Plasma Display
Output devices that generate a visual display with electrically charged particles of gas trapped between glass plates.

Plotter
A hard-copy output device that produces drawings and graphical displays on paper or other materials.

Pointer
A data element associated with an index, a record, or other set of data that contains the address of a related record.

Pointing Devices
Devices that allow end users to issue commands or make choices by moving a cursor on the display screen.

Pointing Stick
A small buttonlike device on a keyboard that moves the cursor on the screen in the direction of the pressure placed upon it.

Point-of-Sale (POS) Terminal
A computer terminal used in retail stores that serves the function of a cash register as well as collecting sales data and performing other data processing functions.

Port
(1) Electronic circuitry that provides a connection point between the CPU and input/output devices. (2) A connection point for a communications line on a CPU or other front-end device.

Postimplementation Review
Monitoring and evaluating the results of an implemented solution or system.

Presentation Graphics
Using computer-generated graphics to enhance the information presented in reports and other types of presentations.

Prespecified Reports
Reports whose format is specified in advance to provide managers with information periodically, on an exception basis, or on demand.

Private Branch Exchange (PBX)
A switching device that serves as an interface between the many telephone lines within a work area and the local telephone company's main telephone lines or trunks. Computerized PBXs can handle the switching of both voice and data.

Problem
A basic condition that is causing undesirable results in an organization or other system.

Procedure-Oriented Language
A programming language designed for the convenient expression of procedures used in the solution of a wide class of problems.

Procedures
Sets of instructions used by people to complete a task.

Process Control
The use of a computer to control an ongoing physical process, such as petrochemical production.

Process Design
The design of the programs and procedures needed by a proposed information system, including detailed program specifications and procedures.

Processor
A hardware device or software system capable of performing operations upon data.

Program
A set of instructions that cause a computer to perform a particular task.

Programmed Decision
A decision that can be automated by basing it on a decision rule that outlines the steps to take when confronted with the need for a specific decision.

Programmer
A person mainly involved in designing, writing, and testing computer programs.

Programming
The design, writing, and testing of a program.

Programming Language
A language used to develop the instructions in computer programs.

Programming Tools
Software packages or modules that provide editing and diagnostic capabilities and other support facilities to assist the programming process.

Project Management
Managing the accomplishment of an information system development project according to a specific project plan, in order that a project is completed on time, and within its budget, and meets its design objectives.

Prompt
Messages that assist a user in performing a particular job. This would include error messages, correction suggestions, questions, and other messages that guide an end user.

Protocol
A set of rules and procedures for the control of communications in a communications network.

Prototype
A working model. In particular, a working model of an information system that includes tentative versions of user input and output, databases and files, control methods, and processing routines.

Prototyping
The rapid development and testing of working models, or prototypes, of new information system applications in an interactive, iterative process involving both systems analysts and end users.

Pseudocode
An informal design language of structured programming that expresses the processing logic of a program module in ordinary human language phrases.

Pull Marketing
Marketing methods that rely on the use of Web browsers by end users to access marketing materials and resources at Internet, intranet, and extranet websites.

Push Marketing
Marketing methods that rely on Web broadcasting software to push marketing information and other marketing materials to end users' computers.

Quality Assurance
Methods for ensuring that information systems are free from errors and fraud and provide information products of high quality.

Query Language
A high-level, humanlike language provided by a database management system that enables users to easily extract data and information from a database.

Queue
(1) A waiting line formed by items in a system waiting for service. (2) To arrange in or form a queue.

RAID
Redundant array of independent disks. Magnetic disk units that house many interconnected microcomputer hard disk drives, thus providing large, fault-tolerant storage capacities.

Random Access
Same as Direct Access. Contrast with Sequential Access.

Random Access Memory (RAM)
One of the basic types of semiconductor memory used for temporary storage of data or programs during processing. Each memory position can be directly sensed (read) or changed (write) in the same length of time, irrespective of its location on the storage medium.

Reach and Range Analysis
A planning framework that contrasts a firm's ability to use its IT platform to reach its stakeholders, with the range of information products and services that can be provided or shared through IT.

Read Only Memory (ROM)
A basic type of semiconductor memory used for permanent storage. Can only be read, not "written," that is, changed. Variations are Programmable Read Only Memory (PROM) and Erasable Programmable Read Only Memory (EPROM).

Real-Time
Pertaining to the performance of data processing during the actual time a business or physical process transpires, in order that results of the data processing can be used to support the completion of the process.

Real-Time Processing
Data processing in which data are processed immediately rather than periodically. Also called online processing. Contrast with Batch Processing.

Record
A collection of related data fields treated as a unit.

Reduced Instruction Set Computer (RISC)
A CPU architecture that optimizes processing speed by the use of a smaller number of basic machine instructions than traditional CPU designs.

Redundancy
In information processing, the repetition of part or all of a message to

increase the chance that the correct information will be understood by the recipient.

Register
A device capable of storing a specified amount of data such as one word.

Relational Data Structure
A logical data structure in which all data elements within the database are viewed as being stored in the form of simple tables. DBMS packages based on the relational model can link data elements from various tables as long as the tables share common data elements.

Remote Access
Pertaining to communication with the data processing facility by one or more stations that are distant from that facility.

Remote Job Entry (RJE)
Entering jobs into a batch processing system from a remote facility.

Report Generator
A feature of database management system packages that allows an end user to quickly specify a report format for the display of information retrieved from a database.

Reprographics
Copying and duplicating technology and methods.

Resource Management
An operating system function that controls the use of computer system resources such as primary storage, secondary storage, CPU processing time, and input/output devices by other system software and application software packages.

Robotics
The technology of building machines (robots) with computer intelligence and humanlike physical capabilities.

Routine
An ordered set of instructions that may have some general or frequent use.

RPG: Report Program Generator
A problem-oriented language that utilizes a generator to construct programs that produce reports and perform other data processing tasks.

Rule
Statements that typically take the form of a premise and a conclusion such as If-Then rules: If (condition), Then (conclusion).

Rule-Based Knowledge
Knowledge represented in the form of rules and statements of fact.

Scalability
The ability of hardware or software to handle the processing demands of a wide range of end users, transactions, queries, and other information processing requirements.

Scenario Approach
A planning approach where managers, employees, and planners create scenarios of what an organization will be like three to five years or more into the future, and identify the role IT can play in those scenarios.

Schema
An overall conceptual or logical view of the relationships between the data in a database.

Scientific Method
An analytical methodology that involves (1) recognizing phenomena, (2) formulating a hypothesis about the causes or effects of the phenomena, (3) testing the hypothesis through experimentation, (4) evaluating the results of such experiments, and (5) drawing conclusions about the hypothesis.

Secondary Storage
Storage that supplements the primary storage of a computer. Synonymous with Auxiliary Storage.

Sector
A subdivision of a track on a magnetic disk surface.

Security Codes
Passwords, identification codes, account codes, and other codes that limit the access and use of computer-based system resources to authorized users.

Security Management
Protecting the accuracy, integrity, and safety of the processes and resources of an internetworked E-business enterprise against computer crime, accidental or malicious destruction, and natural disasters, using security measures such as encryption, fire walls, antivirus software, fault-tolerant computers, and security monitors.

Security Monitor
A software package that monitors the use of a computer system and protects its resources from unauthorized use, fraud, and vandalism.

Semiconductor Memory
Microelectronic storage circuitry etched on tiny chips of silicon or other semiconducting material. The primary storage of most modern computers consists of microelectronic semiconductor storage chips for random access memory (RAM) and read only memory (ROM).

Semistructured Decisions
Decisions involving procedures that can be partially prespecified, but not enough to lead to a definite recommended decision.

Sensitivity Analysis
Observing how repeated changes to a single variable affect other variables in a mathematical model.

Sequential Access
A sequential method of storing and retrieving data from a file. Contrast with Random Access and Direct Access.

Sequential Data Organization
Organizing logical data elements according to a prescribed sequence.

Serial
Pertaining to the sequential or consecutive occurrence of two or more related activities in a single device or channel.

Server
(1) A computer that supports applications and telecommunications in a network, as well as the sharing of peripheral devices, software, and databases among the workstations in the network. (2) Versions of software for installation on network servers designed to control and support applications on client microcomputers in client/server networks. Examples include multiuser network operating systems and specialized software for running Internet, intranet, and extranet Web applications, such as electronic commerce and enterprise collaboration.

Service Bureau
A firm offering computer and data processing services. Also called a computer service center.

Smart Products
Industrial and consumer products, with "intelligence" provided by built-in microcomputers or microprocessors that significantly improve the performance and capabilities of such products.

Software
Computer programs and procedures concerned with the operation of an information system. Contrast with Hardware.

Software Package
A computer program supplied by computer manufacturers, independent software companies, or other computer users. Also known as canned programs, proprietary software, or packaged programs.

Software Piracy
Unauthorized copying of software.

Software Suites
A combination of individual software packages that share a common graphical user interface and are designed for easy transfer of data between applications.

Solid State
Pertaining to devices such as transistors and diodes whose operation depends on the control of electric or magnetic phenomena in solid materials.

Source Data Automation
The use of automated methods of data entry that attempt to reduce or eliminate many of the activities, people, and data media required by traditional data entry methods.

Source Document
A document that is the original formal record of a transaction, such as a purchase order or sales invoice.

Source Program
A computer program written in a language that is subject to a translation process. Contrast with Object Program.

Special-Purpose Computer
A computer designed to handle a restricted class of problems. Contrast with General-Purpose Computer.

Speech Recognition
Direct conversion of spoken data into electronic form suitable for entry into a computer system. Also called voice data entry.

Spooling
Simultaneous peripheral operation online. Storing input data from low-speed devices temporarily on high-speed secondary storage units, which can be quickly accessed by the CPU. Also, writing output data at high speeds onto magnetic tape or disk units from which it can be transferred to slow-speed devices such as a printer.

Stage Analysis
A planning process in which the information system needs of an organization are based on an analysis of its current stage in the growth cycle of the organization and its use of information systems technology.

Standards
Measures of performance developed to evaluate the progress of a system toward its objectives.

Storage
Pertaining to a device into which data can be entered, in which they can be held, and from which they can be retrieved at a later time. Same as Memory.

Strategic Information Systems
Information systems that provide a firm with competitive products and services that give it a strategic advantage over its competitors in the marketplace. Also, information systems that promote business innovation, improve business processes, and build strategic information resources for a firm.

Strategic Opportunities Matrix
A planning framework that uses a matrix to help identify opportunities with strategic business potential, as well as a firm's ability to exploit such opportunities with IT.

Structure Chart
A design and documentation technique to show the purpose and relationships of the various modules in a program.

Structured Decisions
Decisions that are structured by the decision procedures or decision rules developed for them. They involve situations where the procedures to follow when a decision is needed can be specified in advance.

Structured Programming
A programming methodology that uses a top-down program design and a limited number of control structures in a program to create highly structured modules of program code.

Structured Query Language (SQL)
A query language that is becoming a standard for advanced database management system packages. A query's basic form is SELECT . . . FROM . . . WHERE.

Subroutine
A routine that can be part of another program routine.

Subschema
A subset or transformation of the logical view of the database schema that is required by a particular user application program.

Subsystem
A system that is a component of a larger system.

Supercomputer
A special category of large computer systems that are the most powerful available. They are designed to solve massive computational problems.

Superconductor
Materials that can conduct electricity with almost no resistance. This allows the development of extremely fast and small electronic circuits. Formerly only possible at supercold temperatures near absolute zero. Recent developments promise superconducting materials near room temperature.

Supply Chain
The network of business processes and interrelationships among businesses that are needed to build, sell, and deliver a product to its final customer.

Supply Chain Management
Integrating management practices and information technology to optimize information and product flows among the processes and business partners within a supply chain.

Switch
(1) A device or programming technique for making a selection. (2) A computer that controls message switching among the computers and terminals in a telecommunications network.

Switching Costs
The costs in time, money, effort, and inconvenience that it would take a customer or supplier to switch its business to a firm's competitors.

Synchronous
A characteristic in which each event, or the performance of any basic operation, is constrained to start on, and usually to keep in step with, signals from a timing clock. Contrast with Asynchronous.

System
(1) A group of interrelated or interacting elements forming a unified whole. (2) A group of interrelated components working together toward a common goal by accepting inputs and producing outputs in an organized transformation process. (3) An assembly of methods, procedures, or techniques unified by regulated interaction to form an organized whole. (4) An organized collection of people, machines, and methods required to accomplish a set of specific functions.

System Flowchart
A graphic diagramming tool used to show the flow of information processing activities as data are processed by people and devices.

System Software
Programs that control and support operations of a computer system. System software includes a variety of programs, such as operating systems, database management systems, communications control programs, service and utility programs, and programming language translators.

System Specifications
The product of the systems design stage. It consists of specifications for the hardware, software, facilities, personnel, databases, and the user interface of a proposed information system.

System Support Programs
Programs that support the operations, management, and users of a computer system by providing a variety of support services. Examples are system utilities and performance monitors.

Systems Analysis
(1) Analyzing in detail the components and requirements of a system. (2) Analyzing in detail the information needs of an organization, the characteristics and components of presently utilized information systems, and the functional requirements of proposed information systems.

Systems Approach
A systematic process of problem solving that defines problems and opportunities in a systems context. Data are gathered describing the problem or opportunity, and alternative solutions are identified and evaluated. Then the best solution is selected and implemented, and its success evaluated.

Systems Design
Deciding how a proposed information system will meet the information needs of end users. Includes logical and physical design activities, and user interface, data, and process design activities that produce system specifications that satisfy the system requirements developed in the systems analysis stage.

Systems Development
(1) Conceiving, designing, and implementing a system. (2) Developing information systems by a process of investigation, analysis, design, implementation, and maintenance. Also called the systems development life cycle (SDLC), information systems development, or application development.

Systems Development Tools
Graphical, textual, and computer-aided tools and techniques used to help analyze, design, and document the development of an information system. Typically used to represent (1) the components and flows of a system, (2) the user interface, (3) data attributes and relationships, and (4) detailed system processes.

Systems Implementation
The stage of systems development in which hardware and software are acquired, developed, and installed; the system is tested and documented; people are trained to operate and use the system; and an organization converts to the use of a newly developed system.

Systems Investigation
The screening, selection, and preliminary study of a proposed information system solution to a business problem.

Systems Maintenance
The monitoring, evaluating, and modifying of a system to make desirable or necessary improvements.

Systems Thinking
Recognizing systems, subsystems, components of systems, and system interrelationships in a situation. Also known as a systems context or a systemic view of a situation.

Tangible Benefits and Costs
The quantifiable benefits and costs of a proposed solution or system.

Task and Project Management
Managing team and workgroup projects by scheduling, tracking, and charting the completion status of tasks within a project.

Task Management
A basic operating system function that manages the accomplishment of the computing tasks of users by a computer system.

TCP/IP
Transmission control protocol/Internet protocol. A suite of telecommunications network protocols used by the Internet, intranets, and extranets that has become a de facto network architecture standard for many companies.

Technical Feasibility
Whether reliable hardware and software capable of meeting the needs of a proposed system can be acquired or developed by an organization in the required time.

Technology Management
The organizational responsibility to identify, introduce, and monitor the assimilation of new information system technologies into organizations.

Telecommunications
Pertaining to the transmission of signals over long distances, including not only data communications but also the transmission of images and voices using radio, television, and other communications technologies.

Telecommunications Channel
The part of a telecommunications network that connects the message source with the message receiver. It includes the hardware, software, and media used to connect one network location to another for the purpose of transmitting and receiving information.

Telecommunications Control Program
A computer program that controls and supports the communications between the computers and terminals in a telecommunications network.

Telecommunications Controller
A data communications interface device (frequently a special-purpose mini- or microcomputer) that can control a telecommunications network containing many terminals.

Telecommunications Monitors
Computer programs that control and support the communications between the computers and terminals in a telecommunications network.

Telecommunications Processors
Internetwork processors such as switches and routers, and other devices such as multiplexers and communications controllers that allow a communications channel to carry simultaneous data transmissions from many terminals. They may also perform error monitoring, diagnostics and correction, modulation-demodulation, data compression, data coding and decoding, message switching, port contention, and buffer storage.

Telecommuting
The use of telecommunications to replace commuting to work from one's home.

Teleconferencing
The use of video communications to allow business conferences to be held with participants who are scattered across a country, continent, or the world.

Telephone Tag
The process that occurs when two people who wish to contact each other by telephone repeatedly miss each other's phone calls.

Teleprocessing
Using telecommunications for computer-based information processing.

Terabyte
One trillion bytes. More accurately, 2 to the 40th power, or 1,009,511,627,776 in decimal notation.

Text Data
Words, phrases, sentences, and paragraphs used in documents and other forms of communication.

Throughput
The total amount of useful work performed by a data processing system during a given period of time.

Time Sharing
Providing computer services to many users simultaneously while providing rapid responses to each.

Total Quality Management
Planning and implementing programs of continuous quality improvement, where quality is defined as meeting or

exceeding the requirements and expectations of customers for a product or service.

Touch-Sensitive Screen
An input device that accepts data input by the placement of a finger on or close to the CRT screen.

Track
The portion of a moving storage medium, such as a drum, tape, or disk, that is accessible to a given reading head position.

Trackball
A rollerball device set in a case used to move the cursor on a computer's display screen.

Transaction
An event that occurs as part of doing business, such as a sale, purchase, deposit, withdrawal, refund, transfer, payment, and so on.

Transaction Document
A document produced as part of a business transaction. For instance: a purchase order, paycheck, sales receipt, or customer invoice.

Transaction File
A data file containing relatively transient data to be processed in combination with a master file. Contrast with Master File.

Transaction Processing Cycle
A cycle of basic transaction processing activities including data entry, transaction processing, database maintenance, document and report generation, and inquiry processing.

Transaction Processing System (TPS)
An information system that processes data arising from the occurrence of business transactions.

Transaction Terminals
Terminals used in banks, retail stores, factories, and other work sites that are used to capture transaction data at their point of origin. Examples are point-of-sale (POS) terminals and automated teller machines (ATMs).

Transborder Data Flows (TDF)
The flow of business data over telecommunications networks across international borders.

Transform Algorithm
Performing an arithmetic computation on a record key and using the result of the calculation as an address for that record. Also known as key transformation or hashing.

Transnational Strategy
A management approach in which an organization integrates its global business activities through close cooperation and interdependence among its headquarters, operations, and international subsidiaries, and its use of appropriate global information technologies.

Turnaround Document
Output of a computer system (such as customer invoices and statements) that is designed to be returned to the organization as machine-readable input.

Turnaround Time
The elapsed time between submission of a job to a computing center and the return of the results.

Turnkey Systems
Computer systems where all of the hardware, software, and systems development needed by a user are provided.

Unbundling
The separate pricing of hardware, software, and other related services.

Uniform Resource Locator (URL)
An access code (such as http://www.sun.com) for identifying and locating hypermedia document files, databases, and other resources at websites and other locations on the Internet, intranets, and extranets.

Universal Product Code (UPC)
A standard identification code using bar coding, printed on products that can be read by the optical supermarket scanners of the grocery industry.

Unstructured Decisions
Decisions that must be made in situations where it is not possible to specify in advance most of the decision procedures to follow.

User-Friendly
A characteristic of human-operated equipment and systems that makes them safe, comfortable, and easy to use.

User Interface
That part of an operating system or other program that allows users to communicate with it to load programs, access files, and accomplish other computing tasks.

User Interface Design
Designing the interactions between end users and computer systems, including input/output methods and the conversion of data between human-readable and machine-readable forms.

Utility Program
A standard set of routines that assists in the operation of a computer system by performing some frequently required process such as copying, sorting, or merging.

Value-Added Carriers
Third-party vendors who lease telecommunications lines from common carriers and offer a variety of telecommunications services to customers.

Value-Added Resellers (VARs)
Companies that provide industry-specific software for use with the computer systems of selected manufacturers.

Value Chain
Viewing a firm as a series, chain, or network of basic activities that add value to its products and services and thus add a margin of value to the firm.

Videoconferencing
Real-time video and audio conferencing (1) among users at networked PCs (desktop videoconferencing), or (2) among participants in conference rooms or auditoriums in different locations (teleconferencing). Videoconferencing can also include whiteboarding and document sharing.

Virtual Communities
Groups of people with similar interests who meet and share ideas on the Internet and online services and develop a feeling of belonging to a community.

Virtual Company
A form of organization that uses telecommunications networks and other information technologies to link the people, assets, and ideas of a variety of business partners, no matter where they may be located, in order to exploit a business opportunity.

Virtual Machine
Pertaining to the simulation of one type of computer system by another computer system.

Virtual Mall
An online multimedia simulation of a shopping mall with many different interlinked retail websites.

Virtual Memory
The use of secondary storage devices as an extension of the primary storage of the computer, thus giving the appearance of a larger main memory than actually exists.

Virtual Private Network
A secure network that uses the Internet as its main backbone network to connect the intranets of a company's different locations, or to establish extranet links between a company and its customers, suppliers, or other business partners.

Virtual Reality
The use of multisensory human/computer interfaces that enable human users to experience computer-simulated

objects, entities, spaces, and "worlds" as if they actually existed.

Virtual Storefront
An online multimedia simulation of a retail store shopping experience on the Web.

Virtual Team
A team whose members use the Internet, intranets, extranets, and other networks to communicate, coordinate, and collaborate with each other on tasks and projects, even though they may work in different geographic locations and for different organizations.

VLSI: Very-Large-Scale Integration
Semiconductor chips containing hundreds of thousands of circuits.

Voice Conferencing
Telephone conversations shared among several participants via speaker phones or networked PCs with Internet telephone software.

Voice Mail
Unanswered telephone messages are digitized, stored, and played back to the recipient by a voice messaging computer.

Volatile Memory
Memory (such as electronic semiconductor memory) that loses its contents when electrical power is interrupted.

Wand
A hand-held optical character recognition device used for data entry by many transaction terminals.

Web Browser
A software package that provides the user interface for accessing Internet, intranet, and extranet websites. Browsers are becoming multifunction universal clients for sending and receiving E-mail, downloading files, accessing Java applets, participating in discussion groups, developing Web pages, and other Internet, intranet, and extranet applications.

Web Publishing
Creating, converting, and storing hyperlinked documents and other material on Internet or intranet Web servers so they can easily be shared via Web browsers with teams, workgroups, or the enterprise.

What-If Analysis
Observing how changes to selected variables affect other variables in a mathematical model.

Whiteboarding
See Data Conferencing.

Wide Area Network (WAN)
A data communications network covering a large geographic area.

Window
One section of a computer's multiple-section display screen, each of which can have a different display.

Wireless LANs
Using radio or infrared transmissions to link devices in a local area network.

Wireless Technologies
Using radio wave, microwave, infrared, and laser technologies to transport digital communications without wires between communications devices. Examples include terrestrial microwave, communications satellites, cellular and PCS phone and pager systems, mobile data radio, and various wireless Internet technologies.

Word
(1) A string of characters considered as a unit. (2) An ordered set of bits (usu-ally larger than a byte) handled as a unit by the central processing unit.

Word Processing
The automation of the transformation of ideas and information into a readable form of communication. It involves the use of computers to manipulate text data in order to produce office communications in the form of documents.

Workgroup Computing
Members of a networked workgroup may use groupware tools to communicate, coordinate, and collaborate, and to share hardware, software, and databases to accomplish group assignments.

Workstation
(1) A computer system designed to support the work of one person. (2) A high-powered computer to support the work of professionals in engineering, science, and other areas that require extensive computing power and graphics capabilities.

World Wide Web (WWW)
A global network of multimedia Internet sites for information, education, entertainment, E-business, and E-commerce.

XML (Extensible Markup Language)
A Web document content description language that describes the content of Web pages by applying hidden identifying tags or contextual labels to the data in Web documents. By categorizing and classifying Web data this way, XML makes Web content easier to identify, search, analyze, and selectively exchange between computers.

Name Index

Company Index

Subject Index